American Jewry

Documents

Eighteenth Century

American Jewry · Documents

Eighteenth Century

PRIMARILY HITHERTO UNPUBLISHED MANUSCRIPTS

Jacob Rader Marcus

DIRECTOR, AMERICAN JEWISH ARCHIVES
ADOLPH S. OCHS PROFESSOR OF JEWISH HISTORY
HEBREW UNION COLLEGE-JEWISH INSTITUTE OF RELIGION
CINCINNATI

THE HEBREW UNION COLLEGE PRESS
CINCINNATI
1959

Publications of the American Jewish Archives   No. III

Jacob R. Marcus, *Editor*

772

PUBLISHED ON

THE NEUMANN MEMORIAL PUBLICATION FUND

OF THE

AMERICAN JEWISH ARCHIVES

Library of Congress Catalog Card Number: 58–12928

Distributed by University Publishers, Inc.

Manufactured in the United States of America

To Irene

Preface

This book is a collection of hitherto unpublished manuscripts dealing with eighteenth-century North American Jewry, including Jews in Canada, the "fourteenth colony." There are a few exceptions to the statement "hitherto unpublished," such as a number of contemporary newspaper accounts and advertisements, and three or four documents that have already appeared in print. For instance, I have reprinted a brief entry from a published minute book of Congregation Shearith Israel of New York (*Publications of the American Jewish Historical Society,* XXI, 113) in order to provide background for the unpublished manuscript that follows it. After compiling this book, I permitted workers in special fields to publish certain items. And finally, as every historian knows, "hitherto unpublished" is a phrase that must be used with caution. One never knows whether an "undiscovered" document has appeared in print. There can be no question, however, that at least 90 per cent of the material in this work is published here for the first time.

American Jewry · Documents · Eighteenth Century is not a typical source book including within itself the basic records of American Jewry of that period. It is not intended to serve as such. For example, *none* of the *published* texts, such as George Washington's letters to the Jews, are included. But it is a source book in the sense that all its materials can be helpful to the historian of the Jewish and general scene.

The papers which have been edited are divided into four sections: The Personal Life, The Religious Life, The General Community, and Commerce and Trade. On occasion, as the reader will note, the assignment of a letter or a record to one or another category is arbitrary. The business letters exchanged between eighteenth-century Jewish merchants frequently touched on religious and personal matters. Life was of one piece.

It is hoped that the section on personal life will throw light on the day-to-day activities of the colonial and early American man. The section on religion is intended to portray not only the practices and spiritual hopes of the individual but also the nature of Jewish communal-religious organization.

In one respect, at least, American Jewry differed from the Jewries of most European lands, with the possible exception of Holland and England. Though denied full political equality, the Jew in the North American colonies participated in the life of the general community about him. This fact is documented by the records included in Section III, which touch on the Jew as part of the larger society.

The section on economic life emphasizes the rich diversity of the activities of the Jews of that period in their efforts to make a living. Most of them were engaged in one or another form of commerce and trade. The wording and phrasing of the documents recording their transactions constitute, as it were, a "formulary" for the businessman of that period. The economic historian also should find them of interest.

Most documentary works deal with political history on the highest level and limit themselves to compacts, charters, constitutions, or pronouncements of national significance. Others are specialized works dealing with vice-admiralty courts, municipal courts, and the like. This is one of the few reference books that portray the actual day-to-day living of the urban businessman in early America. In this respect, I believe, this work is unique.

It is questionable whether any body of men, no matter how small their number, are completely atypical of a culture as long as they participate in the life of an urban community and do not live in close settlement. Because the conduct and dealings of the Jew in early America are in many respects typical, he is a microcosm of the whole. Thus, a study of the Jew may well serve as a measuring rod to judge and understand the lives of those settlers who were engaged in commerce and trade. If in any sense—outside the religious, of course —the Jew presents deviations from the "norm," then it might be well for the historian to re-examine his concepts of that which is typical in American life.

It will be noted that every item in this source book is preceded by an appropriate introduction. Inasmuch as the same dramatis personae recur frequently in the documents, there is some repetition of biographical data. This is done deliberately so that each source may stand by itself. This is a reference book, not a continuous narrative as was my two-volume *Early American Jewry*. Those who seek more data on a specific individual will do well to consult the Index.

Most source books are very chary of detail in introducing their selections. I have striven for amplitude and have not hesitated to include epitomes of many of the documents. This has been done intentionally, primarily to aid the amateur historian, the beginning student, and the nonprofessional reader, who, I hope, will use this work. Without detailed explanations, the religious documents, because of their terminology, would pose considerable difficulty for even the most competent of craftsmen. It is also my belief that historians, by scanning the introductions, will be able to determine more quickly whether the documents themselves offer them anything of interest. Thus it is hoped that the frequently calendarlike prefatory notes to the different items may prove to be a most welcome aid to the harassed researcher.

Following a procedure employed in previous works, I have incorporated all explanatory notes into the text itself, distinguishing them by square brackets. There is no need to glance at the bottom margins or to thumb laboriously through the pages at the end of the book. No glossary has been compiled. Foreign words are re-explained in every document, for I am fully aware of the fact that many readers will not know or recall the most common Hebrew terms.

The "style" employed in editing this collection is based on that adopted by the American Historical Association's Committee on Legal History. Punctuation, capitalization, and paragraphing are modernized. No unjustified liberties have been taken with the original text. Spellings, of course, remain as in the originals. *Words are retained as they are misspelled.* Most Jews in colonial America were immigrants from non-English-speaking lands, where they had been denied practically all secular training. What they learned they picked up themselves, and this lack of proper training in English is reflected in their letters and other writings.

Naturally, the faulty Hebrew and Yiddish transliterations in original texts are *not* changed. This, of course, may at times be confusing to the reader who finds the same word transliterated differently (and correctly). Editorial transliterations follow the style set by the Jewish Encyclopedia, omitting, however, the diacritical marks. All foreign words in the text are italicized, save when *Webster's New International Dictionary* accepts a Hebrew or Yiddish word as English. Actual translations of all foreign words are enclosed in quotation marks; paraphrases are not. Biblical quotations given in the original Hebrew are translated and italicized.

This work has been made possible by the Eda K. Loeb Fund for works of American Jewish historical interest. Mrs. Loeb, in whose memory this fund was established, was born in Cincinnati, Ohio, on September 13, 1867, one of ten children of Samuel and Regina Wise Kuhn. On April 3, 1895, Eda Kuhn married Morris Loeb, the distinguished chemist. Mrs. Loeb, her husband, and her brother-in-law James Loeb represented the high cultural standards of many of the leading families of the time. James Loeb, a student of ancient Greece, was the founder of the Loeb Classical Library. Morris Loeb was a competent amateur violinist, while Mrs. Loeb, a patron of music, counted among her friends such notables as Frank Damrosch and Fritz Kreisler. A member of several boards of directors, Mrs. Loeb displayed particular interest in the Loeb Convalescent Home and the Henry Street Settlement. She died on November 17, 1951.

A work such as this is in many respects a co-operative enterprise. It requires the co-operation of a host of historical societies, libraries, and interested individuals who are ready to make their collections available to the research historian. I express my thanks to the following individuals and institutions, and to their staffs and associates, for their constant courtesies and for permission to publish manuscripts in their possession: The New-York Historical Society, New York; American Jewish Historical Society, New York; Rhode Island Historical Society, Providence; Newport Historical Society, Newport, R.I.; Rhode Island State Archives, Providence; Newport County Court House, Newport, R.I.; Massachusetts Historical Society, Boston; Georgia Historical Society, Savannah; William L. Clements Library, Ann Arbor, Mich.; The Library of Congress; The Library Company of Philadelphia; Colonial Williamsburg, Inc.; Duke University Library, Durham, N.C.; Yale University Library; Baker Library, Harvard University; Connecticut State Library, Hartford; New York State Library, Albany; the Library of Girard College, Philadelphia; The New York Public Library; Séminair du St. Joseph, Three Rivers, Canada; the archivist of the Montreal Courthouse; Historical Society of Pennsylvania, Philadelphia; The John Carter Brown Library, Providence; Boston Public Library; State Historical

Society of Wisconsin, Madison; Public Archives of Canada, Ottawa; Pennsylvania Historical and Museum Commission, Harrisburg; State Department of Archives and History, Raleigh, N.C.; Department of Archives and History, Atlanta; Archives du Séminaire de Québec; Historical Commission of South Carolina, Columbia; Chicago Historical Society Library; Public Record Office, London; Registrar's Office, Bridgetown, Barbados; University of Virginia Library, Charlottesville; Cincinnati Public Library; Cincinnati Law Library; University of Cincinnati Library; Historical and Philosophical Society of Ohio, Cincinnati; Deutsches Zentralarchiv, Merseburg, Germany; Congregation Shearith Israel, New York; Congregation Mikveh Israel, Philadelphia; Congregation Mickve Israel, Savannah; Congregation Shaar Hashamaim (Bevis Marks), London; Congregation Shearith Israel, Montreal; Congregation Mikveh Israel, Curaçao; Emily Solis-Cohen, Philadelphia; Edwin Wolf 2d, Philadelphia; the late Lee M. Friedman, Boston; Mr. and Mrs. B. H. Levy, Savannah; Mr. and Mrs. Henry S. Hendricks, New York.

Finally, it is my pleasant task to express my gratitude to those at the American Jewish Archives who have worked closely with me in the preparation of this book: Dr. Selma Stern-Taeubler, the former archivist; Rabbi Stanley F. Chyet, the Harrison Jules Louis Frank and Leon Harrison Frank Research Fellow; Miss Jeanette Weiss, my editorial assistant; my secretaries, Mrs. Etheljane Callner and Miss Sarah Grossman; and Mr. Emil Oberholzer, Jr., of New York City, my editorial aid. Mr. Maxwell Whiteman, of Philadelphia, was kind enough to read the manuscript and to offer many helpful suggestions. Rabbi Malcolm H. Stern, of Norfolk, the Archives genealogist, generously put himself at my service at all times. My classmate Rabbi Abraham I. Shinedling carefully read and corrected the typescript and prepared the Index. Dr. Nelson Glueck, the president of the Hebrew Union College-Jewish Institute of Religion, and Dr. Samuel Sandmel, the provost, evinced a deep personal interest in the publication of this book. To them, and to the others whom I have mentioned, and to the many unmentioned who were helpful to me in the preparation of this work, my most heartfelt thanks.

American Jewish Archives
Cincinnati, Ohio

JACOB R. MARCUS

Contents

I The Personal Life

No. 1   Peddlers—1753–1787

In the following account (Document A) copied from a New York paper, Benjamin Franklin tells of a Jewish peddler who took advantage of a farmer's wife. The betrayed woman revenged herself, however, by destroying the peddler's pack. In all probability this is not a true story but one of those wandering folk tales found in the literature of many peoples. The moral is entirely too pat: the deceiver is deceived.

This anecdote may be fictitious but it reflects a fact known from documentary sources: young Jews peddled their wares (and occasionally their charms!) in colonial days. As early as 1670, Jacob Lucena, an itinerant trader from New York, while journeying through Connecticut, was arrested and convicted of having been "notorious in his lascivious dalience and wanton carriage and profers to severall women," for which he was heavily fined.

Another peddler who was far from fictitious was Solomon Raphael, for whom President Franklin of Pennsylvania signed a license in 1787 (Document B). In many respects Raphael's career was typical. Somehow or other he had saved enough money to rise in the economic hierarchy from "foot" peddler to "horse" peddler; no longer did he have to carry his pack and jewelry box on his back. Raphael was married by 1788, and within a few years he rose to become a shopkeeper selling watches. For a time he also kept a coffeehouse. That was in Philadelphia. By 1796 Raphael was in business in Baltimore, and later in the decade he moved to Richmond, where he became a respected merchant, a tavernkeeper, and

1

auctioneer. His career in Virginia may well have been furthered by his brother-in-law Solomon Jacobs, a prominent businessman who served as acting mayor of Richmond and became Grand Master of the Masonic Lodges of his state.

SOURCE. Document A: *The Pennsylvania Gazette,* March 13, 1753; Document B: American Jewish Historical Society Library, New York, Rosenbach Collection.

A [NO. 1]

New York, February 26 [1753].—We have an account from the country of the following comical affair, which lately happened, viz.

A Jew pedlar went into a house where he offered his goods for sale, but the good man being out, and all his family, except his wife, who told the pedlar that she could not buy any thing, for her husband had got the key of the money. The pedlar, then, finding that the woman was entirely alone, offered to make her a present of a piece of calicoe upon condition of her giving up her charms to him. The bait was very alluring, for the thoughts of sporting with a young man, and having a new gown in the bargain, made her readily yield to his desires.

He accordingly gave her the calicoe and, after taking a repast in the banquet of love, went about his business, but had not gone far before he met with her husband, and having some knowledge of him, said: "Sir, I have sold your wife a very cheap piece of calicoe, and on six months' credit." With that the poor man stood amazed, and said: "I wonder at my wife's ill conduct in running me in debt, when she knows that I have a considerable sum of money to pay in a few months' time, and can't tell how to make it up." He then persuaded the pedlar to go back and take his piece of calicoe, which he readily consented to, and, when they came to the house, he [the husband] ordered his wife to give the pedlar his calicoe again, which she did, after privately concealing a coal of fire in it.

The pedlar took the calicoe and put it up in his pack (which was a wallet slung across his shoulders) [and] so marched off, pleased with the thoughts of his success. But for his sweet meat he soon found sour sauce. He, not suspecting the cheat, jogged along till he met with a countryman, who, seeing his pack on fire (and which was then just ready to blaze), cryed: "Hay, friend, from whence came you?" *"From Hell,"* replied the pedlar. "So I perceive," says the countryman, "by the flames at your back." The pedlar then looked behind him, and to his great surprize found all his goods on fire, which made him stamp and rave like a mad man and curse his folly in cuckolding the poor man.

B [NO. 1]

By the Supreme Executive Council
of the
Commonwealth of Pennsylvania.

Whereas Solomon Raphael, the bearer hereof, intending to follow the business of a pedlar within the Commonwealth of Pennsylvania, hath been recommended to us as a proper person for that employment, and requesting a license for the same:

We do hereby license and allow the said Solomon Raphael to employ himself as a pedlar and hawker within the said Commonwealth, to travel with one horse and to expose and vend divers goods and merchandize until the twenty first day of March next;

Provided he shall, during the said term, observe and keep all laws and ordinances of the said Commonwealth to the same employment relating.

Given under the seal of the Commonwealth, at Philadelphia, the twenty third day of March, in the year of our Lord one thousand seven hundred and eighty seven.

B. Franklin, president

Attest:
James Trimble,
for John Armstrong, Junior, secretary

No. 2 Circumcision of Babies and Marranos—1753–1767

Benjamin Gomez (1711–72), a New York merchant, was very friendly with his cousin's husband, the Newport businessman Aaron Lopez. Both were Sephardim, Jews of Spanish and Portuguese origin, and both were devoted to their ancestral traditions.

Gomez was a native New Yorker, the son of a Spanish refugee; Lopez was a Portuguese émigré who fled the Inquisition with wife and family and settled in Rhode Island. When Lopez became the father of a son in 1753, he hastened to inform his friend Gomez. Lopez was then about twenty-two years of age and had been in the colony for a year. Apparently he was still struggling along. Much time was to elapse before he would become one of America's great merchants. In the 1770's, however, he was the outstanding merchant-shipper of pre-Revolutionary Newport, and one of the greatest in his field in all New England.

Since Gomez, a pillar of the New York synagogue, occasionally performed the operation of circumcision, Lopez was eager to have him present in Newport in 1753 at the circumcision ceremony of what was probably his first-born son. Lopez knew full well that Gomez, like any good Jew, was eager to pile up religiously meritorious deeds, and officiating at a circumcision was not the least of such religious opportunities. Document A is Gomez' answer, translated from the original Spanish, to the invitation of his Newport friend.

Years later, in 1767, when Gomez received a letter for a Mr. Abraham Pereira Mendes addressed in his care, he sent it at once to Aaron Lopez of Newport, knowing that Mendes was the son-in-law of the Rhode Island merchant. In his covering letter, Gomez, after expressing the hope that Lopez was enjoying the High Holydays, congratulated his friend on the arrival of a brother, Abraham Lopez, from Lisbon. The brother and his three sons had arrived in Newport on July 11, in a ship which Aaron had sent to Portugal for the express purpose of fetching his brother and nephews. Escape from Portugal and the Inquisition may have been easy at that time because the anticlerical Marquis de Pombal was then in power. Because of his skill and experience in the field, Gomez felt competent to advise Lopez on the circumcision of the recently arrived New Christians or Marranos.

Note that Gomez' letter of September 28 (Document B) arrived in Newport no later than the thirtieth, for Lopez answered him on that day (Document C). It was only an overnight trip by boat from New York to Newport.

SOURCE. Newport Historical Society Library, Newport, R. I., Lopez Letters.

A [NO. 2]

New York, 28 May, 1753.

Mr. Aaron Lopez.
Dear Sir:

I have received your esteemed letter, in which you so kindly inform me that our Lord has given you a son. For this I extend the due felicitations to you, to your wife, my cousin, and to the rest of the family. May God permit you to rear him in great joy, together with the rest of your dear ones.

I am very grateful for the favor that you do me in offering me a part in the circumcision ceremony. I would accept most willingly, were it not that my business affairs do not permit it. I have no doubt that my brother

Daniel will try to send someone who can. I, on my part, shall do what I can in this regard, and I shall always be honored to serve you in anything within my power.

Praying to God that this letter finds you and your wife, my cousin, and the rest of the family enjoying perfect health—may it come to me [also] soon—and may God preserve you for many years.

Yours sincerely,
Benjamin Gomez

B [NO. 2]

New York, September 28th, 1767.

Sir:

The inclosed [letter for a Mr. Mendes] received this week from Jamaica. As there is no person of that name here, conclude it must be intended for your son in law, who, am imformed, is gone to Jamaica. Wish him safe there, and that this may find you in health in company of your spows [spouse], his, and the rest of your famley [family], as mine is at present.

Announcing you the compliments of the [Holiday] season, and that you may all be recorded in the books of life, I am, sir,

Your most humble servant,
Benjamin Gomez.

I congratulate you on the safe arrivall of your brothers, whome, I understand, intend to undergo the [circumcision] operation. Pray take care to have a good surgeon present, as it will require some judgment to stop the blood and cure the wound. My compliments to them, allso to Mr. Reveira and famley.

Mr. Aaron Lopes.

C [NO. 2]

Newport, September 30th, 1767.

Mr. Benjamin Gomez.
Sir:

I received your esteemed favour of the 28th inst., covering a letter for my son in law, Mr. Mendes, who left this port the 24th ult. for Jamaica and hope is safe arrived there before now. Your forwarding his letter lays me under an obligation, as also the good wishes and kind expressions you are pleased to pronounce on the arrival of my brother and his family from Portugal.

I duly notice the hints you are good enough to give in regard to the safety of the operation.

May you enjoy the approaching holy days and many others to come with perfect health and uninterrupted felicities, in which sincere wishes Mrs. Lopez and rest of my family joins me. Being most respectfully, sir,

Your very humble servant,

[Aaron Lopez]

No. 3   Aaron Lopez Buys Three Lottery Tickets—1753

When Aaron Lopez received the letter printed below, he was a newcomer to Newport, Rhode Island, and to this continent. There is every reason to believe that at that time he was only a struggling shopkeeper.

Lopez' correspondent in this letter was Naphtali Hart Myers (*ca.* 1711–88), an American businessman who had been active as a merchant in several towns. Myers had been in the country since the 1740's. Later, before the Revolution, he returned to London, where he became one of the leaders of Ashkenazic Jewry. In 1753 Myers was temporarily in London on a business and pleasure trip, and, as we shall read, brought a bride back with him.

Note Lopez' and Myers' interest in lottery tickets and the pleasant admixture of business and social amenities.

SOURCE. Newport Historical Society Library, Aaron Lopez Letters.

London, November 16, 1753.

Mr. Aaron Lopez.

Sir:

I have the pleasure to informe you that your kind wishes in your favour [letter] per Mr. Solomon Hart are accomplished, and long since acknowledged the receipt of your favour per Mr. Pimentel with the 7 half-johanesses [Portuguese coins] which are invested in 3 [lottery] tickets that cost 15s. 6d. per piece. And if wishes can influence their good fortune, you will then reap all the advant[age] they or any other undertaking can possibly be attended with.

Your books I shall have the pleasure of conveying you when I have the happiness of returning to America with her I'm to be united with next February.

My respects to your lady, the old gentleman Mr. [Jacob] Rivera and his consort, and all friends, and with my sincere wishes for your prosperity, subscribe, sir,

Your friend and servant,

Naphtali H. Myers

It is some [time] since I transmited the numbers of [your] lucky tickets to Mr. Rivera.

No. 4   Members of Libraries—1754–1773

American Jews joined and supported the semipublic libraries that were being established early in the eighteenth century. Benjamin Franklin organized the Library Company of Philadelphia in 1731, and within a quarter of a century David Franks, the Philadelphia merchant and socialite, was admitted to its membership (Document A).

In Newport, where the Redwood Library had been established in 1747, Moses Lopez, a merchant and interpreter, became a member within two years, in 1749. Other Newport Jews joined the library in later years; some passed their rights on to their children. Jacob Rodriguez Rivera, the merchant, joined in 1758. Years later, in 1773, he offered library privileges to Abraham Lopez, a refugee from the Portuguese Inquisition (Document B). Lopez was something of a student, for in that very year he translated a Spanish sermon into good English. Maybe that is why he wanted to use the library!

SOURCE. Document A: Boston Public Library; Document B: Yale University Library, New Haven, Conn., Stiles Papers.

A [NO. 4]

At a meeting of the directors of the Library, February 11, 1754. Present:

P. Syng	S. Rhodes
Hugh Roberts	Joseph Stretch
Evan Morgan	James Mifflin
T. Cadwalader	B. Franklin

David Franks applying to be admitted a member, it was unanimously agreed to.

B [NO. 4]

Newport, June 17th, 1773

Please to let Mr. Abraham Lopez have any book he shall require out of the library, on my right, conforming to the rules, and you'll oblige, sir,

Your humble servant,

Jacob Rodrigues Rivera

To the Reverend Mr. Styles, Librarian of Redwood's Library.

No. 5   The Libraries of Nathan Levy and Samuel Judah—1754–1785

Nathan Levy was the real founder of the Jewish community of Philadelphia, where he settled about 1735. At the time of his death, in December, 1753, he was a merchant and shipper of note.

Included in the inventory of his household goods are a number of books that had been stored "in the closet in the front parlour," and which, in all likelihood, constituted his personal library. The list (Document A) includes eight "Spanish Hebrew" books. If this statement is to be taken literally, the works were in Ladino, an old Spanish dialect usually written in the Hebrew script. This would substantiate the family tradition that Levy's father was born in Spain. It is far more probable, however, that these were standard liturgical works, printed in Spanish and Hebrew, such as were used by the American Jews who were members of the colonial synagogues, all of which followed the Sephardic rite.

The inventory, in addition to listing these tomes and a number of dictionaries, gazetteers, lawbooks, and other reference works, also includes a violin, a violin case, and some books of music. When Dr. Alexander Hamilton, the Maryland physician, visited the Music Club in Philadelphia in 1744, he reported that "one Levy there played a very good violine." That was our Nathan Levy.

Like Levy, Samuel Judah, of Montreal, was a merchant who, as many of his contemporaries, was also engaged in the fur traffic, with an operational base for the Indian trade at Detroit. At times he lived in Three Rivers, Quebec, where his brother-in-law was the town's leading businessman.

In addition to his mercantile interests Judah was something of a student. Among his papers is an inventory of the books he owned in May, 1785. To this list (Document B) should be added twenty-one volumes of Bell's *British Theatre* and a fifteen-volume edition of Smollett's *History of England,* both of which are known to have been in his possession in the spring of 1784.

It is noteworthy that there is not one book of Jewish interest in the whole lot, but no hasty or false conclusions should be drawn from this fact. His branch of the family remained Jewish for another generation or two, and though his grandson Samuel Judah, the Indiana politician, married out of the faith, there is no proof that the latter became a Christian. The literary interest of the earlier

Judah was carried on by the later one. Samuel Judah, of Vincennes, had a fine library, and was known for his proficiency in Greek and Latin.

SOURCE. Document A: Register of Wills, City of Philadelphia, Administration Papers, No. 58, Book F, 527; Document B: Séminaire du Saint Joseph, Three Rivers, Canada, Hart Papers.

A [NO. 5]

An inventory of the household goods, etc., of N. Levy, deceased. . . .

In the closet in the front parlour . . .

2 Vollumes Chambers's Dictionary [Cyclopaedia] . . .

History of England by Rapin [Paul de Rapin-Thoyras] . . .

Carkess Book Rates [Charles Carkesse, The Book of Rates] . . .

Cowley's Law Dict. . . .

Merchant's Map of Commerce . . .

Laws of Massachusetts . . .

2 Religion [of Nature] Delineated by Wolasten [William Wollaston] . . .

Stevensen's Spa[nish] Dict. . . .

3 Old Bibles in English . . .

Lingua Franca Dict. . . .

Coles [Elisha Coles, the Younger] Lattin and Eng. Dict. . . .

Dutch and French Dict. . . .

[Nathan] Bailey English Dict. . . .

Newhouse on Navigation . . .

Mathematical Tables . . .

11 Historical Registers . . .

4 Lock[e] on Human Understanding . . .

3 [Humphrey] Prideaux Connect [Old and New Testament Connected] . . .

Mathematick Lessons . . .

Jure Maritimo . . .

3 Plutarch's Lives . . .

4 Statutes Abridged . . .

Voyage Round the World . . .

2 Gazetteers . . .

Arithmetick . . .

Magistrate's help . . .

Eng. and Dutch Grammer . . .

Confession of Faith . . .

Treasury of Mathematicks . . .

De Ritz Memoirs . . .
Rider's Almanack . . .
Lex Mercatoria . . .
[Matthew] Prior's Poems . . .
Bible in Hebrew, Greek, and Latin . . .
Hebrew and Latin Dict. . . .
22 Hebrew Books . . .
 8 Span[ish] Hebrew Books . . .
25 Musick Books . . .
A parcell of pamphlets . . .

Philadelphia, April 20th, 1754

B [NO. 5]

List of Books [in Samuel Judah's Library]

Postlethwaite's Dictionary, 2 vols.
Watson's History of Philip the 2d, 2 vols.
Hutchinson's History of Massachusetts Bay, 2 vols.
Abbe Reynall's History of the East and West Indies, 5 vols.
Gibbons's History of the Roman Empire, 1 vol.
Saxby's Brittish Customs, 1 vol.
Baldwin's——ditto, 1 vol.
Spectator, 8 vols.
Tour through Britain, 4 vols.
Life of John Bundo, Esq., 4 vols.
Remembrancer, 13 vols. in 8 books
The Profest Cook, 1 vol.
Malcolm's Arithmetick, 1 vol.
2 vols. of Shakespear, 3rd and 4th
The Universal Gazetteer, 1 vol.
Salmon's Geographical Grammar, 1 vol.
Two of Bayle's Dictionaries
Bailey's English Dictionary
Town and Country Magazine, for 1781 and 1782
Annual Register, 2 vols., for 1779 and 1780
Parliamentary Register, 2 vols., No. 1 and 3
Swift's Works, 2 vols.
Gentleman's Magazine, 1 vol., for 1776
Commodore Walker's Voyages, 1 vol.
The Grecian Courtezan, 1 vol.
Nature Displayed, 1 vol.
Tryal of Doctor Sachaverell, 1 vol.
Pope's Works, 1 vol.

Peregrine Pickle, 1 vol.
Don Quixote, 1 vol. in French
The Young Man's Book of Knowledge, 1 vol.
Lady Chudleigh's Poems, 1 vol.
Court Calendar, 3 vols., for 1776, 1780, and 1781
Adventures of a Jesuit, 1 vol.
History of Canada, 1 vol.
Earl of Warwick, a Tragedy
Peerage of England, 3 vols.
German Grammar, 1 vol.
Acts of Parliament, 1 vol.
Trials for Adultery, 5 vols.
Death of Abel, 1 vol.

No. 6   A Postscript for the Folks Back Home—1759

An ambitious young businessman who came to New York about 1755, during the French and Indian War, was the Dutch-born emigrant from England, Uriah Hendricks. His letter book for the years 1758 and 1759 shows the merchant and importer hard at work buying English manufactures through his family and one or two large wholesalers and suppliers, and bartering the goods against American raw products, primarily West India sugar. One of his suppliers was Moses Franks, a large wholesaler, who was born in New York and was sent "home" to London to help manage the family's mercantile and financial interests in that center.

Most of Hendricks' correspondence was with his family; with a brother-in-law, who resented the fact that Americans were "slow-pay," with a brother Abram, and with his father Aaron, apparently his chief supplier.

Occasionally Uriah Hendricks bought on his own account; most of the time he sold on commission. He speculated in shares in privateers, did a thriving business in lottery tickets, and became a merchant-shipper in order to participate directly in the lucrative sugar trade with the non-British sugar islands. Later in life he became an ironmonger, establishing a successful metal business, which his descendants carried on down into the twentieth century.

In religious practice he was very observant and devout, looking contemptuously on those army sutlers who desecrated the Sabbath and ate forbidden food. In 1791 he was president of Congregation Shearith Israel.

Although he was devoted to his family, his voluminous correspondence with them was nearly always strictly limited to business matters. In the following postscript of a letter to his brother Abram, dated May 14, 1759, the twenty-eight-year-old Uriah steps out of his usual role as the harassed merchant and chats with the family—but only for a brief moment.

SOURCE. Uriah Hendricks Letter Book, 1758–59. Copy in the American Jewish Archives.

P.S. I made a *misheberack* [blessing] in our shul ["synagogue"] on your account and offered 18s. currency towards the building of a new shul in Rhoade Island, for which have made your account current debtor.

My sincere love to all our sisters, and in perticular to Rosy, to whom you'll please to give on my account one guinea as pocket money.

You'll please to mention to me per first [opportunity] what kind of a boy our cousin Abram is, our Aunt Cohen['s] son, if he is a boy of capacity, etc., as I may be servicable to him in case his mother consents [to his coming to the American colonies].

I hope our cousin Sally and sisters, etc. is well, and shoud be glad to hear from them by way of letter of themselves, as likewise of our cousin Myer of whom have several times inquired of but not heard of.

I wish you, my honored one, lots of luck in the lotteries. May you attain all the desires of your heart, and may it also be God's will.

No. 7 The Will of Judah Hays—1763

Judah Hays (1703–64), of New York, was one of six brothers who came to this country from Holland in the early part of the eighteenth century. He was quite successful as a merchant, shipper, and owner of privateers. But if Hays lacked business worries, he had his share of family problems. As far as we know, he had nine children, seven girls and two boys. His domestic problems are reflected in the following will, signed in 1763 and admitted to probate in the following year.

His son Michael, who was incompetent in business matters, was given the interest from a trust fund; Rachel, who married the Canadian trader Levy Michaels without parental permission, was cut off with five shillings, while Caty, who had married Abraham Sarzedas, a merchant, was, like her brother Michael, limited to the interest from a special fund. Apparently Hays had no confidence in Caty's husband either.

The testator appointed his wife Rebecca, his son Moses Michael, and William Smith, Jr. as executors. The latter, no doubt, was the famous jurist and historian. After some initial difficulties Moses became a very rich and respected businessman in Boston, carrying on the best mercantile traditions of the family.

SOURCE. Surrogate's Court of the County of New York, Wills, Liber XXIV, 524.

In the Name of the Eternal God of Israel, Amen.

I, Judah Hayes, of the city of New York, merchant, being a little indisposed at present, but injoying the free exercise of my understanding as in a season of health, think it proper to make my will, and it is in these words:

Imprimis, I order my remains to be interred in such manner and at such an expence as my wife in her discretion shall think proper to direct; and I bequeath to her absolutely all my plate and linnen and all my household furniture.

Secondly, having frequently taken very just offence at the disobedience and general conduct of my son Michael, who owes me above four hundred pounds, and having no opinion of his prudence, I have some times resolved to give him no part of my estate. But by the advice of a friend and upon mature consideration, thinking it my duty to make some provision for him, I do hereby forgive his debt and ordain that the capital sum of three hundred pounds New York money be [put] out at interest upon land and personal security by my executors, who are also directed anually within twenty days after the interest becomes due, to give the said Michael a power to demand and receive the same to his own use; and upon default of payment, I direct them to sue for the same and put out the capital in other hands for the preservation of the annual interest for his use during life.

Thirdly, the said capital and all other my estate, both real and personal, I devise and bequeath to my wife and the rest of my children (except my daughter Rachel, to whom I give only five shillings, as she married contrary to my will and disire), equally to be devided between them, my wife taking no more than one of the children, and each to hold his or her part of the real estate as tenants in common in fee simple, and what I have above devised and bequeathed to my wife is in lieu of her dower.

Fourthly, the share of such of my children as may die before full age, unmarried and without issue, I devise and bequeath to the surviving children, to be equally divided between such survivors as tenants in common in fee simple.

Fifthly, I empower my executors and the major part of them, and the survivors or survivor of them, to sell all my real estate and turn the same into money for the more easy distribution of my estate and compliance with this will; and I ordain that the share of each child under age at my decease be put out at interest for his or her maintenance till full age, or if a girl, till marriage or full age, when the capital share shall be paid to them, respectively.

Sixthly, notwithstanding any thing in my will to the contrary, I devise and bequeath and ordain that the share and estate of my daughter, now the wife of Abraham Sarzadas [Sarzedas], be put out at interest by my executors as soon as the same can be liquidated after the settlement of my estate, that the annual interest when received be paid to her as long as she lives, and that her receipt covert or discovert [married or unmarried] shall be their discharge, and that after her death leaving issue, the said interest be employed to maintain and educate such issue till their full age when the capital shall be given to such issue in equal shares.

Lastly, I revoke all former wills and declare this only to be my last will and testament, whereof I appoint my wife Rebecca, my son Moses M. Hayes, and William Smith, Junior, to be the executors.

In testimony whereof, I have hereunto set my hand and seal this twenty second day of July in the year, according to the Christian account of time, one thousand seven hundred and sixty-three.

Judah Hays

No. 8   Hayman Levy, Bankrupt, Is Given New Hope—1765

A number of Jewish merchants were economic casualties of the French and Indian War and of the Indian uprising under Pontiac. Among these was Hayman Levy, a Hannoverian immigrant, who had come to New York in the 1740's, a young man in his twenties, and had speedily identified himself with the local congregation. During the French and Indian War he was active as a merchant, as a speculator in privateering expeditions, and as an army purveyor. In all probability he was the Levy of Levy and Solomons, a consortium of Jewish businessmen engaged in furnishing supplies to the British army of conquest. By 1765 Levy was bankrupt.

The following letter reflects Levy's effort, at the age of forty-four, to start life over again. Getting in touch with his former Rhode Island correspondent, Aaron Lopez, he asked for consignments of that profitable staple, spermaceti candles. Although Lopez and his father-in-law Jacob Rodriguez Rivera were unable to comply because they were committed to a New York agent, they went out of their way to send Levy some candles under circumstances that would allow him a decent profit and would, at the same time, require no advance payment on his part.

What is significant is that Lopez began his letter to Levy with words of encouragement and sympathy, conscious that his fellow merchant had just gone through the harrowing experience of bankruptcy. The kindness and solicitude expressed by Lopez were typical of him.

SOURCE. Newport Historical Society Library, Aaron Lopez Letters.

Newport, February 28th, 1765.

Mr. Hayman Levy.
Dear Sir:
Your favor of the 28th ultimo I duly received, and though it is a long time (as you observe) since our correspondence dropt, do most sincerely assure you [I] have felt with true concern the deplorable narration you give me of your present circumstances, which after a long, close, and industrious application proves so unfruitful.

It is indeed a severe tryall, but when you come to reflect the instability of human affairs, and consider how often instances will present to our sight of the like nature and that they are the decrees of a just [and] wise Ruler, who directs all events for our own good, [it] will no doubt furnish consolation to aleviate your grief and strengthen your thoughts with fortitude to launch prudently into the world again. It gives me great satisfaction to see you have settled your affairs to the content of the generality of your creditors, and that you have acquitted yourself with honour.

I make no doubt but when you come to put together your indefatigable industry with the advantageous experience you have acquired, [it] will soon enable you in solid establishment, a confirmation of which will give me singular pleasure.

Agreeable to your desire, have shipped you 6 boxes spermacety candles as per inclosed invoice, amounting to £24.11.7½ now passed to your debit. I have charged them at a price that will leave you a full allowance for the commissions I pay at Newyork, which may fully answer you the same purpose as if I addressed them for my account. I would readily comply with your request on the commission way, but my works requiring such a large stock has brought me under an engagement with Mr. Ludlow, which I can't violate, and your good friend, Mr. Rivera, being under the same tyes, makes it impracticable to either of us. However, I shall be willing to furnish you, on your own account, with candles whenever I have them by me and to supply you with one advanced parcell till it is sold, so as you be not in any disbursement.

Mrs. Lopez joyns with my sincere assurances of esteem to you, Mrs. Levy, and rest of your family, being respectfully, dear sir, etc.

[Aaron Lopez]

P.S. I have no candle moulds that will make candles of 6″ the way you desire.

No. 9 Hannah Paysaddon Appeals to Aaron Lopez for Charity—1770

Aaron Lopez, of Newport, was known for his philanthropy to both Jews and Gentiles. Ezra Stiles, president of Yale, said of Lopez: "His beneficence to his family connexions, to his nation, and to all the world is almost without a parallel." It was not unusual, therefore, for persons of different faiths to write to him for aid.

The following appeal came from a New York woman, Hannah Paysaddon (Bensadon?), probably a Jewess. If this woman was really in need, and if she was a Jewess, she would certainly have received help from the local Jewish community. Apparently she was not given a grant by the synagogue Shearith Israel, for her name does not appear in its records. However, for some reason or other, she may have hesitated to turn to her coreligionists for aid.

SOURCE. New York State Library, Albany, N. Y., Champlin Collection.

Newyork, July 26, 1770.

Dear Sir:

I take the liberty once moor of troubling you in the letter way, which I hope you'l pardon. Necesseaity drives me to it. I am now in years and unable to do anny thing for my self. It's comeing to quarter [rent] day, and I am affraid I shall be troubled. I am helpt by my friends, but it is not sufficent to keep me from disstress. So, dear sir, I hope your heart, which is naturly tender, will be moved with kind compassion for a poor fellow creature who is labouring under greater distress then it's possible to express. What ever you do for me, I hope God will doubly return.

So, remain with great respect,

Your obedient servant,
Hannah Paysaddon

No. 10 Two Cantors Exchange Pulpits—1770

Isaac Touro, a native of the Netherlands, came to the American colonies about 1758 and was appointed hazzan, or cantor, of the Newport congregation. That community was then undergoing a rebirth, and by 1763 the Jews of the town had erected a beautiful synagogue.

In 1770 Touro made a trip to New York. It seems to have been a visit for pleasure, if we may judge from the following letter, written originally in Portuguese, to his Newport friend, Aaron Lopez. And apparently this was also an "exchange of pulpits": Touro officiated in New York, and, as we know, Cantor Gershom Mendes Seixas, who was then visiting in Newport, conducted services twice in that city.

The Reverend Dr. Ezra Stiles went to hear Seixas and wrote: "How melancholy to behold an assembly of worshippers of Jehovah, open and professed enemies to a crucified Jesus!"

SOURCE. American Jewish Historical Society Library, Rosenbach Collection.

New York, August 22, 1770.

My dear friend and sir, Aaron Lopez:

Yesterday I reached my house at one o'clock in the day, a time very appropriate in which to arrive after a journey of 30 hours. I could not have had better weather than that which I had, since it was wonderful. Thus when I arrived in this [city], the parnas ["president"] begged me to pray [conduct the services], and since it was agreeable to me, I accepted the offer. My friends received me with very much affection, especially my friend Mr. Is. Sexyas, and in every respect I had to accept [hospitality and favors] from him.

I do not regret the resolution which I made to go to New York, and especially to you [I give thanks] for the encouragement which you gave me, thanking you for all the favors, thinking that you are enjoying health in the company of all your families, not even making an exception of my intimate friend, your father-in-law. Despite the fact that I am not writing to him, it is not because I do not want to, but rather out of a desire that he should not say that it [my letter] is brief. I know the Portuguese. But although this letter is singular, I call it plural, because it is intended for your cousin just as much as it is for you.

I would request, Mr. Aaron, that you give my regards to the gentlemen, your brothers, as well as to all the gentlemen of my congregation. May God prosper and increase them, Amen. And peace from your friend, as to whom you can depend upon it that he wishes for you everything good.

Ishac De Abraham Touro

N.B. Many remembrances to my friend Osborn and to Hazan Sexyas. P.S. I assure you that New York [is worth] the trouble to be here, to see the deference which you have, especially in the factories [offices].

No. 11   The Longest Way Around Is the Shortest Way Home—1770

Merchants in colonial days were only too happy to help one another, and never forgot the maxim that one good turn deserves another. Thus a Jewish merchant in the West Indies did not hesitate to ask a stranger on the mainland for a favor.

Here we have a letter from Jacob Melhado, of Jamaica, asking Michael Gratz, of Philadelphia, to forward an enclosed note to the Dutch island of St. Eustatius. Although this island and Jamaica were less than 300 miles apart, there was no regular service between them. It was quicker to send a message from Jamaica to St. Eustatius by way of Philadelphia, a round trip of over 2,000 miles.

SOURCE. The Library Company of Philadelphia.

Kingston, Jamaica, 22th August, 1770.

Mr. Michael Gratts.

Sir:

Through the recomendation of my friend Mr. Abraham de Isaac Deleon, have inclosed you a letter to forward to a brother of mine who resides in St. Eustatia, which beg you'l send per first opportunity for that place, as I find it very inconvinient to convey letters from this place to any of the Windward Island[s].

Shall beg leave now and than [then] to trouble you in forwarding a letter or two as directed. If [I] can be of any service to you this way, please to lay your commands, and you may assur yourself they shall be punctually executed by, sir,

Your unknown and most humble servant,
Jacob Melhado

P.S. If any [letters] for me [are] directed for your care, shall be much obliged to you to forward them by first opportunity for this place.

No. 12   Joseph Lopez Writes a Letter to His Father—1772

Aaron Lopez, the Newport merchant, had at least seventeen children, including Joseph (1754–1822). The latter was born in Newport before a circumciser had arrived there; hence the operation was not performed until he was three. Abraham I. Abrahams, of New York, who finally initiated Joseph into the Abrahamitic covenant, came up to Newport in 1757 to circumcise the child and his cousin on the same day. Such wholesale operations in outlying towns and hamlets were not uncommon.

In 1772 Joseph was in New York City, recovering from what seemed to be a mild case of smallpox. In the following letter he reported to his father on the state of his health and also conveyed the good wishes of the Gomezes, one of whom had married his sister Esther.

Note the formal mode of address used even by a son to his father. The style was not specifically Portuguese-Jewish, but was characteristic of the time.

None of the Lopez sons seem to have acquired their father's mercantile abilities. Apparently they were not successful businessmen.

SOURCE. New York State Library, Champlin Collection of Autographs, No. 617.

New York, November 10, 1772.

Honoured Sir:

Your most esteemed and agreeable letter of the 21st ulto. was duly handed me by our mutual friend, Doctor Wigneron.

I have now the pleasure, thank God, to advise that I am perfectly recovered of the small pox after a very disagreeable sickness of 3 days; and a great number of pox broke out, were very tedious, but they proved to be of the favourable sort.

This will be handed you by Cousin David, and should be exceeding glad could I have accompanyed him; but, being prevailed on by Messrs. Gomez and several other friends that they think it very imprudent in me for to venture [to go out] as yet, and none of my cloths [clothes] being clensed sufficiently, I thought it best to tarry about 6 or 8 days longer and have them properly done, which you may depend, sir, that I shall use all precaution in being very particular so as not to carry the infection, which God forbid.

I have, according to your request, presented your respectfull compliments to Messrs. Dan. and Mor.[decai] Gomez, who desires in return that you'll accept of their best respects.

Time does not permit enlarging, the vessell just pushing off, save that you'll be pleased to present my duty to honoured mama, love to sister Mendes, and the rest of the sisters and brothers, and to all the family in general.

I am, with greatest respect, honoured sir,

Your dutifull son,
Joseph Lopez

P.S. My kind compliments to Mr. Mendes [my brother-in-law], and for want of time, could not do myself the pleasure of writing per this conveyance.

———

No. 13   Gershom Mendes Seixas, Rejected Suitor?—1774

Gershom Mendes Seixas was the first native-born American to serve as "rabbi" of a congregation in this country. In 1768 he was appointed hazzan, or cantor, of Shearith Israel in New York.

The following letter was written to thank Aaron Lopez, after Seixas had visited that wealthy Newport shipper. Much that Seixas wrote is very cryptic, but it all takes on meaning if we assume that the rabbi went to Newport to try his luck with one of the Lopez girls. Apparently (and this is all assumption) he was turned down. But his optimism came to the fore and he expressed the hope that God and time would "one day bless me with what my heart most earnestly desires." The Lord and time did not do so well by him as far as one of the Lopez girls was concerned; in less than a year he married a Miss Elkalah Cohen.

SOURCE. Newport Historical Society Library, Lopez Letters.

New York, 27th November, 1774.

Mr. Aaron Lopez.
Respected Sir:

Permit me to address this sheet to you as a testimony of my gratitude for the kind, the hospitable treatment received of you whilst at your place, and the indulgencies allowed me under your blessed roof.

Conscious of my own unworthiness, I scarcely dare presume on this liberty, but convinced of your natural good disposition, your benevolence, your affability and humanity to all who have the honor of your acquaintance, [I] am encouraged to proceed, even in opposition to my own reason, entirely following the genuine dictates of my inclinations, those at present must not think to mention; therefore very unwillingly omit them.

Hard state, indeed, where a man dare not act agreable to his will when founded on the most solid bassis of virtue, of honor. However, trusting to the most benign Creator, am yet in hopes he will, from the many marks of his clemency alredy experienced, one day bless me with what my heart most earnestly desires. All I pray of him at present is to grant me fortitude to resist the ills of life and health to persevere in every necessary occupation. Time may effect what all human power is incapable of.

May you, most worthy sir, in conjunction with your amiable deserving spouse, be ever exempted from all the calamities of this transient state, the only sublunary happiness man can possess, and may you long enjoy that serenity of temper you now have, so essentially necessary to conduct us thro' life, free from the cares, the vicissitudes of fortune. May your children live to be a comfort and happiness to you in old age, and may your days be spent in every earthly felicity, is the sincere prayer of, respected sir,

Your much obliged well-wisher and very humble servant,
Gershom Seixas

No. 14   Samuel Jacobs Fiddles and Reads Plays—1778

Samuel Jacobs (d. 1786), probably an Alsatian Jew, had come to Canada with the British troops, as a sutler or as an army purveyor, during the French and Indian War. He transported his wares on his own schooner. When Quebec and Montreal were captured by the British (1759–60), Jacobs decided to remain in the conquered province and, making the transition from army to civilian supply, became a general merchant.

Some time after the conquest of Canada, Jacobs settled in St. Denis on the Richelieu, north of Lake Champlain, where he operated a country store. The language of his letters is often better suited to the barracks than to the countinghouse. It is something of a shock, therefore, to find in the following letter that Jacobs was a fiddler and a reader of plays.

Jacobs' correspondent, Jer. [emiah?] Fish, was probably an officer of the British forces. At the time the following letter was written, Jacobs was a British commissary, doing business with many officers and outfits. The vermilion which Fish sought was intended probably for the Indians who fought on the side of the English and harried the American frontier.

SOURCE. Public Archives of Canada, Ottawa, Samuel Jacobs Letters.

January 28, 1778

Dear Jacobs:

I was extreamly sorry [that] the hurry we left St. Dennis in prevented me [from] doing myself the pleasure of seeing you before I set off. I would be obliged to you to let me know how much I am indebted to you per bearor, and will take the first opportunity of sending it to you. My servant brought away your fiddle in a mistake, but will take care of it for you.

You remember I was speaking to you about a small bag of vermillion. I would be glad you'd send me one and set it down with the rest. I send you by the bearor the salmon I promised you and a book of plays. If you have read the others you may give them to the man.

I am, dear Jacobs,

Yours sincerely,
Jer. Fish

This is a miserable place we are in. Therefore, Captain Dobin and I would be much obliged to you if you could send us some mutton, beef, veal, or any provission you can get.

No. 15   Isaac M. Seixas Exchanges Gossip with Aaron Lopez—1779

War has its own way of scattering people and of further disrupting the uneven tenor of life. When the British took Newport in December, 1776, the Whigs left. Aaron Lopez made his headquarters ultimately at Leicester, Massachusetts, and Isaac Seixas fled to Stratford, Connecticut.

Seixas (1709–80) was a native of Lisbon and came to New York via England and Barbados in the 1730's. Although he had some aristocratic pretensions, he married into the less aristocratic but more wealthy Levy-Franks family. (Some of the Frankses were not happy about the marriage.)

Isaac Seixas was a merchant who was never particularly successful and lived off and on in New York and Newport. He reared a large family. Gershom, one of his sons and the rabbi of Shearith Israel, joined his father in exile when the British marched into New York City. On January 27, 1779, another son, Benjamin, married Zipporah Levy, the daughter of Hayman Levy, the Indian trader. The marriage took place in Philadelphia, the Whig capital, where everyone was congregating in those days. Gershom went there to perform the marriage, carrying with him a letter from Mrs. Aaron

Lopez to her husband, who was then in Philadelphia seeking to regain some of his ships seized by unscrupulous American privateers. This is the background of the following letter of Isaac Seixas to Aaron Lopez.

SOURCE. Newport Historical Society Library, Lopez Letters.

Stratford, February 2d, 1779.

Dear Sir:

Your most welcome favour under date January 18th received by the post, and was, you may be assured, extremely rejoiced that you was safely arrived there the day before and had your health, which I sincerely wish you, and every other blessing. We are all here well.

Mrs. Seixas and family devoutly join with me in our respectfull salutations to you, and affectionate congratulations on the happy birth of your grandson, and the welfare of his amiable mother, praying the Lord he may live to be the joy of his worthy parents, as well to your self and all his dear relations.

Good Mrs. Lopez honoured me with her command to forward a letter to you, which accordingly I did by our son Gershom, and hope you have received it, as we are imformed by his letter to his wife, he arrived at Philadelphia the 20th ulto. at night. I did not flatter my self he could over take you as you had so much the start of him.

My gratefull thanks are due for your kind, friendly, and honourable expressions concerning our dear son Benjamin, and your hearty wishes for his happiness. We hope he was last Wenesday made so with his lovely bride, and we bessech the Allmighty may be pleased to bestow his binediction on the happy couple, and grant that you may live to see all yours in the same state, and to sit like olive branches round your paternall table for ages innumerable.

The last letter I had the honour to recieve from the best of friends, your most worthy and venerable father in law, Mr. Jacob Revera [Rivera], was dated the 22d January, when I was made happy in being assured by him all the family was well, which hope will be confirmed by this day's post.

I heartely wish you a prosperous success in your law suit and every other undertaking, and a safe return to your own house, in the way to which we hope, if you take the Stratford Road, to be honoured with your most aggreable company for some time, in doing which you will add to the many favours already received by, dear sir,

Your sincere friend and most obedient, humble servitor,

Isaac Seixas

Excuse bad writing.
Mr. Aaron Lopez.

No. 16   Samuel Jacobs, Jr.: Problem Child—1780–1785

Samuel Jacobs (d. 1786), a merchant of St. Denis, Quebec, Canada, desired that his children receive a good education, which was impossible in the little country village. Two of his daughters were sent to the Ursuline convent in Quebec, while one of his sons, Samuel Jr., boarded at the home of Elias Salomon and studied at the private school of John Reid in Quebec.

On November 2, 1780, Salomon billed Jacobs for the son's board and lodging. Since the boy was growing up, Salomon told Jacobs that he would have to raise his charges and suggested that Samuel's allowance be increased. Young Jacobs, then sixteen years of age, was allowed sixpence a week (Document A).

Salomon and Jacobs quarreled over the bill, and, probably early in 1781, Samuel was removed from Salomon's care and placed in the hands of Reid. On December 3, 1781, however, Reid asked Jacobs to remove his son because he had committed a burglary (Document B).

In another letter sent the same day the merchant Charles Grant, a friend of the family, who had been keeping a watchful eye on Samuel Jr., informed Jacobs that the boy was running wild and warned that something had to be done (Document C). The father took Grant into his confidence and, in a letter written in February of the following year, rather pathetically commended his son to Grant's care, adding a postscript for the wayward youth (Document D).

That Reid was prevailed upon to give the boy another chance is indicated in Document E, Reid's bill for the period from May 1 to July 15, 1782.

Evidently the family attributed Samuel's downfall to Elias Salomon, who, on October 16, 1782, was induced to sign a promise to leave the boy severely alone (Document F).

About two months later Jacobs informed William Grant, a friend, that the prodigal son had returned penitent and had been received back into the bosom of the family (Document G). All's well that ends well—for the time being.

After almost three years, young Samuel, under the prodding of his critical father, determined to try his luck in Jamaica. The last two documents (H and I), letters from Samuel to his father, written before his departure for the West Indies and telling of his plans, are touching. Although the boy was twenty-one by this time, he was not very grown up. To his aggressive and shrewd father the son must have been a sore disappointment.

SOURCE. Public Archives of Canada, Samuel Jacobs Papers.

A [NO. 16]

Quebec, 2d November, 1780.

Mr. Samuel Jacobs.
Dear Sir:

You have [herewith] inclosed the account of your son, S. Jacobs', amounts to £69 2s. 8d. currency, which when examined and found right, should be obliged to you for the amount. I should have write to you sooner, but expected to have had the pleasure of seeing you in Quebec when I would have been able to explained my sentiments to you better. You'l observe, the board I charge you is much under the current prices of this place, and likewise should wish to observe that as your son is grower [growing] larger than smaller, you'l will naturally emagine I shall expect more, and also the care taking by me and my wife ought to be considered by you.

Your son, Jacob[s], is much grown; nay, indeed, almost to the size of a man. As such, I think the allowance I have hitherto allowed him of 6d. per week for pocket money is much to little, as it's naturally to be expected that a youth of his age is desirous of having a few shillings in his pocket at his own disposal. You'l please write me what sum you think proper to be allowed him for the future.

My wife and two daughters join with me in compliments to you.
I am, dear sir,

Your most humble servant,
Elias Salomon

B [NO. 16]

Quebec, 3d December, 1781.

Sir:

It is with real concern that I am constrained to inform you of a recent circumstance in your son's conduct which obliges me to request that he may be immediately removed from my family. The dissipated turn of mind he has lately given into has prompted him to commit an action which really shocks me to mention.

On Tuesday night last, the house of Mr. Solomon, of this place, was broke open, and a watch discovered to have been stolen therefrom. In the course of a few days, the watch in question was seen in the possession of a person who declared that he had purchased of your son. Upon examining farther into the matter and desiring to know how he came by it, the boy made an ample confession, declaring that he himself was the person who broke open the house and stole the watch.

I need not, sir, aggravate your feelings by pointing out the extreme danger there is of the unhappy youth's falling a victim to public justice should he remain any longer in this place, where, nothwithstanding every effort of mine to reclaim him, he has connected himself in such a chain of acquaintance as must necessarily prove his ruin.

This inclines me to request that you would come down here with all convenient speed and concert some plan for the boy's future destination, as well as to accommodate the affair with Mr. Solomon, who seems inclined to prosecute.

I have endeavoured for your sake, as well as the young man's, to keep the matter as much as possible a secret, that a chance may be still given him to reclaim. My friend, Mr. Grant, will write you by this post, and, I believe, agrees with me in judging your presence here indispensibly necessary.

I am, with much esteem, sir,

Your most obedient, humble servant,
J. Reid

Mr. Samuel Jacobs.

C [NO. 16]

Quebec, 3d December, 1781.

Dear Sir:

I am exceedingly sorry to have occasion to write to you on a subject which must be so disagreeable to a feeling parent. Your son Sam has contracted a set of acquaintance here which soon must prove his ruin, if not immediately removed out of the place.

Last week he commited an act of so horrid a nature that Mr. Ried came and consulted me on the point in question, which Mr. Ried at my desire wrote to you the particulars of by this day's post. I am convinced Mr. Ried paid every attention to his morals and had a watchful eye over his conduct, but, of late, it has been discovered that young Samuel got out in the night time, when the family were all at rest, and indulged his vicious inclinations amongst his idle acquaintances.

It is now so near post hours that I have only time to inform you your daughters are well, and that I remain, with great regard, dear sir,

Your sincere friend,
Charles Grant

Mr. Samuel Jacobs.

D [NO. 16]

Worthy Sir, and the most generous of friends:

Your esteemed faveur revived our drooping spirits to find their are hopes in that unhappie boy. I did my duty, left the sole management of him to Mr. Reid, and had he but once hinted that the youth inclined to bad company or frequented Mr. Solomon's, I might have prevented the thunder clap that distroys our queite [quiet], for when we come to a certain age, our joyes consistes only in laying a foundation for the welfare of those that are near and tender to us. You, my friend, knows the world. Idleness in youth is the fore runner of mischeif. Let us request on our knees your friendly protection. Manage him as you please, and receive for thanks the prayers of a fond mother, a tender father, and his help less children. My heart is full, stops me from dictating. There is hope in relying on him [Charles Grant] to whom I and my family ever am in gratitude bound, dear sir,

Yours sincerly to command,
[Samuel Jacobs]

St. Dinnis, 15th February, 1782.

N. B. To obey my friend in saying some thing to the anhappie boy, the lines under neath are for his perusal, if you think proper. (Mr. Grant's letter sent per favour of Mr. Suiter.)

St. Dennis, 15th February, 1782.

Mr. Sam:

I was your father and did my duty. Your conduct has made it void and null. If your future behaviour merits every good man's esteem and pity, your past folly [and] repentance opens your eyes, I then with joy and tenderness will own you again as my child. Till then I am only your well wisher.

[Samuel Jacobs]

E [NO. 16]

Mr. Samuel Jacobs to John Reid, Dr.
For boarding and educating his son from

1st May to 15th July, 1782	£8	6s.	8d.
1 new beaver hat	1	15	
1 ruler and pencil		2	6
7 pair fine thread stockings [@] 7s. 6d. ..	2	12	6
2 pair shoes @ 11s. 8d.	1	3	4
Paid for making 12 stocks		12	6

Writing books, pens, and ink		5	9
Washerwoman's bill	1	18	4

Currency	£16	16s.	7d.

F [NO. 16]

I, Elias Solomon, of Quebec, merchant, do hereby bind and oblige myself towards Mr. Samuel Jacobs of St. Dennis, merchant, as follows, vizt.:

That I, the said Elias Solomon, shall not hereafter, on any account or under any pretence whatsoever, either harbour, or advance, or furnish any money, goods, or effects, or other things whatsoever to Samuel Jacobs, Junior, son of the said Mr. Samuel Jacobs. Neither shall I be any wise accessary to any other persons harbouring or advancing any moneys, goods, or effects, or other things to the said Samuel Jacobs, Junior.

Dated at Quebec this sixteenth of October, one thousand seven hundred and eighty two.

Elias Salomon

Passed in the presence of J. Blackwood, Robert Russell

G [NO. 16]

St. Dinnas, 18th December, 1782.

Worthey Friend:

Your favour of 8th instant was delivered me by my son Sam in an humble poster [posture], holding out your letter. . . . Nature overcame resilution, and I took him to my arms. He is very sorrowful and seems to repent past follies. He has been neglected by Mr. Read and [had] no person to look after him or advise him for his good tel [till] you took him under your friendly care.

I asked Sam what he intended to do now, as there was no time to be lost. He answered, if he was under your care to write [become a clerk] in your office, he was shure to learn and improve himself. His reply gave me satisfaction, and to make him the fitter, will endeavour to get a French school master here for the winter, as it seems you have no present accation [occasion] for him. But should you at any time incline to take him under your protection, where he may receive your friendly instruction, I will with pleasure send him [to] you at a moment's warning, and think my self very happy to have him plased under your eye.

Mrs. Jacobs joyns in her kindest acknowlegement with him who is, dear sir,

Yours sincerely,
[Samuel Jacobs]

The Honourable Wm. Grant, Esq., at St. Helen, Montreal.

H [NO. 16]

St. Dennis, 14th September, 1785.

Honoured Sir:

As I see you have no more buisiness for me at present, and [as] I want to be in a way of getting my livelihood, the soonner I go off the better it will be. Would be very sorry to propose this, if I thought that you, or the family, would want me. But as you proposed your self for my departure, if you think proper to procure a passage, as I believe there is vessels going off to the place where you mentioned, I should be happy to go, as I am certain I'll have friends there in a short time by my good behaviour, and shall often peruse they [the] good advise you have given me.

I am certain you will not be sorry for my departure when you'll hear of my welfair, and shall try to be in buisiness for my o[w]n account as soon as possible. Should I tell you the reason, you would laugh at my wakeness [weakness], but still is the only recourse [?] that can make me happy. Shall say no more on the subject. I am, and shall ever be,

Your most effectionate and dutiful son till death,

Samuel Jacobs

Mr. Samuel Jacobs,
Present [in this city].

I [NO. 16]

Quebec, 30 October, 1785.

Mr. Samuel Jacobs, Merchant,
St. Denis.

Honored Father and Mother:

This is to let you know that I am to go to Jamaica as they [the] vessel is bound their [there], commanded by Captain Garnner, which he sales [sails] to day or to morrow. Mr. Fraser and Dalton agreed for my passage, which a mounts to twenty guineas. I think it is a high price; I said nothing to them about it.

Mr. Fraser, he is to give me a letter, and yours to him inclosed in it, for Mr. Grant, a capital merchant, and the Chief Justice's brother of that place, which he is an intimate acquaintance of yours, as they say, and has been a merchant here. . . .

Now, my dear father, I take fare well of you and of the family, which, I hope to God, I shall see you and them again in good health, but God knows when. Let me be where I am, or in what station I shall be, you shall here of me by every opportunity and shall all ways be happy to hear of my loved parents, and I hope I shall deserve their attention, as I shall do nothing but what is becoming of a gentleman.

I hope this voyage will make a man of me. But, my dear father, do remember your dutiful son (that wishes all they happiness to you and to my dear and tender mother), which I hope shall be all ways in your good openion. Cannot help to make my self some reproches to see that I have been such an expence and I have been so little use. The time past ca[nnot] be recalled. I hope the future it will be [better?], as I go upon a good desire, and hope there is no fear of one that wance [wants] to do well, and [h]as the fear of God before him.

You shall here more of me when I'll arrive to Jamaica, which I hope I will. My love to my sisters and brothers. Now, my dear father and mother, fare well again, and do remember

Your most effectionate and dutifull son till death,
Samuel Jacobs

No. 17   Tory Social Life in Occupied New York—1781

David Franks, the son of Jacob Franks, was one of the earliest Jews to settle in Philadelphia. There he married into a well-known Gentile family and moved in the highest social circles. When the Revolutionary War broke out, Franks, at that time a very successful merchant, maintained his loyalty to the Crown. At various times charges were preferred against him by the Pennsylvania and Continental authorities, and finally he was banished into the British lines. When he went into exile in New York City in December, 1780, his daughter Rebecca, a brilliant, witty, but somewhat flighty young lady of about twenty-one, went with him.

During the Tory occupation of Philadelphia in 1777 and 1778, Rebecca had been among the best-known members of the younger social set, and when the great fete of the *Mischianza* was staged there on May 18, 1778, she was one of the outstanding participants. However, her wings were clipped when the Americans returned to Philadelphia and tried her father for corresponding with the enemy.

In the Tory-occupied New York of 1781 Rebecca was again in her element. A number of her letters from that period are extant. The one printed below was sent to her sister Abigail (Mrs. Andrew) Hamilton 3d and bears the pseudonym "Emma," but there is hardly any question concerning its authorship. Rebecca may have used the pseudonym, as well as initials to refer to her friends, in order to confuse the Whigs, should the letter fall into their hands. "Woodlands," the home of Abby Hamilton, was then in Whig territory.

The note shows that food, letters, and other messages were constantly being shuttled between the American and British lines. In the breezy and breathless gossip of its pages there is a vivid reflection of the social life of the wealthy Tories of New York City.

Less than six months after the date of the letter Rebecca married Lieutenant Colonel Henry Johnson, of the Seventeenth Foot Regiment. Her grandfather Jacob Franks (d. 1769), an observant Jew, was bitterly opposed to intermarriage; her father David, an indifferent Jew, had married out of the faith, and Rebecca went to church as a Christian.

SOURCE. Massachusetts Historical Society Library, Boston, Livingston II Papers.

Broad Way, Monday, July 23d, 1781.

Mrs. Andrew Hamilton,
Corner 3d and Wallnut Streets,
Philadelphia.
Dear Abby:
You'll think I live at General R.[obertson's] as the three last times I've wrote I have been going there, and the same to day. He knows the town is hot and disagreable, and is good enough to make parties for us every week by way of refreshmint.

We go in Captain Elphinston's barge. I wish I could introduce him to your acquaintance. You would, I am sure, agree with me in thinking him as agreable a young man as you ever knew. You may remember seeing some letters of his in the Philadelphia papers, about the little *quail,* wrote with great humour. 'Tis just as he talks. I regret that his duty will oblige him to leave us very shortly, as we seldom now adays meet with such rational animals.

If I do not write to the girls [my nieces], tell them 'tis not for want of inclination but time. Nothing give me so much pleasure as when my time is imployed in their service.

I am sorry you did not see Nairn. We hear he is going to Boston. I hope he'll recieve my letter first. B.B. and your letter wrote by B.L., I recieved yesterday. I can't think where they have lain all this while, as I received one (from you and B.L. of the 13th and 15th of this month) last week.

A note from General R., disapointed of a chaperon. Of course, we do not go, as here a single lady never appears without one. We Philadelphians, knowing no harm, feared none and never looked for a married lady. But here the case is different, and I am in an ill humour, tho that you'll know and say is too often the case.

But the agreable Captain, or the Warwick shire Lad, is come, and even he can't alter my temper, but, on the contrary, makes the disapointment greater as he tells me the handsome Captain Montague is to be of the party.

Papa's come in and sais he thinks where ever he goes, we may; and as our enclinations are the same, we readily agreed and off we've sent the Warwick shire Lad to let the General know we've changed our minds.

You'll wonder who I mean by we. Cornelia Van Horn has been with me this week past. I wish Andrew [your husband] knew her; she'd make him laugh by the hour. As she's looking over me, I'll say she's a monstrous fool. You'll know how to take me, as females all ways go by contrarys. She wants to know who Andrew is, and is sure I am beging for a remission of my sins, or I'd never address an *Abby*.

Adieu. Tell Mrs. Swift Mrs. I. is well; I heard from there yesterday. Billy A. I gave the letter to yesterday. He was here just as I recieved it. Tell B. H. he can't wish more for my company at his *teas* then [than] I do to be at them. One party at the W-d L-ds ["Woodlands"] would make me happy for a month. I'd skim the *cream* and leave the milk for vulgar minds. (I had nearly forgot how to spell cream.) The crackers and ham not yet arrived. When I write to the [blank], I'll not forget you. R. Marston again abroad, but Heathcote still confined.

Adieu, ma chere seour ["Good-by, my dear sister"]. Love attend you all.

Tell Mrs. R. I was again at church yesterday. Yellow Peter . . . [a Negro messenger?] is now talking with Papa. He came in a few weeks ago, and white Peter came in last week. He sais he was at your house a few days before he left Philadelphia, but did not tell you he was coming.

Tell Mento her news of Flora I can, with pleasure, contradict. Thank God, she has no such thoughts. Let Mr. Amid know all his family are well. Mrs. Armstrong moved for the summer to Bedford [Westchester County] a Friday, where I intend paying her a visit very soon. Thursday I go to Flat Bush for a few days.

Once more, adieu. Let not fears of any kind disturb your peace. We know none.

July the . . . th. In spite of all things, we [had] a delightfull day yesterday. The Capt. Montague is charming. Such eyes! [But] I haven't time to expatiate. Tell the girls I wish't for them: three honourables, one with 26 thousand [pounds] a year. A Major Demerson, of 2d Milton's, I last night had a letter from. He was well the 18th of this month and in good spirits.

Adieu, the bearer waits.

Emma.

No. 18   Joseph M. Myers Loses His Temper and Apologizes—1781

Joseph M. Myers was a very prominent Mason and took an active part in the affairs of that order in several states during the Revolutionary period. A merchant by occupation, he was closely associated with Michael Gratz, the Philadelphia merchant and fur trader. The two were probably partners in joint ventures in Virginia for a while, but even friends can fall out where money is concerned. Bitter words were exchanged between them, and Gratz sued Myers.

In the following letter Myers made his apologies to Gratz, begged him to withdraw the suit, and promised to settle the differences.

SOURCE. The Library Company of Philadelphia.

Philadelphia, 16 September, 1781.

Mr. Michael Gratz, Present [in this city]
Sir:

I some time since wrote your brother Barnard from Lancaster, acknowledgeing the pain our unfortunate quarrel gave me, and offered at the same time to give you every gentleman like sattisfaction, and that I would discharge the note in dispute as soon as I am in cash.

I am now goeing down the countery to dispose of some goods, and hope shortly to have it in my power to settle our matters to your sattisfaction. Be ashured that I am sorry my passion carried me to the lenghts it did, and I hope, when you consider I had provacation, and that we ware on the most brotherly footing prior to that unhappy dispute, that you will forget what is passed, and that there will be no farther anemosity between us.

I must take the liberty to reminde you that I am goeing down the countery, and that it will be a great dittirement [detriment] to my affaires to be obliged to attend court. I therefore solicet that you will withdraw your suit against me, and I will order some person to discharge the costs of court.

I am, sir,

Your most humble servant,
Joseph M. Myers

P.S. I will be much obliged to you if you favour me with an answer before I go out of town, which I purpose to do at three o'clock this afternoone.

No. 19   Samuel Jacobs' Daughters—1781–1786

Samuel Jacobs, the St. Denis merchant, had several daughters. One of them, Marie-Geneviève, a former student at the Ursuline convent in Quebec, had left school and was staying with the family of Charles Grant. Her younger sister, Marie-Anne, was a student at the convent in 1781. In December of that year a Scotsman named Bryce M. Cumming, a friend of Jacobs but not of the nuns, wrote to Jacobs and advised him to remove Marie-Anne from the care of the religious (Document A).

In June, 1783, Jacobs received a formal letter from an officer on duty with the Brunswick German mercenaries who were fighting for the British. In his note the officer asked for the hand of Jacobs' daughter in marriage (Document B). The letter fails to state the girl's name; it referred probably to Marie-Geneviève.

About seven weeks later Jacobs received a letter from Nathaniel Day, a commissary officer and Jacobs' superior. (During the Revolution the St. Denis merchant went back to his old job as an army supplyman.) Day suggested that Jacobs come to Quebec, for his daughter needed him. Day suspected that there was a man in the offing (Document C).

Three years later another crisis occurred in the young lady's life (if it was the same daughter). In July, 1786, Polly (Marie-Geneviève) wrote a letter to her father, indicating that she was in great distress. There had obviously been a conflict between her and her father with respect to her marriage. Polly apparently wanted to marry a Captain Stanislaus Vigneau. Papa said "No," and he meant it, for his will provided that she was to be cut off with one shilling if she married this man (Document D). There is reason to believe that she married him.

SOURCE. Public Archives of Canada, Samuel Jacobs Papers.

A [NO. 19]

Dear Jacobs:

I have a very great regard for your oldest daughter because she is like her mother, and I have still as mouch regard for your second, because she is like you. I don't think you mean to make her a nun. Therefor must beg that you would give orders to those that has the care of her to lett her come out at least once a week. She wishes it mouch herselfe. And I think it would be of services to her. The alteration is so mouch for the bettor in your oldest daughter since she went to Mrs. Grant, that I think if you once seed her, that you would never think of confining your second [daughter] amongest a parcel of d——d idle, usles [useless] b——tchs! Since her sister went out, they won't so mouch as lett her speak to any body at the grate, and I am affriad that the litle creator [creature] will break her heart.

My old woman would take it very kind if you would send orders for her to have leave to come out and stay with her for the holy days. You may depend on her being well taken care off. If you are so kind as grant this request, it will be estaimed a favour; and if you come to Quebec, I hope you will give us a call.

I am sorry to inform you that I don't think your frind Charles Grant is in a good state of health. His close attendance at his warff all summer, and offten standing with wate [wet] feet, has not been of service to him. I hope you'll find the gentleman of the 44 [regiment] agreeable neghtbours, and begs my best respects to them all, not forgetting good Mrs. Jacobs. And beleave me to be with estaime,

Your very humble servant,
Bryce M. Cumming

Quebec, 9 December, 1781.

B [NO. 19]

Sorel, June 10th, 1783.

Sir:

You will certainly find it extraordinary to be addressed by a person who has not the pleasure [of] a particular acquaintance with you, the more [so] as this letter is written upon no common subject of a very intresting nature. But a character [as] plain and honest as yours will not look upon m[ere] forms, but disregard trifles if after mature del[iberation] he finds the matter worth his attention.

For this reason, I will defer my apologie untill [a] personal conversation gives me a better opportunity. Though not personally known to you, sir (if you except a few times I called at your house du[ring] my stay in the province), I flatter my self that my person and character [are] as well known and established as any gentleman['s] ought to be, that would make a proposal like [that] I am going to make to you, sir.

The personal accomplishments joined to the be[auty and] education of your eldest daughter have procu[red] her a general estime, and are inducements enough to desire her person as a partner for life. If you, sir, will intrust me with her hand, I shall study to make her as happy as her many good qualitys deservent.

I do not mean, nor could I with propriety expect, a decisive answer upon such a proposal. A further acquaintance after such an explication will be necessary to decide upon a matter of such consequence. If a fair character, a respectable rang [rank] in the world, and an honest intention to make your daughter happy can have any weight with you, I will give you convincing proofs that anything less as interested views have directed my choice.

Give me leave, sir, to add a few words more. If you are yet pertial for your country, I am a countryman of yours, but equally versed in the English, French, and German languages. My present employment in the army I am tired of, and as I intend to remain in the province, I shall, either as a lawyer or as a civil officer under goverment, appear in a light you should perhaps your daughter wish to see in. I should not desire her hand if I could not give her my own in a public character.

I am not rich, but have no debts and a few thousand livres in my pocket. I love a quiet country life if my circumstances would allow, and therefore, do not care for riches myself. If you, sir, have no *particular reason* to decline any further explanation upon the subiect, I wish you would only let me know what time I can have the pleasure of a personal conversation with you, should the first be the case. I trust to your hon[our] and well-known honesty, you will be pleased to remit this letter into my hands.

I am, with particular estime, sir,

Your most obedient, humble servant,
Sinet [Signed] Charles Thomas,
Judge Advocate of the Brunswick Troops

[Answer]

St. Denis, 11 June, 17[83].

Sir:

I was favoured with your esteemed [letter] of the 10 instant. If a[ny] time your buisiness lies this way, should be glad to take a cheerful glass with you *an [en] passant*. I am, with respect, sir,

Your most humble and obedient servant,
[Samuel Jacobs]

C [NO. 19]

Quebec, 31st July, 1783.

Dear Sir:

Calling Tuesday last at friend Charles Grant's, Miss Jacobs followed me to the door and told me she should be glad to see her father. Seeing her in some emotion, I asked if any person had been talking to her of marriage or [had been] rude to her. She answered No, but something else that made her uneasey, on which occation she would be glad to see her father, and I promised her to write this letter in order to apprise you of her wish. And if you thought it required your presence for the good of your child, you have my leave to come down, as I am certain you will leave things at St. Dennis in such a manner as the service cannot be hurt by your absence.

I remain, with my best compliments to Mrs. Jacobs and family, dear sir,

Your sincere friend and humble servant,
Nathaniel Day

Mr. Samuel Jacobs.

D [NO. 19]

St. Dennis, 6 July, 1786.

Dearest Father:

It would give me undoubted gratuity [gratitude] could I speak to you reather than to write, but I am in such a situation that it would be impossible for me to tell you what my heart suscribes. Let me then, with cander and truth and the help of the education you have given me, request of you the tenderness to look on your poor Polly as your child, to give your blessing, not your curse, on such occasion as present. It is true I have acted in this affair very ill in not telling you my mind, but as I suffer by your taking all away from me, don't make me misarable by rejecting me as not your child.

Lett me with the greatest sincerity assure the [you], it is not [from] in gratitude [ingratitude], nor for want of love for you, that I marry. Be persuaded that it is the sincere love I have for him. Lett me implore your good wishes—on my knees I begs it of you—and be persuaded, if ever I am happy, it will be by your blessing. This is all I want, and was it to be refused, then I am mesarable indeed. And one thing more, is that you must think and beleive me sincere, for it comes from my heart and soul. And if I am so happy as to posses[s] what my heart wishes, that is your benediction, then you shall see your poor Polly as happy as it is possible to be in this world. I ask your pardon for all the antiety [anxiety] I have put you in since that affair. I can't say no more—my heart is too full—but this, that I am and shall for ever be

Your sincere and loving daughter till death, and

Your very humble servant,
P. Jacobs

No. 20   Celery in Lieu of Radishes—1781

Colonial families, even though they were many miles apart, were neighborly. Samuel Jacobs, of St. Denis, Canada, sent the following friendly note to Uriah Judah, a Montreal merchant. There are no more horse-radishes. Won't you accept some celery? And can we expect you here this winter?

SOURCE. Public Archives of Canada, Samuel Jacobs Papers.

St. Dennis, 18th December, 1781.

Dear Sir:

Pray be pleased to excuse me to Mrs. Judah for not being able to send her some horse raddishes. The gardner, not having collected so many as he expected, planted a new bed with the remainder, to produce more next year. Make our kindest respects agreable. Hopes she will favour us on exceipting [accepting] fifty bundles of sallery [celery]. Shan't we have the pleasure our beating up [of your being up at] our quarters this winter?

Mrs. Jacobs joins in her complements with, dear sir,

Yours sincerely to command,
[Samuel Jacobs]

Mr. Uriah Judah, Montreal.

No. 21   The "Resurrection" of Samuel Jacobs—1782

Charles Grant, the son of a Scottish laird, was a well-known and respected Quebec merchant. In 1780 he wrote a report on the fur trade for Governor Frederick Haldimand.

Grant and Samuel Jacobs, the St. Denis merchant, were very good friends. Hence it was a shock to the former when he heard that Jacobs had passed away. But, as we shall see from the following letter, the report was "greatly exaggerated."

SOURCE. Public Archives of Canada, Samuel Jacobs Papers.

Quebec, 29th April, 1782.

Mr. Samuel Jacobs, Merchant,
St. Denis, River Chambly.
Dear Jacobs:

With great pleasure I always received your letters, but you never wrote one to me that gave me so much satisfaction as the last of the 17th instant. A few days before I got that letter, a Mr. Hollowell, from Montreal, came down here and reported in town that poor Jacobs was no more. On hearing of this report, I immediately sent out to know the fact from himself. He returned me for answer that you dyed on Friday, the 12th of this month, that he had the accounts of it from Uriah Judah before he left Montreal.

When he geve me his authority, I began to consider how little confidence ought to be put in the author as well as the bearer of the news. Of course, I set it down as a palpable falsehood. At same time, I was not a little alarmed at the probability of the report, knowing the situation I left you in. Now you may judge how happy I was in receiving on Friday last your letter above mentioned and an other letter from you of the 20th to Mr. [John] Blackwood, which came to hand yesterday, by which all my fears about you are removed; and I hope you will not alarm me again on like occasion and in like manner for these twenty years to come. After that you may take your departure in peace and cost no person a thought about the matter. . . .

Your children here are all well. None of them heard any thing concerning you but Samuel, on whom, I am told, the report had no small effect. Your letter to [Elias] Solomon I delivered and advised him to trouble you with no more of his letters till you come down. His claim on you [for boarding your son Samuel] I would have discharged long ago, but as my doubts about the justness of his demands are not cleared up, I will let the matter stand as it is till you enquire into the merits of it yourself.

After four weeks' confinement with bealed breasts [tumors], my wife [the former Jane Holmes] got out of her room for the first time only yesterday. She joins me in compliments, etc., and I remain always

Your sincere friend,
Charles Grant

No. 22 "We Are Delivered from a Cursed, Proud Nation"—1783

On April 15, 1783, Congress ratified the provisional treaty of peace with Great Britain. By April 20 the news had reached Charlestown, South Carolina, and Sheftall Sheftall (1762–1847), a veteran of the Revolutionary War, sent the good tidings to Savannah to his father Mordecai Sheftall (1735–97), one of the patriot leaders of Georgia.

Sheftall Sheftall had been his father's deputy during the Revolution and, although only sixteen years of age, had served as an assistant commissary of issues. In 1780, as a lad of eighteen, he was put in charge of a mercy ship, the flag-of-truce sloop *Carolina Packett,* which carried money for the relief of the imprisoned General William Moultrie and his soldiers in British-held Charlestown. Obviously Sheftall Sheftall was an able young man, but the promise of his youth was never fulfilled. He became an attorney but achieved no distinction. As an old man he lived in the memory of past glories; one of the last survivors of the Revolution, he was known in Savannah as "Cocked Hat Sheftall."

Included in the son's note were reports of all the ships that had come to town. Reporting ship arrivals was not idle gossip; it was important for merchants to know what boats were in or due to arrive. Peace would flood the American markets with goods; war prices would collapse; inventories would lose much of their value—and the Sheftalls were merchants.

SOURCE. The Mr. and Mrs. B. H. Levy Collection of Sheftall Papers, Savannah, Ga.

Charls Town, April 20th, 1783,
Sunday evening, 7 o'clock.

Honored Sir:

Since writing this morning, a packett schooner is arrived from Philadelphia in six days, with official accounts of peace. Inclosed is a hand bill; it will speak of it self. I sincerely congratulate you on the great and happy event. We are delivered from a cursed, proud nation, Britton [Britain].

A vessell arrived here last night from St. Eustatia [West Indies]. There is in this harbour a brig from the port of Embdin [Emden, Germany] and wears the Prussian flag. Fifty sail of vessels are expected here every moment from different places.

A letter is here for you in the post office from Mr. Hollingsworth. It came in the packett. I have been four times for it this afternoon and the man is not att home.

My duty to mama, love to brothers and sisters, and I remain

Your dutifull son,
Sheftall Sheftall

No. 23   "A Jew Broker" Replies—1784

In February, 1784, Robert Morris, one of the founders of the Bank of North America, recorded in his diary that a group of persons, among them Miers Fisher, a Quaker lawyer and former Tory exile, was making an effort to obtain a charter for the Bank of Pennsylvania, a potential competitor of the Bank of North America. Fisher appeared before the Pennsylvania legislature, which then met in Philadelphia, and unsuccessfully sought to obtain the desired charter. Among his arguments on behalf of the proposed bank was the contention that its establishment would reduce the rate of interest, thus protecting the people against the exactions of Jewish brokers.

Fisher's anti-Jewish remark may have been intended as an indirect smear against Robert Morris and the semiofficial Bank of North America, which had received support from Jews. Nor is it improbable that by accusing the Jewish Whigs, Fisher and his associates, most of whom had been Loyalists or neutrals during the Revolution, attempted to exculpate themselves from their Toryism by inciting prejudice against the Jews. This diversionary maneuver was even then a common device of Judaeophobes. By writing against Jews and encouraging others to do so, they directed attention away from themselves and from their guilt. In the same year a Georgian pamphleteer, in all probability a Loyalist, went out of his way to strike at the Jews of that state, most of whom had been Whigs. The anti-Jewish Georgian maintained that the Jews were enemy aliens and hence had no rights in a court of justice.

The Independent Gazetteer of Philadelphia printed the reply of one of the Jews whom Fisher had denounced. In all likelihood the writer, who signed himself "A Jew Broker," was the patriot Haym Salomon. Edwin Wolf 2d and Maxwell Whiteman, in *A History of the Jews of Philadelphia,* have demonstrated that Salomon might well have been aided in his reply by Colonel Eleazer Oswald, the editor of the paper.

SOURCE. *The Independent Gazetteer,* Philadelphia, March 13, 1784.

[March 13, 1784.]

To Miers Fisher, Esquire:

I must address you, in this manner, although you do not deserve it. Unaccustomed as you are to receive any mark of respect from the public, it will be expected that I should make an apology for introducing a character, *fetid* and *infamous,* like yours, to general notice and attention. Your conspicuous *Toryism* and *disaffection* long since buried you in the silent grave of *popular* oblivion and contempt; and your extraordinary conduct and deportment, in several other respects, has brought and reduced you to that dreary dungeon of insignificance, to that gulph of defeated spirits, from which even the powers of *hope* "that comes to all" cannot relieve or better you.

In this most miserable of all situations, principally arising from an obstinate, inflexible perseverance in your political *heresy* and *schism* (so detestable in itself, so ruinous and destructive to our country, and obnoxious to all around us), you are now left quite destitute and forlorn! Unhappy and disappointed man! Once exiled [September, 1777] and excommunicated by the state, *as a sly, insiduous enemy;* severred and detached from the generous bosom of *patriotism* and *public virtue; shunned* and deserted by *faithful friends,* in whom you once so safely trusted; since, debarred and prevented from *your practice* by rule of court as an attorney at the bar; *and excluded* from every other essential and dignified privilege of which the *rest of citizens* can boast—with the wretched remains of a *wrecked* reputation—you exhibit so complete a spectacle of distress and wretchedness, as rather excites one's tenderness than vengeance, and would soften and melt down dispositions more relentless and unforgiving than mine!

But whatever claims of mercy you may demand, on these accounts; whatever I should think, were I to judge of you as your *personal* enemy in *private* respects; yet the *forward* and unexampled advances and steps you have lately taken in the concert of *public* affairs; the high-cockaded air of *fancied* importance you now assume; the petulant, discontented humor you have manifested for establishing *a new bank;* your longings and pantings to approach our *political vineyard,* and blast the fruits of those labors for which you neither *toiled nor spun;* and more particularly, the indecent, unjust, inhumane aspersions, you cast so indiscriminately on the *Jews* of this city at large, in your arguments of Wednesday week, before the honorable legislature of the commonwealth—these circumstances, if my apprehensions are right, preclude you from any lenity or favor, and present you a fair victim and offering to the sacred altar of public justice.

You are not therefore to expect any indulgence, because you merit none. I daresay you experience it not in your own feelings; nor have you any right whatever to hope for the least tenderness from me. You shall not have it; and if you are cut and smarted with the whip and lashes of my reproach and resentments, if I lay my talons and point out the *ingrate,* if my tongue is clamorous of you and *your odious confederates,* and I should pain the tenderest veins of their breasts—remember, you first gave birth to all yourself, that it arose entirely from you; and in tracing of events hereafter to the source you will, perhaps, find to your sorrow and cost that you are only blameable for whatever consequences have or may arise on the occasion.

You not only endeavoured to injure me by your unwarrantable expressions, but every other person of the same *religious* persuasion I hold, and which the laws of the country, and the glorious toleration and *liberty of conscience,* have allowed me to indulge and adopt. The injury is highly crimsoned and aggravated, as there was no proper reason or ground for your invectives. The attack on the *Jews* seemed wanton, and could only have been premeditated by such a base and degenerate mind as yours. It was not owing to the sudden sallies of passion, or to the warmth of a disconcerted and hasty imagination. I cannot, therefore, place it to the account of meer human frailties, in which your *will* and understanding had no concern, and for which I am always disposed to make every compassionate allowance. And though an individual is not obliged to avenge the injuries of particular societies and sectaries [sects] of men, he is nevertheless called upon, by every dear and serious consideration, to speak his mind freely and independently of public transactions and general events, to assert his own share in the public consequence and to act his part fairly on the social theatre.

Permit me, then, with this view of things, to take notice of these terms of reproach and invective which, considering you as a friend to good manners and decorum, you have heaped on our nation [religious group] and profession with so liberal and unsparing a hand. I am a Jew; it is my own nation and profession. I also subscribe myself a broker, and a broker, too, whose opportunities and knowledge, along with other brokers of his intimate acquaintance, in a great course of business, has made him very familiar and privy to every minute design and artifice of your *wiley colleagues* and associates.

I exult and glory in reflecting that we have the honour to reside in a free country where, as a people, we have met with the most generous countenance and protection; and I do not at all despair, notwithstanding former obstacles [the disabilities imposed by the Pennsylvania Constitution of 1776], that we shall still obtain every other privilege that we aspire to enjoy along with our fellow-citizens. It also affords me unspeakable satisfaction, and is indeed one of the most pleasing employments of my thoughtful moments, to contemplate that we have in general been early uniform, decisive Whigs, and were second to none in our patriotism and attachment to our country!

What but Erinnys (the name of the Furies of Hell) itself could have thus tempted you to wander from the common path of things, and go a stray among *thorns and briars*? What were your motives and inducements for introducing the Jews so disrespectfully into your unhallowed and polluted lips? Who are you, or what are you (a meer *tenant at sufferance*, of your liberty), that in a *free* country you dare to trample on any sectary whatever of people? Did you expect to serve yourself, or your friends and confederates [Tories and pacifist Quakers]—these serpents in our bosom, whose poisonous stings have been darted into every *patriot* character among us?

In any other place, in managing another cause, you might have had patience to attend to the consequences of such unpardonable rashness and temerity. But here you thought yourself safe, and at full leave to take the most unlicensed liberties with characters, in regard of whom you can in no respect pretend to vie! You shall yet repent, even *in sackcloth* and *ashes,* for the foul language in which you have expressed yourself. And neither the interposition of some well meant though mistaken Whigs who, I am sorry to think, have joined you, "nor even the sacred shield of cowardice shall protect you," for your transgressions. Who knows but the beams of that very denomination whom you have traduced may, on one day, perhaps not very remote, warm you into the most abject servility, and make you penitentially solemnize what you have done?

An error is easily remedied, and there may be some compensation for actual injuries. But a downright insult can neither be forgiven or forgot, and seldom admits of atonement or reparation. It is our happiness to live in the times of enlightened liberty, when the human mind, liberated from the restraints and fetters of superstition and authority, hath been taught to conceive just sentiments of its own; and when mankind, in matters of *religion,* are quite charitable and benevolent in their opinions of each other.

Individuals may act improperly, and sometimes deserve censure; but it is no less unjust than ungenerous to condemn all for the faults of a few, and reflect generally on a whole community for the indiscretion of some particular persons. There is no body of people but have some exceptionable characters with them; and even your own religious sectary [the Quakers], whom you have compelled me to dissect in the course of this address, are not destitute of *very proper subjects* of criticism and animadversion.

Good citizens who nauseate, and the public who contemn, have heard your invectives against the Jews. Unhappily for you, a long series of enormities have proved you more your own enemy than I am. To you, then, my worthy friends and fellow-citizens (characters teeming with strict candor and disinterestedness), do I turn myself with pleasure from that steril field, from that *Grampian* desart, which hath hitherto employed me.

It is your candor I seek; it is your disinterestedness I solicit. The opinions of *Fisher* and his adherents, whether wilful in their malignity, or sincere in their ignorance, are no longer worthy of my notice. His observations are low; his intentions are too discernable. His whole endeavours centre in one point, namely, to create a *new bank.*

To effect this end, he has spared neither pains or labours. He has said every thing that artifice could dictate, or malice invent. He has betrayed himself in a thousand inconsistencies, and adopted absurdities which, supposing him a man of sense and observation, would have disgraced the lips of an idiot.

And for whom is the new bank meant and intended? For the benefit of men like himself, who have been in general averse and opposed to the war and common cause: for the insurgents against our liberty and independence; for *mercenary* and *artful* citizens, where selfish views are totally incompatible with the happiness of the people; for bifronted political *Janus's*, the meer weathercocks of every breeze and gale that blows.

Who traded with the enemy? Who first depreciated the public currency? Who lent our enemies money to carry on the war? Who were spies and pilots to the British? Who prolonged the war? Who was the cause of so many valuable men losing their lives in the field and *prison-ships*? Who did not pay any taxes? Who has now the public securities in hand? Who would not receive our Continental money? Who has purchased *Burgoyne's* convention bills? Who depreciated the French bills? Who depreciated the bills of the *United States* on Paris? Who slandered the institution of the *Bank* of *North-America*? Who refused taking *bank-notes* when they fi[r]st issued? Who discouraged the people from lodging money in the bank? And are these the characters who talk of instituting a bank for *the good of the public*? Are these the people who want a charter from our legislature? Shall such a bastard progeny of freedom, such jests and phantoms of patriotism and the social virtues be indulged in their wishes? For shame! For shame! Surrender the puerile, the fruitless pretensions! Public honor and public gratitude cry aloud against you, and says, or seems to say, as earnest as your endeavors have been, you shall not have your charter.

From such a *medley* and *group* of characters (an impure nest of vipers, the very *bloodhounds* of our lives and liberties) we have every thing to hazard, and nothing to expect. Suspicion shakes her wary head against them, and experience suggests that the sly, insinuating intrigues and combinations of these persons are to be watched and guarded against as much as possible. Though the *proposals* are generous and captivating, their practices, I will venture to affirm, cannot correspond; and however *fascinating* they may be *in appearance*, their designs are *deep* and *wiley*. With the soft and soothing voice of *Jacob* they may exercise the *hand*, the *hairy* hand of *Esau*!

I shall not inquire whether two banks in a commercial country would not clash with each other, and prove exceeding detrimental and injurious to the community. Having only ventured to give an account of the leading characters who compose the new bank, allow me in conclusion to rectify an error of Mr. Fisher's, who publicly declared, "the Jews were the authors of high and unusual interest." No! The Jews can acquit themselves of this artful imputation, and turn your own batteries on yourself. It was neither the *Jews* or *Christians* that founded the practice, but *Quakers*—and *Quakers* worse than *heathens, pagans,* or *idolaters;* men, though not Jews in *faith,* are yet Jews in *traffic;* men abounding with avarice, *who neither fear God, nor regard man.*

Those very persons who are now flattering themselves with the idea of a new bank, first invented the practise of discounting notes at five per cent. I have retained an alphabetical list of names, as well as the other brokers, and can specify persons, if necessary. In the language of Naphtali [Nathan] to David, I have it in my power to point at the very *would-be* directors, and say: *"Thou art the man."* I can prove that it were these people, unwilling to venture money in trade during the war, who first declined letting out money on the best mortgage and bond security.

Were they now gratified in their expectations, would they not display the same undue spirit and degrade the dignity of a bank with practices unbecoming a common broker? Is it not in their power to finess at the bank, and refuse discounting notes on purpose to gripe [harm] the necessitous part of the people, and extort improper premiums out of doors [secretly]? And have we not reason to expect this would be the case?

A Jew Broker

No. 24 Moses Michael Hays Introduces Paul Revere—1789

Moses Michael Hays (1739–1805) left his native New York and settled in Newport about 1769. He was a merchant and shipper but had little success. When the Revolution broke out, he, like other Newport Whigs, had to leave. He spent some time in Philadelphia, one of the few large cities still in the hands of the patriots. By 1782 he was in Boston, where he remained for the rest of his life. Although one of the great cities of the country, Boston did not have a permanent Jewish community until about 1840.

In Boston Hays became a successful merchant and maritime underwriter. However, his distinction does not lie in his business successes but in his importance as one of the promoters of Masonry in the American colonies and states. In 1788 he was grand master of the Massachusetts Grand Lodge, succeeding the patriotic Dr. John Warren, one of the founders of the Harvard Medical School. In all likelihood it was through Masonry that Hays came to know Colonel Paul Revere. In 1791, when Hays was again re-elected as grand master, he appointed Revere his deputy.

In September, 1789, Revere needed some iron for his foundry. Hays sent him to Providence with a personal note of introduction to Brown & Benson and guaranteed any purchases the colonel might make (Document A). Revere was back in Boston within a few days without having achieved his purpose. Hays thereupon, on September 14, wrote another note to Brown & Benson, urging them to let Revere have the metal (Document B). The next day the Providence firm answered Hays, regretting that they could not supply Revere with the quality of goods he required (Document C).

SOURCE. The John Carter Brown Library, Providence, R.I., Brown Papers.

A [NO. 24]

Boston, 9th September, 1789.

Messrs. Brown & Benson,
Providence.
Gentlemen:

Colonel Paul Revere will hand you this. His business to Providence is to purchase five or six tons of pig metal, which he wishes to have at three or four months credit, understanding that it is the usual terms you sell pig metal. Colonel Revere will punctually comply with his contract for such a quantity, and for which I will by this letter be his guarantee.

I am with respect, gentlemen,

Your humble servant,
M. M. Hays

B [NO. 24]

Boston, September 14, 1789.

Gentlemen:

Colonel Revere returned on Friday, but seems yet uncertain if you can supply him with any pig metall. He wishes much to have the furnace under way, which he cannot do with out some aid from you. And if you can furnish him with from two to six tons of pig metal, you will oblidge him and me also very much. And I will see that you are punctually paid. Reply per first opportunity, if you please.

I am with respect, gentlemen,

Your most humble,
M. M. Hays

The time of payment will not exceed two months.
Messrs. Brown & Benson.

C [NO. 24]

Providence, 15th September, 1789.

Sir:

We should have addressed Colonel Revere before this time on the subject of his letter, but as there are a number of proprietors to the furnace, and one of them, Capt. [Rufus] Hopkins, resides 12 miles from town, we cannot always obtain their immediate opinion relative to any proposals for pig iron. In reply to yours of the 14th current, now say that there are no pigs of the quality which Colonel Revere wants. This information we received this day by Capt. Hopkins' son, who is [come] directly from the furnace.

With due esteem we are, sir,

Your obedient friends,
B. & B.

Mr. Moses M. Hays,
Boston.

No. 25 Aaron Hart and His Children—1790

Aaron Hart (1724–1800) came to New York in 1759 or 1760 as a sutler or quartermaster with the British army. He participated in the conquest of Canada and settled in Three Rivers on the St. Lawrence. There he engaged in the fur trade, acquired large tracts of land, operated a general store, and turned his hand to small-scale merchant shipping. At the time of his death he was the wealthiest Jew in Canada and probably the most important merchant of his city.

Hart had a number of sons and daughters and, like most successful and aggressive men, he kept a watchful and paternalistic eye on his family. Although he had lived in a French-speaking Roman Catholic village with few and sometimes no Jewish associates, Hart remained true to the faith and practices of his ancestors and was meticulous in his observance of the Passover. Thus it was that on March 28, 1790, he wrote to his oldest son, Moses (Mo) Hart (1768–1852), advising him to return to Three Rivers for the Passover holiday. Had Mo stayed at William Henry (Sorel) on the St. Lawrence, he would have had to remove all leaven from the house, a burdensome process.

The father also told his first-born that he had written to the United States to summon his younger sons, Benjamin, age eleven, and Alexander, age eight, home for the summer. These boys were probably in Philadelphia, receiving a Jewish and general education, for Hart was determined to rear his children as Jews. The younger boys were to return home by way of New York, the Hudson Valley, and Lake Champlain. Mo would meet them near the lake, at Kingsbury probably, where Aaron's brother Harry was in business. With the children was Uriah Judah, a brother of Mrs. Hart. Judah served as an escort until Mo could assume charge of his younger brothers (Document A).

About June 20 the father wrote to Ben and Alex. The boys evidently had their own room in Philadelphia, but since they were returning home, their uncle was to sell the furniture and give the money to the boys. That the two boys had made progress in their Hebrew studies is shown by the fact that they had or were to receive Hebrew prayer books (Document B).

Because Hart's English is at times almost beyond comprehension, the letters printed below are followed by transcriptions into intelligible English.

SOURCE. Séminaire du Saint Joseph, Hart Papers.

A [NO. 25]

Dear Mo:

I se no way for you to keep *Pesah* at William Hanry thear fore you had batter come over hear the Sunday before than you neat not due any thing to your house to git the *hamez* out of your house. It will be attanted with no lass as its all holy dayes that pople boy noting.

I have wrote to H. Judah and to Ben and Alex to sett of for New Yark the 1st of May next as I am determent to have tham hear. If you cane at any rate go across the lakes for tham I will pay all expence you may be at. As I hope you well not faile being hear *Pesah* than shall say more to you on that jurny. It well save you truble and expence of baking of *mazot* to come heur.

I had only one letter by December pachit of PES of 5th December. Noting new the full not than arrived haveng further to mention tell I se you and am d[ea]r Mo your loveng father

Aaron Hart

28th March.

[Paraphrase of Document A—No. 25]

Dear Mo:

I see no way for you to keep Passover at William Henry. Therefore, you had better come over here the Sunday before. Then you need not do anything to your house to get the leaven out of your house. It [closing the store] will be attended with no loss, as it's all holydays when people buy nothing.

I have written to H. Judah and to Ben and Alex to set off for New York the 1st of May next, as I am determined to have them here. If you can, at any rate go across the lakes for them; I will pay all expenses you may be at. As I hope you will not fail being here Passover, shall then say more to you about that journey. It will save you trouble and expense of baking unleavened bread if you come here.

I had only one letter by the December packet from Phyn, Ellice & Co., of the 5th of December. Nothing new, the full [post?] had not then arrived. Having [nothing] further to mention until I see you, I am, dear Mo,

Your loving father,
Aaron Hart

28th March.

B [NO. 25]

Dear Benjamen and Alexander:

Your letters of 29th May I receved last post it came by post not by ship. I cane not say you write better than when you went frome hear I mean Ben. Whe ware all glade to hear you ware will and I hope you bote like the cangre[gation?]. Master Ben, you will let your unkill know what your g[rand]mother bought for you went to house keeping that them things may be sold. The money thay sell for is for you and Alex. Master Alex, I will send you some money and write to London for a set of prayers same as Mo bought for Ben. I know you will mind your larning and all wayes wase a good boy. God bless you both and dear Ben and Alex your laveng father,

A. Hart

Pray write me by first post you will both write in one lether when you write by post.

[Paraphrase of Document B—No. 25]

Dear Benjamin and Alexander:

Your letters of the 29th May I received last post. It came by post, not by ship. I cannot say that you write better than when you went from here. (I mean Ben.) We were all glad to hear you were well, and I hope you both like the congregation.

Master Ben, you will let your uncle know what your grandmother [Judah] bought for you when you went to housekeeping, in order that those things may be sold. The money they sell for is for you and Alex.

Master Alex, I will send you some money and write to London for a set of prayer books, the same as Mo bought for Ben. I know you will mind your learning, and you always were a good boy. God bless you both, dear Ben and Alex.

Your loving father,
A. Hart

P.S. Pray write me by the first post. You will both write in one letter when you write by post.

No. 26 Jewish Life in Virginia—1791

Hyman Samuel, who married Rebecca Alexander, was a silversmith and watchmaker, living in Petersburg, Virginia, Baltimore, and Charleston, S.C. During the last decade of the eighteenth century Rebecca described Jewish life in Petersburg in two letters to her parents, who were then living in Hamburg, Germany. The Samuels, who were probably of German stock, had apparently spent some time in England, and looked with contempt upon the uncouth German Jews they found in this country.

Rebecca Samuel's letters are among the most significant that we possess for this period, inasmuch as they touch, albeit lightly, on the vital questions of anti-Jewish prejudice, acculturation, the religious education of children, the separation of church and state, the absence of craft guild restrictions, and the larger opportunities available in this country for the common man.

Mrs. Samuel writes of the tobacco trade, of which Petersburg was then a center. We know from other sources that Samuel Myers was then buying tobacco there for Stephen Girard of Philadelphia.

The two letters of Rebecca Samuel printed below were written in Yiddish. The first unfortunately is incomplete. The second, though not dated, was written probably within the same decade, for we know that the Samuels were still in Petersburg in 1792. By 1796 they had moved to Richmond.

SOURCE. American Jewish Archives, Cincinnati, the Henry Joseph Collection of Gratz Papers.

A [NO. 26]

Petersburg, January 12, 1791, Wednesday, 8th [7th?] Shebat, 5551.

Dear and Worthy Parents:

I received your dear letter with much pleasure and therefrom understand that you are in good health, thank God, and that made us especially happy. The same is not lacking with us—may we live to be a hundred years. Amen.

Dear parents, you complain that you do not receive any letters from us, and my mother-in-law writes the same. I don't know what's going on. I have written more letters than I have received from you. Whenever I can and have an opportunity, I give letters to take along, and I send letters by post when I do not have any other opportunity. It is already six months since we received letters from you and from London. The last letter you sent was through Sender [Alexander], and it was the beginning of the month of Ab [July, 1790] when we received it. Now you can realize that we too have been somewhat worried. We are completely isolated here. We do not have any friends, and when we do not hear from you for any length of time, it is enough to make us sick. I hope that I will get to see some of my family. That will give me some satisfaction.

You write me that Mr. Jacob Renner's son Reuben is in Philadelphia and that he will come to us. People will not advise him to come to Virginia. When the Jews of Philadelphia or New York hear the name Virginia, they get nasty. And they are not wrong! It won't do for a Jew. In the first place it is an unhealthful district, and we are only human. God forbid, if anything should happen to us, where would we be thrown? There is no cemetery in the whole of Virginia. In Richmond, which is twenty-two miles from here, there is a Jewish community consisting of two quorums [twenty men], and the two cannot muster a quarter [quorum when needed?].

You cannot imagine what kind of Jews they have here [in Virginia]. They were all German itinerants who made a living by begging in Germany. They came to America during the war, as soldiers, and now they can't recognize themselves.

One can make a good living here, and all live at peace. Anyone can do what he wants. There is no rabbi in all of America to excommunicate anyone. This is a blessing here; Jew and Gentile are as one. There is no galut ["exile," rejection of Jews] here. In New York and Philadelphia there is more galut. The reason is that there are too many German Gentiles and Jews there. The German Gentiles cannot forsake their anti-Jewish prejudice; and the German Jews cannot forsake their disgraceful conduct; and that's what makes the galut.

[Rebecca Samuel]

B [NO. 26]

Dear Parents:

I hope my letter will ease your mind. You can now be reassured and send me one of the family to Charleston, South Carolina. This is the place to which, with God's help, we will go after Passover. The whole reason why we are leaving this place is because of [lack of] *Yehudishkeit* [Jewishness].

Dear parents, I know quite well you will not want me to bring up my children like Gentiles. Here they cannot become anything else. Jewishness is pushed aside here. There are here [in Petersburg] ten or twelve Jews, and they are not worthy of being called Jews. We have a shohet here who goes to market and buys terefah [nonkosher] meat and then brings it home. On Rosh Ha-Shanah [New Year] and on Yom Kippur ["the Day of Atonement"] the people worshipped here without one sefer torah ["Scroll of the Law"], and not one of them wore the tallit [a large prayer shawl worn in the synagogue] or the *arba kanfot* [the small set of fringes worn on the body], except Hyman and my Sammy's godfather. The latter is an old man of sixty, a man from Holland. He has been in America for thirty years already; for twenty years he was in Charleston, and he has been living here for four years. He does not want to remain here any longer and will go with us to Charleston. In that place there is a blessed community of three hundred Jews.

You can believe me that I crave to see a synagogue to which I can go. The way we live now is no life at all. We do not know what the Sabbath and the holidays are. On the Sabbath all the Jewish shops are open; and they do business on that day as they do throughout the whole week. But ours we do not allow to open. With us there is still some Sabbath. You must believe me that in our house we all live as Jews as much as we can.

As for the Gentiles [?], we have nothing to complain about. For the sake of a livelihood we do not have to leave here. Nor do we have to leave because of debts. I believe ever since Hyman has grown up that he has not had it so good. You cannot know what a wonderful country this is for the common man. One can live here peacefully. Hyman made a clock that goes very accurately, just like the one in the Buchenstrasse in Hamburg. Now you can imagine what honors Hyman has been getting here. In all Virginia there is no clock [like this one], and Virginia is the greatest province in the whole of America, and America is the largest section of the world. Now you know what sort of a country this is. It is not too long since Virginia was discovered. It is a young country. And it is amazing to see the business they do in this little Petersburg. At times as many as a thousand hogsheads of tobacco arrive at one time, and each hogshead contains 1,000 and sometimes 1,200 pounds of tobacco. The tobacco is shipped from here to the whole world.

When Judah [my brother?] comes here, he can become a watchmaker and a goldsmith, if he so desires. Here it is not like Germany where a watchmaker is not permitted to sell silverware. [The contrary is true in this country.] They do not know otherwise here. They expect a watchmaker to be a silversmith here. Hyman has more to do in making silverware than with watchmaking. He has a journeyman, a silversmith, a very good artisan, and he, Hyman, takes care of the watches. This work is well paid here, but in Charleston, it pays even better.

All the people who hear that we are leaving give us their blessings. They say that it is sinful that such blessed children should be brought up here in Petersburg. My children cannot learn anything here, nothing Jewish, nothing of general culture. My Schoene [my daughter], God bless her, is already three years old. I think it is time that she should learn something, and she has a good head to learn. I have taught her the bedtime prayers and grace after meals in just two lessons. I believe that no one among the Jews here can do as well as she. And my Sammy [born in 1790], God bless him, is already beginning to talk.

I could write more. However, I do not have any more paper.

I remain, your devoted daughter and servant,
Rebecca, the wife of Hayyim, the son of Samuel the Levite

I send my family, my . . . [mother-in-law?] and all my friends and good friends, my regards.

[Postscript of Hyman Samuel, the husband:]
I, Hayyim, send my regards to you both and all my good friends. I do not have any time to write much. We shall, however, write another letter to you soon. We received letters from. . . . I should write to Raphael and my nephew. In the first place, they defamed me innocently, and if they don't write to me first, I can assure them they will receive none from me; they will perhaps say they are not interested in me. I say the same thing. Further, I remain your devoted son,
The humble Hayyim, the son of Samuel, of blessed memory.

[A sentence scratched out.]
[Additional postscript of Rebecca:]
Hayyim wanted to write impudence, so I crossed it out.

[Additional postscript of Hyman Samuel:]
You can note my son's pretty fingers in the letter. If you want to write us direct to Charleston, my address there will be: Hyman Samuel, Watch and Clock, Charleston, South Carolina.

You will see and hear that we are leaving Petersburg honorably. I will send you a newspaper from which you will see that I am not writing you any lies.

To Mr. Aaron Alexander,
On the New . . .
Hamburg.

No. 27   The Bride Leaves Home—1791

On October 26, 1791, Rachel Gratz (1764–1831), the only surviving child of Barnard Gratz, married Solomon Etting (1764–1847), a Baltimore merchant and the son of Elijah Etting, who had come to York, Pennsylvania, in pre-Revolutionary days. Elijah was a merchant and Indian trader, doing business with Joseph Simon of Lancaster. One of Simon's daughters had previously married young Etting but died soon thereafter. Thus Rachel Gratz was Solomon's second wife, and by marrying her Solomon Etting remained in the Simon clan, for another one of the Simon girls had married Barnard Gratz's brother and partner, Michael.

Solomon Etting and Rachel Gratz were married in Philadelphia and at once moved to Baltimore. Printed below are two letters of November 13, sent to Barnard Gratz by his daughter and son-in-law. Both of them wanted him to come and visit them.

The gossip in the two notes throws light on the beginnings of Baltimore Jewry. There were too few Jews to create a community and, as can be seen, there was dissension even within the same family.

The Mrs. Levy mentioned in Rachel's letter is evidently the aristocratic and assimilated Mrs. Benjamin Levy, of Philadelphia, a member of the Levy-Franks family. The Josephsons were well-known Philadelphia Jews; Manuel Josephson signed a letter sent by the Jews of New York, Philadelphia, Richmond, and Charleston, congratulating George Washington on his accession to the Presidency. The Cohens are probably "Rabbi" and Mrs. Jacob Raphael Cohen, of Philadelphia, while the Salomons are Mrs. Elijah Etting's brothers Isaac and Levy, who had once lived in the Dutch island of St. Eustatius.

It is interesting to note that the socially prominent Levys were friendly, while the Salomons, flesh and blood, were not. That is why Jewish communities did not grow up in a hurry.

SOURCE. The Historical Society of Pennsylvania, Philadelphia, Etting Papers.

A [NO. 27]

Baltimore, November 13th, 1791.

My ever honoured parent:

I was made very happy on Fry day last, on the receipt of your welcome letter. As an assurance of the welfare of my dearest father is the first wish of my heart, continue to favour me frequent, there by affording much satisfaction to me, and [I] flatter my self with the pleasure of soon embraceing you and convinceing you verbally, how very happy I am situated, and the wish of entertaining my dear father is the most earnest of my solicitations. Do not disappoint me, my best of paren[ts]. Tho[ugh]t of your not accompanying me was painful; [I] therefore entreat you will not prolong your stay, but hasten to make perfectly happy your grateful daughter.

I this morning was favoured with a visit from Mrs. Levy, who was very pressing in her invitations to me. Amidst the many I have received from the people here who have called on me, one of the number was an old acquaintance of yours, a Mrs. Hunter, who was very particular in her enquiries about you and wishes much to see you. From what little I have seen of this place, think I shall like it very much, as it far exceeds my expectations.

My dear Sally [Etting] is well and intends writeing to you. Mrs. [Elijah] Etting and family beg their best respects to you, as does Mrs. Salomons. It is now late and am fearful of missing the oppertunity [of sending this]. Must conclude, with my most ardent wish for your health and contentment.

[I] remain your most affectionate and dutiful daughter,

Rachel Etting

Please to present my best regards to Mrs. and Mr. Josephson, Mrs. and Mr. Cohen, with all other friends. . . .

B [NO. 27]

Baltimore, November 13th, 1791.

Honored Sir: . . .

I writ you the evening of our return and mentioned uncles Isaac and Levy visiting us. The next day a very numerous and respectable circle of acquaintance come to welcome my return, and take a repast with us, but those two gentlemen, altho invited, did not make their appearance. On Fryday, Rachel and myself, by particular invitation requested their company to dinner this day, but [it was] not favored. I *thought, to[o]*, all friendship [was] at an end with them and not worth noticing.

It would have given my dear Rachel and self infinite pleasure to have had you amongst us: a fine circle of family connection and the day spent with the greatest satisfaction, my mother enjoying herself like the old hen amongst her chickens. Permit me to reiterate my wish of seeing you in Baltimore as soon as convenient, and I flatter myself we will be able to make your stay agreeable to you. No pains will be wanting to render it so.

My letter to you by post was brief, owing to fatigue. We were blest with beautifull weather and agreeable company, and the time past [passed] very pleasantly. In the preist [priest] we found a most excellent travelling companion and a remarkable clever fellow. My dear Rachel stood the ride amazingly and arrived less fatigued considerably than I did. So did Becky [Gratz?]. I am pleased beyond measure to inform you my sweetest Rachel is so much taken with the place, but when I begin to reflect she has only seen two streets and them the best and handsomest, I fear when she sees the rest, she'l unsay all again.

The things I sent, as well the bundle of beds, are safely arrived. We have not got them yet, but am informed by the boats that they are on board. The bearer returns in a very few days. Write us by him and omit no oportunity, as nothing will be more pleasing than to hear of your health, etc.

I am, dear sir, with respect [and] in haste,

Your affectionate son[-in-law],
Solomon Etting

No. 28 Moses Sheftall Announces His Forthcoming Marriage—1791–1792

Early in November, 1791, Dr. Moses Sheftall (1769–1835), a disciple of Dr. Benjamin Rush, the famous Philadelphia physician, returned to his master's city from his native Savannah. He had come to see the girl he was determined to marry, Elkali (Nelly) Bush (1772–1830), a sister of the Revolutionary veteran Dr. Solomon Bush.

In a letter of November 16, 1791, Moses asked his father Mordecai Sheftall, a Savannah merchant and well-known patriot, for his opinion concerning his "lovely little girl." The parents were not pleased with Moses' selection. One reason was that Dr. Bush had married out of the faith. More exasperating was the fact that the girl and her brother had apparently paid no attention to the letters sent to them by the family. Moses, however, proceeded to explain away all difficulties. He loved Nelly.

To augment his income Dr. Sheftall made the rounds, trying to get a federal appointment, probably at the port of Savannah. To this end he called on Senators James Gunn, of Georgia, and Pierce Butler, of South Carolina. Knowing his father's interest in politics, he reported, on December 1, that Congress would, in February, consider the charges of fraud in the Georgia congressional elections, which had been preferred by General James Jackson against General Anthony Wayne. Since Mordecai Sheftall was still trying to collect on some claims arising from the Revolution, Moses also reported that he had deposited with the authorities some important receipts signed by Richard Wyley (Wylly), the deputy quartermaster general of the Georgia troops (Document A).

On February 16, 1792, the doctor wrote to his mother Frances Sheftall, announcing his forthcoming marriage to Nelly on Wednesday, March 20 (Document B). Actually, the marriage did not take place until May 21.

SOURCE. The Mr. and Mrs. B. H. Levy Collection of Sheftall Papers.

A [NO. 28]

Philadelphia, December 1st, 1791.

Honored Father:

A few days have elapsed since I wrote you by Capt. Collins—which you will receive ere this can possibly come to hand—in which I gave you an account of my affair with Miss Bush. As letters from here have frequently miscarried which were directed to our family, I must again beg leave to relate each particular circumstance relative to this business.

On Thursday I arrived in this city, and being informed that two of the ladys were in town, namely Miss Peggy and Miss Nelly [my sweetheart], you therefore must suppose it was natural for me to wish to see her. However, I waited untill the day after when I saw the Doctor [Bush], who, you may rely on, was closely interrogated why I had been thus used. The manner of my usage he could not understand, as he declared upon his sacred honor that he had wrote, as well as his sister, and in particular an answer to your letter. Some went by the way of Charleston; others, he thinks, went in a vessel bound for Savannah. All this may be true, as Samuel Hays informed he had wrote, as likewise my land lord [Levy Phillips], S.[imon] Gratz, Mr. [Thomas] Leaming, and others who were much surprised at my not having received their letters.

Upon this information and by his request I called on his sister who was at his house and there I beheld the object of my love; whenupon, entering into a conversation with her and asking her similiar questions as I had asked the doctor, [she] made similiar replys. She declared that her affections for me where the same and that she was ready to convince me of it by going with me now, or whenever I thought most convenient, to Georgia. Therefore, I shall now anxiously wait your determination, should you think proper to give me something to begin the world with.

And [with] my own industry, I think, it will be in my power to maintain this amiable lady, and will bring her out with me in the spring, if you should approve of the step.

To leave her hear [here] again is what I do not wish, as in my former letter I mentioned something respecting her religion, which I think proper to explain. Bad examples are very apt to be catching, and as she frequently comes to town to her brother's, she may possibly come into some of his mode of living. I would not have you suppose from what I have said that I am afraid her affections are placed somewheres else. Know, sir, I believe her affection for me is too sincere ever to be eradicated by any thing but time alone. However, it seems to be her wish to come out with me in the spring, and my most sincere wish to bring her.

On that subject I think I have been pretty full; therefore, hope you will be the same, and, least [lest] an early opportunity should not offer, write me by post under cover to Col. Gunn. Let all the letters which the family may write be enclosed to Col. Gunn, as they will then be sure of coming safe to hand.

And now with respect to my appointment, nothing as yet has been done, but Col. Gunn tells me they will surely take it up. He thinks I stand upon the best foundation of any who can apply for it. I have his word, Mr. Tew and Major Butler's, for their interest in my behalf, as likewise Doctors [Benjamin] Rush and [William] Shippen. Should I get it, it will be of great service to me.

Generals Wayne and Jackson's business is to be determined on the first Tuesday in February next. I have been introduced at a levee to the President by Col. Gunn. Gunn's attention to me is very pleasing, I assure you.

Not being able to procure any sour crout [sauerkraut], you will receive by Capt. Burrous a barrel of very excellent cyder, marked M. S. [Moses Sheftall], which I request you will substitute for the crout. My land lord says if you b[u]y him a hundred weight of coppers, he will allow at the rate of 6d. sterling a pound. He wants them for small change.

The following is the price of funded paper: 6 per cents 22s. 6d., 3 per cent 12s. 6d.; 3 ditto deferred 13s. 6d. Wylly's receipts for papers deposited 14s.

My respects to General [Lachlan] McIntosh. My duty [to] my mama. I remain, honored father,

Your ever dutifull son,
Moses Sheftall

M. Sheftall, Esq.

If the coppers can't come this winter, they will not do.
My reason for not having wrote to Sheftall is that expect he has left home before this.

B [NO. 28]

Philadelphia, February 16th, 1791[2].

To the[e], my honored mama, would I now attempt an apology for my former apparent neglect, but having wrote you some time since, via N. York, and in that having offerd every apology I had to offer, I deem it unnecessary now to make any more, as I am confident my honored parent will forgive all my misconduct heretofore acted.

In full relyance of this, permit me to inform you that the Wednesday after Purim [March 20th] is the day alotted to make your son happy by his being united to the dear object of his affections, and, in behalf of that dear girl, [to] receive the gratefull acknowledgements of both our hearts for your kind wishes towards us; and with truest and most sincere duty do we acknowledge thy proferrd service of becoming a mother to the intended partner of your son's heart, whose constant study will ever be to merit a continuance of your kindness towards her.

Happy shall we be on the day which makes us one. Thrice happy should we have been could it [have] been possible for my honored mama to have been present. You will excuse the shortness of this, and believe me to be, dear mama,

Your ever dutifull and affectionate son,
Moses Sheftall

Mrs. F. Sheftall.

_____

No. 29   Aunt Shinah Offers Advice on the Right Man—1791

Joseph Simon, the Lancaster trader, had a large family. One of his daughters, Shinah, married Dr. Nicholas Schuyler, of Troy, N.Y. Although she married out of the faith, Shinah appears to have been happy. Both she and her husband maintained good relations with the Simons.

Shinah's sister Miriam married Michael Gratz, the Philadelphia merchant. Two of their children, Richea, seventeen, and Frances, twenty, became favorites of their childless Aunt Shinah.

In the following gossipy letter Aunt Shinah, writing probably from Troy, expresses herself on the selection of a husband.

SOURCE. Duke University Library, Durham, N.C., Jacob Mordecai Papers.

December 17th, 1791.

Miss Richea Gratz,
Lancaster.

I received my dear Richea's two aggreeable letters with inexperssable [inexpressible] pleasure. . . .

My dear Richea, I sincerly thank [you] for all the news. Why, my dear, your information was quite from the matrimonial budget. . . .

And when, pray, do you enter the list of matrimony? Seriously, my love, I must be your confident; however, my dear Fanny [Frances] must enter her claim first. You have my most cordial prayers for both your happiness whenever that happy period arrives. I would advise you not to be too percipitate, unless an extraordinary and worthy man solicits that honor, and your heart can accompany the gift. Never, my lovely girls (for I address you both), alter your situation but by uniting your selves to a worthy man and one you can love and esteem. Should even adversity be your lot, their will be a consolation experienced which your marrying for wealth will never yeild [yield] you, and compleat your misery with an undeserving man. Let esteem for virtueous principles be the first basis for love, and then your happiness will be perminant. That both of you, my dear girls, may marry agreeable to your parents, and each have a worthy husband, I sincerely wish, tho' I would still advise you to continue single. Your both young, and two or three years more will be sufficent for to think of altering your situation.

I am in exceeding good health and spirits; indeed, few have less reason to complain. I have a very dear, good husband. I think few, very few, can say they live happier, and, thank God, he's exceedingly hearty and has constant employ in either writing or visiting his patience [patients] and chatting to his little wife, for, you know, I will have some attention paid to me.

Well, Richea, where do you spend your winter? I hope you'll attend the Lancaster [dancing] assemblys. We have refused subscribeng to the Albany assemblys as it will interfear too much with the doctor's business, but he seems a strenious advocate for having them here; if so, I must attend, tho' to speak truth, I would rather not this winter. We have some very elegant women in this place, and they dress too much for my indolent disposition, for I have an utter aversion to dress unless it's to be clean and neat.

I wish you was here, my dear; I long to see you. Let me hear from you soon. How are my dear mamy's eyes? I hope both my dear parents enjoy their health. My most affectionate love to my dear sister. Tell her I wish she lived near me.

I once lived in the same town with my dear [sister] Bell [Mrs. Solomon M. Cohen], tho' I was deprived of her society. [The sister probably ignored Shinah, who had married a Gentile, and may even have become a convert to Christianity.] Believe me, my dear, at this moment my eyes are filled at the bear [bare] recollection. I think if she had not a heart of stone she would have stole to see me when their [there], tho' I forgive her. Pray let me know how she does and what her situation is. I would write to my dear sister but as I write to you, my dear Richea, it will answer every purpose.

Do write by the post. I shall expect you will, as it will be impossible to convey a letter in any other manner. The river will be closed shortly [because of the ice]. Write long letters. The postage is the same if you inclose two letters so that it don't appear, which may easely be done by folding them exactly of a size. I have wrote so fast that my fingers are perfectly crampt. God bless you, my dearest girl. May you enjoy an [un]interrupted serees [series] of happiness is the sincere prayers of your affectionate friend and aunt,

Shinah Schuyler

My love to my dear sister Fanny Simon, etc., etc. My dear old man desires his best love may be acceptable to you. We both join in compliments to the Mr. Gratzes.

I insist on your writing by the post. Could you have them conveyed and put in the [post] office in New York? If not, put them in the Lancaster or Philadelphia office. It's impossible to send by private conveyances, and I am very an[xious] to hear from you often. Write long letters an[d the ne]ws; every circumstance of my family [and] friends will be agreeable. Tell my dear sister [Fanny] to write likewise. Don't laugh at my long poscript. God bless you, my dearest girl, and grant you every laudable wish of your little heart.

No. 30   Small Profits and Quick Returns—1792

Mordecai Sheftall, the Savannah merchant, sent his son Sheftall north in 1792. As we know from the family correspondence, the young man was given a number of tasks. In Philadelphia he was to see Secretary of the Treasury Alexander Hamilton and to secure repayment of the £1,900 due Mordecai from the days when he was commissary general for the American forces in Georgia and South Carolina. Young Sheftall was also to buy goods in the market and to ship them back home in a hurry.

The following letter from the father to his son throws light on several aspects of the economic, religious, and cultural life of the times: on the business relations between the North and the South, on the attempts of slaves to seek their freedom through flight, on Hebrew books, and on synagogal and ritual practices.

SOURCE. Copy in the American Jewish Archives, The Nathan-Kraus Collection.

Savannah, the 10th August, 1792.

Dear Sheftall:

Yours by [Capt.] Collins I rec[eive]d, and was really surprised to see that you where [were] still in Philadelphia, but much more so to finde that you had not sent forward the goods as orderd. Good God, at what time are they to arrive? The summer season is now gone, and I fear if you are as neglectfull as you have been, the winter season will allso elapse.

To what purpose do you keep such a considerable sum of money, as you must still have in your hands, idle? Had I directed the money to be sent to Eaurope, I should by this time have been furnished with an assortment, and you, that are so near at hand, cannot finde any thing to invest the money in that will turn to an advantage. Your orders where [were] in a great measure discretionel, so that you might have invested it in such articles as would have afforded a small profite, if you could not got such [an investment] as would have yeilded a large one. You certainely ought, at this time of life, to know that small profits and quick returns makes a heavy purse, but money laying in a man's chest will not afforde a gaine, but may waste away. . . .

Should this reach you at New York, I want you to look out for a mulato man who calls himself Edward Cole. He pretends he is a free man, thoe I have understood, since he ran away from here, that he is a slave to a gentleman in Port Auprince [Haiti]. He went from here in the brig *Eliza,* Capt. ——, that used to come to Mr. John Fisher, and carried from here a Negroe woman slave, the property of a Mr. Cadine, in Port auprince. I came to the knowledge of her being a slave and the property of Mr. Caudin from [Cole] the fellow himself, who was taken up under a warrant from me, and committed to goale [gaol] on an application of one Armstronge, who came with them here from Jam[a]ica, particulars of which you will see by the affadavites, which I forward to Mr. B. Gomez. When I found that Armstronge was a villan, and that he wanted to make the wench his property, I took her from him, with an intent to have her secured for her owner, and, in mercy to the wretch, I permitted her to stay in your brother, the doctor's [Moses Sheftall's] yard, as I thought that confineing her in goale would be attended with a very great expence to her owner, besides the risque of her dying in goal at this inclement [yellow fever] season of the year.

She is a very black girle, speaks no English, dresses intierly in the French fashion. She is likely [pretty]; her name is Marian Vile. The steward of Capt. Burnham, who is a free mulato, knows them both and will assiste you in the apprehending them. The fellow plays very well on the violine and speaks good English. He pretended to me that he was borne in Connecticute. I am very anxious to have them brot back, least

[lest] the owner of the wench may blame me for my humanity. I am determined to prosecute the captaine of the brig [*Eliza*]. It is the brig that Capt. King used to come here in. . . .

We had liked to have [we almost] lost Lolly [one of the Sheftall girls]. She was suddenly taken in fits. They continued on her on and off, from Monday morning till Tuesday after noon. There was every medical aide got for her that could be procured. I sent Ben [Sheftall] out for Doctor McCleod, who came at the first notice and remained in town all night. When I offerd to pay him, he declined takeing any thing and appeared happy to have it in his power to render her assistance.

Thank God, she is perfectly recoverd, and I thinke better than she has been ever since she has been here. 'Tis easier for you to immagine how I felt during her illness than for me to describe. She was so far gone that we had prayers for her in snogau [synagogue], and I do thinke she began to mend from the time the prayers where finished. . . .

I finde that not only the Kippure ["Atonement"] book, but the Sucoth ["Feast of Tabernacles"] book, is wanting in the sett [of David Levi's *Form of Prayers*] you sent me. I should be glad to have a sett of the *Lingua Saera* [*Sacra;* Levi's three-volume Hebrew dictionary and grammar], as I thinke they must be very usefull books, especially for a person not well versed in the Hebrew. Get the Kippure and Succoth books to compleat the setts.

Is the lotterys drawn, in which you interested me? If they are, what is the fate of my tickets? Why are you not more particular on this subject? In short, it is my wish that, as you have been indulged in every-[thing] that you asked for, that you will carefully over look [look over] all the letters I wrote you and endeavour to complie with them as nearly as possible. I shall write you to Boston, by Capt. Ripely, who sailes for there next week, and in whom [in whose ship], I understand, that Isaac Polack goes passanger.

Your uncle Levi [Sheftall] has the goute, poor fellow. He and all his family give theire love to you, as does Many [Emanuel Abrahams] and family, Cardoza and ditto, Curvoise and ditto, Gen. McIntosh and ditto; in short, all your freinds. Your brother Ben and sisters wishes to know wether 'tis the polite ton[e] that you have learnt, since you have left home, that induces you to call them master and misses. They wish you well, as does your mother, allthoe she is angry at your neglecting her orders. I am,

> Your affectionate father,
> Mordecai Sheftall

Mr. Sheftall Sheftall,
Councellor at Law,
New York.

No. 31   Richea Gratz and Her Sweetheart Samuel Hays—1793

Some time in the summer of 1793, Richea Gratz (1774–1858), the daughter of Michael Gratz, the Philadelphia merchant, became engaged to Samuel Hays (1764–1838). The Gratzes had done their best to give Richea a good education and had entered her at Franklin College (later Franklin and Marshall) the year it was opened. She was probably the first Jewess in the country to matriculate at an American "college."

Hays, her fiancé, a very respectable young merchant and broker, was a member of the widespread Hays family of New York, which had come to this country in the first third of the eighteenth century. He had been a clerk under Haym Salomon, the Polish Jewish Whig, and thus had the advantage of training at the hands of a master. Hays, an observant Jew, was a loyal member of the Philadelphia congregation.

On August 5 Richea received a congratulatory note from an older brother, Simon, or Simmy, as he was called. The letter was couched in a rather pompous and formal style, but we may be sure that it was well meant. The description of the ideal wife that Simon painted most likely reflected his own wishful thinking. Simon at that time was all of twenty and spoke, no doubt, out of the fullness of his own inexperience (Document A).

During the engagement Samuel Hays bombarded his sweetheart with letters. Richea had returned to the old Simon homestead in Lancaster, for the yellow fever was then raging in Philadelphia. Hays had gone to see her but was back in town by the morning of Friday, November 22. He was eagerly awaiting her return and in the meantime solaced himself with frequent letters. One of these, written in Philadelphia a few hours after his return from Lancaster, was brief because the Sabbath was approaching, and he would not willingly desecrate the day by writing. The epidemic was almost over, he told Richea, as he eagerly awaited her return to town— and to him (Document B).

The marriage between Samuel Hays and Richea Gratz, on January 8, 1794, was in all likelihood solemnized by the local minister, Jacob Raphael Cohen (ca. 1738–1811). Cohen, probably a native of the Barbary States, had been the hazzan in Montreal but, after a quarrel with the Jews there, had served the Loyalist congregation in New York and then, changing pulpits with Gershom Mendes Seixas in 1784, had gone to Philadelphia.

As we see from a letter written to Richea on November 27, 1793, Hays did not like the rabbi. His dislike may have been a prejudice carried over in part from Uncle Manuel Josephson, who was "feuding" with the congregation. As likely as not, the poor rabbi was caught in the middle. In this letter Hays tells Richea not only what the rabbi preached, but also what he practiced (Document C).

A note dashed off the next day gives a good description of Philadelphia's recovery from the yellow fever (Document D).

SOURCE. Duke University Library, Jacob Mordecai Papers.

A [NO. 31]

Lancaster, August 5th, 1793.

Miss Richea Gratz,
Philadelphia.

The letter of the 1st instant from my dear sister I now seat myself to accknowledge. Its contents I duly note. The subject it treats on is of the most interesting nature, and I hope my dear sister gave it the consideration due.

You are now about to enter into a state wherein I hope and pray you may experiance nothing to give you pain but, on the contrary, enjoy perfect happiness and tranquility. But, my dear, you must remember that to ensure to yourself and to the man you love a lasting continuance of happiness, you must ever make it your constant duty and study to please. In short, copy our amiable and virtuous mother; act as she does, and you will ensure to yourself and to all about you contentment. But as a preliminary to all happiness, lett a due sence of relegion, and a proper attention to the precepts and commands of the great God always actuate you, and place your sole confidence and trust in him.

Be pleased to remember me affectionately to Mr. Hays. I shall be down at Philadelphia immediately after the [Jewish] hollowdays, and shall then spend some time with you. Grandpa [Joseph Simon] desires his love to you and begs you would write and inform him how Aunt Leah [his daughter] is, as his greatful son-in law, Mr. [Levi] Phillips, has not thought proper to write him a line this 5 months.

I shall write to you again shortly, but in the intrem, belive me to be, with constant prayers of your happiness,

Your ever affectionate brother and well wisher,
Simon Gratz

Hyman [our brother] desires his love to you and can't write this week.

B [NO. 31]

Philadelphia, Friday, 22nd November, 1793.

Miss Richea Gratz,
at Mr. Joseph Simon's, Merchant,
Lancaster.

Have just time, before Shabath sets in, to acquaint my dear and amiable girl of our getting here this forenoon in good health. The city seems more lively then I ever remember it, all the shops open, and business transacted as usual. I have heard nothing mentioned of the fever.

[Benjamin] Nones and family are in town and is just the same as ever, much benefitted in his looks. They insist on Simmy and me supping with them tonight. He has shewed us a rock [a precious stone?] of 20 odd pound [worth 20 odd pounds].

The markets lookt to me today as if it had been market day. In short, nothing is thought more of the past disorder, and I should entirely forget it, was but my d[ear] girl here [if only you were here]. I anticipate the moment. Interim, am in haste hers, etc.

S. Hays

My respects to your honored parent, Fanny, etc. Nancy opened the house to day. I wrote from Mrs. Miller's per F. Lauman. Have a great deal to say, but Shabath will not admit [permit it].

C [NO. 31]

Philadelphia, 27th November, 1793.

Miss Richea Gratz,
Lancaster.

It is now a week since I left Lancaster, and not a line have I received. Hope my dear girl is in health. I saw Phila [Phillips] at Mr. Nones's last evening. She said I might expect the pleasure of seeing you next week, as she had a letter informing [her] you would set of [off] next Tuesday.

You may now come with safety. Nothing is mentioned about the past disorders, and [I] believe [they are] entirely forgot by many. The city is more lively than I ever knew it, and [I] believe more dissipation. The dress of the ladys are more extravagant and [there are a] great number of new faces, English ladies. The gentlemen here say they surpass all the American ladies they ever saw. They forget my friend Fanny [Gratz, your sister]. Tell her it is time for her to return to retrieve the credit of the Americans, and to convince the gentlemen here they are not surpassed in beauty or other accomplishments by any nation on earth.

Our worthy pastor, Mr. Cohen, is not yet returned and does not come till next week. He has sent the children down to air the house. He, like other persons of his cloath, gives precepts they don't mean to follow. One afternoon he was at Jonas Phillips's and preached for half an hour to put their trust in the Almighty, that there was no such thing as flying from His hand, that He would protect those who put his trust in Him, and that he meant to stay, which made Mr. Phillips conclude to do the same. When, behold, the first thing Mr. Phillips heard next morning was that Mr. Cohen, with all his morality, had flewn and left his congregation to put their trust in that Being, [whom he] himself put no faith in. Myer Hart has killed [the cattle according to the ritual] ever since, for Mr. Cohen thought fasting as well as prayer would have a good effect on the yellow fever.

Mr. Nones and family are in good spirits, different from what I expected from his letter to me. I said then their [there] was no faith to be put in it. He, as well as Mrs. N., brag of their living in New York. Every one of the family have new cloaths, and by all accounts made a great par[a]de their [there]. She had her private purse for playing lew [loo, a game of cards], weares an elegant gold watch by her side with a gold chain that he says cost seventy dollars, and has purchased a dozen of prints [intaglios?] at a guinea a piece. She says we only breath here, that N. York is the place to live. In short, to appeerence, he must have found the philosopher's stone.

This will be handed [to you] by your worthy brother. He can tell you more than will bear writing. Tender my unfeigned respects to your honored parents, Mrs. Simons [your grandmother], etc. My affectionate regards to my friend Fanny.

Am impatient till the stage arrives. Am going to endeavour to get my hair dressed. The fever has made such a havock among the mechanicks that their is no getting a barber or a taylor to do any kind of work. Adieu, my dearest girl, and believe me, unalterably

Yours,
S. Hays

D [NO. 31]

Philadelphia, 28th November, 1793.

Miss Richea Gratz,
at Mr. Joseph Simon's, Merchant,
Lancaster.

With heart felt pleasure did I receive my dearest Richea's kind and affectionate letter per Dursh's stage, as it conveyed the pleasing intelligence of her being in health, which blessing, pray, she may many, many years enjoy. Also the pleasing information that I may hope to embrace, the ensuing week, what I hold most dear on earth. Believe me, the time appears long, long, and would be insupportable if I was not engaged in procuring many things I yet want, on an occassion I hope is not far distant.

The city is just the same as if nothing had happened. We walk without dread through every part; no apperence of smelling bottles and spunges. Buildings going on. That of Cook's [Cooke's Folly, on Third and Market Streets,] is grand and magnificent and a great ornament to the city.

I have been so engaged that I have been at Mr. [Jonas] Phillips's but once. Phila [his daughter], I think, looks as formely, as also Mrs. Phillips. Intend going to see them this evening. Simmy, am sorry to see, has a disagreable day to travel. He would leave us yesterday. Uncle Josephson has just sent for me, to do some business for him.

Mame and Reyne [My mother and my sister Reyna] request their love to my dear girl. Tender my respects to your good parent. Tell Fanny we shall have a great deal to say when she comes down, but beg her to spare you in my absence, and that I'll bear her raillery and satire for three months to come on myself without murmuring.

Adieu, my amiable girl. May we soon meet, never more to be seperated, is the fervent prayer of your

S. Hays

No. 32   Dr. Moses Sheftall Discusses a Medical Problem with Dr. Benjamin Rush—1795

Dr. Moses Sheftall (1769–1835), the son of Mordecai Sheftall, the merchant and Whig of Savannah, was a great admirer of Dr. Benjamin Rush, of Philadelphia, under whose tutelage he had studied during the years 1790–92. By 1792 Dr. Sheftall must already have been a practicing physician, for in that year he pulled General James Jackson through a severe illness.

In 1793 a yellow fever epidemic struck Philadelphia. Many of its victims looked to the ministrations of Dr. Rush, who had concluded that the fever, caused in this instance by poisonous gases exuding from rotting coffee, was of the inflammatory type. As a cure, he advocated copious bloodletting and the use of calomel and other drugs. A year after the epidemic, when Rush published *An Account of the Bilious Remitting Yellow Fever, as It Appeared in the City of Philadelphia, in the Year 1793*, Sheftall wrote to his former teacher and ventured his own opinion on the nature of the disease.

In the letter printed below Sheftall also sought Dr. Rush's advice on how to fight the fever, offered his condolences on the death of the doctor's sister, aligned himself with the Philadelphia physician in his medical battles with Dr. Adam Kuhn and others, and last, but certainly not least, attempted to secure Rush's aid in obtaining a federal appointment at the port of Savannah.

Sheftall's friendship for Rush was well known, and when in 1813 Rush fell a victim to typhus fever, an intimate acquaintance of Sheftall, Richard Leake, hastened to notify him of the death of his "friend and patron, the accomplished scholar, the real gentleman and true republican." Leake concluded his sad tidings with this couplet:

> Rush rests for ever and no longer fears
> The critics censure or the coxcomb's sneers.

SOURCE. The Library Company of Philadelphia.

Savannah, January 24th, 1795.

Doctor Benjamin Rush.
Sir:

It is with pleasure I have perused your publication entitled, *An Account of the Bilious Yellow Fever*, as it appeard in your city in the year 1793. 'Tis not for me to comment or say much upon it, but, sir, the world, I think, must ever feel herself obligated to you for introducing into practice what has been by some called the new mode of healing the yellow fever.

I beg you'll excuse me for not proceeding in a regular manner through your publication on that epidemic, as it was but a hasty view that I had of it. I had long ago, from publications which I frequently seen in the news papers, of yours as well as other gentlemen of the faculty, felt my self satisfied that the disease then spoke of was one of those diseases that might be truly called inflammatory. But, sir, when I come to see the volume published by you, giving an account of the other diseases, such as the mumps, the scarlatina, etc., putting on those inflammatory appearances, had there been the least doubt on my mind, it must have been immediately removed, for the previous heat and dryness of the weather no doubt contributed greatly to increase the inflammatory disposition of the diseases. Doctor Sydenham attributes a highly inflammatory state of the small pox to a previous heat and dry summer. These observations, and many others, that are mentioned in your piece with the method of cure, must fully convince every reasonable man that the disease was of the inflammatory kind.

It will do well to observe here that I do agree with you in opinion with respect to the name of this disease, [for] which you say you've adopted the term *yellow,* from its being most frequently used. I am of opinion that a more proper and suitable one might be found, for I can assure you that almost every fever which prevails in this country, in the lower parts of it particularly, where there is low and swampy grounds and with easterly winds, there is a yellowness of the skin or, too [to] appearances, a suffusion of bile. It surely would be the height of imprudence for the safety of our citizens and peace of their minds to call those fevers the yellow fever. I beg you'll excuse my suggesting to you, whose many years' experience in the science of medicine must long since have put it out of the power of so young a practitioner to suggest any thing new or entertaining, but from my knowledge of your disposition to listen with attention to such as may address you, and put them to rights when they err, I have ventured to call this the inflammatory bilious fever.

This new name alone would induce practitioners of medicine in different places to immediately have recourse to the antiphlogistic [against inflammation] remedies laid down by you. Then this vague and absurd idea of putrefaction of the circulating blood would not be thought of, but every man of any medical information would know that, unless this inflammatory affection was speedily removed, it would fall on some vital part and there, in a short period of time, would undergo the same changes that all other inflammations do. He would not think of pouring in bark, wine, and laudanum from his knowledge of the impropriety of such remedies in those diseases. Although it would be more proper at some other time to bring into view the authors referrd to by you, I must beg leave here to say that, with all respect to tertians [fevers] spoke of by Doctor Cleghorn, whose own words I will here insert:

> These tertian fevers have as a good right to be called contagious as the measles, small pox, or any other disease, for although in that season there certainly is a peculiar disposition in the air to effect [affect] numbers in the same way, yet those who are much conversant among the sick are most liable to catch the distemper. (Page 132.)

I must differ with him that tertian fevers are not contagious. I would prove by asking this question: Are not persons much conversant among the sick of any disorders always more liable to take that disease than any other, by being much debilitated by fatigue, anxiety, night-watching, etc.? If so, surely tertians are no more contagious than pleurisys, peripnewmonys or any other complaints that occur during the year. Your fever, I think, was takeing by exhalation from the coffee and then propagated by contagion, as appears plainly from Mrs. [Thomas] Leaming's takeing it from her sister.

It is impossible for me to travel through your history of the yellow fever and give it its just merits. The calumnies raised against you by many of the medical faculty can only, in my opinion, tend to endear you more to your fellow citizens, as they are fully convinced of the utility of the mode of treatment pursued by you and the destruction brought on by a contrary mode of practice.

As for Doctor Kuhn's conduct on the occasion, I know not what to compare it too [to], but that of a general officer flying from his standard. I think he should be brought to a court martial and tried for desserting his post in time of danger. Was I one of his court, I should surely cashier him and render him incapable of ever serving in the field of medicine.

These lines, sir, are intruded on you from no vain motives. They are wrote for the purpose of receiving a letter of instruction and information in return for them, as they can afford no further satisfaction than to know that your former students, who attended your medical and usefull lectures (however distant they may be), always feels a pleasure when they peruse a work done by you, particularly where they so plainly see the difficulty which you must labourd under, and the satisfactory manner in which you triumphed over your enemies, and the readiness with which you forgive them for the calumnies they raised against you. 'Tis truly expressive of your goodness of heart.

Permit me to beg your attention for a moment to my business. As 'tis generally believed that Congress will, in their present session, make some arrangement with respect to hospitals for the reception of sick seamen in the different ports of the United States, I must beg of you to use your best endeavours to get me appointed visiting physician for this port. My recommendations have been laying for some time in the hands of my brother-in-law, Doctor [Solomon] Bush, to whom I have wrote, requesting him to deliver them to a Mr. [Abraham] Baldwin, a member of the House of Representatives from this state. If you can serve me, I shall ever gratefully acknowledge it.

Before I bring this to a conclusion, permit me most sincerely to condole with you on the loss of your amiable sister and worthy students, losses which no doubt must long make a lasting impression on your mind of the fatality of your late contagious fever.

With my best wishes for your future health, and may the Great Author of all beings long preserve and protect you, and increase the number of your years, that you may long be a lasting evidence and scourge to pestilential fevers should your city be ever again visited, which Heaven forbid, is the sincere and ardent prayer of, sir,

Your most obedient and very humble servant,
Moses Sheftall

P.S. Be pleased to present my best wishes to Doctors [James] Mease and [James] Woodhouse, and tell either of them I will be thankfull if they will forward me Mr. Seybart's [Adam Seybert's] *Inaugural Dissertation* and other late medical publications, particularly that of the College of Physicians of your city, with the cost, and I will by the first opportunity remit them the expense of the same.

No. 33   A Future State Senator Writes a Letter—1795

In 1795 Ephraim Hart, of New York, wrote the letter printed below, introducing his son Samuel to Aaron Hart, of Three Rivers, Canada.

Both Harts, though not related, were fabulous characters. Aaron Hart (1724–1800), a Bavarian by birth, was an army supplyman during the conquest of Canada (1759–60). By 1795 he was, without doubt, the richest Jew in Canada and, in all likelihood, the most influential businessman in Three Rivers.

Ephraim Hart, also a Bavarian, came to the colonies in the early 1770's, and by 1795 was seemingly the richest Jew in New York City. A pillar of the local synagogue, he served as its president in 1794, showed a great deal of intelligent interest in the Hebrew school, and was one of the founders of a sick-care and burial society. He was a land speculator and one of the original members of the stockbrokers' guild, out of which grew the New York Stock Exchange. In 1810 he was elected to the New York State Senate.

Samuel Hart, one of Ephraim's sons, hoped to settle and make his way in Canada. If he ever reached that province he did not remain long, for he died within the year. After the turn of the century, Harriot, Ephraim's daughter, married a son of Aaron, thus uniting the two families.

Aaron and Ephraim Hart, German immigrants, had many things in common, including a German-accented phonetic English, as the following letter amply demonstrates.

SOURCE. Séminaire du Saint Joseph, Hart Papers.

N. York, 16th March, 1795.

Dear Sir:

It is longe since I wrote to you, beeing in expectation of receiving a letter from you as promised by you and Ezekiel [your son]. However, I'll not stay for punctilies [punctilios; I shall not stand on ceremony]. Shall at all times be happy to renter you and yours every servis in my power.

My famely have been this 7 weeks much deranged on account of my secount son, Asher, beeing sick that time, and God knows wheter he ever will recover his former health. [This] provented my giving more attanion [attention] to my friends.

I have from time to time regolar forwarted your letters for England and will ever take care that your orders shall be punctaly attendit do.

The bearer of this is my oldist son, Samuel, who beeing willing to see som part of the world and fint a place where he may be able to do bussines for him self, he not beeing very partial to N. York, I have consented to his going to Canada, or ware ever he should fint more agreable to him self, when I shall be willing to assit him, what in my power, to promod his interest.

I therefor recomant him to you and Mrs. Hart attendion. And beg any advice or service you can give him, you'll not spare of doing it, for which I shall at all times be oblige to you, and in return do the same to any of your offspring.

So with wishing you, Mrs. Hart, and the rest of your good family health and happiness, and *simhat y[om] t[ob] ad meah shanim* ["may you have joyous holidays for a hundred years"],

Remain your friend and humble servant,
Ephraim Hart

Pray give my best wishes to Mrs. Hart, your son Moses, Ezekiel, and Fanny, and the rest of your good family. Excuse hast.

No. 34 Jacob Mordecai, Child Pedagogue—1796–1798

Jacob Mordecai (1762–1838) was a native American, the son of the German Jewish merchant Moses Mordecai (1707–81), who came to this country about 1750. Jacob received a rather good religious (Hebrew) and secular education and improved upon it by extensive reading. He was a man of considerable culture.

In 1774, when the difficulties with the British government became acute, young Mordecai, an ardent patriot of twelve, belonged to a boys' military group that made itself useful—and conspicuous— by escorting the delegates of the First Continental Congress into Philadelphia on that momentous September day.

He was not a successful businessman. After clerking for David Franks during the Revolutionary War, he lived briefly in several towns and hamlets, including New York, where in 1784 he formed a partnership with Haym Salomon. Finally, however, he settled in

Warrenton, North Carolina, as a country merchant and dealer in tobacco and grain.

It was in that village that his wife, the former Judith Myers, died in January, 1796. A few weeks after her death, the local Masonic lodge met, wrote him a note of condolence, and informed him of his election to office in the lodge. Document A is his answer to this kind gesture.

After the death of his wife, Mordecai sent two of his little girls, Rachel and Ellen, then seven and six years of age, to live with their uncle Samuel Myers in Richmond. Little Caroline, a child of two, was sent to another aunt in the same city.

It was during that period, before Mordecai's remarriage in 1798, that he maintained a constant correspondence with his two little daughters in the Virginia capital (Documents B through E).

In these letters the father set about purposefully to inculcate proper rules of conduct and ethical behavior in his little ones. His letters are ponderous and didactic. What could they have meant to lonely little girls who were just learning their letters? Very likely he felt that it was his duty as a good father to concern himself seriously with the proper rearing of his motherless children.

In one letter (Document D) Mordecai forgot his copybook morals and wrote a child's letter, giving us good reason to believe that behind his starched dignity was a real human being.

In his emphasis on reading and studying and in his dogged devotion to the intellectual development of his children, he was not typical of the Jew of his generation.

SOURCE. Document A: State Department of Archives and History, Raleigh, N. C., Pattie Mordecai Collection. Documents B through E: Duke University Library, Jacob Mordecai Papers.

A [NO. 34]

Warrenton, January 27th, 1796.

Dear and respectable Brethren:

Your kind note of condolence was handed me by Brother Richards. The commisseration you are pleased to express for the recent loss I have met with, evinces your adherence to those great principles of our order which teaches us "in all cases of distress and affliction, to cherish, console, and releive each other," and claims in return for this "cordial testimony of your fraternal affection," every thing that a grateful heart can suggest.

While I deplore the stroke that has bereft me of life's greatest comfort, and know death to be the irrevocable law of our nature, and that man among the rest of creation, when called by Providence, must submit to part with the life that was given him, still, my friends, I find there is no reasoning down our feelings when the heart is corroded by affliction. I will endeavor to "resist the shock" with becoming fortitude, and to bear this affliction with a rational composure.

The better to evince the desire I have of according with your wishes so flattering to myself, I will, as speedely as is consistent with the "solemn occurrence," accept the seat you have honored me with; and my best exertions shall zealously be made to promote the prosperity of the lodge. In the execution of this important duty, I pleasingly anticipate your kind cooperation, that by our mutual endeavors we may support the name of a respectable, regular, and uniform society.

That the Grand Architect of the universe may prosper you in every walk through life and guard you from its unfortunate vissicitudes is, my dear brethren, the sincere wish of

Your affectionate and obedient,
Jacob Mordecai

To the Wardens and Brethren of Johnston Caswell Lodge.

B [NO. 34]

Warrenton, December 10th, 1796.

My dear Rachel and Ellen:

I was very agreeably surprised, on the receipt of your good Uncle Samy's letter the other day, to be informed of the progress you made (and the pleasing reward attending that progress) in your learning.

The satisfaction your friends derive, the pleasure resulting to yourselves, and the advantages attendant on education will no doubt all conspire to impell you with ardor steadily to pursue this pleasing avocation. You must not be discouraged if at times you meet with little difficultys. They can be overcome by perseverance and attention, and your pleasures will increase with your knoulege of things, which will become more generally familiar as you progress in learning. Be, therefore, attentive to your preceptor, and I have no doubt the specimen you have given, and considerd by your friends as a presage of more considerable improvement, will in due time be confirmd. How pleasing must the reflection be to yourselves, how desirable to all who love you! Proceed, therefore, with confidence, and your endeavors will assuredly be attended with success.

Your dear brothers have wrote to you. They are all well and have a great desire to see you, but the season is too severe. In the course of the ensuing year, perhaps, they may visit you, and as you can hear frequently of each other, that must suffice, for you know it would be a great disadvantage for them to leave their studys for any length of time, and short visits would be painful to you all. It's therefore best to be satisfyed with the knoulege of each other's welfare. Theirs I will often communicate, and your dear Uncle Samy will inform me of yours. Kiss dear Caroline for me, and be kindly attentive to each other. . . .

Your father,

J. M.

Miss Rachel and Ellen Mordecai,
Richmond.

C [NO. 34]

Warrenton, August 13th, 1797.

My dear Rachel must not suppose from my long silence that I have been unmindful of the promise I made to acknowlege the letter she deliverd me in Richmond.

I have received it with pleasure. It assures me of your affection and convinces me of your improvement. The former I will always endeavor to preserve, for you are very dear to me; and I am certain you will merit mine, by attending to the advise I may occasionally give and strictly observing that which you frequently receive from your dear aunt and uncle.

Inattention to the council [counsel] of our friends who are zealous to promote our welfare is at all times and in every situation inexcusable. It is a species of ingratitude that will tend to alienate their affections, for when their well meant endeavors to form the mind, cultivate the manners, and improve the person are either obstinately opposed or carelessly attended to, their attempts ceasing to be a pleasure, disgust ensues, and we become almost indifferent to the welfare of any one capable of making an unkind, improper, and painful return for our good intentions.

Those general observations will, I trust, have your attention. Examine your conduct. If they apply, correct your errors. The goodness of your heart will ensure you success and secure the esteem of your kind patrons. Be obedient to their councils. Impress them upon your mind. Persevere in attempts to improve your personal carriage, so justly the object of animadversion. Difficulties always decrease when we encounter them with firmness, and what at first view appears very difficult, soon becomes familiar, easy, and agreeable.

Cultivate the affections of your sister. Be kindly attentive to that dear blessed infant, my Caroline, and whilst under one roof, daily attend to my former request. Let politeness distinguish your conduct to every one. Nothing excuses rudeness, even to a domestic.

Your brothers are well and send a great deal of love to you, their sisters, and frends. They have not time to write by this opportunity which leaves town immediately. I send you a book; it is well spoken of. Peruse it with attention; give me your opinion. Read it for Ellen, to whom my love, which I would confirm with many kisses. . . .

My affectionate regards to grand ma, aunts, uncles, etc. God bless you, my dear Rachel. In haste, I am,

Your,

J. Mordecai

D [NO. 34]

My dear Rachel and Ellen:

You don't know how much I was pleased when your Uncle Samy came to see me and told me you were very good girls and attended to the advise he and your uncles Moses [Mears Myers] and Samson [Mears Myers] give you; that they all love you very much, and you in return, I am sure, love them so well that whenever you are told of any thing you do amiss, you will not do so again.

You must write to me very soon and tell me how your grand mama [Joyce Mears Myers] and Aunt Richa [Myers] were when you left them, for I suppose you will be in Petersburg very soon after Uncle Samy gets home. Your dear brothers and little Caroline send a great deal of love to you and want to see you very much. Little Solly [age five] and Caroline call you every day, and they all love you both very much. Uncle Samy will give you the chest of drawers I forgot to send with your other toys.

Be good girls, mind your reading and writing, that you may be able to send me letters often, for I love you so dearly that I shall always be pleased when you can write to me. God bless you, my dear children. Love each other and mind your dear uncles and then you will always afford pleasure to your papa.

I participate with you at this remote distance in the pleasure that will attend the recet [receipt] of these few lines which will be deliverd by your belovd brother Moses. He will give you all the news and every information respecting your brothers, who are in health and both send an abundance of love to you. Solly says he is going to Petersberg next week to see his sisters and has several horses in readiness.

I hope my dear Rachel has received the book I sent to the care of Uncle Samson some time past. The bearer has another in charge from me, with some other trifles which you will accept as a mark of my love for you, my dear girls. Tell Ellen my lips have not diminished in consequence of the kisses she gave me, and that I long to press her to my heart.

You are all equally dear to me and shall never know an abatement of my affection while you continue to merit my tenderness, and that, I am sure, will be as lasting as your lives.

God bless you, my dear children, and preserve you from every ill, is the wish of

Your affectionate father,
J. M.

Kiss dear Caroline for *me* whenever you visit her.
September 4th, 1797.

E [NO. 34]

Warrenton, July 31st, 1798.

It is a long time since I heard from you, my dear Rachel, but as no direct opportunities have offered, I know it has not proceeded from inattention. The satisfaction I have in writing to you would be a sufficient inducement, but as I believe you also receive equal gratification, I shall take every private opportunity of informing you that we are all in good health and that you are verry dear to me and beloved by your good [step]mama, brothers, and Caroline. Ellen equally shares our affection, and you are both the daily subjects of conversation.

I please myself with the progress you make in your studies, the attention you pay to cleanliness and a neat disposition of your dress, the obedience you pay to your protectors, and improvement in those things that will make you agreeable to your friends, and, of course, [I am] well satisfyd with yourselfs, which I am sure cannot be the case when any part of your conduct is disapproved. We have all our foibles. When they are apparent to ourselves, which a little self examination will point out, or made known to us by the gentle admonition of our friends, it becomes a duty to remove the cause and never to persist in any act that is improper.

Write to me as often as you conceiveably can. You need not wait till an opportunity is immediately offering. Take any leisure time and give me a specimen of your improvement in that necessary art.

Caroline spells and grows a verry fine child. She often gives me a kiss for you and Ellen and says she will make me a pretty night cap.

My love to grand mama, aunts, etc. When Uncle Sammy comes home, I hope they will be pleased with your conduct during their absence. Nothing equals the pleasure I receive when informed that you are both good girls. Accept an abundant share of love from

Your father,
J. M.

Miss Rachel and Ellen Mordecai,
Richmond.

No. 35   Tom, a Slave, Seeks His Old Master—1796

Mordecai Sheftall (1735–97) was the outstanding Jew in Georgia during the Revolutionary period. His father Benjamin had come to Savannah only a few months after James Oglethorpe, and Mordecai had grown up in the colony. Very early in life he became a successful businessman. Among his enterprises were one or two "cowpens," or ranches. In 1772 his five children were the owners of the 5S ranch.

Mordecai, one of the leading Whigs in his colony, was chairman of the committee created to further the Revolutionary cause in Christ Church Parish (county), which included the colony's largest city, Savannah. It was only natural, therefore, that when Tories such as James and Daniel McGirth attacked the Whigs and ran off with their slaves, Sheftall would not be spared. Many years after the raids, Sheftall received a letter from James Seagrove, a Camden County politician, informing him that one of his slaves, carried off by the McGirths, was ready to return to his old master. The following letter describes what happened to the Negro.

SOURCE. The Mr. and Mrs. B. H. Levy Collection of Sheftall Papers.

Town of St. Mary's [Georgia], 5th October, 1796.

Mordecai Shifftal, Esq.,
Savannah.
Dear Sir:

About a week past, a negro man, who calls himself John, but says he was formerly named Tom, came to the garrison at Colerain [near St. Mary's] from St. Augustine. The account he gives is that he and his brother were taken from your cowpen near Briar Creek, during the [Revolutionary] War by the noted McGirt and carried to Florida and there sold; that he has had several masters, but the one from whom he run at this time is named McEnery, living in St. Augustine. He tells me that all his family belonged to you.

I brought him with me from Colerain, as the fellow was confined there. He is at my house, where, he says, he will remain until I hear from you, and to know whither [whether] you consider him as your property. I shall be glad to hear from you and to have a state of facts relating to this negro. With esteem, I remain,

Your humble servant,
James Seagrove

No. 36   A Letter from a Retired Businessman—1798

By 1798 Barnard and Michael Gratz, pioneer merchants in the trans-Allegheny trade, were "old" men. Sick and tired, they were incapable of sustained effort, although the older of the two was only about sixty years of age. Life in early America, especially on the frontier, wore people to the bone.

Barnard Gratz at that time had already retired from business in Philadelphia and had moved to Baltimore, where he lived with his only child, Rachel (Mrs. Solomon Etting). In place of the old firm of B. & M. Gratz, a new business had arisen, conducted by Michael's two sons, Simon (Simmy) and Hyman, who had received their early mercantile training from their grandfather Joseph Simon, of Lancaster, a pioneer in the Pennsylvania fur trade. In 1798 Simon and Hyman Gratz were transacting business in the house on Market Street where in 1776 Thomas Jefferson had lived and written the Declaration of Independence.

The brothers suffered some severe financial setbacks, but did well in later years and were among the earliest supporters of the Pennsylvania Academy of Fine Arts. In 1798, however, they were only beginners, concentrating their mercantile efforts in the field of wholesale groceries. Long after Hyman's death in 1857, Gratz College, a school for the education of Jews, was established in Philadelphia (1893) from the funds of his residuary estate.

In the following letter, written by Uncle Barnard to his nephew Simon, the retired merchant writes with painful effort about a number of matters. Barnard had hoped to go north to his old home in Philadelphia to be present when his nephew Joseph was formally inducted into Judaism as a Son of the Commandment [bar mizvah], but unfortunately was compelled to forego the pleasure, no doubt because of his infirmity. Barnard also urged Simon to speed up the liquidation of the estate of Joseph Henry, a close relative who had died in 1793. Joseph Henry's father in Silesia was pressing for payment of his inheritance, and embarrassed the American branch of the clan by naïvely writing to the President of the United States and to the mayor of Philadelphia about the estate.

In the postscript Barnard Gratz sent his affectionate regards to the "dear son" of Mr. and Mrs. Samuel Hays. That child Isaac, then about two years of age, was to grow up to become one of the two men who wrote the code of ethics of the American Medical Association.

SOURCE. The Edwin Wolf 2d Collection of American Jewish Documents, Philadelphia.

Baltimore, March 7, 1798.

Mr. Simon Gratz, Merchant,
Philadelphia.
Dear Simmy:

Your favor of the 25th ultimo with the deed of Joseph Henry's land, by Mr. Kope, I duly received and hope you will take care to secure the remainder of the payments so that we may be shure to gett payment in due time without any truble, either by mortgage, or bonds and secuerity.

I am sinceerly sorry for been dissoppinted of injoyment of Jose [Joe's] *bar mitzwa* [confirmation ceremony]. Hope he performit well in reading his *parsha* [portion of his Pentateuchal reading], of which I hope to hear in your next letter. And [I] hope Hy will meet with good sucess in his colliction, which I sinceerly wish.

I should have been glad to have heard [your grandfather] Mr. Simon's answer to your mother's letter. I supose it is the Englishman's written [reply] in regard to my been [being] home for *Pesah* ["Passover"], [which] I fear will be out of my power as am told [the] Susquahanna is froze over yett and dangers crossing yett. The posts dose not come in reguler yett to this place.

I just now returned from seeng [Mrs. Reuben Etting, your sister,] Fany who is, thank God, getting better from her rumettick pains. Her children [are] very well and desires there love to you all, in which Reuben joynes. He talks of comeing up to Philadelphia with little Gratz [three-year-old Elijah Gratz Etting], as soon as Fanny is out of her laying in, and perhaps Fanny too.

I have nothing more to write at pressent, only my affectsoin to your father, mother, sisters, and brothers, and wish you all a great deall joy on Joe's account. May you all live to see him grow [up to be] a good man and see him marriad, in which my Rachel and Solly and there children all joyn me in [wishing] to you all.

I hope your good mother will excuse me of not writting to her, as she will see by this writting how trublesome it's for me to write, and believe me to be, dear Simmy, as usual,

Your affectionate uncle, etc., etc.,
Barnard Gratz

My compliments to Mr. and Mrs. Gootsholkson [Solomon Gottschalkson], Mr. and Mrs. Aaron Levy, Mr. and Mrs. Hazzan ["Cantor"] Cohen. My affectionate love attends Mr. and Mrs. Samuel Hays and the dear son [Isaac], etc. Hope they [are] all well.

———

No. 37   Rebecca Franks Hears from a Long-Lost Brother—1799

The Frankses, of London, came from Germany in the latter part of the seventeenth century. Some time after 1700 one of the sons, Jacob, came to New York, followed by members of other branches of the family. Judging from the recurrence of the same common given names (Abraham, Isaac, Jacob, David, John, Moses, Rebecca, etc.), most of the Jewish Frankses were related, although there is no positive proof to that effect.

The following letter was sent by a Rebecca Franks of Philadelphia to her brother John of Quebec. (The writer is not to be confused with her famous namesake, the brilliant if somewhat flighty daughter of David Franks, the Philadelphia Loyalist.) Her father may have been a John Franks who did business with Halifax in the 1750's, and it is possible that Colonel David Salisbury Franks was her brother. Evidently the family moved to Canada while Rebecca was very young. Two of her brothers, John Jr. and Moses, went with her, but Moses ultimately returned to Philadelphia, where he made a home for himself and his sister. It is very likely that he was the Moses Franks who, after the siege of Boston in 1776, was one of the three men selected by John Hancock and the Continental Congress to convey $250,000 in coin to General Washington.

John remained in Canada and became a merchant of some stature. In 1784 he joined a group of Canadians who petitioned for a representative government based "on fixed and liberal principles," and later he became the first chief of the Quebec fire brigade.

At the time Rebecca wrote to John, her other brother, Moses, who had sailed to the West Indies, had been gone for almost two years, leaving his sister alone in Philadelphia. It must have seemed a miracle to Rebecca to receive word from John, whom she had given up for dead, saying that he was in Canada. His promise to send some money was particularly welcome news in her present state of privation.

Rebecca's letter is interesting because it emphasizes an aspect of American life that only too frequently is ignored or overlooked: the hard lot of the woman in early American economic life. True, there was little comparison between the lot of the woman on a pioneer clearing, bowed down under the yoke of work and a brood of children, and the fate of a mother, sister, or wife in Philadelphia, the country's largest city, enjoying all the comforts and luxuries of a thriving metropolis. Still, the life of the women in a merchant's family was by no means an untroubled one, for the man she loved was often away from home for months or even years, braving the dangers of the Indian trail, the threat of pirates, or the devastating power of the Caribbean storms.

SOURCE. State Historical Society of Wisconsin, Madison, John Lawe Papers.

Philadelphia, February 5th, [1799].

My dear brother:

I realy am at a loss to find words to express my joy in addressing my long lost brother. Be assured, I never had the most distant idea of ever hearing from you, for I had long thought you had gone to that bourn from whence no traveller returns, but, thank God, I have been *most* agreeably surprised.

Oh brother, it is many years since we have been with each other. I suppose you have no recollection of me and I *am sure I have none of you.*

I have gone through many scenes since I was in Canady. I was a very young adventurer, an[d], I may say, am still; but I trust in God, I have vearly [verily] done and that I shall shortly be settled with or near you, for at present I feel friendless and deserted, without parents, without connection, for my brother Moses is never with me. If he was, my situation would be far more agreeable, but he is sometines gone for 2 years when he tells me it [is] probable he will be back in the course of 6 or 8 months, and in that time he never writes one line to [enable me to] know where he is. I some times by chance hear. This last voyage he has nearly been gone two years and has never wrote once to me.

My feelings are sensibly wounded, for he knows my sole dependance is on his bounty. I have been under the disagreeable necessity of applying to a friend of his for money to pay my board and get necessaries, for I am obliged to appear genteel. I cannot think his slight is for whant [want] of affection, but the whant of thought, for untill now he has ever been kind and attentive. I have wrote twice lately, but have received no answer.

Had I done any thing to cause his displeasure, I should not be surprised, but, *thank God,* I have never done any thing to occasion a blush in either of my brothers' faces. It would be a very great happiness to me was I capable of doing somthing for my self, but I am not; therefore, I must be content.

I pay at the rate of five dollars per week for my board, and [that] is as cheap as I can get it. I am with a very worthy couple who are adva[nced] in life without children. They do all they can to make me comfortable, but you know that is not like being with or near our own relations. Their [there] is but three of us left, and I think it a very great pity that we could not all be to gather; but instead of that, you are in Canada, my brother Moses in the West Indias, and poor me in Philadelphia.

It would have been a very great gratefication to me had I seen Mr. Levy, but I immagine he must have been here at the time of the dreadfull malady [1793], and every person at that time where [were] obliged to fly for their lives, which will be the case again this summer, for we have many instances of it now. It is plain to be seen that the c[old weather?] has only checked it, that as soon as the warm commences it [will return?] with as much violence as ever; but I have not heard the [news?] of Mr. Levy's being hear [here].

I will not fatigue you by [sending you?] too long a letter. I will accept of your generous offer. [You may be?] assured I never wanted it more then at present, for the little I had is nearly spent, and I have no person that I can apply to, for the gentleman who advanced me the last sum said that he could not think of doing it again, as he had not received orders from my brother. I have been very particular in . . . every thing, maby more so then I ought to be.

All [I can?] say is to request you to write soon as you can [to me] for I am very anxious to hear from you.

May every wished for[tune] attend; this is the sincere wish of [your]

Affectionate sister,

[Rebecca]

Direct to Philadelphia, South Second Street, between C[hestnut? and] Walnut, at Mr. Blackburn's. *Do pray write soon.*

II   The Religious Life

No. 38   The Beginnings of the Newport Synagogue—1754–1764

In all likelihood Jewish religious services were held in Newport as early as the 1670's, and a small congregation may even have existed there at the time. If there was an organized congregation, however, it did not last very long, possibly not more than a decade. In the 1740's Jews began to resettle in Newport in greater number and by 1754 there were enough to constitute a formal religious organization.

The Newporters called themselves Nephutse Israel, "The Scattered of Israel," taking their name, like the Jews of Barbados, from the Messianic verse, Isaiah 11:12: "And God will assemble The Dispersed of Israel [Barbados], and gather together The Scattered of Judah [or Israel, Newport]." A decade or so later the congregation called itself Jeshuat Israel, or The Salvation of Israel.

In 1754 the Newport congregation appealed for financial help to the mother synagogue of the Sephardic Jews in England. In their reply, in Spanish (Document A), the leaders of the London congregation extended their good wishes to the newly organized group, but stated that they were unable at that time to comply with their request. However, they later sent a contribution. Undeterred by many handicaps, the Jews of Newport continued their efforts toward realizing their dearest hope, the erection of their own house of worship. This dream became a reality when, in December, 1763, they dedicated the synagogue which Peter Harrison had designed for them. Still standing, it is now a national historic site.

The need for a place of worship was not the only motive for the

86

erection of the synagogue. In later correspondence it is revealed that the Newport congregation lived up to the traditional command to provide a place for prayer, study, and philanthropy, stressing not only worship, but also the education of the children and the dispensing of charity.

The synagogue, a beautiful Georgian structure, cost the little Jewish community about £2,000 sterling, part of which was defrayed by a mortgage. After the French and Indian War (1764) money became tight, and again the congregation had to appeal to others for financial aid. Among those to whom they turned was the seventeenth-century Curaçao Congregation Mikveh Israel. It is interesting to note in the appeal to Mikveh Israel (Document B), translated from the Spanish, that Frederick De Wit, a member of a well-known Christian Curaçao family, served as mediator between the two congregations. Inasmuch as there are no extant Newport or Curaçao congregational records for the middle eighteenth century, it is difficult to determine whether the cry for help was answered.

SOURCE. Document A: Congregation Shaar Hashamaim (Bevis Marks), London, Minute Book; Document B: Congregation Mikveh Israel, Curaçao, Manuscript Records.

A [NO. 38]

London, the —— August, 1754.

New Port, Road Island
Very illustrious gentlemen of Congregation of
Nephuse Israel:

We received your very esteemed letter of the 6 Sebat [January 29, 1754] of this year, in which you request this whole *kaal* ["congregation"] of Saar a Samaim [Gate of Heaven] to cooperate in aiding you to establish and form a synagogue in this place, so that in it, with greater decorum, they may keep their *sepharim* ["scrolls"] and make their prayers. May God accept from you such a faithful and religious desire!

We, on our part, praise you very much, and after we had read your letter in the full *mahamad* ["board"], we resolved also to place it before a meeting of the elders of this *kaal*, and considering well your circumstances, it was resolved that at the present time it would not be convenient for us, nor are we able to comply with your request.

May God be the One who assists all, and of whose grace we would desire that he give to you as he is able, and may he prosper you in your pious plans!

Moseh de Jacob Franco, *gabay* ["treasurer"]

B [NO. 38]

To the honorable members of the K. K. Mikveh Israel:

Cheered by the hope offered us by the kind protection of Mr. Frederick De Wit, we, through the offices of the above gentleman, request the liberal assistance of your worthy congregation, so that we might be able to repay the obligation and mortgage which we were forced to place on our building, and so that we might be able to pay the workmen who constructed it.

For two years we have just about managed to collect enough to pay the interest at eight per cent, an expenditure which, when added to the annual expenses involved in the maintenance of the synagogue, has proved extremely difficult for this small congregation in such adverse times. The third annual due date of the mortgage having arrived, and . . . [in view of the fact] that it will be impossible for us not only to pay the principal, but even the interest, we find it necessary to appeal to our brethren, and to inform them of our deplorable situation, especially when we consider the great risk of eventually losing our valued building.

Mr. De Wit, who has personal knowledge of our plight, has graciously encouraged us, offering to supervise and sponsor a campaign for funds to save the synagogue, and, being an effective speaker, proposes to open the drive for this campaign—an offer which we can hardly commend highly enough, and one which is characteristic of noble thoughts.

We flatter ourselves that since the practice of mitzvot is so deeply ingrained in your spirit, you will unanimously agree to come to the aid of this effort. May God lead you to such action and may he be pleased to recompense your large congregation with long life, increased favor, and prosperity for many years.

Your very humble and obedient servants,

Aaron Lopez, parnas	Jacob Hart
Moses Seixas	Isaac Hart
Jacob Rodriguez Rivera	Moses Lopez
Naphtali Hart, Jun.	Isaac Elizer
Ishac de Abraham Touro, hazan	

Newport, Kahal Kadosh Nephutsé Israel, Tishri 7, 5525 [October 3, 1764].

No. 39   Old-Age Pensions and Loans to the Needy—1761–1765

Although the Jewish congregation of New York City was relatively small, it devoted a substantial part of its income to the care of the poor, the sick, and the old. Old-age pensions were granted to those who had no other means of support.

Moses Louzada, of New Jersey, died in 1750, leaving his wife Hannah and his children a very small estate, if any. The name of the Widow Louzada appears in the ledgers of the Gomezes of New York, indicating that for a while she attempted to carry on some sort of business. Obviously she was not successful, for in 1756 she appealed to the congregation for help. Although the original grant was for four weeks only, she remained on its pension rolls, and in 1761, too ill to go to the city, she wrote to the congregation in phonetic and almost unintelligible English, asking for her usual grant (Document A). As late as 1774 she was still being supported by Shearith Israel.

The congregation occasionally loaned money to persons in need to tide them over a period of trouble. Levi Michael was such a suppliant for financial aid. In 1759, Michael, then living in South Haven, Long Island, married Rachel, the daughter of Judah Hays, the well-established New York merchant-shipper. There can be no question that the latter had no use for his son-in-law, and when Hays's will was probated in 1764 it was found that he had cut his daughter off with five shillings for marrying contrary to his desire. By that time Michael had moved to Canada, where he remained for the rest of his life, active as a merchant and fur trader.

In all likelihood it was some time in 1764 that Michael returned to New York, apparently because of a misfortune that had befallen his daughter. In need of money to get back to Canada, he petitioned Shearith Israel for a loan (Document B).

SOURCE. American Jewish Historical Society Library, Lyons Collection, Document A: No. 77; Document B: No. 131.

A [NO. 39]

New Brunswik, 9 November, 1761.

Sir:

I take the liberty to wright to yow now. I think the at [that] is time for yow to get my wenters [winter's] . . . provisions, likewise a little money to bay some wood for the wenter. I woud a come down my self to feetchet [fetch it], but ben desebled, my legs heving swelds [swellings]. But y [I] hope, sir, that at ensent [that ancient proverb] not aut a sigt aut of mind [will apply to me].

Sir, hier y [I] lay sufering for the vant of wood and provisions.
Y [I] remende, sir,

Your most humble servent,
Hanne Lezade

Remember my love to your espowse . . . and the reste of your familly. . . .

B [NO. 39]

To the President and Elders of the Synagoga in the City of Newyork:

The petition of Levy Micheals of the city of Mountreal in the province of Cannada most humbly sheweth:

That the petitioner, being alarmed with the unexpected and disagreeable situation of his daughter in this city, induced him to leave home and come to Newyork in the month of November last, and being unhappyly detained here beyound the time he had fixed, has caused his money to become nearly exhausted.

Labouring under the most pressing diffeculties and a heavy expence for his support, and the great distance he has to travel home, lays him under the necessity of takeing this method to lay his diffeculty before you, and humbly prays you to take his case into consideration and grant him such a sum of money, upon loan, as you in your wisdom shall see meet, and, as in duty bound, etc., which sum shall be returned as soon as possible after his ariveal home.

Levi Michaels

No. 40   Abraham I. Abrahams, Circumciser
and Schoolteacher—1767–1769

Although the New York Jews were never very successful in carrying on their own religious and secular schools, they were interested in providing an education for their children. In 1762 they hired Abraham I. Abrahams (1720–96) to serve as a teacher. His contract specified that he was "to keep a publick school in the *Hebra* [the community building], to teach the Hebrew language and translate the same into English, also to teach English, reading, writing, and cyphering." On frequent occasions he officiated also as a volunteer rabbi and circumciser.

In September, 1767, Aaron Lopez, the Newport merchant, asked Abrahams to come to Rhode Island and to circumcise Abraham Lopez, Aaron's older brother, and his three adult sons. Abraham

Lopez, his wife, and his children were Marranos, secret Jews who pretended to be Christians in order to escape the wrath of the Inquisition, and they had just arrived from intolerant Portugal.

Abrahams could not get away until October, but on the twenty-seventh of that month he performed the operations at Tiverton. Abrahams stayed on, enjoying the hospitality of the Lopezes for almost a month, and returned to New York in the middle of November. Then, in a letter to Aaron Lopez (Document A), he announced his safe arrival at home and informed his host that Isaac Adolphus, a New York merchant, was sending some prayer shawl fringes (*zizith*) for the newly circumcised Lopezes. Abrahams himself sent a gift of some fringes for the children of Mrs. (Moses?) Lopez, Aaron's sister-in-law. In Document B, Aaron acknowledged the receipt of the gifts and sent his thanks on behalf of the family.

As a rule, Jews who lived in a community where a synagogue existed were very faithful in their adherence to Jewish law and ceremonial. Before his employment as a tutor, Abrahams was a merchant and manufacturer of liquor and snuff, and in all probability he continued in business even after becoming the community teacher and circumciser. But with all his trade he could not support his thirteen or more children and appealed, about 1769, to the elders of the synagogue (Document C) to permit him to occupy one of the congregational "parsonages."

SOURCE. Documents A and B: Newport Historical Society Library, Lopez Letters; Document C: American Jewish Historical Society Library, Lyons Collection, No. 48.

A [NO. 40]

New York, November 28th, 1767.

Mr. Aaron Lopez.
Sir:

I arrived safe here last Fryday week, after a very fatiguing, tedious passage, having laing at Fisher's Island several days. And at last came home by land from Huntington [Long Island], which was attended with no small expence. However, hope all is for the better. I long to hear of your brother and family. Beg it by the earliest opportunity.

Herewith send four double setts *tsitsiths* for them, being a present from Mr. Isaac Adolphus. He has no tephilim ["phylacteries"] to spare or would send some. Also four setts for Mrs. Lopez, her sons, with my compliments to her.

I found my family all in health, who join their best wishes to you and yours, with, sir,

Your most humble servant,
Abraham I. Abrahams

B [NO. 40]

Newport, December 4th, 1767.

Mr. Abraham I. Abrahams:

Your esteemed favour of the 28th ulto. released us from the anxiety we felt on the event of your fatiguing passage, and are exceeding glad you was at last restored in safety to your dear friends, whom [I] have the pleasure to learn, you found in health.

I delivered your kind message with the *tscissiths* to my brother Abraham, who, with his wife and children, thanks you for your friendly enquire [enquiry] after them, and likewise to Mr. Adolphus for his religious present; I also delivered [to] my sister in law the *tscissiths* for the boys, with your kind compliments.

Please to recive in return an ample and round salutation from the whole family, who, thanks to the Almighty, is well. My brother and his family did not return from Tevertown till last Monday. They are all breavily [brave] and full of devotion. God may increase it in them and in all our brethren, that we may cordially join to praise His mercifull regard for us.

I am, with particular esteem, sir,

Your most humble servant,
[Aaron Lopez]

C [NO. 40]

To the Gentlemen Parnasim and Elders of K. K. Sheerith Israel.
Gentlemen:

Having served this congregation in the capacity of a Ribbi upwards of seven years, and having a numerous family to support, have been obliged to try several ways to do the same honestly, as the pay I get for the same is far too short.

Therefore, as the house next the synagogue that I lived in, was not fit to carry on any business, and Mr. [Isaac Cohen Da] Silva, the former hazan's health would not permet his living far from the synagogue, I propos[ed to] the gentlemen parnasim and elders to give me the [sum?] allowed him for rent and I would remove, on which I was allowed fifteen pounds towards the same, which allowance was taken from me last year, yet was in hopes to been able to do without it. But as times are so bad and little to be done, if you gentlemen will be so kind as to take it into consideration to put the house in proper repair [and] fit for my family, and will let me have it again [to] dwell in, you will very much oblige, gentlemen,

Yours and the congregation's most humble servant,

Abraham I. Abrahams

No. 41 A Slaughterer Certifies Kosher Meat—1768

The Jews of North America exported relatively large quantities of meat to the West Indies and to Surinam in South America. In order to guarantee that a shipment was ritually acceptable, the firkins or barrels were accompanied by a statement certifying that the contents were kosher. Congregation Shearith Israel of New York supervised the export of such meat from the first half of the eighteenth century and levied an export tax to raise revenue for the congregation. To prevent frauds on the part of meat dealers and shippers, the barrels enclosing the meat were branded and sealed, and, as an added precaution, the meat itself sometimes carried a lead seal.

The following form was used in the eighteenth century by a Philadelphia shohet. This slaughterer was evidently engaged in certifying kosher meat to be exported to the Dutch island of Curaçao. In spite of its faulty spelling, the meaning of the certificate is clear.

Edwin Wolf 2d and Maxwell Whiteman, in their *History of the Jews of Philadelphia*, say that this certificate was prepared by a shohet working for Michael Gratz, of Philadelphia. The latter, as we know, was engaged in the exportation of meats to the West Indies about 1767.

SOURCE. The Library Company of Philadelphia.

Form for to make the certeficat

Mr. .... send by this vessel caled [called] ....
whereof [is] Capt. .... bound to Coracoa ....
...... furhins [firkins] ...... market [marked] ...... From No. .....
till .... Insides market [marked] with a strengh [string] seal and wax [with special markings] ...... I testefy by this that I have kill de [the] meat and examine[d] the same, as being *Sohet* ["slaughterer"] of this place, and that in considration of that, all our brothers, the House of Israel, may eat of the same.
In witness thereof, I sign my hand, Philadelphia, the .... 17...

No. 42   The First Philadelphia Synagogal
Constitution—*ca.* 1770

Individual Jews settled in Philadelphia and other locations in eastern Pennsylvania early in the eighteenth century. The first Jewish burial plot in Philadelphia was purchased in 1738, and, according to tradition, there were enough Jews in the city for occasional religious services during the 1740's. There is definite evidence that an informal synagogal group was in existence at that time, but it was not until the 1760's that they began to organize a congregation and even to talk of building a house of worship. In 1771 the Philadelphia Jews announced that a house of worship had been opened in Cherry Alley. By this time also a body of synagogue officials was functioning, and a congregational fund had been established to help unfortunate coreligionists and impoverished itinerants.

An organized congregation must have its constitution, and the following document, translated from the original Yiddish, is probably a draft that had been prepared for the Philadelphia Jewish religious community. (Its character as a draft is proved by the fact that repetitious material had not yet been eliminated.) Inasmuch as in the middle eighteenth century practically all the Jewish Philadelphians who were vitally interested in regular religious services were German immigrants, it is not surprising that their synagogal ordinances were originally written in Yiddish, interwoven, of course, with Anglicisms. The misspelling of the Hebrew words employed demonstrates eloquently that the writer certainly, if not the congregation, was unlearned in Hebraic lore.

However, though these Philadelphia German Jews wrote their first constitution in Yiddish, they followed the prevailing Sephardic organizational pattern. The Spanish-Portuguese liturgy and religious way of life had become typically "American." As a matter of fact, a comparison of the concepts and wording of the New York Shearith Israel "Rules and Restrictions" of 1728 with this organic statute lends credence to the belief that the Philadelphians had a copy of the New York constitution before them as they sat down to write. These Philadelphia regulations were written probably no later than 1770, and perhaps even as early as the 1750's. When the congregation was reconstituted in 1782, it called itself Mikveh Israel ("The Hope of Israel").

SOURCE. American Jewish Archives, The Henry Joseph Collection of Gratz Papers.

Since we are concerned about the matter of creating an organized community, it is important that we exercise prudence in selecting communal leaders.

The members who select the Board of Five are hereby warned to be careful to choose people who will dispense justice.

And when the Board of Five choose a president, the ruling is that he must first have served as *hatan torah* and *hatan bereshit*. ["Bridegroom of the Law" and "bridegroom of the beginning." These men were given the honor of closing and beginning the annual cycle of the Pentateuchal readings in the synagogue.] In addition, the Board of Five shall be careful, when they select a president, to see that he is neither quarrelsome nor tyrannical, but that he is a God-fearing man who is desirous of according justice to everyone.

If it should happen that a person has been a *hatan torah* and a *hatan bereshit,* and his turn arrives to become president, and it is known that he is quarrelsome and tyrannical, then that man is not to be made president. The Board of Five shall then elect another person, one who is respected here, to serve as president, even though he has not been either *hatan torah* or *hatan bereshit.*

Every householder is obligated to pay heed to what the president orders in the synagogue and, God forbid, not offer him any affront.

If there is a quarrel among the members, then the one in whom the quarrel centers must go to the president and to the Board of Five, and they must settle the matter. If however the litigant will not present himself, then the president has no right to give him a seat nor show him any religious courtesy in the synagogue, not to him, nor even to his children (as long as the children are subject to the litigant), until he submits to the president's decision. For the president is required to rent out the seats in order to support the synagogue. If, however, a person does not want to pay for his seat, then he has no right to a seat, nor to any congregational religious courtesy, not even to make a single donation in public.

If a person has insulted the synagogue and does not wish to submit, and the president decides that that man has done wrong, and that the affronter is to have no religious courtesy as long as he, the president, is in office, when, later on, another president comes to power, the new president is not to accord that man any religious courtesy until that offender has been examined by the new president and the Board of Five, to determine whether he was guilty or not.

Every householder is obligated to do that which is right, to submit to any orders of the president in the synagogue.

The president has the right to summon the Board of Five together whenever the need arises.

If a householder is of the opinion that the president has done him an injustice, then that man has the right to go to the Board of Five and to lay his case before them, and the Board of Five shall listen to both disputants to determine who is right. If, however, the Board of Five cannot settle the matter, then they are to summon a number of householders in order to settle the dispute between the parties.

If it is known that a person has desecrated the Sabbath, that person has no right to receive a religious courtesy in the synagogue until he hears what his sentence is to be.

If the president accords a religious courtesy to anybody in the synagogue, that person is obligated to accept; if not, he has to pay a fine.

If a person has a religious obligation to fulfill at a morning service, he is obligated likewise to come to the afternoon service. If not, he has to pay a fine. [If the community has arranged a special weekday service in the morning for a man, others may want his presence for a religious quorum in the afternoon. Let him appear!]

If a stranger comes to town, he is not immediately to be accorded a religious courtesy in the synagogue. He has to be here in town for at least several weeks, unless it happens that there are people here in town who know him. Then he is entitled to religious courtesies at once.

If there are people in the community who do not want to make any contribution, and separate themselves from the group, and do not want to help to support the community, when they die they [their heirs] have to pay for the cemetery lot, as much as the president and the Board of Five think that the lot is worth. They can demand much or little.

If a stranger [dies in town] and has means, he [his heirs], too, must pay for his burial lot. [Strangers who were impoverished itinerants were not expected to pay for their burial lots!]

––––––

No. 43   Passage to Surinam for a Poor Man—1770

In the spring of 1770 a Jew arrived in Newport from the Dutch island of St. Eustatius. He had once been wealthy but having lost his money, set out to seek relatives in Surinam, South America. Eager to help him, Jacob Rodriguez Rivera, the Newport merchant-shipper, wrote and asked Nicholas Brown & Company, of Providence, whether they would give the man passage in one of their ships (Document A). That firm specialized in the Surinam trade and nearly always had a vessel headed in that direction.

The Browns answered that they had a ship, but the passenger would have to embark at Providence. Rivera sent him at once and told the Browns that the man was carrying his own provisions, kosher food most likely (Document B). A few days later Rivera received a brief note confirming the man's departure (Document C). Helping an impoverished coreligionist make his way to a different city or country was a relatively common occurrence in the eighteenth-century American Jewish community.

SOURCE. The John Carter Brown Library, Brown Papers.

A [NO. 43]

Newport, May 21st, 1770.

Messrs. Nicholas Brown & Co.
Gentlemen:

There is one of our [religious] society who arrived here yesterday from St. Eustatious, in order to git a passage for Surinam where he has very able relations that have sent for him. His family I knew well in the West Indias, and [they were] some of the principal [members] of our society, but by the frowns of fortune are reduced [in circumstances]. I am informed you have a vessel bound to Surinam. I shall be glad [if] you'll let me know by first boat if he can have a passage in her, when she will sail, and whither she is to stop here before she sails, or if he must goe to Providence.

If you can oblige me in this, I shall thankfully acknowledge the favour, and am very respectfully, gentlemen,

Your humble servant,
Jacob Rodrigues Rivera

B [NO. 43]

Newport, May 25th, 1770.

Messrs. Nicholas Brown & Co.
Gentlemen:

Mr. Lindsey sent me word that you had desired him to inform me that your vessel would sail for Surinam next Sunday, and that you was so obliging as to allow the bearer a passage in her, but must be there by Sunday. He therefore goes up with this boat and will wait on you. He carries his provissions with him, and [you] will add greatley to the favour if you recommend him to your captain. I cannot but return you my thanks for this favour, and would return the same whenever you put it in my power.

I am with great respect and regard, gentlemen,

> Your most obliged servant,
> Jacob Rodrigues Rivera

C [NO. 43]

May 29th, 1770.

Mr. Rivera.

Sir:

Yours of the 25 instant is before us. Captain Sheldon in our brigg sailed last Sunday for Suranam, by whome your friend went passenger.

> We are your humble servants,
> [Nicholas Brown & Co.]

No. 44   Barrak Hays: Stormy Petrel—1772

Early in the eighteenth century a family of Dutch Jews named Hays emigrated to New York City. Barrak Hays, a son of one of the many brothers who made up the clan, was very probably born in this country.

One Sabbath morning in February, 1772, during the services, Hays insulted Hayman Levy, the president of the congregation, and consequently was denied certain religious privileges. That punishment constituted a mild form of the ban (Document A). Evidently the religious censure did not serve to deter the offender, for Levy was compelled to sue Hays in order to secure a public retraction (Document B). It seems, however, that the public apology did not end the quarrel, for litigation in the case was still pending before the Supreme Court of New York in July of the following year.

Such insults, quarrels, and suits were not uncommon in the early American Jewish communities. Competition, petty rivalries, and the difficulties inherent in life in "frontier" communities tended to exacerbate difficulties and to distort personal relationships.

SOURCE. Document A: Although this minute was printed in the *Publications of the American Jewish Historical Society*, XXI (1913), 113, it is reproduced here in order to explain the succeeding item; Document B: New York Historical Society Library, New York, The John Tabor Kempe Papers.

A [NO. 44]

At a meeting 2d Nisan 5532 [April 5, 1772], the repeated insults offered the parnas by B.[arrak] H.[ays] were considered, particularly that of Sabat *Teruma* [Sabbath, February 8] while the said parnas was officiating in his duty which evidently appeared to many of the congregation.

Resolved, therefore, that the said B. H. shall have no mitzva [religious honor], nor any benefit appertaining to the sinagogue, neither shall the hazan make an offering for him or in his name, till he pays a fine of ten pounds.

B [NO. 44]

Advertisement and acknowledgement signed by Barrak Hays at Brock's Tavern, New York, 26th October, 1772.

Whereas I, Barrack Hays of the City of New York, merchant, have heretofore at sundry times maliciously abused the charecture of Hayman Levy of the said city, merchant, for which he has justly brought an action at law against me, this is therefore to assure the publick in general that there is not the least truth in the abuses uttered by me as aforesaid, and that I made use of the same in the heath of passion, for which I now ask Mr. Levy's pardon.

This advertisement is published as Mr. Levy has condescended on this condition to withdraw his action and on my paying all the costs accrued on the suit.

Signed,
Barrak Hays

Witness:
Samson Simson
Jabez Johnson

The witnesses to the above advertisesement, Mr. Samson Simson, is deceased, and Mr. Jabez Johnson is absent. These [the following] gentlement being present at the same time and seen the advertisement signed:

Mr. David Jones, the person that wrote the advertisement.

Gregory Springall	Solomon M. Cohen
Moses D. Gomez	Isaac Moses
John Simons	Samuel Judah

Barrak Hays offered, by Mr. Samuel Judah, to give me one hundred pounds if I would not advertise him.

No. 45 The Redemption of Captives—1773

Among the several categories of traditional Jewish philanthropy is the "redemption of captives." Later generations interpreted this concept more liberally and offered aid to prisoners who were worthy of support.

The following letter is a case in point. Michael (Meir) Jacobs, imprisoned probably for debt, appealed to the New York congregation for help. Jacobs, whose Hebrew name was Meir, signed the letter both in English and Hebrew.

At a board meeting held nine days later the congregation responded by returning to the suppliant the money he had contributed to the synagogue.

SOURCE. American Jewish Historical Society Library, Lyons Collection, No. 122.

City of New York,
New Goal [jail], 9th September, 1773.

To Mr. Solomon Simson of the City of New York, merchant.
The petition of Michael Jacobs, of the said city, shopkeeper, most humbly sheweth:

That your poor distressed petitioner has been confined in this goal for upwards of twenty-six weeks, which has so reduced him that he is no longer able to support under it, and connot afford himself the common nessary's of life.

Your petitioner, therefore, most humbly prays that you and the congregation will be favorably pleased to take it into your generous consideration and grant him such relief in the premises as to you shall seem meet.

And your petitioner, as in duty bound, shall ever pray, etc.

his
Michael Meir Jacobs
mark

———

No. 46 Messengers from Palestine—1774–1778

Like most of their coreligionists, the Jews of America had a deep attachment to the Holy Land. Ever ready to support its schools and to aid its distressed inhabitants, the Diaspora gave large sums of money for Palestine, through messengers sent out to solicit contributions. One such collector, Rabbi Moses Malki, was at work in New York and Newport as early as 1759. Somewhat later another solicitor, Samuel Cohen, appeared on the American scene.

Cohen, a native of Palestine, started out on his philanthropic mission early in 1772. His primary concern was to secure funds for the Hebron community, which, along with other cities in the Holy Land, was in a state of constant crisis because of the exactions of the local Turkish pashas.

By the end of April, 1773, Cohen was in Amsterdam, where the Sephardic leaders of the community, one of the most influential in all Europe, gave him permission to issue a general appeal to the Jews in America. On May 5, 1773, Cohen appeared in London, where the Sephardic congregation authenticated his credentials and gave him a letter of recommendation, in Spanish, to the American congregations (Document A). Continuing his tour, Cohen reached Barbados early in 1774, and after making the rounds on the island, he secured a letter introducing him to the outstanding Jew of the Newport community, Aaron Lopez (Document B).

Since Cohen did not reach Newport until June, 1775, it is likely that he visited not only some other islands, but Surinam as well. After his arrival in Newport he met Ezra Stiles, the Congregational minister who was to become president of Yale University. In July, Cohen preached a fast-day sermon in the local synagogue, using as his text Numbers 25:11–12, which includes the phrase "covenant of peace." At this time Boston was under siege by General George Washington, and the Newport merchants, like many others, hoped that the quarrel with the mother country would soon be patched up.

Moses Levy, the president of the Newport congregation, forwarded Cohen's credentials to Congregation Shearith Israel in New York, suggesting that the two groups share equally the expenses of the Hebron messenger's return to London. The host communities were certainly eager to get him out of the war zone as speedily as possible, and in all likelihood Cohen sailed for Europe at the first opportunity. It cost the congregation over £31, a considerable sum of money in those days.

Other emissaries from Palestine came to America in the decades immediately after the Revolution. In 1786 two Algerians, "dressed in the Moorish habit," arrived in Virginia and traveled overland to Charleston, South Carolina. They may well have been solicitors who had originally come from the Holy Land.

Two years later another couple of agents, also seeking aid for the Jews of Palestine, landed in Philadelphia. A local newspaper appealed to Christians as well as to Jews to contribute toward the redemption of the Jews who were under Turkish oppression (Document C). The sympathy of Christians for Jews, and their desire to help them, were typical of the spirit of tolerance and understanding that distinguished many Gentiles in the United States of that generation. In the same year a group of non-Jews contributed toward the relief of Congregation Mikveh Israel of Philadelphia, which was in danger of losing its sanctuary for failure to meet payments on a mortgage. It is doubtful whether there was another country in the world at that time in which the Jew was accepted as he was in the United States.

SOURCE. Document A: Congregation Shaar Hashamaim (Bevis Marks), London, Minute Book; Document B: Newport Historical Society Library, Lopez Letters; Document C: *The Pennsylvania Packet,* August 16, 1788.

A [NO. 46]

Most worthy gentlemen, parnessim ["presidents"], *gabaim* ["treasurers"] of the holy kehilot ["congregations"] of America:

Having seen the contents of the letter which was signed by the gentlemen *hahamim* ["rabbis"] of the city of Hebron, in the Holy Land, and addressed to us, and since it is clear to us that the wretchedness and misery are true which are happening to our brothers in Palestine, caused by the civil wars, which, alas for those regions, as also for their safety,

Now you will please take note that we have granted the request which the same gentlemen made of us in the above-mentioned letter, and we recommend to all our brothers, the gentlemen parnassim deputes [officers] and *yehidim* [members] of the various kehelot of America, that the Great God have mercy on the misfortunes and miseries of our brothers of Hebron, and that they respond to this call for aid with their generous assistance to their messenger, the gentleman R.[abbi] Samuel Cohen, bearer of this letter, for the relief and refuge of the said people of Hebron; and may He [God] reward this pious work with an increase in His good gifts as the culmination of His goodness bestowed upon this K. K. of Saar Asamaim ["Holy Congregation, Gate of Heaven"] in London, the 5 of May, of Sivan 5533 [1773].

Signed by the following gentlemen:

Abraham Aboab Osorio, President,   Charles Serra
Isaac Israel Nunes   Isaac Serra, *Gabay* ["treasurer"]
David Abarbanel

B [no. 46]

Barbados, April 17th, 1774.

Mr. Aaron Lopez.

Dear Sir:

Your kind and polite letter I had the pleasure to unfold the 1st instant per Capt. [John Peters]. The contents [I] have duely noticed, and for the many very kind expressions I stand greatly indebted. Should any thing offer this side the water that I can render you or my good friend Mr. Riberro [Jacob Rodriguez Rivera] any services, shall be glad to be commanded.

Dear sir, pardon the liberty I've taken in recommending the bearror, Mr. Samuel a Cohen, who is on an embasy from Hebron. His deportment with us has been praysworthy, and make not the least doubt but his person will be sufficient to recommend. Could you render him any service for and towards that *kaal* [community of Hebron], as it now labours under many dificulties, such favours bestowed shall ever be acknowledged by him who subscribes himself to be, dear sir,

Your honoured and very humble servant.

N.B. My compliments are respectfully offered Mrs. Lopez and family.

July 1st, 1774.

Since the above, have taken my passage for England per Capt. Blackburne. Shall be glad on my arrival to execute any your commands, and are very respectfully, dear sir,

Yours very affectionately,
Isaac Lindo

C [no. 46]

A correspondent says that two Jews, one of whom is a person of distinction, have lately come to this city from Jamaica, and who have not long ago been at Hebron, which is about thirty miles from Jerusalem, and which is their usual place of residence.

Their object is to collect subscriptions for some of their brethren, who have been enslaved by the Turks for not producing a certain tribute at an appointed time. There are some who remember that upon the failure of the payment of this tribute, the Jews at Hebron were seized once upon as slaves by their cruel and insulting oppressors, the Turks.

It would be a laudable instance of generosity and magnanimity in the Christians to contribute according to their ability, as well as the Jews, for the purpose of relieving the oppressed. It has been said that mercy is twice blest, that it blesses those who receive and those who give.

No. 47 Hiring a Religious Factotum—1776

The *Pennsylvanische Staatsbote* announced in its July 30, 1771, issue that a synagogue had been opened in Cherry Alley, Philadelphia. Five years later Congregation Mikveh Israel took a step forward when its leader Michael Gratz, the merchant, hired young Ezekiel Levy to serve in the threefold capacity of ritual slaughterer of cattle and fowl, hazzan or reader, and Hebrew teacher. In the contract he signed, he agreed to instruct six children. Obviously these were the children of the poor whom he contracted to teach without extra charge. There were certainly other Jewish children in town, but he would be paid extra for teaching them. Primary education for all was not a communal responsibility. Compensation was a matter to be arranged privately between the communally subsidized teacher and the parents.

To guarantee that the three-in-one shohet, hazzan, and melammed would stay on the job for at least a year, the congregation saw to it that Ezekiel Levy's father signed the contract and bond. The two witnesses called in to subscribe their names were businessmen. One of them, Alexander Abrahams, worked for Michael Gratz as a clerk. The other, Israel D. Lieben, had been Aaron Levy's personal shohet in Northumberland County, Pennsylvania. Shortly after 1774 he went to Philadelphia and began to assume the duties of shohet, and possibly teacher, for the Gratzes. There was some question about his slaughtering, and a major controversy ensued. Apparently, when that quieted down, the contract between Gratz and the Levys was drawn up.

SOURCE. American Jewish Archives, The Henry Joseph Collection of Gratz Papers.

Articles of Agreement made between Michael Gratz of the City of Philadelphia, for and in behalf of the Jewish Society held here, of the one part, and Abraham Levy and his son Ezekiel Levy of this province, of the other part.

Whereas, the said Michael Gratz for himself and the rest of the society hath engaged the said Ezekiel Levy to act in the capacity of a Jewish killer [ritual slaughterer], reader in the synagogue, and to teach six children the art of reading the Hebrew tongue for one year, for which offices he, the said Ezekiel Levy, is to receive an annual salary of £30, paid him quarterly by the acting *gaboy* ["treasurer"], for the time being with board and lodging,

And the said Ezekiel Levy doth hereby bind himself for and in consideration of £30 to act for the society in the capacities of killer [slaughterer], reader, etc., for the continuation of one year, to commence from the day of the date hereof; and that the said Ezekiel Levy cannot discharge himself after the expiration of the year, without giving one quarter's notice of his intention to the society,

For the true performance of which we, the said Abraham Levy and Ezekiel Levy, have signd our hands to these presents to observe the same in all its due forms, under the penal sum of thirty pounds Pennsylvania currency, for the use of the said society. Given this day, Philadelphia, the 18th June, 1776.

Abraham Levy
Ezekiel Levy

Signed in the ⟩ I. D. Lieben
presence of ⟨ Alexander Abrahams

No. 48   Shearith Israel Synagogue, Montreal—1778–1780

Detailed formal regulations with respect to synagogal administration were rare in early America. One of the few collections of congregational statutes is contained in the minutes of the Montreal synagogue for the period from 1778 to 1780. These records throw a great deal of light on the internal life of a small Jewish community at that time.

Montreal Jewry, according to tradition, was organized religiously in 1768 as Congregation Shearith Israel. Some of its members had certainly come up the Hudson from New York, bringing the name of the congregation of that city with them. At that time the Montreal synagogue was the only one in Canada. Like all the others in the New World, it followed the Sephardic ritual and maintained very close ties with the congregation of the Spanish and Portuguese Jews in London.

David Salisbury Franks, Montreal merchant and American patriot, was reputed to have been president of Shearith Israel about 1775. Two years later, when the congregation had about twenty members, the group erected a building. In December, 1778, the religious community adopted a series of statutes and ordinances which constituted its "code of laws," regulating the life of the congregation.

As in all other American Jewish communities of the eighteenth century, membership was practically compulsory. Strangers who refused to join when invited faced the prospect of being denied essential religious privileges. But although newcomers to Montreal were expected to affiliate themselves with the group, they were accorded only second-class privileges in the management of the synagogue. The charter members reserved to themselves special rights, such as double votes, for it was *their* synagogue.

Since most of the members were engaged in the same competitive field as merchants and fur traders, quarrels and slanders marred their relationships. The prevailing atmosphere of suspicion and recrimination is reflected in the following minutes.

SOURCE. Shearith Israel Congregation, Montreal, Minute Book.

The synagogue built in St. James Street, Montreal, is purchased and built with the money arising from subscriptions and offerings from us, the subscribers, and others. It is therefore the property of us and our heirs jointly, but not individually or separately. Neither can we, on any pretence whatsoever, claim any part separately of the said synagogue further than the privileges here agreed to, hereby revoking all title and claim to the same, as if no money had been given by us,

Provided always the said synagogue, as we all comprehend, is meant for the use and service of all Israelites who conform to our laws and our regulations, and under the management of a parnass ["president"], *gabay* ["treasurer"], and a junto ["board"] of three of the elders, to be annually chosen by a majority of us, the subscribers to all laws and regulations, which shall be made by the consent of the said junto of five persons.

We do, in the name of Almighty God, promise most strictly to abide by [them], in every shape whatsoever, paying every due submission and respect to the said five persons who constitute the junto:

David bar Abraham	Andrew Hays
Levy Solomons	Myer Michaels
Uriah Judah	Myer Myers
Samuel Judah	Abraham Franks

In the name of God. On the 25th of Ellul, 5538 [September 17, 1778], the congregation met to elect a parnass and *gabay* in the room [place] of Mr. David Franks and Mr. Ezekiel Solomons, when the following, having a majority of votes, were accordingly elected: Mr. Levy Solomons as parnass and Mr. Uriah Judah as *gabay* for the ensuing year; as also to chose *hatanim* [honorary officers], when the two following gentlemen were elected and served: Mr. Ezekiel Solomons as *hatan torah* and Mr. Levy Michaels as *hatan bereshith*. [*Hatan torah* and *hatan bereshit*: "bridegroom of the Law and bridegroom of the beginning." These men were given the honor of closing and beginning the annual cycle of the Pentateuchal readings in the synagogue.]

At the above meeting, Mr. Samuel Judah was fined three pounds Hallifax currency for refusing to serve [in] the office of parnass, to which he was elected, as was also the following gentlemen for refusing to serve as *hatanim* to which they was elected:

Isaac Judah fined two pounds and ten shillings
Myer Michaels ...... do. .... do.
Andrew Hays .... do. .... do.

28th Elul, 5538 [September 20, 1778].

The congregation met and confirmed Mr. Levy Solomons, parnass, and Mr. Uriah Judah, *gabay*, for the ensuing year, in the room of Mr. David Franks and Mr. Ez. Solomons. At the same time, confirmed Mr. Ezekiel Solomons, *hatan torah*, and Mr. Levy Michaels, *hatan bereshith*.

11th Kislaf, 5539 [November 30, 1778].

The Israelites of the town of Montreal were this day called together to have the voice of the congregation concerning the death of a son of Mr. Ezekiel Solomons, to know whether he was to be buried according to the rules and customs of Jews, the said child [having a Gentile mother and] not being circumcised. Several circumstances favourable to the said Ezekiel Solomons appeared to us, for which reason we allow his [child] being buried. But at the same time, we do hereby unanimously agree and declare that no man or boy, whomsoever shall be, after sixty days from this date, be buried in the burying place of this congregation unless circumcised.

Dated as above.

3d Tebeth, 5539 [December 22, 1778].

The congregation met to chose a junto of three persons to assist the parnass and *gabay* to make a proper code of laws for the better regulating this *kahal* ["congregation"], when a majority appeared in favour of Mr. Ezekiel Solomons, Mr. Samuel Judah, and Mr. Andrew Hays, who were unanimously appointed.

The above junto, having met, made the following orders and regulations which were laid before the congregation at large, by them agreed to, and signed.

Present:

Mr. Levy Solomons, parnass		
	juntos {	Mr. Ezekiel Solomons
		Samuel Judah
Uriah Judah, *gabay*		Andrew Hays

1st. That the names of every subscriber to the synagogue, with the sums they have subscribed, be made out; for which reason certain privileges to the subscribers, in preference to any others who may hereafter settle here. Agreed unanimously that the present subscribers only shall have, on all occasions, a double vote hereafter for ever, them and all their oldest sons, after they attain twenty one years of age.

2d. No stranger to be entered in this congregation hereafter, but on the following conditions: "To enjoy no office for three years, to have no vote for two years, and then to have only a single vote afterwards, and that every such stranger shall pay ten pounds, Hallifax currency, before he enjoys any such privilege.["]

N.B. The intention of this 2d order is meant to preserve to those, the present subscribers, the founders of this congregation, which has been [so] far established at an expence beyond the bounds of our circumstances, that we may enjoy certain privileges beyond any stranger that may hereafter settle here.

3d. No person whatsoever hereafter to have a vote untill attained the age of 21 years, or married and had a child.

4th. All those laws and regulations to be read annually at the meeting for chosing the proper officers of this congregation.

5th. In mentioning the junto, it is to be understood the parnass and *gabay* are included.

6th. Anyone who compose the junto misbehaving can be expelled, provided it is by the unanimous consent of the other four, who are to chose another to serve the remainder of the year. Provided also, and it is agreed, the expelled member of the junto may have power to appeal to the general body of the subscribers, if he pleases, for a final determination, which shall be decided by the majority.

7th. The seats in the synagogue has already been fixed on for the subscribers and numbered. Resolved: That the names of the persons with the numbers of their seats annexed be entered in this book. Those seats to be kept for them and their sons for ever, and not to be taken away on any pretence whatsoever.

8th. A meeting every three months of all the subscribers, at which time the *gabay* to render accounts.

9th. In the absence of one or more of the junto, the remainder to call in others to act in their stead.

10th. The parnass to have the casting vote in no case but in the choice of parnass, *gabai* and junto.

11th. No meeting to be held unless 12 hours' notice is before given, except by general consent.

12th. The junto to be the established counsell [council] of this congregation, and no other subscribers to be called in but as circumstances may require. Any past parnass to have liberty to attend and speak at any meeting of the junto but not to have a vote.

13th. Any Israelite that will not sign these our laws and regulations (that are inhabitants of this town) within twenty days, and those out of the town [temporarily], within six months, shall for ever be exempted [barred] from having any privilege, honour, or employment in this congregation, and be looked on as no member thereof, except only Chapman Abraham [usually at Detroit] and Benjamin Lyon [usually at Michilimackinac], who are at too great a distance, but allowing them twenty days after their arrival in this town.

14th. We do jointly and separately promise to promote harmony and unanimity amongst us, and endeavour as far as lays in our power to assist each other as circumstances will permit.

15th. The penalty of fifty shillings to be paid by any one who shall expose or devulge the proceedings of any meeting, provided secresy is required.

16th. All monies that may be in hand over and above fifty pounds at the expiration of every year shall be made a dividend amongst the subscribers toward the expence of building the synagogue.

17th. Any person or persons making a disturbance or having the least controversy in the house of God to be liable to be fined; exempted from all mitzvahs [religious honors] for a limited time; his name in capital letters inserted in this book, with the crime he has been guilty of, to deter others from such misbehavour in so sacred a place.

18th. The like fines, exemptions, and insertions to be extended to any persons absenting themselves from the house of God on any frivolous pretence arising from any controversy with others.

19th. Thirty nine shillings' fine to be paid by any person refusing a mitzvah with which he may be honoured by the parnass, *gabay*, or any other person acting as proxy for the parnass.

20th. All punishments, fines, etc., to be settled by the abovementioned adjuntos ["board members"]; and every misdemeanor committed by any member of the congregation, the same shall be enquired into within forty eight hours after such offence be committed.

21st. All fines to be paid within thirty days after judgment be given, in default of which such other recourse to be had as in the wisdom of the above adjuntos shall be adjudged most expedient.

22d. At the annual elections of officers belonging to this congregation, the parnass (then only) to have the casting vote, should there be an equal majority [a tie] of votes.

23d. Any member of the junto not giving attendance at any meeting called by the parnass to pay a fine of forty shillings.

24th. Any member who shall be elected to the offices of parnass or *gabay* and should refuse to serve to pay a fine of twenty dollars.

25th. Any persons who shall be elected to the offices of *hatanim* and should refuse to serve to pay a fine of fifty shillings Hallifax [currency].

26th. Any member who shall presume to say he would have his name erased out of the congregation books, the same to be done and the party to not come to any *dibrah kedusha* [religious courtesy] untill he pays a fine of forty dollars.

27th. Strict obedience and respect to be paid to the parnasim and the elders of this congregation.

28th. No private quarrels to extend so far as to make a disunion in this congregation on pain of severe penalties.

29th. Severe penalties on those who shall be the means of giving a bad name to any of the congregation, by which a disgrace may be brought on any of the Israelites.

30th. All offerings made in the synagogue to be punctually paid to the *gabay* every three months, in default of which such persons to be excluded from any mitzvahs, etc.

31st. The parnass, *gabay*, and junto to be annually chosen before Rosh-ashanah ["New Year"] and the parnasim to be called out [announced] in the synagogue on the first day, as likewise the *hatanim* on the second day of Rosh Hashanah.

32d. The parnas that served the last year to officiate the first day of Rosh Hashonah, and the mitzvahs to be given on the day of Simhat Torah ["Rejoicing of the Law," when the last section of the Pentateuch is read] and *Shabat Bereshith* [the Sabbath on which the reading of Genesis is begun again] by the *hatanim*.

33d. If any dispute should arise between any members of the congregation, they shall be obliged to come before the *mahamad* ["board"] that they may endeavour to settle it before they go to any magistrate, or be liable to such a penalty as they [the *Mahamad*] may think proper.

34th. No person to be admitted without the consent of the junto.

35th. All monies expended by the parnasses (during their acting) out of their own capital, shall be made good by those who are chosen to succeed them.

36th. The shamas shall be obliged to carry each member his account.

37th. The *gabay* shall lay before the junto the monies expended and received, during his acting, the week before Rosh Hashanah.

38th. The parnass is not to lay out any money for the congregation without the consent of the majority of the adjuntos.

We, the underwritten, do hereby most solemnly promise, in the name of the Almighty God, to abide by the above regulations, or to be liable to such restrictions as is herein specified, as witness our hands, the 3d day of our month, Tebeth, 5539.

Levy Solomons, parnass
Uriah Judah, *gabay*

Samuel Judah	Myer Myers
Andrew Hays	David David
David bar Abraham	Heineman Pines
Myer Michaels	Barnet Lions
Abraham Franks	Abraham Judah
	Sam David

12th Adar, 5539 [February 28, 1779].

Present:

Uriah Judah, *gabay*		⌈ Samuel Judah
J.[acob] Franks	adjuntos	⟨ Ezekiel Solomons
Isaac Judah		⌊ Andrew Hays
David David		

A meeting was this day called for by the *gabay*, at the request of Mr. J. Franks and others, when it was unanimously agreed that at any other meeting which may be called by the *gabay*, or any other gentleman who compose the junto, [the above regulations] shall be equally in force as if such meeting had been called for by the parnass, and every such member not giving attendance, the 23d article to be put in force. Agreed to unanimously.

Uriah Judah,
for the gentlemen present.

26th Nisan, 5539 [April 12, 1779].

Whereas, the bretheren of this congregation have, at divers times, most shamefully, maliciously, and wickedly aspersed the characters of each other, by which means shame and disgrace has fell on the reputation of individuals, those proceedings is contrary to our laws and sacred religion, and turning the vengeance of our Almighty God on us, by which means destruction now threatens us and our posterity. In order to prevent in future such misconduct and such abominable practices, we have, unanimously,

Resolved and agreed, first, to take the oath by the Laws of Moses, that we will never hereafter speak against the characters, or prejudice the persons of each other on any pretence whatsoever, by which means any disgrace may be brought on us.

We at the same time agree, and by the above oath bind ourselves, that we shall and will be obliged to make known and discover to the person spoke of or injured by any assertion whatever.

We do likewise, and by the said oath, bind ourselves that we will jointly and separately detest, abhor, and despise any Israelite belonging to this congregation, inhabitants of this town, that will not join with us in this our well meant determination.

We do further agree and bind ourselves by the above oath, that for every time any of us shall be found guilty of [violating] any article that is contained herein, and convicted by the majority of us, that we will pay for every such crime the sum of forty shillings Hallifax currency.

We do hereby further acknowledge our full consent to our having taken the sacred oath above mentioned and singned our names:

Uriah Judah	Levi Michaels
Samuel Judah	J. Franks
Ezekiel Solomons	Andrew Hays
Simon Levy	

A junto was called this day at the request of Mr. J. Franks, on a complaint made by him against Mr. Levy Solomons, when it appeared to the gentlemen present that he had made use of expressions to the manifest injury of this congregation. The following resolve was made and a copy thereof sent Mr. Levy Solomons.

Copy

We, the junto of this congregation, were this day called together on a subject that appeared to us of the greatest consequence to ourselves and the future welfare of our religion in this province. And as there is every reason to suppose that you are guilty of the charge brought against you, we have unanimously resolved that you are suspended acting [as parnas], neither are you to take your seat in the *banco* [official seat] of the said synagogue as parnass, untill you are heard before us on Sunday morning next, at 10 o'clock, at which time you are desired to attend.

To Mr. Levy Solomons.

Uriah Judah	Samuel Judah
Ezekiel Solomon[s]	J. Franks
Andrew Hays	

The junto met and called the congregation at large to deliberate on the above affair. Mr. Levy [Solomons] not appearing, [and] further time by the majority of the gentlemen present being required, Mr. Levy was ordered to attend at 6 o'clock this evening, which he neglected doing, and sent word he would have nothing more to do with us. Whereupon Mr. Uriah Judah was voted to act as parnass the remainder of this year in his room [place].

Mrs. Davis, having in her possession a shofar ["ram's horn trumpet"], refuses lending it to this congregation for Rosh Hashanah, but will sell it for a guinea, which sum has been paid by the congregation at large. Therefore remains their sole property.

24th day, Ellul, 5539 [September 5, 1779].

The congregation met this day in order to chose parnass and *gabay* for the ensuing year, when Mr. Uriah Judah was unanimously elected to both offices.
Present:

Uriah Judah	Samuel Judah
A. Hays	Myer Michaels
A. Franks	Levy Michaels
Simon Levy	David David
Samuel David	

The Portugueze congregation of London thought proper to send this *kahal* ["congregation"], as a present, two safar torahs ["Scrolls of the Law"] which they delivered [to] Mr. Abraham Judah in London to forward in their name. The said safar torahs came out under the care of Mr. Joseph Pines with a third, which was raised by a subscription sett on foot last year.

The following gentlemen subscribed as under:

Uriah Judah	£1 1s.	Samuel Judah	£1 1s. 0d.
Levy Solomons	2 2s.	A. Hays	10s. 6d.
Levy Michaels	10s. 6d.	J. Franks	1 14s. 8d.
Ezekiel Solomons	1 1s.	Ben. Lyon	10s. 6d.
Simon Levy	5s. 6d.	Barnet Lyon	10s. 6d.
Heineman Pines	9s.	Jacob Cohen	10s. 6d.
Isaac Judah	10s. 6d.	A. Franks	10s. 6d.
Myer Michaels	10s. 6d.	David David	5s.
		Total	£[12 3s. 2d.] Sterling

The following gentlemen were by the above congregation elected to the offices of *hatanim*, which they accepted and served accordingly: Mr. Abraham Franks as *hatan torah*, and Mr. Simon Levy, as *hatan bereshith*.

22 Hellul, 5540 [September 22, 1780].

It is the unanimous consent and approbation of the congregation of Jews to accept with satisfaction Mr. Abraham Judah to be a member of this society; that from this day he shall be on the same footing and enjoy the same priviliges as any member belonging to us, the same as if he had been a subscriber from the first establishing of this congregation.

Uriah Judah	Abraham Franks
Andrew Hays	David David
Simon Levy	Samuel Judah
Myer Michaels	Samuel David

Same day. The congregation met in order to chuse parnass and *gabay* for the ensuing year, when Mr. Samuel Judah was unanimously elected parnass and Mr. Andrew Hays, *gabay*. Mr. Abram Franks was chosen *hatan torah* and Mr. Levy Solomons served as *hatan bereshit*. And the junto for this year is despensed with.

21st day, Hesvan, 5541 [November 19, 1780].

This day the subscribers met according to appointment, when it was proposed and agreed on unanimously that the synagogue be finished and the sum not exceeding forty pounds be applied for that purpose; and Mr. Abram Judah and Mr. Levy Solomons were nominated to carry the same into execution, and the *gabay* is hereby ordered to pay the said sum to those gentlemen when demanded.

No. 49   Congregation Mikveh Israel, Philadelphia—1782–1798

When the Revolution broke out, some of the Jewish Whigs who had been driven out of Newport, New York, Charlestown, and Savannah, settled in Philadelphia, the nation's capital, and the émigré merchants, numerically dominant, assumed the leadership of the Jewish community. Until 1782 the congregation had worshiped in rented quarters, but the increased number of Jews in the city compelled them to consider the question of a synagogue building.

Printed below (Document A) are some of the minutes, beginning with the session of March 24, 1782, when the congregation was formally reconstituted and adopted the name Mikveh Israel ("The Hope of Israel"). The name was in all likelihood taken from the old Curaçao synagogue, then the oldest one extant in the Western Hemisphere.

One of the first acts of the members of the new synagogue was to adopt a set of simple parliamentary rules. A committee was appointed to prepare a constitution and bylaws, which, as we shall see in the later minutes, were submitted and adopted. Unfortunately, those statutes of this important Jewish religious organization were not incorporated in the minute books now extant and are therefore lost.

At first Mikveh Israel bought an old house and a plot of ground. Then, after some hesitation, the congregation decided to build a new synagogue on the lot. When the nearby German Reformed (Protestant) Church objected to the Jews as neighbors, the latter acquired a new piece of ground on another street. But their means were not adequate to the task which they had set themselves. It was necessary to raise more money. To accomplish this, as we note in the record, they sold the privilege of laying the cornerstone and wrote letters soliciting funds from American and West Indian communities and individuals.

The following minutes bring to light a number of interesting incidents in the first six months of the history of the congregation. Take the case of the impoverished Mrs. Mordecai, originally a proselyte named Elizabeth Whitlock, the widow of the Philadelphia merchant Moses Mordecai, who died in 1781. When she prepared to marry Jacob I. Cohen, the congregation objected strenuously, for, according to Jewish law, a Cohen, a "priest," was not permitted to marry a proselyte. Then there is an all too brief reference to Ezekiel Levy, who was accused of shaving on the Sabbath in Baltimore. The duties of the sexton, or shamas, are briefly enumerated; he was instructed to attend only those funerals "which are according to our religion." Obviously he was not to participate in the funeral of a Gentile who had married a Jew. A brief outline is given of the ceremony of consecration of the new building and of the transfer to it of the Scrolls of the Law, and there are minutes of the meeting, held after the dedication, to settle the dissatisfaction aroused by the distribution of the seats on that important occasion. A conflict of authority had arisen between the board and a special seating committee, but the difficulty was ironed out and "buried in oblivion."

On January 28, 1798, a new constitution was adopted, the old one having proved inadequate. This document of 1798 is in all probability the oldest extant constitution of the Philadelphia Jewish community which reconstituted itself as Mikveh Israel. Unfortunately, the copy in the congregational archives is not the final one. That copy would probably show some changes, and articles fifteen and sixteen seem to be missing altogether. In this draft constitution (Document B) the parts that were rejected and stricken out are included within parentheses.

SOURCE. Congregation Mikveh Israel, Philadelphia. Document

A: Minute Book, Vol. I, 1781–95; Document B: Minute Book, Vol. II, 1796–1823.

A [NO. 49]

Philadelphia,
Sunday, 9th Nisan, 5542, and 24th March, 1782.

At a meeting of the congregators of the synagogue, by adjournment from Sunday last, the 2nd Nisan and 17th March, which was held by a publick call in the synagogue the Saturday before, in order to receive the report of the committee appointed at said meeting to bring in an estimate of the charges to put in order a certain house then agreed to be purchased for the use of a synagogue, as also to produce a plan of the same.

Present:

Messrs.	Messrs.
Isaac Moses, *segan* [vice president]	Isaac Dacosta
Simon Nathan	Gershom Seixas
Benjamin Seixas	Solomon Myers Cohen
Haym Solomon	Abraham Levy
Mordecai Sheftall	Myer Cohen
Hayman Levy	Barnard Gratz
Michael Gratz	Jonas Phillips
Solomon Marache	Jacob Hart
Jacob Mordecai	Cosman Polack

Mr. Isaac Moses represented to this meeting that a meeting had been held the 2nd of this instant Nisan, who [at which it had been] unanimously determined that a certain house and lot should be purchased for the use of a place of worship. And as we have hitherto congregated according to the custom of other congregations only, but have no fixed rules established by the whole body for its government whereby the rulers hitherto had no right or legal power so to do, and consequently their determinations were not binding on the congregators. We therefore moved that we may now enter into the following resolution, *vizt.*:

That we, the subscribers now met, agree that in order to promote our holy religion and establish a proper congregation in this city, do hereby solemnly form ourselves into a congregation to be known and distinguished by the name of Mikve Israel in the city of Philadelphia. And we, whose names are hereunto subscribed, do bind ourselves one to the other that we will assist if required to form a constitution and rules for the good government of the congregation and strictly abide by the same.

And in order that we may be properly intitled to canvass and transact said business with the greater freedom, and form ourselves as proposed, he, the said Mr. Moses, does hereby abdicate and divest himself from all or any prior appointment of office in said congregation, either as parnas, *segan*, or adjunta man ["trustee"], recommending to the remaining former gentlemen of the junta ["board"] to do the same, in order that we may be enabled to proceed from hence forward with order and regularity. Whereupon the following gentlemen of the former junta seperately rose and abdicated their places and seats in the junta, namely, Messrs. Solomon M. Cohen, Hayman Levy, and Barnard Gratz.

On which it was moved by the body of this meeting that a chairman be appointed to regulate the debates and collect the votes and sentiments of this meeting, and regulate the whole with that order and decency that is necessary in all societies, when Mr. Isaac DaCosta was chosen by a majority and directed to take the chair for that purpose, which he accordingly did.

[At this stage, in all probability, the following regulations were adopted. Obviously they were written by Benjamin Nones, a Frenchman.]

Rules to be observed in this congregation:

1st. Eny membre that has eny thing to propose shall address him selfs to the chair. (Agreed to)

2d. That evry motion made must be seconded and then put to vote, and when carried in the affirmative by a majority, it shall be binding. (Agreed)

3th. In case of equal votes, the Chair man shall have the casting vote. (Agreed)

4th. Enything that is determined by a majority shall no be again repetid in this meeting if on the same subject. (Agreed)

5th. When a membre is up he shall not be interupted by eny other. (Agreed)

6th. That no membre of this society shall not speeck more then tuice on the same subjet. (Agreed)

7th. No *yachid* [member] that is in this present meeting shall live [leave] the room without leave from the chairman. (Agreed)

And, after having premised among ourselves several different matters respecting the mode of our conducting ourselves in this meeting in regard to our addressing the chair, etc. [the above rules], the chairman took up Mr. Moses' motion first abovementioned and read it paragraph by paragraph for debate, after its having been seconded by Mr. Jonas Phillips, when, some time having been spent in debate thereon, the question thereupon being put by the chairman, it was carried in the affirmative unanimously in the manner and form above recited in the said motion. It was moved and seconded that we enter in the following resolution:

Resolved: That one parnass and five adjunta men shall be chosen this day by ballot, who shall rule the congregation to the end of this year or until a new constitution is formed and agreed to by the congregation (as is herein after directed to be done, which[ever] shall first happen); and that they shall, as soon as may be, within the space of this year, prepare a code of laws which, when finished, shall be laid before the congregation for their approbation, and that each one of this congregation shall have a right to give in to the said parnass and adjuntos in writing such rules or regulation as he thinks proper to present. And the said parnass and adjuntas are hereby empowerd and required to receive the same, and therefrom adopt in their code such laws as, in their opinion, would be beneficial to the government of the congregation, which being debated, the question was put thereupon and carried in the affirmative by a great majority.

On a motion which was seconded, it was resolved that until such laws and regulations (as above expressd) are approved and agreed on, we do hereby impower the said parnass and junta this day to be elected, to repair, rebuild, or build anew a proper place for a synagogue, to borrow money in behalf of the congregation, to carry the above plan into execution, mortgage any lands the property of the congregation, collect or receive all monies that has or shall be subscribed or offered for the purpose of building a synagogue, cause decency and good order to be observed, and in every respect rule and govern the said congregation to the best of their abilities. And we, the subscribers, will support the said parnass and adjuntos to the utmost of our power, for the performance whereof we bind ourselves one to the other, under the penalty of being liable to such fine, in case of transgression, as the parnass and junta shall think proper to mulct him. And untill such sentence shall be complied with by such transgressor, he shall not have the rights in the congregation that he would be entitled to was it not for his transgression; neither shall he be permitted to offer nor be offerd for [offer donations or have them offered in his behalf].

On a motion which was seconded, it was resolved that these rules and regulations shall be read in the synagogue publickly on the 1st and 2nd days of the approaching holidays of Pesah ["Passover"]; and anyone being inclined to become a member of this congregation, who is not present at this meeting, shall apply to the parnass and junta within fifteen days from the date of the publication, who [the parnass and junta] are to be judges wether he shall be admitted or not.

On a motion seconded, resolved that whoever shall be elected this day parnass and refuses to accept said office, shall pay the sum of five pounds said currency.

Moved and seconded, that evry gentleman present pledge their honour one to the other to sign the above resolutions, or any others that may be enterd into this day, that have already or may be carried in the affirmative by a majority of votes; agreed to, n.[emine, "no one"] c.[ontradicente, "contradicting"].

In pursuance of the above resolution, to elect one parnass and five adjuntas this day, the members present proceeded to elect [vote] by ballot, for one parnass. And the chairman having examind the ballots, and the majority being in favor of Mr. Isaac Moses, he therefore was declared to be parnass-elect, to serve the time specefied in one of the above resolutions, after which the members proceeded to elect the five adjuntas, and the ballots being examined by the chairman, the majority being in favor of the under mentioned gentlemen, vizt.: Messrs. Bernard Gratz, Hayman Levy, Jonas Phillips, Benjamin Seixas, Simon Nathan. So that they were declared adjuntas-elect, for the time specefied in one of the above resolutions, all whom are to be publickly proclaimed in the synagogue in the morning of the 1st day of Pesah ensuing.

Moved and seconded, wether the old building on the lot bought for the use of a synagogue should be repaired and put in order for a place of worship, or should we agree to build a new one? And on examination of the different estimates of the repairs of the old building and those for building a new one, and finding that a new building would not cost much more than the repairs of the old one, it was resolved, n.c., that a new synagogue be built, and now that the parnass and adjuntas are elected, [it is they] who are authorized to transact that business and which is recommended to their care and attention.

Signed:

Isaac DaCosta, Chairman	Solomon Marache	Henry Marks
Benjamin Seixas	Solomon Myers Cohen	Lyon Nathans
Michael Gratz	Haym Solomon	Benjamin S. Judah
Simon Nathan	Hayman Levy	Ashar Myers
Jonas Phillips	Gershom Seixas	Judah Myers
Isaac Moses, per David	Israel Jacobs	Isaac Abrahams
Abraham Levy	Moses Nathan	Benjamin Noneez
Barnard Gratz	Bernard Moses Spitzer	Mordecai M. Mordecai
Jacob Mordecai	Jacob Myers	Isaac Moses
Mordecai Sheftall	Manuel Josephson	Mordecai Levy
Coshman Polack	Ezekiel Levy	Myer M. Cohen
Jacob Hart		Jacob Cohen
		Lazarus Barnett

Monday, 10th Nisan, 5542, and 25th March, 1782.

At a meeting of the congregators of the synagogue name Mikve Israel in the city of Philadelphia, held this day by a written notice from the chairman. . . .

On a motion made and seconded, Mister Solomon M. Cohen was nominated and appointed by this meeting to be *gaboy* ["treasurer"] for the *sedaka* [treasury] of this congregation, and Mr. Simon Nathan to be *gaboy* for the building of the synagogue of this congregation, who accepted their different offices. . . .

The parnass represented that Mr. Jacob Cohen had applied to him to sign the rules, and it was unanimously agreed he should be admitted. . . .

Mr. Isaac DaCosta mentioned that as we are now assembled and gone through the business that we were called for, in order to avoid the necessity of calling another meeting for the matter he intends to propose, he begs leave to be permitted to do it at this meeting, which being agreed to, he moved that the laying of the four corner stones of the new synagogue, as also the two stones that support the door posts thereof, may now be agreed to be sold at publick sale to the highest bidder for ready money on Sunday next in the synagogue, for which purpose notice may be given in the synagogue on the approaching Sabbath. [These privileges were sold to help pay the building costs.] And that the purchasers thereof shall be entitled to have a *misheberach* [blessing] in the new synagogue on the day of the dedication of the same and also on evry Kipur [day of "Atonement"] night and on evry anniversary day of the dedication during their natural life; and after their demise, they shall be entitled to have an *escoba* [a memorial prayer] on each anniversary day of the dedication and on evry Kipur night forever.

Which being debated, it was proposed by Mr. Mordecai Sheftall and seconded by Mr. Hayman Levy, that the words *ready money* in the above motion be left out, and in their stead insert *at three months' credit*, which amendment being by the parnass put to the vote whether the motion shall stand as made, or with the amendment, and it was carried by a great majority that it remain, as in the original motion. Afterwards the motion itself was put to the question, and it was carried in the affirmative by a great majority. . . .

16th Sivan, 5542, and 29th of May, 1782, at a meeting of the parnass and junta. . . .

Mr. Moses informed the junta that Mrs. Mordecai had applied to him for money to enable her to pay her rent, nine pounds, as also for Hannah Levy's rent, being a smaller sum. Resolved: That the above sums be paid.

The parnass acquainted the junta that Mr. Jacob Cohen of Virginia had applied to him to become a *yoheed* [member]; therefore, moved that he may be permitted. But, on examineing the law passed the 9th of Nissan, it was found that no provison was made for a stranger or any other person that did not apply within fifteen days after the publication. The parnass and junta were therefore of opinion that they were not a[t] liberty to admit Mr. Cohen without the consent of the whole congregation untill a proper code of laws shall be enacted. Resolved: That a copy of the above minutes, together with the note relating to the admission of members, be sent him by the parnass. . . .

30th June, Sunday, 18th Tamuz, 5542 [1782]. . . .

Resolved: That Mr. Mordecai M. Mordecai be requested by the parnas to write a letter in Hebrew to the congregation at Surinam, requesting their aid and contribution to our new synagogue, and that the parnas be desired to write to Rhode Island and Lancaster, requesting the assistance of our brethren at those places for the same purpose. . . .

At a meeting of the junta the 24th Ab [August 4, 1782]. . . .

Resolved: That proclamation be made next Sabbath that a *shamas* ["beadle"] is wanting and whoever intends to apply for that place to give in their names and condition to the parnas and junta, that they may be laid before the congregation at their next meeting.

The parnas informed the junta that Mr. Henry Marks refused to pay his offerings. Resolved: That Mr. B. Gratz wait on him and know his reasons, also what he has done with the money taken out of the charity box.

The committee are desired to inform themselves what it will cost to purchase some lamps, crowns, etc., for the new synagogue. . . .

At a meeting of the junta the 2d Elul, 5542 [August 12, 1782]. . . .

The parnas informed the junta that he had spoken to Mr. [Manuel] Josephson and Mr. Isaac DaCosta, who refused to enter on the subject in question respecting the marriage of J. Cohen. They told him what the *din* [rabbinic law] was (as a private person), which is that no Cohen can marry a woman situated as the Widow Mordecai is [a proselyte]. Resolved: That we will not take any further notice at present respecting said marriage unless said Mr. Cohen applies in writing to the parnas and junta, agreeing therein to abide by their decision. . . .

Mr. Phillips requested something might be provided for a poor French boy. Resolved: That he be releived by subscription. . . .

The mode of consecrating the new synagogue being again considered, the following is to be observed, *vizt.:*

To meet at the old shull ["synagogue"] at three o'clock and say minha [afternoon prayers] till after Amidah [the "standing" prayer]; the parnas then to give out the following mizvahs [religious honors]:

Opening the new synagogue door
Portes echall in d[itt]o. [opening the doors of the ark]
Persons to carry the *sepharim* ["Scrolls"]
Companya [accompanying the scrolls when they are taken out and returned to the ark]
To walk in procession to the new synagogue, stop at the door and afterwards at the *taba* [reader's desk]; then to carry the *sepharim* six times around the same; the seventh time to deposit them in the *echall* [ark]; afterwards to make the *hanothen* [prayer for the government] and *mishebarachs* for those who are intitled to have them; then whoever has a mind to make any offering, to go before the *echal*, where the hazan will attend. . . .

At a meeting of the junta Sunday, 8th Elul [August 18, 1782]. . . .

Resolved: That the salary of a *shamas* be eighty dollars per annum and that he be allowed his mazoths ["unleavened bread"]. Mr. [Jonas] Phillips objected to the eighty dollars per annum salary, and thinks £25 sufficient.

Resolved: That it is necessary the duty of a shamas be explained, that any candidate offering [himself for the position] may know what he undertakes and what the congregation expects of him. He is to keep the shull and every thing belonging to it clean and in good order. He is to make all the candles, light them when they are wanted, and see them properly put out. He is to attend whenever there is prayers, and see the shull secured [locked] afterwards. He is to obey all orders of the parnas, and in his absence, the *gaboy* and any of the adjuntas. He is to see that the [eternal] lamp is kept constantly burning. He is to attend all circumcisions, weddings, and funerals which are according to our religion, and no others. . . .

The parnas moved that Mr. B. Seixas write a letter to Cape François [Cap Haitien] in order to solicit their assistance towards compleating our place of worship. Mr. B. Seixas requested Mr. Jonas Phillips might be added with him. Resolved: That Mr. Phillips and Mr. Seixas be a committee to write said letter.

Adjourned till four o'clock this afternoon. Met according to adjournment. . . .

The committee appointed to write a letter to Cape François brought one in, which, being read, was approved of, and ordered to be entered on the minutes and signed by the parnas and junta. Ordered that a copy of said letter be wrote and addressed to our brethren at St. Thomas, St. Croix, and Rhode Island. Copy of a letter wrote to Cape François, etc., etc.:

A small number of our brethren who have, during this calamitous war, fled here from different parts for refuge, in conjunction with those in this city, undertook to build a place of worship that we might meet to offer up our prayers to the Holy God of Israel, having hitherto substituted a room for that purpose, from which we were compelled to move by the owner.

Our ability to compleat the building is not equal to our wishes, from many recent losses. We are under the necessity to ask the assistance of our absent brethren. Amongst them, we look *up to you and the rest of our brethren with you,* not doubting but you'll readily contribute to so laudable an undertaking.

We pray the Almighty Father of the universe, the Lord God of Abraham, Isaac, and Jacob, to take you all under his holy protection, and grant you long life, health, and happiness.

We are respectfully, etc. . . .

Mr. B. Seixas moved that the parnas and each junta [board member] pay into the hands of the treasurer twenty-five dollars for carrying on the building of the new synagogue as a further advance thereto, and that the treasurer give a receipt to each one who has advanced money, specifying the sum received. Agreed to.

At a meeting of the junta, 15th Elul, 5542 [August 25, 1782]. . . .

The parnas presented a letter from the hazan, which he read, and moved that Mr. M. Mordecai and Mr. Israel Myer be sent for. Agreed to. . . .

Mr. Mordecai and Mr. Myer attended, and the parnas informed them of the point in question: Can Mr. Jacob Cohen marry the Widow Mordecai according to our law? After they had debated some time, Mr. DaCosta was requested to attend, which he did accordingly; and after a full hearing [of] the *dinim* [rabbinic "laws"] relating thereto, agreed to adjourn till four o'clock, requesting the same gentlemen's attendance, and also desired Mr. Jacob Cohen to attend. . . .

The gentlemen attended that were desired to attend this morning, and a great while was spent in debating and hearing of the *din*. Messrs. DaCosta and Mordecai proved by the *din* that it is contrary to our law to suffer such [a] marriage. The parnas then requested to know the determination of the junta and what answer should be given the hazan.

Mr. B. Gratz moved, seconded by S. Nathan, that a letter be wrote to the hazan, in answer to the one received, to forbid him to marry Mr. Cohen to Mrs. Mordecai, and not to mention his name in synagogue. After some time spent in debating thereon, the following letter was agreed on:

Sir:

In answer to your letter of 24th August, we now inform you that you are not to marry Mr. Jacob Cohen to Mrs. Mordecai, neither are you to be present at the wedding. And you are hereby strictly forbid to mention the said Cohen or his wife's name in any respect whatsoever in the synagogue.

We are, sir,

Your very humble servants,

Signed by I. Moses   B. Seixas
B. Gratz   S. Nathan
J. Phillips

Reverend Gershom Seixas

Mr. B. Seixas moved, seconded by Mr. Jonas Phillips, that the congregation be informed on Tuesday next that the parnas and junta have forbid the hazan to mention the name of Jacob Cohen and wife in shull, and that they be acquainted likewise that his wedding is contrary to the *din*, and all who are present at the same are liable to the same punishment.

A debate arising thereon, the question was put and the motion was lost.

For the motion:	Against it:
Jonas Phillips	Barnard Gratz
Benjamin Seixas	Simon Nathan
	Isaac Moses

The parnas then moved that as a full and decided opinion was this day given respecting the *din* on the marriage now in question, that it is the duty of the junta to enter into a pointed [point of] law respecting the said marriage, setting forth what punishment will be incurred by those that marry the parties or attend the same, and that the said law be published on Tuesday next.

A debate arising thereon, the question was put, and carried in the manner following:

For the motion:	Against the motion:
Jonas Phillips	Barnard Gratz
Benjamin Seixas	Simon Nathan
Isaac Moses	

Adjourned till tomorrow evening. . . .

At a meeting of the congregation by order of the parnas and junta, 17th Elul, 5542 [August 27, 1782]. . . .

The parnas informed the congregation that there were three candidates for the office of shamas, *vizt.:* Lyon Nathan, Mordecai M. Mordecai, and Abraham Cohen. Mr. Hart moved that the salary for shamas be enlarged to £37..10 per annum. Agreed to by a great majority. Mr. DaCosta moved, in addition to his salary he be allowed to receive any gifts or offering that may be made him by any of the congregation. Agreed to unanimously.

Mr. B. Seixas moved, seconded by Mr. DaCosta, that the candidates be asked before the election "whether they are satisfied with the salary and are willing to perform the duties as laid down by the parnas and junta." Agreed to unanimously. They were then severally asked the question and all answered in the affirmative.

Mr. DaCosta moved, seconded by the parnas, that Abraham Cohen be not included as a candidate for *shamas*. A debate arising thereon, it was carried in the affirmative. [The motion was lost.]

The congregation then proceeded to the election of a *shamas* and, the ballots being taken, were as follows:

M. M. Mordecai   – 4
Lyon Nathan   – 5
Abraham Cohen   – 4

Mr. Lyon Nathan was declared duly elected.

Mr. Solomon M. Cohen appeared. The parnas moved that Abraham Cohen be allowed thirty dollars for his [past] services. Agreed to unanimously. . . .

Resolved: That the congregation be called together on Sunday next at nine o'clock in the morning, and that publick notice be given in the synagogue next Sabbath to have such laws as the junta have adopted laid before them for their approbation, and to reject such as they do not approve of.

Resolved: That the parnas apply to Mr. Moses Gomez and request the loan of his *sepharim* and *remonim* [Torah ornaments] on the day of the dedication of the new synagogue, and that we will return them to him when required.

Mr. Solomon M. Cohen attended the junta and requested their acceptance of a new *tabah* [reader's desk] cloth for the use of this K. K. Mikveh Israel which he should deliver before the day of dedication.

Mr. Jonas Phillips acquainted the junta that he intended making his *sephar* holy on the day of dedication of the new synagogue, and for the use of the K. K. Mikveh Israel. [He would "dedicate" it as a gift to the synagogue.] . . .

At a meeting of the congregation called by order of the parnas and junta on Sunday, 22d Elul [September 1, 1782]. . . .

The parnas informed the congregation that the junta had prepared eleven laws, which he would read to them, and afterwards take them up singly, for their assent or dissent. . . . Here, it is presumed, the laws should be inserted, but as the whole when finished will be entered, reference must be had to the constitution, as it now stands, and it is recommended that it be taken care of and tacked to this book. . . .

The parnas informed the congregation that Mr. Phillips had offered his *sephar* to the new synagogue, and Mr. S. Cohen had presented a new *tabah* cloth, and recommended their having a *mishebarach* every *kipur* night and on every anniversary of the dedication, for ever. Agreed to unanimously.

The parnas read a letter he had received from Mr. Joseph Simons, requesting that he might be admitted to become a *yahid* of this K. *Kadosh* ["Holy Congregation"] Mikveh Israel. Resolved unanimously: That Mr. Joseph Simons be admitted as a *yahid* of this K. *Kadosh* Mikveh Israel. . . .

At the meeting of the parnass and junta on Thursday morning the 4th of Tisra, 5543 [September 12, 1782]. . . .

A petition from Lyon Moses desiring to become a *yahid* referred to the next meeting. A letter directed to the parnass and junta from Messrs. Barnard Gratz, Jonas Phillips, Gershon Seixas, Benjamin Seixas, Simon Nathan, committee for superceeding [supervising?] the building of the synagogue, informing them that the new synagogue is so far finis[h]ed [as] to be concecrated tomorrow, the 5th of Tisra, in the afternoon.

Voted: That the committee be appointed to wait on the governour and council [of the State of Pennsylvania] with an address. Resolved: That Messrs. Gershom Seixas, Jonas Phillips, Barnard Gratz, Isaac Moses be the committee appointed to wait on the governour, etc. . . .

At a meeting of the parnass and junta on Sunday, the 7 Tisra, 5543 [September 15, 1782]. . . .

The parnass represented to the junta that he was informed by Mr. Mordecai M. Mordecai that Ezekiel Levy, contrary to our laws, shaved on a Sabbeth at Baltimore. The motion was put by the parnass to send for Mr. Ezekiel Levy, and being put to vote that Mr. Levy be send for: Yeas: the parnas, Hayman Levy, Michael Gratz, Simon Nathan; nays: Solomon Myers Cohen, Solomon Marachey. Mr. Simon Nathan then made a motion, seconded by Solomon M. Cohen, that Mr. Mordecai should be send for. Agreed to unanimously.

Mr. Levy appearing, the matter was represented to him, on which he desired that the accusers might appear, which was accordingly done, who attented, and being asked wuther he knew from his own knowledge that Mr. E. Levy did shave on a Sabbeth, replied that his information was received from Mr. Isaac Abraham at Baltimore. Therefore, it is resolved that the matter be purponed [postponed], and the parnass is requested to write a letter to Mr. Abraham for his full information respecting the same. Adjurned. . . .

At a general meeting of the congregation on Wednesday, the 17th of Tisra [September 25, 1782], held in consequence of a letter received from Messrs. Benjamin Seixas, Isaac Moses, and Isaac DaCosta, directed to the parnass, requesting the congregation may be convened. . . .

On motion of the parnass, seconded by Mr. Spitzer, that each person is not to speak longer than a quarter of an hour, but may get up three times in his turn and speak: determined in the negative by a great majority.

Messrs. Simon Nathan, Solomon M. Cohen, and Benjamin Seixas where each of them fined two shillings and six pence for speaking out of their places.

Mr. Benjamin Seixas, seconded by Mr. Spitzer, [moved] that the congregation determin whether any gentlemen who is admisted [admitted] to be a *yahid* have a right to speak in congregational meetings, alltho he has no right to vote: determined in the negative.

Mr. Parnass [the president], having read a letter from Messrs. Benjamin Seixas, Isaac Moses, and Isaac DaCosta, complaining of arbitary proceedings in the junto, he requested that the congregation would form it self into a committee of the whole house, in consequence whereoff the parnass lift [left] the chair, and Mr. Mordecai Sheftall was chosen by a great majority to act as chairman for this particular business, who, having accepted the chair, and a considerable time having been taken in debate by the accusers and the accused. . . .

Mr. Isaac Moses made a motion, which was seconded by Mr. Benjamin Nones, vizt., whether the parnass and junto had a right in referring to the committee for regulating the seats in the new synagogue, after they, the committee, had giving out the numbers of each seat for the respective persons on the day of dedication. Several of the members being desirious to speak to the above motion, and it being late, it was resolved to adjourn till tomorrow, five o'clock in the evening.

At a general meeting of the congregation agreable to adjournment. . . .

Mr. Coshman Polock moved, seconded by Mr. Spitzer, that as it appears that nothing criminal had been done either by the committee appointed to distribute the seats in the sinagogue, nor by the parnass or junto, but that many irregularetys have been committed from a misconstruction of the constitution since their election, therefore recommended that every thing that has happened be buried in oblivion. Which was carried by a majority of votes.

B [NO. 49]

Whereas the constitution heretofore established for the government of the congregation by the name of K. K. Mikve Israel, established in the city of Philadelphia, for divers causes has been found to be inadequate thereto, with a view to lessen or totaly obviate all inconveniencies arising therefrom, we, the subscribers, members of the said congregation, have altered and amended the same, and have now adopted the following constitution.

Section 1. The officers of the congregation shall be one parnass ["president"], three adjuntos ["board members"], and one *gabay* ["treasurer"], to be elected by the congregation by ballot on the first Sunday after *Rosh Hodes* [the first day of the month of] Elul in every year, to serve for one year from Rosh Shashonah ["New Year"]. And the congregation at the same time shall elect by ballot one person to serve as *haton torah,* and one person to serve as *haton beresith.* Agreed. [*Hatan torah* and *hatan bereshit:* "bridegroom of the Law and bridegroom of the beginning." These men were given the honor of closing and beginning the annual cycle of the Pentateuchal readings in the synagogue.]

Section 2. The congregation shall meet once in every three months or oftner if required by the parnass, who shall call special meetings at the request of any four members. Seven members shall form a quorum to transact business. Agreed.

Section 3. The parnass and adjuntos shall meet at least once in every month to transact such business as may be necessary during the recess of the congregation, not otherwise provided for. The parnass and two adjuntos shall be a quorum, and when the parnass is absent, the three adjuntos shall be a quorum. Agreed.

Section 4. The *gabay* shall keep account of all offerings, and collect and take charge of all monies belonging to the congregation. He shall pay all orders of the parnass, who is not to draw at any one time for more than 3 dollars for any one person without the consent of the adjuntos. The *gabay* shall render a just account of all receipts and expenditures to the parnass and adjuntos once in every three months, and his books shall be open to their inspection. And [he] shall pay all monies and deliver up all books and papers belonging to the congregation to his successor as soon as may be after his election. Agreed.

Section 5. The hazan, rabbi [teacher], *sochet* ["slaughterer"], and *shamas* ["beadle"] to be chosen by the congregation and to be amenable for their conduct in their respective offices to the parnass and adjuntos, with the priviledge of an appeal to the congregation; their salaries to be established by the congregation and paid quarterly, but no reduction shall be made in the saliries of either [any] of the above mentioned officers untill three months after it shall have been resolved (previous to the expiration of the year). Agreed.

Section 6. The parnass shall precide at all meetings; in his absence a chairman shall be appointed. All questions shall be decided by a majority of votes. Should the number be equal, the parnass or chairman shall have the casting vote. In all elections the parnass or chairman shall vote, and when the number of votes is equal, the choice to be determined by lot. Agreed.

Section 7. The parnass shall keep in a book for that purpose fair records of the transactions of the congregation and adjuntos at all their meetings. Agreed.

Section 8. Any person not heretofore a member of this congregation and not now residing in the city of Philadelphia, Northern Liberties, or district of Southwark, may, when approved of by the parnass and adjuntos, become a member of this congregation on paying three dollars, and signing his name to the constitution (in a book to be kept for that purpose), and any person heretofore a member and not now residing in the city of Philadelphia, Northern Liberties, or district of Southwark, shall sign his name to the constitution (in said book) on his comeng to reside among the congregation. Agreed.

Section 9. [The following sections in parentheses were crossed out in the original text.] (Any Jew that buys, sells, or works, or keeps open store on a Sabbath or on hollidays shall not be intitled to any of the priviledges of this congregation. His name shall be erazed from the books, and in case he should die, he shall not be interred in the burial ground belonging to the congregation nor shall any of their officers or members be aiding or assisting at said burial, etc.) Provided, unless the person so offending shall have first made concessions (and payed such a fine as the parnass and adjuntos) as the congregation may have thought reasonable. Agreed.

Section 10. Any Jew (or Jewess) who shall marry any other person than one of his (or her) own religion (and any one who shall be assisting thereto shall be subject to the same penallty contained in the last section . . .) shall forfeit his membership and his name shall be erased from the books (of the congregation) and shall not be entitled to any of the privaleges of this congregation. Agreed.

Section 11. The parnass and adjuntos shall not alter or revoke any law passed by the congregation, but shall from time to time recommend such laws and regulations as they may think necessary. Agreed.

(Section 12. All deeds, mortgages, and leases to be given by the congregation, or all papers obligatory on them, shall be signed by the parnass and adjuntos, the consent of the congregation first to be granted at one of their stated meetings, and not otherwise.)

Section 12. Every Jew not residing in the city of Philadelphia, the Northern Liberties, or district of Southwark, but occasionally or on holy days frequenting the synagogue, shall contribute and pay towards the support of this congregation a sum not less than three dollars per annum, and any one refusing to pay the same shall (be subject to the same penalties contained in the 9th section with the benefit of the proviso therein.) not be entitled to any mitzvas [religious honors], provided notice thereof be first given him. Agreed.

(Section 13. No person shall be a member of this congregation under the age of —— years.)

Section 14. The congregation [is] reserving to themselves the right of altering and amending this constitution with the consent of two thirds of the members composing the congregation, but no alteration or amendment shall take place unless proposed in writing at one stated meeting and agreed to at another with the consent of two thirds of the members of the whole congregation. Unanimously agreed. . . .

17. We the subscribers, members of the congregation by the name of K. K. Mikve Israel, who have hereunto signed their names have agreed to the foregoing written constitution for the good government of the said congregation, and that we will seperately and jointly use the utmost of our endeavours to have the same fulfilled, and that we will from time to time contribute such sums as our abilities will allow for its support. And for the true performance of this, we bind ourselves one to another in firm belief that this, our transaction, will be for the benefit of the Jewish religion.

Done in the city of Philadelphia, this 10th Sebat, 5558, corrisponding with the 28th January, 1798, one thousand seven hundred ninety eight. Agreed.

————

No. 50   Gershom Mendes Seixas Returns to Shearith Israel, New York—1783–1784

After April, 1783, when the provisional treaty of peace between the United States and Great Britain was ratified by Congress, it was quite evident that the Revolutionary War was over. It was only a matter of time before the British-occupied cities would be evacuated. The Whig Jewish merchants who had fled to Philadelphia during the Revolution began to make plans to return home. It was obvious that if they left, Congregation Mikveh Israel, whose synagogue building was heavily mortgaged, would be faced by a crisis. The rabbi, Gershom Mendes Seixas, realized the threat to his security, for the man who had guaranteed his salary, Isaac Moses, had already returned to New York. Accordingly, in November, 1783, the apprehensive minister wrote to the president and board of the Philadelphia synagogue, asking them how they were going to meet their financial obligations (Document A). He pointed out that individuals who had advanced money for current expenses and for the building fund had compensated themselves by not paying their congregational offerings, and therefore the treasury was depleted. Nor, wrote he, could he ask the new president, Simon Nathan, to guarantee his salary: Nathan was his brother-in-law.

During the following month, the New York congregation, where Seixas had officiated before the war, asked him to return. In his reply the rabbi asked whether the congregation would institute certain administrative reforms and, in addition, grant him a living wage. By January, 1784, the trustees of the congregation indicated their willingness to pay him well, and Seixas, in turn, agreed to go back. In February he wrote to the Philadelphia board and presented his resignation (Document B).

The members of Mikveh Israel were indignant that their rabbi intended to leave them on such short notice, and Seixas wrote President Hayman Levy of New York, asking for permission to remain until after the Passover holidays. With the winter thaw the roads would be in bad shape (Document C). Levy politely but firmly said "No" to the Philadelphians (Document D). If Mikveh Israel wanted a man, he suggested, the congregation might get in touch with Jacob R. Cohen, who ministered in New York during the war while Seixas was in Philadelphia. (The congregation took Cohen.) Levy insisted on Seixas' return, and early in April he was back at his old post in Shearith Israel.

The four letters throw light on the problems of the New York and Philadelphia synagogues as they struggled to keep alive in a post-war world of impending economic adjustment.

SOURCE. Archives of Congregation Mikveh Israel, Philadelphia.

A [NO. 50]

Philadelphia, 10th November, 1783.

Gentlemen:

Mr. Isaac Moses, who was bound to me for the payment of my salary as hazan of this congregation, and being now gone to reside in New York, is thereby released from the obligation, as it was only for the time he remained here.

As I have before experienced the inconvenience of relying on the public, hope your honors will not take it amiss in me for applying for some individual security, more especially as I observe that several gentleman who owed money to the *tsedeka* [treasury] have paid themselves by ballancing their accounts with monies advanced towards the *binyan a bait* ["building fund"], thereby giving a sanction to the present *gabay* ["treasurer"] to follow the same mode of reimbursing himself to a considerable amount, which he has really advanced and perhaps ought to have been repaid ere this.

The connection between the parnass and me is, I think, a sufficient plea for my not accepting of him to enter into any contract for the purpose. Have therefore to request your honors to take the matter into your serious consideration, and to provide accordingly.

I am, gentlemen,

Your most obedient servitor,

Gershom Seixas

Reader and Notary of the Holy Congregation Mikveh Israel

Honorable Parnass and *Mahamad* ["board"] of K.K.
["Holy Congregation"] Mikve Israel.

B [NO. 50]

Philadelphia, February 15th, 1784.

Gentlemen:

Being called to my former place of residence (and the place of my nativity), have to inform you that my quarter expires here on *Ros Hodes* Nisan [the first of Nisan, March 23], at which time have engaged to return to New York. That you may not lose the opportunity of providing yourselves with a suitable person for the office of hazan, beg leave to recommend a speedy application to those whom you think worthy. And I will on my part do every thing in my power for the benefit of the K.K. Mikve Israel, to whom I acknowledge myself greatly indebted for the many kind and generous favors that I have received during my stay amongst them, and shall ever make it my study to render every possible service in return.

May the Great God of Israel vouchsafe to hold you under His holy and divine protection. May you increase and prosper in peace and tranquility, most devoutly prays, gentlemen,

Your much obliged and very humble servitor,

Gershom Seixas

The Honorable Parnass and *Mahamad,*
K.K. Mikve Israel.

C [NO. 50]

Philadelphia, 15th March, 1784.

Dear and worthy Sir:

The unsettledness of the weather almost makes me despair of being able to accomplish my contract with your congregation at the time appointed, which was to have been to morrow sennight [seven nights, or a week, from tomorrow]. Have some small hopes to be with you the week after; but as I understand from information that a letter is to be sent to you and the junta for permission for me to stay here till Ros Hodes Iyar [the first of Iyyar, April 22], will wait the result of your answer to it.

If you can by any means indulge this congregation, you will at the same time greatly oblige me, as I can by that time get every thing ready to take my family and effects with me, and sooner I have not the least prospect. Should the prayer of the letter not be thought elibible [eligible?], you will please to let me know by post, and I'll be with you for *Shabbat Ha-gadol* [the Sabbath before Passover, known as "The Great Sabbath," April 3] and leave my family till after Pesah ["Passover"], though you must allow it to be a great hardship for a man to be without his family of a Pesah.

Several letters have passed between the parnass and junta and me. They condemn me for not having given them timely notice of my intention to quit them. Have said every thing I could to justify my conduct. The matter now rests entirely with you to say go or stay.

Should have wrote to you before, but was in such continual and violent pain upwards of a fortnight after my return home that I could not even speak without encreasing the pain.

With the greatest respect to Aunt Levy, in which my wife unites, and salutations to the rest of your worthy houshold and connexions, am, dear and worthy sir,

Your obliged and affect[iona]t[e] humble servitor,
Gershom Seixas

Mr. Hayman Levy.

D [NO. 50]

New York, 22nd March, 1784.

Gentlemen:

Your letter of 14th inst. only reached us this morning. The time is so short that we have hardly [had] sufficient [time] to answer you with that precision we should otherwise do. We shall therefore answer the most material without going to particularities.

We are much surprized that you should complain of short notice, given you by Mr. Seixas of his *intention*. Those who have been obliged to take up their residence in Philadelphia while this place was in the power of the British always expected Mr. Seixas would return, and to your candor we submit, when we ask you, did you expect otherwise?

As to the gentleman who now officiates here, we make no doubt he will, when properly invited, pay you a visit. *Perhaps* the congregation of Mikve Israel may approve of him.

With regard to Mr. Seixas's removal befor or after Pesah, we cannot conceive it will affect you in any material degree; a few days cannot be of that consequence. We therefore, when we say we cannot agree to your request, hold ourselves clear of any imputation whatever of being detrimental to the interest or prosperity of your synagogue (which we sincerely wish) unless we sacrifice that of our own.

With wishing you the enjoyment of many happy festivals, I am in behalf of the junto, gentlemen,

Your most obedient, humble servant,
Hayman Levy, parnas

The Honorable Parnass and Junto
of the K.K. Mikve Israel.

No. 51   Petition for the Building of a Ritual Bathhouse—1784

Manuel Josephson (*ca.* 1729–96), an emigrant from Germany, was one of the best-educated men in the Philadelphia congregation. A sometime sutler during the French and Indian War, Josephson became a merchant in New York and finally settled in Philadelphia. He was a good Hebraist and was interested in general culture; in religious matters he was a fervent traditionalist.

In 1784 Josephson presented the following petition to the board of Mikveh Israel, asking that a ritual bathhouse (*mikveh*) for the women of the congregation be built. His motivation is classical in its orthodoxy: inasmuch as the American Jew had been blessed with desirable privileges, it was incumbent upon him to thank God by scrupulously observing the Divine Law. If he failed to do this, all the curses threatened in Holy Writ would descend upon the transgressor.

By 1786 the ritual bathhouse was erected and placed under the supervision of the zealous Josephson.

SOURCE. Archives of Congregation Mikveh Israel, Philadelphia.

It having pleased the Almighty God of Israel to appoint our lot in this country, the rulers whereof he has inspired with wisdom and a benevolent disposition toward us as a nation, whereby we enjoy every desireable priviledge and great preeminence far beyond many of our brethren dispersed in different countries and governments,

And in order to manifest our gratitude for those peculiar favors and blessings, we ought, in a very sincere manner, observe a strict and close adherence to those laws and commandments ordained by Him and delivered to our master Moses, of blessed memory, which have been handed down to us in a regular succession to the present time, wherein we are told (Exodus 19:5: "Ye shall be a peculiar treasure unto me above all people"), that the Almighty has made choice of our nation in preference of all others, on condition (ibid., "If ye obey my voice and keep my covenant") that we hearken unto his voice and observe his covenants; and on the other hand, if we neglect our duty, He has denounced (Leviticus 26:14, etc., etc.) severe and tremendious sentences against us, to avoid which we should endeavour with all our might to regulate our conduct in every respect conformable to His Holy Law, rectify every deviation therefrom, and supply every omission so far as in our power.

In order thereto, we, the subscribers, having taken these matters to heart and duly reflected on the many defects this congregation called Mikve Israel in Philadelphia labours under, and to our great regret and sorrow we find one in particular, which strikes us most forcibly and cannot but affect with astonishment and horror every judicious and truly religious mind. This is the want of a proper *mikve* or batheing place, according to our Law and institution, for the purification of married women at certain periods. The necessity of having and using such place will readily appear from the text (ibid., 20:18) where a transgression of this ordinance is highly criminal to both husband and wife. Nor does it rest with them only, but the very children born from so unlawful cohabitation are deemed *bene niddot* [children conceived during the menstrual period], which makes this offence the more hoeinous [heinous] and detestable, in as much as it effects not only the parents, but their posterity for generations to come. And should it be known in the congregations abroad that we had been thus neglectful of so important a matter, they would not only pronounce heavy anathemas against us, but interdict and avoid intermarriages with us, equal as with [a] different nation or sect, to our great shame and mortification.

Now, therefore, in full consideration of the foregoing, we have unanimously agreed that a proper *mikve* or batheing place for the sole use of our congregation be forthwith built, and that no delay may be made in accomplishing so necessary and laudable a work. We do hereby, each of us for himself, most solemnly and religiously engage and promise to pay such sum of money as is annexed to our respective names, without any hesitation or demur whatever, unto such person or persons as shall hereafter be nominated for the purpose of receiveing the said subscription money and to see the said work carried on and compleated. And we flatter ourselves that evry married man will use the most persuasive and evry other means, to induce his wife to a strict compliance with that duty so incumbent upon them, that so the Almighty may look down in mercy upon us, and send the Redeemer to Zion in our days. Amen, so be it.

Philadelphia,   21st May, 1784.
                        Rosh Hodesh Sivan (the first of Sivan), 5544.

No. 52   The Jews Observe Their Holydays—1784

The following letter by "A Protestant" appeared in a Philadelphia newspaper. The writer lamented the fact that Christians were more concerned with their worldly pursuits than with the observance of Good Friday, and pointed out that Jews, in contrast, were meticulous in celebrating the Passover, which usually occurs about the same time. It is possible that the writer (probably the Reverend Charles Crawford) had no particular group of Jews in mind, but it is more likely that he was thinking of the Jewish community of Philadelphia which clustered around its synagogue Mikveh Israel.

SOURCE. *The Pennsylvania Packet, and Daily Advertiser,* December 23, 1784.

Though I do not pretend to such an outward shew of religion as our modern inthusiasts, yet I flatter myself I am never the worse Christian. However, I cannot help being extremely shocked, when I observe the day of our blessed Saviour's death [Good Friday], appointed by the church (as no doubt it ought to be) so strict and solemn a fast, treated, by all ranks of people, with that unchristianlike levity and concern, which casts a reproach upon our country.

That day, in my opinion, ought to be observed, if possible, more holy than the Sabbath, that we poor sinful mortals, instead of following our worldly concerns on this most sacred day, might have the opportunity of attending before and sending up our praises to God, for giving his only Son to die an ignominious death upon the cross, as an expiatorial sacrifice for our sins. Certainly one day's abstinence from the concerns of this world cannot be any injury whatsoever.

The Jews set us the example; who, at the time of their Passover, refrain from the tempting lucre of gain during the course of almost a week. Let not us Protestants be behind all other nations [religious groups] in shewing respect to the dying day of Jesus Christ. Wherefore, I think, to promote such a due observance of that day as is requisite, I humbly propose that the clergy exhort their respective congregations to attend the service of the church, and keep holy that day, which certainly would not fail to be acceptable both to God and thousands of Christians [indentured servants?], who at this present are debarred, against their inclinations, in conformity to a custom contrary to all the rules of religion and right reasoning. I have nothing more to add but my prayers that this plan may be carried into execution, and I remain in hopes,

Yours,
A Protestant

No. 53   Michael Judah Leaves His Estate to Jewish Charities—1784

Michael Judah was a small-town merchant who left New York to settle in Norwalk, Connecticut, in all probability because the competition in that town was less keen. There is a record of a petty loan made available to him by Congregation Shearith Israel. It may be that the £5 the trustees of the congregation lent him in 1745 set him up in business.

Judah married out of the faith. His son David, who became the ancestor of General Henry Moses Judah and of Theodore Dehone Judah, the Pacific Coast railroad promoter, was a Christian. Michael Judah, however, was a loyal and observant Jew. He seems to have attempted to keep a kosher household, brought the mohel from New York to circumcise his son, and, as we shall see from the following will, bequeathed the bulk of his very modest estate to Jewish charities.

The Solomon Simson mentioned in the will was a well-known New York merchant and one of the founders of the Democratic Society. Captain Eliakim Raymond, the executor, was related to Michael's late wife, Martha Raymond Judah.

The testament reflects the attempt of a Jew to maintain his religious loyalty in an overwhelmingly non-Jewish environment.

SOURCE. Connecticut State Library, Hartford, Connecticut Archives, Norwalk District, No. 3498.

Know all men by these presents that I, Michalel Judah, of Norwalk, in the County of Fairfield and State of Connecticut, being weak in body and sick, and caling to mind the frailty of human nature and that it is appointed for all men to die, and being sound in mind and memory, and having a desire to dispose of the little interest which it has pleased God in his providence to endow me with, do hereby make this my last will and testament, revoking all other wills heretofore by me made.

And my will is, first, that after paying my just debts and funeral charges, I give and bequeath to my son, David Judah, five pounds lawfull money as his part of portion in my estate,

And the remainder of my estate to be given, equally divided and given, the one half to the Sinagouge in Newyork, and the other half to the poor widows and orphans of my own nation, living in Newyork, to be distributed at the discretion of Mr. Solomon Simson of Newyork.

And I do hereby make, ordain, constitute, and appoint Capt. Eliakim Raymond to be my executor of this, my last will and testament.

In witness whereof I have hereunto set my hand and seal this 31th day of December, A. D. 1784, in prisents [the presence] of

> Aron Abbott
> Matthias Abbott   Michel Judah
> Stephen Abbott

Fairfield County, in Norwalk. Personally appeared Michael Judah, signer and sealer to the above written instrument, and signed, sealed, published, and pronounced the same to be his last will and testament, before me, the day and date above written.

Elephalet Lockwood, Justice of Peace

No. 54   The Burial of Benjamin Moses Clava—1785

According to the records, Benjamin Moses Clava, a Jewish merchant, was a business partner of Barnard Gratz in the 1750's. His death on March 15, 1785, and the burial which it necessitated, ordinarily matters of routine, created a problem for the members of Philadelphia's Mikveh Israel.

Like many other peddlers and merchants who lived in obscure villages and hamlets, Clava had fallen in love with a Gentile woman, and their marriage had been solemnized by a civil official. Here was a poser for Philadelphia Jewry. Was he entitled to proper Jewish burial? Three years before his death the members had needed his help in building their synagogue. His name was not found on the list of donors, and it appears that he did not belong to the congregation.

As we shall see below (Document A), the members decided that

Clava might be buried in consecrated ground, but without shrouds or benefit of ritual cleansing. Other sources indicate that he was buried in a corner of the cemetery, and when the actual burial took place, some members disregarded the congregational decision and interred Clava with the proper rites and ceremonies. Document A is copied as it is found in the records. For the sake of clarity it is followed by a version in modern English.

Even after the members of the congregation had decided the issue some uncertainty remained. Had they done the right thing? Where could they obtain guidance for action in future cases? There was not a single qualified rabbi in all of North America at the time; all the officiating "rabbis" were readers of the service. Faced with a baffling question and with no one in the vicinity to answer it, the congregation decided to refer the matter, in a Yiddish letter, to the rabbis of Amsterdam and The Hague (Document B).

SOURCE. Document A: Congregation Mikveh Israel, Philadelphia, Minute Book, Vol. I, 1781–95; Document B: Congregation Mikveh Israel, Correspondence.

A [NO. 54]

At a meeting held of the congragation on the 5th [of] Nison, 5545, or 16th March, 1785.
Present:

Messrs. Asher Myers	Moses D. Nathons
Manuel Josephson	Benjamin Nones
Henry Marks	Manuel Noah
Jonas Philips	Moses Nathan Levy
Moses Jacobs	Samuel Hays
Mordicai Levy	Myer Derkom
Jacob Cohon, hazzan	M. Gratz

When the parnass acquainted the gentlemen that in concequaince of a letter received from Mr. Jonas Philips, Henry Marks, and Moses D. Nathons recquaisting to have the congregation calld imadeatly as is of great portencee in a present case, for the genaril good of the sasiaty. When the letter was read setting forth that there is to be a burell of one B. M. Clava who was marrid to a *goy* [Gentile] by *goyim*, and as many *to our sorry* are in the same preditement, that some mode of buriall aught to be adapted from the comon way of good *yehudim* ["Jews"]. Wher on it was debaited and agreed on, with out a desanding voice, that a *din towrah* [*din torah*, an authoritative decision] should be asked and oboydid by. When Messrs. Manuel Josephson, Moses D. Nathons, and

Joseph W. Corples was chosen to give the *din* ["law"] or wordeek in writig but as the corpse or *mes* was laying to be burried, there ansure is at present that B. M. Clava and all such persons in fewture is to be entiard with out washing and clothing, but put in the corphin as he now lays, and carried to the grave. Agreed unanimously.

[Paraphrase of Document A—No. 54]

The parnass acquainted the gentlemen that, in consequence of a letter received from Messrs. Jonas Phillips, Henry Marks, and Moses D. Nathans, the congregation had been called immediately to discuss the present case, a matter of great importance for the general good of the society. Whereupon the letter was read, setting forth that there was to be a burial of B. M. Clava, who had been married to a Gentile woman by Gentiles. Since many, to our sorrow, are in the same predicament, some mode of burial ought to be adopted different from the usual way of burying good Jews.

Whereupon the question was debated, and it was agreed upon, without a dissenting voice, that a legal ruling should be asked and abided by. Messrs. Manuel Josephson, Moses D. Nathans, and Joseph W. Carpeles were chosen to give the verdict in writing, but, since the corpse was waiting to be buried, their answer at the present was that B. M. Clava, and all such persons in the future, were to be interred without ritual washing and clothing, but to be placed in the coffin as they were, and to be carried to the grave.

Agreed unanimously.

B [NO. 54]

Philadelphia, Sunday, 9 Nisan, 5545 [March 20, 1785].

To the honored . . . Rabbi Saul [Loewenstamm] of the Ashkanazic Community of Amsterdam. . . .

Last Tuesday, the fifth of this month [Tuesday was the fourth: March 15, 1785], there died here a man named Benjamin Moses Clava, who left a Gentile woman whom he had married in a civil ceremony. He had with her two daughters who are also still living. He was said to be a man of great Jewish learning. After he had married the Gentile woman, he became blind and had to stay in. His Gentile wife provided for him and the Jews sometimes sent him kosher food. On Tuesday it became suddenly known that he had died and that no Jews had been with him at the time of his death. (About a year before his death he called several Jews and recited the confession of faith before them, but continued to live with the Gentile woman till his death.)

There was a lot of speculation in our congregation about his burial.

The president and the leaders and a majority of the members of our congregation met to agree on the matter, and it was finally left to a religious court for a decision. The congregation appointed as a court Moses Nathan and the two undersigned with instructions to send you a copy of our decision in English. Here, for the record, is a brief resume:

The dead man shall be buried in a corner of the cemetery, without ritual washing, without shrouds, and without a ceremony, but four boys shall carry him to the grave and bury him, and the shrouds that have been prepared shall be put into the casket, but he shall not wear them. Whoever shall disregard this decision, and render any service to the dead man, shall be excluded from all religious functions until he submit to the congregation and accept whatever punishment be imposed upon him. This decision shall be permanently enforced and applied to all transgressors who shall marry out of the faith. This is the outline of the decision.

Now the president went to the place where the body was kept to see whether there were any irresponsible people who would attend the body in disregard of our decision, and he found there several irreverent and irresponsible men, among them [Moses] Mordecai. The president warned the men, in the presence of Mordecai, not to attend the body, but Mordecai paid no attention to his words, and, on the contrary, quoted rabbinic laws against him. And they washed the body and clothed it in shrouds, that is to say, the president anticipated that and cut the shrouds almost completely into pieces, but they [the malcontents] did what they wanted. The congregation will shortly decide what to do to these men.

All this goes to show the conduct of Mordecai, who is ready to destroy good ordinances that were made to meet the needs of the moment because of the great lack of discipline that prevails in our generation. Now, those unrespectful men who attended the body unlawfully claim that the decision was improper. We, therefore, request of you to answer . . . about this decision, whether it was properly made to meet the need of the hour.

May the mouths of those who speak falsehoods be closed, may they be put to shame and receive their just deserts from the Lord; and may we soon see the coming of the Redeemer, so that Israel's authority will be as of old to punish those who rebel against God and his law. Then the Lord will be One and his name will be one; and there will be reward for those who labor for the Lord and his law.

We are looking forward to your reply and are ready to observe your instructions as slaves obey their masters, and disciples their teachers. With best wishes, etc.,

Manuel Josephson
J. W. Carpeles

No. 55 The Gentiles of Philadelphia Help the
Synagogue—1788

After the Revolution Congregation Mikveh Israel of Philadelphia found itself in debt to the extent of £800. Its new building had cost a considerable amount of money, and many of the Jews on whose help the congregation had counted had returned to their New York or Charleston homes.

In an effort to save the synagogue the congregation experimented with a variety of expedients, including an appeal to the non-Jews of the city. This appeal, which was circulated among local Gentiles, is given below. Among the subscribers who responded to it were Benjamin Franklin, David Rittenhouse, William Bradford, Thomas McKean, William Rush, Charles Biddle, and one of the Muhlenbergs. Although the synagogue failed to raise the necessary amount on that occasion, its problem was solved in 1790 when the state authorities permitted Mikveh Israel to run a lottery.

Knowing the men whose help they sought, and having done business with them frequently, the Jews did not hesitate to solicit their subscriptions. Equally, if not more important, however, was their conviction that in an "enlightened" age Gentiles could not object to aiding men of a different faith in worshiping according to the dictates of their consciences.

SOURCE. The appeal was published in abbreviated form in J. T. Scharf and T. Westcott, *History of Philadelphia*, II, 1439–40. It is reprinted here in its entirety, except for the signatures, from the original in the Archives of Congregation Mikveh Israel, Philadelphia.

To the humane, charitable, and well disposed people, the representation and solicitation of the good people of the Hebrew society [community] in the City of Philadelphia, commonly called Israelites.

Whereas, the religious order of men in this city denominated Israelites were without any synagogue or house of worship untill the year 1780 [1782], when, desirous of accommodating themselves and encouraged thereto by a number of respectable and worthy bretheren of the Hebrew society then in this place (who generously contributed to the design), they purchased a lot of ground and erected thereon the buildings necessary and proper for their religious worship;

And whereas, many of their number at the close of the late war returned to New York, Charleston, and elsewhere their homes (which they had been exiled from and obliged to leave on account of their attachment to American measures), leaving the remaining few of their religion here burthened with a considerable charge consequent from so great an undertaking;

And whereas, the present congregation, after expending all the subscriptions, loans, gifts, etc., made the society by themselves and the generous patrons of their religious intentions, to the amount of at least £2,200, were obliged to borrow money to finish the building, and contract other debts that is now not only pressingly claimed, but a judgment will actually be obtained against their house of worship, which must be sold unless they are speedily enabled to pay the sum of about £800; and which, from a variety of delicate and distressing causes, they are wholly unable to raise among themselves;

They are therefore under the necessity of earnestly soliciting from their worthy fellow-citizens of every religious denomination their benevolent aid and help, flattering themselves that their worshipping Almighty God in a way and manner different from other religious societies will never deter the enlightened citizens of Philadelphia from generously subscribing towards the preservation of a religious house of worship. The subscription paper will be enrolled in the archives of their congregation, that their posterity may know and gratefully remember the liberal supporters of their religious society.

Philadelphia, April 30th, 1788.

———

No. 56   Salomon Raffeld (Raphael) Asks for Permission to Be Married—1788

American Jewish congregations of the eighteenth century required a couple to submit a formal request to the president before the marriage could be solemnized by the hazzan or minister. By granting or withholding approval the community leaders attempted to control intermarriage, inevitable in sparsely settled countries where young Jewish women were scarce.

A typical example of such a request is the following petition, which Salomon Raffeld addressed to Levy Phillips in October, 1788. This Raffeld is identical with Solomon Raphael, a merchant and auctioneer, who at various times did business in Philadelphia, Baltimore, and Richmond.

Unfortunately, Raffeld's letter does not speak for itself. Because the English is almost unintelligible, it is followed by a paraphrase.

SOURCE. Archives of Congregation Mikveh Israel, Philadelphia.

To the anerable, the presedent, and the genthelman jauntay:

Weer as I have pramis mie selleff in matteri mony whit one gall, the dogter of Mr. Barent Jacob, in the Norderen Libberthes in Philladelpia; and I would bie werry happay that jour anerable budday would order to Mr. Jacob Kohon as gasan of the congragashis of Mikvy Israel to give mie goupa and kadousin agins Dousday. Ther for, genttelman, I pray one ansver of jour shentel man to mourow . . . the 12 day of Tisri at 11 o'clok and, by soo douing, your pertisnar will eiver pray.

Froom jour omble sarwint,
Salomon Raffeld

To Mr. Levy Phillip, President of the K.K. Mikvy Israel,
Philadelphia, Sonday, the 11 day of Tisri, 5549.

[Paraphrase of Document No. 56.]

To the honorable, the president and the gentlemen [of the] junta:

Whereas I have promised myself in matrimony with one [a] girl, the daughter of Mr. Barent Jacob, in the Northern Liberties [section] in Philadelphia, I would be very happy if your honorable body would order Mr. Jacob Cohen, as hazzan ["cantor"] at the congregation of Mikveh Israel, to give me *huppah* and *kiddushin* [a legal and ritually proper Jewish marriage] against [next] Tuesday.

Therefore, gentlemen, I pray one [an] answer from you gentlemen tomorrow, the 12th day of Tishri at eleven o'clock and, by so doing, your petitioner will ever pray.

From your humble servant,
Salomon Raffeld

To Mr. Levy Phillips, President of the Holy Congregation Mikveh Israel,
Philadelphia, Sunday, 11th day of Tishri, 5549 [October 13, 1788].

————

No. 57   Beth Shalome, Richmond: Frontier Congregation—1789

Few Jews went to Virginia in the days before the Revolution, for the colony's plantation economy was not conducive to Jewish settlement. There were no large cities and no vigorous middle-class merchant groups. Toward the end of the Revolution, however, Jews began to drift in, and by 1789 the little town of Richmond had enough Jewish male adults to permit the establishment of a congregation.

These men, interested in furthering the "Israelite religion," adopted a simple constitution on August 24, 1789 (Document A). It was not written in polished English; most of the subscribers were immigrants. Because the congregation was small and the defection of even one family might endanger its existence, the sensitivities and privileges of every member were clearly kept in mind. It was a "democratic" document; the protest of a single member sufficed to subject any decision of the board to review by the entire congregation. The limitation of membership to "free" men was probably not directed against the Negro slaves of Jewish masters but against white indentured servants. The congregation took the name Beth Shalome, "House of Peace."

About three months after the organization of Beth Shalome, President George Washington proclaimed the first national Thanksgiving Day. In preparation for the service held at the synagogue, Jacob I. Cohen (1744–1823) wrote a special prayer for the welfare of the government (Document B). Cohen, a leader in the local Jewish community, was a partner in the mercantile firm of Cohen & Isaacs. Although the prayer that Cohen prepared borrowed phrases from the traditional supplication for the preservation of the civil authorities, it seems to have been an original composition.

SOURCE. The Emily Solis-Cohen Collection of Leeser Papers, Philadelphia.

A [NO. 57]

New moon of Ellul, 5549, August 24, 1789.

We, the subscribers of the Israelite religion resident in this place, desirous of promoting the divine worship which, by the blessing of God, has been transmitted by our ancestors, have this day agreed to form ourselves into a society for the better effecting the said laudable purpose, to be known and distinguished in Israel by the name of B'eth Shalom, *beth shalom.*

It is necessary that in all societies that certain rules and regulations be made for the government for the same as tend well to the proper decorum in a place dedicated to the worship of the Almighty God, peace and friendship among the same. We do, therefore, agree that the following rules be adopted and be continued in force until a majority of the congregation propose to alter or amend the same.

1. Every free man residing in this city for the term of three months, of the age of 21 years and who congregates with us, shall be a *yahid* ["member"] of the kehilla ["congregation"] and entitled to every right and privilege of the same.

2. The first Sunday before Rosh Hashana ["New Year"] in every year, a general meeting of the *yehidim* be made, and by a plurality of votes a parnas and 2 assistants and 2 *hathanim* [honorary officers] be chosen to serve the ensuing year. The parnas and assistants shall not be connected in family or in partnership in trade, in order to preserve an equal and an independent representation.

3. The duty of the parnas shall be to preserve decorum and good order in the synagogue, distribute the mitzvoth [religious honors], and to provide everything necessary for our religious worship. When [Then?], with the advice of his assistants, [he] shall from time to time propose such regulations as may be necessary for the good government of the society.

He shall be obliged to call his junta ["board"] the first Sunday in every month and keep a book of their proceedings, wrote in a legible hand and good manner, which book shall be laid before the members at large whenever he is requested to do it by a majority.

No rules or regulations shall be considered as binding on the congregation until it is read 2 Shabbath or holidays separately in the synagogue. Should any member object to the same, it must be by a letter to the parnas within 24 hours after the last publication, who shall be obliged to call a meeting of all the members in toto. When [there is] a majority present at such meeting, which must be ⅔ of the members in town, [it] shall deterim [determine] the same, and the [de]teremination shall be binding on the objecting member and all the rest.

He [the parnas] shall give four copies of the laws now made, with the proceedings of the juntas, [which] shall be delivered to his successor with all books and papers belonging to the congregation.

He shall, when a *yahid* has a son born, give him the distribution of all the mitzvoth on the following Shabbath, and [the father] must be called to the *sefer* [reading of the "Scroll"]. And when his wife comes to shul ["synagogue"] after lying-in of a son or a daughter, [the husband] must be called to the *sefer*.

4. The duty of the assistants shall be to assist the parnas in the execution of his office. They shall be obliged to attend him on the fourth Sunday of every month and report to the congregation *any improper conduct that they may observe by him,* and such complaint to be laid before the *yahidim* for their determination.

5. In the absence of the parnas the senior assistant shall officiate, and so in rotation, [including] . . . the *hathan torah,* and in his absence the *hathan bereshith. [Hatan torah* and *hatan bereshit:* "bridegroom of the Law and bridegroom of the beginning." These men were given the honor of closing and beginning the annual cycle of the Pentateuchal readings in the synagogue.]

B [NO. 57]

A Prayer for the *Medina* ["country"] by Order of the Congress of
America November 26th, 1789, Kislev fifth [seventh]
day, Thursday

When we call on thee, O righteous God, answer us.
Hearken to the voice of our cry and show us grace.
Have compassion on us and hearken to our prayer.
For thou, Most High God, hast removed distress far from us.
O gracious God, thou has[t] delivered us from all our enemies;
Thou has[t] redeemed us from those who rose up against us;
Thou has girded us with strength to smite the pride of our enemies;
In shame and disgrace they fell beneath our feet.
O God of Hosts, thou has set peace and tranquility in our palaces
And has set the President of the United States as our head [ruler?],
And in prayer we humble ourselves before thee, oh, our God.
Unto our supplications mayest Thou hearken, and deliver us.
A *mind* of wisdom and understanding set in the heart of the head
of our country;
May he *judge* us with justice; may he cause our hearts to rejoice
and be glad.
In the *paths* of the upright may he lead us;
Even unto old age may he administer and judge in our midst.
Pure and upright be the heart of the one who rules and governs us.
May God Almighty hearken to our voice and save us.
We will prolong our prayer before God, our Redeemer.
May he guard and keep the Vice President, senators, and repre-
sentatives of the United States.
May he give good sense and understanding to the officers of the
courts.
May the hearts of our governors be upright and faithful.
May he prosper and bless our country,
And deliver us from the hand of outside enemies.
May our sons in their youth be like growing plants.
May our daughters be like [cornerstones?]
May our storehouses be full and bursting from end to end, multi-
plying in our streets.
May our cattle be fat and may there be no breach and no————
in our broad places.
May our God bless all friends of our country and their judges,
And give glory to the Lord God, our Redeemer.
May Judah be saved and Israel dwell securely,
And may the Redeemer come to Zion, and let us say, Amen.

Signed

I, the small one, Jacob son of R.[abbi] Joshua Cohen(?), Richmond, Virginia.

No. 58 The Constitution and Bylaws of Congregation
Shearith Israel, New York—1790

Congregation Shearith Israel was incorporated on June 4, 1784, shortly after the legislature of the state of New York enacted a statute providing for the incorporation of religious societies. Although we cannot be altogether certain, it is very probable that six years elapsed before the congregation finally adopted a constitution and a series of bylaws. Pursuant to the 1784 Charter Act, as the congregation referred to it, the members were to elect a board of trustees to administer the property and finances of the synagogue. Spiritual matters, on the other hand, were in the province of the parnas, or president, and of the junta (also called adjunto), or board. Thus the control of the synagogue was divided into two separate realms.

Congregation Shearith Israel was the largest and most influential synagogal organization in the United States in 1790. Its rules and regulations are therefore of importance, since they throw light not only on its structure and organization but also on the community's socioreligious ideals.

Document A, below, may well be the 1790 constitution, which was adopted on May 30 (the 17th of Sivan), although conclusive evidence for this assertion is lacking. The fair copy seems to have disappeared; what we have is an undated rough draft. The opening paragraphs are reminiscent of the high idealism of the Enlightenment and of the all-embracing liberalism of the American and French revolutions. In all likelihood they are the work of Solomon Simson, a radical Whig, who in 1790 was one of the congregation's presidents and who later in the decade became president of the Democratic Society of New York. An interesting feature is the absence of any reference in the document to *yehidim*, or first-class members. But in spite of its equalitarian appearance, the constitution prohibits the admission of indentured servants to synagogue membership.

Document B, also undated, appears to be a sort of bill of rights. Like Document A, it opens with a liberalistic genuflection to the social contract theory of Rousseau. The rights and privileges of first-class members (*yehidim*) are touched upon in the first few articles, and the document continues in the ante-Revolutionary tradition of distinguishing between these and the less privileged congregants. It is by no means improbable, however, that *yehidim* refers to the typical members, while the others are members *in potentia*. Perhaps no definite distinction between two different classes of members was envisaged. Only a part of this document is reproduced here because the extant copy has been hopelessly mis-arranged by an early copyist.

The bylaws adopted on June 6 (the 24th of Sivan) fortunately are dated (Document C). These deal with the rights of members and the duties of paid officers: cantor, beadle, ritual slaughterer, and teacher. It is interesting to note that the regulations for the beadle were copied almost verbatim from those enacted in 1768. Of con-siderable interest also are the rules for parliamentary procedure, adopted in 1790. The repetition in Document C of some of the regulations in Documents A and B would seem to imply that the constitution finally adopted differed in some respects from the draft materials in Documents A and B.

Document D, dated July 11 (the 29th of Tammuz), describes the ratification of the constitution and bylaws by the trustees, as well as the bylaws regulating certain financial aspects of synagogue ad-ministration, which were adopted concurrently.

Document E, dated August 22 (the 12th of Elul), contains a number of disciplinary enactments, covering the abuse of dietary laws and the observance of the Sabbath and of the Passover holiday.

SOURCE. Congregation Shearith Israel, New York, Minute Book.

A [NO. 58]

In the name of the Lord, the God of Israel. Amen.
New York.

We, the members of the K.[ehillah] K.[edoshah, "Holy Congregation"] Shearith Israel, met this day by a legal summons from the junta (or associate elders) published in the synagogue two Sabbath days succes-sively, do by these presents in the most solemn manner, in the presense of the Almighty and of each other, agree to form such rules to serve for and be considered as a constitution, and to accede to such other institu-tions, rules, and regulations as may be conducive to the general good of this congregation.

And we, whose names are hereunto subscribed, do severally engage fully to perform all such acts, institutions, and regulations as shall from time to time be thought expedient and necessary to be for the support of our religious and holy divine service.

In a state happily constituted upon the principles of equal liberty, civil and religious, the several societies, as members of that government, partaking of that blessing, being free to adopt the best means for preserving their privileges, and for entering into such compact for regulating and well ordering the internal institutions for the administration of the affairs of their several communities as may be most likely to attain that end,

The congregation of *yehudim* ["Jews"] in this city, convinced of the propriety, only comply with their duty to themselves and posterity by entering into an agreement and covenant for the purposes aforesaid, and, accordingly, on the day and year above mentioned, declare the following rules shall serve for and be considered as a constitution:

First. That every man, except a bound or hired servant, professing to be and living as a Jew, being of the age of twenty one years and upwards, who is not married contrary to the rules of our religion, and subscribing and conforming hereunto, shall be entitled to every right and privilege belonging to this society and are [is] hereby declared to be in every respect on an equality with those now convened.

Secondly. That a book shall be opened wherein shall be transcribed a fair and correct copy of this constitution, and whoever chuses to subscribe thereto within three months from the date hereof, being qualified according to the preceding articles, shall hereby become a legal member of this congregation, in as full and ample manner as those who now sign these presents for that purpose, excepting the children of the subscribing members, and those who are born in this place who shall be admitted without paying any admission fee upon application to the persons appointed for that purpose, and they being qualified agreeable to the preceding article.

Thirdly. Any person residing at present in this city who does not chuse to become a subscribing member within the time limitted above shall not be admitted thereafter, except by a proper application in writing to such person or persons as shall be appointed for that purpose, and shall pay such sum of money as shall be fixed for the admission of strangers.

Fourthly. Any person who comes to reside in this city hereafter, and is desirous to become a member of this, our congregation, shall not be admitted as a subscribing member untill he has resided at least three months, then to make application in writing to such persons as shall be appointed for that purpose; and if deemed to be a person proper to be admitted, shall pay the sum of two and a half Spanish milled dollars to the *tzedaka* [treasury] for his admission.

Fifthly. That so soon as any person has subscribed to become a member of this congregation, he shall be entitled to every right, privilege, and immunity whatever appertaining to a member thereof.

Sixthly. That all the members of this congregation shall annually meet at the *hebra* [community building] on the first day of the week preceding Rosh Hashanah ["New Year"] except it should be the day before the holyday (in which case the anticedent [antecedent] first day of the week); then and there to elect by ballot from among the subscribing members who have served in this congregation either as parnasim or ajunto ["board members"], three ajuntos or associate elders to serve for one year, whose employment shall be:

First. To meet at the *hebra* on the first Sunday in every lunar month (festivals excepted) and at any other time when legally summoned to attend, which summons must be sent to their respective place of abode in writing.

Secondly. To observe that the institutions and regulations made by this congregation be duly attended to, and that none of the members of this congregation have any of their rights and privileges infringed or violated.

Thirdly. To meet at the *hebra* at least three days before Rosh Hashanah in every year with the parnassim of this congregation, then and there to elect, conjunctively with the said parnasim, two parnasim for the year then next ensuing (from among the subscribing members who have served in this congregation as parnasim, ajuntos, or either of the *hattanim* [the *hatan torah*, or "Bridegroom of the Law," and the *hatan bereshit*, or "Bridegroom of Genesis"]), and the two *hattanim* from among the said subscribing members at large, also to serve for the year then next ensuing. Those who have been elected as *hattanim* without having accepted but did pay their fines, are considered as having served and [are] eligible for parnasim.

Fourthly. In case either of the parnasim elect refuse serving, the senior associate elder [adjunto] is then to officiate in his stead, which seniority is hereby declared to be seniority in office heretofore.

Fifthly. To be judges with the parnasim of persons proper to be admited [as] subscribing members of this congregation, and to make such rules for their own board as they think convenient.

Sixthly. In case either of the *hattanim* elect refuses to serve, then to appoint another, and if he also declines serving, then the elders to draw lots who shall serve in his place, and the same mode in case both *hattanim* refuse serving.

And for the better government of the community and [that] the several institutions may have their full effect, there shall be two parnasim, the senior parnass to serve from Rosh Hoshanah untill Pesak ["Passover"] and the junior parnass untill the next Rosh Hashanah, the acting parnas to be titled president, and the other the vice president.

The Duty of the President

First. The president shall dispense of all mesvoth [religious honors] given out in [the] synagogue, excepting particular cases only, which will be enumerated in the bill of rights [bylaws?].

Secondly. To take care that divine service be performed with decency and decorum, to admonish any person behaving amiss in the synagogue, to dispose of any vacant seat to any transient person or persons of either sex, to suspend any of the servants of the congregation (that is, the hazan, the rabbe ["teacher"], shochet ["slaughterer"], and *shamas*) either for neglecting duty or being guilty of mall practices [malpractices]. But on any suspension, the parnass shall convene the congregation within forty eight hours, if aproved, to be valid, otherways to be taken off (Sabaths and holydays excepted). [Suspensions are invalid if not approved by the congregation within forty-eight hours.]

Thirdly. To summon the associate elders to meet whenever he sees fitt, and when met with the vice president, to form the junto ["board"] of the Kahal Kadosh Sheerith Israel or *maamad* ["board" of] K. K. Shearith Israel; and all adresses [formal communications] to them are to be directed to the parnassim and ajuntos.

Fourthly. The parnassim and associate elders shall have full power to frame and propose all the institutions and ordinances for the well governing and discipline of this congregation as they shall judge proper from time to time, and to alter or amend any institutions or regulations now not repugnant to the constitution in being, provided always that no such rules, order, or institution shall be deemed obligatory untill it has been published in the synagogue two Sabbath successively; then, if not objected to within one week after such publication, to be of equal validity with those now in being.

[There was apparently no fifthly.]

Sixthly. In the absence of the presiding parnas, the parnas vice president to act in his stead, and in the absence of both the parnassim, then the senior associate elder to officiate as parnas with the same authority and power as appertain to the parnas.

Seventhly. In the absence of the parnassim and ajunto from synagogue either of the *hattanim* to officiate as parnas, that is, the *hattan torah* ["Bridegroom of the Law"] first, and if he be absent, then the *hattan bereshith* ["Bridegroom of Genesis"]; in the absence of the *Hattan Bereshith* the oldest man present (officers and persons not entitled to vote agreeable to this constitution excepted). The parnas or person officiating as such in his stead shall on any occasion deemed necessary by three members, convene the congregation, to lay before them such matters as may require their consideration, and every member of the congregation, when thus convened or at other usual meetings, shall have full right to speak his sentiments freely on any subject, proposal, or on any occasion whatever. And if a motion be made by any member and seconded, the parnas or other person acting as chairman to [of] that meeting shall be obliged to put the question; but if not seconded it shall pass unnoticed.

Eightly. The establishment of this congregation, having always been *keminhag Sephardim* ["according to the Sephardic ritual"], is hereby confirmed and declared to be the constitution of the same, and that no language [is] to be made use of in synagogue but Hebrew, except the offerings.

Ninthly. In order to promote decency in [the] synagogue where we meet to worship the Almighty God, to support respect and decorum in a place dedicated to His service, and to prevent any insult being offered to the parnassim and assistants, or any of the congregation, it is agreed that any person who shall by word or act behave in such manner as to come under the above description, or refuse to follow the order or derection of the parnassim for the time being (or, in his absence, the person officiating in his stead), shall, upon trial, if found guilty in any respect, forfiet to the trustees, for the use and benefit of this congregation, not less than two dollars, nor more than twenty dollars, which shall be decided in the manner following:

Upon any dispute happening, the parnass and junta shall summon the parties, who shall choose two persons, each unconnected with either one, according to our religious system, which four persons shall meet in the presence of the parnasim and elders; and if they cannot agree, [they are] to choose a fifthe person; and after they have determined [made their decision], the parnassim and elders [are] to confirm such judgment, and to make report of every fine incured to the chairman of the trustees, which judgment shall be binding on the parties.

And any person offending, and being duly summoned to choose arbitrators, and not attending in time, the parnass and junta to proceed and choose four persons who shall proceed and determine in the same manner as if the person offending had attended. And any person chosen to decide upon any dispute, and not attending at the time he is summoned, shall be cited to appear before the parnassim and ajuntos to asign his reasons for non acceptance, which if not deemed sufficient, shall forfiet and pay to the *sedaka* the sum of three pounds four shillings for such refusal, which said fine shall be recovered before any magistrate, and the parnass or person officiating as such to be subject to the same trial in case of any complaint against him, which complaint shall be to the junta; and they shall be obleged to conform and summon arbitrators in [the] same manner as mentioned in the forgoing.

Tenthly. Any person elected to serve as parnass and [who] refuses to accept shall pay a fine of ten pounds. And any person elected to serve as adjunta and [who] refuses to accept shall pay a fine of three pounds four shillings; and any person elected to serve as a *hatan* and refusing to serve, shall pay the sum of five pounds.

Elevnthly. If a parnass dies or resigns during the time of his administration, or shall leave the city to reside elsewhere, the vice president shall officiate in his stead the remainder of the year; and the oldest adjunta shall become vice president, and they shall summon the congregation to meet immediately after such death, resignation, or departure, to choose another ajunta, so that the parnassim and associate elders shall form a board of five persons, three of which (the presiding parnass always being one) to be a quorim for transacting business, without which any business done at such meeting shall be deemed illegal, and no meeting to be deemed legal without [unless] all the members are summoned. And any associate elder who neglects his duty shall be tryed by the subscribing members of this congregation and, on sufficient proof therof, shall pay a fine of three pounds four shillings.

Twelfthly. Every person called to *sephar* [the reading of the "Scroll"] shall offer at least sixpence for the presiding parnass; and any person who has any mitzvoth given him, and refuses, shall pay a fine of six pounds eight shillings. And no person shall have any right to a mitzvoth in the synagogue under pretence or claim of *hazaka* [prior right], but every mitzvoth shall be included as at the disposal of the parnass. All fines [are] to be recoverd by the trustees upon the parnassim and adjunta furnishing them with an account of the same; and no person who refuses to pay his fine shall be entitled to any right, privileges, or benefits whatever appertaining to a member of this congregation untill such fine is paid, nor shall he offer [make a public contribution] or be offerd for, or his name mentiond in synagogue.

Lastly. This constitution is to remain in full force for the term of two years, at which time, if three fourths of the subscribing members think proper to continue or revise the same, the whole congregation are to be convened, and by the decision of the majority it shall be settled.

B [NO. 58]

Whereas in free states all power originates and is derived from the people, who always retain every right necessary for their well being individually, and, for the better ascertaining those rights with more precision and explicitly, frequently from [form?] a declaration or bill of those rights. In like manner the individuals of every society in such state are entitled to and retain their several rights, which ought to be preserved inviolate.

Therefore we, the profession [professors] of the Divine Laws, members of this holy congregation of Shearith Israel, in the city of New York, conceive it our duty to make this declaration of our rights and previleges, *vizt.*:

First, of Jews in general. That every free person professing the Jewish religion, and who lives according to its holy precepts, is entitled to worship the God of Israel in the synagogue, and by purchase or gift to have a seat therein, and to be treated in all respect as a brother, and as such a subject of every fraternal duty.

Secondly. Of those who have been for a length of time members of the K. K., though not reputed *yehadin* ["members"]: That all those who have formerly and now continue to be members of this *kahal kodosh* ["holy congregation"] at large, not having subscribed to the constitutions of the aforesaid congregation, but living as worthy professors of our holy law, are entitled to the several privileges in the foregoing articles, and shall be called to *sepher* [the reading of the "Scroll"] when not interfering with the [prior] rights of a *yahid*.

Thirdly. Of the *yehidim*: The qualifications of the *yehidim* being defined in the constitution, reference is to be had thereto.

Of Their Rights

[Firstly]. They are entitled to all the privileges in the preceding articles.

Secondly. Every *yahid* is entitled to vote for the adjuntas and for the several officers and servants of the congregation, according to the mode prescribed in the aforesaid constitution. However, as this is a right, it by no means obliges either their attendance at a junto [congregational meeting?] or to vote, it being at their own option.

Thirdly. Any *yahid* who is desirous of having a copy of the constitution aforesaid may have one.

Fourthly. In ordinary, to have the preference of being called to *sepher* and in all the metzvots [religious honors].

Fifthly. When a *yahid* has a son born, he shall have the distribution of the metzvots the Sabbath preceding the berit ["circumcision"], provided it be to such as may by the constitution be lawfull; and if he has a daughter born, he shall be called to *sepher* the Sabbat after, and if he acquaints the acting parnas in time, he shall be also called to *sepher* on the [first] day his wife comes to synagogue [after she has given birth].

Sixthly. In case of death in his family, the hazan ["cantor"] and *shamas* ["beadle"] shall attend the funeral at the place appointed, provided the *shamas* has due notice given him (whose duty is to acquaint the hazan), and, if requested, the hazan shall mention in synagogue the time of the funeral, the place of meeting at and after the funeral, the hazan to perform the usual duties of his function.

Seventhly. In case of the marriage of a *yahid* or any of his family, the hazan shall officiate, and the *hatan* [bridegroom] shall have the distribution of all the metzvot the Sabbath next ensuing said marriage, to such persons as by the constitution it is permitted, and provided also that the marriage is consonant to our holy law, and the persons concerned be not under any disqualification otherways by the constitution.

Eightly. Every *yahid* is entitled to be chosen *hatan torah* ["bridegroom of the Law"] or *hatan bershit* ["bridegroom of Genesis"], and those who have been before [this in the office of] either of the *hattanim*, or paid their fine for non acceptance, are entitled to be chosen parnassim, and such as have served as parnas or adjunto may be elected to any of the before mentioned offices, subject nevertheless to the penalties for non acceptance as declared in the constitution.

Ninthly. In all general meetings . . . or any other usual meetings, every *yahid* has and ought to have a right of debating on any subject whatsoever with decency, yet to deliver his sentiments without restraint, and freely to give his opinions and advice concerning any matters in question, or to open a new subject in order, at his own option.

Tenthly. That every *yahid* has and ought to have a right to make his offering in synagogue in the Hebrew language or in the Portugese, and in those languages only (the latter having been practiced from the establishment of this congregation), as he shall think proper to do, and this article to extend to all and every person who makes this *misheberach* or offering, but always avoiding any thing satirical, offensive, or otherways indecent.

Elevently. If any number of *yehedim* (not less than three) have any thing to propose to a general junta ["meeting"], the parnasim and adjuntas are to be applied to, and if they are desirous of a general junta to be called, and they adduce sufficient reason for it, the parnas shall summon such general meetings as soon after as may be convenient. . . .

C [NO. 58]

Peace unto Israel
Congregational By Laws
Commenceing 24th Sivan, 5550 [June 6, 1790].

Whereas, the preamble of our constitution confirms the prescribed rules of the society, in order in some measure to explain the same at this, our first meeting, it is agreed on by the *yahidim* of the congregation that our religious customs is to be in no manner or ways infringed on, and whatever acts have been done by the executive authority of the society shall be deemed valid and good;

And that the said constitution continue without any alteration for one year from the day of its being first entered into. At the expiration of which term, if three-fourths of the *yahidim* should agree to enter into a revision of the same, they may, provided whatever alterations, additions, or amendments may take place in the revision aforesaid—that the same shall be mutually acceeded to by three forths of the *yahidim* then societing with the congregation, signing their names to the same. But that all laws respecting the government of the said society, that have heretofore been made prior to our constitution aforesaid, shall be and are hereby repealed and made null and void, and the following by laws enacted in their stead:

1st. That a meeting of the *yahidim* shall be held on the second Sunday in Elull yearly, to chuse the parnasim particularised in the constitution. Commencement of the first parnas entering into office on the first day of Roshashona, and to rule from that time untill Pesach; then the second to the end of the year; and any *yahid* being nominated and refuseing to act shall pay unto the *zadaca* [treasury] five pounds. And the parnasim, on or about the time aforesaid, shall appoint a *hatan torah* and a *hatan berasheath;* and any *yahid* refuseing to act as a *hatan* on his being nominated shall pay the sum of two pounds; and on vacanceys in consiquence of such refusals, the parnasim and adjunto may appoint anew, in order that *hatanim* may serve as customary.

In case of the absence of the parnasim and adjunto from synagogue (if the *hatanim* should be *yahidim*) the *hatan torah* may distribute the mitzvot; and in case of the absence of the *hatan torah,* the *hatan beresheath* may officiate in giveing out the misvot; and in the absence of the parnasim and adjunto aforesaid, then the eldest *yahid* present always takeing prefference by seniority.

2nd. Every person congregateing with the congregation of Shearith Israel is to behave orderly and accept the mitzvot apointed him, and when called to *sephor* shall offer at least six pence for the acting parnas and *k. kadosh* ["holy congregation"].

3rd. Every *yahid* shall be intiled [entitled] to distrebute the mitzvot the Sabath after his marriage; and when he has a son born, he shall have the distrebution of the misvot on the Sabath following before the circumcision (provided those intitled to distribute the mitzvot shall duly acquaint the parnas and give a written paper particulariseing in what manner he will wish to have the honors distributed). And if a daughter [is] born, [he] shall be called to *sephor* the first Sabath after, and also on the first day of his wife's going to synagogue [after childbirth].

In case of death in his family, he shall have a right to have the hazan and *shamas* to attend the funeral at the house appointed for it; the *shamas*, haveing due notice given him, whose place it shall be, to acquaint the parnas and hazan. And the hazan is hereby enjoined to perform the usual cerimonies. And in case of the marriage of a *yahid* or any of his family, the hazan shall offeciate (if such marriage is not contrary to our religion), provided always any *yahid* claiming the above honors shall not be, at the time of his claiming the same, impeached or under fine for infringing on the congregational by laws, by not makeing the demanded satisfaction for the same, or if he does not regulary discharge his *zadaca* bill as hereafter mentioned.

And it is hereby declared that none but *yahidim* are or shall be intitled to the aforesaid prevelidges, unless on special occassions sanctioned by the approbation of the parnasim and adjunto (on application to them), who shall give their approbation to such applicant, provided they judge proper; and if the hazan should attend on any occassion aforesaid without such approbation being previously obtained, he shall forfeit to the *zadaca* for every such offence five pounds; if the *shamas*, three pounds; and if the shochet, two pounds.

4thly. If three *yahidim* should at any time be desirious of laying any matter of business before the congregation, they must in writing set forth their reasons, and if the parnas deems them sufficient, he may call a meeting, and, if not, and they three persists in their request, the parnas is then to convene his adjunto, who is to determine the same according to the form or custom they may fix for makeing descisions in their board. And if then given against the parnas, he is hereby bound to call a meeting under the penalty of three pounds for neglect, according to the request of the said *yahidim*.

5thly. All insults offered or given to the parnasim, adjuntos, or other officers of the congregation dureing their offeciateing in their respective offices will be considered as insults given to the congregation at large; and the same offender or offenders shall each and every [one] of them be fined seperately a sum not exceeding thirty nine shilling. And in case of any indecency or disturbance dureing our holy service, the parnas or acting ruler for the time being is hereby desired calmly to admonish the offender or offenders, and if he or they, notwithstanding, persists and continue to offend, the parnas on the first proper day following may convenes his adjunto, and, if they judge proper, either bring him or them to trial before their board, in which case they, or either of them so offending, on conviction shall be fined a sum not exceeding five pounds; or, if the nature of the case requires it (which should never be in force unless at the last extremity), seek redress by applying to the laws of the land.

6thly. On a general meeting of *yahidim* being proclaimed conformable to the constitution, all non-attendants shall be fined one shilling, unless a reasonable excuse [is presented], such as may be accepted by the meeting following.

7thly. And for the more securing the revenue of the synagogue, it is recommended that the trustees pass a bylaw settling accounts with every congregator that is in arrears, demanding of them a settlement of thir accounts by given a bond for the ballance that may be due the synagogue prior to the first day of Nison last [March 16, 1790], payable in four years, one-fourth part annually (to the trustees or their successors), and to begin the books intirely on a new score. And every delinquent who shall hereafter be six months in arrears shall forfeit the rights and prevelidges of a *yahid*. Any person who shall be refractory in the payment or settlement, it is recommended that the trustees use ways and means that they may judge necessary to compel them or either of them. For it will be considered the highest offence and insult that can be offered to the Supreme Being, whom we worship, for any person to openly declare to a falshood by makeing a freewill offering and refuseing to make payment of the same.

8thly. The accounts and books of the income and expenditures of the public money shall be laid before the congregation at their annual meeting, previously audited by three *yahidim* that shall or may be appointed for that purpose. And no person whatever shall be deemed eligable to be elected to any office of honor or trust, in or belonging to the congregation, without first paying his bill for the year, or any other demand the congregation shall or may have on him contracted after the formation of our constitution.

9thly. In case the officers of the congregation under pay should in any manner or ways misbehave by not performing their duty, the parnas shall or may suspend them or either of them, not to exceed one month, within which time he shall bring them or either of them to trial before the parnasim and adjunto, who at their discretion, according to the nature of the offence, shall fine them or either of them, on conviction, a sum not exceeding five pounds. But if the offence should appear of such that the parnasim and adjunto cannot take cognisance (which will be considered of such a nature that the offender or offenders should be dismissed), the parnas must call a meeting of the *yahidim* and lay the matter before them, if relateing to the *shamas* and schochet; but, if the hazan, before a meeting of the electors who must be convened for that purpose.

10thly. In case any congregator who shall or may infringe on the congregational bylaws, the offender or offenders shall be cited to appear before the parnasim and adjunto by a written citation served by the *shamas* to the offender or offending in person; and if they or either of them should not appear accordingly, a non-appearence shall be considered as confession of the crime [they are] accused of, and judgement shall be given against them or either of them accordingly. But if, on appearing, they or either of them should object to leaving his or their accusation intirely to the parnasim and adjunto, the accused shall have liberty to chuse three *yahidim* from the body at large, and the parnasim and adjunto shall chuse three also, which six *yahidim* shall chuse a seventh, and they shall be considered a jury to determine by a majority according to evendence whether guilty or not. In which case, the parnasim and adjunto shall either pass judgement or acquit. (The seven *yahidim* shall be on oath, if required.)

And in case any parnas or adjunto should, dureing his or their administration, infring on or breake the bylaws of the congregation, he, they, or either of them, on their leaving the office they were appointed to, shall be subject to trial in like manner and form aforesaid. And further, to prevent partiality, no relation as nigh as father or son, brother, uncle, or nephew, shall sit in judgement or give a vote for or against each other, unless brought forward on evidence, and then on oath if required.

11th. Any person leaving a legacy to the society, not less then five pounds, or their relatives or friends paying a sum not less then aforesaid: If the parnasim and adjunto should conceive the deceased to have been a worthy member of this or any other Jewish society, which will be confirmed by the parnasim and adjunto for the time being, [upon] receeving the same for the benefit of the *zadaca*, [the deceased] shall have an *escoba* [a prayer in memory of the dead], as hath hitherto been customary in the society.

12th. That no satyrical or malicious *mishaborach* [blessing] shall be made in synagogue, and in case the hazan should, at the request of any one, violate this law, he shall forfit for every offence, on conviction, twenty shillings. And in addition to the punishments heretofore named, it shall be at the discretion of the parnasim and adjunto, when convened, to forbid the name of any offender or offenders to be mentioned in synagogue, and to curtail him or them of all mitzvot or honors that are or hath been customary in the society, or publish his or their name in writing in synagogue to public view, or forbid a name being given their children in synagogue, or any other matter or thing appertaining to our honorary custom, which are not to be put in force unless the delinquent should refuse to make the satisfaction required of him or them conformable to the congregational by laws, and then not untill the process particularised in the tenth section of these our by laws.

13th. Any person hereafter marrying a *goiah* ["Gentile woman"], or otherways contrary to our custom, without the approbation of the parnasim and adjunto, shall forfit the right of a *yahid,* and shall not be

The aforegoing laws and regulations were duly enacted at a meeting of *yahidim* held on the 24th day of Sivan, 5550 [June 6, 1790].
Attest: Isaac M. Gomez, clerk.

> Isaac Moses, parnas presidente [president for the first half of the year]
> Solomon Simson, parnas residente [president for the second half of the year]

D [NO. 58]

At a meeting of the trustees on Sunday, the 29th Tammuz [July 11, 1790]:
Present:

Solomon Simson	Benjamin S. Judah
Manuel Myers	Isaac H. Levy
Uriah Hendricks	

The committee who were appointed to prepare the ratification of the congregational bye laws, and to form other bye laws to cooperate with the same, reported as follows, which, being read paragraph by paragraph, were unanimously agreed to:

Charter By Laws

Whereas, the Congregation of Shearith Israel did at a general meeting held on the 17th day [of] Sivan, 5550, corroborateing with the 30th day of May, 1790, enter into a solem league and covenant which, being duly executed, was pronounced and declaired, together with the charter act [the New York State Religious Societies Corporation Law] (passed the 6th day of April, 1784), to be the constitution of the society [Shearith Israel];

And whereas, consistent with the aforesaid constitution, at another general meeting held by the *yahidim* of the congregation aforesaid, on the 24th day of Sivan, 5550, corroborateing with the 6th day of June, 1790, were enacted a code of by laws for the civil and religious government of the said society, "whereupon it is recommended that the board of trustees ratify and confirm the same, in order that they may have their full force and energy"; reference thereunto had, will more fully appear.

And in order to conform to the said recommendation, we, the trustees of the said society, do repeal all by laws enacted by this board antecedent to the 17th day of Sivan, 5550, that were formed for the regulation and government of the said society. And in their sted do ratify, confirm, and enact for the civil and religious government of the society aforesaid (as far as our charter act empowers this board) the aforesaid constitution and congregational by laws.

And we do ordain that the same be, and are hereby considered, the by laws of this corporation in all things, whether they effect our temporalities [synagogue possessions] or otherwise. But, nevertheless, that all legal acts and deeds that have been performed and executed, conformable to the resolves and by laws that are hereby repealed, shall remain good and valid. And in order more fully to comply with the requsition aforesaid, we do enact, in addition, the following charter by laws:

1st. Whereas, all the temporalities of the society are vested in the trustees of this corporation, it is ordained that all property of this society in the posession of members of the congregation (or otherwise) are only held at and dureing the pleasure and will of this board (unless in cases w[h]ere an express leese has been given). And that every person, both male and female, occupiing and posessing seats in the synagogue, are hereby declaired to hold and occupy the same dureing the will and pleasure of this board. And on all occasions as it may seem meet unto us, we hold and retain the right of reposessing and disposeing of the same.

2nd. That the acting parnas may at his discretion present a vacant seat to a stranger as a temporary posession, but that the right of granting seats to congregators be held by this board.

3rd. That conformable to the intention of the charter act, resolved that there be a clerk, treasurer, and collector, and that the clerk provide proper books and make a fair entry relative to the proceedings and accounts of the society,

That he attend this board when convened, and take down and record the proceedings thereof, and that he make out and deliver all accounts for collection to the collector, the clerk signing the same, takeing the collector's receit for the accounts, particulariseing their sums, on the delivery of the same,

That the collector deliver up no account [surrender no statement] unless the debtor pay and discharge the same; and that all monies collected shall be immediately paid into the hands of the treasurer, takeing the treasurer's receit for the same; and that the treasurer pay away no monies without a warrant signed by the parnas presidente worded in the following manner:

To the treasurer of the congregation of Shearith Israel.
(Seal) No. .... Pay M. .... or order currencey, being for .... and for so doing, this shall be your sufficient warrent.

Witness the seal of the corporation
New York, the ... day of ... 17...
Parnas Presidente

The books and accounts of the treasurer shall be audited and signed by a committee to be appointed for that purpose once every six months; and if adjudged right and just, to be signed by the parnas presidente.

4th. That the parnas presidente may at his discretion dispose of the sum of three dollars without the consent of this board, but that he issue no warrent to exceed that sum (unless it should be for the express payment of the salary and wages of the officers of the congregation that are or should be legally allowed, in which case he must distrebute in equal proportions, as monies may be in the hands of the treasurer, and according to the different salaries that may hereafter become due, or for prepayment of wax and oil or other necessaries that may be purchased for the use of the synagogue) without the concent and approbation of this board.

5th. That the parnas presidente, and, in case of his absence, the parnas residente (provided [they are] trustees), preside at this board. But if neither of the parnasim have a seat as trustee, in that case, the senior trustee presides, and that each member be warned by the *shamas* [to be present], by order of the acting parnas or senior trustee as aforesaid, at least one hour before the time of meeting.

6th. That obligations [personal bonds] be taken from the debtors to this society, conformable to the 7th section of the congregational by laws; and should any debtor or debtors refuse to give obligations accordingly, it will be considered that the person so refuseing intends defrauding the society, in which case the parnas presidente is to apply to the laws of the land to compel the payment of the claim the society may have against such refractory person, but not untill a general report is or should be made by the parnas to this board of the person's so refuseing, as the trustees would not wish to take such disagreable measures unless compeled by the perverseness of the debtors.

Passed this 29th day of Tammuz, 5550, corroborateing with the 11th day of July, 1790.

Isaac Moses	Uriah Hendricks
Solomon Simson	Ben S. Judah
Manuel Myers	Isaac H. Levy
	trustees

Resolved that the order and regulations [for the parliamentary conduct of affairs], containing 9 articles, that are set down for the government of all meetings of the congregation [in Document C] be and are hereby adopted for the order of this board, to which the following is added:

10th. That no person be permitted to rise more than three times to speak on the same subject except leave be first obtained.

It was moved and seconded that a committee be appointed to take obligations from the debtors of this congregation agreeable to the 6th section of by laws entered into this day, and that Messrs. Benjamin S. Judah and Isaac H. Levy be that committee.

Report made by Ben S. Judah respecting Mr. Solomon Simson's account which was admitted and passed, *vizt.:*

In consiquence of my appointment, I waited on Benjamin Siexas, clerk, and examined the within account and find that the debits and credits were right, but am of an opinion that the charge of six shillings was improper to pay for writing three letters when there was a clerk to the society under pay, whose province it was to have wrote the same. Also that there is some difficulty in examining and passing accounts w[h]ere no vouchers are produced.

Sunday, July 11th, 1790.

Signed: Ben S. Judah.

It was observed that Mr. Judah was under a mistake, for at that time there was no clerk to the board—Mr. B. Seixas not acting as such—and that this board approve of the charge noted in the above report for writing three letters.

Adjourned.

E [NO. 58]

At a meeting of the *yahidim* held on Sunday, the 12th of Elul, 5550 [August 22, 1790], the following by laws were duly enacted:

1st. That any *yehudi* ["Jew"] violating our religious laws by eating trafa [nonkosher food], breakeing the Sabath, or any other sacred day, shall not be called to *sephor,* or receive any mitzva [religious honor], or be eligable to any office in the congregation.

And on information being lodged or layed before the parnasim and adjunto, the person so informed against shall be subject to the like trial as provided by the 10 section of the congregational by laws. And should any person acting as parnas give mitzvas to such persons as above described, he shall forfit to the *sedaca* ["treasury"] forty shillings.

2nd. That in order to prevent *chometz* ["leavened"] flour being made use off in the bakeing of masoth ["unleavened cakes" for Passover], it is resolved that the parnasim annually provide flour and permit no other to be used in bakeing but such as shall be provided as aforesaid. And each family or person receiveing the flour as aforementioned shall pay at the rate it is purchased by the parnasim, and no advanced price to be demanded. And any person obstinately attempting to violate this law shall not make use of the bakeing implements.

Done in the *hebra* [community building] the day and year aforesaid.

Isaac Moses, parnas presidente

Solomon Simson, parnas residente

No. 59 American Jewry Prepares to Write to President Washington—1790

From all parts of the country congratulatory notes poured in on the nation's first President, George Washington. The Jews of the United States were as eager as anyone to show their respect and admiration for the great leader who symbolized the achievements and hopes of the American patriots.

New York Jewry deemed it advisable to present but one address on behalf of all the American Jews, for they had been given to understand that Washington preferred to answer one letter rather than many. To accomplish this end, Isaac Moses and Solomon Simson, two eminent Whig merchants, who were then the presiding officers of Congregation Shearith Israel, circularized the four other Jewish communities in the country, Newport, Philadelphia, Richmond, and Charleston, on June 20, 1790. Savannah Jewry had already taken the bull by the horns, much to the chagrin of the Jewish leaders in New York, who resented such individualism. The New Yorkers believed that they were particularly well qualified to handle this affair because New York was the nation's capital at that time and Washington was living in their city.

As soon as the Philadelphia congregation received the letter from Shearith Israel, a meeting of the group was called, which approved in principle the New York plan for a joint greeting to the President. The Philadelphians, however, used the occasion to reproach Shearith Israel for its embarrassing delay. Their letter to the New York congregation is printed below.

The Charleston community, too, was prompt in its answer to the New York letter, and on July 15 sent a draft which they hoped would serve as the basis of the joint address. This paper, however, was intended to be no more than a draft, and it never reached the President.

In the meanwhile, on July 2, 1790, almost two weeks before the Charleston draft reached Shearith Israel, Moses Seixas (1744–1809) of Newport sent the New Yorkers a dignified but scorching letter in response to their circular. Seixas pointed out that the Gentile organizations of the country had already written the President, and that the Jews of the land were a year late. In effect, his rebuke asked: What plea can the Jews now make for their "neglect which almost amounts to disrespect?" As far as the Georgia Jews are concerned, they had a perfect right to act as they did. They waited long enough for you to organize the presentation of the address to the President.

In the letter Seixas and the Newport Jews signified their willingness to join in a common greeting. The following month, however, Seixas and his friends changed their minds. In the course of his journeys through the country to study the state of the Union, Washington visited Newport on August 17–18. On the morning of the eighteenth, right after breakfast, various groups called on the President to pay their respects. Naturally the Jews were not absent, and on that occasion Seixas, speaking for Congregation Jeshuat Israel, presented an address to the distinguished official.

The New York congregation continued to move at a snail's pace. By November little progress had been made in framing the joint letter. In the meantime, the capital and the President had returned to Philadelphia, where the members of Congregation Mikveh Israel were impatient and intended to write a separate note. Their leader Manuel Josephson (ca. 1729–96) knew how to get things done. Now it was their turn to ask the New York Jews if they wanted to join in the Philadelphia address. On November 25 Solomon Simson answered on behalf of Shearith Israel, agreeing to the Philadelphia proposal and asking that Richmond and Charleston also be included, for these towns had already sent in their authorizations. The President was to be informed that the Jewish greeting had been delayed because the Philadelphians were waiting for authority to include "all our bretheren on the continent." At last the Philadelphians were ready to act, and some nineteen months after the inauguration, American Jewry succeeded in pulling itself together so far as to agree on an address to the President, even though the paper spoke for only five of the seven congregations. On December 13 Josephson went to see Washington and presented the letter to him in person.

The Jews of the country had certainly not yet learned to work as a united group on a national basis.

SOURCE. Congregation Mikveh Israel, Philadelphia, Correspondence, Vol. I, 1781–95.

At a meeting of the [Philadelphia] congregation, Sunday, 15th Tammuz, 5550, being 27th June, 1790.
Present:

Manuel Josephson	Moses Nathan
Michael Gratz	Isaac Moses
Jonas Phillips	Samuel Hays
Solomon Lyons	

Mr. Josephson informed the meeting that he received a letter from the parnasim and junto ["board"] of the congregation at New York, dated 20th instant, which letter he produced, purporting that they (the congregation at N. York) are desirious to address the President of the United States in one general address, comprehending the different congregations in the Union, and whether this congregation was willing that they should be included in that address.

The question beeing put by Mr. Josephson, does this meeting agree to be included in an address to be presented by the congregation at N. York to the President of the United States, it was determined in the affirmative. And [it was further decided] that the parnasim and junto at N. York be requested to favor this congregation with a draft of the intended address previous to its being presented, which will afford an opportunity to insert some expressions that might have been omitted in the first draft and such as may be mutually approved of. It was also resolved that Mr. Josephson be, and he is herewith, desired to correspond with the parnasim and junto at N. York on this business.

(To be signed) S.[amuel] Hays, clerk pro tem.

It was agreed that Mr. Josephson should signify to the congregation at N. York our approp[b]ation in being included, and that they should forward the copy of the address to him, previous to its being presented, in order to his making such alterations or additions as he may think proper and which may be mutually agreed on.

Philadelphia, 28 June, 1790.

Gentlemen:

By the preceeding copy from the minutes of a meeting of this congregation held yisterday, you will please to observe my beeing desired to correspond with you on the subject of an address to the President of the United States. As the sense of the congregation on that behalf is sufficiently set forth in said minutes, it only remains for me to second their request that you will please to forward us a draught of the intended address, and whatever may occur to be added shall be communicated with candour and submitted to an impartial decision. We entertain no doubt of your acquiescence, considering we are the smallest and youngest congregation.

The conduct of the Georgians seems to be displeasing and hurtfull to your feelings. Amongst us it is not considered in that light, for they certainly had reason to expect your congregation would long since have seen the propriety of addressing the President and inviting others to join (as it now appears you have done), but finding your inactivity, they stept forward to show the exemple, and I hope it will not give offence to suggest that even at this late hour you have been roused to action by the Georgians' officiousness, as you are pleased to call it, though we think it spirituousness.

It is confessed it gave us a little disgust, not what they had done, but that we (your [congregation] and this congregation) should be left in the rear through a neglect on your part, for on 17th January last the matter was suggested from here, of the propriety to prisent an address, and on 28 of the same month was repeated, when a very slight and inadequate excuse was made, and the business left dormant and neglected till now. However, that is not to be recalled. Let us now join and go hand in hand to repair that neglect by framing a decent and plausible reason for our appearant tardiness. I shall be speedy and punctual in replying to any communications you may honour me with.

In behalf of this congregation, I remain, gentlemen,

Your obedient, humble servant

[Manuel Josephson]

The parnasim and junto of K. K. Sheerith Israel, New York.

No. 60   The Will of Philip Jacob Cohen, of Savannah—1790

At a meeting of the local congregation of Savannah, held on August 29, 1790, Mordecai Sheftall, the dominant figure of the Jewish community, moved that the group apply for a charter for the synagogue. One of the original trustees and incorporators appointed by the congregation was Philip Jacob Cohen, a German who had come to Charlestown by way of England and who had served as a militiaman during the Revolution.

Within a few weeks after his election as a trustee Cohen died. His will, printed below, throws light on the religious attitude of a man who was closely identified with the local congregation.

SOURCE. Office of the Ordinary of Chatham County, Savannah.

Georgia.

In the Name of God, Amen. I, Philip Jacob Cohen, of Savannah, in the State of Georgia, merchant, do make this my last will and testament.

First, it is my desire to be buried after the Jewish custom and no other, and I will that all such debts as I justly owe at the time of my decease, together with my funeral charges and expences, be paid by my executors herein after named.

And as to my estate, both real and personal, I dispose thereof as follows, that is to say: it is my will that all my estate, real and personal, be sold by my executors herein after named, and also my stock in trade, in such way and manner as my said executors, or such of them as may qualify and act as such, may think proper, and that such money as I owe to the synagogue be paid as soon as possible after my decease.

Also it is my will that as soon as my just debts are paid, I do hereby give to Elizabeth Stronach my young Negro wench named Bessey or Betsy, and also the sum of fifty guineas for her care and attention to me during my long illness.

Lastly, I do hereby nominate and appoint my trusty friends, Adam Tunno and Israel Joseph, of Charleston, and John Glen, of Savannah, attorney at law, or such of them as shall qualify and act as my executors or executor, executors and executor of this my last will and testament.

Hear, O Israel, the Lord our God, the Lord is One.

In testimony whereof, I have hereunto set my hand and seal, the sixteenth day of September, one thousand seven hundred and ninety.

Philip Jacob Cohen

Signed, sealed, published, pronounced, and declared by the testator, as and for his last will and testament in the presence of us, who in his presence, in the presence of each other, and at his request, have subscribed our names as witnesses hereto:

Levi Sheftall, Isaac Polock, James Glen

No. 61   The Problem of the Itinerant Suppliant—1790

The Jewish community in Europe had no developed, constructive techniques of dealing with the itinerant poor. When a wanderer arrived in town he was given food, lodging, a few pennies, and frequently transportation to the next Jewish settlement. The same practice was followed on the North American mainland in the eighteenth century. In the early days, when towns were few and far apart, the expense of sending a man from one town to another, to Europe, or to the West Indies, was a serious drain upon a congregation's resources. Yet rarely was a suppliant denied some aid.

In October, 1790, when two Polish Jews appeared in Philadelphia and asked for help, a meeting of the whole congregation was called to discuss the needs of the men. Only eight members responded. The minute, printed below, describes the action taken.

SOURCE. Congregation Mikveh Israel, Philadelphia, Minute Book, Vol. I, 1781–95.

16th of Hesvan [5551].

At a meeting of the Congregation M. I., at the Congregation House, Sunday, October 14th, 1790, Mr. Manuel Josephson in the chair. Present:

Mr. J. Philips	Mr. M. Nathan
Mr. S. Lyon	Mr. M. Noah
Mr. L. Phillips	[Mr.] S. Etting
Mr. B. Nones	Mr. M. Hamburg

The meeting took into consideration the case of two gentleman from Poland, who having stated their distresses and requested the congregation to afford them assistance, the business was considered. And it is agreed on, that the finances of [the] congregation are small, and out of their power to render them the assistance demanded. The disposition of all present would be to assist, if 'twere possible, out of the cash belonging to the stock [treasury]. [The] congregation have at same time agreed to pay their expence already accrued in this place and to pay their passage from hence to New York.

———

No. 62 The Charter of Congregation Mickva Israel, Savannah—1790

The first Jews in Georgia arrived but a few months after General James Oglethorpe landed there in 1733. They held services at the time but with the decline of the colony around 1740, the Jewish community also died out. Later services were held about 1750, in 1774, and again in 1790. In the latter year the congregation, Sephardic in its ritual, was reconstituted as Mickva Israel ("The Hope of Israel"). The name was in all likelihood taken from that of the Philadelphia congregation, although the Curaçao synagogue, the oldest in the New World, also was known as Mikveh Israel.

In 1790, shortly after the adoption of a state constitution that gave Jews equal rights, and the enactment of a statute permitting the incorporation of synagogues, Savannah Jewry applied for and received the charter printed below. Mickva Israel, thus organized in 1790, has survived to this day.

SOURCE. Charter. In the records of Congregation Mickva Israel, Savannah.

On motion by Mr. Mordecai Sheftall and seconded by Mr. David Cardozo that application be made to his Excellency the Governor, for to incorporate this congregation as a body politick by the name of Mickva Israel, and that the trustees be as follows: Levi Sheftall, President, Sheftall Sheftall, Treasurer, Philip Jacob Cohen, Emanuel De La Motta, Abraham Depass, Joseph Abrahams, and Mordecai Sheftall, members of this congregation and their sucessors, which being put to the vote, was carried in the affirmative.

Savannah, 29th August, 1790.

Ordered that Mr. Coshman Polack be nominated as one of the trustees in the charter intended to be applyed for in the room of P. J. Cohen, deceased, as per resolve of the 29th August, 1790.

Savannah, 26th September, 1790.

Resolved: That Mr. Mordecai Sheftall be requested to make application to his Excellency, the Governor, to have this congregation by the name of Mickva Israel incorporated as a body politick agreeable to a resolve of the general ajunto of the 29th August, and that the charter be filled as follows:

Levi Sheftall, president
Sheftall Sheftall, treasurer
Coshman Polack
Joseph Abrahams } members of this congregation
Mordecai Sheftall
Abraham Depass
Emanuel De La Motta, and their successors.

Sir: Being informed you are agoing to Augusta, I am requested by the *mamad* ["board"] to inclose you their resolution in having this congregation incorporated, and request you will apply to have the same done, knowing your attatchment to the wellfair of this congregation; hope you will not think the trouble too much. In behalf of the *mamad,* I am, sir,

Your obedient, humble servant,
Signed: Levi Sheftall, parnos
Savannah, 25 November, 1790.

M. M. Sheftall.
Georgia

By His Excellency, Edward Telfair, Governor and Commander in chief in and over the said state.

To Messieurs Levi Sheftall, Sheftall Sheftall, Coshman Polack, Joseph

Abrahams, Mordecai Sheftall, Abraham Depass, and Emanuel D. L. [De La] Motta:

Whereas by an act of the General Assembly of the said state passed the twenty third day of December in the year of our Lord one thousand seven hundred and eighty nine, entituled "An Act to Incorporate the Episcopal Church in Savannah, called Christ's Church, and the Independent Congregational Church or Meeting House at Medway in Liberty County, and to Authorize the Governor to Grant Charters of Incorporation to Other Religious Societies," it is amongst other things enacted

"That it shall and may be lawfull to and for his excellency the governor at any time or times hereafter, on application in writing of any religious society belonging to any church or place of worship now erected or that may be erected hereafter, to grant under his hand and the great seal of the state usual and customary charters of incorporation to such members of the said churches or places of worship, and to authorize such bodies politic or corporate to sue and be sued, and to have and to hold all lands and tenements, monies, and other goods and chattels that already belong to such religious societies, or which may hereafter be given, granted, or bestowed, and the same to have and receive to the proper use and behoof of such churches or places of worship, in such manner as the members and supporters of such church or place of worship shall point out in their application for such charter, or the principles of this act, and with the same priveledges and advantages as are granted, given, and secured to any church or religious society incorporated by this act."

And whereas application has been made to me by and in behalf of the Hebrew Congregation (who have erected a place of worship in the city of Savannah in the state aforesaid), requesting that the said Levi Sheftall, Sheftall Sheftall, Coshman Polack, Joseph Abrahams, Mordecai Sheftall, Abraham Depass, and Emanuel De La Motta may receive a charter of incorporation as parnas [president] and adjuntas [board members] of the Hebrew Congregation.

Now know ye that in consequence of such application, and in virtue of the said act, and withal being willing to promote religion and virtue, I do by these presents declare you, the said Levi Sheftall, Sheftall Sheftall, Coshman Polack, Joseph Abrahams, Mordecai Sheftall, Abraham Depass, and Emanuel De La Motta, to be, and you and your successors shall, and are hereby, declared to be, a body corporate, by the name and style of "The Parnas and Adjuntas of Mickva Israel at Savannah." And you, the said Levi Sheftall, Sheftall Sheftall, Coshman Polack, Joseph Abrahams, Mordecai Sheftall, Abraham Depass, and Emanuel De La Motta, parnas and adjuntas as aforesaid, and your successors in office are hereby invested with all manner of property both real and personal, all monies due or to grow due, gifts, grants, hereditaments, priveledges, and immunities whatsoever which now do, or may belong, is, or may be transferred to the said Hebrew congregation of Mickva Israel, to have and to hold the same for the proper use, benefit, and behoof of the said congregation of Mickva Israel.

And I do hereby declare that you, the said parnas and adjuntas, shall hold your said offices until the first Monday in September next, and I require on that day and on every first Monday in September thereafter annually, the members of the said congregation shall convene at the place of worship (Mickva Israel) aforesaid, and there between the hours of ten and two o'clock, elect from among themselves seven fit and discreet persons as parnas and ajuntas aforesaid who shall be, and are hereby declared to be, vested with all necessary powers to carry the purposes of this charter fully into effect.

And you, the said parnas and adjuntas, and your successors in office shall be, and you and they are hereby declared to be, capable of sueing and being sued, and of using all necessary and legal steps for recovering or defending any property whatever which the said congregation (Mickva Israel) now doth or may hold, claim, or demand, and is herein secured or otherwise, and also with power to make all necessary regulations not repugnant to law, and to recover in your own name, or in the name of your successors or otherwise, as well the monies as other property with all rents, issues, and profits of the same, or of lands, houses, or other estate belonging thereto or any part thereof.

Given under my hand and the great seal of the said state at the State House in Augusta, this thirtieth day of November in the year of our Lord one thousand seven hundred and ninety, and in the fifteenth year of the independence of United States of America.

By His Excellency's command.

Signed: John Milton, secretary

[Edward Telfair, Governor]

At a meeting of the ajunto at the house of the Parnos:
Present:

Levi Sheftall, parnos	Coshman Polack
Sheftall Sheftall, *gaboy*	Abraham Depass
Joseph Abrahams	Benjamin Sheftall, Jr., secretary

The parnos presented to the ajunto the charter for the congregation, which was read. Resolved, that the same be read in the snoge [synagogue] on Saturday next before the *seipher* ["Scroll"] is taken out.

Savannah, 19th December, 1790.

The parnos informed the congregation that he thought it necessary a new code of laws should be made for the government of this congregation, which was unanimously agreed to.

Resolved: That a committee of five be appointed for that purpose, and to report to the parnos and ajunto as soon as they had framed the same, and that the following persons be that committee: Mordecai Sheftall, Coshman Polack, Levi Sheftall, Emanuel De La Motta, and Joseph Abrahams.

Savannah, 10th January, 1791.

———

No. 63 Code of Laws of Congregation Mickva Israel, Savannah—1791–1792

Within six weeks after its incorporation, Congregation Mickva Israel appointed a committee of five members to prepare a new code of regulations, replacing the congregational rules which had evidently been in effect before the incorporation in 1790.

The following body of laws (Document A) was adopted on July 31, 1791. The administrative structure was simple: a board, a president, a treasurer, and a secretary. Democracy expressed itself in the provision that any three members could appeal from an action taken by the board and could submit the issues directly to the congregation. Apparently no separate "benevolent society" was established, for charities were handled by the president and the trustees.

The influence of the environment may be seen in the code. Offerings by strangers were to be collected at once. Most of these were businessmen who came by boat and most likely left on the next one. There were no facilities to bill them, and it therefore behooved the congregation to collect synagogal offerings as soon as possible. Also indicative of local conditions is rule fifteen. A number of the members spent much time on their plantations or in the countryside, inevitably collecting mud on their boots. Such persons were not to mount the pulpit in their customary footgear.

Whatever influence the environment had, loyalty to the ancient Law was not neglected. Intermarriage under congregational auspices was forbidden, and, under rule twelve, Sabbath violators were to be denied synagogal honors. The seriousness with which the congregation viewed such ritual offenses is evidenced by Document B, which describes the trial of Isaac Polack, who was accused of keeping his store open on the Sabbath.

SOURCE. Congregation Mickva Israel, Savannah, Minute Book, Vol. I, 1790–1851.

A [NO. 63]

At a meeting of the congregation of the synagogue, agreeable to order of the 25th July, inst. [1791]
Present:

Levi Sheftall, parnos	Abraham Depass
Sheftall Sheftall, *gaboy*	Coshman Polack
Mordecai Sheftall	Levy Abrahams
Joseph Abrahams	Emanuel De La Motta
Ralph Depass	Abraham Abrahams
David Cardozo	Moses Sheftall
Benjamin Sheftall, Senior	Benjamin Sheftall, Jr., secretary
Samuel Mordecai	

The parnos opened the business when Mr. Levy Abrahams was put in the chair and the laws read paragraph by paragraph and approved of as follows:

Rule 1st.

That this congregation be continued by the former name of Mickva Israel, and that the mode of worship be according to the Pourtuguese minhauge ["rite"], and that all [money] offerings shall be made in Hebrew, and that the money so offered shall be nominated in the name of the coin, as named in the state.

Rule 2d.

That their shall be chosen on every third Monday in August annually, from the *yehadim* [members] of this congregation (whose ages shall exceed twenty-one years), one parnos and six ajunto [board members], and their [shall] be chosen by the *yehadim* one person out of the said ajunto to act as *gaboy* ["treasurer"], and that they have power to regulate this congregation and inflict pennalties on all transgressors of the following rules.

Rule 3d.

That the said parnos, *gaboy*, and ajuntomen and a secretary, being elected by ballot and having a majority of votes, shall be considered as such. And if the parnos elected refuse to serve, he shall pay a fine not exceeding forty shillings; the *gaboy*, thirty shillings, and each ajuntoman, ten shillings. And if in case a parnos, *gaboy*, or any of the adjunto be re-elected, and do not chuse to serve, neither of them shall be liable to pay the fine specified. On refusal of the new elected parnos, *gaboy*, or ajunto, the old officers to serve untill a new election take place, which shall be within three days after said general election, and that the officers elected shall take their seats on the first day of Rossanah ["New Year"].

Rule 4th.

That the *hatinim* [honorary officers] be drawn from the *yehadim* (exceeding the age of twenty-one years) within twenty four hours after the general election, by the presiding parnos and ajunto, when the parnos shall notify the same to the persons so drawn, who shall be obliged to declare his or their acceptance or refusal to the parnos within forty eight hours after; and should any decline serving, shall pay a fine not exceeding forty shillings each; and [if] in proceeding through the whole of the above disscribed *yehadim,* none will accept, then each pay the above mentioned fine, and in such case, the acting parnos and *gaboy* be obliged to serve.

Rule 5th.

Should the parnos be absent at any time, then the *gaboy* shall precide; and in case of the absence of both, then the members of the ajunto shall act by seniority.

Rule 6th.

Should the conduct of the officers or any of the adjunto be at any time reprehensible, in such case, on complaint in writing from a *yehid* or congregator, he or they shall be called to account by the remainder of the ajunto. But should the detirmination of said adjunto be not satisfactory to the complainant, on application of said person, signed by at least three *yehadim* (not allied by consanquinity of blood) to the parnos and adjunto, to have a general meeting of the *yehadim* called, they shall in such case be obliged to convene them within one week; and should the *yehadim,* so met, think their was no just cause of complaint, they, the *yehadim,* shall have it in their power to inflict a f[ine] [on] the complainant or complainants.

Rule 7th.

That a decent beheavour be observed by every person during service, no person to raise his voice above, or disturb the reader, or hold any conversation either in the synagogue or places adjacent. And in case any person so offending, on being called to order and still persisting, shall, for every such offence, pay a fine not exceeding forty shillings.

Rule 8th.

That any person refusing a mitzwa [religious honor] shall not be entitled to another untill he can give a sufficient excuse to the parnos. Also, any person who is called to [participate in reading the] *seipher* shall be obliged to offer for the parnos [money for the congregation], and that no offering be less than six pence.

Rule 9th.

That the parnos shall call the adjunto once a month and oftner if requisite.

Rule 10th.

That any person fined for a violation of these rules shall not be intitled to receive any mitzwa, or have any offerings made for him untill he has complyed by paying such fines.

Rule 11th.

That the *gaboy* keep a proper set of books, collect all offerings and fines, shall ballance said books yearly, and render accounts to the *yehadim* and congregators quarterly, and to strangers weekly and sooner if requisite. That the secretary keep proper books, in which shall be inserted the rules and proceedings of the ajunto and congregation. Also, that the *gaboy* and secretary be obliged to bring up their books [to date] at delivering the same to their successors in office. Any neglecting so to do, shall be liable to a fine not exceeding five pounds, and that the books of both *gaboy* and secretary be kept in English.

Rule 12th.

That every person professing the Jewish religion (either *yehid* or congregator) who shall violate the Sabbath or holydays, on information being given to the parnos of his or their so acting, he or they shall be called before the ajunto within four days, if the accuser and the accused be in town. If not, then the business to remain untill both parties be present. And should such person or persons be found guilty, he or they shall be deprived of every honour in the synagogue untill he or they make such concessions as may appear satisfactory to the parnos and ajunto.

Rule 13th.

That the parnos shall have power to bestow charity of the monies in [the] fund to the amount of twenty shillings; and in case a larger sum be wanted, he shall consult the ajunto.

Rule 14th.

All persons hereafter desireous to become a *yehid* of this congregation shall notify the same by letter to the parnos, who shall, within one month after receipt of such letter, call a general ajunto before whom such letter shall be layed, and who shall ballot for such applicant. And if a majority of votes are in favour of the applicant, he shall be considered as a *yehid* on his paying one guinea towards the charity fund of this congregation, and having been a resident six months previous to his making application.

Rule 15th.

That every person shall appear in synagogue in as decent apparel as his abilities will admit, and that no person shall be called to [the] *seipher* in boots.

Rule 16th.

All persons intending to have a wedding in their family shall notify the same to the parnos, requesting the attendance of the hazon [reader], who shall be desired to attend provided the wedding be with a female of our religion. Also, in case of births, such persons shall be obliged in like manner to inform the parnos, in order that they may have those honours paid them that is customary. Any person neglecting to inform the parnos shall not be intitled to receive those honours that is accustomed; also that the hozon shall not attend in such cases.

And lastly, Rule 17th.

We, whose names are hereunto subscribed, do solemnly promise upon our sacred honours, each for ourselves, and not one for the other, to abide by and consider ourselves as bound by the foregoing rules untill they shall be altered or amen[d]ed by three-fourths of the *yehadim* present.

Mordecai Sheftall, Levi Sheftall, Joseph Abrahams, etc.

The business being closed, the chairman resigned the chair when the parnos closed the meeting.

Savannah, 31st July, 1791.

B [NO. 63]

At a meeting of the parnas ["president"] and adjunto ["board"] at the house of the parnas.

Present:

Mordecai Sheftall, Jr.	David Cardozo
Levi Sheftall	Benjamin Sheftall
Emanuel De La Motta	Benjamin Sheftall, Jr., secretary

The parnas informed the adjunto that his reason for calling them together was in consequence of information being given him of Mr. Isaac Polack keeping his store open on the Sabbath.

Orderd, that the said Isaac Polack be summoned to attend the parnas and adjunto on Tuesday evening next, at 6 o'clock, in the synagogue, to shew cause, if any he has, why the 12th rule of this congregation should not be put in force against him. Order that this adjunto do meet on Tuesday evening next, at 6 o'clock, in the synagogue. There being no other business proposed, the adjunto closed.

Savannah, 11th March, 1792.

At an extra meeting of the parnas and adjunto at the synagogue, agreeable to order of the 11th instant,

Present:

Mordecai Sheftall, parnas	Emanuel De La Motta
Levi Sheftall	Benjamin Sheftall, Sr.
David Cardozo	Benjamin Sheftall, Jr., secretary

The parnas informed the adjunto that agreeable to order he had delivered the secretary a citation for Mr. Polack which was in the words following:

City of Savannah,
K.K. Mickva Israel

Mr. Isaac Polack:

Information being given to the parnas and adjunto that you did, contrary to laws of God and the rules of this congregation, keep your store open on the Sabbath, you are, therefore, hereby summoned to be and appear before the parnas and adjunto of this congregation on Tuesday evening next, at 6 o'clock, at the synagogue, to show cause, if any you have, why the 12th rule of this congregation should not be put in force against you.

Given under my hand at Savannah this 12th day of March, 1792.

Signed: Mordecai Sheftall, parnas of K.K.M.I.

By order
Benjamin Sheftall, Jr., secretary

Mr. Polack attended, agreeable to summons, and confessed his store was open on the Sabbath, and alleaged for [the] reason that it was unavoidable, as he had sundry goods consigned to him from Charleston, and the captain of the vessel sent them to his house without his knowledge, and he ordered his clerk to store them. The opinion of the adjunto being taken, [they] wher [were] of opinion that Mr. Polack had not voilated [violated] the 12th rule.

Nothing further being proposed, the adjunto closed.

Savannah, 13th March, 1792.

No. 64   Collection of Funds for a Nonsectarian
Orphan Asylum—1791

Some time in the early 1770's Gershom Cohen, an emigrant from Europe, came to America. Evidently he had a good Jewish education, if we may draw any conclusion from his ability to write a beautiful Hebrew hand. This skill is reflected in the Hebrew initials of his name which were encircled in the curlicues of his florid English signature.

While still in his twenties, Cohen became a merchant in Charleston, South Carolina, served as a militiaman in the Revolution, and married Rebecca Sarzedas, whose brother was a Revolutionary officer. When Cohen died, at the age of fifty-four, he left behind a widow and nine children.

By 1791 Cohen's community of Charleston was well on its way to overshadow the Jewish group in New York. Charleston was rapidly becoming the chief center of Jewish life in the young republic. There were over fifty Jewish families in the town.

In February of that year, acting under the influence of a new and more liberal state constitution, the synagogue obtained a corporation charter. Three reasons, the Jews wrote, motivated the incorporation of their institution: their wish to exercise their religion publicly; the desire to provide for their poor; and, finally, the need to support and educate their orphans. It was their proud hope, as they expressed it in the petition for incorporation, that their future religious and political conduct would prove the wisdom of that article in the new South Carolina constitution of 1790 giving them the right to participate on equal terms with others in the religious life of the community.

The members of the Jewish community were determined to put their best foot forward. When therefore in August, 1791, the officers of the city orphan asylum asked them, along with all the other churches, for aid, they responded to the appeal. This action required a real sacrifice on their part, for the Jewish community had just extended itself to buy a lot for a proposed new synagogue. Apparently little money was left for the building itself.

On Sunday morning, August 21, the Reverend Mr. Abraham Azuby conducted a service; and, following an address by Joseph M. Myers, a collection was taken up on behalf of the orphans. Myers was a state deputy inspector general of Masonry and, according to a contemporary Christian clergyman, was a well-educated man. In the cordial note of thanks which a Mr. Vander Horst wrote in the name of the commissioners of the Orphan House, he voiced their "warmest acknowledgements for the very excellent discourse delivered."

It would seem that Cohen carried on a correspondence about this service with a number of his friends. Writing to a very observant coreligionist in New York City, Cohen defended Charleston's Jewry against the charges of imitating the Christians by having the services on a Sunday. Cohen's defense was that Sunday was the most appropriate day for a gathering of Jews and Christians, and that the contribution to a general orphan asylum would go far toward cementing Jewish-Christian relations.

In another letter, the one printed below, Cohen jubilantly described the details of the service to his friend Mordecai Sheftall, of Savannah. It is important to note that Cohen emphasized and re-emphasized the decorum of his fellow Jews. He dwelt with obvious relish on the good music, the English prayers, the English address, and the substantial sums gathered for a Gentile or nonsectarian charity.

SOURCE. The Mr. and Mrs. B. H. Levy Collection of Sheftall Papers.

Charleston, 29th August, 1791.

Mr. Mordica Sheftall,
Dear Sir:

[I] inclose you the form of prayers translated from the Hebrew, and a religious discourse delived in English at the synogoge on Sunday, the 21st August, by Mr. Joseph Myers to a large and respectable audence, after which a collection was made to amount £58 15s. 0d. and 20 dollars, afterward making in the whole, £63 8s. 4d. sterling, a very large collection for our small congregation, and the day very much against us indeed.

With a deal of satisfaction, I assure you, I neivour [never] saw more decoram and decent beheavour in a place of worship in my [life?]. The whole was conducted so as to give unive[rsal satisfac]tion. A committe was apointed for that perp[ose . . .] neivour was more decoram observed [in our] synogoge. The hazan and four men and four boys perform all the prayers. The singing was regular (they having practiced for a whole week), and the tunes delightfull pretty. In fact, the performance has occationd [occasioned] honor to our little society and respect to our [Jewish] nation at large. Neivour was aney sett of men so well satisfyed as the Board of Commistioners (say the intendent and City Councle), which they manefested by a vote of thanks to Mr. Azube, Mr. Myers, and the wardens and elders of the synogoge. Excuse my inlargien [enlarging] on the subject.

Last week two Polish rabies arrivid here from Philidlephia. They apear to be decent men. They intend for Rhode Island to gitt a passage to Surriman [Surinam]. . . .

Our children are very poorly. Mrs. Cohen [my wife], thank God, well, but much furteaged attending the children. With pleasure acquaint you and famely, Mrs. Cohen was, on the 27th of July, delivered with a fine girl, whome we named Rebecca. Hope this may meet you and famely injoyin health. Mrs. Cohen joines me with our best of wishes to your self, Mrs. Sheftall, Miss Perla [Sheftall], and every branch of your famely, and, bleive me to be, sir,

Your asshured freind and well wisher,

Gershen Cohen

N.B. The persons assisting the hazen was

Mr. J. Dacosta	Boys:
Mr. Joseph Myer	Aaron Lauzarus
Mr. H. Zuns	David Cantor
Mr. A. W . . .	Isaac Scaixas, and
	Philip Cohen

In my last [letter] to you, I sent by Mr. Dacosta sundry papers, for which gave a receipt to your son Benjamin, which will thank you to return. Please make my complements to your brothir and famely.

No. 65 Congregational Discipline—1792–1793

Many Jews in the eighteenth century considered it incumbent on all professing coreligionists in the community to rally to its support and to help maintain its institutions. If they refused to do this, they were to be coerced, in one way or another, by the denial of religious privileges to them and their dear ones.

As we see from Documents A and B, printed below, Philadelphia Jewry acquiesced in this commonly held view. The harshest threat employed to force recalcitrants into line was denial of burial according to the Jewish rite.

On occasion members of the synagogal community were remiss in the payment of their dues, either neglecting or refusing to pay what they owed or what they had pledged. The congregation bided its time—the Church can wait!—and when (God forbid!) a death occurred in the family of the offender, burial was denied until the bills were paid. How effective that threat was may be determined from Document C, printed below.

SOURCE. Congregation Mikveh Israel, Philadelphia, Minute Book, Vol. I, 1781–95.

A [NO. 65]

At a meeting of the congregation K.K. ["Holy Congregation"] Mickvey Israel, held 15th of Elul, A. M. [*anno mundi*, "the year of the world"], 5552, coresponding with 2d day of September, 1792.

Present:

Messrs. B. Nones	Jonas Philips
Barnard Gratz	Levy Philips
Sol. Lyons	Moses Nathan
Samuel Hays	Josiah Nathan

. . . On motion of the parnass, seconded by Mr. Levy Philips, that the parnass and adjuntas ["board members"] shall make or cause to be made an *ascamah* [law] or an irevocable resolve of this congregation in the must expresive languauge, the same to be publickly reed [read] and made known in synagogue on next Rosh Hanah ["New Year"], that any one professing Judaism and does not or will not contribute for the suport of our congregation, shall not be considered in publick or in private as Jeus [Jews] during life and be regarded and treated in the same manner when dead. The same motion, being duly considered, was carried in the affirmative.

No other business offering, this meeting was closed till next *Sum Gathailah* ["Fast of Gedaliah," September 19].

B. Nones

B [NO. 65]

In junto [board meeting], Monday, 16 Ellul, A. M., 5552, corresponding to the 3d day of September, 1792.

Present:

Messrs. Benjamin Nones, parnas
    Manuel Josephson
    Barnard Gratz   } juntos
    Solomon Lyon

. . . The board then proceeded to the subject matter contained in the second motion of yesterday's meeting, and having duly considered the same, came to the following resolutions, *vizt.*:

Resolved, that whereas there are several persons in this place who profess Judaism, attend publick wo[r]ship whenever they incline, have the advantage of the shochet ["slaughterer"] to parchase casheer [kosher] meat whenever they chuse, and on many occasions (such as mariages, circumcisions, and funerals) avail themselves of the benefits appertaining to this congregation without contributing, as they ought, to the support thereof, which requires a considerable sum and is borne by [a] few individuals that have the well fare and maintenance of our holy religion and worship at heart, [and] who with much reason consider it a great hardship to bear the burthen, whilst those who refuse a just and proportionable contribution partake of every advantage equally with themselves;

Therefore, in order to remedy the same, as much as in the power of the congregation to prevail on such as persist in withholding their aid towards its support, that it be resolved, and it is hereby resolved, that all and every person professing Judaism, and refuses to contribute a just and equitable proportion toward the support of the synagogue, shall be deemed as not belonging to our society [religious community], either in publick or private. Nor shall they be noticed in any concerns peculiar to the rites and ceremonies thereof, on any occasion whatever, and in case of death of themselves or any of their family residing within their dwelling, they shall not be intitled to the aid or attendance usual on such occasions from any person belonging to the congregation.

And in order to deter any member or members of this congregation from acting or doing any thing contrary to the sense and meaning of the aforesaid resolve, thereby to counteract and render the sane [same] void and of non effect,

It is further resolved that every such person shall be considered and held in the same light, and proceeded against in every respect, as the person or persons against whome the aforesaid resolve was originally intended to operate.

And that no one may pretend ignorance of the aforesaid regulations, resolved, that the parnas order the same to be publickly read at synagogue on the first day of Rosh Ashana now next ensuing, after the morning service, before taking out the *sepharim* ["Scrolls"], that all persons may know the same and regulate themselves accordingly. *"And all the people shall hear and fear"* [Hebrew, Deut. 17:13].

C [NO. 65]

At a meeting of the parnass and junta held at Philadelphia the 25th Yar [Iyyar], 5553, corresponding with 7th of May, 1793.
Present:

> Messrs. Benjamin Nones, parnass
> Jonas Philips ⎫
> Levy Philips ⎬ juntas
> Moses Nathan ⎭

The parnass open the business of the meeting by informing his junta that an application had been made him from Solomon Raphael and requested [?] permission to have his child burried.

On motion [made] and seconded, resolved, that burrial be permitted to the child of said Solomon Raphael, in such place as the parnass may direct, on condittion, nevertheless, that said Solomon Raphael pays unto the hands of the parnass, for the use of said congregation, his 2 years' contribution toward the support of the shoehet, at 30s. per annum, also the sum of two pounds 5s. for his free will offerings, at the time his child was circumcise.

Resolve also, that he shall also paid the sum of five pounds for the bracking [breaking] the grownd of said burrial place and the money last mentioned to be apply toward the repairing of the *beth a haiim* [cemetery].

On motion and seconded, resolve . . . that in case of none compliaine [noncompliance], that the right of burrial be denied. The same being duly considered, the whole of the withiny resolved was duly carried in the affirmative.

Philadelphia, May 7th, 1793   B. Nones, parnas

Jonas Phillips ⎫

Levy Phillips ⎬ adjuntas

Mosese Nathans ⎭

On application by the parnass in person to Solomon Raphael, to whom he informed of the resolve of this congregation, said Solomon Raphael made answer that it was right and requested Mr. S. Lyon to pay for him to the parnass the sum of two pounds 5s., the amount decreed by the junta, which said Solomon Lyon did comply with, and I have received said money.

Philadelphia, May 7th, 1793.

Benjamin Nones, parnass

———

No. 66   A Problem of Intermarriage—1793

Intermarriage was a problem in the colonies from almost the first day. Communities were small, individuals lived in the countryside, social relations were easy and natural, and intermarriage was inevitable. The typical Jewish settler wanted a home and children, and when there were no Jewish women, he married a Gentile.

The fact that a Jew married out of the faith did not necessarily mean that he himself deserted the religion of his fathers. There can be no doubt that on numerous occasions the Jewish village merchant held to his ancestral faith to his dying day and would gladly have brought his Gentile wife into town for conversion had he been given any encouragement by the Jewish community, but conversion was frowned upon by the congregations.

As early as 1763 Shearith Israel in New York passed a law forbidding the acceptance of proselytes or marriage with a proselyte. It is not too difficult to understand the motivations of these early Jews.

They may have maintained—in defense of their attitude—that they did not have the proper religious authorization to admit converts; they may have argued, with some cogency, that English Jewry had promised the civil authorities that they would not engage in proselytizing and that they were merely following current English synagogal practice, but all this was certainly a rationalization. Underlying the taboos was the desire on the part of the struggling young community to maintain itself in the face of powerful assimilatory influences. Once they let down the bars, they knew or believed that they would be lost as a Jewish group. Back of it all was their grim and almost fanatical determination to survive as a distinct religious entity.

In 1793 a member of the Philadelphia community, Moses Nathans, brought his problem of intermarriage before the congregation. He and the Gentile mother of his children had never been married according to Jewish law. However, she was willing to become a Jewess and sought the privilege of conversion and of a Jewish marriage. The husband's friends were sympathetic to the request. Nevertheless, they felt that they could do nothing on their own account and referred the matter to the ecclesiastical court of the Spanish-Portuguese synagogue in London. Accordingly, the president, Benjamin Nones, sent the following letter. Very likely a similar note was dispatched to The Great Synagogue (Ashkenazic) in the same city. In the meantime, the man concerned—a member of the board!—was, from the point of view of synagogal ritual, looked upon as unmarried.

The hazzan's records show that he married the woman in 1794 in accordance with Jewish ritual.

SOURCE. Archives of Congregation Mikveh Israel, Philadelphia.

Philadelphia, August 7th, 1793 (5553).

To the *beth din* of K. K. Shagnar a Shamaim ["court of the Holy Congregation Gate of Heaven"], of London, whom God augment.
Gentlemen:

We, the parnass and adjuntas ["board members"] of K. K. Mickvey Israel, of this city, have the honor to address your respectable board on business of importance to Jewdaisme at large, and to our young and rising congregation in particular, and we flatter ourself you will, as soon as it may be convenient, favor this congregation with your answer and advice.

The case is this: A *yahid* [member] of this congregation has lived in a public way with a goyah ["Gentile"] woman who has kept house for him about eight years and has had by her three childrens, two of which are boys, which he had *nimmolim* ["circumcised"] at the 8th day. The same person *now* applies to us, with the consent of the woman, to make her a *giyyoret* ["convert"], as also to grant him permission to marry said woman with *huppah u-kedushin* [Jewish ritual marriage].

We must say in favor of the above *yahid* that he has and does keep up, as far as we know, to our rules and contributes toward the support of our congregation as others do.

We have represented, to the best of our knowlidge, the case and conduct of the person, and therefore request your opinon on the subject and what we have to do. Your answer will much oblige this congregation, in whose behalf we are, gentlemen,

Your most obeidient, humble servants,
Benjamin Nones, parnass

––––––

No. 67 The Duties of the Minister of the New York Congregation—1795

Gershom Mendes Seixas (1745–1816) had been elected hazzan, or reader, of the New York synagogue in 1768. Actually he was the "rabbi," although he was not trained or ordained in the traditional sense for that position.

In the winter of 1795 Seixas' salary was raised to £200. A parsonage went with the office, and of course there were also occasional perquisites. About the same time a committee brought in a report on his duties. Nothing was said about preaching. Sephardic congregations of the eighteenth century were not interested in a preaching minister. Practically the only time a hazzan delivered an address was when the colonial or state or federal government called on all citizens to celebrate a military victory or a day of thanksgiving, or when it asked them to collect money for the victims of a war.

Many of the duties of the hazzan were of a purely ritual nature and his authority even in the service was carefully delimited. Unlike the hierarchical churches, the early American Jewish congregation was completely dominated by the lay leaders. The Jewish officiant was a paid functionary who had little prestige and still less power.

SOURCE. Congregation Shearith Israel, New York, Minute Book.

At a meeting of the trustees of K. K. S. I. on Sunday, the 8th November, 1795, corresponding with the 25th Hesvan, 5556. . . .

Mr. Ephraim Hart and Mr. Alexander Zuntz were appointed a committee to draw up rules to be signed by the chazan for the due performance of his duties in consideration of his salary and [to] lay the same before this board on Sunday next, and the clerk was ordered to draw up an agreement for the purpose against the said time.

Adjourned S. D. [*sine die*]

At a meeting of the trustees of K. K. S. I. on Sunday, the 15th November, 1795, corresponding to the 3d Keslav, 5556. . . .

The minutes of the last meeting were read and confirmed. Mr. Ephraim Hart and Mr. Alexander Zuntz, the committee appointed for drawing up the duties and services which are to be performed by Mr. Gorsham Seixas as chazan to this *Kaahl* ["congregation"], gave in the sane [same], which, being read, after due deliberation and amendment, are as follows:

Duties and Services to Be Performed by the Chazan

1st. Whenever the synagogue is opened for the performing of divine service, it shall be the duty of the chazan to be there within a quarter of an hour after the limmitted time for beginning of the same, and remain during the continuance thereof, unless prevented by sickness, except when a person shall have *yotzitt* [*yahrzeit*: the anniversary of the death of a relative] and neglect to notify him in proper time.

2d. It shall be the duty of the chazan to see that the *zimroth* ["songs"] be read in proper time, and if the person to whom the same may be given to read should neglect to perform it, it shall be his duty to read the same so that the service may be performed, as customary in our places of worship.

3rd. It shall be the duty of the chazan to peruse the *parza* [*parasha*: portion] of the week in the same *sepher torah* ["Scroll of the Law"] which is to be read the succeeding Sabbath or holiday; and that he be allowed 2s. 6d. for each error he may find out and correct in the same, by the owner thereof, and pay a fine himself of 5s. for any error that may be discovered in the same when read in public by any person.

4th. It shall not be in the power of the chazan to appoint any person to perform service on the Sabbath or holiday, as chazan, except the *zimroth;* neither shall he give the *haph torahs* ["prophetical portions"] of the following days, to wit, the 1st and 2d days of Roshah Shonah ["New Year"], the two *haph torahs* of *Kipur, Shekal, Zochor, Parah, Hahodesh* [holiday and special Sabbath readings], the three preceding Sabbaths before the 9th day of *Ab,* and the said 9th day of *Ab,* without leave of the acting parnass.

5th. The chazan shall comply with such directions as shall be from time to time authorized and enacted by the parnasim and adjunto, which may be required of him in writing by the acting parnass, appertaining to the services and customs of the synagogue.

6th. The chazan shall not marry any person whatsoever, nor attend in his official capacity on any barette [berit: "circumcision"] if forbidden by the acting parnas.

7th. It shall be the duty of the chazan to attend every funeral in this congregation and perform the functions of his office in the usual mode unless ordered to the contrary by the acting parnas.

Ordered that the clerk do forthwith furnish Mr. Siexas with a copy thereof and that the president be requested to carry the contract into execution.

No. 68 Misconduct in the Synagogue—1796

Sometimes worshipers in the synagogue were anything but decorous. They were boisterous, insolent to the president, or downright pugnacious. Document A concerns itself with an Abraham Pinto, who evidently refused to accept a religious honor accorded him in the synagogue.

Document B deals with the case of a Mr. Philips, who created such a disturbance during the service that the members had him sent to jail. One suspects that he was more than slightly inebriated. His wife, apparently pregnant, solemnly promised the indignant board that she would keep him out of the synagogue. It is to be hoped that the worthy officers, sensing the tragicomedy of her request, exercised the quality of mercy by withdrawing the charges which they had preferred against her husband.

SOURCE. American Jewish Historical Society Library, New York, Lyons Collection, Nos. 108 and 119.

A [NO. 68]

[Mr. Abraham Pinto.]
Sir:

I am directed by the parnassim and junto ["board"] of K. K. ["Holy Congregation"] Shearith Israel to inform you that they consider your behaviour to the acting parnas on Saturday, the 26th of December last, [not only] as an insult to him in his office, but a direct infringement of the ninth article of the rules and regulations formed for the good government of the congregation and insuring their mitzvas [religious honors] and privileges to them from the acting parnass;

And that you will lay under the punishment of that rule until you do away the breach thereof, by complying with what is required.

These regulations were read in synagogue, but least [lest] you should be at a loss for the contents, I enclose an extract.

I am, sir,

Your very humble servant,
E. Lyte, clerk, K. K. S. I.
February 2d, 1796.

Article 9th

If any person decline the acceptance of a mizvah, or in the performance thereof does not conduct himself acarding to the usual mode, the parnass shall not be permitted to give him any mizvah, nor shall his name be publickly mentioned in synagogue until he has made such concession to the parnas as the adjunta ["board"] shall think proper.

B [NO. 68]

To the Pornas and Trustees of K. K. S. Israel.
Gentleman:

I beg you will take into consideration my present situation and destress I am in at this present tine from the behaviour of my husband. I acknoledge he deservd some punishment, but as you have punished him with confinement, I hope it will be the means of his better conduct in future. I beg the favour of you gentleman to release him from confinement, being the first offence. I do promise in future to keep him from going to synagoge any more. Consider, gentleman, I am left without a husband and a friend to provide for me nesesirais [necessaries] of life in my present situation.

By complying with the above you will oblige your destresed friend,

G. Philips

New York, April 26th, 1796.

———

No. 69   New York Jewry Hires a Shohet—1796

One of the prime requirements of a Jewish community is kosher meat, and ever since they first came to New Amsterdam, the Jews managed to satisfy their needs. In the eighteenth century the shohet ["slaughterer"] was a paid officer of the congregation; the butchers or dispensers were usually Gentiles who handled also terefah ["nonkosher"] meats. Frequently the community had to cope with incompetent or careless slaughterers and butchers who attempted to palm off nonkosher meat. In 1796, for instance, the Common Council of the City of New York, upon complaint of the congregation, met and deprived Nicholas Smart of his butcher's license. Smart, a non-Jew, tried to live up to his family name and "fraudulently affixed Jewish seals to meat for sale in the Public Market." His license was restored to him several weeks later, and he was a chastened, if not a wiser, man.

In February of that year Shearith Israel elected a new shohet, Mark Solomons (1763–1830), a native of London. The congregation very likely secured him in Philadelphia, for he came to the copresidents of the synagogue with a letter of introduction from Levy Phillips, a member of the Simon-Gratz family of Philadelphia and Lancaster (Document A).

At the time of his appointment Solomons received a statement specifying his duties as shohet (Document B). One of the articles of the agreement required him to give the board three months' notice if he desired a raise in pay. That was one provision that he lived up to religiously: less than four months after he began his work, Solomons petitioned the Board of Trustees for an increase in salary. He began with an annual remuneration of £20 and tongues; by 1820, less than a quarter century later, he was drawing £80 and tongues.

SOURCE. American Jewish Historical Society Library, Lyons Collection, Nos. 215 and 262.

A [NO. 69]

Philadelphia, February 8th, [17]96.

Messrs. Simon Nathen and Alexander Zuntz.
Gentlemen:

I wrote you the 3d instant by post which hope came safe to hand wherein refer too.

The bearer hereof is Mr. Mark Solomon, your intended shochet. At the same time permit me to recommend him to your perticuler notice. I think him worthy of your attention and any service rendred him shall be acknowledged. I have advanced him by your order £3 for his passage and expences which please to give him as he'll stand in need of, been [being] in a strange place. I hope he will meet the merit of the congregation, which is my sincere wish.

With presenting my kind regard to both your ladys, I remain, gentlemen,

Your friend and obedient servant,
Levy Phillips

B [NO. 69]

Copy of Letter and Agreement with Mr. Solomons, Shochet K. K. S. I.

By request of the parnass and adjunto ["board"]: Enclose you a copy of your agreement with the congregation, and am desired to inform you that is expected you will pay particular attention in removing the seals in proper season [if the meat becomes ritually unfit] (as there has been a complaint of neglect in this respect), and also to seal the hind quarter of small [lamb, etc.], as well as large [beef] meats.

[To] Mr. Solomons

Copy of Agreement

Mr. Solomons agreed to except [accept] of the office of shochet and to observe the following rules:

1st. He shall supply the merket with a sufficiency of large and small meats for the congregation.

2d. The seals shall be plain and placed on different parts of the hind as well as the forequarter.

He shall also remove the seals from the meat whenever he thinks it becomes trepha. The crantz [permitted] fat shall be sealed [thus permitting its use] when requested by the butcher or a congregator.

He shall also be re-examined at the expiration of 12 mo. by such persons as may be appointed by the adjunto.

That three month notice shall be given to the trustees whenever an alteration in the salary appears necessary.

———

No. 70   Moses Gomez Steps Down—1796

In June, 1796, the board of Shearith Israel in New York received a brief note from Moses Gomez, Jr., asking for a cheaper seat in the synagogue. Circumstances had forced a leading member of the congregation literally to take a back seat.

In the early part of the eighteenth century the Gomezes could share with the Frankses the honor of being the most influential and wealthy family in the congregation. During the Revolution some of the members of the Gomez family took refuge in Philadelphia, but Moses junior remained loyal to the Crown. Some time after the war the shadow of the family diminished considerably. Moses Gomez, Jr. suffered financial reverses and was compelled to retrench. It is doubtful whether this was the aftermath of his Tory sympathies, for twenty years had elapsed since he took his stand with the Loyalists, and in such matters the patriots had very short memories once the war was concluded. A few years after he sent the following request to Shearith Israel, Gomez, in a letter asking a friend to support his application for appointment as auctioneer of the City of New York, attributed his difficulties to "losses and bankruptcy."

It was certainly not easy for the Gomezes to step down. The original American member of the family, Luis Moses Gomez, had fled from Spain and France and had come to the colonies, by way of England, almost a century before. Three, or possibly four, generations of the family had lived and died in New York. Evidently Moses junior was a cultured gentleman who wrote and spoke very good English, but his reverses constrained him to give up his choice seat and to ask the parnasim, one of whom was a former German commissary officer who spoke a broken English, for a cheaper location. Gomez' brief note unemotionally documents the financial decline of a branch of a once powerful and wealthy family.

SOURCE. American Jewish Historical Society Library, Lyons Collection, No. 202.

New York, June 19th, 1796.

Gentlemen:

Permit me to request the favor of discharging me from the seat I occupy in the synnagogue, in lieu thereof to allot me one not exceeding the price of 40s. per annum. My reduced circumstances and the arrears I am in for my present seat will not justify my continuing it. When ever in my power I shall, as I always have, consider my self bound to contribute to the support of our holy worship.

I am, gentlemen,

Respectfully your humble servant,
Moses Gomez, Jr.

Trustees of the K. K. ["Holy Congregation" of] S. Israel.

No. 71 Relief for Sufferers from the Yellow Fever—1798

Yellow fever was a scourge in the North American colonies from the middle seventeenth century, and it was to remain an ever-recurrent threat to the colonies and states into the second half of the nineteenth century.

In the summer of 1798 the malignant fever struck in New York City, carrying off over 2,000 persons. At least ten Jews died of the disease at that time. Because the poor and the stricken in the local

Jewish community needed financial help during the plague, a number of men met in the congregational booth during the harvest Festival of Booths (Sukkoth, September, 1798) and organized a relief society called *kalfe sedaka mattan basether* ("The Collection for Charity Given Secretly").

One of the managers of the fund, Samuel Lazarus, died less than three weeks after he assumed office. Lazarus was a great-grandfather of Emma Lazarus, whose sonnet "The New Colossus" is inscribed on the base of the Statue of Liberty.

In the course of a month over £41 was collected, and when the trustees of the congregation who had taken refuge in the countryside during the epidemic returned, they placed their stamp of approval on the new organization. The fund continued to exist and to grow, serving the impoverished and afflicted into the nineteenth century. One of the founders of this philanthropy, Cantor Seixas, proposed in 1805 that the funds collected be used to establish a hospital, but it was to be almost half a century before his suggestion bore fruit. Not until 1852 was the Jews' Hospital (Mount Sinai) incorporated.

SOURCE. Congregation Shearith Israel, New York, Minute Book.

Meeting of the trustees of Sheareth Israel on Sunday, the 18th November, 1798. . . .
Present:

Manuel Myers, pres.	Benjamin Seixas
Isaac Moses	Bernard Hart
Joshua Isaacs	

Mr. Moses moved, and [it] was seconded that the treasurer is authorized to deduct the offerings of the [paid] officers from the amount of their respective salarys quarterly.

The board, having taken into consideration the suffering of the officers during the late calamity, resolved that their [there] should be paid to the hazan ["cantor"] fifty dollars, to the shochet ["slaughterer"] twenty-five dollars, to the *shamas* ["beadle"] twenty-five dollars, to the clerk ten dollars, the money to be paid in the following manner, *viz.*:

Mr. Isaac Moses to advance fifty dollars to the hazan, Mr. Joshua Isaacs to advance twenty-five dollars to the shochet, to be deducted from the amount of their bills for the year 5559, the treasurer to pay the clerk and shamas out of the first monies collected after his ballance is paid.

Resolved, that the clerk give notice of the same to the respective officers.

Mr. Bernard Hart presented the following proceedings of a number of the congregation during the late epedemic which, being read, is as follows, viz.:

1st day of Sucoth, 15th Tisri, 5559.

Several members of the congregation (Shearith Israel in New York) being assembled in the *sucah* ["booth"] the hazan requested their attention to what he had to propose, which was nearly in the words following: That it had been suggested by some of our congregators to establish [a] fund abstractedly [apart] from the *sedaha* [treasury] to assist such poor or sick persons of our society as might be in want during the time our trustees should be absent from the city; and as the power vested in the *segan* [vice president] were very inadequate to any extraordinary matter, it would be necessary to appoint at least two members from the congregation [at large?] to be his associates in council, to superintend the direction of this institution; that the hazan had written to his brother Benjamin and had informed him of the problem[?], that he, Mr. Benjamin Seixas, had mentioned it to Mr. Moses, the parnas presidente of the congregation, who had written to the hazan; that he had no objection to such an institution being established, provided that the[re] should be but one offering only made to that fund; and in order to commence a fund for that express purpose, he would give five pounds thereto; and that he had nominated Mr. Samuel Lazarus as a proper person to be joined in the direction, upon which Mr. Lazarus was nominated and approved of unanimously. Mr. Isaac Abrahams was then proposed for the other associate and was also approved of unanimously. Mr. Barnard Hart, the *segan*, having likewise approved of the institution, he desired the hazan to ask the members chosen if they would accept of their appointment. They having replied in the affirmative, the following conditions were discussed and agreed to unanimously *viva voice [voce]*.

Conditions made and entered into by the members of our congregation assembled this day (as before recited) to establish an institution for the assistance of the poor or sick of our society:

1st. That every person be allowed to make one single offering at any proper time in the synagogue to any amount, or for any particular appreciation.

2dly. That the gentlemen appointed to act in counsel with Mr. B. Hart, the *segan*, be a committee to appropriate any sum or sums of money of the fund to such purposes as they judge proper, without being accountable to the contributors for their expenditures, and [that] the said committee continue in office untill the trustees of our congregation return to the city and be enabled to form a quorum.

3dly. If the trustees, when assembled, do not approve of the institution and should deprive them of the liberty of offering in the synagogue, then the contributors should meet and determine by a majority of voices in what manner the residue of the money which shall then be in stock shall be disposed of.

4thly. That the committee meet by themselves and chuse one of themselves to be their cashier, and any two of them be competent to determine in all cases, and any one of the three be allowed to dispend any sum not exceeding twenty shillings for any charitable purpose without being obliged to consult the other two, provided it be a case of emergency, and to draw on the cashier for that amount.

The whole of the preceeding was unanimously agreed to and G. Seixas offered his service to keep the account of offerings made to the fund and to collect the monies and pay such sums to the cashier, which was accepted of by the members.

2d day of Sucoth, 16th Tisri, 5559.

The *segan*, Mr. B. Hart, desired the hazan previous to the taking out of the *sepharim* ["Scrolls"] to acquaint those gentlemen who were not at the meeting yesterday of the design and usefulness of the institution, which he did, and to commend [commence] the fund contemplated in the foregoing by offering the fi[ve] pounds which Mr. Moses, the p. p. [parnas presidente], ordered in his letter to the hazan of 14th Tisri, which was followed by oferings of Messrs. Joshua Isaacs, p[arnas] presidente, B. Seixas, and B. Hart, as in the following list. *Viz.*:

16th Tisri, 5559.

Isaac Moses	£ 5 0 0	Simon Adler	£ 1 0 0
Joshua Isaacs	2 0 0	D. Valentinus	0 8 0
Benjamin Seixas	2 0 0	Henry Daniel	0 8 0
Barnard Hart	1 0 0	J. B. Kursheid	0 5 0
Samuel Lazarus	1 0 0	Moses Leon	0 5 0
Moses Lazarus	1 0 0	Isaac Abraham	0 5 0 . . .

[1]8th Hesvan, 5559.

In consequence of the demise of Mr. Samuel Lazarus, Mr. B. Hart, the *segan*, desired the hazan to inform the contributors to the fund that it was necessary to appoint another manager in place of our deceased friend and requested the gentlemen to attend after divine service for that purpose, which they did, and Mr. Kursheidt was nominated and approved of unanimously to continue in office for the time limited in the 2d article of the conditions agreed to in the *sucah* on the 15th Tisri last. The hazan then read the conditions which he had committed to paper by memory and refered them to their consideration to know if they corresponded with their ideas of the business, and having received their assent thereto, the meeting adjourned, *sine die.*

The foregoing institution, having been submitted to the trustees of the congregation, is hereby confirmed and approved of on the conditions therein specified so long as the trustees do not find it injurious to the *sedaka* [treasury] of Shearith Israel, reserving to themselves the power of prohibiting the offerings made thereto in synagogue whenever they find it necessary.

In conformity to the foregoing, resolved, that the hazan be requested to inform the congregation on Saturday next that a meeting will be held at the *hebra* [community building] on Sunday following, at 10 o'clock in the morning, in order to appoint managers for the said fund, one of which must be chosen out of the board of trustees who is to continue as a manager during the time he is a trustee, and whenever his seat is vacated by the time of his election having expired, and not being re-elected, or by a resignation, another trustee is to be elected in his place.

Meeting of the congregation of Shearith Israel on Sunday, the 25th November, 1798, agreeable to proclamation for the purpose of appointing managers for the charitable institution. Present:

Benjamin Seixas	J. B. Kursheidt
Joshua Isaacs	Mordecai Myers
Moses Lazarus	Naphtali Judah
Gershom Seixas	Bernard Hart
Jacob Hart	Isaac Abrahams
Cary Judah	

Mr. Joshua Isaacs unanimously elected chairman.

On motion made and seconded, resolved, that the managers be chosen to serve untill the first Sunday in Tamus, 5560 [1800]. And in case there should be any reason or in the course of the year by absence or otherwise, then the contributors to meet and chuse another in lieu of the person absent. And in case of a trustee being absent or his seat vacated at the board, another trustee to be chosen in his place so that the managers shall always consist of one trustee and two contributors; and should the managers or ei[ther] of them be elected a trustee during the time they were elected to serve out of the number of contributors, then a new election must be held to choose another in his or their steads.

On motion made and seconded, resolved, that this meeting proceed to chuse by ballot three managers, conformable to the above, and that the ballots be taken singly for each. First, Mr. Bernart Hart, trustee, was ballotted for and elected a manager; secondly, Mr. Isaac Abrahams; and thirdly, Mr. J. B. Kursheidt, all of whom were elected managers by a majority of votes.

III The General Community

No. 72 Moses Lopez Becomes a Naturalized Citizen—1741

In 1740 Parliament passed an act for the naturalization of foreign Protestants and others. The motivation of this break with history and the toleration of dissenters and Jews is reflected in the opening statement of the law: "Whereas the increase of people is a means of advancing the wealth and strength of any nation or country, etc." Among those included under the benefits of the act were Jews who had resided in the colonies for a period of seven years. They were exempted from the requirement of receiving the sacrament of the Lord's Supper, and in taking the oath they were permitted to omit the phrase "upon the true faith of a Christian." Mercantilism was ready to throw the mantle of charity over the Jews in the colonies.

Naturalization did not, however, grant Jews complete equality. Political office was frequently dependent on a religious test. In essence, naturalization was a form of denization, granting in a formal fashion the right of settlement and the privilege of doing business. For the time being the Jew had to be content with these gains; they were more than he could hope for in most European lands, even in England.

The naturalization certificate printed below is probably the oldest one granted to a Jew that is extant in North America. Its recipient was Moses Lopez (*ca.* 1706–67), a New York merchant.

Lopez was a Portuguese émigré who fled to this country, arriving here or in one of the West India colonies in the 1730's. As far as we know, he was the first of his clan to come to the North American mainland. José, as he was called in Portugal, changed his name to

Moses when he came among Jews. In 1752 he was joined by a younger half brother, Duarte, who took the name Aaron. By that time Moses was in Newport, whither he had moved in the 1740's. He was one of the pioneers of its reconstituted Jewish community, and there he was to remain until his death.

During the generation he lived in that New England city he was a merchant, a translator, and a potash and candle manufacturer. During the 1760's he was also working for his brother Aaron, who within a decade was to emerge as one of the great merchant-shippers of New England. Apparently Moses was never too successful.

SOURCE. American Jewish Archives, the Nathan-Kraus-Van Praag Collection.

George the Second, by the Grace of God of Great Britain, France, and Ireland, King, Defender of the Faith, etc. To all to whom these presents shall come or may concern, greeting:

Know ye that it appears unto us by good testimony that Moses Lopez, of the city of New York, merchant, being a person professing the Jewish religion, hath resided and inhabited for the space of seven years and upwards within some of our colonies in America, and that the said Moses Lopez, on the twenty third day of October last, betwixt the hours of nine and twelve in the forenoon of the same day, in our Suprem Court of Judicature of our Province of New York, before our judges of our said court, did take and subscribe the oaths of allegiance and supremacy and the abjuration oath, pursuant to the directions of an act of our Parliament of Great Britain, made and passed in the thirteenth year of our reign, entitled "An Act for Naturalizing Such Foreign Protestants and Others therein Mentioned as Are Settled or Shall Settle in Any of His Majesty's Colonies in America," and that the said Moses Lopez's name is registred as a natural born subject of Great Britain, both in our said Supreme Court and in our Secretarie's office of our said province, in books for that purpose severally and particularly kept, pursuant to the directions of the aforesaid act.

In testimony whereof we have caused the great seal of our said Province of New York to be hereunto affixed. Witness our trusty and well beloved George Clarke, Esq., our Lieutenant Governor and Commander in Chief of our Province of New York and the territories thereon depending in America, etc., the thirteenth day of April, *Anno Domini* 1741, and in the fourteenth year of our reign.

George Joseph Moore, deputy secretary

No. 73 A Lottery for the Relief of an Imprisoned Debtor—1748

A man named Joseph Fox, probably a scrivener by profession, had been thrown into prison at Newport for debt. His pitiable condition invited the compassion of his neighbors, for he had no means and his wife and children were dependent on him. A number of men therefore petitioned the General Assembly of Rhode Island to license a lottery for the purpose of raising money for the release of the unfortunate prisoner.

Among the 112 signers of the appeal were but two Jews, Abraham Hart and Moses Lopez. This is not surprising, however, for there was no Jewish community in Newport at the time. The Jewish merchants were to come in during the following decade.

SOURCE. Rhode Island State Archives, Providence, Petitions to the General Assembly, VII, 33.

To the honourable the General Assembly of His Majesty's Colony of Rhode Island, etc., to be held at Providence, within and for the colony aforesaid, on the last Wednesday of October, A.D. 1748:

We, the subscribers, being sensible of the difficult circumstances of Joseph Fox, who has been in Newport Prison above a year and a half, upon a judgment obtained at the suit of Messrs. Hardman, Ogden and Company, merchants in Liverpool, in Great Britain, for about the sum of three thousand pounds, a debt truly another's and not his own, beg leave to represent in his behalf to this Honourable Assembly that, as he is well known to many of us, we are assured that it is impossible he should ever be able to raise that sum, so that in all likelyhood, he must remain in prison during his life, and his wife and children suffer unless relieved by the charitable disposition of the publick, private charities being too small ever to raise that sum, and all he can get by his pen (his only way of getting a penny, being hardly enough for to provide for his wife and children) is not, or can be, any foundation to build hopes of relief on.

Therefore, we are willing, and doubt not most men who know or have heard of his hard measure are well inclined to contribute to his discharge, provided a fit way could be found out to raise a sum sufficient for that purpose, which has by some of us been thought on. And therefore [we] pray this honourable Assembly to grant liberty for a charitable lottery to be set on foot in Newport for that end, according to a scheme to be offered herewith for your Honours' approbation (or any better or other scheme this Assembly shall determine on), under the direction of certain gentlemen to be by your Honours chosen for the management of it.

And, as this is a method heretofore used by other governments on the like occasion, to wit, that of charity to a distressed person and his whole family, we doubt not of Your Honours' allowance of [it].

And, as in duty bound, will ever pray, etc.,

Joseph Scott, . . . Abraham Hart, . . . Moses Lopez, . . .

No. 74   Sir Alexander Cuming Plans to Settle Jews in the Cherokee Mountains—1750

In the middle of the eighteenth century Sir Alexander Cuming, of Culter, a Scottish nobleman, came forward with a strange scheme. Claiming that the family of the reigning House of Hanover owed him £50,000 for services rendered, he asked that the British government pay this debt. In return he offered to use his influence as ruler of the Cherokees—whom he had visited twenty years earlier—to establish a bank in the Cherokee Mountains. Then he would settle 300,000 Jewish families in the area and would pay the national debt of £80,000,000.

When Cuming wrote the letter in which he set forth his project to the Duke of Bedford, the secretary for the Southern Department (who had charge of colonial affairs), he was a debtor imprisoned in the Fleet. Obviously Sir Alexander was not completely sane. But what lay behind his weird proposal?

Throughout the period, and particularly in the 1730's and 1740's, humanitarians, mercantilists, and Anglican ecclesiastical imperialists were working together to settle the colonies with impoverished Protestants. They felt that economics, religion, and politics would be served by mass immigration and large-scale settlement. The colonies would be stocked with people, the Carolinas would be protected from the Spanish in Florida, the social problem would be solved, raw materials would pour into England, manufactured goods would stream out, and God would be glorified by the expansion of Christianity. Out of this confluence of notions came the settlement of Georgia in 1733.

English Jews, too, were enraptured by such a solution of their social welfare problem, and during the entire period Anglo-Jewish leaders nursed the hope of sending large numbers of their impoverished coreligionists to Nova Scotia, the Carolinas, and Georgia.

A small number actually sailed for Georgia in 1733 and became the Jewish founding fathers of Savannah.

SOURCE. Department of Archives and History, Atlanta, Ga., Colonial Records of Georgia. Originals in the Public Record Office, London.

> From his Majesty's Prison, the Fleet,
> London, May 24th, 1750.

My Lord Duke:

If twenty years esperience may be deemed sufficient to convince me that I ought to lay claim to the Cherokee Mountains and to the territories thereunto belonging, as an inheritance bestowed upon me by the favour of Providence and the unanimous consent of a free people, whose minds, although savage, seemed to have been influenced by His overruling Spirit to chuse a Christian for their lawgiver, their leader, and chief, I cannot but conceive that this was intended as a rational means to propare the way for bringing in the Gentiles, and for the conversion of the Jews to the purity of the Christian faith.

As my deceased father was made the instrument of Providence to save his present [the late?] Britannick Majesty [George I] from being lost, and had thereupon assurances of being raised to the first honours of this kingdom if his Majesty had lived to have power in England; as a salary of three hundred pounds [per] annum was settled upon me for secret services (contrary to my inclination and contrary to my judgment), and was to pass as a security through the hands of the late Duke of Argyle, commencing at Christmas, 1718, and to be continued until I should be otherwise provided for to my satisfaction; as the payments of this salary have been discontinued from Christmas, 1721;

I humbly conceive that the damages I have sustained from thence ought to be charged to the administration of government, as a debt of honour and conscience, which no administration in this kingdom can ever get fairly rid of until the said damages shall be made good to me, with interest, so long as his present Majesty, or any person descending from his royal loins, shall sit upon the throne of these kingdoms [Great Britain and Ireland].

My damages, computed at a very moderate rate, amount now to fifty thousand pounds sterling, with which sum (if it should be allowed to me by Mr. Palham [Henry Pelham] and the ministry as a publick debt and secured to me as such by the British Parliament) I should propose not only to discharge my own debts, but would also propose, with the blessings of Providence, to discharge eighty millions of the national debts of Great Britain in sixteen years, upon the supposition of being also encouraged, at the same time, by the said authority, to set up a bank in the Cherokee Mountains, as an inducement for three hundred thousand families of Jews to settle there for the improvement of those lands, as industrious, honest subjects to the legislative authority of the British nation, under the direction and protection of God himself as their Supreme Lawgiver, the great Ruler and Governor of this world, and who must be acknowledged by them and by all men to be the King of Judah and Israel, when his kingdom, the kingdom of righteousness, shall at last be established upon earth.

Whether this plan be approved of or rejected by your Grace and the ministry, I beg you will honour me with an answer and favour me with your commands hereupon, who am, with esteem and great regard, my Lord Duke,

Your Grace's most obedient and most humble servant,
Alexander Cuming

To His Grace, the Duke of Bedford, one of his Majesty's principal secretaries of state.

No. 75   Moses Lopez, Spanish Interpreter—1750

By virtue of the fact that most Jewish immigrants to the colonies came from non-English-speaking lands, they were at least bilingual and therefore able to serve as interpreters.

As early as 1695 John Archdale, governor of the "Pleasant Province of Carolina," had a Jew as a Spanish interpreter. Zachariah Polock was a Dutch interpreter in Rhode Island in the 1740's; Haym Salomon, the Whig patriot, was released from a British jail in New York in the course of the Revolutionary War in order to serve the German mercenaries, whose language he understood; and in the post-Revolutionary period Isaac Pinto served as Spanish interpreter for the federal government.

Moses Lopez, a Newport merchant, was already engaged as a Spanish interpreter for the Rhode Island Vice-Admiralty Court in 1743. The record shows that when called upon to act in an official capacity, "Mr. Moses Lopez, being a Jew, was sworn on the Five Books of Moses in court to give a true interpretation in this case." In all probability he was paid for his services.

Lopez was employed also by the colonial authorities of Rhode Island as an interpreter. In 1750 he addressed a petition, printed below, to the General Assembly of that colony, pointing out that although he was the government's Spanish interpreter, he had never accepted any pay. As a reward for his services, however, he asked to be exempted from all personal duties or obligations. His petition was granted.

SOURCE. Rhode Island State Archives, Petitions to the General Assembly, VII, 130.

To the Honourable the General Assembly of his Majesty's Colony of Rhode Island, etc., now conveied [convened] at Newport in said colony.

The humble petition of Moses Lopez of Newport aforesaid, merchant, sheweth:

That your petitioner hath for several years past translated divers letters and papers from the Spanish into English for the use of the government, which he declined being paid for, inasmuch as it was for the use aforesaid, and is ready and willing at all times to do the like, and desires no other gratuity than only to be exempted from all other personal duties in said colony during his residing in the same.

Therefore, your petitioner humbly prays that your Honours would maturely consider the same and grant that your petitioner may be exempted from all personal duties in said colony during his continuance in the same, the above mentioned [translations] only excepted.

And your petitioner, as in duty bound, will ever pray, etc.

Moses Lopez

Newport, August 24th, 1750.

No. 76   Alexander Schomberg Reports on the Fighting at Quebec—1759

During the eighteenth century it was very difficult, though probably not impossible, for an unbaptized Jew to serve as a high-ranking officer in the British navy. That Alexander Schomberg (1716–1804), although he was probably a convert to Christianity, could make a career for himself in the British armed forces of that period is evidence of the spirit of toleration that manifested itself after the Glorious Revolution. Out of this toleration was to come in the next century the principle of equality of rights, both in Britain and in the United States.

Captain Schomberg was a native of Germany and the son of Meyer Löw Schomberg, a Jew. His father, a physician, emigrated to England and soon became one of London's outstanding practitioners. Alexander entered the navy and by 1759 was in command of the frigate *Diana,* under Admiral Charles Saunders. In July and August of that year he participated in the attack on Quebec.

In the letter to Admiral John Forbes, printed below, Schomberg described the fortunes of war to one of his superiors in England. During the battle his ship had been driven onto the rocks and, it may be assumed, was taken back to Boston, Massachusetts, for repairs. Schomberg intended to convoy a fleet of ships, carrying masts from the king's woods in New England, from the Bay Colony back to England. Less than two weeks after Schomberg had written the letter Quebec surrendered to the British.

SOURCE. The Library of Congress, Division of Manuscripts. Original in the British Museum, London; Hardwicke papers, Add. MS 35893, folio 237–38.

Boston, Sept. 5, 1759.

Sir:

It is probable that the letters which I wrote to you from the [St. Lawrence] River have not yet come to your hand. I therefore send this by a merchantman which is this morning going to run it for England.

I am just arrived, and left the fleet and army the 11th of August. The admiral [Saunders] and general [James Wolfe] were continuing their operations, and every thing was *going on.*

The enemy is entrenched from the River Charles to the Fall of Montmorency [near Quebec City], and Gen. Wolfe has taken post on the eastern side of the Fall. Brigadier [Robert] Monckton is encamped on the Point Levi [Levis] side [opposite Quebec], and with his batteries (about 1,200 yards from the lower town) he has done much mischief to both the upper and lower town of Quebec.

The *Sutherland* and *Squirrel* are both above the town. I was attempting to pass it July the 19th at night, by the admiral's direction, but a sloop most unfortunately ran me on board, and I could not disengage myself from her 'till I was forced into an eddy tide which carried me on the rocks.

I was but barely out of gun-shot from Quebec, which occasioned the sending the floating batteries out to insult us. However, they did not prevent out [our] working, nor did they do us any material mischief; but had they been more enterprizing, I think they might *at first* have destroyed us, for we lay with our larboard streak exposed.

The wind is westerly and I must dispatch my letter. Aug. 1st a descent was made at the entrenchments of *Beauport,* but it was ineffectual. As my ship was *hors de campagne* ["out of the field"], I had offered myself for any service if the admiral thought I could be usefull, and he gave me the landing of Monkton's brigade.

The fire was very extraordinary, nor did I imagine that the fire of musquetry could have been kept up so uninterruptedly and do so little damage. The enemy's being above us can only account for it. We lost about fifty and, I guess, about 200 wounded. I have mislaid the return, but I think that was the number.

On the retreat, our troops were very regular, and retired across the Falls and to the boats with a sullen pride and in good order. The general thinks [they retired] in better order than when they first got on shore, and he taxes his grenadiers with too much ardour. I can write no more of this day.

In short, sir, the enemy's situation is very advantageous, and his number very superior. General Wolfe appears in his conduct more like *Fabius Maximus* [cautious] than *Achilles,* notwithstanding what has been said of his impetuosity by his enemies and rivals.

When refitted, I shall take upon me the charge of the mast ships, and conduct them to England.

I am, sir, with great respect, etc., etc.,

Alexander Schomberg

————

No. 77   The Naturalization of James Lucena—1761

In 1761 James Lucena petitioned the Rhode Island General Assembly for the privilege of naturalization (Document A). The petition was granted and Lucena took the necessary oaths (Document B).

Lucena, a cousin of the Lopezes of Newport, was in reality a Jew. He was born in Portugal where, of course, he had to live as a Marrano, a Christian. It was fear of the Inquisition that probably drove him to a more tolerant land, but the fact that he fled did not necessarily mean that he wished to live as a Jew. In Portugal he was subject to suspicion, arrest, and even torture, merely by virtue of his Jewish origin. When tortured, almost any Marrano would admit to Jewish practices, whether guilty or not. Many a Marrano, therefore, after safely arriving in a land of tolerance, continued to remain Christian because he had no real interest in Judaism. He had fled merely to escape the actual or potential menace of the Inquisition, which threatened his life and property. Lucena was obviously such a refugee; he was certainly not an émigré for conscience' sake. Thus, when he took the oaths, he did not hesitate to swear "upon the true faith of a Christian." Unlike his cousin Aaron Lopez, he was not interested in taking the oath prescribed for Jews by the tolerant Naturalization Act of 1740.

Lucena, then an Anglican by religion, settled in Savannah in the middle 1760's, became a justice of the peace, remained loyal to the Crown during the Revolution, and returned to Portugal, where he died, as he had been born, within the Roman Catholic Church.

SOURCE. Rhode Island State Archives, Petitions to the General Assembly, 1758–61, X, 147.

A [NO. 77]

Rhode Island, SS.:

To the Honourable General Assembly of the Colony of Rhode Island, now sitting in East Greenwich, in the County of Kent. Humbly sheweth:

James Lucena, now of Newport, in the county of Newport, merchant, that some time ago he came into this colony with his family and brought his estate with him, with a design to settle here, and prays that your Honours would be pleased to pass an act for his being naturalized upon his taking the necessary oaths. And as in duty bound will ever pray, etc.

James Lucena

February 26th, 1761.
To the House of Magistrates.
Gentlemen:

Resolvd that the above petition be granted and that an act be drawn up accordingly. Voted and past.

Per order, J. Lyndon, clerk

Read on the 27th in the Upper House and concurred.

By order, Henry Ward, secretary

B [NO. 77]

I, James Lucena, do sincerely promise and swear that I will be faithfull and bear true allegiance to his Majesty, King George. So help me God.

James Lucena

And I do swear that I do from my heart abhor, detest, and abjure, as impious and heretical, that dam[n]able doctrine and position, that princes excommunicated or deprived by the Pope, or any authority of the See of Rome, may be deposed or murdered by their subjects, or any other whatsoever. And I do declare that no foreign prince, person, prelate, state, or potentate hath, or ought to have, any jurisdiction, power, superiority, pre-heminence, or authority, ecclesiastical or spiritual, within this realm.

So help me God.

James Lucena

I, James Lucena, do truly and sincerely acknowledge, profess, testify, and declare in my conscience, before God and the world, that our sovereign lord, King George, is lawfull and rightfull king of this realm and all other the dominions and countries thereunto belonging.

And I do solemnly and sincerely declare that I do believe in my conscience that the person pretended to be Prince of Wales during the life of the late King James, 2d, and since his decease pretending to be and taking upon himself the stile and title of King of England, by the name of James, 3d, or of Scotland by the name of James, 8th, or the stile and title of King of Great Britain, hath not any right or title whatsoever to the crown of this realm, or any other the dominions thereunto belonging.

And I do renounce, refuse, and abjure any allegiance or obedience to him; and I do swear that I will bear faith and true allegiance to his Majesty, King George, and him will defend to the utmost of my power against all traiterous conspiracies and attempts whatsoever which shall be made against his person, crown, or dignity.

And I will do my utmost endeavours to disclose or make known, to his Majesty and his successors, all treasons and traiterous conspiracies which I shall know to be against him or any of them. And I do faithfully promise, to the utmost of my power, to support, maintain, and defend the succession of the crown against him the said [King] James, and all other persons whatsoever, which succession by an act entituled, "An act for the further limitation of the crown, and better securing the rights and liberties of the subject," is and stands limited to the late Princess Sophia, Electress and Dutchess Dowager of Hanover, and the heirs of her body, being Protestants.

And all these things I do plainly and sincerely acknowledge and swear, according to the express words by me spoken, and according to the plain and common sense and understanding of the said words, without any equivocation, mental evasion, or secret reservation whatsoever. And I do make this recognition, acknowledgment, abjuration, renunciation, and promise heartily, willingly, and truly, upon the true faith of a Christian. So help me God.

James Lucena

Taken and subscribed this sixth day of March, 1761, and in the first year of his Majesty's reign in the presence of his Honour the Deputy Governor and the Secretary.

Henry Ward, secretary

J. Gardner, deputy governor.

No. 78   Newport Inhabitants Ask for More Equitable
Proportioning of Taxes—1762

The Naturalization Act of 1740 encouraged Jews in the British
colonies to seek naturalization. In spite of this tolerant attitude of
Parliament, some of the colonies found ways to circumvent the intent of the law. Rhode Island, for instance, naturalized no Jew who
refused to take the oath "upon the true faith of a Christian."
Nevertheless, the Jews were encouraged to take an active part in
the life of the larger, non-Jewish community, and they did.

The petition printed below is a protest by seventy-eight Newport
inhabitants against what they considered an unjust form of assess-
ing taxes. Ten of the signers were Jews. The list included practically
every Jewish householder in the community.

SOURCE. Rhode Island State Archives, Petitions to the General
Assembly, XI, 37.

To the honourable the General Assembly, setting by adjournment at East
Greenwich, in the County of Kent [Rhode Island], on the twenty third
day of August, 1762:

The petition of us, the subscribers, inhabitants of the Town of Newport, humbly sheweth:

That the Town of Newport in June last ordered a rate to be made of
£12,000, to discharge the town debts:

That Messrs. James Tew, Charles Spooner, and Elisha Gibbs, Junior,
were appointed rate-makers for the town, who accordingly assessed said
rate and delivered the bill in, to have it collected; which bill, in the
humble opinion of your petitioners, is very unequally proportioned, and
besides, upwards of one hundred persons [are] not rated, many of whom
are freeholders and freemen of the town, as appears by a former rate-bill.
And your petitioners have the highest reason to beleive, that from so
great a number of persons being omitted, and comparing the sums against
the names of those who are rated, that said rate is assessed in a very
negligent, careless, or partial manner.

Therefore, your petitioners humbly pray that your Honors would take
this matter into consideration and pass an act to make void said rate and
discharge said rate-makers from their office, and appoint for the remainder of the year, one merchant, one farmer, and one tradesman
[craftsman], or impower the town to chuse them; and that one merchant,
one farmer, and one tradesman be annually chosen rate-makers at the
town election;

That the rate-makers for the future shall have power, upon complaint, to redress, alter, and confirm any rate in the rate-bill which shall be made [and] appear to them to be over or under charged; and that they shall appoint and give notice of the time and place to hear any complaints that shall be made, and rate any person that may be omitted within one month after the rate is assessed.

And your petitioners further pray that when the collector receives the new rate-bill for the aforementioned rate, that he may immediately inform every person his or her rate, and those who shall have already paid him be authorized to receive from, or return to, each person the difference that may appear to be in their respective rates.

And your petitioners, as in duty bound, shall ever pray.

Silas Cooke, . . .	Jacob Isaacks, . . .
Naphtali Hart, Junior, . . .	Moses Levy, . . .
Naphtali Hart, . . .	Aaron Lopez, . . .
Isaac Hart, . . .	Isaac Elizer, . . .
Issachar Polock, . . .	Nathan Hart, . . .
Jacob Rodrigues Rivera, . . .	

No. 79   Hospitals for Smallpox Inoculations—1763

Smallpox was one of the greatest scourges the American colonists had to face. About 150 of Newport's substantial citizens, or freemen, were convinced in 1763 that inoculation (variolation) was God's— and man's—answer to that problem. Accordingly, they petitioned the Rhode Island General Assembly to establish government hospitals where people could be inoculated voluntarily.

There was only one Jew among the signers: Jacob Isaacks. Apparently the other Jewish merchants were not asked to sign because, unlike Isaacks, they were not native-born Americans.

SOURCE. Rhode Island State Archives, Petitions to the General Assembly, XI, 1771.

Colony of Rhode Island.
To the honourable the General Assembly of the colony, to be holden at Newport, within and for said colony, upon the second Monday of June, A.D., 1763:
We whose names are under written, freemen of the said colony, desire leave to represent to you that it is now known and very generally admitted, that of all the diseases with which Almighty God has been pleased to visit or afflict mankind, there is not one more universal[ly] wasting or unavoidable than the small pox.
It is also now manifest and very certain that the finger of Divine

Providence has at last clearly pointed out a safe method of alleviating the distress and diminishing the ravage or loss in the natural small pox by engrafture or inoculation, the salutary and sure effects of which method has been largely and faithfully experienced through out Europe, and advantageously proved by many persons within this colony.

Moved, therefore, with commiseration of our selves and many others who are earnestly desirous of partaking the benefit of inoculation, but [who can do nothing] for want of opportunity and incapacity of circumstances, with many other considerations too tedious to enumerate and not necessary to particularize to the General Assembly,

We, therefore, very humbly petition and pray that Gold Island, Coasters Harbour, or some other proper safe, detached place may be fixed upon and appointed by authority of the General Assembly for erecting a fitt publick and well-accomodated hospital, under proper government and direction, for inoculating all such persons as are willing and qualifyed subiects for it, whereby the terrors and loss from this cruel distemper may be prevented, and large sums of gold and silver money saved and kept within the colony.

And your petitioners, as in duty bound, will ever pray.

Martin Howard, Jr., . . . Jacob Isaacks, . . .

No. 80   A Number of Rhode Island Merchants Ask for the Regulation of Customhouse Officers' Fees—1764

After the French and Indian War (1754–63), the British government sought to strengthen the bonds of empire by enforcing old trade laws and by enacting new ones. Furthermore, the colonies were to pay their share of the war debt of £140,000,000, largely incurred in the cause of driving the French out of North America. Imperial control was tightened, particularly with regard to international commerce. The trend is reflected in the Sugar Act, which went into effect in 1764, the year in which the following petition was submitted to the Rhode Island General Assembly.

Evidently the customs officers in Rhode Island had already begun to enforce the existing regulations and apparently demanded excessive fees. In any event, the days of "salutary neglect" in customs enforcement were a thing of the past. The Rhode Island merchants objected strenuously to the course pursued by the customs officials. Times were bad and the merchants sought to pay as little as possible in duties and fees. They therefore requested the colonial Assembly to legislate with respect to fees.

Any such action of the Assembly would obviously assert the colonial prerogative as against the imperial prerogative; it would assert the right of self-government against Whitehall's trend toward centralization. Hence the petition reflects in a modest fashion the growing struggle between the colonies and the mother country.

The Upper House acted cautiously. A joint committee of both houses was to investigate the matter and report its findings and recommendations to the Assembly.

Of the forty-six merchants who signed the petition, five were Jews. Yet when the break came in 1776, only one of the five seems to have been an out-and-out Whig.

SOURCE. Rhode Island State Archives, Petitions to the General Assembly, XI, 144.

To the honorable the General Assembly, to be holden at Newport, within and for the Colony of Rhode Island, on the last Monday in July, 1764:

The subscribers, in behalf of themselves and the trading part of the colony, beg leave humbly to represent to your Honors:

That without trade it will be impossible for the inhabitants of this colony to procure themselves any tolerable subsistence;

That at this time, when our commerce is restrained and circumscribed within very narrow limits, and under the most discouraging situation, our circumstances are rendered still more deplorable by the grievous exactions of his Majesty's custom house officers, who without any pretence of law or equity have burthened our trade with the most unreasonable and extravagant impositions;

That by these means the trade of the colony is in danger of being entirely ruined, and the coasting trade especially is so oppressed that several coasters have already been obliged to lay up their vessels, as their whole freight in some instances will not pay their port charges in Newport.

And, therefore, we pray Your Honors to pass an act for regulating the fees of the custom house officers in this colony, and restricting them from taking any greater fees than they shall be allowed by law, under such penalties as shall be thought sufficient to put a stop to this evil, which will be so fatal in its consequences to this colony.

And your petitioners, as in duty bound, will ever pray, etc.

Peleg Thurston, . . .	Naphtali Hart, Junior, . . .
Isaac Elizer, . . .	Moses Levy, . . .
Issachar Polock, . . .	Aaron Lopez, . . .

No. 81   The Affair Walker—1764

From the time of the British conquest until 1764 Canada was under the government of the military, who ruled with a high hand. Typical of the experiences of civilians under such rule was that of Thomas Walker, an Englishman who had come to Canada about 1763. In 1764, while he was a justice of the peace, soldiers broke into his home, brutally assaulted him, and cut off one of his ears. The civilian population, greatly exercised by this outrage, appealed to Governor James Murray for redress. Among the responsible signers of the petition, printed below, was Ezekiel Solomons, who very probably signed not only for himself but also for his Jewish associates.

Solomons, a Jew from Berlin, had come to Canada with the British troops. He was a member of a combine of five army purveyors and, after the fall of New France, turned to fur trading, operating primarily at Mackinac. It was there, in June, 1763, that he was captured by Indians who seized the fort. Subsequently ransomed, Solomons was the first Jewish settler of present-day Michigan.

When the Americans invaded Canada in 1775, Walker, a victim of great injustice, went over to their side; Solomons, like most Canadian merchants, remained loyal to the Crown. Although the majority of English and Jewish Canadian merchants were not in sympathy with the British attempt to placate the French Roman Catholics, and resented the disregard for Anglo-Saxon traditions of self-government, they stood with their mother country against the Americans.

SOURCE. Archives du Séminaire de Québec.

To His Excellency, James Murray, Esq., Captain General and Governor in Chief of the Province of Quebec, Vice Admiral of the same, etc., etc., etc., and to the honorable the members of his Majesty's Council for the said province, etc.:

The remonstrance and petition of us, his Majesty's loyal subjects, the merchants, traders, and others of the city of Montreal, humbly sheweth:

That whereas, on Thursday, the sixth inst., at about the hours of eight and nine at night, a number of persons, disguised and masqued, forcibly entered the house of Thomas Walker, Esq., merchant of this city, and one of his Majesty's justices of the peace for this district, and did there bruise, cutt, and maime, in the most inhuman manner, the aforesaid Thomas Walker, Esq., also one of his servants, who providentially made his escape and alarmed the city, notwithstanding which neither the guards or centinels took the least notice, or lent any aid or assistance;

That on application being made to Brigadier Ralph Burton, commanding the troops, concerning the same, the quarters were ordered to be searched, if possible to find out who were absent; but we are sorry to say that so salutary and well timed [an] order had not its intended effect;

That on the eighth inst., the inhabitants of this city assembled and made a subscription for a reward to any one who would inform against any person or persons concerned in this intended massacre, and at the same time presented a letter to Brigadier Burton, begging his assistance in recommending it to the officers of the army in general to do their utmost in aiding and assisting to find out the perpetrators of this most horrid act; and that in case it should be a soldier who should give such information, and a party concerned, that he might have his discharge, and be sent without punishment to any of his Majesty's colonies whe[re] he should choose to go; in consequence of which letter, we received for answer the fullest assurances of his Excellency's assistance; and he accordingly recommended the same to the officers in general, and we did not doubt but that [we] should soon have the satisfaction to bring the authors to justice.

But how great is our disapointment to find that every method is taken to frustrate the discovery of the delinquents; that when soldiers are taken up on suspicion or information, they are encouraged and supported by some of their officers, and not suffered to be examined any other way than before said officers, and that in public. These are steps so unprecendented in affairs of this nature, which are only found out by private and cross examination, that we are under the greatest apprehensions for our liberties.

There is now in custody one Serjeant Rogers of the 28th Regiment, who, from sundry circumstances and proofs, we have all the reason to think was a principal, and who is in the most open manner supported and encouraged by sundry officers of said regiment. We were even under the apprehension of a rescue, and from the threats of both officers and soldiers who, from the encouragement the latter meet with, breath death and distruction to us, more particularly the civil majistrates, that we are not secure even in our houses, but are under hourly apprehensions, and the necessity of accompanying each other in the streets, and defending our houses by night in rotation, which prompts us to beg the protection of your Excellency and the honourable the members of the Council, and that such salutary measures may be taken as in your great wisdoms may be judged most proper to releive us, in this our most melancholy situation.

We furthermore humbly pray that some speedy and effectual method may be taken for the support of the civil majistrates in the execution of their duty, who are discouraged from it by menaces and avowed threats, a glaring instance of one having been put in to execution, insomuch that at this present we have only two majistrates who dare act, and that at the risque of their lives.

We would beg leave further to add that Brigadier Ralph Burton has lent all the assistance possible, as well as recommending it in the strongest manner to those under his command, for which at a general meeting we returned a letter of thanks, being highly sensible of his Excellency's readiness and eager desires to discover the assassins, and also that Thomas Lamb, Esq., has, notwithstanding the very ill state of his health, acted with such firmness and taken such indefatigable pains since this most melancholy affair, in order to find out the delinquents, that the inhabitants of this city in general could never think of parting with so good a majistrate, and at so critical a juncture. And we humbly hope that the present calamitous affair will plead an excuse for his not obeying your summons.

And your petitioners will for ever pray.

James Crofton, Ezekeil Solomon & Co. . . .
Montreal, December 12th, 1764.

No. 82   Petition for a Lottery to Pave a Street—1768

As we have already seen, the Jews were on occasion invited to participate in the life of the larger community, even though they were not granted full political rights in any colony in the eighteenth century. Their political disabilities were primarily connected with officeholding, which was made difficult for Jews because of a Christian test oath.

Thus it was that the Jews of Rhode Island, who were not completely enfranchised until well into the nineteenth century, were invited in 1768 to sign a petition asking the General Assembly to authorize a lottery, the proceeds of which were to be used to pave a street in Newport. After considering the petition, the Assembly licensed a lottery to raise the sum of $500.

Of the twelve signers of the following document, three were Jews. One of them, Isaac Hart, seems to have been the outstanding member of the Newport Hart clan. He was a wealthy merchant of some culture. During the French and Indian War he was very much interested in privateering. When the Revolution broke out, he remained a stanch Loyalist and, though he was a civilian, was shot and killed by the Whigs in a guerrilla foray (1780).

SOURCE. Rhode Island State Archives, Petitions to the General Assembly, XII, 125.

Colony of Rhode Island, etc.

To the honorable General Assembly, to be holden at East Greenwich on the last Monday in February, 1768:

The petition of the subscribers humbly sheweth that the street named Kings-Street in Newport is a very publick street and much used, that it hath never yet been paved and in the winter season is almost impassable, and that the paving of it will accommodate many people.

Wherefore, they humbly pray Your Honors to grant a lottery for raising five hundred dollars, in one or more classes, as the directors shall think best to be applied to paving said street, and that Messrs. John Mawdsley, John Jepson, Pardon Tillinghast, William Gyles, James Taylor, and Benjamin Greene may be appointed directors of said lottery, they giving bond according to custom.

And your petitioners, as in duty bound, will ever pray, etc.

John Banister, . . .	Isaac Hart,
Isaac Elizer, . . .	Jacob Isaacks, . . .

———

No. 83   Coal for America—1768

The following memorial was presented to the Privy Council's Committee for Plantation Affairs at London by Isaac Levy, an American merchant and probably a member of the Levy-Franks family, of New York, Philadelphia, and London.

In 1754 Levy had purchased a half interest in two of the Georgia Sea Islands from Thomas Bosomworth, an Anglican clergyman and the husband of Mary, "Queen of the Creeks." Six years later Bosomworth sold the islands to the Crown without consulting his partner. Levy maintained that the sale was illegal, that he had not been consulted or compensated, and that Bosomworth had colluded with Governor Henry Ellis.

In his memorial Levy asked for redress. He suggested that he be granted the right to exploit a coal mine on Cape Breton Island, Nova Scotia, as compensation for his loss. In the petition he argued the pros and cons of coal as a fuel, with special reference to colonial industry and to English mercantilism, which did not encourage manufacturing in the colonies. The document thus throws light on the commercial theory and practice of England in the eighteenth century.

SOURCE. The Library of Congress, Division of Manuscripts, Memorials 1768–71, Vol. I. Copied from the Public Record Office, C.O. 5:114, pp. 13 ff.

To the right honourable the Lords of the Committee of Council for Plantation Affairs:

The memorial of Isaac Levy sheweth that your memorialist in the year 1759, being at that time resident in Philadelphia, presented by his agent his humble petition to his Majesty [King George II], praying to be restored to a moiety [an equal share] of 2 islands, called Ossaba and Sapalo, on the coast of Georgia, of which he was illegally dispossessed by collusion between his Majestie's late governor of Georgia and one Thomas Bosomworth;

That your memorialist, finding that there were great delays in prosecuting his claim before the lords of trade, thought it necessary to come himself to London, where he has been for four years, soliciting for relief in the premises;

That your memorialist begs leave to inform your Lordships that he should not have persevered in his solicitation to his Majesty for relief, but from a firm opinion that upon a proper representation of his case, his Majesty would have been most graciously pleased to have given such relief to your memorialist as the nature of his case required, without his being subjected to the delay and expence of recovering his just right by proceeding at law for the same, more especially as an appeal to his Majesty in Council must ultimately have determined any suit brought about the premises by your memorialist in Georgia;

That your memorialist, being encouraged to hope that he might have some compensation made him for the moiety of the said islands by some other grant from the Crown, he was therefore advised, and did a second time petition, that his Majesty would be most graciously pleased to order a restitution of a moiety of the said islands to your memorialist, or otherwise to grant him some lands in the ceded islands in the West Indies or the coal mine in the Island of Cape Briton [Cape Breton, Nova Scotia], and for a term of years and under such other conditions as his Majesty thought proper, which petition his Majesty was pleased by an order of Council to referr to Your Lordships, and Your Lordships were pleased to referr the same to the Lords of Trade and Plantation to consider thereof and report their opinion thereon;

That in February last, the Lords of Trade and Plantation did report their opinion thereon to Your Lordships, and are thereby pleased in substance to admitt the hardship of your memorialist's case; but for the reasons therein contained, take exception to either of the modes of relief pointed out in your memorialist's last mentioned petition to his Majesty; yet [they] say that upon some less exceptionable proposal your Lordships might probably think fit to recommend him to the royal favour in consideration of his losses, etc.;

That your memorialist, being at present incapable of pointing out any other mode of relief in the premises, or laying any other proposal to your Lordships other than what is in your petitioner's former petition and herein after mentioned, your memorialist is thereby left remediless in the premises, in consideration whereof your memorialist begs leave humbly to represent to Your Lordships:

That, as to the grant of the coal mine in Cape Breton, your memorialist is informed that the exception made to the granting it is that it will be prejudicial to Great Britain; for that it has been urged [that] if the Americans can be supplied with coals at a moderate price, it will enable the Americans to rival England in the iron manufactory.

Your memorialist begs leave to represent, first, that the expence of labour in America is at present near double of what it is in England, and if, in course of time, the expence of labour should decrease, yet the colonies will absolutely be unable to manufacture iron in any proportion so cheap as in England, because of the want of slitting mills, plating forges, and steel furnaces, which, by an act of Parliament of 1750, are absolutely prohibited from that time to be erected in the colonies; and therefore they are thereby totally disabled from becoming competitors with England, as they have at present but two slitting mills on all the continent which were erected before the year 1750.

In the next place, your memorialist begs leave to represent that he conceives that opening the coal mine at Cape Breton will tend to the advantage of Great Britain, because it will enable many ships that sail from England to America, which now proceed in ballast (especially such as go to South Carolina, Virginia, and Maryland), to load coals, and thereby making a tolerable freight, which now they cannot do, because coals are not vendible, except small quantities (in capital towns) to black smiths, and in the interior towns, charcoal is substituted in the place thereof.

Your memorialist apprehends that as soon as the Americans find the advantage of burning coal, they will certainly prefer it to wood in most places, because it will be less expensive and has many other advantages, experience of which is only wanting to give it the preferrence and make it the general fuel. And in order to bring the Americans to this experience, coals must be supplied them at a very moderate price for two or three years, after which the price may be advanced. And in this case most of the ships that go from England will find their account in loading coals, when they can readily sell them, which at present they cannot.

Your memorialist must observe to Your Lordships that coals from Cape Breton cannot be carried to any part of America and there sold (a place or two excepted) for a less price than coals can be carried from England, because no advantage of a freight from any place in America to Cape Breton can be made or had. But ships must go there in ballast, whereas many ships from England can load coal in prosecuting their voyage to America without going much out of their way and at little or no expence on that account.

Your memorialist therefore begs leave to lay before Your Lordships his proposals of the terms and conditions on which he is ready to take a lease of the said coal mine:

For a grant or lease of 30 years, your memorialist humbly proposes for the first ten years thereof to pay only a pepper corn annually, and for the remaining 20 years thereof to pay the Crown one shilling and six pence per chaldron [equal to 32 bushels] for every chaldron to be there dug for sale.

For a grant in fee [full title], to pay the Crown two shillings and six pence for every chaldron to be dug there for sale.

That your memorialist likewise begs leave humbly to represent that the publick have been already benefited by the sale of your memorialist's property, and your memorialist has been at a very considerable loss and expence by staying in London in order to solicit a compensation for the same for the space of 4 years last past. And therefore your memorialist humbly submits to Your Lordships whether it would be an unreasonable request for your memorialist to ask as a satisfaction for such his expence, a grant from his Majesty of the Island of Becouia [Bequia], one of the Grenadines [in the Windward Islands], more particularly, as your memorialist is credibly informed that the said island has not been put up to sale, as being considered of little or no value, on account of its not being fit for a sugar plantation and being subject, by reason of its defence-less situation, to devastation and plunder of the enemy in case of a war.

No. 84 Lopez and Rivera Help Build a College and a Church—1770–1775

Nicholas and Joseph Brown, of Providence, were anxious that Rhode Island College be located in their city. When the college moved there in 1770, it was in no small part due to the generosity of the Browns and to their successful efforts to induce others to join in support of the school. Jews, too, contributed to the institution. When the Reverend Hezekiah Smith visited Charlestown, South Carolina, in 1769 to raise funds, a number of Jews responded generously, and one in particular was very much impressed by the fact that the college guaranteed liberty of conscience.

Closer to home, the Browns approached Jacob Rodriguez Rivera and Aaron Lopez, of Newport. The two merchants each promised to donate 5,000 feet of lumber. The boards were needed immediately (March, 1770), because the first building of the college, now University Hall, was then being erected. In a letter dated March 22 (Document A) Lopez informed the Browns that the lumber was being forwarded as promised, although delivery was somewhat inconvenient at that particular time.

Five years later Nicholas Brown turned to Rivera once more and asked him to buy tickets for the Baptist Meeting House lottery. Rivera's response (Documents B, C, and D) is interesting, for he dwells on the motivations that prompt him to subscribe to a worthy cause. Let it not be forgotten that this man Rivera, who was ready to "forward every publick building" in America, fled as a child from Inquisition-ridden Spain.

The fact that Jews contributed to general philanthropic causes is not insignificant. In large parts of Europe where discrimination and disabilities still prevailed, Jews were not inclined to aid the institutions of a society that rejected them. In America, however, the reverse was true. American Jewish interest in the welfare of the larger community is documented ever since a number of New York Jewish merchants contributed money toward the building of the steeple of Trinity Church (1711).

SOURCE. The John Carter Brown Library, Brown Papers.

A [NO. 84]

Newport, March 22d, 1770.

Messrs. Nicholas Brown & Co.
Gentlemen:

In compliance to your request in [your] favour of the 15th current, I delivered its bearer the 5 M [thousand] feet boards of my subscription, and tho' inconvenient for me to gratify at this juncture, [because of] your zealous attention to forward building the college, and to answer Mr. Rivera's wishes, I delivered him 5 M feet more on his [Rivera's] own account, which compleated the 10 M, and hope will please the concerned.

I shall have occasion in about three weeks for 40 tons pigg iron. Should it suit you to supply that quantity and receive payment for the amount thereof in such goods as I have at present by me, on the same terms as we have bartered heretofore, please to signify it to me per return of the boat for my government [guidance].

I have as yet a tollerable good assortment by me of checks, ⅞ Irish linens, dowlas [coarse linen cloth], callicoes, stockings, breeches patterns, cloths, etc., which will easily run up to ballance this transaction.

I am, very respectfully, gentlemen,

Your most humble servant,
Aaron Lopez

B [NO. 84]

Newport, March 20th, 1775.

Mr. Nicholas Brown.

Sir:

By a list I have seen of the 4th class of the Baptist Meeting House lottery, I find that six out of the seven tickets you last sent me are prizes.

I have now sent them by the bearer, Mr. Raphael Jacobs, and for which please to give my account credit.

If you please, you may forward me five or six more in the 5th class and debit my account for the same.

I am, with all possible respect, dear sir,

Your obliged humble servant,
Jacob Rodrigues Rivera

There are but five prizes as No. 748 and 751 blanks.

C [NO. 84]

Newport, April 3d, 1775.

Mr. Nicholas Brown.

Sir:

Your very obliging favour of the 27th ultimo came safe to hand and note your having received the five prize tickets sent you by Mr. Jacobs. And that the other which I took to be a prize, proved a blank.

The seven tickets in the fifth class, you was pleased to send me by Mr. Jacobs, he will deliver me when he comes down, which will be next week. The numbers [I] note are from No. 1653 to 1659 inclusive. And as it's allways my greatest pleasure to be [a] promoter of every publick [building], I cannot but chierfully accept the proportion you have allotted me, to whom I am greatly obliged, not only for the honour you do me in ranking me amoung the number of your friends abroad, but also for your kind good wishes for their success.

I have the pleasure of subscribing with the greatest respect and esteem, sir,

Your obliged friend and very humble servant,
Jacob Rodrigues Rivera

D [NO. 84]

New Port, June 12th, 1775.

Mr. Nicholas Brown.

Sir:

Your ever obliging favours of the 2d and 3d current came safe to hand, inclosing seven tickets you was pleased to send me in the sixth class of the Baptist Meeting House lottery, numbers from No. 469 to 675 inclusive, which [I] have noted accordingly, as well as the four tickets prizes in the 5th class which I now return you.

Am very sensible of your good wishes for their success, but if they don't turn up as fortunate as we both wish, yet these two points I shall certainly have considered, *vizt.*, that of pleasing the very worthy Mr. Brown, which I wish ever to do, and, secondly, my great inclination to promote and forward every publick building to the utmost of my extent, and when those two points are answered, am very easy about the success.

If, on the drawing of this last class, I should still prove as unfortunate as I have in the former classes, you'll please to send me down an account that I may immediately send you the ballance. . . .

I have the pleasure of subscribing with the greatest sincerity and respect, sir,

Your very obliged friend and very esteemed humble servant,

Jacob Rodrigues Rivera

P.S. I have sent the seven tickets of the 5th class, that you may cut out there the prizes to prevent their being lost by being seperated here. . . .

No. 85   Petitions for a New Road—1770

On November 10, 1770, one hundred and fifty-seven inhabitants of Lancaster County asked the governor and council of Pennsylvania and Delaware to approve of a new road already laid out between Philadelphia and Strasburg. Describing the need for a better road in detail, the petition emphasized the economic advantages which would accrue from its construction (Document A). In a complementary petition (Document B), about ninety Philadelphia merchants supported the Lancastrians' appeal. The latter, though brief, is an excellent summary of the value of good roads in a province which could boast of but a few navigable rivers.

Document A lists only two Jewish signers, Joseph Simon and Isaac Solomon; Document B, too, contains but two Jewish signatures, those of Benjamin Levy and David Franks. The paucity of Jewish signers in the Lancaster petition is not surprising, although there were some other Jewish businessmen in Lancaster and its neighborhood at the time. In the case of the Philadelphia petition, the absence of the name of Michael Gratz is puzzling. (Barnard Gratz was in London on a business trip.) It is possible, of course, that these Jewish merchants were considered small fry, but this may be doubted.

Although some inhabitants of nearby Chester County opposed the petition, the council decided to confirm the road in question as a king's highway. It was to be sixty feet wide.

SOURCE. Pennsylvania Historical and Museum Commission, Harrisburg, Pa., PP. XXXIX, 55–56.

A [NO. 85]

To the Honourable John Penn, Esquire, Lieutenant Governor of the Province of Pennsylvania and Counties of New Castle, Kent, and Sussex on Delaware, and his honourable Council:

The petition of divers inhabitants of the County of Lancaster humbly sheweth:

That the great road from the upper parts of the said county, especially from the borough of Lancaster to Philadelphia, is, by the constant use of it with heavy loaded carriages and by its being laid in many places over very bad ground, now rendered almost impassable, and is attended in many parts of it with such danger and difficulty that the waggoners in many seasons are under the necessity, when heavy loaded to or from the Philadelphia market, of travelling in parties, that they may afford each other assistance.

That notwithstanding the great labour, care, and expence used in repairing the said road, it is constantly in bad order and, as the trade and commerce of the province increases and it is more used by heavy carriages, will be still more troublesome and difficult.

That another road, upon better ground and nearer by some miles, may be had and is now absolutely necessary for the accommodation of the back inhabitants of the said county in their commercial intercourse with the city of Philadelphia. The want of a good road seems to threaten a diversion of the valuable trade of this county, or some parts of it, to other places, and now not only actually prevents many farmers from attending the city markets, but puts them under the disagreeable necessity of trusting and giving comissions to others, to carry the produce of their farms to market, by which many have suffered greatly. Whereas, were the roads good and safe, their own horses and carriages might be employd for that purpose, and would take back for them salt and other articles for their home consumption, which they could purchase most reasonably in the city.

That a king's highway or publick road hath lately been laid out by order of the Governor and Council, from the Middle Ferry on Schuylkill [River] to the sign of the Ship in Chester County, and, from thence along or near the old Gap-Road as far as the village of Strasburg in Lancaster County. This road, your petitioners beg leave to say, is laid out on much better ground than the old road, is some miles shorter, and, your petitioners conceive, is the best, straitest, and most convenient road for the back inhabitants, and will be of great utility to the trade of Philadelphia. The inhabitants of Lancaster, and such as shall choose to pass through that town from the remote parts of the province, will have an easy road from thence to the said publick road, whereby they will shun eight or ten miles of hills and bad ground, which are upon the old road between the town and the sign of the Ship. And those whom it may best suit to take the back road, from Harris's by the Dunker Town (formerly called Peter's Road), may enter into the said new laid out road, near the north branch of Brandywine Creek, and by that means have an easy, safe, and shorter carriage from thence to Philadelphia.

Your petitioners therefore pray the Honourable the Governor and Council to take the premises into consideration, and, as the said new road seems to have been laid out chiefly with design to encourage and secure the trade of the inhabitants of the interior parts of the province to the city of Philadelphia, and is the best road yet pointed out for that purpose, to confirm the said new laid out road as a king's highway or publick road, and to order that the same may be forthwith opened and cleared.

And your petitioners will pray, etc.

Johannes Miller, . . .	Joseph Simon, . . .
Benjamin Poultney, . . .	Isaac Solomon, . . .

[November 10, 1770]

B [NO. 85]

To the Honourable John Penn, Esq., Lieutenant Governor of the Province of Pennsylvania, and to the honourable the members of his Council:

The petition of divers inhabitants of the city of Philadelphia most respectfully sheweth:

That your petitioners are informed a new road from the city to the village of Strasburg, leading to the borough of Lancaster, is by your order lately laid out; that the ground over which it is laid is good and suitable for the purpose; that the said road is much shorter to the said village and to a number of well settled back townships than the old road now in use, or than any other ground of equal goodness will admit of, and that notwithstanding these facts great opposition is raised against a confirmation of the said road.

Your petitioners, therefore, beg leave to represent to the Governor and Council:

That it is of great importance to the people of this province to have such roads as may promote the trade thereof, being the best communication in their power between the capital city and the back inhabitants, and thereby lessen the expence of bringing the produce of the country to market and supplying the back counties with such foreign commodoties as they may require;

That trade and commerce, on which the welfare and happiness of every community depend, is in this province supported under disadvantages which several of the neighbouring colonies are free from, their water carriage affording their remote inhabitants an easy transportation of all commodoties for market, while ours are discouraged by a length of road laid generally on bad ground, crooked, and ill supported.

Your petitioners therefore pray the Governor and Council to take the premises into their consideration and confirm the said new-road.

John Wharton, . . .   Rob't Morris, . . .
Benjamin Levy, . . .   David Franks, . . .

―――――

No. 86   Eleazar Levy Seeks Justice—1774

Eleazar Levy, a New York merchant, went to Canada in 1760, at the time of the British invasion of the country, and after the conquest decided to remain there. By 1763 he had moved from Quebec to Montreal, where he became the agent for the trustees of Thomas Wilson, a bankrupt merchant. Lieutenant Daniel Robertson, an army officer, came to see Levy, demanding payment of a considerable sum of money which Wilson allegedly owed him. Levy had not yet liquidated Wilson's estate, and when he refused to meet the officer's demands, the plaintiff appealed to General Ralph Burton, the Governor of Montreal. The general issued a warrant ordering the seizure and sale of Levy's goods to pay the sum claimed by Robertson. Levy then appealed to the civil courts for justice, eventually taking his case to the Privy Council in London, the highest court of appeals for colonial cases. For ten years he was entangled in litigation, and though the final judgment was in his favor, he never collected a cent.

Levy later moved to New York City. The injustices he had experienced in Canada turned him against the British, and when the colonies revolted in 1775, he became an avowed Whig, fleeing to Philadelphia when the English occupied New York. He died in 1811, a helpless, impoverished old man, a pensioner of the New York Jewish community.

The following petition, containing a summary of his trials and tribulations, was addressed to the Earl of Dartmouth.

SOURCE. Public Archives of Canada, Q 10.

To the Right Honourable William Legge, Earl of Dartmouth, Viscount Lewisham, his Majesty's Secretary of State for the Plantations, etc., etc.:

The humble petition of Eleazar Levy, merchant, sheweth: that your petitioner did, in May, 1760, go from New York to Quebec, carried with him a large quantity of various goods and merchandizes, did there establish himself, and followed merchandizing.

In 1763, your petitioner established a store or warehouse in the city of Montreal, in the Province of Quebec, wherein he had for sale divers goods and merchandize to a very considerable amount.

That on or about the 20th of January, 1764, the late General Ralph Burton, Esquire, since deceased, was military governor of Montreal. The said General, by a most arbit[r]ary act of power, did cause, by warrant under his hand, the goods, wares, and merchandize belonging to your petitioner to be seized, taken, and carried away from his store, to the amount of £700 and upwards, and no part thereof has ever been restored your petitioner.

That in October, 1764, civil government was established in the province of Quebec, and proper courts of judicature were erected. Your petitioner brought a joint action against General Burton and the officers that seized the goods under his authority and warrant of seizure.

The defendants pleaded their several justifications and authority, and issue being joined by plaintiff and defendents, the cause was tried in the Supreme Court of judicature of the province, at the city of Quebec, the 24th day of August, 1765, before the Honourable William Gregory, Esq., Chief Justice of the Province of Quebec, and a special jury, when council [counsel] was heard for both partys and several witnesses examined. A verdict was given in favor of your petitioner for £500 sterling, damages and costs, which costs were afterwards taxed by the court at £26 17s. 8d. and judgement signed for £526 17s. 8d. sterling.

The defendents, in order to avoid payment and to vex and deprive your petitioner of the benefit of his judgement, appealed from the verdict and judgement of the Supreme Court to the Governor and Council of Quebec, and proceeded therein till the same was ready for a hearing. They then dropped their appeal, it being ordered by the Governor and Council to be quashed, and brought a writ of error [a method to have a judgment reviewed on the basis of errors in the lower court] on the aforementioned judgement, also returnable before the Governor and Council of Quebec, as no precedent could be found of an appeal from the verdict of a jury in civil causes.

Your petitioner, being put to great expence in defending said appeal, did by his council [counsel] move in the court of the Governor and Council, praying they would be pleased to order your petitioner [to] be paid his charges in defending the appeal, before deffendents [General Burton and officers should] be admitted to proceed in their writ of error, which [was] not only being equitable, but usual in like cases. The Governor and Council refused to order said payment, saying all cost would be paid on the determination of the suit.

The cause in error came to a hearing at Quebec, the 18th of May, 1767, before Governor [Guy] Carleton and the Council of Quebec, when they reversed the verdict and judgement of the Supreme Court, and ordered the same should be null, void, and of no effect.

Your petitioner, being advised there was not any material error in the record and proceedings of the Supreme Court to warrant setting aside the verdict and judgement; that if any error there were, it was only mere forms of law, omitted by your petitioner's attorney, and not in any matter affecting the merits of the cause, which ought to have been amended by the Court of Errors [the Governor and Council], more especially as the courts were newly erected, and the forms of their proceedings not as yet firmly established and fixed.

Your petitioner, therefore, agreable to his Majesty's instructions and order of the mode of proceeding established in the colonys, and thinking himself aggrieved by the judgement of the Court of Error[s], appealed from the said judgement of the Court of Errors to his Majesty and [Privy] Council, for which purpose your petitioner in few weeks after left Quebec and came to England and entered his appeal, which was attended with great expence and loss of his business.

The appeal was heared [heard] at the Cockpit [the Privy Council room], Whitehall [London], the 31st of July, 1771, before a committee of lords of his Majesty's most Honorable Privy Council. When council [counsel] was heared for both parties, their lordships were pleased to reverse the judgment in error of the Governor and Council of Quebec, of the 18th of May, 1767, and confirmed the judgement of the Supreme Court of Quebec, of the 24th of August, 1765, in favor of your petitioner. Report thereof being made to his Majesty in Council, his Majesty was pleased to approve thereof and confirm the same, and the governor, lieutenant governor, or commander in chief of his Majesty's said Province of Quebec for the time being, were ordered to take notice thereof and govern themselves accordingly.

The decree of his Majesty and Council, with the privy seal thereto affixed, was transmitted to Quebec, and your petitioner's council [counsel] presented an humble petition to the Governor and Council of Quebec on behalf of your petitioner, praying they would settle and ascertain the costs in this ten years' litigation. The vouchers and papers were then and there ready to be laid before them, which the Governor and Council refused to do [consider], and Mr. Hey, the Chief Justice, and one of the Council answered that the cost must be settled by the King and Council.

Your petitioner's attorney, on issuing a *scire facias* [a writ based on a matter of record] against General Burton's bail, in order to recover the judgement obtained in the Supreme Court of Quebec, found, in the course of his proceeding therein, that the bond had been delivered by Mr. Hey, the Chief Justice, to the obligors [the persons who put up the security] in the said bond, which was by them distroyed, and, as they termed it, was judicially destroyed.

By cancelling the bond, your petitioner is deprived of all means of recovery, and must sit down with the loss of his goods seized and taken from him in January, 1764, value £700 and upwards (and the interest thereon due for ten years at 6 per cent, being the established and lawful interest of said province, amounts to £420), no part of which goods has ever been restored to your petitioner, and also the heavy sums of money expended by your petitioner in law and other charges, in a ten years' litigation, amounting to £600 and upwards, exclusive of two voyages made by your petitioner from America at a great expence; and is also deprived of his judgement obtained in the Supreme Court at Quebec, in August, 1765, of £526 17s. 8d. and interest thereon, together with extraordinary costs usually allowed when writ of error is brought on a judgement of a court of judicature, and as several acts of Parliaments in such case directs, to which your petitioner apprehends himself entitled to receive. Your petitioner is hereby damaged to upwards of £2,500 sterling, exclusive of his loss of time and absence from his business and family.

The bond was the only security your petitioner had for proceeding in his appeal. The securitys in error [the bondsmen] are bound to pay the condemnation money, and rendring the bodys of the principles [principals] in discharge of the bail is not admissable where writ of error is brought on a judgement were the principles living, and could [they] be come at, which is not the present case, as it is well known that General Burton and Major [Daniel] Disney, two of the principles, had left the province of Quebec some considerable time before the cause in error came to a hearing, and [that they were] out of the jurisdiction of their courts. Consequently, your petitioner could appeal under the security of the aforesaid bond only.

Your petitioner apprehends and is advised that the Chief Justice who took the recognizance [the bond governing conditions of forfeiture] and in whose possession the same was deposited, should not have delivered it to the obligors thereof, nor should [it] have been cancelled, but ought to have remained with the Chief Justice untill the final end of the process, and should have been entered on record; that though deligent search has been made by your petitioner's attorney, a council [counsel] at Quebec, no copy of said bond can be procured, nor [is] any mention thereof to be found in any of the records at Quebec.

That though your petitioner is possessed of every judgement in his favor, yet is in a much worse situation than those against whom such judgement stand[s], he [being] dispossessed of his property and interest thereon due, which they have possessed and kept upwards of ten years. No part thereof has ever been restored him, and as, your petitioner has been informed, the greatest part of his goods, taken from him as aforesaid, has been distroyed by two fires at the military provost martial's [marshal's] house at Montreal, and what little yet remained in 1770 are by time, neglect, and the moth rendered of no value.

Your petitioner is informed, and verily believes, that [the] government has paid the representatives of the late General Burton a considerable sum of money, to the amount of several hundred pounds, for the reimbursement of the law charges they expended in this long litigation.

Your petitioner, from this circumstance, hopes and beleives [the] government means to releave [relieve] your petitioner on proper application made, which mode of application your petitioner apprehends, is in Your Lordship's department. He therefore humbly presents to Your Lordship this his petition and case.

As the Governor, and also the Chief Justice of the Province of Quebec, are at this present time in this kingdom [Great Britain], who transacted the greatest part of the business, as set forth in this, your petitioner's case, and, as your petitioner is informed, are shortly returning to Quebec, your petitioner, apprehending Your Lordship may think their information necessary on the subject of your petitioner's case,

Your petitioner therefore most humbly prays Your Lordship will please to appoint a short [not too distant] day for examining into his case, as it is from Your Lordship's humanity and justice, as well as in support of his Majesty's most gracious decree in your petitioner's favour, he hopes to obtain such relief as his case requires, and to Your Lordship shall seem meet.

And your petitioner will ever pray . . .

Eleazar Levy

13th August, 1774.

———

No. 87 Georgia Jews: Liberty People and Violent Rebels—1775–1781

One of the leaders of the Revolutionary movement in Georgia was Mordecai Sheftall (1735–97), the chairman of the rebel Committee of Christ Church Parish, which included Savannah, the colony's largest city. Associated with him were his brother Levi (1739–1809) and a friend, Philip Minis (1733–89), probably the first white male child born in Georgia who survived to manhood.

The activity and importance of these men as rebel leaders, particularly of Mordecai Sheftall, are documented in the following letters and depositions. The two letters printed below (Documents A and D) were written by Sir James Wright, the governor of Georgia for the largest part of the period, from 1760 to 1776 and from 1779 to 1782. It was he who referred to the Whigs, rather contemptuously it would seem, as "liberty people."

SOURCE. Department of History and Archives, Colonial Records of Georgia (MSS). Document A: XXXVIII, Part 1, 562–64; Document B: XXXVIII, Part 1, 626–27; Document C: XXXVIII, Part 2, 32–33; Document D: XXXVIII, Part 2, 484–88.

A [NO. 87]

Savannah, in Georgia,
the 17th of August, 1775.

My Lord: . . .

We have received an account here that an armed vessell or two, fitted out from Charles Town [South Carolina], proceeded to the bar of St. Augustine [Florida], and there met with a vessell bound to that port, which had a great quantity of gun powder and king's stores on board, part of which had been sent on shore, but that they took out of her 15,000 weight of the gun powder which they had landed safe at Beaufort, Port Royal, South Carolina.

The conduct of the people here [in Savannah] is most infamous. One Sheftall, a Jew, is chairman of the Parochial Committee, as they call themselves, and this fellow issues orders to captains of vessels to depart the king's port without landing any of their cargoes, legally imported. And fresh insults continue to be offered every day, and no sloop of war arrived yet. . . .

James Wright

To the Earl of Dartmouth.

B [NO. 87]

The deposition of Richard Bissell, master of the ship *Clarissa*, belonging to Rhode Island, but now lying in Savannah River, taken on oath the 12th day of September, 1775, before the Honourable Anthony Stokes, barrister at law, Chief Justice of the said provence.

This deponent, being duly sworn on the Holy Evangelists of Almighty God, maketh oath and saith:

That he arrived in this province on or about the twenty fifth day of July last, from the island of Jamaica, having on board the said ship ten hogs heads of melasses, and sundry other goods;

That this deponent, about the middle of August, advertized the said melasses for public sale; that soon after the said advertizement appeared, one Stephen Biddurph, messenger to the Parochial Committee in Savannah (as this deponent has been informed and verily believes), came to this deponent and told him that the committee ordered him to appear before them;

That when this deponent went before the said committee, he there saw sitting in the chair one Mordecai Sheftal, of Savannah, Minis, of Savannah, both which persons profess the Jewish religion; one Platt who acts as secretary to the said committee, one Lyons of Savannah, blacksmith, one Tondee of Savannah, tavern keeper, and several others, whose names this deponent doth not know;

That the said Mordecai Sheftal told this deponent that the aforesaid melasses could not be landed in this provence and that they must be carried back to Jamacai or abide by the consequences;

That this deponent hath since been obliged to sign a bond, at the Custom House, for the delivery of the said melasses at the island of Jamaica aforesaid.

Richard Bissell

Sworn the day and year aforesaid: Anthony Stokes
A true copy: Preston & Pryce

C [NO. 87]

I, David Montaigut, Deputy Collector of his Majesty's customs for the Port of Savannah, in the province aforesaid, do hereby declare and certify:

That upon the third day of October of this present year, 1775, the sloop *Charlotte* (Suthey Miles, master), from Rhode Island, reported in ballast at his Majesty's Custom House; but it afterwards appearing that she had goods on board, consisting of onions, barrels of apples, etc., which were that same day landed and hawked about town, the comptroller and myself, being confined to our houses with sickness, ordered her immediately to be seized, which was done accordingly, and a waiter [watchman] put in possession of her; but the said master would not permit him to remain aboard and continued to dispose of his cargo as before;

That upon the twenty fifth day of said month, betwixt the hours of 3 and 4 in the afternoon, several of the inhabitants of Savannah, calling themselves Committee Men, amongst whom were Oliver Brown, Alexander Phoenix, Mordecai Sheftall, Levy Sheftall, Thomas Sherman, Seth John Cuthbert, Ebenezer Platt, George Basil, Jacob Oates, Powell Griggs, Joseph Farley, Junior, and others, whom the deponant could not well distinguish from the crowd present, came to his Majesty's Custom House and there demanded that the register [important ship's papers] of the said vessel, then under prosecution in the Court of Admiralty (since condemned and run away with by the mariners), should be delivered up to the master, which, having been repeatedly refused by us, proceeded with iron instruments to force open the locks of the desks and drawers in the office, and after rumaging for the space of two hours, got possession of the said register which they carried off with them.

And, this deponant apprehends, had not the said committee men succeeded in their attempt, evil consequences would have happened in this town, considering the inability of the magistrates to support [the] government and protect the officers, by reason of the then turbulent disposition of this colony, which [hath] shewn itself on former occasions both at Sunbury and Savannah when seisures were violently rescued.

David Montaigut

Georgia,
Parish of Christ Church.

Signed and sworn to before me, the 16th November, 1775.

Henry Preston, J. P. [Justice of the Peace]

D [NO. 87]

Savannah, in Georgia,
the 9th of March, 1781.

Duplicate

On the 6th inst., I did myself the honor of writing to your Lordship, in which I gave your Lordship some account of the situation of affairs in this province. . . .

On the 6th inst., my Lord, I assented to five bills, and have the satisfaction to acquaint your Lordship that one of them is entitled: "An Act for Granting to His Majesty, Certain Dutys upon All Goods, Wares, and Merchandize of the Growth or Production of This Province, Which May Be Exported from Hence, as the Contribution of Georgia to the General Charge of the British Empire. . . ."

Another is entitled: "An Act for Securing His Majesty's Government and the Peace of This Province, and for the More Effectual Protection of the King's Loyal Subjects Here against the Wicked Attempts and Designs of the Rebels and Other Disaffected Persons, and for Other Purposes Hereinafter Mentioned." From the great number of sculking rebels and disaffected persons remaining in this province, I saw, my Lord, that it was impossible for his Majesty's loyal subjects to remain in any tolerable degree of peace or security, and therefore proposed this law to enable the inhabitants to take up and secure all rebels and persons guilty of harbouring, concealing, aiding, or assisting rebels and plunderers, or giving them intelligence [information], and to compell them to remove out of the province.

I judged it also necessary to prevent the Jews who formerly reside[d] here from returning, or others from coming to settle here. For these people, my Lord, were found to a man to have been violent rebels and persecutors of the King's loyal subjects; and, however this law may appear at first sight, be assured, my Lord, that the times require these exertions, and without which, the loyal subjects can have no peace or security in this province. . . .

[Letter from Sir James Wright, apparently to Sir George Germaine, his Majesty's Principal Secretary of State for America.]

———

No. 88   Haym Salomon Is Certified as a Patriot—1776

In June, 1776, Leonard Gansevoort (1751–1810), a young lawyer and well-known Whig leader of Albany, New York, wrote a note to Major General Philip J. Schuyler (1733–1804), commanding the Northern Department of the Continental Army. In the letter Gansevoort had a good word for a Jewish peddler: he certified that the Jew's sympathies were with the Americans.

The peddler was Haym Salomon (ca. 1740–85), a Polish Jew who had come to the colonies about 1775 and was a sutler with Schuyler's troops at Lake George. He then returned to New York, only to be imprisoned as a rebel when the British took possession of the city. When he was released to serve the Hessians as a commissary, he continued to work underground for the Whigs. Discovered, he fled for his life and managed to make his escape to Philadelphia. There, after a few years, he became the chief broker to Robert Morris, the Superintendent of Finance, helping him to dispose of bills of exchange and the like. James Madison, then a congressman, gratefully recorded in his correspondence that "our little friend in Front Street" lent him money at a critical period.

A fervent devotee of liberty, Salomon was the leader among the Philadelphia Jews in urging that the Pennsylvania Council of Censors give its Jewish fellow citizens equal political rights. When Mikveh Israel built its synagogue, Salomon was its most generous benefactor. After the war he became a broker and merchant, but survived the peace only two years, leaving behind a young wife and four children, all under the age of seven.

SOURCE. New York Public Library, Division of Manuscripts, Schuyler Papers.

New York, June 12th, 1776.

Honoured Sir:

I am just this moment arrived here and have not yet heard the news.

The bearer hereof, Mr. Haym Solomon, tells me he has laid in stores to go suttling [peddling among the soldiers] to Lake George, and has been informed that the General admits none, but such as have a certificate of their being friendly to our measures, to suttle there.

I can inform the General that Mr. Solomon has hitherto sustained the character of being warmly attached to America.

I am, in great haste, dear General,

Your very humble servant,
Leonard Gansevoort

The Honourable General Schuyler.

No. 89 Moses Levy Chooses the United States—1776–1783

When Moses Levy, born in New York in 1763 (?), was quite young, his father sent him into the royal navy. During the Revolution, Levy, still in his teens, secured his discharge while in Jamaica and boarded a vessel for British-held New York. He was determined to return to the mainland and to become a citizen of the new United States.

While bound for New York, the captain and crew of the ship carrying Levy decided to divert the vessel and brought her into

Wilmington, North Carolina, then in American hands, as a prize. Levy then went to South Carolina and, in the following appeal, petitioned for citizenship. There is every reason to believe that his request was granted, for he is recorded as purchasing 528 acres of land in the Charleston district in 1785.

SOURCE. Historical Commission of South Carolina, Columbia, S.C.

To the Honorable John Lloyd, Esq., President, and the honorable members of the Senate:

The petition of Moses Levi most humbly sheweth that your petitioner was born in New York and was by his father put on board a British ship of war while a lad, since which your petitioner, having arrived to a certain age by which your petitioner could form with some degree of certainty the merits of the contest between the British nation and the United States of America, and for which purpose obtained a regular discharge from the said service while in Jamaica;

And in order to carry your petitioner's intentions into executions, he shipt himself on board the ship *Dawes*, Capt. Eves [commanding], bound from Jamaica to New York. However, fortunately for your petitioner, the master and crew of said ship agreed to carry her into one of the ports of the United States of America, and to which your petitioner chearfully acquiesced in the said proposal, and carried the said ship and cargo into Wilmington, in the State of North Carolina, where your petitioner sold his share of said ship and cargo, and proceeded to this state with the full intent of becoming a citizen thereof.

Your petitioner therefore craves you'll please take his case into your serious consideration, and grant him such protection as the case of his situation requires, particularly of admitting him a subject thereto.

And your petitioner will for ever pray.

Moses Levy

No. 90 Sheftall Sheftall Describes His Career as a Revolutionary Soldier—1777–1783

In 1777 or 1778 Sheftall Sheftall, only fifteen or sixteen years of age, was appointed Assistant Deputy Commissary General of Issues to the Georgia troops. Captured with his father after the fall of Savannah in December, 1778, he remained a prisoner until he was exchanged in 1780. In that year, then a young man of eighteen, he was put in charge of a mercy ship, the flag-of-truce sloop *Carolina Packett*. His mission, which he carried out successfully, was to bring money for the relief of the imprisoned General William Moultrie and his soldiers in British-held Charlestown.

Shortly after his seventieth birthday in 1832, Sheftall made the following affidavit, testifying to his war service, in support of a pension claim. The document is instructive because it throws light on the career of a man who served his country, and served it well, in positions of responsibility, although he was only twenty-one at the end of the war, after about five years of service as a soldier and prisoner of war.

SOURCE. Georgia Historical Society, Savannah.

Georgia }
City of Savannah }

Sheftall Sheftall of the said city, being duly sworn, saith:

That some time in the latter part of the year one thousand seven hundred and seventy seven, or the beginning of the year seventeen hundred and seventy eight, this deponent was appointed by John B. Geredeau [Geradieu] Esquire, Deputy Commissary General of Issues of the Continental troops in Georgia, to be an Assistant Deputy Commissary of Issues in his office;

That he continued in that station for some months when Mr. Geredeau resigned, and this deponent's father, the late Mordecai Sheftall, Esquire, was appointed Mr. Geredeau's successor; that this deponent was reappointed to his said office by his father, and that he continued in the office untill the British troops took Savannah, which was on the twenty ninth day of December of the said year seventeen hundred and seventy eight, when they took this deponent and his father prisoners, and a few days after put them on board of a prison ship, say, the second day of January, seventeen hundred seventy nine;

That on the twenty sixth day of March following, his father was admitted to his parole; that on the twenty-sixth day of June of the same year, this deponent was admitted also on his parole. On his landing, he was sent to the town of Sunbury, a distance of forty miles from Savannah, where his father and a number of Continentall officers were on parole; that they continued theire [there] untill the month of October following (the British garrison having been previously withdrawn to reinforce Savannah);

That the American and French army, under the command of General Lincoln and Count D'Estaing, laid seige to Savannah; that while in that situation, a Tory armed party that was hovering about the country threatened to kill the American officers and did actually kill Captain Hornby of the Fourth Georgia Continental regiment; that in this situation, the officers applied to the commanders of the Allied army, what they were to do, who, in reply, recommended to them to remove to a place of safety, but to consider themselves as still on parole;

That this deponent, his father, and several officers embarked [October, 1779] on board of a brig in the harbour of Sunbury, which had been taken in the said harbour by a small American privateer, for to proceed in her to Charles Ton [Charlestown], in South Carolina; that on their passage, they were taken by a British frigate called the *Gaudaloupe,* who bore away and carried them and landed them in the island of Antigua; that some time in the month of November, that after being their [there] between five and six months, their [they] were admitted to a parole to return to America;

That this deponent and his father arrived in Philadelphia (via St. Eustatia) on the twentieth day of June, seventeen hundred and eighty; that a few days after their arrival, they were introduced to the Board of War, which consisted of General Thomas Mifflin, Colonel Timothy Pickering, Colonel [Robert Hanson] Harrison, and Richard Peters, Esquire, their secretary, by Colonel George Walton, one of the signers of the Declaration of Independence;

That the Board of War directed Mr. [Thomas] Bradford, Commissary of Prisoners, to send away two Englishmen, natives of Antigua, by the name of Jacob Jarvis and his brother, John Swinton Jarvis, for to be exchanged for this deponent and his father;

That some time in the early part of the month of December following, certified copies of their paroles, with certificates of their exchange for the said gentlemen, were received by this deponent and his father, by which means they were released from being prisoners of war;

That a few days thereafter, this deponent was sent for by the Board of War, and informed that he must proceed in a sloop called the *Caroline Packett,* commanded by Captain John Derry, [under] a flag of truce, as flag master to Charles Ton in South Carolina, for to carry goods, flour, and money for to be delivered to General Moultrie or the senior officer of the Continentall troops, prisoners of war at that place;

That he proceeded on the voyage agreeable to his instructions; that owing to storms and head winds, he did not arrive in Charles Ton harbour untill the seventh day of February following, when the aforesaid articles were delivered to a person appointed by General Moultrie and by his order; that he was detained by the British untill some time in April, when he was permitted to pursue his voyage back;

That he arrived in Philadelphia on the twenty third day of April; that on his arrival, he delivered up to the Board of War all his papers and vouchers, and, in particular, got a receipt acknowledging the delivery of the money, agreeable to the orders of General Moultrie, which receipt was signed by a Mr. Charlton or Carlton [Joseph Carlton], Paymaster of the Board of War and Ordinance;

That about three years agoe, a fire broke out in this city, in his neighbourhood; that he moved his furniture and things for safety into the street; that among them was the certificate of his exchange, the instructions from the Board of War, and the receipt for the money, [all of which] was unfortunately lost;

That the deponent continued in the service untill the close of the Revolutionary War, and that this deponent's pay was sixty dollars per month, exclusive of rations, and that on the eight[h] day of September last past, he was seventy years of age.

No. 91   Mordecai Sheftall Seeks Confirmation of an Army Appointment—1778

Some time in 1777 Mordecai Sheftall, the Savannah merchant, rancher, and patriot, was appointed Commissary General of Purchases and Issues to the Georgia militia. The following year General Robert Howe, commanding the American forces in the Southern Department, appointed him to be Deputy Commissary General of Issues to the Continental Troops in South Carolina and Georgia. Sheftall, eager to have his appointment confirmed by the Continental Congress, asked Henry Laurens, its president, to intercede on his behalf. It is surprising that Laurens, a Charlestown merchant, had never met Sheftall. True, they moved in different social circles, but they had a common friend in Isaac DaCosta.

Before Congress could take any action, Sheftall was captured at the Battle of Savannah, December 29, 1778.

SOURCE. The Library of Congress, Division of Manuscripts, Papers of the Continental Congress.

Savannah, 19th August, 1778.

Sir:

I take the liberty to inclose you an extract from general orders appointing me to act as Deputy Commissary General of Issues in this state, in the room [place] of J. B. Gerrideau [Geradieu] Esq., whose bad state of health has oblidged him to resigne.

Not haveing the honor of a personal acquainetence with Your Excellency, my freinds, Mr. Gerrideau, Mr. [Joseph] Clay, and Colonel [George] Walton, have favoured me with letters of recommendation on which I presume to ask your freindship in obetaineing me a commission from the Honorable the Congress, confirming me in the above appointment. Should a further knowledge of me be necessary, an applictation to General McKintosh [Lachlan McIntosh], now with you, will lead to it, should I be so fortunate as to obetaine the appointment.

My inclination to do eaqual justice in the office I now act [hold] induces me to request very full and particular instructions for my government [guidance]. Many matters remaine to be explained in any [instructions] I have yet seen; and I have my doubts that we have allready run into some errors, particularly in the rations at present drawn by the soldiery, of which I inclose a list.

I have the honor to be, with the greatest respect,

Your Excellency's most obedient, humble servant,

Mordecai Sheftall

His Excellency, Henry Laurence, Esq.

No. 92   David Franks, Loyalist—1779

In 1775 the Americans appointed David Franks, of Philadelphia, to supply their British and Tory prisoners. Three years later, in October, 1778, Franks was removed from office on suspicion of being a Loyalist. The evidence against him was a letter from him to his brothers, Moses and Naphtali, in London, which had been intercepted by the Continental Congress. Dated October 18, the letter told of his work as a purveyor. Arrested as an alleged Tory, Franks was released a month later, for Congress found no basis on which to try him.

The provisioning of the prisoners was at the expense of the British Treasury, which worked through the London firm of Nesbitt, Drummond, and Franks, of which David's elder brother, Moses, was a member. Franks advanced large sums for the rations he and his associates furnished to the prisoners and logically expected reimbursement by his employers in London. The firm in turn looked to the Treasury for payment, but the officials in Whitehall referred the matter to the British in America. There, Sir Henry Clinton, the commander in chief, refused to reimburse Franks by drawing on his contingency fund, or even by ordering payment to be made in England. When the firm failed to receive compensation, it refused to honor Franks's drafts and left him holding the bag for large amounts of money. In Document A the company told Franks why it would not pay him.

Franks's release from prison did not satisfy the radicals, and his case became a football in state politics, in the struggle between the radicals and the moderate Whigs, between the Constitutionalists and the anti-Constitutionalists. The two parties used the Franks affair as a pretext to belabor one another. Franks was a wealthy aristocrat, allied through the marriage of his daughter Abigail with the Hamiltons and the Allens, and even with the Penns. Thus he was fair game for the radicals. After Sir William Howe's evacuation of Philadelphia in June, 1778, the radicals vigorously prosecuted a good many Tories and confiscated their estates. It was inevitable, therefore, that they should turn their attention to Franks.

Some time after the Continental Congress had freed Franks, the Constitutionalists rearrested him and in April, 1779, tried him before a Pennsylvania court on the charge of traitorous correspondence with the enemy. When the jury acquitted the defendant, the radicals were furious. Among the latter were Timothy Matlack, secretary of the Supreme Executive Council of the state, and Jonathan D. Sergeant, the attorney general, who had prosecuted Franks. Matlack and an associate anonymously published the "incriminating" correspondence, along with some comment, in *The Pennsylvania Packet or The General Advertiser* on April 29, 1779 (Document B). Matlack italicized those phrases which in his belief demonstrated Franks's treason.

Some readers construed criticism of the acquittal as a reflection on the jury system. In the May 1, 1779, issue of the paper, Davis Bevan, one of the jurors, defended his vote of "not guilty" (Document C). Three days later, on May 4, the newspaper printed both an attack on Franks by "A Citizen" and a defense of him by "Sidney" (Document D). Two days after that "A Juror" pitched into the attorney general, whom he mistakenly accused of publishing Franks's letters. The "Juror" was indignant at Sergeant, whom he accused of interfering with the rights and prerogatives of jurors (Document E).

An excellent résumé of this *cause célèbre* appeared on May 13 in a defense both of Franks and the jury that had acquitted him (Document F). From this and other letters it is quite clear that the pro-Loyalists and the conservative anti-Constitutionalists bitterly resented the Constitutionalists' Tory-hunting. The conservatives suspected that the radicals had "taken advantage of the times to gratify their vengeful passions upon their private enemies." In the same issue "Cato" answered Davis Bevan, seeking to demonstrate Franks's guilt (Document G). The Philadelphia newspapers printed additional comments on the trial, but lack of space prevents their republication here.

In October, 1780, Franks was subjected to his third and last arrest and was banished to New York, then in the hands of the enemy.

SOURCE. Document A: William L. Clements Library, Ann Arbor, Mich., Sir Henry Clinton Papers; Document B: *The Pennsylvania Packet or The General Advertiser*, Philadelphia, April 29, 1779; Document C: *Ibid.*, May 1, 1779; Document D: *Ibid.*, May 4, 1779; Document E: *Ibid.*, May 6, 1779; Documents F and G: *Ibid.*, May 13, 1779.

A [NO. 92]

London, 6th March, 1779.

David Franks, Esquire,
Philadelphia.
Sir:

A very tedious interval has passed since we have had the pleasure of hearing from you, except by letters of advice (down to the 4th December last), which have accompanied some of your drafts on us, and by which we observe you had drawn as far as No. 126. The amount we are not able to say exactly, as two of these drafts, No. 105 and No. 106, are not yet presented, nor have we yet received the letters of advice. But we are truly concerned to tell you that we are under the disagreeable and painful necessity of suffering the drafts . . . to be returned protested, for the reasons hereafter mentioned. Though we are fully convinced that you will have immediate redress on Sir Henry Clinton, or whoever may be the Commander in Chief, the Lords of the Treasury have repeatedly given directions to the Commander in Chief to settle and pay the expence of the service for victualling the prisoners out of the army contingencies.

We are already in advance [in arrears] for this service of victualling the King's prisoners upon bills of your drawing, etc., about seven thousand pounds sterling, exclusive of the last bills, and as you have not transmitted any certificate for what you have delivered since the 24th of May last (the date of your last certificate), we presume in your particular situation that you neither could obtain permission from the Congress to proceed to New York yourself, where the General [Clinton] is, nor be permitted to send your clerk to settle the vouchers and to procure certificates for the quantities you had delivered, which, in December last, exceeded 500,000 rations.

Under these circumstances, and considering that if you could not go to the head-quarters in the season when the General was in your vicinity and at rest, it will be almost impracticable to follow or find him in the season when the army was in motion; therefore it would be imprudent to the highest degree to engage farther by accepting bills for a service altogether precarious and tedious, and which, though the Lords of the Treasury had repeatedly ordered the General to fix and settle a price with you for the ration[s], yet to this day it has not been effected.

Add to this that, having stated the matter litterally, as it stands, to the Lords of the Treasury, and entreating their assistance by granting an imprest [an advance] on account, as far as we are in advance [in arrears], and to give directions about accepting these bills, they [the Lords of the Treasury] have thought proper to decline doing either, and instead of giving us relief, as in justice we expected, their Lordships are pleased to tell us that they have ordered their Commander in Chief to settle and pay you upon the spot, and that they have insisted upon his compliance, while on our part, we utterly refuse accepting the proposition of being paid in America; nor can any consideration induce our consent to that mode of payment.

We, therefore, must decline accepting your drafts, and as you are to apply and be paid at head-quarters, you, we hope, can not suffer by it, as the holders of the bills will see what it is that presses you to this fatality [necessary step]. For it can not be expected that we, as individuals, should maintain the King's Army, which is the case, in fact, if in the present situation of affairs we agree to any mode of payment but here, in London, at and by the Treasury.

You are in equity, law, and honor entitled to the charges of protest of 20 per cent, the common custom of bills under protest in America, and therefore must recover it.

We hoped from the circumstances of this business and our and your having engaged in it on good faith, that it would have had another determination [outcome]; but our best and earnest and, we may add, indefatigable, solicitation at the Treasury has not been in the least effectual, nor had any attention, so that what we do is compulsive, and our conduct towards you is truely distressing; but, as we said above, we are not to blame, for we neither can or will take upon us to maintain an army.

What we have else to desire is that as soon as you have settled with the Commander in Chief the price of the ration[s], that you will instantly signify it to us, as hitherto the certificates you have transmitted have been estimated only at so low a rate as sixpence per ration, which was a regulation to serve untill the settlement should be made on your side; and, even on those certificates, at that price, we have received but partial payment.

You will be mindful that we hold ourselves entirely disengaged from any further connection in this business. If you proceed in it, we wish you prosperity.

In case you have obtained a certificate and sent it to us, you may then draw upon us for the amount of the bills which may be returned.

We are truly, sir,

Your obedient, humble servants,
For Messrs. Nesbitt, Drummond & Franks,
Richard Rowland

B [NO. 92]

[April 29, 1779.]

For *The Pennsylvania Packet:*

On Saturday last came on before the Supreme Court the trial of David Franks, of this city, on a charge of misdemeanor in giving intelligence to the enemy at New-York. The jury sat 'til Sunday morning, eight o'clock, and then brought in their verdict: Not Guilty.

On the trial Mr. Franks confessed that he wrote the letters upon which the charge was founded. As the intelligence which those letters contained is become, by length of time, of no consequence to the enemy, they are laid before the public for their information, as every thing which relates to the interest of the state ought to be. This case certainly deserves very serious attention.

Mr. Franks's compliments to Captain Thomas Moore; hopes he is well, and begs his particular care of the inclosed. The family's respects to him. His friends are well, and acquaints [him] that last night about twelve o'clock Billy Hamilton [the brother of my son-in-law], after a twelve hours' trial, was *honourably acquitted,* the jury about two minutes absent, which [I] beg Mr. A. Allen [his kinsman] may be acquainted with. It appeared an *ill-natured prosecution;* [he was] charged with having a superintendent's commission for keeping the Middle Ferry.

The inclosed [letter to my brother Moses] for London to be forwarded per first opportunity.

October 18th, 1778, Philadelphia.

To Captain Thomas Moore, of General [Oliver] DeLancey's regiment in New-York.

Philadelphia, October 18, 1778.

Dear Brothers:

The opportunity of prisoners going [back into the British lines] gives me the satisfaction of addressing you, and enquiring after yours and good family's health, and presenting our sincerest and best loves to you, yours, and all the good family, as [I] cannot at these times write to all.

I did yesterday write the boys [my sons], *and thought all the prisoners then in town were gone.* This goes in an hour or two. I desired you might be made acquainted that, in [the] next week, I hope myself or clerk may be permitted to go for New-York to procure a settlement and get a certificate [for what is due me]. It will be a large one, and as the price of provisions have risen very high in the country, hope you may be able to procure me at least one shilling sterling per ration; they, I think, won't be less for some time past than 2s. 6 [our currency] per ration at an average. *The agents for the French are giving in Virginia and Maryland 60s. to 80s. per cent* [hundred pounds] *for flour for* [the] *French fleet, and meat in proportion.*

The contractors' [your firm's] accounts will go when I go or send. No opportunity trust-worthy has offered, nor would it be proper they should be inspected by [I] don't know who [British general headquarters]. *This goes by stealth per soldiers,* and suppose letters will not be *so frequent on account the French war.*

I acquainted [my son] Moses that his friend Billy Hamilton was acquitted Friday after a trial of twelve hours, a prisoner at the bar, for high treason. *People are taken and confined at the pleasure of every scoundrel. Oh, what a situation Britain has left its friends!*

Sister Richa, I shall next address my love, etc. [to you]. I pray the Almighty to give you every wished-for blessing, and me and mine join heartily in the prayer, being, with the most sincerest gratitude, my dear brothers'

Most affectionate, obliged brother and servant,
David Franks

Flour in town 100s. per cent.
Beef in market 2s. 6 to 3s. lb.
And every article in proportion.
European goods almost any price.
Good broadcloth £15 to £20 per yard.
A good beaver hat 50 dollars to 70 per hat.
Men's shoes 7 to 12 dollars per pair.
Linens almost what you'll ask.
And all for liberty.
Butter 7s. 6 to 10s. lb.
7th day [calf?] at market 12s. 6 to 15s. lb.

Moses Franks, Esquire.

Will it be credited in Europe or by posterity that in a time of open war, the above letter should be deemed innocent? And with what security may our intestine enemies betray our councils and situation, if impunity is thus held forth to offenders? It is vain to think of carrying on war consistent with civil government, if the same transaction before a civil jurisdiction can be pronounced inoffensive, which by a military trial would be punished with death. For had this letter been wrote from General Washington's camp, the writer would have been hanged as a spy, and we should all have approved the sentence. Does the place where it was written alter the nature of the offence? And what confidence will our allies place in us if, disregarding all those rules of justice and necessity which prevail among other nations, we thus permit persons holding office and growing rich by their connections with their and our avowed enemies to communicate to those enemies our situation, circumstances, and abilities to carry on the war.

A juryman, as such, is a public character; and as it is the privilege of the people to scrutinize public measures and characters, they must expect to submit to the same tribunal with others, and have their conduct upon such interesting and important occasions open to the public eye.

It is usual in other countries, in all important trials, to publish lists of the jury. I wish it may be now done; and if there are any upon this occasion whose public conduct has suddenly altered to a very favourable turn towards these offenders, let them be known to their country; and if there are any who have been urged by hard necessity to yield their judgment to the demands of suffering nature, they will have an opportunity of removing the impressions which have been made on the minds of all those who duly consider the malignity and dangerous tendency of such correspondence.

Nothing now remains but for the community to express that detestation of Mr. Franks's conduct, which his attachment to the enemies of this country and the known disaffection of him and his connections upon all occasions must necessarily create, by treating him, and them, with the contempt they so justly deserve.

C [NO. 92]

[May 1, 1779.]

Mr. [John] Dunlap [publisher].
Sir:

Your publishing the following in your paper will much oblige your humble servant,

Davis Bevan

Perusing your paper of the 29th, I find some harsh sentiments thrown out against the jury who sat on the trial of David Franks, as he says, for a misdemeanor. Was it not more in regard to the public (who, I hope, will always stand forth in behalf of juries, who are and ever have been esteemed as the bulwark of justice and liberty) than to the chimerical observations of any hot-headed scribbler in this or any other place?

He [Timothy Matlack] says it was on a charge of giving intelligence to the enemy at New-York, a construction that never was admitted by the jury, nor, I believe, will by the public. This gentleman is totally unacquainted with business, as from the contents of David Franks's letter to his brother it must appear he never intended they should be known in New-York at all, as the consequence must have totally ruined his scheme of getting the ration raised [by the British] to one shilling sterling, though the contents of the letter were totally disapproved of by the jury.

But I beg this great censor to let me ask him a few questions. First: If he had a mind to give the enemy at New-York intelligence, why not mention the price current of goods to Captain Thomas Moore? Secondly: Whether he would find a man guilty where there was no law known or given for the offence? Where there is no law there is no transgression.

Another thing I have to mention, that the charge in the bill of indictment was so high, or otherwise contained what the law of this state would have stiled misprision of [misdemeanor akin to] treason, but the grand jury brought it in misdemeanor. Now, sir, I beg to ask you, whether you would have had us make a law, or leave it to a superior body, our Assembly?

The work you have undertaken is beneath the character of a friend to this commonwealth, as it has a tendency to destroy the strength of juries, and touch men's characters who were on oath to do justice to the best of their knowledge. It appeared very clear that we could not, from the letters as you have quoted, find they would support the charges . . . [and] have mentioned the words hard necessity that was the reason of so long delay. You are mistaken, for after it was dark we could do nothing as we were deprived of candle by order of the court, or the matter would have been determined as it is before ten o'clock.

I do not mean to give you these reasons; they are to the public, as I think you or any other man beneath my notice who would so far censure either this or any jury that may sit hereafter. I am, with due respect,

> The public's humble servant.
> One of that jury.
> Davis Bevan

April 30, 1779.

P.S. It must appear to every man of business that the letter to M.[oses] Franks was not for the purposes mentioned by this censor, but a letter of negotiation for private emolument, and not to injure the states.

D [NO. 92]

[May 4, 1779.]

For *The Pennsylvania Packet.*

As it is my wish to support the laws of the country, so likewise I conceive it my duty to support the interest of our allies, the magistracy of the state, and the incorporated dignity of its citizens.

The jury have acquitted Mr. David Franks, and I submit to the decision, though with some reluctance, because to counteract it would be an unsafe precedent. But there is something due to our allies as well as to our laws, and on their part I wish to express my contempt of a man who, getting his living among us, and that by our permission, should dare to inform their and our enemies of any transactions which those allies may at particular times find it necessary to take for the support and victualling a fleet destined to act in conjunction with us.

"*People,*" says Mr. Franks in his letter, "*are taken and confined at the pleasure of every scoundrel.*"

I answer, no man can be taken and confined here but according to the written laws of the country, and therefore, according to Mr. Franks's phrase, every citizen is a scoundrel who acts in conformity to law. *Query:* Is it either safe or decent that Mr. Franks should continue among us?

A Citizen

[May 4, 1779.]

Mr. Dunlap:

In your paper of April 29th I find an *attack* upon *juries,* the first that ever was made upon them in a free country. I wish the author of that publication would speak out and tell us at once that he means and wishes that juries should be abolished as troublesome restraints upon our rulers, and that a few *Tory-hunters* should hang, burn, or gibbet all who do not *think* with themselves, without law, judge, or jury.

Sidney

E [NO. 92]

[May 6, 1779].

To Mr. Jonathan Sergeant,
Attorney General of the State of Pennsylvania.
Sir:

Having seen in Mr. Dunlap's paper of April 29th, 1779, a publication of Mr. Franks's letters with many injudicious and scandalous insinuations against the jury who sat upon his trial, calculated solely to prejudice the minds of the people against them, I take it for granted that you are the author, from some warm expressions you were pleased to make use of when you were officiously listening at the window where the jury sat, that you "would publish his letters," and your exclaiming against their [the jury's] supposed opinion in a loud manner when you returned to court by saying, "it was not worth your while to indict any person hereafter," for that "*you knew* how the verdict would go, etc."

The mode of your obtaining this *knowledge* [by eavesdropping], when a strict direction was given by the court to the contrary, casts a shade upon your integrity, and shews the malignity of your temper, in a case which was at that moment in the utmost state of doubt and suspense.

Now, sir, if your remarks meant any thing, they conveyed this idea: that a part of the jury were perjured, and you have artfully called upon them to retract the verdict which they gave before the court, and that, too, upon their qualifications. Do you really think, because *you* are *attorney general,* that you have a *right* to insult, in the public newspapers, the freemen of this state, especially those who are upon oath to do justice between the Commonwealth of Pennsylvania and a person whom *you* thought proper to prosecute? Be assured, sir, you shall not, nor shall this insult upon the rights of citizens pass with impunity.

The first bill you drew up against Mr. Franks was for high treason; it was presented to the grand jury, and they returned it ignoramus [no true bill]. You then preferred another, for misprision of [misdemeanor akin to] treason, in which the jury likewise refused to gratify you, for they could not make it more than a misdemeanor. You pledged your *word* and *honor* to the jury that you would support your *favourite bill,* by a law enacted by the legislature of this state, for punishing high treason and misprision of treason, which law the jury took with them when they left the bar [courtroom to consider the case]. But when they came to consider the circumstances relative to the case before them, they found that neither the evidence, nor the law you dwelt so tediously upon, would support them in finding Mr. Franks guilty, agreeable to your bill of indictment.

And will you *dare* to say that the jury had not an undoubted right to determine the fact, that is, whether Mr. Franks did or did not commit the crimes charged against him in the bill? And whether any twelve honest men upon their oaths could, consistent with their conscience, find him guilty upon that indictment? Whether you ought to say it, I leave to those who are better acquainted with the law than I am to determine.

And now, give me leave to tell you, sir, if there was any crime in Mr. Franks's acquittal, it is a crime chargeable upon *you,* and not upon the jury. If public justice appears to *you* to have been eluded, it must be ascribed to the errors of *your* head, and not the defection of *their* hearts;

for by *your over*charging the bill, you have effectually *dis*charged the prisoner.

I am, sir,

A Juror

Philadelphia, May 5th, 1779.

F [NO. 92]

[May 13, 1779.]

To the Public:

The malignant attempts of some late publications to blacken the characters of Mr. David Franks and of the jurors who sat upon his trial must excite the indignation of every friend to his country, every friend to trial by jury, and every lover of good order in society. Had Mr. Franks's letters been published without any comment upon them, neither my acquaintance with, or friendship for him, would have induced me to trouble the public with a single thought about either of them. But the base attacks, which I complain of, are not simply made against him but are levelled, with a wicked intent, against the bulwark of our liberties, *trial by jury*, as well as against the safety of every citizen who may hereafter be acquitted by the laws of his country and the judgement of his peers.

For what security can any freeman have in the due administration of wholesome laws, if it is in the power of prejudice to raise the resentment of the people against both him and the jury who acquitted him, by publishing to the world such parts of the evidence only as operated against him, and suppressing whatever made in his favour? Do not our courts of justice furnish daily instances of what appears the strongest evidence brought in support of prosecutions, vanishing like air, when it comes to be explained by the defendant's witnesses? By halving and frittering away evidence in this manner, may not the plainest logical deductions be made the most nonsensical absurdities? And may not impiety, by practices of the like kind, turn every page of holy writ into blasphemy?

In order fully to understand the state of Mr. Franks's case, and the principles on which an honest jury founded their verdict, it is necessary to observe that many years before the wageing of the present war between Great Britain and America, Moses Franks, Esq., of London, contracted with the Lords of the Treasury to supply the British troops in America with rations at a stipulated price, and appointed his brother, Mr. David Franks, of this city, his agent to manage such parts of the business for him as were to be transacted here.

When, by the prowess of American arms, large numbers of the enemy were made prisoners of war, and became very expensive to the country (no British commissary residing here to supply them with necessaries), Mr. David Franks was by a resolve of Congress authorized to continue in his former capacity of agent to his brother and as such to supply, at the expence of the enemy, their troops confined as prisoners among us.

This he continued to do in the most unexceptionable manner, till the month of October last, when the price of provisions took such a sudden and rapid rise, owing to many causes, that Mr. Franks, the factor, saw his brother could no longer afford to supply rations purchased here, at the former rate. To prevent his brother and employer who had reposed a confidence in him from being ruined in his fortune, it was the duty of the agent, as a part of his business, and for the omission of which he must have been highly culpable in the eye of every reasonable man, to give as early information of this as possible to his employer. Accordingly, in the line of his business, he wrote the letter in question directed to his brother, but very prudently declined sending it in the usual manner, by a flag [of truce ship] and unsealed, since in such case it must have been open to inspection at [British] head quarters in New-York, and would not only have conveyed intelligence improper to have been communicated there but *his plan of enabling his brother to better his contract* must in all human probability have been defeated, since Mr. Franks must have been an ideot indeed, if he could suppose the commander in chief at New-York would be so inattentive to his master's [the king's] interest as to have suffered a letter of this kind, after perusing it (which would have been done by him or his proper officers), to pass to London.

In order, then, to ensure the letter a safe passage to his brother, *without being examined, and consequently stopped at New-York*, he sealed it up, and sent it by a soldier, inclosed to Capt. Moore, an officer of his acquaintance at New-York, in whom he could confide. Although it must be admitted to be improper, on most occasions, to send a letter within the enemy's lines by a soldier, yet when the circumstances of this case are attented to, it will appear quite different, since this was the best plan that ingenuity could form to prevent the letter being *intercepted at New-York*. And if it contained nothing improper to be communicated to the person for whom it was intended, the sending of it by a soldier cannot make it a crime.

That David Franks did not wish the contents of the letter to his brother to be known at New-York is evident, not only from what was his brother's interest, *which alone he had in view*, but from his intrusting it *sealed up* to an officer [General Oliver DeLancey], with whom he had been long acquainted, and who was also related to his family, with a request that he would *take particular care of it, and forward it to London by the first opportunity.*

The same is also evident from his giving no account of prices in his note to Capt. Moore, which he would have done, had he wished to give intelligence to any person at New-York.

It is true Mr. Franks desired Captain Moore to inform Mr. A. Allen that Mr. Hamilton had been honorably acquitted, after a trial of 12 hours, the jury about two minutes absent, and concludes with calling it an *ill-natured prosecution*. But this does not tend to betray America into the hands of the enemy, and is therefore neither prejudicial to the former or beneficial to the latter, but indifferent as to both and consequently no offence in the eye of law or reason. It was natural for Mr. Franks, whose daughter [Abigail] is married to Mr. Hamilton's brother, to embrace an opportunity of acquainting Mr. A. Allen, who is Mr. Hamilton's first cousin, with his welfare. And it is nothing extraordinary that so near a connection should call the prosecution an ill-natured one, since Mr. Hamilton's innocence was so evident that a sensible jury did not take *two minutes* to deliberate upon their verdict of acquittal. Thus the letter to Captain Moore is not only harmless in itself, but was necessary to procure a conveyance for the other to his brother *without the enemy's* knowing the contents.

If it should be thought that the letter to Moses Franks contains the current prices of other articles than were to be purchased by Mr. Franks, and supplied as rations, the public should be informed that by the evidence of Mr. Cottringer and Mr. Mordecai it was proved to the jury that Mr. Franks supplied the prisoners not only with beef, pork, bread, butter, etc., but with hats, shirts, stockings, shoes, and other cloathing, which brings the list of articles nearly within his proper business as factor. Another part of the letter said to be exceptionable is that which mentions that Mr. Franks "had the day before wrote the boys," but as it did not follow that because a father, moved by paternal affection, had written to his *two sons*, who had long been absent from him, that his letter contained treasonable matter, the jurors were men of better understanding, and paid a more sacred regard to their oaths than to presume it.

By an unaccountable distortion of language, ignorance or envy has construed the expression in the letter, "that the agents for the French were giving in Virginia and Maryland 60s. to 80s. per cent. [hundred pounds] for flour for French fleet, and meat in proportion," into traiterously giving intelligence to the enemy, injurious to our allies, when it is plain and obvious to the understanding of any man of common sense that he only mentions this to his *employer* (not to any person at New-York) as the reason of the sudden rise in the prices, and does not leave his brother to form the unfavourable conjecture (which might otherwise have taken place) that it was owing to an approaching famine, or the fall of our monies credit. Yet we find this innocent expression pitifully wrested to raise the resentment of the French gentlemen [allies], by endeavouring to impress an idea that Mr. Franks wished the supplies for the French fleet should be intercepted, though this letter was not to be read *till it reached his brother in London,* long before which time the provisions would be supplied if at all.

What has probably kindled the zeal of these censors against Mr. Franks is the wound which they receive from this expression in the letter, "that people are taken and confined at the pleasure of every scoundrel," and I must confess that if, by any rule of fair construction, it could be extended to the government or court where the trial was had, it would be highly censurable. But the words are not descriptive of either, but naturally relate to such bad men as history, the key of knowledge and experience, the touchstone of truth, tell[s] us have at all revolutions taken advantage of the times to gratify their vengeful passions upon their private enemies, till relief can be obtained from the justice of the country in the courts of law. And, indeed, so far was Mr. Franks from casting any reflection on the seat of justice, that he gives it the credit of honourably acquitting Mr. Hamilton, the moment his case was enquired into.

To use the words of one of these fathers of wisdom (who assumes the privilege of condemning jurors for daring to exercise their own understandings), "will it be credited in Europe or by posterity," that the following expression, "Oh, what a situation Britain has left its friends!" has been construed into criminality against the country? when reason and candor must agree that it is charging our enemies with ingratitude and want of humanity, who by all the arts of cunning and deception, by denouncing vengeance against their foes, and promising protection to their adherents, seduced some to join them, and others to think and speak favourably of them, and then abandoned them without settling, or endeavouring to settle, any terms of oblivion or amnesty in their favour. Have not *good Whigs* exulted over the Tories, often, by using the same or like expressions, "see what a situation your British friends have left you in, who spare neither friend or foe in their ravages"?

The letter to Moses Franks, then, so far as it relates to the price of provisions, appears to be strictly justifiable; and though there is one expression in it which had better have been left out, yet, as it is not a violation of any law, it could be taken no notice of by any human tribunal.

That the public may see no particular lenity has been shewn to Mr. Franks, they should also be informed that a bill for high treason was sent against him to the grand jury, who returned "ignoramus" thereon. Upon this the attorney general did not think proper to send a bill for misprision of treason, since such a prosecution could not be supported without a traiterous attempt to give intelligence to the enemy being made appear, and of this there was little expectation, from the first bill being returned "ignoramus." However, to make a conviction certain, by leaving the matter at large to a jury, this expedient was luckily hit upon: to send a bill for a misdemeanor, without charging a breach of any act of Assembly or known law, or even without containing a charge *of giving or attempting to give intelligence to the enemy,* but simply disturbing the peace of this commonwealth, by raising sedition within it, etc., *though the contents of the letter were not to be seen till it reached his brother in London.*

The trial was had by a struck jury of reputable citizens, several of whom had faced the enemy in the hour of danger, and whose characters are too well established to be hurt by the feeble efforts of narrow minded men "who suffer prejudice to get in the judgment seat, and pronounce sentence in the place of reason." Upon the trial no violated law could be shewn to support the prosecution but, on the contrary, the 4th volume, page 5, of the learned Judge Blackstone's Commentaries was read, to prove that a "misdemeanor is an act committed or omitted in violation of a public law, either forbidding or commanding it," and no such thing appeared in the case of Mr. Franks. As the jury did not sit in a legislative capacity to *make* laws and convict upon them at the same time, but were bound to determine according to the laws already in being, and as the safety of a free people requires that the laws respecting treason, and treasonable practices, should be known and settled, so as to leave no constructive engines of oppression in the hands of power, they found Mr. Franks *not guilty,* as by the law and their oaths they were bound to do.

What, then, are we to think of the most unfair publications, made with the corrupt view of exciting the resentment of the people against a citizen who has been fairly acquitted from a groundless prosecution, after every nerve had been exerted to punish him even capitally? What security has any man in the law, or safety in living up to its rules, if after an acquittal by a jury of the neighbourhood, the severest of punishments are to be inflicted by the disatisfied and ignorant, who, being actuated by mobbish [?] principles, neither reverence the law or regard its decrees? How disagreeable must the situation of jurors be if, after being compelled by law to serve in that office, and after giving a verdict according to the honest dictates of an upright conscience and well informed judgment, they are to be held up to the world as "suddenly changing their conduct to a very favourable turn towards offenders of a traiterous kind"; and their countrymen are to be deceived into a belief of this being the case, by having only the most unfavourable part of the evidence to judge from?

Wherein does the excellency of trial by jury consist, if by practices of this kind jurors are to be intimidated into convictions against both law and evidence, in order to support the character of Whigs? How much longer will this mode of trial be revered as sacred, if it is to be calumniated in public by profane tongues? What kind of logic is it, that because, if a person departing from the line of his business and duty should send such a letter as Mr. Franks's, from General Washington's camp, to give intelligence to the enemy at New-York, he would be hanged as a spy, that Mr. Franks therefore, who meant to *give no intelligence* at all, except what was proper to his brother and employer in *a distant country,* should also be hung? With what astonishment must the reasonable and unprejudiced part of mankind hear that it ever entered into the imagination of an attorney general to commence a prosecution upon such a groundless and trifling foundation? And with what an honest zeal of abhorrence must the fired bosom of every patriot glow, who reads in the public papers libels upon a mode of trial which secures the liberty of the subject against all the machinations which tyrants can form against it!

These observations in favour of the jury and in favour of trial by jury are submitted to the consideration of the impartial public by a friend to that mode of trial.

A. B.

G [NO. 92]

[May 13, 1779.]

For *The Pennsylvania Packet.*

Mr. Dunlap:

The examination of any measures affecting the public safety and interests is too important to be relinquished, though it may in its course disturb the tranquility of those who happen to be the objects of such discussions. We have seen the first characters in the community, and men holding the first offices, in this situation. The jury, therefore, in Mr. Franks's case cannot reasonably object to such company. They were called upon to discharge a public duty, under the sanction of an oath— the question is, whether they have done it faithfully. Is not this the case of all public officers? Are they not also sworn and under equal obligations? Why may not they, therefore, claim equal exemptions from enquiry and censure?

Jurymen must expect, like all other men acting on public occasions, to stand or fall in the public opinion by the rectitude and wisdom of their decisions. They have no other protection from the censure of doing wrong, than by doing right. What other protection would a reasonable man in a free country desire? There is no magick in the letters which compose the word jury that should charm or awe men into silence. They have the common right of all men, and especially when called to public office, to be treated with decency and candour, but their title extends no farther. The juryman [Davis Bevan], therefore, in a late paper, will do well to consider that passion and resentment always prejudice a man in the eye of the public, and that an argument may by that means be made worse, but can never be made better. As he, therefore, justifies the verdict, I shall consider his reasons, and though they are not very accurately or intelligibly expressed, they are reducible to the following:

First: That Mr. Franks did not intend to convey any intelligence to New-York, but to his brother in London.

Secondly: That there was no law, and consequently no transgression.

Thirdly: That the letter was innocent in itself, as being a letter of negotiation for private emoluments—not to injure the states.

In answer to the first: The crime was corresponding with the enemies of the United States, the guilt of which cannot depend upon the spot of the enemy's country where they happen to reside. A letter wrote to a secretary of state in London would be equally criminal as to Sir Henry Clinton in New York, in many instances more so. But there is not the least excuse, even on this ground, because this letter was to be sent to New-York, to a refugee officer [General DeLancey] in arms against his country. By this means the paper and its contents were to be conveyed to the enemy, liable to be made use of against us. And whether the letter was sealed, or not, is of no consequence to the writer or sender, either in law or reason, as the malignity of the letter cannot depend upon its being sealed or not, any more than the quality of merchandize depends upon the store in which it is kept, being locked or open.

The plain fact was that the letter was enclosed to an enemy in New-York, to be forwarded to an enemy (Moses Franks) in London, a contractor; wrote by his brother, also a contractor, and both engaged to feed and supply the British troops, while they are employed in the conquest and destruction of this country.

It is said that it appears from the letter that David "did not intend it should be known in New-York, as it would have defeated his intention of advancing [increasing] the ration." This is paying a wretched compliment to Franks's honesty, as it supposes he intended to deceive his employers by concealing the price of provisions from those in this country, who might be presumed to know better, and so obtain an unfair advance in England. But whoever reads the letter will see that Mr. Franks grounds his expectations of this advance on the real price of provisions; and as a proof tells what the French then gave for flour, and meat in proportion, so that it was not his design to conceal the facts from those in New-York.

Do Franks's intentions appear that the contents of the letter should not be known in New-York, by not sending it there? No, for it was found on a person going there, enclosed in a letter to Thomas Moore, residing there, and he [was] desired to forward it. Why, then, these harmless intentions must appear from his sealing the letter. And did the jury think a seal so sacred a thing in time of war and ground their verdict thereupon? The supposition would affront them, unless they resign all pretentions to common sense. But it is asked why he did not send the prices to Moore? I answer, he gave the letter which contained them, and by that means enabled him to know what they were. It will perhaps be said, this was in order to conceal them from the people in New-York; I confess I have nothing to say to such reasoning. But I ask in turn, who is Moses Franks, and where does he reside? To him the letter was directed, and he had an unquestionable right to break this sacred, this hallowed wax. Why, if it was not otherwise known, the letter describes him to be an officer in the enemy's service, of course, an enemy residing in the capital of the greatest enemy America has on earth, George the Third, King of Great Britain, and telling his brother such facts as would afford and does afford the greatest encouragement the enemy have to carry on the war, by enumerating the current high prices of the principal articles and conveniencies of life. But it seems to be forgot that London was in the enemy's country, and that Moses Franks was a subject of that country; and if future juries can forget it too, any one may write what he pleases to London, by way of New-York, and all that he has to do is to take care to seal the letter.

Now as to the second point: That there is no law against it. This I totally deny. There is every law against it. The law of reason, the law of self preservation, the law of nations, and the law of the land. But as the latter is the law I suppose referred to, I shall prove that there was law sufficient. It is evident the prisoner's council [counsel] thought so, or they would have demurred to the indictment, and brought the question of law before the court in a proper manner, but they knew better. They knew the ground would fail them. And it must be remembered that the court laid down the law clearly and fully that it was a misdemeanor, punishable by fine and imprisonment. Blackstone, page 119, speaking of misprisions of treason, says that a misprision is contained in every treason whatever, and that if the king so please, the offender may be proceeded against for the misprision only. And that every misprision contains a misdemeanor, upon which the delinquent may be censured, as happened in the case of the Earl of Rutland, etc.

If the jury had no reason to doubt the integrity and abilities of the court, why did they not give their opinion its due weight, in a point to which they, from their law knowledge, must be deemed more competent? Or why did they not find a special verdict, declaring the facts, and putting it upon the court to pronounce the law? This would have eased their judgements and put the matter upon a proper footing; as if it had been possible for the court to say that there was no law against corresponding with an enemy in time of war. There would have been then some ground for the legislature to have framed one. But if such a law was to be now proposed, whatever the gentlemen of the profession might think it necessary and convenient to say at the bar, those in the house [Assembly?] would hold a different language, and tell them there was law enough, if juries would do their duty.

The last point, and which probably was a governing one, is of the utmost importance to us, and therefore deserves to be seriously considered. The jury in this case seem to have held an opinion that correspondences between subjects of different nations in time of war may be innocent, and that this was so. Both positions are erroneous. By the customs and laws adopted among all civilized nations, in time of war all intercourse with the enemy, but [except] under the sanction of public authority, is illegal and unjustifiable. And this is highly reasonable, for if it was otherwise, every person holding such intercourse must be the judge of what would or would not be prejudicial. Now in many cases information apparently innocent might be of the most fatal kind; besides that being contrary in its nature to a state of war, it would open a door to all manner of dangers and abuses. Hence it has been adopted, as a general rule, that all intercourse with an enemy, but by special permission, is improper, and therefore letters of the most private kind, and uninteresting to the public, are transmitted open, and pass through the hands of persons in authority. So that the court were fully justified in saying that all correspondence with an enemy, but by special license, is improper and illegal.

With respect to this particular letter, it is really doing violence to the common reason and understanding of mankind to call it an innocent letter, and only wrote for private emolument. It appears, in the first place, to have been designed to be conveyed by stealth. It informs what prices our allies were then giving for flour for their support; then a false and infamous reflection upon the government and people of the state, "that people are taken up and confined at the pleasure of every scoundrel." Then follows a list of prices, holding forth an idea either of a great necessity and scarcity, or a depreciation of our money, which, though true, no one has a right to communicate, as either will naturally prove powerful inducements to our enemy to prolong the war. Yet, as it is said, this was a letter of private emolument, I ask what referrence had the reflection on the government, or the price of broad cloth and linens, to his emolument; or how could such information tend to promote it? They might shew a seditious spirit, and disclose our wants and distresses, but how they could promote Mr. Franks's interest remains to be shewn. And yet we are told, not only gravely but angrily, that all this is innocent, and can do our country and cause no harm. Fie upon it!

And now, my fellow-citizens and countrymen, permit me to address a few lines to you. The happiness and safety of government immediately depend upon a just and faithful execution of the laws. You are called frequently, as jurymen, to perform an important part of this duty. Be not eager to decide too much; where you can have confidence in the judges, repose it. Respect their opinions in points of law; they are sworn to assist you in matters of law, you to assist them in matters of facts, and though you have a power to engross both, you should consider that in so doing you stand responsible to God and the world; and that ignorance is a miserable plea for errors you may thus commit. Your office, though not sacred as some seem to wish, is highly respectable, and it depends upon you to make it more so by caution in your decisions and chastity in your recommendations for mercy. The frequency of such applications has very much lessened their weight, and even you yourselves must be convinced that had pardons been as frequently granted as they have been asked and solicited, neither your lives, liberties, or properties would have been equally secured.

Consider also that you are carrying on a war with a bitter and implacable nation, that we have many intestine enemies who earnestly wish and pray for their success and give them all the assistance and intelligence that they dare. Consider that you have allies who look with an attentive eye upon every transaction which affects the common interests of the war. Consider that you have a brave and gallant army exposing themselves to danger and death, that these expect from you vigilance and jealousy to guard, and justice to punish traitors at home, while they are meeting open force abroad; and they have an equal claim upon you to guard them against the secret machinations of the common enemy, as you have to expect their brave and open exertions in the field.

The issue of the trial on which I have made these observations has given great and general dissatisfaction. I trust they will have some weight in future. For it is plain as the face of day itself that we must either give up the war, or pursue the necessary means to close it with success, one of which is the detection and punishment of such practices.

CATO

No. 93   The Sheftalls: Prisoners of War—1779–1780

Mordecai and Sheftall Sheftall, father and son, two Continental army commissaries, were captured when Savannah fell to the British in December, 1778. Both men were put on a prison ship, but toward the end of March, or the beginning of April, 1779, the father was paroled to Sunbury, Georgia. The son had to remain behind.

Mordecai Sheftall was almost frantic in his concern for his son, who was not quite seventeen at the time. (Although looked upon by his father as a "lad," Sheftall was a very self-reliant young man.) The father wanted the son paroled and sent to Sunbury. To this end Mordecai Sheftall wrote a letter on April 12, 1779 (Document A), addressed to Colonel Samuel Elbert, his immediate commanding officer, and to Major John Habersham, both of whom shared Sheftall's fate of a prisoner of war. The writer asked the officers to urge General Benjamin Lincoln, the American commander of the Southern Department, to intervene with the British in order to obtain young Sheftall's parole to Sunbury. Mordecai also wanted Elbert and Habersham, should they themselves be exchanged, to remind General Lincoln that he too wanted to be exchanged.

Mrs. Mordecai (Frances) Sheftall, probably in the same month, also wrote to General Lincoln, pleading that he make an effort to secure her husband's exchange (Document B). At first Mrs. Sheftall had drafted a bitter note to the general, but fortunately she did not dispatch it. In her draft she held General Robert Howe responsible for her husband's capture and alleged that he had wanted her husband to be taken prisoner.

Whether Mordecai Sheftall's associates interceded for the young man is not known, but by June of that year the son was paroled and joined his father in Sunbury. However, although the two were reunited, their troubles were by no means over. After Count Jean Baptiste d'Estaing's failure to recapture Savannah in October, 1779, the Tories and some irregular troops threatened the parolees at Sunbury. The Sheftalls and their friends fled for their lives. When next heard from they were all in St. Johns, Antigua. Document C, a copy of a letter to the president and members of the Continental Congress—in the handwriting of Mordecai Sheftall—tells how they got to the West Indian island.

Document D is a letter sent by Mrs. Sheftall to her husband and son in Antigua. In it she described her efforts to help them, and because they were hungry for news, she regaled them with gossip and wrote that she was in business and was doing well. All this, however, may have been a device on her part to keep their spirits up. Perla, their seventeen-year-old daughter, wrote this letter for her mother.

SOURCE. The Mr. and Mrs. B. H. Levy Collection of Sheftall Papers.

A [NO. 93]

Sunburry, 12th April, 1779.

Dear Sir:

I have now been here a week and cannot learn wether my son is to be permitted to come here or no. I thinke if I could make freinds to applie to the General in his behalf, that he would hardly refuse him the indulgence granted to every other Continental officer, as I know of no charge that has or can be brot againste him. Whatever may be said of me, he was taken in the line of his duty as every other officer was; therefor, it is astonishing to me why he should be pointed at in so particular a manner. You must suppose that it is very grevious to me to have the lad kept from me in the manner that he is. Therefor, must request of you and Major Habersham to use what interest you may have to get him on his parole to this place. It will be laying me under a lasting obeligation to you both, never to be forgot.

It is reported here that you and the major have obetained leave to go to New York. If so, I hope if you write to General Lincoln, that you will mention me to him in such manner as you may thinke will induce him not to forget me. I should be happy to here from you and the major befor you go; and if you go, I wish you boath a happy and prosperous voyage and speedy return to your freinds and your family. You'l pleas to present my compliments to our fellow prisoner, Mr. Freasure [Lieutenant John Frazier], allso to the Miss Minis's. And am very respectfully, sir,

Your mosst humble servant,
Mordecai Sheftall

Sam'l Elbert Esq.

B [NO. 93]

Honored Sir:

Permit me to address you in behalf of my husband, Mr. Mordecai Sheftal, taken with his son at Savanna, now at Sunbury. (My son still remains at Savannah.) Hope it is in your power to have Mr. Sheftal speedily exchanged, as many sorrowful circumstances require it to relieve his distrest family, who most earnestly stands very much in need of it. I would have waited personally on your Excellency, but it is entirely out of my power.

Mr. Sheftal's manner of being taken was singular from others; he could have escaped, but stayed by General Howe's order, and the son would not leave his father, though now obliged to be apart, my son being on board a prison ship at Savanna. Have just now seen a gentleman who made his escape from the same vessell, and by this gentleman have heard that my husband has wrote several letters to your Excellencey to beg by some means to be relieved from his imprisonment.

Honored Sir, [I] hope from your benevolent heart to me and my children, who never knew what want was, some step for his liberty may be found [and] taken to restore him to us, or we too soon shall require it [help], as I have not it in my power to support him during his imprisonment. My unhappiness is not to express on this most afflicting occasion; your Excellencey's compliance [?] to relieve my husband will ever have the prayers and thanks of myself and children from, honored sir,

Your most [humble and obedient servant],
Francis Sheftal

C [NO. 93]

St. Johns, Antigua, 16th December, 1779.

May it pleas Your Excellency:

We, the subscribers, Continental officers and citizens of America, now prisoners of war in this island, beg leave to lay befor Your Excellency and the honorable members of Congress the following narritive, which we humbly hope you will be pleased to take into consideration and grant us such relife [relief] as the nature of our sittuation requiers.

We are some of those unfortunate men who became prisioners of war at the time the British troops entered and took possession of the state of Georgia, where we remained on paroles at the town of Sunburry, in said state, untill the 17th day of October last, when we where [were] left without any kinde of protection or any thinge to subsiste upon. [We were] subject to the incursions of the savages [Indians] and the depradations of the irregulars, who had fled at the approach of the American army, and who returned as soon as his Excellency General Lincoln had called in his out posts, threatening vengeance on all those who should fall in theire hands.

In this sittuation, haveing first obetained his Excellency General Lincoln['s] letter approveing of our removal from the then local circumstances of the state and the sittuation of the combined army befor the town of Savannah, then, for the reasons befor recited, we embarked on board the briganteen *Betsey,* commanded by Captain Samuel Spencer, bound for Charls Town in South Carrolina, and sailed over Sunburry Barr on the 24th day of October, and on the next morning where [were] taken by a British frigate called the *Gaudaloop* and by her brot to this port, where we are detained by the governor, who has admitted us on our parole, restricting us to the limits of this town, and who informs us it is not in his power to exchange us, unless he should receive orders from his sovereign for that purpose. This, togather with the want of every necessary to make life comfortable, is our deplorable sittuation, there being no cartels [agreements for the exchange of prisoners] settled hare, nor any prospect of exchange. And as we are informed, upwards of seventy of our countrymen now confined in goal [jail], for whose sittuation we truly feel, and whose distress we have it not in our power to aleviate.

We therefor pray Your Excellency and the Honorable Congress will be pleased [to] endeavour to facelitate our exchange with the commanding officer of the British troops in New Yorke, upon whose notice of such exchange, signefied to the governor of this island, our libration may be effected, and we once more permitted to return to our native country and freinds.

We are, with all due deference and respect, Your Excellency's most obedient, humble servants.

[Mordecai Sheftall, . . .
Sheftall Sheftall, . . .]

D [NO. 93]

Charls Town, March 3th, 1780.

My dear Sheftall:

I had the pleasure to receive your laste letter, with my son's, by Mr. Coshman Polack by the way of North Carolina, and was glad to here [hear] that you and my son injoyed your healths, a continuance of which I sincerely whish you. But [I] was verry miserable to hear that you and my dear child was in so much distress. I would have endeavoured to have sent something for your reliefe, but the enemy now lay off of the bar, so that it is not in my power to do any thing for you at present, but the first safe oppertunity you may depend on my sending you whatever is in my power.

Their is a Jew gentleman gone from here to North Carolina, by the name of Mr. Levy. He has promised me to buy up six halfe johanases [gold coins] theare [there] and to send them to you with a letter, as thay are much cheaper thare than [they] are here.

I had not the pleasur off seeing Mrs. Walton, as the vessel she came in was obliged to put in to North Carolina. Mr. Coshman Polack has been to St. Eustatia and was passenger with Mrs. Walton, since whitch he has arrived here. He likewhise told us that he wrote to you, but that he never received an answer. Your brother has shewn your letter to Genaral [Benjamin] Lincoln, and he has assured him that he will do all in his power in your behalfe as soon as times is a little more settled here.

You must tell my son that I would have answered his letter in full, but it is Friday afternoon and very late. But he may depend that I will whrite him by the next oppertunity. Our friend Mrs. Whrite is here and has been with me some time. She sincerely wishes to see you. Our old friend, Miss Sally Martin, is dead, and likwhise poor Mrs. Brady. Old Mrs. Mines [Abigail Minis] is here with all her family and is settled here. They all desire to be kindly remembered to you. I hav the pleasure to inform you that your brother's wife is safely delivered off a fine son and he is called Isaac. Mr. Jacobs and wife, in company with Mr. Cohen and wife, desire to be kindly remembered to you. Mr. Cohen's family is likely to increas shortly. I can assure you that Mr. Jacobs is been a father to your children and a great friend to me. I had like to [I almost] forgot to mention to you that I have received the 2 thousand pounds of Mr. Cape, with which I make exceeding well out by doing a little business. Your children all go to school. I have no more at present, but that I and all the children are in good health, and am, my dear Sheftall,

Your loving wife,
Frances Sheftall

Pearla begs that you will excuse this scrool, as she has wrote it in great haste and our Sabbeth is coming on so fast.

The children all desire their love to their brothe[r] and their duty to you. They all long for to see you.

No. 94   Two Savannah Merchants Advise Count d'Estaing—1779

The capture of Savannah by the British forces in December, 1778, was a severe blow to the American cause. Held by the Americans, Savannah was the bulwark of the Carolinas to the north; in British hands it was a threat to the Southern states. Unless the enemy was driven out, there was a risk that Georgia would drift away from the cause and make a separate peace with the mother country. Therefore, in order to save Georgia for the Continental cause, Count Jean Baptiste d'Estaing, the French commander who had come to the aid of the Americans, was asked to recapture the city.

Early in September, 1779, the French fleet and troops under d'Estaing appeared off Savannah. The commander hoped that with the aid of the Americans under General Benjamin Lincoln he would be able to drive the British out of Georgia. In order that he might learn the lay of the land, d'Estaing called upon a number of local patriots to advise him. Among them were two Jewish merchants of Savannah, Philip Minis and Levi Sheftall. They pointed out to the French commander where he could disembark his troops and station a part of his fleet to the best advantage. The report given by the French of their interview with the two men is printed below.

D'Estaing followed the advice of the local patriots and accepted the guidance of the two men. But in spite of the men's assistance, the long siege and the final assault of October 9 failed miserably. General Lincoln and his troops retired after suffering heavy losses, and the French sailed away.

Levi Sheftall (1739–1809) was a merchant, butcher, and rancher in Savannah. As a patriot, he suffered civil disabilities at the hands of the Tories of Georgia. Two years later the Whigs of the state denounced him, if only temporarily, and apparently unjustly, as a Tory.

Philip Minis (1733 [1734?]–1789) fled to Charlestown after the siege and was denounced by the Tory government of Georgia. As early as 1776 he had served the troops in the South as a commissary general and as acting paymaster. In the latter capacity he had advanced money to the Continental forces fighting in his native state of Georgia. More fortunate than others, he got some of his money back.

Both Sheftall and Minis were very active in the Jewish community of Savannah and served in the office of parnas, or president, of the local congregation.

SOURCE. B. F. Stevens, *Facsimiles of Manuscripts in European Archives Relating to America, 1773–1783*, Siege of Savannah; information given by two merchants, etc., MS. No. 2013. The copy used is in the Chicago Historical Society Library.

Siege of Savannah.

Information given by two merchants of Charlestown . . . [relative] to places of landing for the French troops under Count d'Estaing.

September, 1779.

Mr. Philips Minis, a merchant at Charlestown: said to be thoroughly acquainted with the neighbourhood of Savannah for a distance of fifteen miles, with all the roads and dwellings. He is able, within this distance, to guide any party, even through the woods.

He says that the house of Mrs. Morél at Bioulay is the best place for landing, on account of its facilities both for disembarking and for forming any number of troops. The roads which lead to Savannah are good, and fit for the carriage of artillery.

He says it is to greater advantage to anchor an armed ship inside the Straits of St. Catherine, or at Sunbury, to intercept the retreat of the enemy, than at Sapello, since if that alone is held, it cannot hinder vessels leaving by the Straits of St. Catherine.

Mr. Sheftall Levi [Levi Sheftall], merchant at Charlestown, a native of Savannah, is of the same opinion as the preceding with regard to the place called Bioul[a]y to effect the landing. But believing that frigates can pass over the bar, he thinks it would be well to make, at the same time as at Bioulay, a second landing at Tonder [Thunder] Bolt, sending the boats up the north side of the Savannah River to St. Augustine's Creek, which they would enter in order to reach Thunder Bolt. It is supposed that a battery might be made at this place, as one had already been commenced by the Americans for six cannon. Thunder Bolt is four miles from Savannah. The English have cut down the wood for a mile around the town.

He says that the best means of cutting off all communication with Savannah is to hold Bioulay, to intercept the high road from Savannah to St. Augustine, and that from Savannah to Ebenezer at the spot called Cherokee, about eight miles from Savannah. In order to take possession of this point, the house of Stephen Melen, etc., must be passed.

The two guides, Philips Minis and Sheftall Levy, will conduct the force when ordered to do so.

No. 95 Isaac Franks Complains that West Point Is Being Short-Weighted on Hay—1780

The forage master at West Point in 1780 was Isaac Franks (1759–1822), a native of New York and probably a nephew of the wealthy merchant, Jacob Franks.

Isaac Franks joined the army as a volunteer in 1776. He was captured when the British took New York City, but a few months later managed to escape by crossing the Hudson River to the New Jersey shore in a small and leaky skiff with but one paddle. After serving in the quartermaster general's department from 1777 to 1781, he was commissioned an ensign in the Seventh Massachusetts Regiment, with which he remained until 1782, when he resigned for reasons of health. The title "colonel," by which he was frequently known, derived from a postwar appointment in the militia.

After the Revolution Franks settled in Philadelphia as a broker and land speculator. Toward the end of his life, when reduced circumstances compelled him to seek a position, he became prothonotary of the Supreme Court of Pennsylvania.

Although he was the son of observant Jews, Franks himself, as far as we can determine, had no Jewish interests. (The one exception was a contribution to the building fund of Mikveh Israel, Philadelphia, in 1782.) He married out of the faith and reared his children as Christians.

In the following letters Franks complained to General Benedict Arnold, the commander at West Point, about the hay that he received. Obviously somebody was cheating the government. In view of Arnold's record in Canada and Philadelphia with respect to private gain, it is not impossible that he was privy to the cheating. Arnold had already been in the employ of the British for about a year.

SOURCE. The Library of Congress, Division of Manuscripts, Washington Papers.

A [NO. 95]

West Point, September 3, 1780.
Honored Sir:

Hay comes in to this post very fast, and greate quantities are on the way. The hay, as it comes in now, does not appear to me to be above two thirds as much as is mentioned in the invoices that is sent with the same. I have no scail to weigh it. I have applied from time to time to the quarter master to errect one, all to no purpose.

Beg Your Honour would please to order a committe to judge the different quantities after they are unloaded. I will report to them when ever a quantity arives; if some such meathud is not taken, the public will be [w]ronged greatly. I shall be under the necessity of receipting agreeable to the invoices.

I find by my books as I have receipted, according to the invoices, the hay has been deficiant five and six hundred out of every ton that I have received.

I am, honored sir,
Your most obedient and very humble servant,
Isaac Franks
G.F.M. [Garrison Forage Master]

The Honorable Major General Arnold.

B [NO. 95]

West Point, September 22, 1780.
Honoured Sir:

I sent yesterday two tons of as good hay as I had here for the use of your horses. I am affraid they won't eat it. I never saw so much bad hay in so large a quantity as I have here. Severall quantityes that is sent here is not worth unloden.

I have acquainted Colonel Hay of the quallity of hay I have here. I am collecting the best hay out of all I have into a barn for the use of your horses. I shall be able to send over six or seven tons in a fue days. I don't here [hear] of any grain.

I remain, honoured sir,

Your most obedient and very humble servant,
Isaac Franks, G.F.M.

Honourable Major General Arnold.

No. 96   The Sheftalls in Philadelphia—1780-1781

By December, 1780, both Mordecai Sheftall and his son Sheftall Sheftall, former prisoners of the British, had been exchanged and liberated. Like many other Whigs who could not return home, they settled in Philadelphia. Their home towns, Savannah and Charlestown, were still in the hands of the enemy.

In Document A, printed below, the father appealed to Congress for a settlement of his pay accounts and for reimbursement for the money he had advanced to the army while a commissary officer.

While the father was pleading his cause, Sheftall Sheftall was approached by members of Congress to undertake a mission for the government. They wanted him to go to Charlestown in a flag-of-truce ship and to deliver a sum of money and food supplies for the relief of General William Moultrie and his imprisoned men. In Document B young Sheftall told his state representatives in Congress why he required compensation for his services.

In the spring of the following year Mordecai Sheftall succeeded in bringing his family from Charlestown to Philadelphia, but to pay for their passage he incurred a debt. In a petition to Congress he suggested that inasmuch as the owners of the ship that had brought his family were indebted to the government, he might recompense himself in part, if Congress permitted, by collecting from the shipowners what they owed the United States (Document C). This request was denied.

SOURCE. The Mr. and Mrs. B. H. Levy Collection of Sheftall Papers.

A [NO. 96]

Philladelphia, 21st November, 1780.

His Excellency, Samuel Huntington, Esq.,
President of Congress.
Sir:

Being informed by the delegates of the state to which I belong that my application for depreciation of pay cannot now be considered, I must intreat the Honorable Congress to have some consideration for a man who has sacrificed every thing in the cause of his country. I want nothing but justice, to be repaid my advances for the publick.

It is impossible for me to go to the southward to settle, because I am not able to purchase the means of going or to defray the expences of traveling. Therefore, referring me there is declining to pay what is my due. Besides, the sittuation of that country does not look much like settling accounts at present.

I have heitherto bore the character of an honest man, and I trust I can have people of reputation to say [so]. I am willing to swear that my account is just, and if it cannot from any rules of buisness be now settled and liquidated, I beg that the Honorable Congress will order me a sum of money eaqual to its amount, upon account.

I will only add that I am about sending to Charls Town for my family, which I have not seen for two years past, and fear that it will be much longer befor I shall have the happiness to see them, unless I am assisted by Congress.

I have the honor to be,

Your Excellency's most obedient servant,
Mordecai Sheftall

B [NO. 96]

Philladelphia, 22d December, 1780.

Gentlemen:

I am very sorry to learn that an oppinion has gone forth amongst some of the members of the Honorable Congress that I meant to take the advantage of the publick in demanding an exhorbitant sum for going as flag master in the intended flag [flag-of-truce ship] to Charls Town.

The fact is simply this: when I made application to go, I considered my self as a Continental officer whose duty it was to render his country what services he could. But when I applied to the Board of War for my pay, they tell me that I am not intitled to pay nor rattions as longe as I am exchanged, so that by doing my duty as a good citizen in getting my exchange accomplished, I am put out of office and deprived of a subsistance.

This induced me to request pay of the Board of War for going in the flag. As I have it not in my power to support my self while there, nor even to purchase necessary stores to carrie me there and to bringe me back, notwithstanding which I am still willing to go, provided I have necessary stores provided for me and a sufficient support whilst at Charls Town, so that I may not become [a burden?] to my poor distressed mother who has no other support but what she earnes by washing and ironing.

This is the plaine state of facts. Therefor hope that I shall stand acquited of any imputation of design, and am, gentlemen,

Very respectfully, your most humble servant,
Sheftall Sheftall

Honorable George Walton and
the rest of the Georgia delegation.

C [NO. 96]

Philladelphia, April 24th, 1781.

His Excellency Samuel Huntingdon, Esq.,
President of Congress.
Sir:

It is with the outmost regret that I am reduced to the necessity of makeing application to Your Excellency to request your kinde interposition with the Honorable the Congress in my behalf, as I am really reduced to the outmost necessity. My family are arrived from South Carrolina, and I have it not in my power to pay the owners of the flag [flag-of-truce ship] for theire passage. My wife and children's cloathing where stopt [were held] for theire passage money, but I have with dificulty prevailed on the owner, Mr. Carson, to take my note payable in three days for twelve johanases, which I have no visible means of dischargeing unless relived [relieved] by Congress, as the publick are very considerably in my debt.

The American commissary of prisioners advanced in Charls Town for the use of the flag [flag-of-truce ship] upwards of fifty pounds sterling, which the owners owe the publick, as she [the owners] have been paid the freight for the sloop by the honorable the Board of War. I would therefor wish that I might obetaine an order on said owners for that money, on account.

I am very very respectfully Your Excellency's

Mosst obedient, humble servant,
Mordecai Sheftall

No. 97 Isaac DaCosta Seeks to Redeem Loan Office Certificates—1781

Isaac DaCosta (*ca.* 1721–83) was in all probability the outstanding Jew of Charlestown, South Carolina, in the years before and during the Revolutionary War. He was a member of a very distinguished Dutch and English family of Spanish-Portuguese origin. Apparently a native of England, he received some secular training in addition to a better-than-average Hebrew education. In his later years he was the owner of a small rabbinical library and knew how to use it. On a visit to Newport, R.I., he spent some time with Ezra Stiles, the future president of Yale College, no doubt discussing religious matters with him. On occasion, when religious or ritual problems arose in a congregation, DaCosta was consulted on points of Jewish law.

This founding father of the Charlestown Jewish community came to these shores in the 1740's and soon emerged as one of the leaders of the local congregation which was then in the process of formation. He served as a volunteer reader in the first Charlestown synagogue (1749), and laid out the first Jewish cemetery. Socially accepted in the larger community, DaCosta became a steward of the Palmetto Society and established a Masonic lodge in his state.

Ministering to the Jewish community was a labor of love for DaCosta; he made his living as a merchant and shipper, and all indications point to his success. He served as the Charlestown correspondent for Aaron Lopez, of Newport, and at times engaged in the slave trade.

With the outbreak of the Revolution, DaCosta became an ardent patriot. Consequently he was forced to leave Charlestown when the British forces occupied the town in 1781, and went to Philadelphia, where he associated himself with the local Jewish religious group. His flight had left him without means of support, hence he appealed, in the following petition, to the Continental Congress for the redemption of some Loan Office certificates that had fallen due.

SOURCE. The Library of Congress, Papers of the Continental Congress, 136, V, 205.

To His Excellency the President [Samuel Huntington] and the honourable members of the United States in Congress assembled:

The petition of Isaac DaCosta humbly sheweth:

That your petitioner was an inhabitant of Charles Town, in the State of South Carolina; and, on the enemy's landing in said state, your petitioner retired from thence with his family, rather than fall in their hands, and was obliged to leave all his property, both real and personal, behind, which has been taken possession of by the enemy, and only brought off with him some Continental money and a few Continental Loan Office certificates;

That the money he brought is entirely expended, and he has nothing to support himself and family with but the said certificates;

That two of the said certificates have become due the 7th instant, amounting to about 1,050 or 60 specie dollars, including the 3 years' interest;

And that, on your petitioner's applying to Mr. [Michael] Hillegas [the Treasurer of the United States] for the discharge of principal and interest thereof, he informed your petitioner that he could not do it, for want of orders to that purpose, as also for want of cash.

Wherefore your petitioner humbly prays that you will be pleased to take his distressfull circumstances into consideration and order him the payment of the two said certificates.

And, as in duty bound, will ever pray,

Isaac DaCosta

Philadelphia, 13th March, 1781.

————

No. 98   Rachel Myers, a Loyalist, Appeals for Help—1781

While Newport, Rhode Island, was held by the British (1776–79), the Loyalists were secure enough, but when the French forces, commanded by the Count de Rochambeau, came in 1780, many of them found it advisable to leave.

Among the refugees was the widow Rachel Myers, one of whose sons, Benjamin, had been an active Tory. Taking her large brood of children with her, Mrs. Myers went to New York City, which had been under British occupation since 1776. There, without means, she appealed for aid to Sir Henry Clinton, the commander in chief of the British forces in North America.

After the evacuation of New York in 1783, the widow and her family were once again forced to flee. They spent some time in Canada, and then, when the acerbities engendered by the war had been dulled by the passage of time, they returned to the United States. One of the boys, Mordecai, served as an officer in the War of 1812.

SOURCE. College of William and Mary, British Headquarters Papers (Carleton Papers), No. 3427.

To His Excellency, Sir Henry Clinton, Knight of the Most Honorable Order of the Bath, General and Commander in Chief, etc., etc., etc.

The petition of Rachel Myers, late of Newport, widow, humbly sheweth:

That your petitioner was for many years an inhabitant of Newport, where she supported, by her industry, a large family of children;

That from the decissive part her son, Benjamin Myers, took with the associated refugees and other loyalists at Rhode Island, she was obliged to leave that place after it was evacuated by his Majesty's troops and come to this city in a flag of truce [ship] with all her family, consisting of nine children;

That she has in the maintenance of her family struggled with many difficulties, and from the assistance she has derived from a few benevolent friends, hitherto been able to support, tho indifferently, her children. But all her industry is not now sufficient to afford them the necessaries of life, which constrains her to implore your Excellency to extend her some relief from government, by permitting her to receive for her family such rations of provisions, etc., as may be thought necessary.

And your petitioner, as in duty bound, shall ever pray.

Rachel Myers

New York, April 3, 1781.

———

No. 99   Major Franks in the Diplomatic Service—1781

David Salisbury Franks, a native of Philadelphia, moved to Canada, where he engaged in commerce. During the American Revolution, while living in Montreal, he expressed his sympathy for the colonies, for which he suffered imprisonment. After the fall of Montreal he joined the patriots and, more important, furnished them with goods, money, and services. Later, when the northern army retreated, he fought with it as a volunteer until General John Burgoyne's surrender. The arrival of Count Jean Baptiste d'Estaing in 1778 enabled him to serve on the staff of the French allies, whose language he had doubtless learned while trading in Montreal and Quebec. In 1779 he was an aide to General Benjamin Lincoln in Charlestown, South Carolina. A year later, when Benedict Arnold deserted to the British, Franks was in the traitor's military family, but was exculpated of all complicity in the treason. Among those who vouched for him was General Henry Knox, the commander of artillery to whom Franks offered his services (Document A).

In the summer of 1781 Robert Morris, the Superintendent of Finance, made use of Franks's services, sending him with dispatches to John Jay at Madrid and to Benjamin Franklin at Paris. He remained in Europe until the following year and then returned home. In 1784 he went abroad once more, taking with him a copy of the ratified, definitive treaty of peace, and stayed until 1787, serving as a consular official, diplomatic courier, and secretary.

During his first visit to France, Franks was arrested while wandering about in the port area of Brest. Bristling with indignation because the French had held him for a while, the major complained to Benjamin Franklin, who was then living at Passy as the American minister plenipotentiary to France. Franklin had been one of the three commissioners sent to Montreal in 1776 to induce the Canadians to take the Whig side. There it was, in all probability, that Franks, "one of the principal leaders of sedition," first had met Franklin.

As we see in Franklin's reply to Franks's complaint (Document B), the wise old philosopher gently chided the major and suggested that Franks had inadvertently committed some indiscretion. Franklin may well have been right. Jefferson, who knew Franks well and liked him, described him to Madison as "light, indiscreet, active, honest, affectionate."

Though Franklin was not, as far as we know, intimate with Philadelphia Jews, he knew many of them. For fifteen years (1738–53) he did business with Nathan Levy, the founder of the Philadelphia Jewish community, whose ship *Myrtilla* brought the Liberty Bell to America. In the Library Company and in the Pennsylvania Society for Promoting the Abolition of Slavery, Franklin came to know a number of the Jewish citizens of his city. The Indiana-Vandalia promoters, a trans-Allegheny land combine in which Philadelphia Jews were heavily interested, employed him as one of their lobbyists in London. He was associated in a business transaction with Benjamin Nones, a revolutionary patriot, signed a peddler's license for a poor Jew, and in 1788 contributed liberally to Congregation Mikveh Israel, which was then in financial straits.

SOURCE. Document A: Massachusetts Historical Society Library, Henry Knox Papers; Document B: Microfilm of the Franklin Papers in the Library of the American Philosophic Society in Philadelphia, original in The Library of Congress, Division of Manuscripts, Franklin Papers.

A [NO. 99]

Capes of Delaware, 17th July, 1781.

My dear General:

Having allways had reason to think you had a friendship for me and interrested yourself in my wellfare, it is with no small degree of pleasure I inform you that I am this far on my way to Spain, employed by Mr. R. Morris on public business; and from the Court of Madrid am to proceed to Paris and then return immediately to this country. I beg you would be friend enough [no]t to mention this as it may injure me if it were [gen]erally known. Mr. Morris has promised to procure [his] Excellency's permission of absence, and if I do this affair with dispatch, it will be a means of introducing [me] into further employment in this way.

I have letters to all our ministers abroad and to some French gentlemen of fashion, which will be a means of introducing me into very good company in Europe. I shall not neglect employing what money I can collect to advantage, and if I find encouragement I may very probably settle as a merchant in France. I should be glad, my dear General, to be of some service to you or to your good lady, whose polite attention to me I shall ever remember with gratitude.

I should be happy to have a line from you directed to me at Paris, which, if sent to Mr. Morris, he will be so kind as to forward. If any thing worthy your notice should happen in the affairs of Europe, you may depend upon having it from me. If Mrs. Knox wishes me to bring her any thing from France on my return, pray let me know it.

I should have informed you of my voyage sooner had I been earlier acquainted with it, but I came off with my knapsack (and that not over burthened with the goods of this world) at two da[ys'] notice. I must now beg you would accept of [my] most grateful acknowledgements for all your [service?] to me, and particularly your friendly interposition in my favor on the flight of [Benedict] Arnold, all which, be assured, have left an indeleble impression in my heart.

I am, dear sir, with respectful compliments to Mrs. Knox and to Major Doughty [John Douty?] and [Captain Samuel] Shaw,

Your very humble and obliged servant,
David S. Franks

Ship rocks, I can scarcely write.

B [NO. 99]

Passy, Dec. 17, 1781.

Major Franks.
Sir:

I received the letter you did me the honour of writing to me acquainting me with your being taken up at Brest, examined, and uncivilly treated. Me thinks you are too ready to suppose this was done with an intention to offend you.

It is the duty of those who have the care of the ports, when strangers appear there, to enquire who and what they are. Brest is an important place, to us as well as to France, and we ought to take their caution in good part, and be pleased that our allies are so careful of their places.

A man may be sensible of his own integrity, of his consequence, and of the respect due to it; but it does not follow that all the world should be sensible of the same at first sight of him.

The French are naturally so civil to strangers that I am apt to suspect you have inadvertently committed some indiscretion that has drawn upon you the treatment you complain of.

By the enclosed letter, you will see that M. [Charles de La Croix] de Castries [Marshal of France] promised to order a passage [to America] for you by the first occasion. As he has not done it, I conclude there has yet been none convenient. Perhaps it may not be convenient at all; and I do not think it proper to press him farther; especially as you wrote that a good ship is soon to sail from [the port of] L'Orient. I wish therefore you would take your passage in her. As your being delayed may occasion your wanting more money, you may draw on me for fifteen louis d'ors which I will pay on sight.

With much esteem, I have the honour to be,

[Benjamin Franklin]

No. 100   Mathias and Solomon Bush in Search of Jobs—1782–1795

Mathias Bush came to New York City from Bohemia in the 1740's, and later moved to Philadelphia or Germantown, where he married into the Simon-Gratz clan and became a leader in the Jewish synagogue established there in the 1760's. An army purveyor during the French and Indian War, Mathias Bush was also a merchant and shipowner.

During the Revolution the Bushes, like Simon and the Gratzes, were Whigs. In a letter Mathias Bush wrote that he had suffered losses because of his devotion to the Continental cause. In need also because of the burden of supporting a very large family, Bush appealed in 1782 to the Pennsylvania legislature for an appointment as vendue master, or auctioneer (Document A).

The most distinguished of Mathias' many children was his son Solomon, an ardent patriot. Eager, as he once said, to "revenge the rongs of my injured country," he joined the army at the start of the Revolution. In 1777 he was appointed a deputy adjutant general of the state militia, but, severely wounded in the fall of that year, he was compelled to retire from active service. When he left the army he was a lieutenant colonel, the highest rank held by any Jew during the Revolution.

After the war Solomon Bush, a very devoted Mason, became a grand master in his state. He probably studied medicine in Philadelphia after his discharge from the service, and later in the 1780's practiced medicine in London. His heart, however, was not in his work. Like many other soldiers and officers of the War of Independence, he wanted a government appointment. As early as 1780 he approached the Board of Treasury for the position of secretary. In 1784 he asked the Supreme Executive Council of Pennsylvania to appoint him health officer of the port of Philadelphia, and five years later sought a consular position in England. In 1793 Bush asked his old commander, then President George Washington, for the post of naval officer at Philadelphia (Document B), and finally, in 1795 he once more wrote to the President, asking for appointment to the office of Postmaster General, succeeding Colonel Timothy Pickering, who had just been promoted to Secretary of War (Document C).

That the son of an immigrant could aspire, with some degree of justice, to a high-ranking position in the administration of the first President of the United States is eloquent testimony to the assimilatory and Americanizing powers of this country.

SOURCE. Document A: Pennsylvania Historical and Museum Commission, R. P. LIII, 53; Documents B and C: The Library of Congress, Division of Manuscripts, U.S. Applications for Office Under Washington.

A [NO. 100]

To the Honorables the Representatives of the Commonwealth of Pennsylvania in General Assembly met.

The petition of Mathias Bush, late of this city, merchant, humbly sheweth:

That your petitioner resided in this city as a merchant near 40 years, and his character during that time is well known to the citizens as well as to a number of the members of your honorable house. During our present glorious contest, your petitioner flatters himself that his conduct will meet the aprobation of every virtuous citizen. Your petitioner, finding your Honors are about regulating the public auctions of this city, humbly requests to be appointed city vendue master, under such restrictions and limitation as your honorable house shall think proper to direct.

And your petitioner, as in duty bound, shall ever pray.

Mathias Bush

Philadelphia, February 19th, 1782.

B [NO. 100]

May it please your Excellency:

The Naval Office for the Port of Philadephia being vacant by the death of Doctor [Frederick] Phile, permit me to solicit the same, assuring Your Excellency that should I be honourd with the appointment, no endeavours shall be wanting in me to give satisfaction, and fill the duties of the office.

I humbly beg leave to call Your Excellency's attention to my present situation, confiding in your well-known goodness for the liberty I take. Some time since I was comfortably established in England in a benificial medical employment in which I continued untill the death of an aged father called me to my country to take charge of three helpless orphan sisters, whose tender years demanded my protection, and to return again to Europe to my practice, when the wounds I receivd in the service of my country became so troublesome as to render it impossible. And during the last winter, I underwent another operation, having half of my thigh bone extracted. This has injured my constitution so much, as to put it out of my power to follow the practice of medicine. Thus am I situated with a wife and family, three sisters, and an unfortunate brother, who was deprived of his reason (in a campaign to the southward under General Green [Nathanael Greene]), all looking to me for support.

Pardon my mentioning theese circumstances, but I trust Your Excellency's well-known goodness will excuse. I should have endeavoured to aid [add] many recomendations from the merchants, and others of the Port of Philadelphia, but at present there is no communication with that unfortunate city [because of the yellow fever], and my friend, Mr. Robert Morris, is at a distance. I beg leave to inclose a letter from that gentleman on a former occasion, when I was in nomination as first Secretary to the Board of Treasury under the former Congress; that Board being dissolved, the appointment fell through. I have [the] honour to subscribe

Your Excellency['s] obedient, humble servant,

S. Bush

Alexandria, October 24, 1793.
His Excellency, The President of the United States

C [NO. 100]

May it please Your Excellency:

As the officue of Post Master General has become vacant by the removal of Col. Pickering, permit me to call Your Excellency's attention to my situation; and should you think I merit the appointment which I respectfully solicit, the obligation shall be gratefully remembered by

Your Excellency's most obedient, humble servant

S. Bush

Philadelphia, 8th January, 1795.

————

No. 101   Robert Morris Writes to Moses Michael Hays
About Finances—1782

Moses Michael Hays (1739–1805), who formerly did business in New York and Newport, settled in Boston toward the end of the Revolution. There he became a very successful merchant and maritime underwriter. In 1782 he corresponded with Robert Morris, the Superintendent of Finance. Unfortunately, his letter to Morris is apparently not extant.

If we can judge from Morris' answer, printed below, Hays was concerned about the question of a good, sound, acceptable currency. By 1782 inflation had destroyed the value of the Continental paper dollar. In order to strengthen the shaky financial structure of the country, Morris, in January, 1782, opened the Bank of North America, and no doubt received a lot of advice—solicited and unsolicited—on how to rehabilitate the American economy. Hays's note may well have been such a letter.

SOURCE. Pennsylvania Historical and Museum Commission, PRP, XXVI, 33(2). A copy of this letter was entered in Robert Morris' Letter Book C, pp. 312–13, which is in The Library of Congress, Division of Manuscripts, Robert Morris Collection.

Office of Finance, May the 20th, 1782.

Sir:

I acknowledge the receipt of your favor of the 6th instant in order to thank you for its contents, and to inform you of my expectations that the taxes to be paid by your state to the United States will certainly establish such a fund of money, as you propose, in the hands of the Continental receiver, Mr. Lovell, so that he will be enabled to exchange money for bank bills or my notes. Or, if your people will not give to these that free circulation which they ought to have, the money must be sent instead of them. Those who consider this matter will see clearly that my plan is calculated to supply you with a solid medium instead of draining it from you.

I am, sir,

Your obedient servant,
Robert Morris

To M. M. Hays,
Boston.

No. 102   Isaac Touro, Rabbi in Newport and New York, Appeals to the British for Aid—1782

Isaac Touro, a native of Holland, was elected hazzan, or minister, of the Newport congregation about 1758. Fifteen years later the "rabbi," no longer a young man, married Reyna Hays, the sister of the Newport merchant Moses Michael Hays. At the outbreak of the Revolution, Touro refused to take the oath of loyalty to the new government, but was able to remain in the city because of the British occupation in 1776. When the royal forces left after about three years, Touro went to New York City, a Tory stronghold, where he served as rabbi to a small group of Loyalists.

Because his flock could not offer him a livelihood, Touro was compelled to augment his income by going into business. Even this did not avail him, and the rabbi turned to the British authorities for aid. In December, 1782, long after the Battle of Yorktown, he realized that there was no future for him in this country and decided to go to the larger Jewish community of Kingston, Jamaica. To accomplish his purpose he petitioned Sir Guy Carleton, the commander in chief of the British forces in America, for funds to finance the trip to the West Indies.

The petition probably was granted, for Touro went to Kingston, where he died about a year later at the age of forty-six. His widow returned to her family, the Hayses, in this country.

The name Touro is remembered in American Jewish history primarily because of the benefactions of Isaac's son Judah, one of the great philanthropists of the middle nineteenth century.

SOURCE. College of William and Mary, British Headquarters Papers (Carleton Papers), No. 6394.

To His Excellency, Sir Guy Carleton, K.B. [Knight of the Bath], General and Commander in Chief, etc., etc., etc.:

The petition of Isaac Tourro, late rector of the Jewish synagogue at Rhode Island, humbly sheweth:

That from the distresses which your petitioner sufferd from persecution for his attachment to [His Majesty's] government, and coming with his Majesty's troops from Rhode Island to this city [New York], he was so reduced in his circumstances, that had it not been for the humane interference of General [William] Tryon, General [John] Marsh, and other respectable persons, he must have sunk under the weight of his affliction and distress;

That from their kind patronage, the bounty of government has been extended to him, and he has made shift to support himself and family;

That the petitioner is now anxiously desirous of removing himself and family to the island of Jamaica, but is incompetent to defray the expences of his passage, etc.;

That the only resource he has left him is Your Excellency's humanity and benevolince, in the hope that you will grant him an advance of one twelvemonth's allowance, which would effectually enable him to accomplish his wishes.

Your petitioner therefore humbly prays that Your Excellency will be favorably pleased to order a twelve month's allowance to be paid to him, to enable him to remove with his family to the island of Jamaica.

And, as in duty bound, he will every pray, etc., etc.

Isaac Touro

New York, the 12th December, 1782.

———

No. 103   Barrak Hays: Refugee Auctioneer in Canada—1783

Unlike the many Whig members of his family, Barrak Hays, a New York merchant and auctioneer, stoutly maintained his loyalty to the Crown during the Revolution. As a known partisan (he had served as an officer of scouts), he found it advisable to leave the country after the war. Influenced no doubt by the fact that his brother Andrew was an established merchant in Canada, Barrak fled across the border. In the following petition to Governor Frederick Haldimand at Quebec, Hays asked, as a reward for his fidelity, for some form of employment, preferably in his profession as a vendue master, or auctioneer.

Barrak's son John Jacob Hays was one of the first Jewish settlers in the territory northwest of the Ohio River, in what is today the state of Illinois. The younger Hays established himself there about 1790.

SOURCE. Public Archives of Canada, Haldimand Papers, B 217, pp. 335–36.

Unto His Excellency, Frederick Haldimand Esq., Capt. General and Governor in Chief of the Province of Quebec, General and Commander in Chief of his Majesty's forces in the said province and the frontiers thereof, etc., etc.:

The memorial of Barrack Hays humbly sheweth:

That your memorialist for some years past resided in the city of New York, North America, and from his fidelity and attachment to the person and government of his Majesty the King of Great Britain, etc., his Excellency, General [Henry] Clinton, was pleased to appoint your memorialist as an officer of guides, for which employment he was allowed five shillings per day. His Excellency, General Clinton, having left New York [1782], your memorialist applyed to his Excellency, General [Guy] Carleton, praying to have his office continued, which was granted, and his pay paid him up to the twenty-fourth of June last. After the peace was settled, your memorialist, from [because of] his loyalty to the best of sovereigns, was obliged to leave New York and retire to some place where he might remain in qui[e]tness with his familey. That he arrived some time ago in this province and has settled his family at Montreal.

Your memorialist, having a very large family to support, would be glad if Your Excellency would be pleased to allow his pay to continue, or give him some appointment in Montreal.

For twenty years by past, your memorialist did act as an auctioneer in the city of New York. He therefore most humbly entreats and prays Your Excellency would be pleased to grant him a commission as an auctioneer in the city of Montreal. And as your memorialist is not so much master of th[e] French language as to speak it, he has proposed to take, as a partner, one Mr. Samuel Davis, a native of this province.

Your memorialist, therefore, most humbly hopes that Your Excellency will take the particular circumstance of his case into consideration.

Barrak Hays

Quebec, 4th August, 1783.

No. 104   The Inhabitants of New Haven Seek Incorporation—1783

As described in the following document, the people of New Haven sought to be incorporated as a town in order to further their economic well-being. The petition for incorporation was granted.

Among the 200 or more men who signed the subjoined petition were the Reverend Dr. Ezra Stiles, president of Yale, and a Jew, Jacob Pinto. The Pintos had been living in Connecticut since the first quarter of the century and were in New Haven no later than the 1750's. During the Revolution they were Whigs, and Jacob's three oldest sons were veterans of that struggle for freedom. The three Pintos had studied at Yale before Stiles was appointed, but they probably knew the clergyman well. As a fervent orthodox religionist he would certainly have had no truck with a family who, as he tells us, had "renounced Judaism and all religion." (They were probably Deists.) And as likely as not, the Pintos, proud citizens of a new republic, had little in common with a man who viewed equalitarianism from the vantage point of theological orthodoxy. In 1762, in recording the denial of naturalization to Jews, Stiles had written with an almost smug satisfaction: "Providence seems to make everything to work for mortification to the Jews, and to prevent their incorporating into any nation, that thus they may continue a distinct people."

SOURCE. Connecticut State Library, Connecticut Archives Manuscript, Towns and Lands, 1629–1789, Series I, Vol. X, Document 1, pp. a–c.

To the Honourable General Assembly to be holden at Newhaven, on the second Thursday of October next, the memorial of a number of the inhabitants living within the limits of the town plat (so called) of said Newhaven, humbly sheweth:

That your memorialists from their local circumstances are utterly unable to gain a subsistence by agriculture. That they, therefore, in years past have been obliged to turn their attention to commerce, which they formerly carried on with some degree of success. But that during the late war, their town being in an exposed situation, they of course suffered all the evils consequent upon a stagnation of business, and also had their property plundered, burned, and destroyed by the incursions of the common enemy.

That, notwithstanding all their sufferings, they are renewing their efforts to extend that commerce so necessary for them, and so beneficial to a large interior country. Yet that many and great inconveniences do arise for want of a due regulation of the internal police of said town, which are sensibly felt, as well by strangers as [by] your memorialists, in almost every mercantile transaction.

That for the promotion of trade, it is needless to inform Your Honours that a full credit and a strict punctuality in performing contracts are absolutely necessary. And that it is a matter of no small importance that wharves, streets, and highways be commodious for business, and kept continually in good repair.

That the abovesaid regulations cannot take place, unless your memorialists have a jurisdiction of their own, subordinate to that of the state, enabling them to enact bye laws for their particular commercial welfare, as occasion may require. Nor can good faith and credit, however essential to a mercantile people, ever be expected in any great degree, unless your memorialists be allowed a court of their own to sit often for the dispensation of justice, and having a concurrent cognizance of causes arising within certain limits, with the courts of common law in the state.

And your memorialists would further humbly suggest to Your Honours that the [geographical] limits they would propose for their jurisdiction are. . . . And they further would pray Your Honours that all that tract of ground, as well that which is covered with water as that which is not, within the aforesaid lines, be within the jurisdiction prayed for as aforesaid.

And your memorialists would humbly pray Your Honours that the inhabitants living within the aforesaid limits may be made a corporation with full power and authority to enact bye laws for the regulation of their commerce and for the general welfare of said corporation.

And that Your Honours would appoint a court to be holden within said jurisdiction with full power and authority to hear, try, and determine all personal actions (where the title of land is not concerned) grounded on any contract made or injury happening within said limits.

And that said court may have a concurrent authority in said causes with the other courts of common law in the state. And that all the aforesaid matters and things be under such restrictions and regulations as shall seem meet to Your Honours, and your memorialists, as in duty bound, shall ever pray, etc. Dated at Newhaven, September 22d, 1783.

Daniel Bishop . . .

Jacob Pinto . . .

No. 105 Balloon Ascension—1784

Yearning to soar through the air ever since he was enviously aware of the flight of birds, earth-bound man poetically voiced his aspirations in ancient Greek and Nordic myth. But it was not until the eighteenth century that desire became a reality. Late in December, 1783, Benjamin Franklin had enthusiastically reported to his fellow Americans the balloon ascension of Jacques A. C. Charles, the French physicist, "one of the most extraordinary discoveries that this age has produced, by which men are enabled to rise in the air and travel with the wind."

In Philadelphia the next year Peter A. Carnes prepared to make an ascension on the Fourth of July. (Actually, he made the attempt —an unsuccessful one—on the seventeenth of that month.) We may assume that it was the desire to aid Carnes, and thus further American science and national prestige, that induced some of the substantial citizens of Philadelphia to make the following appeal for funds. Among the businessmen who accepted subscriptions to finance the flight were three of the best-known Philadelphia Jews.

The first successful flight in this country was made in Philadelphia in 1793. In January of that year the Frenchman Jean Pierre Blanchard made an ascension in the presence of George Washington and traveled for almost an hour before he made his descent in neighboring New Jersey.

The post-Revolutionary generation sensed the significance of the attempt to travel in the air. After Carnes made a successful ascension in Baltimore on June 24, 1784, *The Maryland Journal* the next day said that his flight "could not fail to inspire solemn and exalted ideas in every reflecting mind."

SOURCE. *The Pennsylvania Packet*, June 29, 1784, pp. 2–3.

To the citizens of Philadelphia.

Gentlemen:

You have been lately addressed on the subject of constructing and raising, by subscription, a large and elegant air balloon. The ardor that has been manifested to assist in carrying the design into execution is an argument of the good opinion which is generally entertained of its useful tendency.

To satisfy those who may desire to know what sum of money is required to complete the undertaking, in order to determine whether they will become subscribers, and to what amount, the following particulars are stated:

To construct the body of a balloon 60 feet in height, and 50 in diameter, it will require, of yard wide silk, 1,000 yards. For the crown work, inferior segment, and base, 200. In all, 1,200 yards of silk. The most proper is India Persian.

The net work lining, covering, cords, and boat to be appended, including also the work and ornaments, may amount to a sum equal to one half of that value.

The theatre [the place] and [chemical] apparatus necessary for raising it, with other contingent and unavoidable expences, which in an undertaking so new cannot be exactly estimated, will perhaps amount likewise to half of the price of the first mentioned article. But in this, some latitude must be allowed.

Many persons unacquainted with the expence and difficulty of procuring true inflammable air from iron filings and vitriolic acid, and with that of the apparatus required for its separation from the iron, ought to be apprized that the intended subscription balloon is of so large a size as may render that air too expensive for a first essay.

Wherefore, the undertakers rather advise, together with the large subscription balloon, to have another of 10, 15, or 20 feet diameter constructed, according as the subscriptions may hold out, to be filled with inflammable air. In this, it may be necessary to use gum elastic to cover the silk, if it can be procured, as this air is more penetrating than what is necessary for the former, and requires that the covering of the balloon be more close and dense, to prevent the escape of that air.

For a balloon 60 feet in height and of proportionable diameter, 80 pounds weight of straw and a few pounds of wool will be sufficient to carry it up into the regions of the atmosphere.

The gentlemen who propose to undertake the business, provided an hearty inclination in their fellow citizens to carry it into effect shall be manifested by prompt and adequate subscriptions, think it incumbent to lay these particulars before the public. Because, as they desire that, on the one hand, nothing shall be wanting to carry the design into execution that can do credit to a set of generous subscribers, they wish, on the other hand, to avoid all needless expence.

Two or three weeks, or perhaps less time, according to the spirit and number of the subscribers, will be deemed necessary to determine whether the design is practicable, or in other words, whether it is likely to meet with such a degree of support, as is necessary to proceed with the undertaking.

If subscriptions offer but slowly, or fall far short of the estimate of expences, notice will be given in due time of the deficiency, and the affair will be dropped, without calling any money out of the hands of the subscribers. If, on the other hand, as the seemingly universal desire of the inhabitants of this place to see it carried on plainly intimates, the number and sufficiency of subscriptions give encouragement, it will be announced in the newspapers, and the subscribers will be called upon to pay their respective donations to Mr. John Swanwick, treasurer to the undertaking.

If the amount of the subscriptions exceeds the expence of the undertaking, the surplus will be returned, or disposed of agreeably to the sentiments of a committee of the subscribers, of whom a meeting will be called, to determine the question, and an account be rendered of the expences incurred.

It may not be amiss to repeat in this place that the undertakers (who are amongst the number of subscribers) are no ways ostentatious of taking a lead on this occasion; nor have they any advantage or interest to hope for from carrying on the design. A love of science and the honor of their country are their motives.

They have indeed the promise of assistance from several ingenious gentlemen of the University and Philosophical Society, when called for. But, if other persons more suitable to support the weight of the undertaking shall offer, they will cheerfully give place to, or concur with them, in the arduous pursuit. They suppose the undertaking will stand or fall by the judgment the public may form of their character or ability for the same, from the names of the gentlemen who have consented to receive subscriptions, and with whom lists are left for the purpose, which are as follows:

In Vine Street . . .	Front Street . . .	Market Street . . .
	Benjamin Nones	Jonas Philips . . .
	Haym Solomon . . .	

No. 106   Solomon Simson Submits Proposals for a Mint—1785

Solomon Simson was a very successful New York merchant whose extensive interests embraced also the manufacture of candles. This in turn involved him in the whaling trade. During the Revolution, at the time of the British occupation of New York, he was among the Whigs who sought refuge in Connecticut. After the war he returned to his home, where he achieved some influence in local Democratic politics. His liberal political views were reflected also in the legislation that he helped to enact for the post-Revolutionary Jewish congregation.

John Jay, the New York Federalist statesman, may well have known so prominent a merchant. As the following letter shows, Jay was very happy to submit Simson's proposal to Congress for the establishment of a mint.

The creation of a mint had been under consideration since at least 1782, and Jefferson wrote extensively on the theme. It is regrettable that Simson's memorandum cannot be located, for it would be interesting to determine whether his suggestions influenced the nature of the mint that was finally established in 1793.

SOURCE. The Library of Congress, Papers of the Continental Congress, 80, I, 161.

New York, 10th May, 1785.

Sir:

At the request of Mr. Simson, who sustains the character of a Whig citizen, and an honest man, I take the liberty of transmitting to your Excellency, herewith enclosed, a paper containing proposals for establishing a mint.

The subject appears to me of sufficient public importance to merit the attention of Congress, and this paper, if committed, may possibly be the means of putting that business in proper train.

I have the honor to be, with great respect and esteem,

Your Excellency's most obedient and very humble servant,

John Jay [Secretary for Foreign Affairs]

His Excellency [Richard Henry Lee], the President of Congress.

No. 107   David Franks Seeks Indemnity from the Parliamentary Commissioners—1786

Late in 1778 David Franks (1720–93), the Philadelphia merchant, land entrepreneur, and army purveyor, was removed as a supply officer for the British and Tory prisoners in American hands. At about the same time he was tried as a Tory sympathizer but was acquitted, only to be arrested again on a similar charge two years later, in the winter of 1780. Although he was again acquitted, the fears aroused by Arnold's treason caused the patriots to bundle him off to New York, where he joined his Tory friends. There is not the slightest doubt that Franks was a Loyalist. He remained in New York until the spring of 1782, when he sailed for England, where his son Jacob (John), who had married a cousin, one of the English

Frankses, gave him a home. Jacob, reared as a Christian, was a man of wealth and position.

In June, 1786, Franks sent the following memorial to the commissioners appointed by an act of Parliament to inquire into the losses suffered by the American Loyalists. In the event that his property in the United States was, or was to be, confiscated, he wanted to be compensated by the British Treasury. The government had already granted him an annual pension of £100, but he reckoned that his losses on ration and commissary commissions amounted to at least £1,200 a year, to say nothing of the loss of profits from nonmilitary commercial ventures. The estate he had left behind, he figured, was worth £20,000.

SOURCE. Public Record Office, London, Audit Office Records, Claims, American Loyalists, Series I (No. 12), 1786–88, XLII, 93–101.

To the commissioners appointed by act of Parliament for enquiring into the losses and services of the American Loyalists:

The memorial of David Franks, late of Philadelphia, merchant, now of Isleworth, in the County of Middlesex [England], sheweth:

That your memorialist resided with his family during a long succession of years in Philadelphia and was engaged in a very extensive commerce and in the enjoyment of considerable property and affluence;

That having upon various occasions manifested his loyalty to the British Government, he was in November, 1778, voted by Congress inimicul to their cause, and was by their order imprisoned and afterwards brougt to trial, under a very heavy expence, where every effort was used to substantiate a charge of high treason against him; but he was acquitted and tried afterwards for a misdemeanour in corresponding with, and giving information to, the enemies of the States, but also acquitted;

That the persecution of the violent party still continued against your memorialist with the most inveterate and wanton cruelty, for in the suceeding month of October, immediately after General [Benedict] Arnold joined the King's Army, your memorialist was seized and closely confined in the state prison, by order of the Executive Councel [Council] of Pennsylvania, and without the least form of trial or enquiry was sentenced to almost instant banishment; and to such rancour did the malice of the usurped government extend, that time was not even allowed to your memorialist to collect his debts or settle any of his affairs, but he was exiled in a few days, with his daughter, from the remaining part of his family, his friends, and his estate.

Under these peculiar circumstances of oppression and distress, your memorialist arrived at New York with his daughter, destitute of employment and deprived of every means of support but the benevolence of friends and, conceiving himself to be an American sufferor in the strictest sense, he was induced to apply to the Lords of the Treasury for assistance from the public munificence granted for such purpose. Your memorialist accordingly did apply by memorial, accompanied with the annexed certificates of his loyalty, uniform conduct, and attachment to the King's government.

That the Lords of the Treasury were pleased to refer your memorialist's case to the consideration of the former commissioners Messrs. Wilmot and Cook, who granted him £100 per annum;

That your memorialist, in consequence of the violent proceedings by which he was banished, was thrown out of a very lucrative business in the mercantile line, and also deprived of the emoluments arising from his agency to the contractors, and the advantage resulting from his appointment by Sir W. Howe to the commissaryship for supplying provisions, etc., to such of his Majesty's troops as were prisoners in New Jersey, Pennsylvania, and Virginia, which offices he then held;

That, although your memorialist cannot adduce any accurate proofs of the annual value of his trade, he can with great truth aver, and can support it by the testimony of many of his fellow citizens now in England, that he lived in great ease and affluence, and supported himself and family in a very creditable and reputable manner.

Your memorialist annexes an account of the cirtificates of the rations he furnished the troops as agent to the contractors from the 24th November, 1776, to the 25th February, 1779, being 2 years and 3 months, amounting to £51,793 sterling, which yielded a commission of £2,589, calculated at the rate of 5 per cent, so that he computes his annual income as agent to the contractors only to ammount to £1,000.

Your memorialist thinks it necessary to observe that a fire, which happened in Cornhill [Street in London] in 1778, consumed all the books, accounts, and papers belonging to the contractors, which deprived him of the opportunity of resorting to them for a general account of his commissions as agent to the contractors. The account he now exhibits, however, can be substantiated by the original certificates remaining in the office of the Comptroller of the Army Accounts.

Your memorialist also annexes an account of the money disbursed by him as commissary to the prisoners above mentioned, by which it appears that from the 28th Feb., 1778, to the 8th January, 1779, he advanced the sum of £3,656 9s., on which sum he was also allowed a commission of 5 per cent, which amounted to £182 16s. 5d. sterling, so that he computes his annual income as commissary to the British prisoners, etc., at £200 sterling.

Your memorialist has not yet been advised, nor does he know, whether the Congress has actually confiscated his estate, or whether it is intended to confiscate the same; but if not, the expences he has incurred in defending prosecutions, in removing himself and daughter from Philadelphia to New York, and from thence to England, have been so great that, if he were to be put in immediate possession of his estate, he should find his circumstances extremely straitned and by no means adequate to the purpose of a scanty support for himself and his family.

Your memorialist, however, begs leave to reserve a right to claim a recompence for such real estate in case it now is, or should hereafter be confiscated, notwithstanding the expiration of the time limited for such application by act of Parliament may expire.

Your memorialist therefore prays his case may be taken into your consideration in order that your memorialist may be enabled, under your report, to receive such aid or relief as his losses and sufferings may be found to deserve.

David Franks

[June 12, 1786.]

No. 108   Isaac Pinto, Government Interpreter—1786–1789

Isaac Pinto, of New York (1720–91), was one of the best-educated Jews in eighteenth-century America. By American standards at least, he was a good Hebraist, knew Spanish well, and was conversant with other foreign languages. As early as 1766 he translated a volume of prayers of the Spanish rite from Hebrew into English for the use of English-speaking worshipers. When he died, a New York newspaper referred to him as a "historian and philosopher."

It is a pity that we know so little about Pinto. We do know, however, that he was a good Whig and that in 1770 he was among those New York merchants who wanted to continue the Nonimportation Agreements. He made his living as a merchant, teacher, and interpreter. In 1786 he was appointed Spanish interpreter not only for the Department of Foreign Affairs but also for all the other executive departments and for Congress. The special oath of loyalty and secrecy that he took is printed below (Document A).

In spite of the fact that Pinto was to do Spanish translations for the government, he received but a few pounds for his work in the course of three years. Understandably enough, he wrote to Secretary John Jay in 1789 asking for more money, although he realized that the amount of work available did not justify a permanent appointment (Document B). Jay, who was about to turn his office over to Thomas Jefferson, suggested that Pinto write to the incoming Secretary of State, with which suggestion Pinto complied.

SOURCE. The Library of Congress, Division of Manuscripts. Document A: U.S. Oaths of Allegiance, III, 344; Document B: U.S. Continental Papers, CC, 78, XVIII, 667.

A [NO. 108]

I, Isaac Pinto, appointed by John Jay, Esq., the Secretary of the United States for the Department of Foreign Affairs, to be interpreter of the Spanish language, to translate all such papers as may be referred to me, as well by the United States in Congress assembled as by committees of Congress, the said Secretary for the Department of Foreign Affairs, the Secretary of Congress, the Board of Treasury, or the Secretary for the Department of War, do acknowledge that I do owe faith and true allegiance to the United States of America, and I do swear that I will to the utmost of my power support, maintain, and defend the said United States in their freedom, sovereignty, and independence against all opposition whatsoever.

And I do further swear that I will faithfully, truly, and impartially execute the said office of interpreter to which I am so appointed, according to the best of my skill and judgment, and that I will not reveal or disclose any thing that shall come to my knowledge in the execution of the said office, or from the confidence I may thereby acquire, which in my own judgment, or by the injunction of my superiors, ought to be kept secret.

So help me God.

Isaac Pinto

Sworn this thirtieth day of November, 1786, before me, Charles Thomson, Secretary of Congress.

B [NO. 108]

Sir:

As you are now soon to quit the Office of Foreign Affairs, I beg leave to address you on the subject of my appointment the 24th November, 1786, interpreter of the Spanish language. When I received that appointment, although no salary was annexed, I took it for granted that the employ would have been of considerable advantage to me. You will, sir, be apprized of the little benefit I have derived there from, when I aquaint you that the whole amount for my service is no more than £8 12s. 4d. in very near three years.

As I was legally qualified [sworn in] for this trust, I am considered in my station as a servant of the public. I therefore conceive it no impropriety in me to hope for, or even to expect, some further consideration. I am persu[a]ded you will think what I have received not an object for an appointment from your office. I rest the matter, sir, on your own equity and feelings to fix the compensation, in confidence that it will be agreeable to my wishes. I presume the subject of my request is in your power to grant and will meet with your approbation.

I am, with much respect, sir,

Your most obedient, humble servant,

Isaac Pinto

New York, 18th Nov., 1789.
The Honorable John Jay, Esq.,
Superintending the Department of Foreign Affairs.

No. 109   Sunday Legislation in New York—1788

The first English settlers who came to these shores in the seventeenth century were convinced that they were establishing a religious commonwealth. This was to be a Christian country. For example, in the colony of Virginia, as early as 1610, attendance at divine services on Sunday was compulsory, and the third consecutive violation of this law was punishable by death. Somewhat similar but less drastic compulsory Sunday observance laws were found in all the colonies.

No provision, of course, was made for non-Christians, especially Jews, with the result that as early as 1655 they began to run afoul of the law. On March 1, 1655, Abraham de Lucena was threatened with a fine of 600 guilders in New Amsterdam for keeping his store open on Sunday during divine services. Nor did the laws always take cognizance of the Jewish observance of Saturday as a day of rest. In 1793 Jonas Phillips, one of the leaders of the Philadelphia Jewish community, was fined £10 for refusing to be sworn on the Sabbath.

In 1695 the colony of New York passed an act against the profanation of the Lord's Day, but that law was abrogated probably during the Revolution, when the colony severed its allegiance to Great Britain. After an unsuccessful attempt to re-enact a Sunday law in 1781, a new bill, directed to the same end, was introduced in 1788. It was based directly on the statute of 1695, which was motivated quite frankly by the desire to stop the profanation of the worship of God "to the great scandal of the holy Christian faith." But the bill of 1788 discreetly omitted reference to that motivation, although its obvious intention was to punish those who did not observe the Christian Sabbath. (The attendance of non-Christians at Christian services was, of course, not required.) The new bill was called "An Act for Suppressing Immorality."

The problem of the extent to which non-Christians must conform to police laws enforcing Sunday observance is still a moot one in nearly every state of the Union. Delicate issues of freedom of conscience and of economic discrimination are involved.

In 1788 this very battle was fought out on the floor of the New York State Assembly. Printed below are a copy of the enacting clause of the bill (Document A) and an abstract of the speeches on the subject by some of the assemblymen (Document B). The debate took place on February 12; the bill was passed on February 15.

SOURCE. Document A: *Journal of the Assembly of the State of New York, 1787–1790* (New York, N.Y., February 12, 1788), pp. 66–67; Document B: *The Pennsylvania Packet*, March 8, 1788.

A [NO. 109]

The first enacting clause, being again read, is in the words following, *viz.:*

Be it enacted by the people of the State of New York, represented in Senate and Assembly, and it is hereby enacted by the authority of the same, that there shall be no travelling, servile labour, or working (works of necessity and charity excepted), shooting, fishing, sporting, playing, horse-racing, hunting, or frequenting of tipling-houses, or any unlawful exercises or pastimes, by any person or persons within this state, on the first day of the week, commonly called *Sunday;*

And that every person being of the age of fourteen years or upwards, offending in the premises, shall, for every such offence, forfeit and pay to the use of the poor of the city or town where such offence shall be committed, the sum of six shillings;

And that no person shall cry, show forth, or expose to sale, any wares, merchandise, fruit, herbs, goods, or chattels, upon the first day of the week, commonly called *Sunday,* except small meat, and milk and fish, before nine of the clock in the morning, upon pain that every person so offending shall forfeit the same goods so cried, showed forth, or exposed to sale, to the use of the poor of the city or town where such offence shall be committed;

And if any person offending in any of the premises shall be thereof convicted before any justice of the peace for the county, or any mayor, recorder, or alderman of the city where the offence shall be committed, upon the view of the said justice, mayor, or recorder, or alderman, or confession of the party offending, or proof of any witness or witnesses upon oath, then the said justice, mayor, recorder, or alderman, before whom such conviction shall be had, shall direct and send his warrant, under his hand and seal, to some constable of the city or county where the offence shall have been committed, commanding him to seize and take the goods so cried, showed forth, or exposed to sale, as aforesaid, and to sell the same, and to levy the said other forfeitures or penalties, by distress and sale of the goods and chattels of such offenders, and to pay the money arising by the sale of such goods so seized, and the said other forfeitures or penalties, to the overseers of the poor of the city or town where the said offence or offences shall have been committed, for the use of the poor thereof;

And in case no such distress can be had, then every such offender shall by a warrant, under the hand and seal of the said justice, mayor, recorder, or alderman, be set publicly in the stocks for the space of two hours.

B [NO. 109]

Poughkeepsie, House of Assembly of New-York.
On Tuesday, February 12, 1788.

When the house were in a committee [of the whole] on the bill for the suppression of immorality, after reading the first clause of the bill which is to prevent any servile labour, drunkenness, or any kind of sports on the Sabbath day;

Mr. Benson moved that the 38th article of the constitution should be read.

[Article XXXVIII of the constitution of New York, 1777:

AND WHEREAS, we are required, by the benevolent principles of rational liberty, not only to expel civil tyranny, but also to guard against that spiritual oppression and intolerance wherewith the bigotry and ambition of weak and wicked priests and princes have scourged mankind, this convention doth further, in the name and by the authority of the good people of this state, ordain, determine, and declare, that the free exercise and enjoyment of religious profession and worship, without discrimination or preference, shall forever hereafter be allowed, within this state, to all mankind: *Provided,* That the liberty of conscience, hereby granted, shall not be so construed as to excuse acts of licentiousness, or justify practices inconsistent with the peace or safety of this state.]

Which being done, he [Mr. Benson] moved that the said clause [to prevent labour, etc., on the Sabbath day] be rejected. (Mr. Dongan seconded the motion.) Mr. Benson's reasons for this motion were that he thought the legislature had no power to pass the bill, as it was repugnant to the constitution, and that it was in itself manifestly improper, as the same principle that would establish any particular day for the worship of the Deity might also describe the mode, and this would lead to intolerance and persecution. If there were any of our citizens who neglected that part of their duty, he thought that government ought not to interfere in it, as they were responsible only to the Deity.

He observed that the first law for establishing a particular day of the week as a day of worship had originated in the days of James I, that this law had been adopted by the colony, which, if it had not been virtually repealed by the constitution, would now be in force. By the constitution, not only all religion was tolerated, but every religious sect placed in a perfect equality. The consequence, therefore, of passing the clause would not only be a violation of the rights of others, but of the constitution.

To illustrate this proposition, he said, a Jew, to be consistent with himself, is obliged to keep holy the 7th day of the week, which is Saturday, and to prohibit him from working on a Sunday would be taxing him one sixth part of his time. This was not equal liberty, one of the boasted blessings of our government. He stated that in the year 1781, at Albany, a bill had been brought forward, similar to the one now before the committee, but which, on the ground of its being against the constitution, was not carried through the legislature. If any men from religious motives were advocates for this bill, they mistook themselves; the Great Author of our religion required no human laws to support it [religion].

Mr. Sylvester said the bill appeared to him to be as important as any that had ever been before the house. He did not think the arguments of Mr. Benson were by any means conclusive. He believed it would be difficult for him, by the most forced implication, to shew that the clause in question was contradictory to the constitution; and with respect to people of different religious denominations, they were not compelled to worship on that day.

As this was a subject on which he had great anxiety, he would attempt to shew that it would be an exceeding proper bill, and that the house would do well to pass it. He wished his abilities were more adequate to so sublime a subject. It would be more masterly handled by the clergy, whose study and profession would enable them to expatiate upon topics of this sort, but as there were no men of that order in the house, he hoped it might not be presumption in him to use his feeble efforts in attempting to support so good a law. He then spoke of the constitution. He said it was only intended to give liberty of conscience to all religious denominations, but if by legal or equitable interpretation it would bear a construction so as to repeal the old Sunday law, he thought it would be one good reason for a new constitution.

If there were no pious inducements for the committee to pass this law, he hoped, as they had been so particularly tenacious of every ancient custom, they would not be regardless of a custom (observing the Sabbath) that had been in use in this country from time immemorial, and confirmed by a law of the late colony, especially as no inconvenience or oppression had been complained of in consequence of that law, nor had any abuses been committed by the persons entrusted with its execution. He asked why the legislature of this state and of this country, as well as all courts of justice, omitted doing business on that day, and why it was called the Lord's day, and not a law day. Why should we, said he, pretend to be so much wiser than our ancestors, by abolishing this good custom, this reasonable service to the Deity? Sabbath-breaking is an offence against God and religion, hitherto punished by the municipal laws of this as well as other countries, in opposition to the notorious indecency and scandal of permitting any secular business to be publicly transacted on that day, in a country professing Christianity, and the corruption of morals that usually follows its profanation.

The keeping one day in seven holy, as a time of relaxation and refreshment, as well as for public worship, is of admirable service to a state, considered merely as a civil institution. It humanizes, by the help of conversation and society, the manners of the lower classes of mankind, which otherwise might degenerate into a sordid ferocity and savage selfishness of spirit. It enables the industrious workman to pursue his occupation in the ensuing week with health and cheerfulness. It imprints on the minds of the people that sense of their duty to God so necessary to make them good citizens, but which would be worn out and defaced by an unremitted continuance of labour, without any stated times of recalling them to the worship of their Maker.

In regard to any religious denominations who may have scruples of conscience respecting that day, as to himself, he had no objections to excuse them from the penalty of the law, provided they did not interrupt the public worship of others. . . .

It is likewise evident that the day which the Christian Church has in all ages observed, and doth still observe, which is commonly reckoned the first day of the week, is the day which is the will of Christ we should observe as our Christian Sabbath. It is plain that the apostles and first Christians did religiously observe the first day of the week as the day of their solemn assemblies for divine worship, and that with a regard to the resurrection of Jesus Christ, this day was called the Lord's Day.

It was on the first day of the first week of time that the Blessed Spirit moved upon the face of the waters to produce a world, a world of beauty and plenty, out of confusion and emptiness. And it was upon the first day of another week that he [Jesus Christ] descended on the apostles, and acted them to produce a church. Justly, therefore, is the first day of the week consecrated to the honor of that divine person, to whom we owe both our being, and our new being, in order to our well being.

Mr. Benson said he was not contending against the observance of the Lord's Day; what he wanted was equal liberty and an adherence to the constitution.

Mr. Sylvester said that rejecting the bill would be one of the most imprudent steps the legislature could be guilty of, as disregarding that solemn day would tend to no religion at all, except the religion of nature. The gentleman, he said, had asked what right the legislature had to interfere in divine worship; he did not admit that it was an interference to prohibit them travelling by [past] churches and disturbing congregations. But with respect to Jews and others, he would have no objection to new model [alter] the clause so as not to prohibit them from work in their houses if they made conscience of it, and to do such things as should not interfere with the public worship of others. [Neither] they, nor no one else, were compelled by the law to go there; and that those Jews who were in the state had made no complaints. Why, therefore, said he, should every thing be set afloat, especially as no difficulties had yet occurred? . . .

Mr. Dongan thought that the gentleman (Mr. Sylvester) had not come to the point in question at all. The constitution, he believed, was in direct opposition to the bill, and this assertion had not been confuted. But he did not object to it on this ground alone; he feared that it would lead to oppression.

Mr. Jones begged the indulgence of the committee for a few moments. The bill under their consideration was, in general, a compilation of the old colony laws, which it become[s] the duty of the revisers of the laws to bring forward. The question to be decided was, whether the constitution had abrogated them. If it has, then the bill before the house could not be passed. He would proceed to consider what was the import of that article of the constitution. If, said he, the bill had declared that a man should go to one church or to another, or that he should hear service in any particular language, then it would, in his opinion, be against the constitution. But there was not a thing in the bill about religious worship, unless drunkenness, horse-racing, etc., were deemed acts of religion. Every man was left to worship the Almighty in the way that pleased him, and he might keep what day he pleased; but if he does not chuse to keep the Sabbath, do not let him disturb them that do.

He wished not, however, to consider this bill in a religious view at all. His opinion of the matter was that the legislature were passing this bill for the sake of good order in society, and not as men actuated only by religious motives. There was a power given by the constitution to prevent acts of licentiousness, and many things in that bill were really acts of licentiousness. He was free to declare that the bill did not in any shape militate against the constitution, as it did not give any undue preference, or make any discrimination. This being the case, the single proposition to be considered was, whether it would be proper to enact this clause, or by a solemn act to declare that all men might do just as they pleased on that holy day. For if there was no restraint, there might be horse-racing, etc., to the disturbance of all the serious part of the community, and to the great corruption of their morals. This, he said, was the sense of the community at large, and whether it was confined to one day or to another, yet there should be some assistance of the law to prevent disturbances on that day. On this principle he should vote for the bill.

Mr. Benson said he did not consider the subject as trifling, and he trusted the honorable gentleman last on the floor had also an idea of its importance, though he did not believe he considered it as solemnly as he did. The gentleman had said there was nothing in the bill contrary to the constitution. He [Benson] had declared that in his opinion the act was against the constitution, and from the reasoning of the gentleman last on the floor, he was convinced of the truth of his assertion. If the constitution was taken up and refined upon, as it must be before the bill could pass, the whole might be refined away. The bill did not declare that a man should worship the Deity in the same mode as those who passed it, but it declared that he should do as they did, and it was an indirect way of making one man adopt another man's belief.

He referred again to the situation of the Jews. This was one of his objections. The Jew may not labor on our Sabbath, but on his you permit every body to work. The gentleman who advocated this bill in the first instance had said, let the Jew work in his house. See, said he, what a refinement this is; and such, he said, must take place if the bill passed. The gentleman was mistaken; the idea of fixing a day gave rise to all the persecutions of the age in which it originated. In the writings of the primitive fathers, the gentleman might also have found many errors that they established, and which proved fatal to numbers [many people]. Sir, said he, why is it that we will not do unto others as we would they should do unto us? Suppose a Jew should say, you offend me by working on the Saturday, and for which he will say he has a positive command. Why has he not as good a right to a law to prevent his sect being disturbed, as any other sects in the community? They, by the constitution, are to enjoy equal rights and privileges. It was a fact, he said, that unhappily for these people, to avoid the noise which is common on a

Saturday, they were obliged to have their houses of public worship in retired places.

If the bill was only to prohibit sports and idle diversions, he should have no objection to it. He repeated it again, that passing this bill would be a violation of the constitution. And though in this instance it had for its object the observance of the Sabbath, yet it might go to every act of a man's life. The arguments the gentleman had used to shew the importance of the Sabbath, he did not differ with him about. He would ask the gentleman what he believed was the greatest sin. Why, no doubt, he would say disbelieving, and would not this law affect them that did not believe in revealed religion, though we have nothing to do with them? It was arrogance in any legislature to interfere and make laws to support religion, as the Great Author of our religion has declared that he will take care of it. But it had been said that serious people required it. He wished to know how this could be proved. The gentleman had not yet done it.

Suppose there was a majority of Jews in the state. Upon the same principles that this bill would be passed, they might declare that Saturday should be set apart as a day of public worship, under the same restrictions and penalties. Besides the inconvenience respecting the Jews, there was many others that it would affect. When does the Sabbath commence? In New England, people suppose it to begin on Saturday evening, as did many people in this state. And how was this to be defined? He did not wish to be understood that he was against the observance of the Sabbath. On the contrary, he supposed it to be the duty of every man. If a man supposes he can consistently labor on that day, do not prohibit him. He wished that gentlemen would confine themselves to fair reasoning, and not to declamation. If, said he, this bill is passed, the constitution will be egregiously departed from. He would say no more on this subject, because it was one of those questions on which every man must decide according to those arguments his own mind would suggest. The question, said he, is whether you will pass a law to prevent a man from doing what he conscientiously thinks he has a right to do.

Mr. Sylvester replied that he was confident there could not but be a majority in the house, notwithstanding what had been said. As to defining the Sabbath, there was no mathematician could do it. It was sufficient that a majority of the Christian world had adopted a day, and from which no inconvenience had arisen. As to the constitution being departed from, he could not agree that this bill could have such an operation.

Mr. Jones said he was yet to learn that any thing in the bill militated against the constitution. If it could be made appear, it must be by refinement on refinement; but not a single argument had been yet offered to convince him that it would in the smallest degree affect the constitution. The division was then called for. Affirmative [that the bill be rejected] . . . 5. Negative [that the bill be passed] . . . 34.

———

No. 110 Jacob Isaacks: Distiller of Fresh Water from Salt Water—1790–1791

Jacob Isaacks was a Newport merchant, insurance man, and ship broker. About 1790 he developed a chemical process for the distillation of ocean water. The conversion of salt water into fresh water was important, for sailors who made long trips could not always carry sufficient fresh water for their drinking and cooking needs. On June 8, 1790, Isaacks addressed a letter to the former governor of Massachusetts, James Bowdoin, president of the American Academy of Arts and Sciences, asking that the organization approve of his "discovery" (Document A). When George Washington visited Newport in August of that year, Isaacks gave him a bottle of his distilled water. It was reported that "the President was pleased to express himself highly satisfied therewith."

Early in 1791 Isaacks informed the House of Representatives that he had found a new method of making fresh water from ocean water, and asked to be rewarded for his discovery. The House referred the petition to Thomas Jefferson, the Secretary of State, because of his scientific attainments, and because the Secretary of State handled patents. The Virginia scholar and statesman hoped that Isaacks' method would be an improvement over the processes devised by European chemists, and wrote: "It will be a new flower in the American wreath." In March of that year Isaacks was called to Philadelphia to demonstrate his discovery. On March 26 Jefferson wrote to Dr. Isaac Senter of Newport—a physician of some scientific training—for further information about Isaacks and his method of distilling salt water.

In his reply of April 13 (Document B), Senter gave his opinion on the value of Isaacks' discovery. Senter's rejection of Isaacks' distillation procedure only confirmed Jefferson in the conclusion that he had already reached in March: the method was worthless. In November, 1791, the Secretary of State reported to Congress: "On the whole, it was evident that Mr. Isaacks' mixture produced no advantage, either in the process or result of the distillation."

After hearing the report, Congress ordered it laid on the table. Isaacks' method was no improvement.

Evidence that Jefferson was determined to continue the search for an improved method of distilling fresh water from salt water may be seen in a resolution passed at the first session of the Second Congress (May, 1792). At his suggestion Congress asked that the printed clearance papers, issued at ports by federal officers, contain, on the reverse side, instructions for obtaining fresh water from salt water. Mariners were also asked to publish the results of their experiments in the field. In all likelihood this Congressional resolution was ignored.

Along with Moses Lindo, of Charlestown, South Carolina, David Nassy, of Philadelphia, and Joseph Ottolenghe, of Savannah, Isaacks was one of the few Jews of eighteenth-century America who apparently had some interest in, and knowledge of, scientific experimentation.

SOURCE. Document A: Library of the Massachusetts Historical Society; Document B: Colonial Williamsburg, Williamsburg, Va., Thomas Jefferson Papers.

A [NO. 110]

New Port, Rhode Island, June 8th, 1790.

The Honorable James Bowdoin, Esqr., L.L.D.,
President of the American Academy of Arts and Sciences,
Boston.
Sir:

Impressed with an idea that the primary object of the American Academy of Arts and Sciences is to encourage and promote every discovery which may be of publick utility, and that they will receive every communication with candour and render it as early an attention as possible, emboldens me to inform them, through you, that I have recently discovered a method to extract fresh water from salt water by a simple and easy process so as to procure 8 parts of fresh from 10 of salt water, agreable to the inclosed certificate which I transmit for their present satisfaction, being ready to attend them at any appointed time, and to give them ocular demonstration of the whole of the process, except the ingredient which effects it. Indeed, it is my earnest wish to give that respectable society an opportunity to examine and determine the quality of the extracted water, to obtain their patronage and an attestation of the truth of my pretensions, as also their advice what mode to pursue so as to profit by my discovery. But my situation in life at present with my advanced age renders it imprudent for me to spend a shilling otherways than in support of my family. I therefore trust that after premising thus much, that in case my attendance may be accepted agreable to my proffer and wishes, and that I should prove to the perfect satisfaction of the Academy that my assertions are within my abilities, that they will reimburse me the expenses which may accrue [in my] journey from hence to Boston, during my stay there, and return home to this place.

Should the gentlemen who have affixed their signatures to the inclosed certificate be unknown to the Academy, I then crave leave to refer them to Mr. Moses M. Hays and Mr. Samuel Brown, merchants in Boston, to whom they are well known, and who will vouch for their veracity.

The benefits which may arise from this discovery of rendering sea water fresh and salutary to maritime commercial affairs, especially such as are dependant on lengthy voyages, must appear so obvious to you that it is needless for me to suggest them; but I must mention that the apparatus can be constructed so as to require but very little room and expense, and if properly found, will undoubtedly yeild a larger quantity of fresh water in less time than what is specified in the within certificate.

Should there be any impropriety in addressing this letter to you, sir, I trust that you will readily excuse the same when I assure you it is for the want of knowing the names of the gentlemen whom the Academy have appointed corresponding members, from whom, I flatter myself, I shall speedily receive a full reply to this. In the interim, I am, with every sentiment of respect, sir,

> Your most obedient, humble servant,
> Jacob Isaacks

B [NO. 110]

Newport, April 13th, 1791.

Sir:

I had the honor of receiving a letter from you yesterday, dated 26th March, disiring me to send you some writings of Dr. [James] Lind's [the Scottish naval hygienist] which you could not procure elsewhere, upon the subjecting of distilling fresh water from that of the ocean. It is, sir, with the greatest pleasure that I embrace the first opportunity by the post to comply with your request, as far as is in my power. . . .

Mr. I. [J.] Isaacks is an inhabitant of this town, and early in his business of distillation he brought me a specimen of the water he procured from the ocean water which he had distilled. I very readily discovered that he had made use of either alkaline salt or calcarious substances in the process. I informed him that they were not only unnecessary, but pernicious, and that fresh water might be obtained from the ocean in great plenty by *simple* distillation, as was practized both in the British and French navies.

I heared nothing more of his *supposed* discovery 'till several months after, when he presented me with a letter that he had just received from the late Governour *Boiden* [James Bowdoin], as president of the Academy of Arts and Sciences in Boston government. This was written in consequence of a memorial Mr. Isaacks had presented to the Academy, accompanied with the certificate of several respectable gentlemen in this town, who had seen him go through the process and, not knowing what had been done in Europe in this affair, supposed it a *new* and usefull discovery of the memorialist. In this letter, the President [Bowdoin] treated the subject with that cautious scientific precision which shewed that he was well acquainted with the present state of this important part of chemistry. Several other letters, however, passed between Mr. Isaacks and some of the members of the Academy, by which his expectations were very much raised.

Finally I was requested by a committee of the Academy to attend his process and write them a true state of his proceedings. I did so, and sent the Academy a particular account of it, so much to their satisfaction that the matter was very little more noticed in this part of the continent, and I thought that Mr. I. had given over the pursuit of a shadow after the substance was *demonstrated* to be in the possession of other hands. But in this business he could not be brought to acknowledge that *two* and *two* made *four*.

Mr. Isaacks can distill 8 pints out of 10, that might be used for any culinery purposes, where natural fresh water could not be gotten. But it has an unnatural soft tast[e] and, upon being agitated, exhibites more air bubbles than good water affords. I did not chemically analize it, for I was very sure that what he could do this way was neither a *new* discovery nor an improvement. . . .

Your most obedient and very humble servant,
Isaac Senter

Honorable Thomas Jefferson,
Secretary of State.

No. 111 Jonas Phillips Protests Against Monopolies—1791

Jonas Phillips (1736–1803) was a Hessian who had come to Charlestown, South Carolina, by way of London in 1756. Shortly after his arrival, however, he moved to Albany and then to New York City. There, during the French and Indian War, he catered primarily to the military. After peace had been declared, Phillips found himself insolvent and took the job of shohet, a ritual slaughterer of cattle and fowl, with Congregation Shearith Israel. Several years later, in 1770, he felt secure enough to resign his job and to return to business. Apparently he did better this time and by 1775 was a successful merchant and auctioneer in Philadelphia.

Phillips was a fighter, ready to do battle against injustice—as he conceived it—whether he found it in the synagogue or in the larger forum of the general community.

In September, 1787, he wrote a letter to the federal Constitutional Convention, meeting in secret session, protesting against Article X of the Pennsylvania state constitution. This clause made it impossible for a Jew (or a deist) to accept office unless he professed a belief in the divine inspiration of the New Testament.

It is difficult to determine why he wrote to the federal convention about a disability contained in a state constitution. Inasmuch as he may not have known that Article VI of the Constitution had already been adopted, he may have wished to warn the delegates against the evil of a religious test, or he may have nursed the hope that the federal Constitution would condemn religious disabilities in the several states.

In 1793, when called to testify in court on a Saturday, he refused to be sworn, for he would not desecrate his Sabbath. The court fined him £10.

Two years earlier Phillips petitioned the General Assembly of Pennsylvania on the subject of monopolies. His memorial, printed below, is a vigorous, forthright attack on that evil and is quite characteristic of the man. When his appeal was presented to the state senate, it was tabled.

SOURCE. The Library Company of Philadelphia.

To the honorable the General Assembly of Pennsylvania in Senate and House of Representatives met:

The memorial of Jonas Phillips sheweth that your memorialist has frequintly petitioned the former General Assembly on the subject of vendues, praying that the same may not be monopolized by one or two persons, etc., where by the mercantile as well as the state intrest in general is greatly injured. Your memorialist again begs leave to recall to your memories the various complaints which have resounded from every quarter against the principles of monopoly.

The enlightened individuals who compose every branch of the present legislature need not be told of the unconstitutionality of confining the vendues to the emolument of any man or party. If the vendues are left open for every citizen who can produce good security for the payment of thi [the] state duties and for his integrity in conducting the business between the seller and buyer, it is all your memorialist will require. But ever whilst the business is under the present unnatural, partial, and unconstitutional regulation, your memorialist will feel it his intrest as a citizen to remonstrate against [it], and as a part of the body politic, to condemn [it].

Jonas Phillips

Philadelphia, January 9th, 1791.

———

No. 112   The French Crisis—1798

Conscious of the help they had rendered the Americans during the Revolution, the French people, engaged in their own revolution against the forces of autocracy at home and abroad, confidently looked to the United States for sympathy and assistance. The negotiation and ratification of Jay's treaty with Great Britain, concluded in 1795, deeply hurt the French, who considered it a betrayal. In the following year they began to attack and seize the ships of the Americans who were hauling supplies to Great Britain, the traditional enemy of France. French officials refused to receive the American minister and, in the X Y Z affair of 1797, demanded not only a loan, but a bribe of almost a quarter million dollars as well, before they would even receive the United States commissioners.

The American reaction to this holdup by Foreign Minister Charles Maurice de Talleyrand-Périgard and his lieutenants was quick and spirited. An undeclared naval war broke out in 1798 and measures were taken to organize the American defenses. The Navy Department was established, the seizure of French ships was authorized, and Washington was once again appointed commander of the armed forces, with Alexander Hamilton second in command. Hamilton wanted war, which would give him an opportunity to seize New Orleans and Florida from Spain, France's ally. Fortunately for this country, however, President John Adams did not lose his head and in 1800 made peace with Napoleon in the Treaty of Morfontaine.

In 1798, however, the crisis was at its height; war was desired by many and expected by most of the people. Document A, printed below, is an appeal by Nathan Levy, of Georgetown on the Potomac, for an opportunity to serve under Hamilton. Levy (1759–1846) was the son of Benjamin Levy, of Philadelphia and Baltimore, a well-known merchant of the Revolutionary period and a good friend of Robert Morris. Nathan himself, as far as we know, was not a person of consequence. His letter, however, reflects the popular hope of many Americans of the post-Revolutionary period for a chance to win a share of martial glory.

Document B, also printed below, is a letter of 1798, from Benjamin S. Judah (1760–1831), a New York City merchant and one of the leaders of Congregation Shearith Israel, to Hamilton. Writing from England, where he was transacting business, Judah offered to purchase arms for the defense of his country, pointing out that it would not be difficult to secure loans in London. The British would certainly have been pleased to see the United States at war with France. The letter also reflects the indignation shared by many Americans at the cavalier treatment accorded the young republic by the even younger French Republic.

SOURCE. The Library of Congress, Division of Manuscripts, Alexander Hamilton Papers.

A [NO. 112]

George Town, August 1, 1798.

Major General Hamilton,
Sir:

I have the honor to enclose you, from General [Henry] Lee and General [Uriah] Forrest, letters recommending me to your consideration as an officer in the army. These gentlemen both know my wish is to be immediately under your orders, and that the nearer to your person you can assign me a station, the more I should be gratified. They have both hinted to me the improbability of succeeding in this application, from the desire that prevails with so many men of merit who may attract your attention and obtain your countenance.

I cannot, however, forbear making a tender of my services, and assuring you that upon receiving information that you have been pleased to assign me a duty, I shall repair with the greatest alacrity to execute your orders.

I have the honor to be, with the most perfect respect and consideration, sir,

Your most obedient, humble servant,
Nathan Levy

B [NO. 112]

London, September 5th, 1798.

Dear Sir:

I find by private and public intelligence that my country has been roused to a just sense of dignity and is determined to defend her claims against an insidious foe. I am sorry to think she is likely to sustain the depression of war, but in a cause on which depends her independent existance, every American must feel the ardour of aiding his country to justify her rights, and if I can in the least contribute (as an individual), I shall feel myself happy in my endeavours to do my duty.

I have been in Europe about two years, and probably may continue a year or two longer. From the connections I have both here and on the continent, I trust that I could procure, on the lowest terms, any quantity of arms, etc., that our goverment may want. At foot I note the prices at the foundry at Berlin, transmitted to me by my agent there. I presume I may procure them somewhat lower.

What has led me to this are applications that have been made to me by friends and acquaintances, even the money contractors to this goverment. I am in the habits of friendship and intimacy with several of the principal negotiators. They have informed me that they are ready to aid our goverment with a loan, which I sincerely hope she may not stand in need off.

Not haveing the honor of a personal acquaintance with our President [John Adams], I have not presumed to address him on the subject, but as you do not let the smallest incident escape you that may terminate in the service of your country, if you judge my feeble aid may benefit her, you may, if you think proper, transmit this with what comments or recommendation to him you please.

As a citizen, I have the advantage of being known to you, and if His Excellency requires any further references, at the session of Congress in Philadelphia he will find that opportunity, as I am personally known to General Jonathan Dayton. Speaker; Doctor Wm. [Thomas] Henderson, of New Jersey; General Philip Van Cortlandt, and the members for the city of New York, and several other representatives in Congress.

I am, with every sentiment of respect and esteem, dear sir,

Your most obedient and very humble servant,

Ben S. Judah

My address in London: to the care of Doctor Joseph Hart Myers, No. 8, John Street, America Square; or a letter left at my house in New York will be forwarded.

"24" cannon, brass, wt. 63 C. [hundredweight] at £8 10s. per C   £535.10

    carriage ....   75.
_____
610.10

"12" do. . .   do. , . . . wt. 30 C ....   £8 10s. per C   £255.10

    carriage ....   65.
_____
320.10

IV   Commerce and Trade

No. 113   A Petition to Ship Provisions to Jamaica—1713

Some of the earliest Jewish merchants of New York were active as purveyors to the British armed forces during the intercolonial wars.

The following petition shows that Abraham DeLucena and his Gentile partner, Justus Bosch, ran afoul of an embargo on provisions which had been imposed during Queen Anne's War (1702–13) as a war measure. Two years before the date of the petition, DeLucena had supplied provisions for the joint land and sea attack on Canada. In 1713 DeLucena secured a permit to send his cargo of foodstuffs to Jamaica, but before it went off departure was prohibited. In this petition the two partners ask that the embargo be not applied retroactively.

The Jewish signatory, Abraham Haim DeLucena, is not to be confused with Abraham DeLucena, also a merchant, who was in New York in 1655. The petitioner was a resident of New York during the first quarter of the eighteenth century. During much of the time he served as "rabbi" of the congregation, no doubt as a volunteer. In 1711 he contributed to the building of the steeple of Trinity Church. He died in 1725.

SOURCE. New York State Library, New York Colonial Manuscripts, LVIII, 125.

To His Excellencey, Robert Hunter, Esq., Capt. Generall and Governor in Cheife of the Provinces of New York, New Jersey, and territories thereon depending in America, and Vice-Admirall of the same, etc., in Councill:

The humble petition of Abraham De Lucena and Justus Bosch, owners of the sloop, *Mary and Abigall,* John Smith, master, sheweth:

That before the order made by Your Excellencey and councill the 7th of May last, that the collector should not cleare any vessell in which there was any quantity of provisions, nor take any entry for any provisions to be exported,

Your petitioners had actually cleared and entred their said sloop at the custom house for Jamaica, with twenty tons of flower [flour], bread, and bacon which your petitioners had long before purchased for that purpose, and had then actually shipped on board twenty-six barrells of flower, part of the said provisions, the rest remaineing in your petitioners' warehouse, ready to be shipt on board.

That after the order for the embargo as aforesaid, your petitioners applyed themselves to the collector of the customes for leave to take the remainder of their said provisions on board, who declared his opinion that seeing they were entred and cleared before the said embargoe, your petitioners might ship the same on board; and accordingly, your petitioners proceeded [to] ship the same on board. The _____ of May last obtained Your Excellencie's let pass [permit] for their said vessell to proceed on her said intended voyage, but some obstructions hitherto have retarded your petitioners' said vessell from saileing.

And now, by vertue of Your Excellencie's further order in Councill of the second of June instant, your petitioners' said vessell (being just ready to sayle) was stopt from proceeding on her said intended voyage.

Wherefore, and for that your petitioners will be very great sufferors, and their designed voyage wholly ruined in case your petitioners' said vessell be now stopt, and some other vessells, under the like circumstances with your petitioners, haveing since beene permitted to proceed on their voyage,

Your petitioners most humbly pray Your Excellencey will be pleased to take the premisses into Your Excellencie's consideration and permitt your petitioners' said sloop to proceed on her said intended voyage with the aforesaid loading soe entred and cleared as aforesaid.

And your petitioners shall pray, etc.

Abraham De Lucena, Justus Bosch

New York, 3d June, 1713.

———

No. 114   A Petition for a Reduction of Duties on Wine—1716

Many of the Jews of early New York were merchant-shippers, exporting raw materials in exchange for European manufactured goods. In the following petition Abraham DeLucena asks the governor for a reduction of the duty on some imported wines that had turned sour and were practically unsalable. Such petitions for an abatement of duties were not uncommon; a similar one was made in 1711 by Luis Gomez, another Jewish merchant.

SOURCE. New York State Library, New York Colonial Manuscripts, LX, 96.

To His Excellency, Robert Hunter, Esq., Capt. Generall and Governour in Chief of his Majestye's [King George I] Provinces of New Yorke, New Jarcys, and the teritorys thereon depending, in Amerrica, and Vice-Admirall of the same in Connecticut.

The humble petition of Abraham De Lucena sheweth:

That your petitioner have on the 16th day of December, 1715, entred in his Majesty's custome house eighteen pipes, 2 hogsheads, and three quarter cascks of Madera wine, imported in the sloope *Rachell and Ann* (Solomon Burton, master), from Madera, and accordingly given security for payment of the duttys to the treassurer of this collony.

Your Excellency's petitioner proceeded to remove said wines into his celler, where he desired the officer who attended the onloadeing said wines to be pressent with severall merchants of this place, to view and taste the said wines, in order to [provide for] the releiff of your petitioner, provided any of the said wines proved eager [sour] or otherwise unmarchantable.

And it then appearring to the said merchants and officer that said wines were in generall very defective, and did reasonabley deserve an allowance thereon, and it alsoe appearing by your petitioner's authentic invoyce thereof that said wines cost an equall price with any other at that time sold in the islland of Madera, it is humbly hopped that your Excellency and this honourable board will take this hard case of your petitioner into concideration and make such allowance as in your wisdom shall seem meet.

And your petitioner shall ever pray, etc.

Abraham De Lucena

New Yorke, the 1th of March, 1715/16.

———

No. 115   A Power of Attorney by Mordecai Gomez—1718

In the following power of attorney, Mordecai Gomez, the New York merchant, authorized his brother Jacob to act as his agent in Barbados, the British colony in the West Indies.

The Gomez clan has been referred to as the most powerful Jewish family in the mainland colonies of the eighteenth century. This assertion is open to question, but there can be no doubt that the family was one of great importance. The father, Luis, came to the province of New York from the Iberian Peninsula, probably by way of the British West Indies. By 1703 he was settled on the mainland, but two of his sons married Jamaicans.

The Gomezes were merchant-shippers with extensive interests in the insular colonies, which at the time were more important in the economic system of the British Empire than the Continental ones. That a voyage to Barbados was beset by danger is grimly documented by the fact that in 1722, four years after his trip to represent Mordecai's interests, Jacob Gomez was killed in a Cuban harbor by Spanish marauders. The family memorialized his death by naming one of its ships *Jacob*.

SOURCE. Registrar's Office, Bridgetown, Barbados, "Powers of Attorney."

Know all men by these presents that I, Mordicay Gomez, of the city of New York, merchant, have made, and by these presents do make, ordain, constitute, and in my place and stead . . . [designate?] my trusty and loving brother, Jacob Gomes (now bound to the island of Barbados), merchant, my true and lawfull attorney for me; and in my name, and for my use, to ask, demand, sue for, levy, recover, and receive all such sum and sums of money, debts, goods, wares, dues, accounts, and other demands whatsoever, which are or shall be due, owing, payable, and belonging to me, or detained from me, any manner of ways or means whatsoever, by any person or persons whatsoever; giving and granting to my said attorney, by these presents, my full and whole power, strength, and authority, in and about the premisses, to have, use, and take all lawfull ways and means in my name for the recovery thereof;

And upon the receipt of any such debts, dues, or sums of money aforesaid, acquittances, or other sufficient discharges for me, and in my name, to make, seal, and deliver, and generally all and every other act and acts, thing and things, device and devices, in the law, whatsoever needfull and necessary to be done in and about the premisses for the recovery of all or any such debts or sums of money aforesaid, for me and in my name, to do, execute, and perform as fully, largely, and simply to all intents and purposes, as I my selfe might or could do if I was personally present, or as if the matter required more special authority than is herein given; and attorneys, one or more under him, for the purpose aforesaid, to make and constitute, and again at pleasure to revoke, ratififying, allowing, and holding for firm and effectuall, all and whatsoever, my said attorney shall lawfully do in and about the premises by virtue hereof.

In witness whereof, I have herewith sett my hand and seal, this 28th day of November, being the 5 year of his Majesty's [King George I] reign, *Annoque Domini,* one thousand seven hundred and eighteen.

Mordicay Gomes

Sealed and delivered in the presence of Andrew Law, Naphtali Lopez. Barbados.

Andrew Law, one of the within evidence, personally appeared before me and made oath on the Holy Evangelists of Almighty God, that he did see Mordicay Gomes sign, seal, and deliver the [above?] instrument of writeing as his voluntary act and deed, given under my hand this 17th day of June, 1719.

Edmund . . .

_____

No. 116   A Protest Against an Unlawful Seizure by a Privateer—1720

The losses respectable businessmen incurred at the hands of privateers, even in times of peace, are reflected in the following incident, which shows that privateers unfortunately were often little better than pirates.

In March, 1720, a New York privateer captured and plundered two Curaçao sloops flying the Dutch flag, which had been trading in Spanish-American waters. In spite of the fact that the United Netherlands and the United Kingdom were at peace, the privateersman excused his action on the ground that the sloops carried contraband, and brought the vessels into New York Harbor.

The four Curaçao owners appointed five New York merchants as attorneys to recover the ships and their cargoes, for the sloops were then in the jurisdiction of the Court of Admiralty at New York. The attorneys succeeded in their quest.

Jewish businessmen in trouble never hesitated to turn to their coreligionists in other lands for help and advice, as they did in this instance. (This fellowship had the further advantage of being a means to initiate and strengthen business relations.) One of the owners, Daniel Moreno Henriques, and two of the attorneys, Mordecai Gomez and Rodrigo Pacheco, were Jews. The former attorney was associated with his father Luis and with his five brothers in the merchant-shipping and fur-trading businesses, and was also a snuff manufacturer.

Rodrigo (Benjamin Mendes) Pacheco came to New York City in the early eighteenth century. He was one of the seven Jewish merchants who contributed to the building of the steeple of Trinity Church in 1711. He may be considered as the first member of the Pacheco family in this country, unless Moses Pacheco of Newport, Rhode Island (1677), was a kinsman. Rodrigo's wife was a Seixas. The Seixases were to be well known later in the century, primarily through Gershom Mendes Seixas, the "rabbi" of Shearith Israel Congregation, New York.

SOURCE. New York State Library, New York Colonial Manuscripts, LXII, 116.

To the Honourable Peter Schuyler, Esq., President, and the rest of His Majestie's Councill of the Province of New York:

The humble petition of Robert Walter, Phillip Cortlandt, Barent Rynders, Mordechai Gomez, and Rodrigo Pacheco, in the behalfe and as attorneys to Messrs. Hasse and Coeyemans, Willem Janse Vermeulen, and Daniel Moreno Henriques, of the Island of Curaçao in the West Indies, merchants, sheweth:

That they, the said Hasse and Coeymans, Willem Jansen Vermeulen, and Daniel Moreno Henriques, having sometime in the month of February, now last past, at Curaçao aforesaid, fitted out two sloops, the one called the *Young Katharin* and comanded by Anthony Muller, and the other called the *Young Adrian*, comanded by Ivan Pedro Jansz, and put on board of them very valuable cargoes in order therewith to trade with the Spanjards at Rio De La hache [Riohacha] as they might lawfully do, their High and Myghtinesses, the States Generall of the United Netherlands, their sovereigns, being then in full peace with the King of Spain.

But so it is, may it please Your Honours, that one Capt. John Hickford, comander of a private sloop of warr belonging to this port, notwithstanding the firm peace and amity now subsisting and in full force between his most sacred Majestie of Great Brittain, and the said lords States-Generall [the Netherlands], and contrary to, and in manyfest violation of, the treatyes of marine between his said Majestie and the said lords, the States, did, on or about the 21st day of March, new stile, now last past, in warlike manner and with force of armes, set upon and take the said two sloops, the *Young Catharin* and *Young Adrian* aforesaid, at a place called La Cruz nigh Rio De La hache aforesaid, and the same, together with severall other vessells there, in like manner taken by him, after having by him and his company been plundered of the best part of their cargoes, brought into this port and lybelled [proceeded] against in the

Court of Admiralty, under the pretence of their having traded with counterband goods;

That the petitioners, by certain letter of attorney bearing date at Curaçao the 2d July, new stile, which they very lately received, are by the said owners fully empowered to reclaim the said sloops and their cargoes, and to use all lawfull means to recover the dammages so suffered by reason of the said illegall caption [capture] and taking, as aforesaid, of the said John Hickford, his owners, and all others therein concerned;

And accordingly have caused their reclaim [demand for restoration] to be entred in the Court of Admiralty, and do not doubt but, upon the hearing of the cause, to obtain the like sentence as was by the said court pronounced in the cases of the other vessells taken in like manner by the said Capt. Hickford.

And the petitioners being informed that the said Capt. Hickford has entred into a certain obligation to his Majestie, with securities for the due execution of his commission, which they humbly conceive he has forfeited by attacking and taking his Majestie's friends and alleys [allies], by plundering them and bringing them in as prizes;

They, therefore, humbly pray that the said bond may be prosecuted for the use of the said owners of the said two sloops, the *Young Catharin* and *Young Adrian*, to make good part of the dammages they have sustained by the illegall caption aforesaid.

And Your petitioners, as in duty bound, shall every pray, etc.

R. Walter	Mordecay Gomes
Phillip Cortlandt	Rodrigo Pacheco
B. Rynders	

New York, 21st July, 1720.

No. 117   Petition and Bill to Grant a Porpoise Fishing Monopoly—1726

The following petition and bill reflect the attempt of two businessmen to secure a ten-year monopoly on porpoise fishing in the colony of Connecticut. Such monopolies in industry and manufacturing, granted to encourage entrepreneurs and local trade, were not uncommon in the colonial period. In this instance the Lower House passed the requisite legislation, but the Upper House failed to concur. The monopoly therefore was not granted.

The petitioners were Mordecai Gomez, a Jew, and Isaac Jacobs, very probably a Jew. The latter was a resident of Branford, a flourishing seaport in the eighteenth century and a rival of nearby

New Haven. He may have been the man who in 1723 was indicted for robbery in Westchester, and secured the services of the brilliant New York and New Jersey lawyer, James Alexander, who, although he could not prevent his client's conviction, got him out of the scrape by securing a pardon.

The following documents are among the first to refer to Jews in the fishing trade in America. Later, as we shall see, the Newport merchant-shippers played a significant role in the whaling industry.

SOURCE. Connecticut State Library, Connecticut Archives, Industry, 1708–89, Series I, Vol. I, Docs. 213–14.

To the Honourable, the Governor and Company of his Majesty's Colony of Connecticut, in Generall Court assemblyed on May the 12th, *Anno Domini* 1726:

The humble petition of Mordecay Gomez, of the city of New York, and Isaac Jacobs, of Brandford, in the Colony of Connecticut, merchants, humbly sheweth:

That Your Honours' petitioners have, at great charge, travell, and expence, for a long time maintained and supported a skillfull and knowing person in those parts of the world where the fishery of porpoises is best known and most practised, in order to attain a competent knowledge therein.

And whereas they have now gained a sure method of improving and perfecting the same, which they humbly conceive will be in a short time of great benefit and advantage to the publick, as allso of long duration after your petitioners may have injoyed the same, for such a term of years as to Your Honours shall seem meet.

And as Your Honours are very generous encourragers of arts and sciences and all usefull knowledge, your petitioners presume to hope that trade, so necessary to support them, will receive some share of your favour. And certain they are that, if the prayer of this petition be considered by Your Honours, what they have to propose will very much advance and enlarge the same with respect to Europe.

Your petitioners therefore most humbly pray that Your Honours will give them leave to bring in a bill for granting to your petitioners the sole fishery of porpoises within this colony for the space of ten years, under such restrictions and limitations as upon the face of the said bill will more at large appear.

And Your Honours' petitioners, as in duty bound, shall ever pray, etc.

Mordechay Gomez, Isaac Jacobs

This assembly grants the prayer of the within petition. Past in the Lower House.

Test [witness]: Tho. Kimberly, clerk.
Read and dissented to in the Upper House.
Test: Hez. Wyllys, secretary. May, 1726.

An act to entitle Mordechay Gomez, of the city of New York, in the Province of New York, and Isaac Jacobs, of Brandford, in the Colony of Connecticut, merchants, to the sole fishery of porpoises in the Colony of Connecticut and territories thereunto belonging, and in all rivers, creeks, and harbours of the same, for the space of ten years.

Whereas the fishery of porpoises managed under a skillfull and propper direction will in a short time become a great and lasting benefitt to this colony, and that the same is at present of none or very little advantage to the inhabitants thereof,

And whereas the said Mordecai Gomez and Isaac Jacobs, by their petition to the General Assembly of this colony, have sett forth that they have at great charge, travell, and expence obtained a compleat knowledge of the true manner and method of catching porpoises, as the same is used in their countrys, where a considerable manufacture is thereby improved and carried on,

And for their encouragement humbly prayed that none but they, the said Mordecai Gomez and Isaac Jacobs, their heirs, executors, administrators, and assigns be permitted to carry on the same fishery in the same method and manner, and with the same kind of engines, tools, or instruments as shall be used by the petitioners for such a term of years as the said Assembly should think fitt,

And it being just and reasonable that the first projectors or undertakers in consideration of their great trouble, charge, and expence, and allso of the great benefitt which may hereafter accrue to this colony thereby, should be promoted and encouraged therein,

Be it therefore enacted by the Governour, Councill, and Representatives in Generall Court assembled, and by the authority of the same, that no person or persons whatsoever, from and after the publication of this act, shall presume to exercise or carry on the fishery of porpoises within this colony and territories thereunto belonging, or in any of the rivers, creeks, inletts, or harbours of the same, in the same method and manner and with the same kind of engines, tools, or instruments as shall be used by the petitioners, for and during the full term and space of ten years, to commence on the day aforesaid,

And that they, the said Mordecai Gomez and Isaac Jacobs, their heirs, executors, administrators, and assigns, shall have and hold, for the said term of ten years, the sole right and title to the fishery of porpoises within this colony, and to all benefitt, profitt, and advantages arising therefrom, saving, never the less, all rights of his Majesty, his heirs, and successours.

And be it further enacted by the authority aforesaid, that if any person or persons whatsoever, from and after the publication of this act (other than the said Mordecay Gomez and Isaac Jacobs, their heirs, executors, administrators, and assigns), shall, within this colony or the territorys thereunto belonging, or in any creek, harbour, river, or inlett of the same, practise, exercise, or carry on the same fishery of porpoises in the same or like manner, or with the same kind of engines, tools, or instruments used or employed therein by the said Mordecai Gomez and Isaac Jacobs, their heirs, executors, administrators, or assigns, for and during the term and space aforesaid, such person or persons so doing and practising shall forfeit, become indebted, and pay unto the said Mordecai Gomez and Isaac Jacobs, their heirs, executors, administrators, or assigns the full and just sum of five hundred pounds money of this colony for every such trespass, offence, or misdoing contrary to the true intent and meaning of this act, one half thereof to be applyed to the support of the government of this colony, one fourth thereof to be applyed to such use as his Honour the Governour, Councill, and Assembly shall think fitt, and the other fourth, or remainder thereof, to be to the sole use and benefitt of the said Mordecay Gomez and Isaac Jacobs, their heirs, executors, administrators, and assigns. The whole sum of five hundred pounds to be recovered by the said Mordecai Gomez and Isaac Jacobs, their heirs, executors, administrators, or assigns, or so much thereof as shall be sued for in any court of judicature within this colony, by action of debt, plaint, or information,

Provided allways that in case the said Mordecay Gomez and Isaac Jacobs, or their heirs, executors, administrators, or assigns, do not within the space of twenty-two months from the publication hereof begin to exercise and practise the said fishery of porpoises and employ themselves (or others by them appointed) therein, within some part of this colony or territorys thereof,

That then it shall be lawfull for any other person or persons to undertake and carry on the said fishery, without incurring any of [the] debts, penaltys, or forfeitures mentioned in this act, any thing therein contained to the contrary thereof, in any wise, notwithstanding.

No. 118 A Letter from Jacob Franks in New York to Naphtali Franks in London—1743

Jacob Franks (1688–1769) was one of the most successful Jewish merchant-shippers in New York during the first half of the eighteenth century. He was a well-known army purveyor, serving the king as an agent in New York and in the northern colonies. For many years he was the lay head of the New York Jewish community. His wealth and integrity guaranteed him a place in the community at large, and he and his wife were welcome visitors at the governor's mansion.

The following letter was addressed by Jacob Franks to his son Naphtali, who was serving as his father's representative in London. In the letter the father touched on economic matters, family problems, and incidents of a religious interest. The contents reflect the busy days of King George's War (1744–48), when the Frankses were importing cannon for privateers, sending foodstuffs and building materials to Jamaica, and outfitting General James E. Oglethorpe in Georgia for his attacks on the Spaniards in Florida.

Family affairs appear in Jacob's recital of his troubles with his daughter Phila (not to be confused with Naphtali's wife, also named Phila), who in 1742 had run off and married Oliver DeLancey, a Gentile. Jacob was inclined to make peace with the DeLancey clan, for Oliver's brother James was the chief justice. The Moses Salomon who appears in the letter was a nephew of Jacob Franks. At that time Moses was in Charles Town, South Carolina, where he was detained, probably because of his inability to pay his debts.

SOURCE. Franks Papers in the collections of Lee M. Friedman, of Boston. A copy is found in the Jacob R. Marcus Papers.

New York, November the 22nd, 1743.
Dear Son:

On the 4th ult., I answered severell of your [letters] received this summer, which I delivered to Capt. [Jeremiah] Osberon, who was to go [as a] passanger from Boston with the *Gosport*, man of war. And I allso wrote you the 11th ult. and sent the same to go with said man of war; but, she being sailed, Mr. Salomon Isaacs writes me [that the packet of letters] was put on board a warr shipe [ship]. But for fear [they might be lost], have here inclosed a copey of what I wrote you, and hope you may be able to git us said como[dities?].

Since which, have had the sattisfaction of yours of 13th and 14th September, with the inclosed invoices and bills of loading for tea on board [the boats] of Bryant and Griffith, which have [been] received in good order, and have disposed of eight chests to good people at three and six months cr[edit], . . . though expect to receive some of the mony much sooner. And by Bryant or Griffith will send you the account sales of the last teas and some returns on the same. Fault is found again that the tea does not draw a high couller [color], for that is the tea liked in this place.

As you must believe, it is all ways a great sattisfaction to me and family to here [hear] from you. I realy think you neglect of given [giving] me the same [satisfaction] verry much, for by many wessells arrived this summer and fall at Boston and Philadelphia, and likewise by Mr. Scoot's [Scot's] wessell directly here, [I] had not a single line from you by any of you. Not so much as a news paper (exept by Scot's shipe), which I think very hard, and there[fore] hope you will not serve me so again.

I think your Uncle Isaac or D. Salomon [a cousin] might have wrote me a few lines by yours. Wee are all, thank God, in good health, hopeing this will find you and your [wife] Phila and the rest of our relations in the same, to all whom [I] shall, please God, write and answer their favours by the next shiping, which will soon be, there being no less than five wessells bound to London.

We are now loading the buildings [materials?] for Jamaicoa. One shipe is allready sailled; two [are] now aloading, and shall load the new wessell of mine with the rest. I compute the cost will be about £3,000 our currancey, on which have allready drawn £2,300, and the bread wee are now a shipeing will amount to about £1,500, both of which will soon be completed; when shall send your uncle [Aaron] and yourself bills for the same, and hope shall draw very little on your uncle for the same. And shall in all respects use my honest endeavour to give you both all the encouragment that lays in my power to contine [continue] the tea trade.

Oliver Delancey has bin with me, being the first time since that unfortunet affair hapned, about the £2,000 left [to] Phila [your sister]. I showed him and gave him a copey of that part of your uncle's will. All I can say about it is, and beg that if it can be don[e], so as he may have it, for your Uncle Aaron to doe it; for to me, it seems it is best, as age befalls me.

He [DeLancey] now writes to Mr. Baker to speak to your uncle Aaron about it, and he will give security, that if ever brother Aaron is obligded by law to allow the said £2,000 to the heir at law, that he will then repay the same.

It may seem strange to you that I should desire the same, but if you conceder wee live in a small place, and he is related to the best family in the place, and though your sister has accted so very unduttyfull, yet it would give me and family a great deal of trouble was she to be ill used by her husband or relations, which at present is other ways [otherwise]. But should he be kep[t] from said mony (if it can with safety be paid), it might be other ways. [He might then mistreat her.]

He seems to be a carefull young man and will not spend his estate, all which I would have you mention to your uncle Aaron, to whom I write a few lines by this opportunity, and shall be heartily glad to here [hear] your uncle Aaron complys with my request.

Am told Phila [DeLancey's wife, your sister] writes you by this shipe. I have hardly had the sight of her since she left the family. Am assured she heartily repents what she has don, and therefore offten am inclined to see her and give her liberty to come to see us, but can not bring your mother to it. Therefore [I] desire you to answer her letter and to write your mother about her.

As to your sister Ratcha, she is as good a child as ever lived, yet am resolved she shall go for London—if [there will be] peace—by first good opportunity, and hope you or relations will [not?] be against the same.

I advise wee have not had a line from the commissioners by our wessells. At the same time, am pleased to here by yours that they are satisfyed with our proceedings; and inclosed you have copey of what wee now write them; and you will deliver the packet of advertisements directed for you at the N.[ew] York Coffee House, delivered to Capt. Clarke.

I have sent D. Salomon [in London] at his brother Moses' desire £100 [or £200] sterling by this opportunity, and shall this week write to him about what you and your uncle mentioned, and wish he was clear [in Charles Town]. I shall not have above £400 our mony when all debts come in of his, and great part of his good[s] I sold but lately. When the accounts [are] finished, will send a copey to his brother David [Salomon], that he may see I don him justice.

Shall send the accounts relating to my demands for the goods sunck at Georgia per next opportunity. Inclosed you have the portested [protested] bill of the Generall [Oglethorpe], for he was gon from Georgia before the bill got there, and am in great hopes the Parliament will doe us justice in said affair, and shall be glad to here you have recovered the mony of Capt. Roberts. There is yet a ballance due to me from Col. Cochran. Pray use your endorsers to recover the same for me. Your brother David [Franks] was gon to Georgia, and am concerned to find it is not in his power to comply with your orders.

Lawrence Levy has not made any payment to his credit at Carolina. He kept [store] in the country, but, inded, am told it is not in his power.

Our new governor [George Clinton] seems to be a good sort of a gentleman, but by what I find his cheif delight is in drinking, and if he keps on as he has hereto [hitherto] don, he will dispatch [kill] himself; but kep it to yourself. At least, let not my name be mentioned about it.

As [for] Mr. Asyne, he is great *shoteh* [fool], but on your and my relations' recommendations, have and shall comply with your request. If there be any fault with the horse, your b.[rother] Moses is to blame.

Inclosed is a bill of exchange and letter of advice for £50 sterling on

Mr. John Stanbury, which when paid, please to credit the account of T.S.C. for £30 st., and the £20 pay to Isaac Levy, the servant, by order of your b.[rother] David. Some of his goods Mr. N.[aphtali] Myers has yet unsold. I daily expect another bill from him, as allso from Mr. Gray. All other perticulars shall answer at large in my next [letter].

You are mistaken about my insurance to Georgia if insurars' risque was over 24 hours after the sloop's arrivell at Georgia. But as Generall Oglethorpe would not let the wessell unload, I can not think but they must stand to the loss, for that is the restraint of princes. [Insurers were not responsible for damages incurred after twenty-four hours subsequent to a ship's arrival, unless the authorities interfered: restraint of princes.] However, shall like it much better to git the payment with you than to go to law with my friends here, who the insurars are.

I wish your tea trade to Boston may answer [be satisfactory]. Tea, am told, sold there lately for £24 ready pay.

Guns are in great demand here and would have sold to great advance. Messrs. Crawley desapionted [disappointed] me very much by not sending them as they promiset me, and they give me their reason. Have wrote them about [this] again, so desire you to speak to Mr. Allen about the same. If they will not engage to send them by the return of the next wessell, then [I] desire you to engage for a large percell [parcel] of swewells [swivel guns]. Would have 50/2 [fifty, two-pounders], 30, three, and 20, four pounders, and with shott sutable [suitable] to them. That is, iff the war continues. . . . Ples [Please?] send only the swevell which will all ways sell. I could have had ready mony for the quantity I now write for, but fear other people now have wrote for some. If you find they have, then send but the half. You may send them on your own account if you think propper.

Shall be glad to here you have bought the branches [for the Feast of Tabernacles]. If not, would have you send, as wrote you allready, a small pair of *ez hayyim* [end staves] for the *sefer* [Scroll of the Law].

Your mother and sister will write you per Bryant. They give their love to you and to the rest of our relations, and pray excuse me to them all for not writing at present, for have realy no time without [unless] the shipe stays a day or two longer. All so, excuse me to your uncle Isaac, with my love and service to them all.

[This] is what offers at present; wishing you and your [wife] Phila all the happiness this world affords, and remain, dear son,

Your most affactionate father,

Jacob Franks

My respects to all friends. Wee daily expect wessells from Jamaicoa, when hope to have further orders from the agents who are yet, and hope all ways will be, our very good friends.

Pray, my respects to Mr. Hart. I shall answer his favour per Bryant.

M.[oses] F.[ranks] [Different handwriting.]

Mr. Nap.[thali] Myer gives his service to you and will write you per Bryant.

I can but take notice of what M. Salomons [of Charles Town] writes me in a letter I received from him few days before Capt. Griffith came in from London, which realy gave me some concern, as I had no letters from London for some time before. What he writes is that he had received a letter from his brother David [Salomon], who tells him that his affairs would have bin [been] made up before had not an accedent happned to his uncle Aaron alone, and desires me to let him know what it was; but as your letters by Griffith makeing [make] no mention of any thing like it, made me easy, but at the same time think it is a very od [odd] way of writting. If any thing was in it, pray let me know it.

No. 119 An Order to Discharge Israel Abrahams and Nathan Nathans, Bankrupts, from Jail—1745

Eighteenth-century merchants were constantly faced with hazards their latter-day successors are frequently spared. Among those hazards were rapidly fluctuating prices, unstable currencies, and inadequate credit information concerning clients, while piracy on the ocean highways was a further and real danger. At one time or another in their careers practically all the well-known Jewish merchants were compelled to make settlements or to file petitions in bankruptcy.

In the following document three Gentiles, serving as trustees for a bankrupt Jewish firm, instructed the sheriff to release the imprisoned partners, inasmuch as they had surrendered all their assets.

The members of the insolvent firm were Israel Abrahams and Nathan Nathans. These were among the earliest eighteenth-century settlers of Newport; probably they had come from New York. The original Jewish settlement of Newport, stemming from about 1670, had long since died out. For a time Abrahams served as an interpreter in Spanish and Dutch for the Vice-Admiralty Court of Rhode Island.

SOURCE. Rhode Island State Archives, Public Notary Records, V, 470.

Rhode Island SS.

To Joseph Scott, Esq., Sheriff of the County of Newport, in the Colony of Rhode Island, etc., greeting:

Whereas Israel Abrahams and Nathan Nathans, of Newport, in the County of Newport, merchants, have, in pursuance to an act of the General Assembly of said colony entitled "An Act for the Relief of Poor and Insolvent Debtors," made and passed on the twenty fourth day of September, A.D. 1745, declared, before the Honourable the Governour and Council of said colony, their insolvency, and have exhibited to said Governour and Council inventories of their estates;

Whereupon said Governour and Council have appointed us, William Coddington, Gideon Cornell, and Daniel Updike, all of said Newport, gentlemen, commissioners for the proportioning amongst the creditors of the said Abrahams and Nathans said estate according to said law;

And the said Abrahams and Nathans, having conveyed and transferred their said estate, interest, and property and debts mentioned in said inventory to us, the subscribers, in trust as aforesaid, as far as in them lies,

Therefore, by the authority to us given in and by said law, we, the said commissioners, require you to discharge the said Abrahams and Nathans from his Majesty's goal [jail] in Newport to their full enlargement [release from confinement], any execution or mesne [intervening] process against them for debt notwithstanding.

And this shall be your security, given under our hands and seals in Newport, the thirtieth day of October, in the nineteenth year of his Majesty's reign, *Annoque Domini* 1745.

Wm. Coddington, Gideon Cornell, Daniel Updike

———

No. 120   A Memorandum on Louisiana by Abraham Gradis—1748

Abraham Gradis, of Bordeaux, France, was one of the outstanding merchant-shippers, army purveyors, and bankers of eighteenth-century France. For many years he was the leading member of the firm of David Gradis & Sons, which, during the Anglo-French wars, devoted itself to the unsuccessful task of saving New France (Canada) from British conquest.

In 1748 Gradis organized the highly successful Society of Canada, a trading company that was soon to control much of the commercial life of the country. Together with François Bigot, the rapacious intendant of New France, and a third partner, Gradis practically had a monopoly on Canadian trade. His was a most lucrative enterprise.

In the same year Gradis nursed his hope of establishing a similar company to exploit the agricultural and commercial possibilities of Louisiana. It was obviously his belief that if his large mercantile corporations could dominate the areas at both ends of the Mississippi, he would not only control the trade of the valley, from Canada to New Orleans, but would also be able to enter into commercial relations with the Spanish lands on the Gulf of Mexico. The plan, submitted by Gradis to the French government, was grandiose in scope, but, unfortunately for Gradis, he was not able to implement it. The Society of Louisiana never came into being.

SOURCE. French National Archives, Colonies, C 13A, 32:248–50. There is a copy of the French original in The Library of Congress.

Louisiana: Memorandum of M. Gradis' sons [Abraham Gradis] on this colony.

Among the most appropriate methods of securing an enrichment of our commerce during a period of peace, which the signature of the preliminaries [of the Treaty of Aix-la-Chapelle] informs us is approaching, there is one which can be highly recommended, inasmuch as it does not touch those of our colonies most familiar to the merchant-shippers of our French ports.

The goal envisaged is to place a colony, at present seldom frequented, into a proper condition to produce those advantages which its location and the excellence of its territory render assured, but which has not been productive up to now for the lack of cleared land and agricultural cultivation.

It is Mississippi or Louisiana which we have under consideration. The excellence of its soil, the fertility and the variety of its available products, could soon turn this colony into one of the wealthiest and most fruitful. Once the soil was cleared, it would become valuable, for it would be in a condition to be cultivated. Merely clearing the land itself would be an object worthwhile, if only for the sake of the lumber which is needed by the settlers in this colony, and which could also be shipped out to our other colonies which possess no timber.

Independent of this double advantage there is one specific circumstance: namely, the location of this colony, which seems to make it particularly outstanding. Located on the very same continent as Mexico, it can serve as a convenient and useful emporium for a lucrative trade in all our manufactures with New Spain, a commerce now inaccessible to the French because of the sea. Through overland caravans into this colony, the Spaniards could secure our merchandise and wares in exchange for gold and silver.

But in order to take advantage of all these resources and to attract commerce to this colony, it is necessary to increase the number of settlements and to clear the ground. This is possible only through the transportation of Negroes. The introduction of Negroes into this colony through normal commercial routine, namely, through merchants, or even by means of concessions which his Majesty might accord them, does not seem the best procedure. It would be exposed to too many obstacles and to too many difficulties before one could hope for a successful conclusion. It would be too risky to expose the development of the colony to this uncertainty.

Vessels coming from the African coast, bound for Louisiana with a cargo of Negroes, have to pass in sight of the coast of San Domingo. There is no question that they would put into port here either to load up with water and victuals or to take on experienced pilots. However, if the captains of the vessels have the opportunity to sell these Negroes in the ports which they touched, where they could nearly always make a quick profit, would they not take advantage of the opportunity to sell them at San Domingo? By so doing they would cut down on the greatest risk of their trade, that is, the dread of mortality, and would not subject themselves to the hazards of the trip from San Domingo to Louisiana, a journey which would lengthen the stay of the Negroes in the vessels and thus expose them the more to destruction through sickness.

But there exists another fear, one calculated to produce the same deterring effect. It is the fear of not knowing whether the settlers of this colony would be in a condition to pay for a substantial number of Negroes, with the result that the captains, deprived of the possibility of transporting these Negroes to another colony, would be forced to sell them at a price which the inhabitants would fix and determine. Because of the small number of settlers these prices must inevitably be low, and they would sink still lower in the event that two or three vessels arrived and offered their Negroes for sale at the same time.

The situation would be quite different, and the introduction of Negroes into Louisiana would proceed properly, if his Majesty himself would be kind enough to pay for the Negroes, who are to be imported into this colony, at a rate that he would arrange with the dealers who would be charged with importing them. It would then be up to his Majesty to distribute them, on terms to be arranged, among the settlers of this colony, and to require them to pay the price which his Majesty would deem proper. Individuals could then assume the obligation, on behalf of his Majesty, of introducing ten thousand Negroes into this colony over a period of five years, that is, two thousand every year. Each shipload would be composed or assorted: One-third, men from the age of fifteen to sixteen years and on; one-third, women; and the other third, children, male or female.

The price of these Negroes would not be less than one thousand livres [French pounds] for each one in the assortment which we have just described. But it would be desirable that his Majesty make an advance payment of one-third the amount which the ships would require for this

Negroe trade on the African coast, and for the purpose of transporting to Louisiana, or to their respective ports of destination, the slave cargos which they will have taken on board. However, this advance payment is not to be made until two months after the departure of each individual ship from France for the coast of Africa.

If, however, a boat were to carry a lesser number of Negroes than estimated for a normal trip, it would then be necessary, with respect to the remaining two-thirds due, to credit his Majesty for the overplus of his advance payment. The final balance, however, would not be paid by his Majesty until two months after the report of the Commissioner (*Intendant*) of Louisiana, certifying the number of Negroes brought in by each vessel.

If this proposal should require any further construing of detail, there should be no hesitation in modifying it in order to aid in its implementation.

Of course, in accordance with established custom, there is no intention to deprive persons holding office in this colony of the privileges accorded them in other colonies nor to seek exemption from established obligations when they shall be known.

David Gradis and Sons

Bordeaux, May 21, 1748.

No. 121 Jews in the Potash Industry—1752–1765

In order to clear the land in colonial days the timber was cut down and burned. The resulting ashes were then leached and boiled to produce potash. In the English industry of the day this chemical was used in the manufacture of glass and soap, and was particularly valuable as a bleach in finishing textiles. Mercantilism, then dominant, encouraged the import of raw materials not available in England, to be paid for by remittances in consumers' goods and manufactures.

Among those interested in the production of this commodity was the merchant Israel Abrahams. That businessman appeared in New York, probably in the late 1730's, but, like a number of others, settled in the following decade in the growing town of Newport. After a business failure, he and his partner Nathan Nathans moved from that Rhode Island town to the new city of Halifax in Nova Scotia, where presumably they continued their partnership. By 1752, if not earlier, the partnership was dissolved, and Abrahams turned to the manufacture of potash.

In Document A, printed below, Abrahams asked the Board of

Trade and Plantations, the chief British colonial office in England, to employ him to further the manufacture of potash in Nova Scotia. He supported his request with a detailed estimate of the cost of production and two substantiating affidavits. Only the petition, however, is printed here.

Samuel DeLucena, the son of the well-known New York merchant-shipper and "rabbi" Abraham Haim DeLucena, kept shop in New York for a number of years. By 1765 he had moved to Norwalk, Connecticut, where he invested a considerable sum in the buildings and equipment necessary for the manufacture of potash. In order to protect his investment he petitioned the Connecticut General Assembly to grant him a monopoly on the manufacture of that commodity within a radius of twenty miles of his factory. His plea was that the export of potash to England would serve to pay for the consumers' goods which the colonists sought (Document B).

In a similar petition, made in 1753, Moses Lopez had asked the Rhode Island General Assembly for a ten-year monopoly in that colony. Lopez emphasized the fact that the export of potash would provide "our mother country [with] a commodity which is very much wanted there, would be serving them in a very great degree, and thereby we should gain their favour, and many other advantages would attend the same."

In 1765 Moses Lopez, still interested in the manufacture of that chemical, was ready to trade industrial formulas with Mr. Shrimpton Hutchinson of Boston (Document C). The latter was a brother-in-law of Henry Lloyd, a Boston businessman who served as agent and factor for a number of the Rhode Island Jewish merchants. As we know from later correspondence in the Lloyd letter book, Lopez complied with Hutchinson's request for his "recipe" for making potash.

Lloyd served also as an agent for Samuel DeLucena, who, during the Revolutionary period, was very much interested in securing sulphur, so important in the manufacture of gunpowder. His request for compensation for his search for sulphur mines, however, was not granted by the Board of War (1779).

SOURCE. Document A: Public Archives of Canada, Nova Scotia, A 49, pp. 122–28; Document B: Connecticut State Library, Connecticut Archives, Industry, 1708–89, Series 1, Vol. II, Document 110; Document C: Baker Library, Harvard University, Henry Lloyd Letter Book, 1765–67, p. 34.

A [NO. 121]

Halifax, October 18, 1752.

May it please Your Lordships:

In the month of April last, I tried an experiment in making pot ash of the wood that grows in the Province and made about 60 lb. weight of the Flemish sort.

I acquainted and layd the sample before the Honourable Edward Cornwallis, Esquire [retiring governor of Nova Scotia]. He sends for two men, soap boilers, that had served their times in London, who examined and tried said pot ash, and reported their opinion to the Honourable Edward Cornwallis, Esq.

I made 200 lb. more of the same sort, which I have sent home [to England] to lay before Your Lordships, that Your Lordships may have the same proved by those that are judges in London. I have likewise sent home to Your Lordships the charge that will occur in making one ton weight of this Flemish sort, and likewise beg leave to acquaint Your Lordships the great benefit this branch of trade will be to this new colony. First, it will clear very large tracts of land of the wood, and, 2dly, of consequence that will employ a great number of men in cutting and clearing the same, and, thirdly, will be the means of making large re- mittances home, besides, of course, impoverish those foreigners that has enriched themselves by supplying us with this commodity.

The men that Your Lordships sent over to make an experiment in pot ash arrived here several months after I had made my first experiment, and wanted to put this government to 7 or £800 charge, whereof I have not put the government to £8 charge.

I would have sent an equal sample of pot ash of the same sort as Russia in every degree, but for the want of ability to purchase the proper iron work required was obliged to decline. I have, My Lords, by build- ing works and lost time in making this experiment in pot ash, reduced my circumstances to a very low ebb. There is many here, as well as in other parts of this continent, that has got large tracts of land and would be glad to have so advantages away [advantageous a way] of clearing their woods, and allso to carry on such a manufactory as will make remittance home, but are prevented for want of knowledge in that art.

Therefore, I am willing to make the thing publick that every one as it suits, to instruct them in the buissness of making pot ash, in con- sideration of my being allowed a salary from the government in England for a term of years for the art, trouble, and attendance in instructing them, or allowing me a premium to make the thing publick in such a manner as Your Lordships shall give instructions, as Your Lordships shall be pleased to direct in promoting this great branch of trade, I am willing to assist, and proud of the honour of having it in my power to serve an infant colony.

I am, my Lords,

> Your Lordships' most obedient, humble servant,
> Israel Abrahams

To The Right Honourable and Honourable
Lords of Trade and Plantations.

B [NO. 121]

To the Honourable General Assembly of his Majesty's English Colony of Connecticut in New England in America, to be holden at Hartford on the second Thursday of instant May:

The memorial of Samuel DeLucena, now resident in Norwalk, in the County of Fairfield [Connecticut], humbly sheweth:

That your memorialist was born and brought up a merchant in the city of New York, in America, but finding of late years that it is hard making returns to Europe from whence he had his English goods, and thereupon, Your Honours' memorialist hath now learned the skill of making of pot ash, and for that purpose hath, by the approbation and consent of the good people of Norwalk, actually disbursed and layed out near two hundred pounds lawful money in building and preparing to carry on that business of making pot ash, which buildings are erected at the south end of the Town of Norwalk, which affair, if carried on with success, Your Honours' memorialist hopes may prove of good advantage both to himself and the government in general, in case he can have the approbation and assistance of this honourable Assembly in the case.

Whereupon Your Honours' memorialist humbly prays that this Assembly will pass an act forbidding any other person or persons setting up any work, or carrying on the business of making pot ash in the colony of Connecticut, within the distance of twenty miles of the place where his works is now erected, or in some other way pass some other act that may be for his incouragement, as this Assembly, in their great wisdom, shall think proper for his benefit, that he may proceed without interuption for some certain term of years, as he is the first undertaker [entrepreneur] to carry on that business in this county.

And your memorialist, as in duty bound, shall ever pray.

> Samuel De Lucena

Dated at Norwalk, the 6th day of May, *Anno Domini,* 1765.

C [NO. 121]

Boston, March 30th, 1765.

Mr. Moses Lopez.

Sir:

My brother in law, Mr. Shri[m]pton Hutchinson, desires me to inform you that he will give you a most minute and exact accountt of the process in making potash, that if you should fail in any part when you come to put his directions into practice, that you may then come to town or send any person you can confide in, to see every part performed at his works.

Mr. Hutchinson would be glad you would communicate to him your method of making use of potash for hard and soft soap, and that he may see the process per mord [performed], if he should be at Newport and desires it. He is already made acquainted with [William] Frobisher's method of using potash for hard and soft soap and would be glad to know yours, that he may judge which is most frugal and proffitable. Frobisher is the principal soap boyler in town. As soon as I can procure you a nother barrell of potash will send it. I am

Your most humble servant.

[Henry Lloyd]

––––––

No. 122 Naphtali Hart & Company's Sailing Orders for a Voyage to London—1754

Naphtali, Samuel, Abraham, and Isaac Hart, probably four brothers, were members of the firm of Naphtali Hart & Company, merchant-shippers in Newport. In business from the late 1740's, the firm engaged in extensive commerce and trade, and in the 1760's was among the founding members of the United Company of Spermaceti Candlers. The Hart business collapsed during the Revolution, when the partners, loyal to Britain, were forced to flee from Newport.

The following letter, consisting of sailing orders for one of the company's ships, is unusually brief and precise in its instructions to the captain. The Abraham Hart in England is not necessarily identical with the signatory of the same name. The former may have been a relative who served as the London agent for the firm. It is to be noted that the agent was to dispose of the vessel as well as of the freight. New England ships were frequently sold after their cargoes were unloaded.

SOURCE. Rhode Island State Archives, Public Notary Records, VI, 80.

Newport, Rhode Island, November 8th, 1754.

Capt. John Wightman,

Sir:

The brig *Pelican,* whereof you are at present comander, being now loaded and fitted to go to sea, you are carefully to observe the following orders during the course of her intended voyage, *viz.:*

First. Embrace the first favourable time to go to sea and then make the best of your way to London.

2d. When you are at London, you must punctually comply with all the orders of our Abraham Hart, respecting the cargo and disposition of the vessel, until your return to this port.

3d. Take in pilots at all usual places.

4th. Make protests [if you suffer damage] when and wherever it may be necessary.

5th. Be frugal in all your expences on the vessel.

We wish you a good voyage and are, sir,

Your owners and humble servants,

Naph., Sam., Abram, and Isaac Hart

No. 123   Michael Moses and David Franks Enter into Partnership in the Soap and Candle Business—1757

In the following indenture we note that Michael Moses was the craftsman and David Franks the financier. Though this copy was not signed, the partnership arrangements were completed, and the two remained in business until the death of Moses in 1769.

David Franks (1720–93), a son of the New York merchant Jacob Franks, was one of the outstanding Philadelphia businessmen in the days before the Revolution. He was a merchant-shipper, fur trade entrepreneur, land speculator, and large-scale army purveyor. At the time of the French and Indian War he represented a powerful British consortium that supplied the troops. During the Revolution he was authorized by the British and by the Americans to provide for the needs of the English and Loyalist prisoners in the hands of the Americans. Because of his suspected Loyalism, Franks was finally dismissed and was compelled to betake himself to New York, within the British lines. He died in Philadelphia during the dreadful yellow fever epidemic of 1793.

SOURCE. The Library Company of Philadelphia.

Articles of agreement indented, made at Philadelphia, the first day of January, in the year of our Lord one thousand seven hundred and fifty seven, between Michael Moses of Philadelphia aforesaid, tallow chandler, of the one part, and David Franks of the said city, merchant, of the other part, in manner following, that is to say:

Whereas, the said Michael Moses is desirous and hath requested the said David Franks to enter into a joint trade or copartnership with him, the said Moses, as partners or joint-traders in the trade or mistery of a tallow chandler and soap boiler, to be equally concerned in all profit and loss thereby, which request the said David Franks hath granted and doth consent unto.

Now these presents witness: that in consideration of the trust and confidence which they, the said parties, have and do repose in each other, it is hereby mutually declared, covenanted, and agreed upon by and between the said parties as follows, vizt.:

That they, the said parties, are, shall, and will become and continue partners and joint traders in the trade of making, vending, and selling soap and candles, upon a joint and equal account between them both as to profit and loss, from the [the date agreed upon is missing], for and during and unto the full end and term of five years, if the said parties shall both so long live. Which trade shall be carried on in the City of Philadelphia aforesaid, by the skill, knowledge, diligence, discretion, and labour of the said Michael Moses from time to time, and by him vended, retailed, and sold.

And as a consideration for the labour of the said Michael Moses, he the said David Franks hath, at his own proper costs and charges, purchased and procured all such utensils, tools, implements, and things needful for carrying on the trade aforesaid, which utensils are now, shall be, and remain the sole property of the said David Franks, and shall be delivered up to him at the expiration of this copartnership;

That the workmen or servants employed in the trade aforesaid shall be equally paid by the said parties, and shall be lodged and dieted by the said Moses at and after the rate of five shillings and sixpence money of Pennsylvania per week for each of them;

That the said Moses shall do the utmost of his endeavours in, and by all means possible, with all his skill, knowledge, and power for the joint interest aforesaid, and in making the soap and candles good and merchantable, and in selling and retailing the same;

And shall once a month, or oftner if required, render a just and true account of all tallow, candles, soap, etc., received, made, or sold by him, and of all gain, profit, and increase that shall arise by reason of such trade, and well and truly pay the said David Franks his part and share every three months;

That the books of account relating to such joint trade shall be kept by the said Michael Moses, to which books the said David Franks shall have free access to peruse and examine at all times;

That the said Michael Moses shall not at any time during this copartnership become bound, bail, surety, or any wise engage himself, by assumption or otherwise, with, unto, or for, any person or persons for any debt or duty, matter . . . without the lycense and consent of the said David Franks first had in writing under his hand in that behalf;

That once in three months, or oftner, the said Michael Moses shall make, yield, and render unto the said David Franks a just, true, and perfect account, as well of all profits and increase by him made as aforesaid, as of all losses by him sustained, as also of all payments, receipts, disbursements, and all other things relating to the said copartnership. And the same accounts so made shall and will clear, adjust, pay, and deliver unto the said David Franks at the time of making such account his equal share of the profits.

And it is further agreed that as the utensils, implements, etc., are procured and provided by the said David Franks, that then the said utensils, etc., shall, during the continuance of this copartnership, be maintained, upheld, repaired, and supplied by and between the said parties, part and share alike; and at the expiration of this copartnership, such utensils, etc., as the said David Franks shall be' at the sole expence of purchasing, shall be surrendred and yielded up to the said David Franks, his executors, and administrators;

And that at the expiration of the said term, or other and sooner determination of the said joint trade by the decease of either of the said parties or otherwise, they, the said parties, or their executors or administrators, shall and will make up a full, final, and just account and reckoning between them, of and concerning the same joint trade and stock, and all tallow, soap, candles, monies, debts, and things belonging and owing to and on account thereof, and all profit and loss thereby;

And that upon making up such account, all monies and debts owing on account of the said trade, and charges and damages thereby, shall be first paid or discounted. And all the remaining monies, tallow, candles, soap, debts, and things belonging and owing to, and on account of, the said trade shall be had, received, taken, enjoyed, and divided by and between the said parties equally, part and share alike, and without any benefit or advantage of survivorship to be had or taken by and between the said parties in case of the decease of either of them.

And to the faithful performance of the premisses on the part and behalf of the said parties respectively, each of them bindeth himself, his executors, and administrators unto the other of them, his executors and administrators in the penalty or sum of two hundred and fifty pounds lawful money of Pennsylvania, firmly by these presents, to be paid by the defective party to the party complying.

In witness whereof, the said parties to these presents have interchangeably set their hands and seals hereunto, dated the day and year first within written.

Sealed and delivered in the presence of us.

No. 124   Assigning Payment for a Soldier's Services—1757

The following brief order to pay £30 to Isaac Polock for the services of a soldier reflects a minor banking transaction. Polock may have advanced the soldier's pay and was then reimbursed by the colony of Rhode Island, or the soldier may have assigned his pay to Polock.

Isaac Polock (1700–1764) lived in New York and in 1742 was elected constable of the South Ward before he moved to Newport, where he was closely identified with the Jewish community. He was a member of the local Jewish social club and was one of the leaders in building the synagogue.

SOURCE. Rhode Island State Archives, French and Indian Wars, II, 166.

Newport, November 29, 1757.

Sir:

Please to pay Isaac Polock or order thirty pounds (old tenor) and charge the same to the colony, it being for ten days' service of Ezekiel Saunders, as a soldier in the last expedition [the French and Indian War].

per Benjamin Wickham

To Thomas Richardson, Esq.,
General Treasurer.

No. 125   Sampson Simson Asks for a Commission for a Privateer—1757

As owners or part owners of privateers, Jews seem to appear for the first time during King George's War (1744–48). During the French and Indian and the Revolutionary wars, however, many Jewish merchants tried their luck at this hazardous game. There was always a chance of capturing a rich prize, but more often than not the enterprise was a failure. In the following letter Sampson Simson petitioned Governor James DeLancey for letters of marque.

Simson, a son of the Hebraist and centenarian Joseph Simson, was born probably in New York City. He became a successful merchant and shipper, and in 1770 was among the founders of the local Chamber of Commerce. Three years later, in the same city, he died of consumption.

The little sixty-ton schooner described below carried sixty men. She must have literally swarmed with tough men, and in spite of her size, she must indeed have been a formidable opponent. A few months earlier, in August, 1757, Simson had sought a commission for the *Hardy*, which had forty men aboard, and in the following year the venturesome merchant asked that the *Sampson* be recommissioned. In 1759 he petitioned for letters of marque for the *Union* and the *Polly*, ships of 160 tons burden. The *Union*, however, carried only fourteen men, and the *Polly* only twenty. Obviously Simson was gambling heavily on his privateers, and all indications suggest that the gamble paid off, for he died a wealthy man.

SOURCE. New York State Library, New York Colonial Manuscripts, LXXXV, 58.

To the Honourable James De Lancey, Esq., his Majesty's Lieutenant Governor and Commander in Chief in and over the Province of New York and the Territories depending thereon in America:

The petition of Sampson Simson of the city of New York, merchant, and Company, humbly sheweth that your petitioner and company have fitted out the scooner called *Sampson*, burthen sixty tons, mounted with twelve guns, and manned with sixty men, to be commanded by Telaman Phenix, and propose to send the' said scooner on a cruize against his Majesty's enemies.

Your petitioners therefore humbly pray your Honour will be pleased to grant a commission to the said Telaman Phenix to command the said scooner for the purpose' aforesaid.

And your petitioners, as in duty bound, shall ever pray, etc.

Sampson Simson & Co.

New York, 23d December, 1757.

———

No. 126   A Good Conduct Bond for a Privateer—1758

The Harts, of Newport, seem to have been heavily involved in privateering. During 1758 the various members of that family dispatched at least four of these armed merchantmen to prey on the enemy's commerce.

In order to ensure that the owners and masters who were granted letters of marque would act responsibly and refrain from illegal or piratical attacks, they were expected to provide a bond for good conduct.

SOURCE. Rhode Island State Archives, Bonds—Masters of Vessels, I, 19.

Know all men by these presents that we, Benjamin Hickes, of Newport, in the County of Newport, in the English Colony of Rhode Island and Providence Plantations, in New England, in America, mariner, commander of ship called the *Confirmation*, and Naphtali Hart and Isaac Hart, of the same Newport, merchants, are holden and do stand firmly bound and obliged unto our Sovereign Lord, George the Second, by the grace of God, King of Great Britain and so forth, in the penal sum of fifteen hundred pounds sterling money of his said kingdom, to be paid unto our said lord the King, his heirs or successors, to the which payment well and truly to be made and done, we bind our selves, our heirs, executors, administrators, and each of us and them, for the whole and in the whole, jointly and severally, firmly by these presents, sealed with our seals, and dated the tenth day of January, in the year of our Lord one thousand seven hundred and fifty eight, and thirty first of his said Majesty's reign.

Whereas, the above bounden Benjamin Hickes is authorized by a letter of marque or commission under the seal of the colony aforesaid, bearing even date with these presents, from the Honourable William Greene, Esquire, Governor, Captain General and Commander in Chief of and over the colony aforesaid, to arm, equip, and set forth to sea the ship aforesaid, of the burthen of two hundred and fifty tons, or thereabouts, as a private man of war, under his, the said Benjamin Hick's own command, with men, victuals, ordnance, and ammunition, to set upon by force of arms and subdue, seize, and take the men of war, ships, and other vessels whatsoever, together with the goods, monies, and merchandizes, belonging to the French king, or to his vassals or subjects, or others inhabiting within any of his countries, territories, or dominions, and such other ships, vessels, and goods as are, or shall be, liable to confiscation, pursuant to the treaties subsisting between our said lord the King, and other princes, states, and potentates, excepting only in the harbours or roads within shot of the cannon of princes and states in amity with our said lord the King,

And, whereas, the said Benjamin Hickes hath, with his said letter of marque or commission, recieved certain instructions bearing even date with these presents, for the due and proper regulation of his conduct, as in and by said letter of marque or commission, and the said instructions or copies of the same upon record in the Secretary's office of the colony aforesaid, reference unto the same being had, will fully and at large appear,

Now the condition of this obligation is such that, if nothing be done by the aforesaid Benjamin Hickes, or any of his officers or company, contrary to the true intent and meaning of the aforesaid instructions, but that the commission aforesaid and the said instructions shall and be, in all particulars, well and truly observed and performed, so far as they shall in any way and manner concern the aforesaid ship and commander and company, and if they, or any of them, shall make and give full satisfaction for all and every damage and injury which shall be done by them, or any of them, to any of his Majesty's subjects, or allies, or neuters [neutrals], or their subjects, and also shall duly and truly pay or cause to be paid, unto his Majesty, his heirs, or successors, or to the customers [customs collectors] or officers appointed or to be appointed, to recieve the same for his Majesty, his heirs, or successors, the usual customs that shall be due unto his Majesty, his heirs, or successors, of and for all such ships, vessels, and goods, so as aforesaid taken and adjudged for prize;

And moreover, if the said Benjamin Hickes shall not take any ship or vessel, or any wares, or goods, or merchandizes belonging to the enemy, or otherwise liable to confiscation through consent, or clandestinely, or by collusion, or by virtue, color, or pretext of his aforesaid commission, then this obligation shall be void, and of none effect; otherwise [it shall] stand and be in full force and virtue.

Benjamin Hicks,   Naph. Hart,   I. Hart

Signed, sealed, and delivered in presence of

Thomas Ward, James Coggeshall

No. 127   Indentured Servants—1758–1788

The majority of immigrants who came to the American colonies were "voluntary" bond servants. They had subscribed their names to indentures, contracts binding them to serve for a specific number of years in payment for their passage.

In that category were the redemptioners, who sometimes paid part of their passage in advance, and on arrival were bound for a limited number of years for the balance due the shipper or captain. As a rule, redemptioners worked from two to seven years to satisfy their debt. Other indentured voluntary servants made specific contracts before sailing, agreeing to serve a fixed number of years after their arrival in the colonies.

Involuntary servants, such as criminals and the like, were usually compelled to serve a minimum of seven years.

Most Jews who came to these shores landed without restrictions on their personal services. They were "free." Bound laborers among them were relatively rare, although there were some Jews in all categories of bond servants who came to the American colonies, including even the involuntary type.

On occasion the Jewish community would ransom an indentured servant on or after his arrival. That was in line with the Jewish tradition of *pidyon shebuyim* ("redemption of captives").

Document A, printed below, deals with Isaac Moses, a skilled mechanic who bound himself out to serve for three years only at his specific trade in payment for his passage. Within less than half a year after his arrival he was "redeemed" by the Georgia Jewish leader, Mordecai Sheftall.

In all probability this Isaac Moses settled permanently in Charlestown, South Carolina, for in later years there was a successful and respected member of the Jewish community by that name. However, the name was by no means uncommon in colonial America, and the Georgia indentured servant is certainly not to be confused with the younger Isaac Moses, a famous New York merchant-shipper.

Document B is the indenture whereby Isaac Salimen (Solomon?) bound himself to Aaron Levy for a period of four years in payment for his "freight" from Rotterdam. He was a commodity. The right to Salimen's labors was transferred on his arrival, and he was then bound out to his Jewish master. That was a stroke of luck for that redemptioner.

Aaron Levy was a Hollander, a native of Amsterdam, who arrived in this country in 1760, when he was about eighteen years old. He lived in Philadelphia, Lancaster, and Northumberland. There is a tradition—which need not necessarily be false—that his wife, the former Rachel Phillips, was an indentured servant of the Chew family, and that Aaron redeemed and married her.

Levy was a merchant, a town builder, and a large-scale land agent. In 1786 he founded the town of Aaronsburg, Pennsylvania, which he named after himself. In his later years, in the 1790's, he was busily engaged in land deals; among his clients were Robert Morris and Justice James Wilson of the United States Supreme

Court. Over a period of about two weeks Levy contracted to turn over to Wilson almost half a million acres of land in Pennsylvania.

SOURCE. Document A: The Mr. and Mrs. B. H. Levy Collection of Sheftall Papers. Document B: The Edwin Wolf 2d Papers.

A [NO. 127]

This indenture, made the nineteenth day of May, in the thirty-first year of the reign of our Sovereign Lord, George the Second, King of Great-Britain, etc., and in the year of our Lord, one thousand seven hundred and fifty eight, between Isaac Moses of Hanover, gold and silver refiner of the one part, and Edward Somerville of London, merchant, of the other part, witnesseth:

That the said Isaac Moses, for the consideration herein after-mentioned, hath, and by these presents doth covenant, grant, and agree with [the said] Edward Somerville, [his executors or] assigns, that he, the said Isaac Moses, shall and will, as a faithful covenant servant, well and truly serve the said Edward Somerville, his executors or assigns, in the plantation of Georgia beyond the seas, for the space of three years next ensuing his arrival in the said plantation, in the employment of a gold and silver refiner.

And the said Isaac Moses doth hereby covenant and declare himself now to be the age of thirty years, a single person, and no covenant or contracted servant to any other person or persons.

And the said Edward Somerville, for himself, his executors or assigns, in consideration thereof, doth hereby covenant, promise, and agree to and with the said Isaac Moses, his executors and assigns, that he, the said Edward Somerville, his executors or assigns, shall and will, at his or their own proper costs and charges, with what convenient speed they may, carry and convey, or cause to be carried and conveyed, over unto the said plantation, the said Isaac Moses, and from henceforth, and during the said voyage, and also during the said term, shall and will, at the like costs and charges, provide for and allow the said Isaac Moses [all?] necessary cloaths, meat, drink, washing, lodging [meet?] and convenient for him as covenant servants in such cases are [provided?] for and allowed.

And [for himself?] the said Edward Somerville [doth promise?] and agree that, provided the said Isaac Moses pays him [or his assigns?] for his voyage within one month after his arrival in Georgia aforesaid, then this indenture to be void, or else to remain in full force.

And for the true performance of the premises, the said parties to these presents bind themselves, their executors and administrators, the either to the other, in the penal sum of twenty pounds sterling, firmly by the[se] presents.

In witness whereof, they have hereunto interchangeably set their hands and seals, the day and year above-written.

Isaac Moses

Sealed and delivered in the presence of
  Thos. Hayes

These are to certify that the above-named Isaac Moses came before me, Gyles Lone, deputy to the patentee, at London, the day and year above-written, and declared himself to be a single person, no covenant or contracted servant to any person or persons, to be of the age of thirty years, and to be desirous to serve the above-named Edward Somerville or his assigns three years, according to the tenor of the indenture above-written. All which is registered in the office for that purpose, appointed by the letters patents. In witness whereof, I have hereunto affixed the common seal of the said office.

Gyles Lone D.[eputy to the] P.[atentee]

[The following receipt appears on the back of this document.]

Received of Mr. Mordecay Sheftall the sum of eight pound eight sill-[ing] in full for the within mentioned Isack Moses' servitude. Savanah, December 11, 1758.

Edward Somerville

B [NO. 127]

Philadelphia SS.

This indenture witnesseth that Isaac Solomon, of his own free will, hath put himself servant to Aaron Levy, for the consideration of nineteen pounds 10s., paid to E. Duthil & Co., for his freight from Rotterdam; as also for other good causes, he, the said Isaac Solomon, hath bound and put himself, and by these presents doth bind and put himself, servant to the said Aaron Levy, to serve him, his executors and assigns, from the day of the date hereof, for and during the full term of four years from thence next ensuing, during all which term the said servant his said master, his executors, or assigns faithfully shall serve, and that honestly and obediently in all things, as a good and dutiful servant ought to do.

And the said Aaron Levy, his executors and assigns, during the said term, shall find and provide for the said servant sufficient meat, drink, apparel, washing, and lodging, and at the expiration of his term, he shall give said servant two complete suits of cloaths, one whereof to be new.

And for the true performance hereof, both the said parties bind themselves firmly unto each other by these present[s]. In witness whereof, they have hereunto interchangeably set their hands and seals. Dated the fourth day of January, *Annoque Domini*, 1788.

Bound before me,

Lewis Farmer,

Isaac Salimen

  register

No. 128 Naphtali Hart & Company Supply the Rhode Island Troops with Clothing—1758

The Rhode Island Committee of War bought large quantities of army goods from Naphtali Hart & Company during the French and Indian War. This firm was probably the largest Jewish mercantile concern in Newport during the 1750's. In 1755 Hart & Company sold tent duck, lead, and flints to the committee; three years later they supplied a large amount of clothing.

SOURCE. Rhode Island State Archives, French and Indian Wars, II, 34.

Newport, July 31, 1758.

Sir:

Please to pay Napthali Hart & Company thirteen thousand two hundred and thirty six pounds, seven shillings, and eleven pence, old tenor, it being for cloathing for the use of the expedition, and charge the same to the colony.

J. Gardner } Committee
Thomas Cranston } of War
Peter Bours }

To Thomas Richardson, Esq.,
General Treasurer.

_____

No. 129 Shipowner Jacob Isaacks Gives Bond Not to Carry Away Soldiers—1759

During the French and Indian War the colony of Rhode Island called upon the owners and masters of ships to give bond that they would not carry away soldiers, some of whom were prepared to leave their duties and serve on privateers. The hazards of serving on such vessels were no less, but the prospects of profit in the form of prize money were infinitely more enticing.

In the following bond the shipowner is identified as Jacob Isaacks (ca. 1718–98). Born in New York, he, like some other members of the Jewish community of that city, moved to Newport in the 1740's. During that decade the growth of this Rhode Island port evidently attracted a number of New Yorkers who helped to re-establish the Newport Jewish community.

SOURCE. Rhode Island State Archives, Bonds—Masters of Vessels, I, 44.

Know all men by these presents that we, William Pinniger, of Newport, in the County of Newport, in the English Colony of Rhode Island, and so forth, mariner, commander of the ship called the *Rising Sun,* and Jacob Isaacks, of the said Newport, merchant, owner of the said ship, are holden and do stand firmly bound and obliged unto Thomas Ward, of the same Newport, Esquire, Secretary of the colony abovesaid, in the penal sum of ten thousand pounds current money of the said colony, of the old tenor, to be paid to the said Thomas Ward or to his successors in his aforesaid office; to the which payment well and truly to be made and done we bind our selves, our heirs, executors, administrators, and every [each] of us and them, for the whole and in the whole, jointly and severally, firmly by these presents.

Sealed with our seals and dated the fourth day of April, in the year of our Lord one thousand seven hundred and fifty nine, and thirty second of the reign of his most sacred Majesty, George the Second, by the grace of God, King of Great Britain, and so forth.

The condition of this obligation is such that if the above bounden William Pinniger shall not carry or suffer to go away in the ship aforesaid any soldier or soldiers, that is, are, or hereafter may be inlisted or taken into the service or pay of the colony aforesaid, then this obligation shall be void and of none effect; otherwise [it shall] stand and be in full force and virtue.

Wm. Pinniger, Jacob Isaacks

Sealed and delivered in presence of
George Gardner, Thomas Ward

No. 130 Myer Levy Stocks Up at Barnard Gratz's Expense—1760

In October, 1760, Myer Levy, of Spottswood, New Jersey, departed suddenly with £2,300 in unpaid goods and other assets. He had probably reached the decision to abscond as early as July, but his wife was pregnant and he doubtless postponed his departure until she had been delivered. Among his creditors was Barnard Gratz, a merchant.

In the following letter we read that Levy ordered some wares from Gratz. A notation on the back of the letter informs us that he purchased teaspoons and dry goods. No doubt this was an order for which Gratz never received payment. It was men like Levy who made a great deal of trouble for honest colonial merchants and who helped to keep them poor.

Barnard Gratz (*ca.* 1737–1801), one of the stalwarts of the Philadelphia Jewish community, came to Pennsylvania in 1754. He and his brother Michael, who joined Barnard in 1759, were Germans. They had, however, spent some time in England, where they had relatives, and had become Anglicized. Barnard, the elder of the two, clerked for David Franks and then became a merchant on his own. Later he and his brother established the firm of B. & M. Gratz of Philadelphia, which was particularly active in the Indian trade and in extensive buying and selling of land.

SOURCE. MSS of The Library Company of Philadelphia.

To Mr. Barront Great,
Merchant in Waters Street,
Philadelphia.

Mr. Great:

Pleas to send me the following thinge as per order, as soon as possible you can, sir. I would a come my self by [but I] cannot as long as my wife is in this [c]ondition. I hop I shall be in the fall with you, and I expect after harvest to have mony in.

Pleas to give my compliments to Mr. Franks, and tell [him] to be easy till that time, and then I shall make, I hope, easy things with him, and all that you have not, as [which] I want, [I] shall have of Mr. Franks.

From your most humble servant,

Myre Levy

Spotswood, July 16th, 1760.

Sir, pleas to send my goods down by the Bordentown stage boat and forward it to me.

No. 131   Ransoming a Ship from Privateers—1760

In July, 1760, *The Elisabeth*, a brigantine owned by Naphtali Hart & Company, of Newport, and engaged in hauling molasses and sugar from the Spanish island of Haiti, was seized by English privateers. Apparently the cargo was contraband or it was thought that war was about to be declared against Spain.

In the following formal protest Captain Daniel Newton recounted the details of his capture and the method whereby he ransomed his boat and part of his cargo.

SOURCE. Rhode Island State Archives, Public Notary Records, Folder No. 17.

By this public instrument of protest, be it known unto all whom it doth or may concern:

That on the twenty fifth day of August in the year of our Lord one thousand seven hundred and sixty, and thirty-fourth of the reign of his most sacred Majesty, George the Second, by the grace of God King of Great Britain, and so forth, before me, Thomas Ward of Newport, in the English colony of Rhode Island and Providence Plantation, in New England in America, Esq., secretary and public notary of this colony duly elected and engaged according to the laws of the same, in his own proper person app[e]ared Daniel Newton, master of a certain brigantine, called *The Elisabeth,* of the burthen of twenty five tons or thereabouts by register, navigated by five men and a boy, who (to wit, the said Daniel Newton), being upon the Holy Gospel sworn, doth solemnly depose and declare,

That, on the sixteenth day of July last, he sailed with and in the brigantine aforesaid from Cape François [Cap Haitien] on the Island of Hispaniola [Haiti] for this port with a cargo of molasses and five barrels of sugar; that in prosecution of his intended voyage, being about two leagues north east from the port at the cape aforesaid, he was attacked by three English privateers, one under the command of Edward Bishop of the Island of St. Eustatius in the West Indies in a sloop of eleven carriage guns, a number of swivels, and about thirty hands. A second was commanded by _____ Walters of the said island of Saint Eustatius in a sloop of twelve carriage guns with a number of swivels and about thirty hands. The third was a sloop comanded by _____ Turner, belonging to Saint Croix, of ten carriage guns, about ten swivels, and eighteen hands or thereabouts.

These three privateers took the deponent with his vessel and cargo, put men on board with a copy of Edward Bishop's commission, and beat her to windward as far up as Point Caicus [Mona Island?], where they detained him, the deponent, sixteen days; that as he found no opportunity and had not any prospect of escaping after tarrying ten days, he agreed to ransom his aforesaid vessel for three hundred Spanish milled dollars and, with that view, drew a set of bills of exchange for the sum of two hundred and sixty of the said dollars on his owners, Messrs. Napthali Hart and Company, merchants in Newport aforesaid, he, the deponent, having delivered the captors one hogshead of sugar out of the cargo to make up the whole sum of three hundred dollars, the ransom agreed upon as is aforesaid;

That having thus obtained his liberty, he made the best of his way unto this colony and arrived at a place within the same called Howland's Ferry on Friday night last, and on occasion of what occurred in the voyage aforesaid, requested a lawful protest.

Daniel Newton

And Thomas Olddridge, mate, and James Anderson, mariner, both belonging unto and on board the brigantine aforesaid, from the time of her leaving Cape François until her arrival in this government, being in the like manner sworn upon their oaths, testify that the foregoing declaration made and signed by the aforesaid Daniel Newton is just and true in every respect.

Thomas Oldridge, James Anderson

Wherefore I, the said Thomas Ward, being requested, did and do hereby solemnly and publicly protest against the violent proceedings of the three commanders of the English privateers as herein before related as the sole occasion of all loss, detriment, and damage already suffered or to be hereafter sustained with, in, or about the brigantine and cargo aforesaid by the owners, insurers, shippers, and all others concerned.

Thus done and protested under my hand and seal of office, the day and year in these presents first mentioned.

T. W.

No. 132   Isaac DeLyon, of Georgia, Sends Rice and Deerskins to Barnard Gratz—1760

The Jewish community in Georgia was very small, although Jews had come to the colony only a few months after Oglethorpe's arrival in 1733. Among those who arrived in that year was Abraham De-Lyon, one of the pioneers of vine growing in the colony.

Isaac DeLyon may well have been his son. Isaac was a Savannah merchant who did business with Barnard Gratz of Philadelphia, bartering and selling local products for the English imports the latter stocked. Goods bought and sold were, of course, shipped by boat; more than a century was to elapse before more rapid overland transportation was available.

SOURCE. MSS of The Library Company of Philadelphia.

Savannah, 24 Sept., 1760.

To Mr. Barned Gratz,
Marchant, in Philadelphia.
Mr. Gratz,
Sir:

By Capt. Joseph Howard I have inclosed you an invoiice of sundry [goods] shiped you on my one [own] account: four barrels rice; four bundles of drear [deer] skins, one hundread dressed ones, fifteen onery [ordinary], six in the heir [undressed], which [you] will be good enuph to seal [sell] them to the best advantage. Please to seal them so that I may git the remittence by this schooner, because I don't know when the[re] will be a nother opertunity. Even if you should be oblige to seal them somthing cheepor then the common rate, I should be glad if you would send me an account of the seals [sales] of what I have shiped you in all.

I should be glad if you have' received the money of what you sould for me. If you have, you will be good enuph to remit it by this.

You rote me by Capt. Nezbet to let you know if starch seals heir [here]. It is now from 30s. to 40s.

Pleas to send me the following artcles. You will mutch oblige me' if you do send theme me this time, becaus it will be mutch to my advantage. Pleas to inshure what you send. From

Your most humble servant,
Isaac Delyon

25 lb. chokolet
1 barrel linced [linseed] oiil
1 doz. best black grane [grain] calf skins
9 barrels makarels
1 ditto herrings
150 lb. gingorbread
2 barrels cramberys
10 barrels of apples
If ther is eny thing remaing, pleasd to send it in milk and butter bread if the wether is not low. Could send me' 15 barrels ables [apples], but do let them be the last you put on board, for fear of the frost.

———

No. 133 Joseph Simon, of Lancaster, Asks Barnard Gratz, of Philadelphia, to Purchase Some Goods for Him—1761

Joseph Simon, a merchant, was probably the largest storekeeper in the important frontier town of Lancaster. He was part of a trading group that included David Franks of Philadelphia, the Gratz brothers, and a number of other Lancaster and Philadelphia merchants. The "Mr. Bush" mentioned in this letter, Mathias Bush, was one of the members, and was related to Simon and to the Gratzes by marriage. Lawrence and Nicholson, of whom Simon writes, were no doubt clerks employed by him.

Simon's extensive interests included a number of branch stores managed by Gentile partners. Much of his business was with Indian traders. He supplied the fur traders at Fort Pitt and points west and engaged in the buying and selling of land. As we see in the following note, he was also a distiller.

Barnard Gratz, as this letter evidences, acted as an agent for Simon, selling furs for one of Simon's customers. The sale was then credited to the account of the fur trader, the original customer, who, if he was not already overdrawn on Simon's books, could proceed to secure more goods from Simon at Lancaster or Fort Pitt.

The opening salutation in this letter is formal, in spite of the fact that almost exactly a month earlier Barnard had married an in-law of Simon.

SOURCE. MSS of The Library Company of Philadelphia.

Lancaster, 11th January, 1761.

Mr. Barnerd Gratz,
Merchant in Chesnutt Street,
Philadelphia.
Sir:

I beg you will let me know what you sold the beavor and racoons for, as I must give the people creditt. And as my waggons will be down this week, I beg you will get my things ready that is for the stilling [distilling] bussiness.

You'll be kind enough to buy me half a galloon of lubbage water (Isaac Levy's wife knows where it is to be had), and ½ gall. of cinnamon water, one barrel of good muscavado [unrefined] sugar, 24 lbs. of chocolate, 25 lbs. good coffe, 1 lb. cinnamon, 1 lb. mace, 1 lb. cloves, and one barrel of Mr. Franks's white powder sugar, if he has any.

Please to send me up my deed of a house and lott in Carlisle [Pennsylvania] which I left in your house, and I have a watch at young Biddle's, which get for me. Any thing that you lay out for me in them triffles, don't book it, but let me know the amount and I will send you down the money by next post.

Lawrence has left me and I have kept Nicholson. My wife joins me in her love to you and Mrs. Gratz [my wife's cousin], and Mr. Bush and his wife and family. I am, sir,

Your humble servant,
Joseph Simon

Shall be oblidged to you if you'll send me up two rock fish.

No. 134   Mordecai Sheftall Establishes a Trust to Protect
Himself and His Family—1761

In 1761 twenty-six-year-old Mordecai Sheftall, of Savannah,
Georgia, prepared to marry Frances Hart, of Charlestown, South
Carolina. On the eve of the nuptials he signed a release which created a trust for the protection of himself, his wife, and possible
future children. Thus Sheftall insured himself and his heirs against
almost any financial setback.

In the following document Sheftall conveyed title to lands and
slaves to his friend Isaac DaCosta, a Charlestown merchant, who
was to act as trustee for the beneficiaries. Under the terms of the
release Sheftall was to enjoy the use of the property during his life-
time unless he became insolvent. On his bankruptcy or death his
wife was to receive the yearly interest on £500, which DaCosta
was to raise by selling the property, and upon her death or remarriage the children were to be supported from the interest thus
realized, and were to receive the principal upon attaining their
majority. If Sheftall ever thought it desirable to sell the property
held in trust by DaCosta, he could do so under the terms of the
instrument, provided that the money received was used as directed
in the deed of trust.

Such conveyances as marriage settlements were quite common
among Jews and Gentiles of that time.

SOURCE. Charleston, S.C., Register Mesne Conveyance Office,
Book 0-3, p. 501.

South Carolina

Mordecai Sheftall ⎫
to ⎬
Isaac Dacosta ⎭

Release

This indenture made the twenty eight[h] day of October, in the second
year of the reign of our Sovereign Lord George the Third, by the grace
of God of Great Britain, France, and Ireland King, Defender of the
Faith, and so forth, and in the year of our Lord one thousand seven hundred and sixty one, between Mordecai Sheftall, of the Province of
Georgia, merchant, of the one part, and Isaac Dacosta, of Charles Town,
of the Province of South Carolina, merchant, of the other part, witnesseth:

That for and in consideration of a marriage already a greed [agreed]
upon, and shortly (by God's permission) to be had and solemnized ac-

cording to the Jewish custom, rites, and ceremonies, between the said Mordecai Sheftall and Frances Hart of Charles Town, in the Province of South Carolina, spinster, the daughter of Moses Hart, at present in the Hague, in Europe;

And that the said Frances may be provided of a compleat jointure [a wife's freehold estate] in case she shall happen to survive the said Mordecai Sheftall, and for provision and mentenance for her and her settling the inheritence of the said lands, town lotts, and negroes herein after mentioned, to such use and uses, and upon such trusts and confidence, as are herein declared, limited, or expressed; and for divers other good causes and considerations, him, the said Mordecai Sheftall, hereunto especially moveing, and also for and in consideration of the sum of ten shillings lawfull money of South Carolina, by the said Isaac Dacosta to the said Mordecai Sheftall in hand at or before the sealing and delivery of these presents well and truely paid, the receipt whereof is hereby acknowledged;

He, the said Mordecai Sheftall, hath granted, bargained, sold, aliened, remised, released, and confirmed, and by these presents doth grant, bargain, sell, alien, remise, release, and confirm unto the said Isaac Dacosta, his heirs and assigns, all that parcel of six hundred and fifty acres of land scituate and being in the Parish of Christ Church in the Province of Georgia, lying in or near the village of Aberiom, in different parcels or lots lately purchased by the said Mordicai Sheftall from Samuel Pelton and other, and also all that lot of land in the town of Savannah, in the Province of Georgia, known by the number _____, presently occupied by the said Modecai Sheftall, lately purchased by him of Thomas Barrington, Esq., scituate and being in Broughton Street, and containing sixty feet in front from the east to west and ninety feet in depth, together with the dwelling house and other houses thereon standing;

And also all that other lott of land in the town of Savannah, in the Province of Georgia, known by the number _____, scituate and being in Broughton Street aforesaid, containing sixty feet in front from east to west and ninety feet in depth, and lying between the lott of John Millidge and the lott lately purchases [purchased] by Mrs. Minis from Thomas Parker; together with all and singular the houses, out houses, edifices, buildings, stables, yards, gardens, orchards, ways, paths, passages, lights, easements, profits, commodities, emoluments, hereditaments, rights, members, and appurtenancies whatsoever on the said parcel of six hundred and fifty acres of land and two town lots aforesaid, standing or being or to the same or any of them in any wise belonging or appertaining (all which said premises now are in the actual possession of the said Isaac Dacosta, by virtue of a bargain and sale to him thereof made, for one whole year, by indenture of lease bearing date the day next before the day of the date of these presents, and by force and virtue of the statute for transferring of uses into possession), and the reversion and reversions, remainder and remainders, rents, issues, and profits, of all and singular the premisses herein before mentioned, and of every part and parcel thereof with the appurtenances;

And the said Mordicai Sheftall for the considerations herein before mentioned, hath bargained, sold, and delivered, and by these presents doth bargain, sell, and deliver, unto the said Isaac Dacosta, his heirs, executors, administrators, and assigns, all those three negroe slaves known by the names of Joe, Anthony, and Phillis, together with the future issue and increase of Phillis; and also all his estate, right, title, and interest, whatsoever of, in, or to the before mentioned real estate and every part thereof, and of, in, and to the before named negroe slaves, to have and to hold the said parcel of six hundred and fifty acres of land, and two town lots herein before mentioned, or intended to be here by bargained and sold, and every part there of, with the appurtenances and also the three before named negroe slaves, together with the future issue and increase of the female slave, unto the said Isaac Dacosta, his heirs, executors, administrators, and assigns;

In trust, nevertheless, and to and for the several uses, intents, and purposes, and with and under the several restrictions, limitations, provisoes, and agreements herein aftermentioned, limited, and declared of and for concerning the same, to and for no other use, intent, or purpose whattsoever;

That is to say, in trust, and to and for the use, benefit, and behoof of the said Mordecai Sheftall, untill the said marriage shall take effect, and from and immeadiatly after the solemnization of the said intended marriage; in trust that he, the said Isaac Dacosta, shall and will permitt and suffer the said Modicai Sheftall to have, receive, and take the rents, issues, profits, and income of the said parcel of six hundred and fifty acres of land and two town lots herein before mentioned, and other the premisses with the appurtenances, and also of the three before named negroe slaves, with the future issue of and increase of the female slave, to and for his own use, benefit, and behoof, during the term of his natural life, unless any unforseen accident or misfortune should happen in the trade, affairs, or bussiness of the said Mordecai Sheftall, in which case the said Mordecai Sheftall shall not any longer be permitted or suffered to have the use or enjoyment or to receive the rents, issues, profits, or income of the said parcel of six hundred and fifty acres of land and two town lotts and of the negroe slaves herein before mentioned, but shall from and immediatly after such accident or misfortune being known, permitted [permit] and suffer the said Isaac Dacosta, his heirs, executors, administrators, or assigns to sell or dispose of the said parcel of six hundred and fifty acres of land and two town lotts and the negroe slaves herein before mentioned, and there out or there by raise the sum of five hundred pounds lawfull money of Great Britain, as a jointure for the seperate use and behoof of the said Francis Hart, the intended wife of the said Mordecai Sheftall;

That is to say, that he the said Isaac Dacosta, his heirs, executors, administrators, or assigns shall and will pay and apply the yearly interest and income of the said sum of five hundred pounds to wards the seperate mentenance of the said Frances Hart, during the joint lives of them the said Mordecai and Frances, without the controul, intervention or meddling, claim or demand of the said Mordecai Sheftall or any other person or persons claiming or to claim by, from, or under him; and upon this further trust, that in case no such accident or misfortune shall happen to the affairs and bussiness of the said Mordecai Sheftall;

And that [if] the said Frances Hart, his intended wife, shall happen to survive him the said Mordecai, then in trust that he the said Isaac Dacosta, his heirs, executors, administrators, and assigns shall sell and dispose of the said parcel of six hundred and fifty acres of land and two town lotts and the negroe slaves, herein before mentioned, for the most money that can be got for the same, and thereout and thereby raise the sum of five hundred pounds lawfull money of Great Britain, as a jointure for the use and behoof of the said Frances Hart, the intended wife of the said Mordecai Sheftall;

That is to say, that he the said Isaac Dacosta, his heirs, executors, administrators, or assigns shall and will, after the decease of the said Mordecai Sheftall well and truely pay or cause to be paid unto the said Frances Hart the yearly interest of the said sum of five hundred pounds, during all the days of her natural life, if she remains the widow of said Mordecai Sheftall without intermarrying with any other husband, and after her decease or intermarriage, whichsoever shall happen first;

That he the said Isaac Dacosta, his heirs, executors, administrators, or assigns shall and will well and truly pay or cause to be paid the said sum of five hundred pounds, together with the overplus of the sales of the said estate (if any shall be) unto the child or children of the said Mordecai Sheftall on [of] the body of the said Frances Hart lawfully to be begotten, when they or either of them arrive at the age of twenty one years, and to maintain and educate such child or children thereout in the meantime;

And in default of such child or children, or their happening to dy before they or either of them arrive at the age of twenty-one years aforesaid, in trust that he the said Isaac Dacosta, his heirs, executors, administrators, and assigns shall and will pay and apply the said sum of five hundred pounds, together with the ballance or overplus of the sales of the said estate (if any shall be), according to such uses and purposes as shall or may be directed, limited, and appointed by the last will and testament of the said Mordecai Sheftall; and incase [in case] he shall happen to make no will in that respect, then to the nearest in kin of him the said Mordecai Sheftall, according to the statute of distribution;

And upon this further trust and confidence, that incase he the said Mordecai Sheftall shall at any time or times hereafter judge it more beneficial and advantage[ou]s that the said parcel of six hundred and fifty acres of land and two town lotts and the negroe slaves herein before mentioned, or any of them, should be sold, either intire or seperately, and the moneys arising from the sale of the same applyed to more beneficial purposes, then the said Mordecai Sheftall may sell, dispose of, convey, and make over the same six hundred and fifty acres of land and town lotts and the negroe slaves aforesaid, or any of them, either intire or seperately, as he shall think fit, providing always that the purchase money received therefore be invested in some other purchase, or taken and employed upon the same trusts, uses, and purposes, and under the same restrictions, limitations, agreements, and appointments herein before mentioned, any thing herein contained to the contrary notwithstanding.

In witness whereof the partys to these presents have hereunto interchangeably set their hands and seals, the day and year first above written.

Mordecai Sheftall

Sealed and delivered in the presence of James Ried, James Grindlay, Emanuel Abrahams.

South Carolina }
Berkley County }

To wit, James Ried, Esq., being duly sworn on the Holy Evangelists, maketh oath that he saw Mordecai Sheftall within named duly sign, seal, and deliver the within deed to and for the uses and purposes therein expressed; that the same James Ried subscribed as a witness to the execution of the said deed is [in] the deponent's hand writting, and that James Grindlay and Emanuel Abrahams were also witnesses to the said deed and subscribed their names as such in the deponent's presence.

James Ried

Sworn this 31 January, 1770, before me,

J. Rutledge, J. P. [Justice of the Peace]

Recorded and examined this 1st day of February, 1770.

Henry Rugeley, deputy register [registrar]

No. 135   Captain Rodman of the *Dolphin* Is Granted Letters of Marque—1762

Although we have documentation for the practice of privateering in America from the late seventeenth century on, this activity did not develop into big business until the French and Indian War.

The following document commissioned Captain Thomas Rodman, of the *Dolphin*, to prey upon the commerce of the enemy. The authorization was issued by the governor of Rhode Island, Stephen Hopkins, a politician and patriot who later became a signer of the Declaration of Independence. The *Dolphin* was owned by three partners, one of whom was Naphtali Hart, of Newport.

SOURCE. Rhode Island State Archives, Public Notary Records, VII, 252.

By the Honourable Stephen Hopkins, Esquire, Governor, Captain General, and Commander in Chief of the English Colony of Rhode-Island and Providence Plantations in New England in America. To all unto whom these presents shall come, greeting:

Whereas his late Majesty, George the Second, of blessed memory, did, by his declaration on the seventeenth day of May, in the year of our Lord one thousand seven hundred and fifty six, for the reasons therein contained, declare war against France,

And thereupon gave orders for the granting commissions or letters of marque to any of his loving subjects and others deemed fitly qualified in that behalf, for the apprehending, seizing, and taking the ships, vessels, and goods belonging to France, or to the vassals and subjects of the French king and others inhabiting within any of his countries, territories, or dominions, and such other ships, vessels, and goods as are or shall be liable to confiscation, pursuant to the respective treaties subsisting between his said Majesty and other princes, states, and potentates, and to bring the same to judgment in any of the Courts of Admiralty of Great Britain, or Ireland, or any of the plantations in America, or other the dominions of Great Britain, for proceeding, adjudication, and condemnation to be thereupon had, according to the course of the Admiralty and the laws of nations;

And whereas Naphtali Hart, Francis Honyman, and Gideon Sisson, all of Newport, in the colony aforesaid, hath equipped, furnished, and victualled a certain brigantine called the *Dolphin*, of the burthen of one hundred and forty tons or thereabouts, whereof Thomas Rodman goes commander;

Know ye, therefore, that the Governor above named hath and by these presents doth, in the name of his most sacred Majesty, George the Third, by the grace of God King of Great Britain, and so forth, grant commission unto, and licence and authorize, the aforesaid Thomas Rodman to set forth, in hostile manner, the aforesaid brigantine under his own command,

And therewith, by force of arms during the continuance of this present war to apprehend, seize, and take the ships, vessels, and goods belonging to the French king, or to his vassals and subjects, or others inhabiting within any of his countries, territories, or dominions, and all such other ships, vessels, and goods as are or shall be liable to confiscation, pursuant to the several treaties subsisting between his Majesty and other princes, states, and potentates, and to bring the same to such port as shall be most convenient, in order to have them legally adjudged in some of the Courts of Admiralty of Great Britain, or Ireland, or any of his Majesty's plantations in America, or other the dominions of Great Britain; which being condemned, it shall and may be lawfull for the said Thomas Rodman to sell and dispose of such ships, vessels, and goods so adjudged, and condemned in such sort and manner, as by the course [Courts] of the Admiralty, hath been accustomed, except in such cases where it is otherwise directed by his instructions;

Provided always that the said Thomas Rodman keep an exact journal of his proceedings, and therein particularly take notice of all prizes that shall be taken by him, the nature of such prizes, the times and places of their being taken, and the values of them as near as he can judge, as also of the station, motion, and strength of the enemy, as well as he or any of his mariners can discover or find out by examination of, or conference with, any mariners or passengers in any ship or vessel by him taken, or by any other lawful ways or means whatsoever, touching or concerning the enemy or their fleets, ships, vessels, or parties, and of what else meterial in these cases shall come to his knowledge, of all which the said Thomas Rodman shall from time to time, as he may have opportunity, transmit and give an account to me or such commander of any of his Majesty's ships of war as he shall first meet with.

And in case of the death or absence of the said Thomas Rodman, I do hereby grant the like commission unto, and licence and authorize, the next commanding officer of the said private man of war to have and take the charge and command thereof, with full power and lawful authority to do, act, and perform every matter and thing which the said Thomas Rodman is hereby impowered to act, transact, or perform, subject nevertheless to a due and strict observance of the instructions aforesaid, and every article of the same;

Provided farther that nothing be done or permitted to be done by the said Thomas Rodman, or the next commanding officer of the said private man of war, or any other of the officers, mariners, or company thereof, contrary to the true intent and meaning of the aforesaid instructions, but that the same be by them and every of them (as far as they or any of them are therein concerned) in all particulars well and truly observed and performed.

And I do beseech and request all kings, princes, potentates, states, and republicks, being his Majesty's friends and allies, and all others to whom it shall appertain, to give the commanding officer of the said brigantine, for the time being, with the officers and company thereof, all aid, assistance, and succour in their ports, together with their prizes, without doing or suffering to be done unto him or them any wrong, trouble, or hindrance, his Majesty's offering to do the like when by any of them thereto desired, requesting likewise all his Majesty's officers whatsoever to give them succour and assistance as occasion shall require.

Given under my hand and seal of the colony aforesaid, this eighteenth day of January, one thousand and seven hundred and sixty two, and in the second year of his said Majesty's reign.

Stephen Hopkins

By his Honor's command, Henry Ward, secretary.

No. 136   Anchovies and Wenches—1762

Michael Gratz arrived in this country in 1759, after working in various parts of Europe and in distant India. He settled in Philadelphia, where he was in turn a clerk, shopkeeper, merchant, merchant-shipper, fur trader, and land speculator. Like most merchants, he and his brother Barnard were wholesalers, trading with the shopkeepers in the back country.

Among their customers was Meyer Josephson, probably a native of Jever, in Oldenburg, North Germany, who settled in the German district of Pennsylvania during the early years of the French and Indian War. By 1761 he was married and busy raising a family in Reading, Pennsylvania, where he had a country store. Although there were other Jews in town—merchants and servants—there were not enough for a religious quorum. When the holydays rolled around, he and his friends went to Lancaster or Philadelphia for services.

Josephson sent his wagons, laden with country staples, such as fodder and provisions, to the city. In exchange he purchased finished goods, including leather products for saddlery and harness, and some luxury items, among which were anchovies and cucumbers for his own delectation. As we see from the following letter to Michael (Yehiel) Gratz, originally written in Yiddish, Josephson's relations with his coreligionists, who were also his suppliers, were close and intimate. If our interpretation is correct, the first part of the letter indicates that the Gratzes were thinking of leaving the city for an indefinite period. Apparently Michael and Barnard were not doing so well in those early days.

The second part of the letter deals with the problem of domestics: indentured servants (in Pennsylvania these were usually Germans) and Negro slaves. We know that slavery was not a bed of roses for the enslaved; but judging from this letter at least, it is obvious that the slaveowners too had their problems.

SOURCE. American Jewish Archives, The Henry Joseph Collection of Gratz Papers.

> Reading (with the help of God, may
> God protect it herein),
> Sunday, 5 Ab, 5522 [July 25, 1762].

Peace to my beloved friend, the honorable Mr. Yehiel. May the Lord protect him, and may this letter find his entire household at peace.

Your letter came at a propitious moment, also the books and bills of exchange [?] and one jar [?] of anchovies which was very important and which my wife, may she live long, has already eaten. Of course, I helped her somewhat. So if I could obtain another jar of this kind, will you send it to me, because it is the best I ever saw.

Also, I was very sorry to see from your letter that you, my special good patron, intend to leave Philadelphia, which I had not expected at this time. However, if you think that it is not to your best interest to remain, I cannot blame you. One must do many things for the sake of a livelihood. I wish it were in my power to advise you what is best for you to do and arrange that you would not leave Philadelphia, because your brother, may he be blessed, intends at present to go to London, and you, sir, will leave also, and I'll be a stranger when I come to Philadelphia. I really don't know where I can go!

If you come here for the coming Sabbath Nachmu [the Sabbath of Consolation]—may it come at an auspicious moment!—it would please me very much, because we are presently very lonesome on the Sabbath. And if you could stay here with us for eight days, it would be still better.

I also inform you that I may again sell my nigger wench at a profit. So if a ship with niggers should arrive, or a ship with [indentured] Germans, you will let me know, because I cannot manage without a servant. The wench I now have has two virtues, both bad ones. First, she is drunk all day, when she can get it, and second, she is mean, so that my wife cannot say a word to her. She is afraid of her. How did all this happen? A free nigger here wants to court her and to buy her from me. I don't want to give her away for less than 110 pounds, with her bastard, because I bought the bastard too. At present she costs me 90 pounds. So if I can make out with her, I think it is best to let her go and get another. So if you should have occasion to hear of a good nigger wench, or of a good servant, you will inform me.

I am,

> Your affectionate friend, the humble
> Meir, son of Joseph from Yever,
> scholar of blessed memory

[Postscript in English]
My spouse gives hear [her] complements to you and very much oblige to you for your coucumers.

No. 137   Isaac Elizer Trades in the Guadeloupe Islands—1762

Isaac Elizer (*ca.* 1720–1807) was one of the dozen or so merchants who built the Jewish community of Newport and helped to establish its commercial importance in the days before the Revolution. He was a merchant-shipper and, like many of his friends and associates, occasionally engaged in the slave traffic. Although he was a notable and respected businessman, he was refused naturalization in Rhode Island in 1762, but was granted that privilege in New York in the following year. Elizer continued, however, to reside in Newport. In his later years he was impoverished and was partly supported by the local Masonic fraternity. He died in Charleston, South Carolina, where he and his family had moved.

In 1762 Elizer was half owner of a sloop which he and his non-Jewish partners had loaded with wares for sale in one of the Guadeloupe Islands. Document A, below, a contract between Elizer and his business associates, determines the sale of the cargo, the authority of the supercargo, and the nature of the return load, preferably sugar.

One of the partners was a Frenchman from Guadeloupe named Joseph Sollier (Soullier). He was then in Newport, but before he returned home, he borrowed on his share, mortgaging it to Elizer as security for repayment. Sollier promised to pay the mortgage as soon as the ship arrived at its destination.

Guadeloupe, normally a French possession, was at that time in British hands. It is quite possible that the transaction between Elizer, Peter Simon, and Sollier, recorded in Document B, was an attempt to protect the cargo from privateers. Sollier was undoubtedly a French citizen and, in view of the French and Indian War then in progress, he was technically an enemy alien. Thus his share at least was subject to seizure by British privateers.

SOURCE. Rhode Island State Archives, Public Notary Records, VII, 377–79.

A [NO. 137]

Articles of agreement tripartite, made, indented, and concluded upon this twenty-eighth day of September, in the second year of his Majesty's reign, George the Third, King of Great Britain, etc., *Annoque Domini* 1762, between Isaac Elizer, of Newport, in the County of Newport, in the Colony of Rhode-Island and Providence Plantations, in New-England, merchant, of the first part, being one half part owner of the sloop *Wheel of Fortune,* now in the harbour of Newport aforesaid, whereof Charles Bardine is at present master, Peter Simon of Newport aforesaid, merchant, one quarter part owner of said sloop, of the second part, and Joseph Soullier of Port Louis, on the island of Grandterre, Guadaloupe, in the West Indies, now residing at Newport aforesaid, merchant, one quarter part owner of said sloop, of the third part.

Witness, that as the said sloop is now laden and ready to sail, it is covenanted and agreed upon by and between the said parties that the said Charles Bardine shall, with the first good wind and weather, sail with said sloop and her cargo on board directly to said Grandeterre, Guadaloupe, and upon said vessell's arriving there, the said Charles Bardine (to whom said cargo is consigned) is to dispose of said cargo to the best advantage, and lay out the neat [net] proceeds in the best sugars, and put the same on board said sloop, if to be had. If not, then [he is] to purchase the best goods which can be done [bought] with said cargo, and put the same on board said vessell.

And the said Joseph Soulleir is desired to assist the said Charles Bardine, in the best manner he can, in disposing of the cargo on board said vessell, and in purchasing another, without charging commissions or any other reward, it being at the requist of the other owners, who have done the business at Newport, without any commissions or other reward.

And when said sloop is loaded, the said Charles Bardine is to proceed with said sloop and cargo directly to Newport. And the said Joseph Soullier doth covenant and promise to use his best endeavours to dispatch said sloop, and that he will not act or do any thing which shall have a tendancy to stop, interrupt, or delay the voyage.

And the said Joseph Soullier is to have the liberty at any time to substitute and appoint any person to represent him and do his business respecting said voyage, provided the same does not stop, interrupt, or delay the voyage, or is any disadvantage thereto.

And for the true and faithfull performance of these present articles of agreement, and every clause and article thereof, the said parties bind themselves, their heirs, exec[u]tors, and administrators, each to the others, firmly by these presents, in the penal sum of two hundred and fifty pounds sterling, and have hereunto interchangeably set their hands and seals, the day and year first above written.

Isaac Elizer   P. Simon   Joseph Sollier

Signed, sealed, and delivered in the presence of us:

John Manley, William Sisson

B [NO. 137]

To all people to whom these presents shall come, Joseph Soullier, of Port Louis, in the island of Grandterre, Gaudaloupe, in the West Indies, merchant, now at Newport, in the County of Newport, in the Colony of Rhode-Island, etc., one quarter part owner of the sloop *Wheel of Fortune,* now in the harbor of Newport aforesaid, whereof Charles Bardine is master, together with one quarter part of her tackle, apparell, appertenances, and cargo, and now ready to sail from Newport aforesaid to said Port Louis, in the island of Grandterre, Gaudaloupe, sends greeting.

Know ye that the said Joseph Soullier, for and in consideration of the full and just sum of two hundred and fifty two Spanish silver milled dollars, and one third of a dollar to me in hand (before the ensealing hereof) well and truly paid by Isaac Elizar, of Newport aforesaid, merchant, the receipt whereof I do hereby acknowledge, and myself therewith fully satisfied, contended, and paid, have hypothecated, granted, bargined, sold, conveyed, and confirmed, and by these presents do hypothecate, grant, bargin, sell, convey, and confirm unto the said Isaac Elizer, his heirs, executors, administrators, and assigns, the said one quarter part of said sloop, *Wheel of Fortune,* with one quarter part of all her tackle, apparell, appurtenants, and cargo;

To have and to hold the said quarter part of said sloop, tackle, apparell, appurtenances, and cargo unto him, the said Isaac Elizer, his heirs, executors, administrators, and assignes for ever, upon condition, nevertheless, that if the said Joseph Soullier, his heirs, executors, or administrators shall well and truly pay, or cause to be paid, unto the said Isaac Elizer, his order, factor, or assigns, the said sum of two hundred and fifty two Spanish silver milled dollars, and one third of a dollar at the said island of Grandterre, Gaudaloupe, upon the said sloop's arrival there; or in case the said sloop shall be taken by the enemy, cast away, foundered at sea, or any otherwise lost or destroyed before her arrival at the said island of Grandterre, Goudaloupe, then this present deed of hypothecation or bargin and sale shall cause [cease?], determine [terminate?], be null, void, and of none effect, otherwise to abide and remain in full force and virtue.

In witness whereof, I, the said Joseph Soullier, have hereunto set my hand and seal the twenty ninth day of September, in the second year of his Majesty's reign, George the Third, King of Great Britain, etc., *Annoque Domini,* 1762.

Joseph Sollier

Signed, sealed, and delivered in the presence of us. the words (one quarter part of, said) over the twenty-fourth line of the othe[r] side being first interlined.

Daniel Fourtane, Mary Dupuy

No. 138   Samuel Jacobs Petitions Governor James Murray, of Quebec, to Seize the Goods of Gershon Levy & Company for Debts Due Him—*ca.* 1762

Samuel Jacobs (d. 1786) was a military supplyman during the British conquest of Canada. He remained in the country after the war, and became a general merchant.

Among Jacobs' chief debtors was the firm of Gershon Levy & Company, fur traders operating in the Upper Country, now for the most part Michigan. Jacobs was himself in debt, but he held his creditors off with the promise to pay as soon as Levy & Company brought their furs down from the interior. When the latter consigned their products to another firm, Jacobs proceeded to attach the furs for the debts due him.

The following petition, which describes the situation in some detail, is illustrative of the problems facing merchants and traders at that time.

Jacobs' endorsement of his retained copy of the petition is revelatory of his knowledge of English: "Partigon to Gen'rl Morry in regar of Mr. Levy" [Petition to General Murray in regard to Mr. Levy].

SOURCE. Public Archives of Canada, Samuel Jacobs Papers.

To the Honorable James Murray, Esq., Governor of Quebec, etc.:

The memorialist [memorial] of Samuel Jacobs, merchant, humbly sheweth: that there yet remains unpaid a ballance of £859 15s. 6d., New

York currency, of a note of hand due 9 July, 1761, drawn by Gershon Levy & Co., of Montreal, payable to Alexander Mackenzie and Samuel Jacobs;

Also, to your Excellency's memorialist, by the said Gershon Levy & Co., about £600, New York currency, in notes of hand and book debts, which they promised and assured your Excellency's memorialist that, if he would only have patience untill the return of the canoes from the upper country, he [Jacobs] should be satisfyed, [even] if no more came to hand than sufficient to pay his demands.

On presumption of which your Excellency's memorialist has engaged to satisfy his credetors, who now press him very much, and [it is] out of his power to satisfy them, as Gershon Levy & Co. have, instead of paying him agreeable to their promise, consigned their beavor and other furrs to Isaac Levy of this place, to be sold for their accounts.

Therefore, your mimorialist prays your Excellency will be pleased to grant an order to secure said goods, for the payment of the just debts due by the said Gershon Levy & Co., of Montreal, to your Excellency's memorialist, who, as in duty bound, will ever pray.

No. 139   Naphtali Hart & Company, of Newport, Act as
Attorneys for Curaçao Merchants—1762–1764

In 1762 three Newport privateers, the *Diana*, the *King George*, and the *Keppel*, seized the schooner *King David* and the sloop *Aurora*, belonging to Curaçaoan merchants, probably Jews, and brought the two prizes into Newport harbor. Naphtali Hart & Company represented the interests of the Dutch owners.

In Document A, which follows, the Harts were made attorneys to work for the release of the *Aurora*. (The master of the *King David* may have given them a similar power of attorney to work for the release of his ship.) The Harts were able to secure the return of the *King David*, but were not so successful in their efforts to effect the restoration of the *Aurora*.

In Document B, dated May 30, 1763, Isaak Pardo, the Curaçaoan Jew with whom the Harts corresponded with respect to the captured vessels, acknowledged the return of the schooner *King David*, but refused, on behalf of the owners, to honor a request for payment of moneys disbursed to secure the release of the *Aurora*. The owners, covered by insurance, were no longer concerned with the fate of that ship, but to compensate Hart & Company they surrendered their rights in the sloop to the Newport firm.

Document C, written over a year later, is an affidavit by Isaac Hart, of Hart & Company, to the effect that the Pardo letter, which he had brought into court, was a true copy of the original. Note that Hart was sworn on the Old Testament.

Though the *Aurora* was not restored to the original owners, they apparently retained some rights to it. Inasmuch as these rights had been ceded by them to Hart & Company, the latter in turn, having been compensated by the privateers, surrendered their rights in the sloop to the privateers. The release by Hart & Company is found in Document D.

It is interesting to note that the capture and final disposition of the ships dragged on for a period of about two years (1762–64). This meant, of course, that a considerable amount of capital was tied up and was unproductive.

Hart & Company were glad to step in and help their Curaçaoan friends, expecting, of course, that they would come to their aid under similar circumstances. The Harts took a chance when they advanced money in the attempt to save the two Dutch ships, but fortunately they were able to retrieve the sums advanced. The element of hazard in mercantile shipping cannot be overemphasized.

SOURCE. Rhode Island State Archives, Public Notary Records, VII, 495, 561.

A [NO. 139]

To all people to whom these presents shall come, I, John Elias of Curraçoa, mariner (master of the sloop called the *Aurora*, that Job Easton, commander of the private man of war sloop *Diana*, James Chambers, commander of the private man of war sloop *Kepple*, and David Mumford, commander of the private man of war brig[antine], the *King George*, seized and took together with her cargo on board of her and sent into the harbor of Newport, in the county of Newport, in the Colony of Rhode Island, etc., for adjudication), send greeting.

Know ye that I, the said John Elias, for divers good causes and considerations have made, ordained, constituted, and appointed, and by these presents do make, ordain, constitute, and appoint Naphtali Hart and Isaac Hart, both of Newport aforesaid, merchants, to be my true and lawful [attorneys] for me, and in my name and to my use to ask, demand, sue for, require, recover, and receive, of and from every person and persons whatsoever, the said sloop and cargo that was on board of her at the time of her being seized and taken as aforesaid, and to take and use all lawful ways, means, and remedies for the recovery, receiving, and obtaining thereof, and upon receipt of the premisses aforesaid, or any part thereof, in my name or in their own names to make and give acquittance or other sufficient discharges for the same;

And also for me and in my name to make, answer, prosecute, and defend in any court or courts, of vice admiralty, or in any other court or courts whatsoever, and before any judge or judges, justice or justices, or ministers of the law in any suit, action, matter, cause, or thing whatsoever with me, for me, or against me as the case may require, giving, and by these presents, granting unto my said attornies my full and whole power, strength, and authority in and about the execution and performance of the premisses, and attorney or attornies, one or more under them, to make and substitute for the purposes aforesaid, and again at their pleasure to revoke and generally to do, execute, perform, accomplish, and finish all and every such further and other reasonable act and acts, thing and things, device and devices in the law whatsoever, which shall be needful and nec[e]ssary in and about the premisses as fully, largely, and amply in every respect to all intents and purposes as I my self might or could do, being personally present, ratifying, confirming, and allowing all and whatsoever my said attornies or their substitutes shall lawfully do, or cause to be done, in and about the premisses by virtue of these presents.

And further, I, the said John Elias, for divers other good causes and considerations, do hereby covenant, promise, and grant to and with the said Naphtali Hart and Isaac Hart by these presents that I will not at any time do, act, transact, or perform any act or acts, matter or things whatsoever wherby this present warrant or letter of attorney be any ways vacated or annuled, but that the same shall be, abide, and remain in full force according to the true expression and meaning thereof.

In witness whereof, I, the said John Elias, have hereunto set my hand and seal, the fifteenth day of September, in the second year of the reign of our sovereign Lord, George the Third, King of Great Britain, etc., and in the year of our Lord one thousand seven hundred and sixty-two.

Jan Elias.
Newport, September 21st, 1763.

Sealed and delivered in the presence of us:
Isaac Howland, Jos. Fox

Newport, to wit:
Personally appeared the above named John Elias and acknowledged this instrument or letter of attorney to be his free act and deed.
Befor John Davis, Jr., Justice of the Peace.
Registered and compared, June 1st, 1763.
Witness ———

B [NO. 139]

Curacoa, 30th May, 1763

Messrs. Naph. Hart & Company.

Gentlemen:

As there have not been for this long time any oppertunity [to send a letter directly] for North America, I have done myself the honour to write you per the sloop *Sally*, Capt. Smith [commander], by the way of Jamaica, which I hope came safe to your hands. This present [letter] goes by Capt. Michael deLeon, by the same way, to acquent you that I was honoured with your favor by Capt. John Elias, dated the 11th November last, it being the first I received.

I can't but return you many thanks for your good assistance on the schooner *King David*, which safe arrived in this port. As for the sloop *Aurora*, which was takin and carried to your port, I am sorry that you have takin so much trouble with her, as the amount of vessel and cargoe was insured in this island. So if she had been cleared, the benefit would have been for the insurers.

I therefore, as soon as I received your letter, I called them [the insurers] togeather and presented your account and bills which you drew on me. There [their] answer was that they was satisfyed with the loss of the vessel and cargoe and would not pay any further charges, and they will seed [cede], relinquish, and transport all manner of rights unto you for the charges that you are at. This is the reason of my not honouring your bills.

Therefore, I do by these presents, in my name and in the names of all the insurers, seed, relinquish, and transport unto you all manner of pretince [pretense], right, and tittle [title] that we may have on the said sloop and cargo. Therefore, if she is released in Great Britain (as I wish she may), all and every part shall belong to you as your own property.

I therefore beg you very much, for the future, to not put yourself under any disbursements for me without my writting [written] orders. But whenever you have any from me, I shall take it as a particular favor [if] you'll give your assistance in any case, and then you may depend on sure payment in any part where you shall think proper.

If I can be of any service to you in this place, you may depend on all that lays in my power, and shall be glad if any opportunity to give you proves how much I am, with due respects, gentlemens,

Your most humble servent,

Isaak Pardo

N.B. If I am favoured with any of your letters hereafter, I shall be oblige to let them be wrote in Dutch or Spanish.

C [NO. 139]

Newport, September 26th, 1764.

To Messrs. Naph. Hart & Company,
Merchants, in New York (via Jamaica),
Colony of Rhode Island, etc.

Before me, Henry Ward, Esq., one of his Majesty's justices in commission for the peace of Newport aforesaid, personally appeared Mr. Isaac Hart, of said Newport, merchant, one of the company of Naphtali Hart and Company, and, being a person professing the Jewish religion, made solemn oath upon the Pentateuch that what is written above and upon the preceding page contains a true copy of an original letter received by the said company from Isaak Pardo, of Curacoa, merchant.

Isaac Hart   Henry Ward

D [NO. 139]

Know all men by these presents that we, Naphtali Hart & Company, of Newport, in the Colony of Rhode Island, merchants, by virtue of the power and authority to us given by the foregoing letter, and for and in consideration of the sum of one hundred and forty-nine pounds, 14s., New York currency, to us in hand paid by John Coddington, of Newport aforesaid, merchant, attorney to the owners, officers, and mariners of the brigantine *King George*, a private vessel of war concerned in the capture of the sloop *Aurora*, and of the sum of eighty pounds, New York currency, paid us by the said John Coddington as attorney to the owners, officers, and mariners of the sloop *Keppell*, a private vessel of war also concerned in the capture of the said sloop *Aurora*,

The receipt of which sums we do hereby acknowledge, and ourselves therewith fully satisfied and paid, have, and by these presents do freely, fully, and absolutely release and forever discharge the owners, officers, and mariners of the said brigantine *King George*, and the owners, officers, and mariners of the said sloop *Keppel*, and every of them, of and from all and all manner of actions and suits and causes of actions and suits for damages, costs, and charges of every nature and kind whatever, which we now have or hereafter may have against them, as either or any of them, for or by reason, or in consequence, of the capture aforesaid, and of all proceedings thereupon had, or any other matter, cause, or thing concerning the same.

In witness whereof we have hereunto set our hands and seals this twenty-sixth day of September, 1764, and in the fourth year of his Majesty's [George III] reign.

Isaac Hart, for himself and company

Sealed and delivered in the presence of
                         Caleb Allen, Henry Ward
Registred 26th Sept., 1764, and compared.
Witness: Henry Ward, secretary and public notary.

––––––––

No. 140   Samuel Jacobs Buys Grain and Runs a Country Store—1763

Samuel Jacobs (d. 1786) came to Canada with the invading British troops. After the conquest he settled in St. Denis, a little town on the Richelieu River, located on the Lake Champlain route from New York to the St. Lawrence River. Unlike many of his contemporaries, he did not specialize in the fur trade, although he did occasionally traffic in that commodity. Instead, by 1763 he had a country store; Charles Curtius was its manager.

The following letter reflects some of Jacobs' commercial interests at that time: trade with the troops at Crown Point (the French and Indian War was just ending), and grain. Sometimes Jacobs exported the grain direct to Europe. More often, however, he served as chief purchasing agent for the exporters at Montreal, in which capacity he was assisted by a staff of agents and subagents.

SOURCE. Public Archives of Canada, Samuel Jacobs Papers.

Quebec, June 8th, 1763.

To Mr. Charles Curtius,
Merchant at St. Dennis.
Dear Sir:

I hope these lines will find you and yours in good health. I wish you and yours sincerely joy and happiness on your mariage.

I am so confident in your understanding and integrity of strict honor and honesty, makes one but slow in writing, as I do much depend upon your judgment. [I don't write you often, for I have confidence in your utter honesty, and that you know what to do.]

As to the corn you wrote me about, I have ordered you up a large batoe [*bateau:* "boat"], which you may make use of to bring the corn from sundry places. You'll please to try to get liberty [a license] to send down some corn. I suppose you know how this must be managed. Get the liberty in your own name and don't ask permition for all at once.

I am waiting for a vessel from London and hope to send you up such an assortment of goods as will please you.

You will forward what corn down you possibly can. Take [make] your bills of lading for the corn to Jacobs & Company. Fail not to compleat this off hand [at once].

So conclude in wishing you and your family success, and remain, your assured friend to command,

[Samuel Jacobs]

P.S. The goods you'll receive in the batoe will be for Crown Point. Please to stow them away till I come up.

No. 141 Jacob Isaacks Sells a Ship and Cargo to Issachar Polock, of Newport—1764

In January, 1764, Jacob Isaacks, a Newport merchant, loaded a brig with fish, barrel staves, leather, indigo, rum, tobacco, snuff, meat, and bread, and prepared to dispatch it to the Canaries. However, he sold the brig and cargo to a fellow merchant in Newport. The following document records the sale.

Issachar Polock, the vendee, was one of the many Polocks who appeared in eighteenth-century Newport. As the name indicates, some ancestor originally hailed from Poland. Polock was a New York merchant who moved to Newport, probably in the 1750's. There he took an active part in establishing the synagogue, but also found time to relax in the local Jewish card club of which Jacob Isaacks was also a member.

This document reflects the Newport trade with the Canaries and the type of cargo sent there. On the return trip the ship undoubtedly brought back wines.

The buyer, Polock, probably purchased the brig and cargo on a speculation. He paid down part of the "consideration money" in cash and gave his note for the balance. If the venture was successful, Polock was lucky; if not, it was just too bad, and he would have to scurry around to meet his note.

A business hazard which vendors and vendees probably did not take into account was clerical incompetence. A check of the multiplication in the following invoice will disclose that Isaacks erred to his own disadvantage in the amount of £30, and to his advantage in the amount of £36. Polock, if he accepted the invoice, as he appears to have done, lost £6. And when Isaacks' accountant computed the dollars in pounds sterling, he erred again, to his own advantage, in the amount of about £3.

SOURCE. Rhode Island State Archives, Public Notary Records, VII, 527.

Newport, January 5th, 1764.

Invoice of sundrys shipped and to be shipped on board the brigantine *Rebecca* (John Hyers, master), bound to the island of Teneriffe [Canary Islands], as follows. Shipped by Jacob Isaacks:

To 1,200 quintals of dried cod fish. @ £18	£21,600
To 4 barrells of cod sounds 50	200
To 2 thousand pipe staves [@ £300 per 1,000] 300	600
To 1,500 lbs. leather .... 1 6s.	1,920 [1,950]
To 4 barrels indigo wt. 700 lbs. ... 7 [per lb.]	4,900
To 6 hogsheads rum [?] 650 gal. .. 5 [per gal.]	3,250
To 12 duks [bolts of cloth?] 92	1,140 [1,104]
To 9 hogsheads tobacco wt. 4,500 [lbs.] .... 5s. 6d.	1,237
To 2,000 lbs. Spanish snuff ...... 30s.	3,000
To 7 barrels beef £60	420
To 2 do. pork 110	220
To 12 hundred bread 22	264

£38,751 [38,745]

To the hull of brigantine *Rebecca,* and clearing out, etc.   21,850

£60,601 [60,595]

£60,601 old tenor is at £7 per dollar 8,657 1/3 dollars, at 4/6 sterling is £1,950 8s. sterling.

Jacob Isaacks.

January 5th, 1764.

Know all men by these presents that I, Jacob Isaacks, of Newport, in the County of Newport, and Colony of Rhode Island, etc., merchant, for and in consideration of the sum of nineteen hundred and fifty pounds eight shillings sterling, to me in hand paid, at or before the sealing and delivery hereof by Issachar Polock of said Newport, merchant, the receipt whereof I do hereby acknowledge, and that I am therewith fully and entirely satisfied, have bargained and sold, set over, and delivered, and by these presents do bargain, sell, set over, and deliver, unto the said Issachar Polock, the brigantine called the *Rebecca* (whereof John Hyers is at present master), of the burthen of about one hundred and ten tons, with all her rigging, tackle, furniture, and apparel, boats and oars, and all appurtenances to her belonging and now used, together with all her cargo, as per invoice thereof hereto annexed (reference thereto being had, will at large appear the same), now lying in the harbour of Newport, to have and to hold the hereby bargained [ship], with all the appurtenances thereto, unto the said Issachar Polock, his heirs, executors, administrators, and assigns, to his and their only proper use, benefit, and behoof forever.

And I, the said Jacob Isaacks, do for myself, my heirs, executors, and administrators, [convey] the hereby bargained vessel and cargo and their appurtenances unto the said Issachar Polock, his heirs, executors, administrators, and assigns, against the said Jacob Isaacks and his executors, and administrators, and against all and every person and persons whatsoever lawfully claiming or to claim the same, shall and will warrant and forever defend by these presents.

In witness whereof, I have hereunto set my hand and seal, the fifth day of January, in the fourth year of the reign of our sovereign Lord, George the Third, King of Great Britain, etc., *Anno Domini*, 1764.

Jacob Isaacks

Sealed and delivered in the presence of us:

John Manley   Robert Mumford

Indorsed:

Newport, January 5th, 1764, received of the within named grantee, Issachar Polock, the full sum of nineteen hundred and fifty pounds sterling money of Great Britain, in full satisfaction of the consideration money within mentioned.

Jacob Isaacks

Witnesses:
John Manley
Robert Mumford

Colony of Rhode Island, etc.   Newport, February 17th, 1764.

Personally appeared Mr. Robert Mumford and made solemn oath that he saw Jacob Isaacks sign, seal, and deliver the within bill of sale as and for his act and deed, and that he saw the said Jacob Isaacks sign and acknowledge the above receipt to be his act and deed, and that he, together with John Manley, did sign the said bill of sale and receipt as witnesses at the same time, and that he saw Issachar Polock pay down part of the consideration money, and give the said Jacob Isaacks a promissory note for the balance.

Sworn before Henry Ward, Justice of the Peace.

Newport, February 20th, 1764.

What is written above and upon the preceding page is truly and exactly registred from an original bill of sale and probate thereof, and from an original invoice to the said bill of sale annexed, and is with the said originals duly compared.

Witness: Henry Ward, secretary and public notary.

———

No. 142   Trading Liquor to Canada—1765

A few years after the young Silesian Jewish immigrants Barnard and Michael Gratz had landed in America, they were engaged in ever-growing ventures as merchant-shippers.

By 1765, in a loose partnership with the Mirandas of Curaçao, they had established the firm of Miranda and Gratz. That joint enterprise lasted probably for only a few years. The Mirandas, who had business interests in a number of West India islands, helped to dispose of the flour and bread and ship stores sent from the mainland colonies, while the Gratzes and their associates received in turn specie, fine woods, and, probably, molasses. There is no evidence, however, that the latter were distillers, turning the molasses into rum, although it is known that they bought and sold liquors.

In 1765 they received a letter from a Mr. L. S. Hayne, apparently a French immigrant, who was on his way to Montreal to establish a liquor business. Hayne offered to trade brandy against furs or cash. The "brandy" he had in mind was bourbon whisky. As Wolf and Whiteman point out in their *History of the Jews of Philadelphia* (p. 46), this is one of the earliest known references to this popular American product. It should be noticed that Hayne had met the Gratzes at the home of Hayman Levy, the New York fur trader, and was receiving his mail in Montreal at the home of Eleazar Levy, another fur trader.

SOURCE. The Library Company of Philadelphia, McAllister Collection.

Montreal, the 22 Juny [June], 1765.

To Messrs. Mourendo & Gratz,
At Philodelpha.
Gentlemen:

I have the honour to be whit you at New York. I lodged at Hayman Levy ther. I dit goen [I am going] now to setle me hear [in Montreal] to set op a distill house of all sortes of cordiales. And as I am informed that by you is destillet a sort of English brandy from corn, so I take me the liberty to inquire of you, could [you] send me 4 pipes [barrels] of them for a reasoneable pris? I shall want moer by and by; it is only my begignung. I can sent you some furr or rady cassh for it, so as you order. . . . I hope to have your ansour whit furst uppartunity.

Genhelmens,

I am your most humble and obedient servent,
L. S. Hayne
of the car[e] Mr. Eleazar Levy
at Montreal.

———

No. 143   A Contract to Supply the British Armies in North America—1766

The Frankses, of New York, were probably the most successful and influential Jewish family in business in this country in the mid-eighteenth century. Jacob Franks, the first of the clan to come to these shores, was in business in New York City no later than 1711, and in all likelihood had arrived before that time.

Franks became a purveyor serving as the king's agent for the Northern colonies. By the time of King George's War (1744–48) he and his sons were actively engaged in large-scale supply. Two of his boys, Naphtali and Moses, native-born like all his children, were sent to London, where they became distinguished and wealthy businessmen working closely with their father's brothers and, of course, with the American branch of the family. Naphtali and Moses were merchants; Moses was particularly interested in army supply.

During the French and Indian Wars (1754–63), Moses became the core of an English consortium of wealthy and politically powerful individuals who contracted to supply the British armies in North America. As late as the 1780's, Moses, still interested in providing for the English forces stationed in this country, wrote to the Earl of Shelburne asking "to be continued in a service wherein I have been many years engaged."

Moses' brother David, who made his home in Philadelphia, served as one of the American agents for the British syndicate, looking after the troops in the Pennsylvania hinterland, Fort Pitt, and the Illinois country. Like Moses, of London, he worked with politically influential people.

The following contract is one made by the London syndicate of Nesbitt, Drummond, and Franks with the Treasury Department in

1766. Setting down the conditions under which the troops were to be supplied in North America, it specified the price of rations, the nature, quantity, and quality of the food to be furnished for the men, the details of commissary administration, the problems of transportation, and the difficulties occasioned by Indian uprisings.

From the 1740's into the 1780's the Frankses were involved in government contracts approximating a million pounds sterling. That was big business. The Gomezes, of New York, and Aaron Lopez, of Rhode Island, were successful merchant-shippers, but there can be no doubt that their operations were not comparable to those of the Frankses at the height of their careers during the days of the French and Indian Wars.

SOURCE. The William L. Clements Library, Gage Papers, English Series.

Articles of agreement indented, had, made, and concluded this 14th day of July, 1766, in the sixth year of the reign of our sovereign Lord, George the Third, by the grace of God King of Great Britain, France, and Ireland, Defender of the Faith, and so forth, by and between the Commissioners of his Majesty's Treasury on the part and behalf of his Majesty, of the one part, and Arnold Nesbitt, Adam Drummond, and Moses Franks, Esquires, of the other part.

Whereas, upon the 13th day of April, 1764, a contract was made between the then Commissioners of his Majesty's Treasury and Sir Samuel Fludyer, Adam Drummond, and Moses Franks for supplying with provisions his Majesty's forces stationed in North America, which said contract upon notice already given by the Commissioners of the Treasury on behalf of his Majesty, according to a clause therein contained, will be determined on the 12th day of January next,

And, whereas, proposals have been made to the said Commissioners of the Treasury by Arnold Nesbitt, Adam Drummond, and Moses Franks for victualling his Majesty's forces in the several parts of North America, at the rates and upon the conditions and in the manner and form following, which proposals the said Commissioners have on the part and behalf of his Majesty thought fit to accept,

Now, this indenture witnesseth that the said Arnold Nesbitt, Adam Drummond, and Moses Franks do for themselves, their heirs, executors, and administrators promise, covenant, contract, and agree to and with the said Commissioners of his Majesty's Treasury that they, the said Arnold Nesbitt, Adam Drummond, and Moses Franks, shall and will deliver or cause to be delivered at their own costs, charges, and risques into storehouses to be provided at his Majesty's charge at the following places of deposit:

That is to say, at New York and Albany on Hudson's River, both in the Province of New York, Philadelphia in the Province of Pennsylvania, Charles Town in the Province of South Carolina, Savanah in the Province of Georgia, Boston in the Province of Massechusets, Perth Amboy in the Province of New Jerseys, New London in the Province of Connecticut, Newport in the Province of Rhode Island, or in any sea port or sea ports in North America, as the said storehouses shall be appointed by the said Commissioners of the Treasury or the commander in chief of his Majesty's forces in North America, and at Quebec in Canada, and Montreal in Canada,

Such respective quantities as the said Commissioners of the Treasury or the said commander in chief shall direct, of good, wholsome, and sound provisions of the kinds hereafter mentioned, as will be sufficient to victual six thousand men during the space of six calendar months in the following proportions:

That is to say, for each person to be victualled for seven days, and so for every seven days successively, seven pounds of bread, or in lieu thereof seven pounds of flour; seven pounds of beef, or in lieu thereof four pounds of pork; three pints of pease; one pound of cheese, or in lieu thereof six ounces of butter; one pound of flour, or in lieu thereof half a pound of rice.

And that they will from time to time make, maintain, and keep such reasonable supplies of the said provisions in the said storehouses that there shall always remain magazines of such provisions sufficient for the said six thousand men for the space of six months at least.

And in case any of the said provisions shall be damaged in the transporting or keeping thereof, or shall be found unfit for use or bad in their kind by the three persons to be appointed, as hereafter is mentioned, for inspecting and examining the same, or by any two of them, such provisions shall immediately be removed out of the said storehouses, and the like quantity of the like species of provisions good, wholsome, and sound shall be replaced there at the expence of the said contractors.

Provided, nevertheless, that the said contractors shoud be indemnified for all such provisions as shall have been damaged or spoiled by reason of their having remained in the said storehouses for any space of time longer than six months, upon proof that the same were in good order and condition when first deposited there.

And it is agreed that the said provisions shall be delivered from the aforesaid places of deposit, weekly or monthly, to such officers of each respective company or regiment as shall be appointed by the said commander in chief to receive the same.

And it is hereby agreed that two of the said inspectors and examiners shall be by the appointment of the said commander in chief, and one other of them by the appointment of the said contractors or their agent in North America.

And the said Arnold Nesbitt, Adam Drummond, and Moses Franks, for themselves, their heirs, executors, and administrators, do covenant, contract, and agree that whenever it shall be judged necessary by the commander in chief to remove from the places of deposit the said provisions, or any part thereof, to any other places or parts of North America for the use of the said forces, the said Arnold Nesbitt, Adam Drummond, and Moses Franks shall and will immediately, upon directions being given unto them, or to their agent or agents in North America, by the said commander in chief, deliver out of the said appointed places of deposit such quantities and sorts of the said provisions as the said commander in chief shall direct to be put into waggons, carts, and other carriages to be provided at his Majesty's expence, or on board boats, batteaus, or other vessels to be provided at the like expence, for carrying or transporting by land or by water the provisions so to be delivered from the said appointed places of deposit to any other places or parts of North America as aforesaid.

And the said contractors do hereby further agree that the provisions so to be removed shall be packed in good, strong, and light casks with sufficient headings to bear such carriage or transportation.

And the said Commissioners of the Treasury on the behalf of his Majesty do covenant, promise, and agree that the said Arnold Nesbitt, Adam Drummond, and Moses Franks, their heirs, executors, and administrators, shall be allowed and receive for the service of victualling the forces in the manner aforesaid at and after the following rates, that is to say, at New York, Albany, Philadelphia, Charles Town, Savanah, Boston, Perth Amboy, New London, and Newport, 3¾d. sterling for each man so victualled by the day; at Quebec 4½d. per man per day, at Montreal 4¾d. per man per day; upon producing certificates signed by the commander in chief or by the commanding officer at each place of delivery of such provisions, and by his Majesty's commissary of stores there, which certificates are to specify the quantities of provisions which shall have been so delivered, that the same were delivered in good order and condition, and the numbers of persons victualled thereby and the times for which they shall have been so victualled.

And as to the provisions to be put, as aforesaid, into waggons, carts, and other carriages, or on board boats, batteaus, or other vessells, from any of the magazines for the use of his Majesty's forces, the certificates are to express the species, the exact quantities thereof, and that on the delivery the same were good, wholsome, and sound in their kinds.

And as the provisions for the service of Crown Point are intended to be included in the certificates of the delivery from Quebec, the contractors shall produce vouchers of the exact quantities delivered at Crown Point, and shall maintain a proper person for that purpose, the expence of the transportation thereof to be borne by his Majesty, and likewise all risques and damages, provided the same shall appear to have happened by no fault or neglect of the contractors or their agents.

And the said Commissioners of his Majesty's Treasury do likewise covenant and agree that they will save harmless and indemnify the said Arnold Nesbitt, Adam Drummond, and Moses Franks from all losses and damages that shall happen on shore, or in any island, lakes, or rivers of and to the said provisions either by fire, inundations, enemies, or violence of his Majesty's soldiers, so that such losses and damages shall appear to have happened by no wilful default or neglect of them, their agents, and servants. And also from the payment of any customhouse duties for or upon any of the said provisions to be delivered pursuant to this contract.

And the said Arnold Nesbitt, Adam Drummond, and Moses Franks, for themselves, their heirs, executors, and administrators, do further covenant, contract, and agree to supply such of his Majesty's forces as may be stationed at the several places, hereinafter mentioned, between Philadelphia and Fort Pitt, with the following species of provisions in the proportions and at the rates or prices hereinafter stipulated, that is to say, for each man for seven days, and so for every seven days, nine pounds of flour and eight pounds of fresh meat, or in lieu of the said fresh meat eight pounds of salt beef, or five pounds of salt pork in lieu of eight pounds of salt beef. At Lancaster, Carlisle, and Fort Loudon at 6d. sterling per man per day, at Bedford 7½d. sterling per man per day, at Ligonier at 8½d. sterling per man per day, at Fort Pitt, which is the deposit for all provisions which proceed down the Ohio [to the Illinois country], at 9½d. sterling per man per day. Which said several rates or prices the Commissioners of his Majesty's Treasury agree to pay the said contractors upon their producing certificates signed by the commander in chief and by his Majesty's commissary of stores. Which certificates are to specify the quantities of provisions, that the same were in good order and condition, and also the number of persons victualled thereby, and the times for which they shall have been so victualled. Provided, nevertheless, in case it should so happen that by the rising of the Indians the expence of carriage in these parts shall be increased, such additional allowance shall be made to the contractors as shall be certified by the commander in chief.

It is hereby declared that the forces at Louisbourg [Canada], as well as those in the islands of [New] Providence [Bahamas] and Bermudas, shall be furnished under this contract from the magazines at New York, and those on the Illinois either from Fort Pitt or from Montreal, as the commander in chief shall think proper. And with regard to any supplies in any parts of North America not particularly inserted in this agreement, the contractors to supply from any of the places of deposit as the commander in chief shall direct.

And, whereas, the supplying the forces with fresh meat at some times may be found practicable and expedient and for the good of the service, it is hereby covenanted and agreed, by and between all the said parties, that, notwithstanding any thing herein contained, whenever and for so long time as the commander in chief shall think fit that fresh meat be provided by the said contractors for the said forces, the delivery of provisions of [storage] beef and pork by the contractors, in part or in the whole, shall be suspended, and a proportionable allowance only for the several other species of provisions shall be made unto them as shall be agreed upon and certified by the commander in chief, and the price to be paid unto them for the said fresh meat shall be settled and certified by the said commander in chief, or by the commanding officer or commissary of stores.

And it is hereby declared and agreed by and between the said parties to these presents that the same and the several articles and things contained therein shall continue and be in force for and during the space and term of twelve calendar months, computed from the 12th day of January next, and until the end of 12 calendar months after warning or notice for the determination of such part of this contract as relates to the province of Canada and the communications on the River St. Lawrence shall be given, either by the Commissioners of the Treasury on his Majesty's behalf, or by Arnold Nesbitt, Adam Drummond, and Moses Franks for themselves, and six months notice only for all other parts included in these presents.

And it is further declared and agreed that this contract shall extend to any additional forces that may be victualled by the Crown within the limits thereof, provided nothing in this indenture shall extend to the victualling such of his Majesty's forces as shall be in garrison or stationed in Nova Scotia or Newfoundland, which are now supplied under other contracts.

Lastly, it is covenanted and agreed between all the parties to these presents that the said Lords Commissioners of his Majesty's Treasury, or any of them, shall not be liable in any of their persons or estates to any action of covenant, or other action whatsoever, by reason or means of their being on his Majesty's behalf made parties to this contract.

In witness whereof the said Lords Commissioners of his Majesty's Treasury and the said Arnold Nesbitt, Adam Drummond, and Moses Franks have hereunto interchangeably set their hands and seals the day and year first above written.

Rockingham *(l.[ocus] s.[igilli])* ["place of the seal"]

William Dowdeswell *(l.s.)*   Thomas Townshend *(l.s.)*

John Cavendish *(l.s.)*   George Onslow *(l.s.)*

———

No. 144   A Lead Mine Speculation—1766

Myer Myers (1723–95), a well-known New York goldsmith and silversmith, was president of the local goldsmiths' society during the post-Revolutionary period. Like most competent craftsmen of his generation, he was also a merchant engaged in various forms of trade and commerce, and for a number of years did business as a jeweler.

In the following letter to Michael Gratz, the Philadelphia merchant, Myers discussed the possibility of selling a lead mine to some London businessmen. Myers and Gratz were partners in the enterprise, and there is reason to believe that the Simson family also was interested. (Myer Myers and Solomon Simson were brothers-in-law.) The reference in the latter half of the letter to an enterprise in which Myers, Gratz, and Solomon Simson were partners may be to the mine, or may equally well be to shares in a privateer.

Lead was an important commodity in those days, being used for alloys, the leading of windows, bullets, and other things. Myers had had some training in metallurgy, and later, in 1775, the colony of Connecticut considered employing him to direct the smelting of the lead deposits in the area around Middletown. There is evidence indicating that the mine owned by Myers and his associates was in that area. None of the Middletown mines were big producers and their owners made little or no money from their mining speculation.

A fervent patriot during the Revolution, Myers fled to Connecticut when the British took New York City in 1776. Later he drifted to Philadelphia, where he helped to re-establish Congregation Mikveh Israel. Just before the end of the war, in 1783, he returned to New York City, where he emerged as one of the leaders of the newly constituted Congregation Shearith Israel. In January, 1784, he was one of the three New York Jews who signed the formal note of congratulation to Governor George Clinton, welcoming him back to the city after its evacuation by the British.

SOURCE. American Jewish Archives, the Henry Joseph Collection of Gratz Papers.

New York, November 23, 1766.

Mr. Michael Gratz

Dear Sir:

In my last I mentioned the situation of affairs in regard to the mine and am glad to find by your answer [that] you are so much a philosopher in disapointments. We have now some hopes of being reimbursed, which must be kept a profound secret. Some of the particulars are as follows: one of the richest companies of mines in London has sent orders here to make a purchase of our mine if, upon tryal, the lead yields as they have had some tryed. A gentlemen here has accordingly applyed for some ore and a description of the situation of the mine, all which is gone home [to London] last week. The gentlemen employed here seems to give the greatest encouragement that they will purchase (God grant it). Mr. Housenclever [Peter Hasenclever] went up to view the mine, and had so good an opinion of it that he offered £1,000, but as that is not one third of our cost, his offer was rejected. He is now gone to London and has taken samples of the ore with him; and as he is an enterprising man, I make no doubt he will make a greater offer. So you see, we have two strings to our bow.

But all this will be uncertain till the spring. Meanwhile, my dear Michael, you must assist me. Solomon Simpson has not finished the accounts yet, other ways would send you a coppy, but he tells me a sixteenth will ammount to £240. And were I not in the greatest want, would not ask you for your part, but must make a large payment in ten or twelve days. Your assistance will near do it. If you can send me a good bill of exchange upon London, it will answer full as well as cash [and] it will be easier for you. But let me entreat you to be speedy, as my credit and ease of mind depends on it. I have sold one of your rings for 40½ dollars.

My children join in love to you and all our relations, and am, dear Michael,

Your assured friend, etc.,

Myer Myers

_____

No. 145   A Merchant-Shipper Intercedes for a
Young Beginner—1767

Some time toward the end of the French and Indian War, Aaron Lopez, the Rhode Island merchant-shipper, sheltered and probably employed Enoch Lyon, a young Jew who had just arrived from England.

By 1767 Lyon was in financial trouble because of his inability to meet his obligations. Threatened by a suit, the young man turned to Lopez, and, as evidenced by the following letter, the kindly Newport merchant interceded on his behalf.

Lopez' interesting letter of explanation throws into sharp focus the difficulties incident to trading in those days. There were hazards in the quality and price of goods sent over, to say nothing of their suitability for a specific market. Then came the additional hurdles of payment. If the purchaser was unable or unwilling to satisfy the American merchant, who then would pay the London factor and the original English suppliers, the wholesalers and the manufacturers?

That Lyon was not wholly dependable may be inferred from the fact that he was indebted to others in 1767, and by 1772 he was in debt to his patron Lopez. In order to protect his own interests, the latter at that time attached a ship belonging to Lyon.

SOURCE. Newport Historical Society Library, Lopez Letter Book, 1767.

Newport, February 19th, 1767.

Mr. Erasmus Williams.
Sir:

Captain Langworthy delivered me your favour of the 15th ultimo, advising that by the last packet you received a power of attorney signed by Moses Moravia [of London] against Enoch Lyon of Rhode Island for the recovery of £200 sterling due to said Moravia from said Lyon.

Agreeable to your request, I enquired of this young man the true state of this affair, who (living with me) made no hesitation to give me a direct answer. He says that about two years ago [he] received a parcell of hard ware shipped him by this Moravia, which goods, he assures me, [he] did not write for, and they happen to prove of so improper a sort for this market and so highly charged, that he was not able to dispose of them till lately, being obliged to give long credit and agree to receive West India goods in payment when they shall become due. He adds that having made his complains to Messrs. Lovekin & Co. [the London wholesalers or manufacturers] about the quality and price of these goods, [he] received said gentlemen's reply by letter, of which I directed him to transmit you a copy, and farther advised him to write you fully and explicit on this subject, recommending him to endeavour a settlement with you in an amicable and equitable manner.

All what I can inform you about this young man is that having lived with me about four years, I never found him otherways but strictly honest. Therefore, being a young beginner, [I] take the liberty to recommend your using all the tenderness you can in settling this matter, and you may depend on my giving him the most favorable advice to a speedy conclusion thereof.

I rest, very respectfully,

Your most humble servant,

[Aaron Lopez]

No 146 Whaling: Financing and Merchandising the Catch—1767

At an early stage in his career Aaron Lopez turned to the manufacture of spermaceti candles. It was quite natural, therefore, that he should concern himself with the supply of whale oil, the raw material used in their production.

In the following document Lopez contracts with two other parties for a whaling voyage. The captain and crew were allowed four-eighths of the oil; the owner was given two-eighths for the charter of his vessel, and an additional eighth part for supplying half of the provisions. Lopez, who supplied the other half, received the last eighth of the catch and the privilege of selling the entire return cargo.

As a manufacturer, Lopez obviously would reserve what oil he needed for his factory before selling the rest on the open market. (It is an interesting question whether Lopez himself could use this oil, inasmuch as he was a member of the United Company of Spermaceti Candlers, the "trust" which allotted "proportions" to each member.)

If the cruise was successful, Lopez was assured of a supply of head matter at a fair price, made a profit on his share of the provisions, and collected a commission on the oil which he dispatched to other markets.

It is a commentary on the spelling of that day to note that in the text the ship's owner is called Almy, but signs himself Amy. The captain of the crew is called Reply, but signs himself Replye. In contemporary correspondence Replye was frequently referred to as Ripley and Riply.

SOURCE. MSS of the Newport Historical Society.

Memorandum that we have this 12th May, 1767, delewered into Aaron Lopez's store [warehouse] thirty-four casks spermatety white oil containing eleven hundred and ninety gallons; also twelve casks headmatter equal to four hundred and twenty-seven gallons, both which being the whole fair [fare: catch] obtained the first whaling cruize per the sloop

Marry [*Mary*] owned by Captain Joshua Almy and fitted out for said cruize, the one half by said Almy and the other half by Aaron Lopez.

The conditions of which adventure are as following:

That the vessel shall draw one quarter part of whatever oil or head-matter she obtains or brings home.

That Captain Joshua Almy shall draw one eight part in consideration of his suplying one half of the provissions and whaling implements for this adventure.

That Aaron Lopez shall draw another eight part in consideration of his supling the other half of the provissions, etc., as aforesaid, and

That Captain Joseph Reply with the rest of the hands on board said vessel shall draw the other half of what said vessel obtains upon conditions of allowing for the barrels required for to put in what oil or head-matter bellongs to their share. [The captain and crew are charged for the barrels used.]

And be it known that we have farther agreed that said Lopez shall have the dispossal of the above oil, etc., into his store, on the best terms he can for our advantage, either in this place, [or] ship it to Darthmouth or Boston, as he shall think more advantageous.

Acknowledge the above to be	Joshua Amy
agreable to my concern on	Joseph Replye
the foregoing memorandum.	
Aaron Lopez	

No. 147   Aaron Lopez in the Jamaica Trade—1767

By January 1, 1767, Aaron Lopez, the Newport merchant-shipper, owed his Bristol correspondent over £10,000 and his London correspondent more than £5,000 sterling, and without doubt he was in debt also to others. Lopez was not insolvent; but too many of his customers were slow in paying him. Ultimately they settled their accounts.

Up to this time the Newport merchant had been engaged rather heavily in the slave trade and in the attempt to sell lumber, oil, and vessels in the English market. Now, in 1767, he resolved to concentrate on the Jamaica trade in the hope that the returns would be speedier. His intention was to send whale oil, candles, foods, lumber, and livestock to Jamaica and to bring back specie, molasses, coffee, rum, and sugar. The molasses, sold as it was or distilled into rum, would find a good market in the North American mainland colonies.

In order to effect his purposes Lopez sent his son-in-law Abraham Pereira Mendes to Jamaica to serve as his agent. After the latter arrived in Kingston late in September, 1767, he went to work to carry out Lopez' plan. Two brigs were to be at his disposal to sail to the Bay of Honduras, where he was to barter provisions against logwood, which would either be sold in Jamaica or consigned to Lopez' correspondents in England. While the brigs were thus making money for the Newport shipper, coopers sent from New England were to knock casks together to hold the molasses which would go into the hold as return cargo.

The co-operation of the officers of one—if not of both—of the brigs was to be guaranteed by giving them the "privilege" of bringing in some fish and of exporting a modest quantity of logwood. In other words, they were to be encouraged to engage in financial "adventures" of their own.

This is the background of the following letter from Aaron Lopez to Abraham Pereira Mendes. It is an important letter because it permits us to peer into the mind of a brilliant and daring merchant-shipper and to sense the strategy of his far-flung activity.

SOURCE. Newport Historical Society Library, Lopez Letter Book, 1767.

Newport, September 27th, 1767.

Dear Mr. Abraham Pereira Mendes:
. . . The heavy and continued rains that we have had for 5 days together prevented my dispatching this brigantine [the *Industry*, Captain John Peters] one week sooner, as intended. However, hope it will not be too late to reach a good market for the cargo on board of which you herein have an inclosed bill of lading and invoice to your address.

The brigantine's hull has deceived me and Peters, as I expected she would carry a great deal more dry fish, which being the last article that went on board, I am disappointed in having 10 or 12 hogsheads left behind. She goes also short of shaken [dismantled] casks and no hoops, for which reason, and my being desirous of not keeping you idle while at Jamaica, I have concluded to send you my schooner as soon as she returns from the [whale] fishery (where I learn she has met with tolerable success).

The method I propose is to ship by her all the hoops and shaken hogsheads which I think both brigantine cargoes [of molasses] may require. Shall also send a couple of coopers in order that while these vessells are executing the [Honduras] Bay plan, they may be setting up casks for their cargoes.

I intend the schooner shall touch at Georgia to land some effects, which Mr. [James] Lucena writes me will very well answer there at this season of the year. Therefore have already desired him to prepare a cargo of their large cyprus [cypress] shingles, to which I shall order the addition of some of their horses, hogs, and poultry [all for the Jamaica and Honduras Bay markets]. So much for your government [guidance].

I flatter myself if this brigantine [the *Industry*] meets with moderate weather on her passage and carries well the few horses I have shipped, that your [Jamaican] countrymen will allow them to be as clever a cargo as any shipped this year. If so, I make no doubt, you will jockey a good price out of them. The stallion is called a fine creature. I have sent but sixty sheep on purpose that they have room enough to be well attended. As for the rest of the cargo, believe your good endeavours shall not be wanting to make the best of it, and dispatch Peters as expeditiously as you can [to Honduras], in order to enable Newdigate [commander of the other brig] to execute the plan of two trips from the Bay with each vessell.

I must recommend you to embrace the first offer for your dry fish, as there is many vessells that will soon follow this with the same commodity.

Several of the sailors on board I took out of the goal [jail], and am in a considerable advance for the most of them [I paid their fines]. I have given Captain Peters a strict charge to keep a watchfull eye upon them that they may not give him the slip at Jamaica, especially the Negro fellow [whom] I bought of Benjamin Brenton, [and] who ran away from Captain [John] Pyner's schooner, and never could catch him till about three or four days past near Boston. Therefore, as he is a noted rogue subject to this failing, may, if indulged, do the same at Jamaica.

After having tryed many of the builders up our rivers for to build the fishing smack which your good friend desired, I have at last engaged Old Goddard (the man that built Mr. Rotch's sailing boat). This old man, though he is deemed our first character in the capacity of boat building, undertakes to do her for a quarter part less than any of the builders of an inferior class, and if I mistake not she will turn out within the last limited price your friend perscribed. The season being so far advanced, I shall not be able to dispatch her before the spring when, if God grant us life, you may expect to see her at Jamaica with such a cargo as her small hold will allow us to put into her. Meanwhile, you may inform your friend my particular attention shall be given to see that she is faithfully built.

I come now to express the satisfaction it gave us to hear you were all well on board [the vessel commanded by] Newdigate five days after you left this port, as we had it reported by a vessel that spoke with you at sea. . . .

We are all well, excepting your dejected wife, who mourns too hard your absence. She is most recovered of an ill turn which has reduced her low, but thanks to God mends fast. I would not permit her to write, fearing it may do her hurt, therefore she desires to join her love with Mrs. Lopez's regards and my best wishes for your preservation from evil. My respects to your honoured mother and the rest of the family concludes me,

Your most affectionate well wisher,
[Aaron Lopez]

P.S. I had forgot to mention that Captain Peters is to have 3 tons of logwood priviledge, and John King, the mate, 2 tons, as per agreement with both of them, which please to note. Also that for farther encouragement of Peters I have spared him the hogshead codfish No. 2 of the within invoice, which you may deliver him.

<hr>

No. 148   Aaron Lopez Hears from a Jamaican Correspondent—1768

In the late 1760's Aaron Lopez was emerging as one of the most enterprising merchants in Newport. He had correspondents in practically every important town on the North American mainland and in the West Indies. His agent at Savanna-la-Mar, in the western part of Jamaica (Westmoreland), was Abraham Lopez. In spite of the similarity in the family name, the men were not related and had not even met.

Aaron Lopez, eager to expand his business, frequently corresponded with Abraham Lopez. The letter printed below is one of Abraham's answers. It is not untypical of business letters of the period in its admixture of commercial and personal matters.

Abraham mentions Aaron's offer to send a consignment of his candles to the West Indies. He writes a word about Abraham Pereira Mendes, the West Indian who had married Aaron's daughter Sally, and who had once been Aaron Lopez' chief agent in Jamaica. (Mendes had not been completely successful and had been succeeded by the eccentric but able Captain Benjamin Wright.) He also gives the Newport merchant, for himself or his friends, some useful business information (in those days there were no credit reporting agencies), and refers, in this and other letters between the two men, to the collection of debts: the Jamaican planters were "poor pay"; sometimes they took years to settle their accounts.

Abraham Lopez, who had just been widowed, did not fail to share his grief with his Newport correspondent. His letter also mentions the gifts that Aaron sent to Abraham, and tells how the latter forwarded a small consignment of limes to Newport, as a speculation on behalf of one of his young daughters. Unfortunately the venture turned out poorly. The limes apparently did not arrive in good condition.

It is of interest to note that, because of the nature of sailboat transportation, some letters were not received or answered until about seven months after they had been dispatched by the original sender.

SOURCE. American Jewish Archives, the George J. Miller Papers.

Westmorland, Jamaica, March 11, 1768.

Mr. Aaron Lopez.

Sir:

I am now to acknowledge the receipt of several of your most esteemed favours, which for want of opportunity could not answer before. [I] therefore crave leave to answer them now in due rotation, though I am afraid time will not permit my enlarging so fully as I could wish.

Your 1st favour, of 20th August last, gives me the highest satisfaction, 1st, as it confirms the receipt of several of my humble addresses to you, and 2dly, as you are so kind to approve my opinion respecting your proposed concerns to me in this island.

I endeavoured to explain the nature of our trade from your parts to this country, and if any usefull hints may be gathered or occur to you therefrom, I think myself extremely happy in having it in my power to communicate them. Your kind compliments thereon are far beyond the merit of such trifling services.

Your kind proposals with respect to the candles are, I think, extremely reasonable, but as I have since determined on leaving off business for a twelvemonth or two, to contract my affairs to a narrow compass, obliges me to beg leave to decline your kind offer. Notwithstanding, I shall always think myself honoured in any of your favours, and shall embrace every opportunity of paying my humble respects to you.

Permit me to lay at your feet my sincere thanks for your kind consolation and sympathy on my heavy loss in the best of women. The Almighty has been pleased to support me under it, for the sake of 9 poor (almost all small) children. May you and yours long be strangers to any such fatal separations.

I beg you may accept my best acknowledgment for the honour paid my recommendation infavour Capt. Wright. I flatter myself you will find him deserving the character I have given you of him and am certain he will find his advantage in being admitted to your employ. I wish I may ever have it in my power to retaliate so great a favour. Any services I can render him here on his own account, but preferably on yours, he shall never stand in need of.

I am well pleased at the safe arrival of Capt. Wheeler and that his cargo turned out in tolerable order. No apologies are required for the advance, but I am sorry to acquaint you the outstanding debts are still extant, but shall pay all reverence to your request in assisting your worthy son in law, Mr. Mendes (now here), in collecting them, or any other assistances he may require at my hands.

My eldest daughter begs leave to return your kind compliment and [to] apologize for the trouble given you in her small adventure of the limes. She is well assured you made the most of them and is sorry she was so unlucky as to give you so much trouble therewith. The flour she is greatly obliged to you for, which she received safe, and the ballance due on her account sales, £1 2s. 7d., I have placed to your credit.

Your farther favours, of 23 October, 6 and 8th November, have [been] safely received. The two latter only require my immediate speculation. Capt. Wright safely delivered me them with your kind present of the apples, geese, and turkeys. (The apples met the same fate as did, I am afraid, the 2 bbs. limes.) Please accept my thanks for them and also my congratulation for the good markett Capt. Wright came to.

He has nothing now on hand and is at prisent assiduous in collecting his debts; [I] doubt not his being successfull therein and for which you have my best wishes. Capt. Wright, I make [have] no doubt, will acquaint you [with] the manner of his transacting Messrs. Handy and Bours' orders on me, drawn by Robert Elliott, to which beg reference.

With respect to the negro man, the property of one of my friends, I note what you are pleased to say of him. Give me leave only to say of him, I am convinced he will want for nothing under your auspices, and every expence will chearfully discharge with many thanks. . . .

Inclosed is an open letter for Mr. Gideon Wanton, which must beg, you'll seal and deliver after perusing, in which is all the light I can give him in Andrew Cozzens's affairs. Was I possessed of any other knowledge, be assured I should have made him acquainted therewith, at your request. . . .

Must beg reference for other particulars, etc'a, to Mr. Mendes and Capt'n Wright. And also that you'll be kind enough to excuse brevity for want of time.

I am, with my best wishes, for every felicity's attending you and good family, and with utmost esteem, most respectfully, sir,

Your obedient, humble servant,
Abraham Lopez

To

Mr. Aaron Lopez.

No. 149   Samuel Jacobs Signs a Contract with a London Commission Agent—1768

Some time in the 1760's Samuel Jacobs, the former army purveyor, left Quebec City to settle in the little village of St. Denis on the Richelieu River. There he successfully ran a large general store, bought grain for overseas shippers, and engaged in small-scale industry. He operated a distillery and, it would seem, made pot and pearl ashes for export to England.

Inasmuch as every merchant of stature required the services of a resident buyer in London who would supply him with consumers' goods, Jacobs, through the Quebec firm of Alsopp and Wells, entered into contract with Watson, Olive, and Rashleigh. The latter, judging from their letters, did not actually stock goods, but were primarily commission agents, buying and selling wares for their clients. Because their customers more often than not lacked the cash with which to pay for goods received, obligations were balanced by the raw materials exported to London. Jacobs sent furs and pearl ashes.

Printed below is the agreement between Jacobs and the London firm. By carrying Jacobs' overdue accounts, the firm also served as bankers.

Jacobs' signature was a double one. Under his English signature he wrote "Samuel" in Hebrew: *Shemuel.*

SOURCE. Public Archives of Canada, Samuel Jacobs Papers.

The terms and conditions on which Messrs. Watson, Olive, & Rashleigh transact the business of their correspondents in America. *Vizt.:*
To pay commissions
On all goods bought in London and shipt on their account and risque, and when they have money of theirs in hand to pay for the same: two and a half per cent commission, and half per cent on making insurance.

On all goods bought and shipt on their accounts and risque, when they have not money of theirs in hand to pay for the same: five per centum, and half per cent for making insurance.

On goods ordered by them from any foreign market, for which Messrs. Watson, Olive, & Rashleigh are to pay and forward from England; as above, free from all other charges; that is to say, their commission to be allowed to them and all other charges.

On all effects remitted to, and sold by them: two and a half per cent.

On all bills paid and received and also on all moneys paid and received: half per cent.

On all insurances made: half per cent.

On all other transactions: as customary to America.

The credit they agree to allow

On goods shipped on their accounts and risque is nine months from date of invoice, unless on such goods as are bought with ready money or at a shorter credit than nine months, in which cases interest for the difference of time at and after the rate of five per cent per annum, to be charged in the invoice, so as to make whole amount at nine months' credit.

To pay them interest

On whatever sum or sums of money may remain unpaid for goods shipped on their account, at nine months' credit from the expiration of that time; and on all other sums, from the date of the advance, at and after the rate of five per cent per annum.

The interest account to be settled on the last day of December yearly, and the ballance thereof, if any, carried to the debit of their account current, and from that day [to] be deemed a part of the principle debt, as shall all premiums of insurance, postage of letters, and every other incidental charge.

I do agree to and accept the forgoing terms.

Quebec, November 14, 1768,

Samuel Jacobs
(Shemuel)

For Messrs. Watson, Olive, and Rashleigh:

George J.[?] Allsopp

No. 150   Freighting and Selling Ships—1768

Jacob Rodriguez Rivera (1717–89) was born in Spain and came to the North American colonies as a child. He lived in New York before he finally settled in Newport. By 1748 he was already in that city, and soon turned to the manufacture of spermaceti candles. Although he and his father were pioneers in that field, his commercial interests were much broader. He was a merchant-shipper and was often associated in business ventures with his son-in-law Aaron Lopez.

Rivera was one of the founders and leaders of the local Jewish congregation, a patron of the Redwood Library, and a man of considerable prestige in the larger Newport community.

The following letter is a copy of the sailing orders that Lopez & Rivera issued for one of their ships, the *Cleopatra*, before she sailed for London. The same vessel was used as a slaver in the early 1770's by Aaron Lopez.

SOURCE. Newport Historical Society Library, Newport, R. I.; Lopez Letters.

Newport, December 13th, 1768.

Capt. Waters Hannars:

The ship *Cleopatra*, now fitted for the seas, being under your command, you are to embrace the first fair wind and proceed with her to the port of London. And when, please God, you arrive there, deliver your cargo, agreeable to bills of lading, to George Hayley, Esq., to whom you are to aply for orders during your stay at London.

We are in hopes, from the encouragement you gave us about the probability of disposing of the ship, that Mr. Hayley may have it in his power to obtain a good price for her, and as much depends on your setting her off to advantage.

We make no doubt she may go off for the reasonable price we stipulate for so good a vessel. If we succeed, we have desired Mr. Hayley to treat with Capt. Shand for yours and the people's passage home. But if we don't happen to hit the markett, we have desired our friend to dispatch you soon as possible, with some goods we order and what transient freight falls in the way. In that case, we rely on your alacrity and care to forward her dispatch, using the best frugality and care to avoid unnecessary charges to the ship.

Wishing you a safe voyage, we remain,

Your humble servants,
Jacob Rodriguez Rivera, Aaron Lopez

Acknowledge the above to be a true copy of my instructions which I promise to comply with to the best of my knowledge.

Waters Hannars

No. 151 Smuggling—1769

Like most other shippers, Nicholas Brown and Company, of Providence, had no moral scruples against smuggling. This was particularly true after 1763, when the British sought to implement the existing regulations. Evading payment of British-imposed duties, many Americans thought, was merely a way of self-preservation and hence was justified. Sharing the common sentiments, Aaron Lopez of Newport thought it only neighborly to warn the Browns, as he did in the following letter, when an official customs vessel started snooping in their direction.

SOURCE. The John Carter Brown Library, Brown Papers.

Newport, January 16, 1769.

Messrs. Nicholas Brown & Co.

Gentlemen:

This only serves to advise that our men of warr's tender is this day to visit your river. The business she goes upon are not known to the trading part of this town. Therefore, I have not thought it improper to trouble you with my insinuating you to be upon your gard and to assure you that I am, gentlemen,

Your most humble servant,
Aaron Lopez

No. 152   The United Company of Spermaceti Candlers—1769–1773

Jews participated to a considerable extent in the manufacture of spermaceti candles, made from the head matter (spermaceti) of whales. The raw product was always limited in quantity, and in order to regulate the competition in its purchase and distribution, the New England candlemakers in 1761 formed the United Company of Spermaceti Candlers, in which the Jewish merchants of Newport were very active.

The articles of agreement binding the associates were periodically revised in an attempt to avoid evasions. The company also sought to control the production and price of the finished product. The correspondence in Documents A, B, and C, written within the short span of about a fortnight, bears eloquent testimony to the company's constant efforts to control the price of the raw material.

Because the uncontrolled purchase of head matter by new manufacturers threatened to upset the company's production and price schedules, the associates sought to bring those firms into their combine. After the manufacturers of Newport, Providence, and Boston had been banded together, and before the demise of the company during the Revolutionary War, the New York firms of Isaac Stoutenburg & Co. [Jarvis & Co.] and of Sampson and Solomon Simson & Co. were brought into the "trust." The latter was a Jewish firm, which included not only the two Simson brothers but also three other Jewish merchants. Of the five, four were New Yorkers and the fifth was a resident of Newport.

The New Yorkers indicated their willingness to discuss the conditions of membership in the association in a letter dated May 27, 1773 (Document D). In June, 1774(3?), they signed the articles and joined the United Company of Spermaceti Candlers. Jacob Rodriguez Rivera, the son of one of the pioneers in the use of spermaceti candles in the colonies, played an important role as mediator in the United Company and was responsible for bringing the New York firms into the combine. Therefore it was to him that the New Yorkers wrote: "We are greatly obliged to you, good sir, for the trouble you have taken for us, and agree with you in sentiment that we had better work a small quantity to advantage then [than] a large one to no profit."

SOURCE. The John Carter Brown Library, Brown Papers.

A [NO. 152]

Newport, January 23d, 1769.

Messrs. Nicholas Brown & Co.
Gentlemen:

. . . The wild extreems in which those manufacturers that ware left out in our union run into last year, and considering how much we suffered by their endeavouring to supply themselves [with head matter] at any rate, make it absolutely nessary to prevent, if posible, the like evil the ensuing season, and that some means should be taken in time, and before they have sowed their pernitious orders about.

Messrs. Jos. Rotch & Son [our purchasing agents] have lately been here. They assure me that unless they [the outsiders] are prevented from offering and giving commissions to the ketchers of head matter, as well as to anybody that has a few cask[s] to dispose of, by uniting them all in our articles [by including them in our association], otherwise, it seems to them [to the Rotches] we shall git as wild the ensuing season as ever we ware, and likely worse, as the number of manufacturers is much greater.

From these few hints, I hope, gentlemen, you will, with your usual precation [precaution], point out such methods as may prevent this growing evil, if it does not produce a total distruction of this branch of business. Nothing has ever appeared to have answerd that salutary purpose so effectually as our union.

Therefore, I would recommend this serious affair to your prudent manajement.

I salute you with great respect, and am, gentlemen,

Your most humble servant,
Jacob Rodriguez Rivera

B [NO. 152]

February 2d, 1769.

Mr. Jacob Rodriguez Rivera.

Sir:

. . . .We are fully sencible of the dark prospect of procuring h[ead] m[atter] next season at aney tollorable price unless a generall union of all the manufactorys can be brought about, and this we fear will be a difficult matter, as their is now so many of them, and who lives at such grait distences from each other.

A union of all those in this colony without including all out of the colony will not, in our oppinion, effect the desine. And as the grait distence from Boston to New York will make it difficult to have a general meeting, and indeed such a meeting at this time might not be prudent, as the eys [eyes] of the inspections [inspectors? the curious?] would be upon us, and perhaps cause more works [factories] to be built, therefore we are of the oppinion that it's best to draft a surkeller [circular] letter, one of which to be sent to each manufactorer out of this government [province]. And as it will take a considerable time to git all their answers, we think no time ought to be lost, and desire you'l, as soone as may be, consult all the manufatory [manufacturers] at Newport. And if they agree to this . . . to draft a letter . . . on the subject and forward it to us imediately, on the receipt of which we will cunsult the new manufactores here and indever [endeavor] to git them to join in the matter. We think the price may be stipulated at £100 Boston, o[ld] t[enor], provided every one comes into the agreement, but if anyone will *not* join, the price must be higher. . . .

We think the new manufactorers should be treated with a good deal of caution, as otherwise they may think themselves of too much consiquence, and may raise diffecultys in setting the proportions [of head matter for themselves]. Your prudence will dictate to calculate the letter [latter], principly for their merideon [area], as the old United Company better know from experence what the effect of such a union may be.

We are, wiht grait humility,

Your most esteemed, humble servants,

[Nicholas Brown & Co.]

C [NO. 152]

Newport, February 7th, 1769.

Messrs. Nicholas Brown & Co.

Gentlemen:

I have before me your very obliging favour of the 2d current, and have attentively considered its contents. . . .

As to what respects the important object of our manufactures, I readily join with you that every prudent method aught to be used to invite all the new manufactures into our union, but cannot think that it's so absolutely necessary, for to answer our purposes, that all the manufactorers on the continent from east to west [from Boston to New York] should be joined, though grant it would be best.

We have repeatedly courted the Bostonians into our articles [association], and as often been refused. Their advantageous setuation will ever prevent their given us any proportion of the numerous advantages they have over us. Neither can I see that though they have for many years back been left loose [to buy at their own price], that we have been any great sufferers. They must have their proportion, and that they can easily obtain there. And when they have that, the whole of what remains must centure [center] amoung the United Company. This need not debarr us from applying to them, but I say their refusal aught not to put aside a union of the rest. The Newyorkers' setuation is reather less advantageous then [than] ours, consiquently may easly (if it should be deemed necessary) be brought to join us. Mr. Thomas Stelle proposes going to [New] York next month and offers his servis in applying and endeavour[ing] to git them to join us.

It is the Dartmouth manufacture, those of Mr. Jenks & Co. and Mr. [George] Rome that prove distructive to this branch [controlling the price of head matter], and which we aught by all means to unite if posible. This, I imagine, will be no dificult task, if they are modest in their claims of a proportion. Their own intrest, in my opinion, must make them ready to unite, as the effects of last year must furnish them a specimen of what they have to expect if we are all let loose [to compete with each other], and, to obtain this, I think there is no great necessity of a circular letter, for if you approve of this method, as we all here doe, Mr. Slocum will undertake to treat with the Dartmouth manufature. You can sound [out] and secure the new manufacture at Providence (which I am informed by Mr. I.[saac] Hart they signifyd to him their readiness to unite when he was up there). And I will undertake Mr. Rome, and as soon as the sentements of the whole can be known, a meeting, when you may think proper, will be necessary to close the matter.

I have communicated your letter to all the United Company here, and they are all nearly of my opinion, and should you also be of the same, please to let us know, and at the same time give us whatever you may judge nessisary. Should the Bostonians refuse comming into our measures, I think it highly nessisary that every member of our United Company should be desbard [disbarred] by our articles from purchasing any head matter at Boston. For if they [the Bostonians] meet with no obstructions, they must have it at their own [price], or at least at our limited price. And when they are supplyd, no more will goe that way and must naturely fall into our netts. When, on the other hand, if many purchasers appear at Boston for these and other manufacturies, it must not only tend to raise the price to them, and consiquently to us, with many unnessisary charges, but must naturely oblige them, if debard of gitting their proportions at Boston, to invade our teritorys, which, in my opinion, must prove as pernicious to us as anything whatever. Let them peaceably supply themselves, and I dare say the rest will afford us a handsom proportion.

The weather today is so extreem cold that my fingers are as chilled as the ink that flows from my pen, which obliges me to conclude, but not before I have saluted you with the highest respect, and to assure you that I am in all your commands, gentlemen,

Your much obliged and humble servant,
Jacob Rodriguez Rivera

D [NO. 152]

New York, May 27th, 1773.

Dear Sir:

We received your kind favour of the 14th May, wherein you are pleased to mention a meeting of the manufacturers of spermaceti at Newport, on Monday, the 14th June next, when Mr. Manuel Myers will attend for us, and Mr. Stoutenburg for Messrs. Jarvis & Company, and, we hope, will answer the good purpose intended by our good friend, Mr. Rivera, who will please to accept of our thanks for the trouble he has taken in this affair.

Being with regard, dear sir,

Your most obedient, humble servants,
(is signed)   James Jarvis, for self & Co.,
Sampson & Solomon Simson & Co.

Mr. Jacob Rodrigues Rivera.

No. 153   A License to Trade with the Indians—1769

One of the most colorful Jewish merchants of early Canada was Chapman Abram. (The name appears also as Abraham, Abrahams, or Abrams.) This man came to Canada with the British troops, probably in 1759 or 1760. Originally he and his four business associates were army supplymen, and we may assume that the firm had contracts to provision the troops during the French and Indian War.

After the war the partners remained in the country and turned to the fur trade. For many years the scene of Abram's activities was the town of Detroit, in whose vicinity he was captured by Indians in May, 1763, during Pontiac's Rebellion. According to a somewhat later but still contemporary account, he miraculously escaped from being burned to death by his captors.

Abram's firm became insolvent after 1765, but Chapman Abram still managed to stay in business, and for years, until his death in 1783, his name appears in the records of Quebec, Montreal, and Detroit. During the Revolution he fought in Canada (1775–76) against the invading American rebels, and he seems to have been on friendly terms with Frederick Haldimand, who later became governor of the province. Although he spent much time on the frontier, Abram identified himself with the Jewish community of Montreal and was interested in Masonry.

The document printed below is a copy of a license authorizing Abram to trade with the Indians in the Upper Country. There were a number of formalities with which Abram first had to comply before he and his men could start moving up the St. Lawrence. His cargo, which he was required to invoice under oath, consisted of 300 gallons of liquor, 2 guns, 200 pounds of shot and balls, and 24 bales and bags of merchandise and provisions. Seven men accompanied him, although he started out to take only five. Abram was required to swear allegiance to the king and to sign a double indemnity bond that he would observe the regulations governing the Indian trade. His canoemen, none of whom could sign his name, also had to declare solemnly that they would not stir up trouble with the natives. After Pontiac's uprising in 1763, the government was very apprehensive.

SOURCE. Public Archives of Canada, R. G. 4, B 28, Vol. 110, Chapman Abram.

By his Excellency Guy Carleton, Captain General and Governor in Chief in and over the Province of Quebec, Vice Admiral of the same and Brigadier General of his Majesty's forces, etc., etc.

In obedience to his Majesty's commands, this licence is granted to Chapman Abrams to pass unmolested with one canoe manned with five men (whose names, occupations, and places of abode, and also the quantity of merchandize on board are reported upon oath and specified in the margin), to Michilimackinac, and from thence to such markets or parts as he shall find most advantageous for the disposal of the said merchandize, with liberty to dispose of any such goods and effects as he shall occasionally find a market for in his passage to Michilimackinac aforesaid, he taking care to endorse upon this licence the quantity and quality of the goods so disposed of, and shewing the same to the commanding officer of the next fort.

Provided always that nothing herein contained shall be construed to extend to give any authority to the said Chapman Abrams to do any act or thing or to trade to any place contrary to such regulations as his Majesty may have been pleased to make, or shall here after think proper to make, by him self, or by the commander in chief, or by any person properly authorized to give directions concerning the Indian trade.

Provided also that he, the said Chapman Abrams, and also all and every the master or masters of, and all other persons concerned in navigating the said one canoe, shall first have taken and subscribed the oaths endorsed on this licence in the presence of the commanding officer at Montreal, and shall also have given security to observe and keep the same, and also that he, the said Chapman Abrams, will not take with him or permit any of his people to take with them any other person or persons but such as usually have followed, or intend here after to follow, the occupation of navigating battoes or canoes, and further that he, the said Chapman Abrams, and all such persons as he shall take with him, shall and will immediately, on his or their return to the city of Montreal, present themselves to and personally appear before the officer commanding at Montreal, and take a certificate from him in writing of their having so personally appeared, death or any other unavoidable accidents only excepted.

These securities being given, this licence to be in force for twelve months, otherwise to be null and void to all intents and purposes.

Given under my hand and seal at arms at the Castle of St. Louis, in the City of Quebec, this fifteenth day of April, one thousand seven hundred and sixty nine.

Guy Carleton

By his Excellency's command.
George Allsopp, deputy secretary.

———

No. 154   The Plight of a Poor Businessman—1769–1772

Emanuel Lyon, a German, arrived in Philadelphia from London late in 1768 or early in 1769. There he advertised that he would "teach a few gentlemen the Hebrew language in its purity," and thus became one of the first Jews known to have taught Hebrew in that city. Not succeeding as a teacher, he turned to business. Within a few months he was heavily in debt, as Mrs. Rachel Moses, a kindly person who tried to help him, indicates in her letter (Document A). Apparently the Reverend Richard Peters, an Episcopal clergyman, had also extended the hand of friendship to the wayward Lyon, and, while Mrs. Moses expresses her disappointment, she appeals to Mr. Peters not to forsake Lyon altogether.

There is every reason to believe that Lyon was a poor and unreliable businessman. In 1772, about three years after his arrival in Philadelphia, he and Isaac Jacobs, who had recently come from Ireland, fraudulently secured a stock of goods and fled. After a lapse of six months their creditors realized that they had been fleeced, and inserted a notice in the daily newspapers, offering a reward for the arrest of the absconding peddlers (Document B). It is interesting to note that the prime creditors were Gentiles, not Jews. The latter had had ample opportunity since 1769 to discover that Lyon was a bad risk and would give him no credit.

Many of the wanderers who came to these shores faced seemingly insurmountable obstacles. Some who had failed to make a place for themselves in the old country failed again in the new, because they lacked the capacity and the integrity that were as necessary in a frontier nation as they were in a place of established culture and civilization.

SOURCE. Document A: The Historical Society of Pennsylvania, Peters MSS.; Document B: *Supplement to the Pennsylvania Packet and the General Advertiser*, No. 42, August 10, 1772.

A [NO. 154]

Philadelphia, July 11th, 1769.

Sir:

Your charitable friendship to Emanuel Lyon, a Jew, is praise worthy. I expected he woud endeavour to be honest enough at least to be thankfull to you, sir, and others [of] his friends, among which I account my self one. I have advanced money for and to him several times to redeem his cloaths and goods, as he told me [at least that is what he told me]. Christian Cramer can witness the truth of what I say.

Lyon now, instead of repaying me money, treats me with abusive and threatening language, for which I am determined to have recourse to the law for redress.

I am a Jew and has [have] no rabbin [rabbi] to apply to here. You are a Christian minister of approved character. On your account, and lest you should suffer loss by him, I shall wait some time in hopes you may bring him to reason.

I am, with great respect, sir,

Your humble servant,
Reshil Mosheh [in Hebrew]
Rachel Moses

To the Reverend Mr. Peters,
In Philadelphia.

B [NO. 154]

Philadelphia, July 24th, 1772.

FIVE HUNDRED DOLLARS REWARD

Any person or persons who shall apprehend and deliver to the sheriff of Philadelphia county, Isaac Jacobs and Emanuel Lyon, Jew pedlars, who left this city sometime in February last, shall be entitled to the above reward, or two hundred and fifty dollars for the apprehension and delivery of either of them, as aforesaid, to be paid by the subscribers, who will indemnify such person or persons from any damage he or they may sustain by reason of such apprehension and delivery.

Isaac Jacobs will probably pass in the country by the name of Jacob Isaac. He was born in Germany, is a short, thick set man, of a fair complexion, wears his hair short, which is of a very light colour and much curled. He came from Ireland about two years ago, and has since followed the business of a pedlar.

Emanuel Lyon was also born in Germany, is about five feet ten inches high, of a dark complexion, wears short, black, curled hair, and almost bald on the top of the head. He was for sometime concerned in the soap business in this city, in partnership with Peter Barker; pretends to be a great scholar and to be well versed in the Hebrew tongue.

These men are largely indebted to sundry merchants in this city, and from many circumstances there is the strongest reason to believe that their intentions are to defraud their creditors.

Wherefore, it is hoped that from a love of justice, as well as the above reward (which will be paid with great cheerfulness and punctuality), many persons will be induced to exert themselves in the apprehending two such atrocious villains.

Part of the goods they purchased were sent to Lancaster by a waggon that went from the house of Dietrick Reese, at the sign of the King of Prussia, in Market Street. If the waggoner will give satisfactory proof respecting the person the goods were delivered to, he shall receive twenty dollars for his trouble.

Philip Francis	Edward Batchelor
Thomas Asheton	Henry Kepple, Jun.
Joseph Dean	

No. 155 A Hays & Polock Ship Is Wrecked—1769

Myer Polock (d. 1779) was a Newport merchant who, about 1769, entered into partnership with a hard-working young businessman from New York by the name of Moses Michael Hays (1739–1805). The latter, a native New Yorker, had learned the watchmaking trade but soon turned to merchandising and commerce.

Hays was a latecomer to Newport and was not very successful, for his firm, Hays & Polock, was bankrupt within a year. The two partners experienced a number of misfortunes; one was the wreck of the *Mary*.

The following Documents A and B are "protests," formal declarations by the master and crew setting forth the circumstances under which the *Mary* was wrecked. The purpose of the protests was, of course, to prepare the ground in a legal fashion for the recovery of insurance.

Document A describes how the ship sprang a leak in June, 1769, when she sailed from Honduras for Amsterdam. Document B continues the narrative from the time the brigantine was repaired in Newport until she was wrecked off Conanicut Island in Narragansett Bay.

SOURCE. Rhode Island State Archives, Public Notary Records, VIII, 35.

A [NO. 155]

By this publick instrument of protest, be it known unto all whom it may concern;

That on the thirtieth day of August, 1769, and in the ninth year of his Majesty's [King George III] reign, before me, Henry Ward, Esq., of Newport, in the English Colony of Rhode Island and Providence Plantations, in New England, in America, Secretary and Publick Notary of the said colony, duly elected and engaged according to law, personally came William Augustus Peck, master of the brigantine *Mary*, owned by Messrs. Hays and Polock, Jonathan Fairbanks, mate; Peter Prosser, Jeremiah

Chic[h]ester, Matthew Craw [Macrea], and James Matthias, mariners all, of and belonging to the said brigantine.

And they, said William Augustus, Jonathan, Peter, Jeremiah, Matthew, and James, being upon the Holy Gospel duly sworn, did solemnly depose and declare that, on the twenty sixth of June last, they sailed with and in the said brigantine from the Bay of Honduras, bound for Amsterdam;

That the next day at eight o'clock A.M., they found she made so much water that one pump would but just keep her free; and on the twenty-eighth at two o'clock P.M., got into the bay again, where they stopped the leak as well as it could be done in that place; and the second of July sailed again from the bay, bound to the said port of Amsterdam, the said brigantine being then very tight, and remaining so until the fifteenth instant, when they, being in the prosecution of their said voyage in lat.[itude] 32° 50′ and long.[itude] 73° 50′, the weather being thick and dirty, and it looking like a storm coming on, they got the vessel into the best order they could and hove her too [to], with the wind at east, when there came on a most violent gale of wind, which lasted twenty seven hours and raised a very great sea, in which the said brigantine laboured and strained greatly and sprung a leak again, and made so much water that they could scarcely keep her free; and that, in their opinion, if the gale had continued twenty-four hours longer, she must have foundered;

That they lost the two top masts that were the lee ruff trees, with the timbers and irons and the flying jibb; that they, being obliged to keep one pump constantly going, they thought it impossible to proceed for Europe without repairing the said brigantine and stopping her leak, which could not possibly be done at sea;

And therefore, for the preservation of the said brigantine and cargo, and their own lives, they concluded to put into the first port in America they could reach, to stop the leaks of said brigantine, and arrived here yesterday.

Jeremiah Chichester	Will Augustus Peck
Matthew Macrea	Jonathan Fairbanks
his	Peter Prosser
James ⊗ Matthias	
mark	

Wherefore I, the said Henry Ward, at the request of the said William Augustus Peck, did, and do hereby, publickly and solemnly protest against the violence of the wind and sea above mentioned, as the true cause of the said brigantine's springing a leak, and as the sole reason of the said William Augustus Peck's deviating from his said voyage and putting into this port; and of all loss, detriment, and damage already suffered, or to be hereafter sustained, in consequence thereof, by the owners, shippers, insurers, and all others concerned in the said brigantine or her lading.

Thus done and protested under my hand and seal of office, the day and year first abovementioned.

Henry Ward

Registred by Henry Ward, Secretary and Publick Notary

B [NO. 155]

By this publick instrument of protest, be it known unto all whom it may concern:

That on the ninth day of September, in the ninth year of his Majesty's [King George III] reign, *Annoque Domini*, 1769, before me, Henry Ward, Esq., of Newport, in the English Colony of Rhode Island and Providence Plantations, in New England, in America, Secretary and Publick Notary of the said colony, duly elected and engaged according to law, personally came William Augustus Peck, master of the brigantine *Mary* (owned by Messrs. Hays and Polock), Jonathan Fairbanks, mate; Peter Prosser, Jeremiah Chichester, Matthew Craw [Macrea] and James Matthias, mariners all of, and belonging to, the said brigantine.

And they, the said William Augustus, Jonathan, Peter, Jeremiah, Matthew, and James, being upon the Holy Gospel duly sworn, did depose and declare that, with much difficulty, they got into this port in the said brigantine, from the Bay of Honduras, on the twenty ninth of August last;

That, a number of carpenters having been set to work upon the said brigantine to stop her leaks, who repaired and made her fit to proceed on her voyage to Amsterdam, they, upon the sixth instant, having every thing ready to proceed directly to sea, went with the said brigantine under the Island of Canonicut to be ready to embrace the first wind to sail for Amsterdam;

That, thus waiting for a wind, on the eighth instant, the said brigantine being well and properly moored, there came on a most violent gale of wind at north east, such as hath scarcely been known in the memory of man, and notwithstanding the said brigantine was secured with both her anchors and cables, and they exerted their utmost diligence and industry to prevent the same, she was by the excessive tempestuousness of the wind and sea driven from her anchors and cast ashore upon the said Island of Cononicut, whereby their lives were brought into great peril and danger, although by the good Providence of God, none of them were lost;

That the said brigantine very soon bulged and otherwise received great damage, and now lieth in the same place where she was driven ashore.

Jeremiah Chichester   Will Augustus Peck
Matthew Macrea   Jonathan Fairbanks
    his   Peter Prosser
James ⊗ Matthias
   mark

Wherefore I, the said Henry Ward, at the request of the said William Augustus Peck, did and do hereby publickly and solemnly protest against the violent storm above mentioned, as the sole cause of the said brigantine's being driven from her anchors and cast ashore, and of all loss, detriment, and damage already suffered, or to be hereafter sustained, in consequence thereof, by the owners, shippers, insurers, and all others concerned in the said brigantine or her lading.

Thus done and protested under my hand and seal of office, the day and year first abovewritten.

Henry Ward

Registred by Henry Ward, Secretary and Publick Notary

No. 156 The Rum Was Twelve Gallons Short—1769

When Aaron Lopez, of Newport, bought some Jamaica rum from the Browns, of Providence, in 1769, he checked immediately on delivery to determine if there were any "wants," any amounts of it missing. There were "wants": during the short trip from Providence to Newport, twelve gallons had "evaporated" down someone's throat. The Browns had to chalk that up to loss!

SOURCE. The John Carter Brown Library, Brown Papers.

Newport, Oct. 22d, 1769.

Messrs. Nicholas Brown & Co.
Gentlemen:

This moment your favour of the 21st current came to hand, conveying 5 puncheons Jamaica rum, which [I] have received in good order and their gauge agreeable to the particulars of your letters. But upon taking the wants the moment they were landed in presence of the bearer hereof, Mr. Thomas Lindsey, they fell 12 gallons short, on which you may depend, as we used the greatest accuracy in comparing them. Therefore you'll be pleased to notice the above deficiency with which [we] have accordingly debited your account and credited the whole 523 gs. at 95s. per go. [gallon] agreeable to your letter. As for the terms of payment, they are satisfactory.

My next will inform you whether I want the 10 tons pigg iron which can't as yet determine.

I am, gentlemen,

Your most humble servant,
Aaron Lopez

No. 157 Pig Iron from the Browns—1769

About 1768 Aaron Lopez, the Newport merchant-shipper, began to buy pig iron from Nicholas Brown and Company, a merchant-shipping and manufacturing firm in Providence. Lopez was a heavy buyer of their product; in 1769 alone he purchased over eighty tons from the Brown's Hope Furnace, although not all of it was bought on his own account. Lopez also freighted pig iron for the Browns. Much of what he bought was sent to London; occasionally he shipped a load to the West Indies. When he needed some iron replacement parts for his spermaceti works, or when he had to buy an anchor, Lopez, as we see from the following letter, turned to the same firm. Payment was by barter, for specie was scarce, and Lopez paid for his purchases in imported consumers' goods, flour, and Jamaica spirits.

SOURCE. The John Carter Brown Library, Brown Papers.

Newport, Nov. 8th, 1769.

Messrs. Nicholas Brown & Co.
Gentlemen:

With your favour of 30th ultimo, I received the two iron plates and 4 tons pigg iron which have [been] entered to your credit. I shall be glad to have per first boat 15 tons more pigg iron for to ballast a new vessell, provided the same terms of pay will answer, and shall also be glad to know, per return of the bearer, whether you can supply me with three cables, the one 11 inch, 95 fathom, another 10 inch and 85 fathom, and the last 6 inch, 100 fathom, to be made of good Petersburgh hemp and delivered here by the 25th inst. at farthest. The terms of payment I propose are the same as I practice with the ropemakers in this town, *viz.:* to deliver the same weight in Petersburgh hemp as I receive in rigging, which I shall perform on the arrival of my ship from London.

Your speedy reply will much oblige, gentlemen,

Your most humble servant,
Aaron Lopez.

Mr. Myer Polock is to deliver me an anchor 1,100 lbs, which he tells me is to come from your works. Pray let me know whether I can depend to have it next week on his account, and excuse my prolixity.

No. 158   Hays & Polock Arbitrate Their Differences with the Harts, of Newport—1770

Moses Michael Hays, of New York, and Myer Polock, of Newport, were merchants and shippers in what turned out to be a very short-lived partnership: they were forced into bankruptcy some time in 1770.

Evidently there were differences of opinion between the firm and the Harts with respect to mutual financial obligations. We know that Hays & Polock were at this time involved with the Harts in a dispute concerning the ownership of the ship *Rising Sun*. The following document is an agreement to submit the differences to the arbitration of three well-known Newport Jewish merchants. In similar situations Jews frequently chose non-Jewish arbitrators.

SOURCE. Newport County Courthouse, Newport, R.I., Superior Court Records, Petitions of Insolvency, Book E, pp. 426–27, March, 1770.

Be it remembered that Moses M. Hays, of the city of New York and Colony of New York, merchant, and Myer Polock, of Newport, in the County of Newport, merchant, of the one part, and Naphtali Hart and Isaac Hart, both of said Newport, merchants, of the other part, came into open court, and in their proper persons desired leave to submit all accounts and disputes subsisting between them to arbitration according to the form of the statute in such case made and provided, and to inspect and rectify any and all past settlements, and in pursuance thereof mutually nominated and appointed Messrs. Jacob Rodriguez Rivera, Aaron Lopez, and Moses Levy arbitrators, who are impowered to appoint time and place for meeting and to hear the parties,

And they or any two of them agreeing to give their finall award in and about the matters submitted, and to deliver up the same in writing into the clerk's office of this court, in one month from this day, where judgment shall be entered up thereon in the records of the court as of this term, and also to report when execution shall issue thereon.

And it is further agreed between the parties to this submission that if either of them refuse to appear upon due notice before the said arbitrators, or shall do any thing that may obstruct or prevent the operation of this rule of submission, it shall be in the power of the said arbitrators to settle said accounts ex-parte.

Moses M. Hays	Naph. Hart
Myer Polock	I. Hart

Read in the hearing of the [said] parties and adjudged that the same be made a rule of this court, and the same is hereby declared to be a rule of court accordingly.

No. 159   Aaron Isaacs Bargains with Aaron Lopez—1770

Aaron Isaacs (1724–98), of East Hampton, Long Island, was a successful merchant. He probably was a native of Hamburg, Germany, and lived for a while in New York City, where he was identified with the Jewish community. Some time after 1748 he moved to East Hampton and became a merchant. His activities were varied: he bought farms and houses, owned part of a wharf, and helped to found a local school, Clinton Academy. During the Revolution this ardent patriot fled Long Island to escape from British rule and remained in Connecticut for the remainder of the war.

About 1750 Isaacs married a non-Jewess, Mary Hedges. One of their daughters, Sarah, married William Payne during the Revolution. The son of William and Sarah Payne, John Howard Payne, was the author of "Home, Sweet Home."

Among the merchants with whom Isaacs did business in the 1760's and after was Aaron Lopez, of Newport. In spite of the fact that the two were in frequent correspondence, they evidently were not too friendly. As we see from Document A, Isaacs was a rather direct person, apparently without too much culture, and entirely lacking the finesse so characteristic of an urbane Iberian such as Lopez.

Documents B, C, and D deal with Isaacs' attempt to collect a promissory note signed by Dr. Samuel Gilston (?), a naval physician. In his typically crude fashion, Isaacs in effect wrote to Lopez: "I owe you money. Therefore it is to your interest to collect the enclosed note against Dr. Gilston, particularly since he is now stationed on Nantucket, in your neighborhood."

Isaacs' spelling is all his own, and the orthography of the following notes is quite typical of his writing.

SOURCE. New York State Library, Champlin Papers.

A [NO. 159]

East Hampton, April the 10, 1770.

Sir:

I have sent by Cap.[tain] Read your barrels and beef, the barrels branded "A I" and your beans, as you wil find in your beal [bill] with the ballunc dew [balance due] to me; and as Mr. Hedges is not to peay you tel fawl, I lock upon it [as] resonobel that you should make me an alounce for promp[t] peay; and if you wil send me 2 barrels of tear [tar], 1 barrel of turpentime for the alounce, then it wil be incoregment to trade with you furder. I stand in nead of 1 box of glass, 6 B 8 [6 by 8], 1 deto [ditto] of 7 B 9, and 100 or 50 pownds of 10 penne nales grately. Pleas to send them by the furst oppertunity, and your ancer wil much oblige

Your frind and humbel sarvent,
Aaron Isaacs

P.S. Sir: If you don't see it in your way to send those arteculs I menchend for promp peay, you nead not send the glass nor neals.

B [NO. 159]

East Hampton, Augoust the 14, 1770.

Sir:

Whare as I stand in detted to you sum mony to be peayed next fawl, thare fore I desire the faver you wold send the in closed note to sume of your frinds in Bostun and desire him to prosecute the note a medaitly, by resun he has dissapinted me of peayment. He is a docter and neavel offesur at Nantucket. And your ancer wil much a blige

Your frind,
Aaron Isaacs

C [NO. 159]

East Hampton, September the 4, 1770.

Sir:

I have sent to you by Hamoun a note aganst Docter Samuel Gilstun, which I hope you have sent to Bostun to be put in sute as I don't live in the goverment [colony]. Tharefore I can[not] sue him to Bostun or els whare in the goverment. He hes owde [owed] me the mony three year past. With a grate deal of trobel I got a note of him last year. Your ancer with my acount currunt by the bearre[r], my sun [son], wil much a blige

Your frind and humbel [sar]vent,
Aaron Isaacs

D [NO. 159]

East Hampton, October the 17, 1770.

Sir:

Sume time ago I sent you a note a gainst Docter Gilston; therefore, I should be glad to know whether your frind in Bostoun hes got the mony or not.

I stand in kneed at present of 25 pownd of lath neals, ten pownd of white leed. Should be glad to have them by the furst oppertunity. And if you have won [one] cask of 8 and won cask of 10 peney nales, and can let them go at 8[s.] 6[d. New] York mony, as I have bought of Cap.[tain] Mosele this summer, you may send them, and your ancer wil much a blige

Your frind and humbel sarvent,
Aaron Isaacs

No. 160   The Rhode Island–Jamaica–London Triangular Trade—1770

The following ship's orders of the Newport shipper Aaron Lopez illustrate with unmistakable clarity the nature of the triangular trade between Rhode Island, Jamaica, and London.

In this instance the usual New England cargo—probably cattle, horses, meat, vegetables, and candles—was sold or bartered in Jamaica for molasses, rum, and sugar. Those goods, together with what freight could be picked up, were taken to London on the next leg of the trip and left with a correspondent for sale. On the last part of the trip, back to Newport, the ship would carry a load of English manufactures.

If there was not enough of a cargo to justify the London trip, the captain was to return to Rhode Island with the customary load of island produce. As factor for the owner, the captain received a commission on all sales and freight, in addition to his salary.

SOURCE. Newport Historical Society Library, Lopez Letters.

Newport, October 10th, 1770.

Captain John Heffernan:

The ship *Jacob*, now under your command, being ready fitted for the seas, you are to embrace the first fair wind and proceed directly to Port Antonio on the Island of Jamaica where you are to enter the ship, land the horses you carry on freight, and endeavour to dispose of as much of your cargo as that market will admit.

After which, proceed to St. Anns on said island and compleat the sales of the cargo. But should you find it necessary and of any advantage to go with the ship to any other parish on the island, you may proceed there, as my insurance is ordered accordingly, tho' flatter myself you'll have an opportunity (being an early vessell) to dispose of the whole cargo at the two first mentioned ports without seeking any others.

Soon as you arrive at St. Anns, deliver Captain [James] Potter's letters agreeable to their directions, and from the day you arrive give out that your ship will proceed to London and take such freight as will present [itself] for that market on the usual terms, in procuring and obtaining which, request your best endeavours may be exerted. That you may be the more able to load your ship, I desire you'll invest as much of the cargo you now have on board in such Jamaica produce as will best answer the London market.

If a freight should so readily present [itself] after your arrival, that you have no time to compleat the sales of your cargo, you are in that case (in order to secure the London freight) to deliver whatever goods remains unsold to Mr. William Hull at St. Anns, taking duplicate receipts thereof for all what you leave with him, to be delivered, or their proceeds, to my order, one of which receipts inclose in a letter to me by the first opportunity, together with a bill of lading for what goods you carry on my account, advising at same time what freight you obtain, the time you are to leave Jamaica, and what progress you made in the sales of my effects, in all which desire you'll be explicit for my government [guidance].

The other receipt you are to leave under cover for Captain Potter in some carefull hand, to keep it till he arrives at Jamaica, as he is to follow you about three months hence in order to take charge of the effects, or the proceeds thereof, you may leave behind after your proceeding to London, where, when please God you arrive, apply to Messrs. Hayley & Hopkins, merchants there, and deliver them all my effects, together with all the freight money.

Mean while, I shall instruct those gentlemen to provide you a cargo for the *Jacob* so as to be here early in the next fall at farthest.

But should you (contrary to my almost certain expectations) fail of getting a freight at Jamaica, then you are to go on with the sales of your cargo till you have compleated them, the neat [net] proceeds of which invest chiefly in molasses, and the remainder in rum and few hogsheads best sugars, and return here soon as possible, attending by all means to quit Jamaica before the 26th July next on account of my insurances [which will have expired by then].

Inclosed you have sundry accounts against some people at Jamaica, which desire you'll do your best to collect in such produce as will best suit the London market. And, as I am conscious of your good knowledge of the Jamaica planters, think it unnecessary to caution you to avoid making any bad debts and leaving any of my interest behind.

If Captain Potter arrives at Jamaica before you proceed to London, then, instead of delivering what effects you may have unsold to Mr. William Hull, you are to deliver [them] to Captain Potter, who will take charge of them. Therefore you are to charge me a commission of 5 per cent on what sales you may have made to the time the goods are delivered to either Captain Potter or Mr. Hull. And you'll observe that you are to charge a commission of 2½ per cent on what neat freight you make for London on all goods, excepting those the ship carries for my account, on which no primage [commission] is to take place.

You are also to take notice that from the time you quit Jamaica, your wages are to be at four pounds sterling per month, instead of six dollars. You are also to have liberty to ship in the *Jacob* two puncheons rum as priviledge [on your own account].

What farther instructions I may have occasion to add, shall communicate per Captain Potter. At present think of nothing essencial, save to express my best wishes for your safe arrival at Jamaica, and assure you that I am

Your assured friend and servant,
Aaron Lopez

Acknowledge the above to be a true copy of my instructions, which I promise to comply with to the best of my knowledge.

John Heffernan

P.S.: One of Mr. William Hull's receipts you are to leave under cover for Captain James Potter in the hands of Mr. William White.

A. Lopez

N.B.: When you write me, if by way of Newyork, direct to the care of Henry Cruger, Esq.; if by way of Philadelphia, to the care of Anthony Stocker; and if via Boston, to the care of Mr. Nathaniel Wheatley.

No. 161. Aaron Hart and Isaac Levy Assume Responsibility for the Debts of Uriah Judah—1770

Hart was a common name among Jews and Gentiles in colonial America, and many of the Jewish Harts were not related to one another. The Aaron Hart mentioned here, a Canadian, was the most famous bearer of that name in the eighteenth-century English colonies.

Aaron Hart (1724–1800), originally a sutler with the British

Army, arrived in New York in 1759 or 1760. He took part in the conquest of Canada and settled in Three Rivers on the St. Lawrence, where he became the leading merchant.

In the following bond, Hart and a former Quebec merchant, Isaac Levy, assume responsibility for the debts of Uriah Judah (1714–82), a merchant who did business in Quebec, Three Rivers, and other Canadian towns. His sister Dorothy, or "Dolly," Judah married Aaron Hart.

SOURCE. Public Archives of Canada.

Province of Quebec, SS.

Know all men by these presents that we, Uriah Judah, Aaron Hart of 3 Rivers [Three Rivers, Quebec], and Isaac Levy, late of Quebec, are held and firmly bound unto George Allsopp, Esquire, deputy secretary of this province, in the sum of five hundred pounds lawful money there of, to the true payment where of we bind our selves, our heirs, executors, administrators, and assigns firmly by these presents.

Witness our hands and seals this 29th day of October, one thousand seven hundred and seventy.

The condition of this obligation is such that if the above bounden Aaron Hart and Isaac Levy do well and trully pay, or cause to be paid, all such debts as the said Uriah Judah hath contracted in this province, then this obligation to be void, or else to remain in full force and virtue.

Uriah Judah   Aaron Hart   Isaac Levy

Signed, sealed, and delivered in the presence of

B. Carbonneaux.

No. 162   The Insolvent Isaac Elizer Asks to Be Released
from Debtors' Prison—1771

Like many of his colleagues, Isaac Elizer, a prominent merchant-shipper, suffered reverses and was in prison for debt. In the following petition he asks that the benefits of the Rhode Island bankruptcy law be extended to him.

SOURCE. Rhode Island Historical Society, Providence.

Colony of Rhode Island, etc.

To the Honourable the General Assembly, sitting in Newport, in the County of Newport and Colony of Rhode Island, etc., the second Monday of June, A.D. 1771:

The petition of Isaac Elizer, of Newport aforesaid, merchant, humbly sheweth:

That he hath with unwearied assiduity applied himself to business in the mercantile way, and is, through many unavoidable misfortunes in trade, rendered intirely unable to pay the whole of his just debts, on account of which he now is confined in his Majesty's goal [jail] in said Newport;

That his present unhappy situation renders him also intirely unable to support his large and growing family;

That in order to make all the satisfaction in his power to his creditors, he is willing to surrender up the whole of his estate to the utmost farthing for their use and benefit.

Wherefore he most humbly prays your Honours to extend unto him the benefit of an act made and passed in June, A.D. 1756, entitled "An Act for the Relief of Insolvent Debtors," upon his full complying with all the conditions, restrictions, and regulations therein contained.

And, as in duty bound, will ever pray,

Isaac Elizer

June 11th, 1771.

To the House of Magistrates,
Gentlemen:

Resolved: That this petition be referred to next session of Assembly, and that in the mean time, the petitioner notify all his creditors by an advertisement in the Newport and New York news papers three weeks successively, to appear at next session to answer the same, if they think proper.

Noted and past.

Per order: Josias Lyndon, Clerk

In the Upper House: Read June 15th and concurred.

By order: Henry Ward, Secretary

No. 163 Solomon Marache Goes into the Grocery, Stone, and Glassware Business—1771

Solomon Marache was either born in New York City or came there as a child. By 1749 he was apprenticed to Isaac Hays, a Dutch Jew, to learn the art, trade, and mystery of a merchant. Within five years, by the time of the French and Indian War, he became a full-fledged merchant and a partner of Hayman Levy, a well-known army purveyor, fur trader, and merchant. The partnership, however, did not last long and was dissolved before the end of the war.

Marache disappears from the New York synagogal records early in the 1760's, only to reappear several years later in Philadelphia. As we see from the following letter to his old friend, Aaron Lopez, the Newport merchant-shipper, he had just moved to Philadelphia, where he proposed to sell groceries and glassware. Some of the latter was evidently made for him by local manufacturers, for we note that he made arrangements to fill a special order for Lopez at the bottle works.

Marache was active in the local synagogue, as he had been while he resided in New York. He was among the leaders of Mikveh Israel in Philadelphia at the time the congregation was reconstituted during the Revolution. In his later years, however, he married a Gentile, his second wife, and seems to have drifted away from Judaism.

SOURCE. Newport Historical Society Library, Lopez Letters.

Philadelphia, 18 August, 1771.

Mr. Aaron Lopez.
Dear Sir:

I intended to have given myself the pleasure of paying my respects to my good friend long since, but my hurry in moving prevented it when Capt. [Joseph] Anthony left this last. Therefore, [I] hope you will excuse the omission.

Agreeable to your request, have applyed to the glass manufactory with the memorandum you was pleased to favor me with, and after all the inquiries I could make, must inform you that the bottles you describe can be manufactured here, but not without your furnishing one for a patern. The lowest price will be two dollars per doz., and can be delivered within the time you limit in the memorandum, after application is made. If the terms will suit you and I can be furnished with a bottle for a patern, shall with pleasure execute your order.

I dare say my good friend, Mr. Rivera, has informed you of the establishment I propose making in the grocery business in this city, which, with an assortment of stone and glass ware, I make no doubt, with the blessing of the Almighty, of obtaining a comfortable living. If industry and proper frugality will contribute towards it, they will not be wanting on my side. I like this place much and wish it had been my fortune to have been fixed here years since; nevertheless, will endeavor to make up for losst time.

It will be in my power to dispose of a considerable quantity of spermaciti candles through the course of the year, and [I] doubt not of rendering my friend agreeable sales, should he be pleased to favor me with a consignment of a few boxes per every coaster [coastal ship]. I shall desire his favors no longer than I continue to give satisfaction.

Mrs. Marache joins me in sincere regards to Mrs. Lopez and rest of your good family. Please to accept the same yourself and believe me to be, with real esteem, dear sir,

Your affectionate friend and very obedient servant,

Sol. Marache

No. 164 A Contract for a Slave Ship—1772

The following document is an unsigned memorandum of an agreement by Aaron Lopez to provide Captain Peleg Clarke with a slave ship. Although the captain made a trip to the Guinea Coast that summer, it was not in a vessel supplied by Lopez. The deal described below fell through.

However, this memorandum confirms what is known from other sources: Lopez was active in contracting for the building of new ships which he used for himself or sold in Europe or in the West Indies when the market was right.

The gratings, chains, and handcuffs listed here are grim reminders that slave ships were floating prisons.

The Captain Nathaniel Briggs, of whom mention is made, was a well-known slaver who occasionally made trips to Africa for the firm of Lopez and Rivera.

SOURCE. Newport Historical Society Library, Lopez Papers.

Newport, February 6th, 1772.

A double deck new brigantine about one hundred and thirteen tons burthen to be delivered by the subscriber to Captain Peleg Clarke by all the month of April next, compleatly finished for the Affrican trade, rigged and equipped with such number of sails as the brigantine *Hannah* was when commanded by Captain Nathaniel Briggs on a voyage to the Coast. To be sheathed with inch pine boards or half inch cedar; her cables to be *viz.*, the best bower [anchor cable], eighty fathom, nine and a half inches; the second one, ninety fathom eight and a half inches; a hawser one hundred and twenty fathom, six inches; the anchors to be in proportion. There is also to be a yawl about eighteen foot long. The brigantine to have gratings and air ports as it is usual in a Guineaman, and to be painted in a plain manner.

The awning, a second boat, caboose, colours, small arms, chains, and hand cuffs, with every other small utensil, to be excluded and provided by Captain Clarke.

The subscriber engages to deliver the above described vessell for the consideration of six hundred and ninety pounds sterling, payable by said Captain Clarke in bills of his own drawing on London at thirty days sight; the bills to be computed at parr, say at four shillings and six pence sterling per dollar, and to be delivered to the subscriber hereof at the signing of this memorandum, if required.

No. 165   Aaron Lopez, Building Contractor—1772

On February 18, 1772, Charles Spooner, a Newport, Rhode Island, carpenter, contracted to build a house for Aaron Lopez. Obviously Lopez already had a customer for the house, for eight days later he agreed to deliver the same building to Linn Martin, a local mariner. (Martin may well have made his money in the slave trade, for he was expected on the Guinea Coast early that autumn.)

Lopez was to receive 809 Spanish silver dollars from Martin; but he paid the carpenter the same amount! Where, then, was his profit as a builder? Martin paid the merchant in cash, but Lopez paid Spooner only about 13 per cent in cash and the rest in English goods and materials—at retail prices of course. Therein lay his profit.

The following document is the contract Lopez made with Martin.

SOURCE. Newport Historical Society Library, Lopez Papers.

Articles of agreement indented, made, and concluded upon the twenty-sixth day of February in the twelfth year of the reign of our sovereign Lord, George the Third, King of Great Britain, and in the year of our Lord one thousand seven hundred and seventy-two, between Aaron Lopez of New Port in the county of New Port in the colony of Rhode Island, etc., merchant, of the one part, and Linn Martin of New Port aforesaid, mariner, of the other part, in manner following, that is [to] say:

First, it is covenanted, concluded, and agreed by and between the parties hereunto and the said Aaron Lopez for himself, his heirs, executors, and administrators, doth covenant, promise, and grant to and with the said Linn Martin, his heirs, executors, and administrators by these presents in manner following, that is to say:

That the said Aaron Lopez, his executors or administrators, shall and will build or cause to be built, to and for the said Linn Martin, his executors or administrators, a good, substantial house of the following dimensions, that is to say, thirty-six feet in front and twenty-six feet in width, two story high, with a single pitched roof, to be well clapboarded and shingled with twenty-five good windows in the same, with a good front door and door head, cellar door and windows, and everything to compleat the outside of said house workmanlike.

And the said Lopez is likewise to compleat the inside of said house in manner following:

First, the entry to have a good bracket stair case with two half paces and ballisters [balusters]. The great room [the family living room] to be wainscotted all round as high as the stool of the windows with a large pannell over the chimney. 'Tis likewise to be cornished [corniced] with a handsome china closet in the same; the keeping room [parlor] to have a large pannell over the chimney, and the windows cased fit for shutters. There is likewise to be window shutters in the great room, and all the other part of said house to be finished plain.

The whole house to be finished with good floors, and the doors to be as follows: seven to be six-pannelled, and all the other four-pannelled.

Said Lopez is likewise to cause a good cellar to be built under said house six feet high under the timber; likewise the chimney with six fire-places, and to lath and plaister said house in every part, the garret only excepted.

Said Lopez is likewise to find six brass knobbed locks and the other locks and latches, and all the hinges for the said house, and every material of all and every kind for the finishing of said house, in manner aforesaid, on his own cost and charge. And the whole to be compleated by the last of September next ensuing.

In consideration of all and singular the matters and things, herein before mentioned to be done and performed on the part and behalf of said Lopez, in manner as aforesaid, he the said Martin, for himself, his heirs, executors, administrators, doth covenant, promise, and grant to and with the said Lopez, his heirs, executors, administrators, and by these presents, that he, the said Martin, his heirs, executors, administrators, shall and will well and truly pay or cause to be paid to the said Lopez, his heirs, executors, administrators, the sum of eight hundred and nine Spanish silver dollars on signing these presents.

And for the true performance of the articles and agreements to be performed on the part of said Lopez as aforesaid, he, the said Lopez, doth bind himself, his heirs, executors, administrators, unto the said Martin, his heirs, executors, administrators, in the penalty or sum of five hundred pounds, lawfull money, firmly by these presents.

In witness whereof, the said parties to these presents have hereunto interchangeably set their hands and seals the day and year first written.

Sealed and delivered   Linn Martin
in the presence of us
  Elesabeth Church
  Sarah Martin

No. 166   Barnard Gratz's Negro George Refuses to Be Sold—1772

The demand for labor in Pennsylvania and the other Northern colonies was in part satisfied by the use of white indentured servants and Negro slaves. Many of the latter were house servants.

In the following letter we note that Barnard Gratz was attempting to sell a rebellious slave. Like most Northerners, the Gratzes as a rule kept white servants.

As far as can be determined, Jews of the colonial period were no different from non-Jews in their treatment of Negroes. The wills of eighteenth-century Jews indicate that some of them were good masters. Rare individuals such as Isaiah Isaacs, of Richmond, believed that the slaves should be emancipated because "all men are by nature equally free."

SOURCE. MSS of The Library Company of Philadelphia.

Reading, March 2d, 1772.

Mr. Bernhard Gratz, Merchant in
Philadelphia.
Sir:

I took your negroe George, some time ago, home, thinking I might be the better able to sell him, who, after beening [being] with me a night, behaved himself in such an insolent manner I immediately remanded back to the gaol.

About a week since, I put him up at public sale at Christopher Witman's tavern, where there was a number of persons who inclined to purchase him. But he protested publickly that he would not be sold, and if any one should purchase him, he would be the death of him, and words to the like purpose, which deterred the people from bid[d]ing.

I then sent him back again with directions to the goaler [jailer] to keep him at hard labour, which he refuses to do, and goes on in such an insolent manner that's impossible to get a master for him here.

I therefore request you'll send for him on sight hereof, or send me a line by Drinkhouse, or the first opportunity, what I shall do with him.

He's now almost naked, and if not furnished soon with some cloaths, I fear he'll perish.

Pray let me hear from [you] and, in the mean time, I remain, with great regard, sir,

Your humble servant,
George Nagel

N.B. He's now chained and handcuffed on account of his threats.

No. 167   Naphtali Hart, Jr., Starts Life Over Again in the West Indies—1773

The political and economic quarrels between England and her North American colonies hurt business. Between 1771 and 1773 imports from Great Britain to the American colonies fell 50 per cent, bringing distress to many merchants. This may be the reason that prompted Naphtali Hart, Jr., to move his family from Newport to the West Indies.

Hart, as we see from the following letter to Aaron Lopez, first went to Barbados. He found, however, that he could not establish himself there and blamed his predicament on his fellow Jews. He then moved on to the Dutch colony of St. Eustatius where, according to his report, the Jews again gave him no encouragement. Obviously Hart was an embittered, unsuccessful man.

The fact that the Jewish merchants of Barbados were selling goods at cost reflects the bad times then prevailing.

SOURCE. Newport Historical Society Library, Lopez Letters.

St. Eustatia, 12th March, 1773.

Sir:

I should have wrote to you sooner to acquaint [you] of my arrival, but meeting with many difficultys in my new interprise, that my mind is so disturbed that I cannot fix my mind to write even to those good friends that I ought not to have neglected. Therefore, you will excuse my long silence. I now return you many thanks for the favours you have done me and family.

I was at Barbados six weeks, and finding that there was nothing to be done there, altho there was several Christian merchants who would have readily contributed towards my gitting into buesness [business], could they have proposed any buesness to my advantage. Nor would they advise me to enter in the shop way [into shopkeeping], as many of our society [Jews] there have ruined the trade, selling many times for the first cost in the retail way for the sake of cash.

I thirefore resolved to come here to try my fortune, have been here three weeks, and as yet cannot find any incouragement to git into credit, as they are afraid here of each other. However, I brought a letter from Barbados to Richard Downing Jennius, merchant of great character here, by who's assistance am in hopes of gitting into buesness, with the blessing of God.

My greatest misfortune is that I brought my family with me, which has been a prejudice to me hitherto in gitting into buesness.

What adds more to my griefe is that I have no one to advise with, as there is no sincerity among those of our society, being jealous of each other. As to Mr. Jacob Polack, [he] has kept himself at a great distance since the first moment of my arrival, and allso Mr. [Samson] Mears. [Polack and Mears were both New England Jews.] The reason [I] am unacquainted with, as I have neither asked favour or advice from either as yet. All which I pass un noticed untill a suitable time.

If you should see your way clear to render me any services here, [I] shall esteem it as a particular favour, and what ever might be committed to my care, you may rely on my faithfull endea[vour] to descharge the trust, reposed in me, with honour.

Markets here in general are good, particularly cattle, sheep, poultry, candles, etc., etc.

My wife joins me in our sincere reguard for Mrs. Lopez and the rest of your family. I remain, wishing you and family health and every other blessing. I am, sir,

Your most humble servant,

Naphtali Hart

Our compliments to your brother Abraham and family, and allso [to your son-in-law] Mr. Mendize and his spouse, your brother David, etc.

To Aaron Lopez.

No. 168   Jacob Isaacks, Broker, Advertises—1773

Jacob Isaacks, a native New Yorker, was for a time a successful merchant and merchant-shipper in Newport, but lost his fortune in 1772. After that, it seems, he never recovered financially. He became a broker, sold insurance, and offered to build vessels "on reasonable terms." In later years he experimented with the distillation of fresh from salt water.

The following advertisement, published in 1773, describes his activities as a broker.

SOURCE. *The Newport Mercury,* October 25, 1773.

JACOB ISAACKS

Who carries on the business of a broker, in all its branches, in which he has given general satisfaction,

Has to dispose of, on the best terms,

Several houses and lots of land, in Newport, which will rent for 10 per cent; a ten acre lot, within a mile of Newport, and two good farms on the island; several new vessels, from 60 to 170 tons, all built by good workmen, and can be launched in a month; several old vessels, from 30 to 140 tons; also the best of shop sugars, and some middling ditto, black pepper, tea, coffee, rice per tierce, best French indigo, beef, pork, ship-bread, brandy, Lisbon wine and sundry other sorts, by the pipe or quarter cask, New-England and West India rum, with a variety of other articles, at the most reasonable rates.

N.B. Any persons living in the country, by a letter to said Isaacks, may have any articles bought or sold for them, to the best advantage.

———

No. 169   Chartering a Sloop—1773

Until the Lopez Papers in the library of the Newport Historical Society are carefully re-examined, it will be impossible to determine how many ships flew the flag of Aaron Lopez, when that Newport businessman was at the height of his career in the early 1770's. Some historians estimate that at that time he owned about thirty sail. That figure seems high. As the following document demonstrates, Lopez also chartered ships for voyages.

SOURCE. The Rhode Island Historical Society Library.

This charter party [lease] indented and made this fifteenth day of November in the year of our Lord one thousand seven hundred and seventy three, between John Strange of Freetown in the County of Bristol in the Province of the Massachusetts Bay, mariner, of the one part, and Aaron Lopez of Newport in the County of Newport in the Colony of Rhode Island, etc., a merchant, of the other part, witnesseth:

That the said John Strange, being owner of the sloop called *The King Fisher*, burthen sixty-six tons or there abouts, now in the harbour of Newport aforesaid, hath granted and to freight letten [to hire] and by these presents doth grant and to freightlet [hire] unto the said Aaron Lopez the said sloop together with her rigging, sails, and all other appurtenances necessary for the performance of a voyage to be made from hence to Cape Nichola Mole on Hispaniola [Haiti], and from thence back to Newport aforesaid, as soon as may be, on the sole risque of the said John Strange as to all danger of the seas or any other casualty of an[y] sort, except seizures.

And it is hereby agreed by the said Aaron Lopez to pay unto the said John Strange the sum of nineteen pounds sixteen shillings lawful money per month for the hire of said sloop, and in that proportion for a greater or less time, the hire of the same beginning from the day and year above written, and in case of seizure of said sloop, the said Lopez to pay said Strange the sum of two hundred pounds sterling.

In witness of the aforegoing agreement, we the parties do bind ourselves each to the other in the penal sum of five hundred pounds, lawful money, and have interchangeably set our hands and seals the day and year aforementioned.

Signed, sealed, and delivered
in presence of us   John Strange
  Benjamin Wright   Aaron Lopez
  Daniel Lopez

No. 170   Frederick Haldimand Signs a Warrant for David Franks—1774

The Franks family had been furnishing provisions to the British troops in this country for a generation, as far back as King George's War (1744–48), if not earlier. One of the Frankses, David, the Philadelphia merchant, was the American agent for the London army purveyors, Nesbitt, Drummond, & Franks. The last-mentioned was David's brother and probably the most active member of that important firm.

The company could not collect for the provisions it supplied until a warrant was signed by a responsible military officer. The following certificate bears the signature of Colonel Frederick Haldimand. Since the French and Indian War the latter had had frequent dealings with Jewish sutlers and supplymen, particularly in the Canadian area. As we can see from this document, army purveying was big business.

SOURCE. Public Archives of Canada.

New York, 25th May, 1774

These are to certify [to] the Right Honorable the Lords Commissioners of his Majesty's Treasury, that Mr. David Franks, agent for Arnold Nesbitt, Adam Drummond, and Moses Franks, Esquires, contractors for victualling his Majesty's forces in North America, hath by my orders victualled the said forces in Philadelphia, in the Province of Pennsylvania, with all species of provisions, according to contract, commencing the 25th day of March and ending the 24th day of May, 1774, amounting to seventeen thousand one hundred and ninety two days for one person, as per vouchers examined by his Majesty's Commissary of Stores and Provisions, for which I have signed four certificates of this tenor and date.

                          Frederick Haldimand
                          certificate signed

Francis Hutcheson,
Acting as Commissary General.

No. 171 A Plea by Philadelphia Merchants for a Just Price on Requisitioned Goods—1779

In June, 1778, a group of Philadelphia merchants succeeded in running a cargo through the British blockade. But to their chagrin the goods were requisitioned by the government. In the following January these businessmen learned that the Continental Congress had appointed a committee to report on the price the government ought to pay for the seized wares.

In the following petition the apprehensive merchants, fearing that they would not be adequately reimbursed, pointed out that they had paid for the goods in sterling, that the price on them had advanced since that time, that the cargo had to be run through the blockade, and that they were entitled to a profit.

Among the signers of the petition was Jonas Phillips (1736–1803), a well-known Philadelphia merchant and auctioneer. He was a Hessian, having arrived in Charlestown, by way of London, in 1756.

Phillips was a very observant Jew, acquainted with rabbinic law and deeply interested in the welfare of the local congregation. However, he was headstrong and frequently found himself at odds with his fellow Jews, primarily in matters of ceremonial and ritual. A man of strong convictions, eager to secure complete equality before the law for himself and his coreligionists, he worked to attain the political and civil rights to which he believed all Jews were entitled.

SOURCE. The Library of Congress, Division of Manuscripts, Papers of the Continental Congress, 41, VI, 105.

To the Honorable the Congress:

The memorial of the subscribers, merchants, and others, that had their goods taken from them in June last by the clothier and quarter master generals.

May it please Your Honors: Your memorialists, being informed by the Honorable Wm. H. Drayton [a member of Congress] that Your Honors had recommitted their case to a committee to report to your honorable house the price to be allowed for said goods,

We, your memorialists, beg leave therefore to assure Your Honors that the goods now in question cost us (from the importers) on an averidge, forty per cent sterling advance on the original cost of the same in Europe. Your memorialists therefore cannot doubt but Your Honors will allow they should not be sufferers by running the great risque they did (fifty per cent being offered for insurance) in secreting said goods, but, on the contrary, will allow them to be justly entitled to a profit thereon.

Such profits as Your Honors shall think them entitled to for running the risque and laying out of their money, your memorialists are willing to leave to Your Honors' justice and generosity, which, together with the first cost they paid in sterling, your memorialists are willing to recieve payment for in current money, at the current exchange of European bills, at the time they recieve payment.

Your memorialists, not doubting but their request will appear to Your Honors reasonable, hope Your Honors will grant them the same, with an order for immediate payment.

Philadelphia, January 28, 1779.

Thomas Harper	Jonas Phillips
William Beaver	W. M. Murtrie
John Shields	John Steinmetz
. . . Douglas	James Fisher

No. 172 Daniel Gomez Asks that His Grandson Be Permitted to Go to British-Occupied New York—1779

Daniel Gomez (1695–1780), a son of Luis Gomez, the New York merchant, was one of the men who helped to build Congregation Shearith Israel during the early part of the eighteenth century. As a patriot, the elderly merchant fled from British-occupied New York and went to Philadelphia, leaving everything behind. In 1779 the impoverished exile, then eighty-four years of age, asked the Pennsylvania authorities for permission to send a grandson through the lines to collect rents and take care of some other errands in New York.

SOURCE. Pennsylvania Historical and Museum Commission, Passport Papers, 1779, Division of Public Records.

To the Honourable the President, and the Honourable the Supreem Exicutive Council of Pennsylvania:

The humble address and pitition of Daniel Gomez most humbly sheweth that the said Daniel Gomez has always had a real affection and zeal for the wellfare of this country, and especially has attached himself to the cause in which it now contests, in so much that he has left his property among the enimys of these states and has don every thing that in him lay for the benefit of the said states; and that your pititioner [is] being laid up by infirmitys, and he is sorry to say he is under the most urgent necessity to send to the city of New York to try to procure some rents and other articles of his property.

He therefore most ardently prays this honourable bord to grant permission to his grandson, Daniel Gomez, Junior, to go to the city of New York for that purpose, and that he may return as soon as it is effected.

And your petitioner shall ever pray for the prosperity and indipendance of the thirteen United States, and for Pennsylvania in particular.

Daniel Gomez

Philadelphia, May [1779].

No. 173   Congress Refuses to Compensate Samuel DeLucena for His Search for Sulphur Mines—1779

Samuel DeLucena, whom we met in connection with his petition for a monopoly on the manufacture of potash, was in Philadelphia by 1779. He had spent some money in his search for sulphur mines and asked to be reimbursed. During the Revolution sulphur was in great demand for the manufacture of gunpowder. The following letter is the answer of the Board of War.

SOURCE. The Library of Congress, Division of Manuscripts, Papers of the Continental Congress, 147, III, 537.

At a [meeting of the] Board of War, July 16, 1779.
Present: Col. [Timothy] Pickering,
Mr. [Richard] Peters.

The board, having considered the memorial of Mr. Samuel De Lucena, beg leave to report:

That it does not appear to us that Mr. De Lucena had any personal encouragement for the search for sulphur mines from Congress or any comittee thereof, nor can we find any explicit promises of reward held out to persons who should engage in such enquiries;

That, although the memorialist (being well affected, as we believe, to the American cause) might have been prompted by a desire to serve the public, yet it is reasonable to presume that his predominant views were the private advantage he should gain, had his endeavors proved fortunate, by the high price of the article its scarcity created. And, as by a compliance with the memorialist's wishes, a disagreeable precedent might be established for indemnifying all persons who have engaged in similar persuits from which no advantages have arisen to the public, the board concieve it is expedient and proper that it should be

Resolved, that Mr. Samuel De Lucena has no just claim upon the United States for a reimbursement of his expenses incurred in searching for sulphur mines, as sett forth in his memorial.

By order,
Richard Peters

No. 174 Isaac Moses Asks the Continental Congress to Furnish Gunpowder for His Privateer—1779

With the possible exception of Aaron Lopez, of Newport, Isaac Moses, of New York, was the greatest Jewish merchant-shipper in North America during the Revolutionary period. He was a German immigrant who came to these shores toward the end of the French and Indian War; perhaps his uncle Hayman Levy brought him over. In 1770 Moses married Levy's daughter Reyna. He was a successful merchant-shipper and for much of his business life eminently successful. But, like other men in trade and commerce, he too suffered severe reverses and on two occasions was bankrupt.

While in New York, Moses was a pillar of Congregation Shearith Israel, and when he left that city, because of the British occupation in 1776, he became a leader of Mikveh Israel in Philadelphia. Indeed, he enjoyed the distinction of serving as president both at Shearith Israel and Mikveh Israel.

During the Revolution Moses engaged in shipping on a very large scale, operating branches in Amsterdam and in St. Eustatius in the West Indies. No doubt his foreign offices were established with an eye to running the British blockade. As a large-scale importer Moses was in a position to help the Continental Congress with strategic goods, which he did. We shall see in the following letter that he turned to it, for once, and asked it to do him a favor.

SOURCE. The Library of Congress, Division of Manuscripts, Papers of the Continental Congress, 41, VI, 141.

To the Honorable the Congress of the United States of North America:

The petition of Isaac Moses, now of the city of Philadelphia, merchant, most humbly sheweth:

That your petitioner, having loaded a schooner, letter of marque, and fitted her with every necessary but gun powder, in a warlike manner, has made all the search in his power for that article, but finding himself every where dissappointed, is now under the dissagreeable necessity of troubling Your Honours, and to pray that you would be pleased to spare him, out of the public stores, two or three hundred weight of powder.

He flatters himself his principals as a true Whig and friend to the liberties of this country are so well known to some of your members, that it is needless to mention them here, or to remind your body of the assistance he has afforded these United States from time to time in the importation of divers articles which he spared them, but particularly when he and his partners spared these states upwards of twenty thousand dollars in specie, in exchange for Continental dollars, at the time the Canada expedition was on foot, and for which they received the thanks from or through your then president, the Honourable John Hancock, Esq.

Your petitioner submits to your honourable House to consider how unsafe it would be in him to risk his property at these times on the high seas without having proper means of defence with it, and pledges himself either immediately to pay for the powder, or to reemburse the public with an equal quantity of that article, and that either on the return of his vessel, or at the time that she ought to return.

Your petitioner therefore flatters himself your honourable House will be pleased on these considerations to grant him his request;

And he, as in duty bound, will ever pray.

Isaac Moses

July 27th, 1779.

_____

No. 175   Twenty Thousand Dollars for a Pair of Horses—1779

Philip Minis, the writer of the letter printed below, was the son of Abraham and Abigail Minis, who had landed in Savannah just about five months after General James Oglethorpe's arrival with the first group of colonists. According to a well-authenticated tradition, Philip, born in 1733 or 1734, was the first white native-born child to survive in provincial Georgia. The young Georgian became a merchant and during the early days of the Revolution served as an acting paymaster and commissary general for the Georgia troops.

After the surrender of Savannah to the British in December, 1778, Minis fled and sought refuge in Charlestown, South Carolina. From the vantage point of that haven he corresponded and did business with former Governor John Houstoun, of Georgia, a delegate to the Continental Congress. Houstoun was then staying at Round O, a town about forty miles northwest of Charleston, South Carolina.

The large sums mentioned in this letter, in business deals of no great magnitude, portray only too eloquently the inroads that inflation had already made. American Whig currency, whether state or Continental, was worth little.

SOURCE. American Jewish Archives, Minis Papers.

Honorable John Houstoun, Esq.
Favor of Mr. Jennet,
At Round O.
Dear Sir:

I am sorry that I coud not have sent the [five] Negroes to the vendue [auction], as the weather was very bad the next day after they came, and the holly days [Christmas] has prevented any since. However, I have sold them for £41,666, payable in a month with interest, which hope will meet your approbation.

I have the promise of a schooner to go to the Burrough[s, a town south of Savannah], if I can get a load their (say 100 barrels rice). I have desired Capt. Penang to send your 4 hogsheads tobacco with my 8 barrels.

Mr. Alexander Rose says he wants a pair of good horses but thinks 20,000 dollars is to much. He says he will call next week and see them. If he buys them, Jockey Polock is to have a comission, as he told me of the chap [who had the horses], and I promised it to him.

I am

Your humble servant,
Philip Minis

Charles Town,
31st December, 1779.

No. 176. Phoebe David, a Poor Widow, Seeks Justice from the Governor—1780

The Davids were a well-known Jewish family in Canada. They may have been among the pioneers who entered during the British conquest (1759–60), and the head of the family, the Welsh-born Lazarus David (1734–76), was already doing business as a merchant in Montreal in 1763. Two years earlier, in Rhode Island, he had married Phoebe Samuel (1736–86), who bore him five children, none of whom was over fourteen at the time of their father's death.

Phoebe carried on her deceased husband's business. It was not unusual for a Jewish woman to step into her husband's shoes after his death. A notable illustration of this is Abigail Minis, of Savannah, who successfully ran the family business and reared five daughters and a son after her husband's death.

Occasionally people seek to take advantage of a helpless widow. Phoebe believed that this was the case when she was unable to collect a long-overdue bill for groceries. Accordingly, as we note in the following document, she appealed for justice to General Frederick Haldimand, the governor of Canada.

SOURCE. Public Archives of Canada, Haldimand, B. 217, pp. 125–28.

To His Excellency Frederick Haldimand, Esquire, Captain General and Governor in chief in and over the Province of Quebec, etc., etc., etc.:

The petition of Pheby David, of the city of Montreal, widow, humbly sheweth:

That your petitioner supplied Mr. Deschambeault's house keeper with groceries and other necessaries for his house for a great number of years past, and that he with the greatest punctuality and honor paid the respective accounts as they were delivered in, up to the month of April, 1778;

That from that period [up] to the month of February following, the same house keeper run up another account in your petitioner's shop for groceries for the use of Mr. Deschambeault's house as before, amounting to the sum of thirty seven pounds, five shillings, and fourpence currency, which he now refuses paying under the frivolous though specious pretext of having quarelled with his house keeper;

That your petitioner, having been left a widow with five children, no inconsiderable family to maintain out of the profits of a small shop, her only support, prevailed on her to make use of every lenient and soothing method that could be suggested to her to induce Mr. Deschambeault to pay this account, all of which proved ineffectual;

That the wrong she would have done her children and herself by relinquishing the just claim to so considerable a sum of money obliged her, however reluctantly, to assert in a public manner her right, and for that purpose she commenced an action in the Court of Common Pleas for this district, against Mr. Deschambeault for the amount of her account, with the flattering hopes of obtaining that right (her only request) from a court of justice, which she has every reason to conceive is with held from her by Mr. Deschambeault more by the evil counsel that has been given him than through the dictates of his heart, which ever before she experienced to be honorable;

That unfortunately for your petitioner, upon the hearing of the cause, the two judges, Messrs. [René O. H. de] Rouville and [Edward] Southouse, differed in opinion, by which the determination of the affair was suspended untill the arrival of the Honorable Judge [John] Fraser from England;

That on his arrival, your petitioner's council [counsel] moved for a rehearing of the cause, which was denied by reason of the admirable delicacy of Judge Fraser, who refused hearing the matter on account of his being related to Mr. Deschambeault;

That the cause remains still in this undetermined state, and probably for ever will, unless Your Excellency would be pleased (as in like cases you have already done) to order a commission to issue, authorizing the honorable the judges of the Court of Common Pleas for the district of Quebec to sit in conjunction with the judges of this district, to hear and determine the same;

That from the well-known wisdom and stern integrity of Your Excellency, your petitioner is perfectly convinced that the voice of justice unattended by the prayer of the widow and fatherless would be a sufficient inducement to Your Excellency to the granting of her request, in the full persuasion of which she and her offspring, as in duty bound, will ever pray, etc.

Pheby David

Montreal, 24th February, 1780.

———

No. 177 The Will and Household Inventory of Chapman Abram—1783

Chapman Abram was a well-known Canada merchant and Indian trader identified for years with the outpost of Detroit.

His will (Document A) throws light on his religious and social loyalties, as well as on his relation to his family in Plymouth, England. It is not improbable this his widow Elizabeth became the wife of Moses Myers, the distinguished merchant-shipper of Norfolk.

Document B is a copy of the inventory of Abram's chattels, and may well serve to show what the inside of a merchant's house looked like.

SOURCE. Montreal Old Courthouse, Montreal, Canada; Municipal Records.

A [NO. 177]

In the Name of God, Amen.

I, Chapman Abraham, of the city of Montreal, merchant, being in a weak and low state of body, but of sound and disposing mind and memory, and being desirous to settle my worldly affairs, do make and publish this, my last will and testament, hereby revoking and making void all former wills by me at any time heretofore made.

And first and principaly, I commit and reccommend my soul to God, and my body to the earth, to be decently interred in the burial ground of the Jewish congregation near to the city of Montreal; and I request of my executors hereinafter to be named, that they would invite the bretheren of the Free Mason Lodge of which I am a member, to accompany my body to the grave.

And as to such worldly estate wherewith it has pleased God to entrust me, I dispose of the same as followeth:

Inprimis ["firstly"], my will is that all my just debts shall be first paid by my executors after discharging the expences of my funeral.

Item: My will is that my executors do, as soon as conveniently may be after my decease, pay to my beloved wife Elizabeth, the sum of one thousand pounds, lawful money of the Province of Quebec.

Item: I will and bequeath unto my said wife, the bed, bedstead, curtains, and appurtenances, together with a small table and six chairs, making part of the furniture of her present bed-chamber.

Item: I will and bequeath to my said wife, all my bed and table linnen.

Item: I will and bequeath unto my nephew, Isaac Abraham, of Montreal, all my wearing apparel except my linnen stocking, shoes, and buckles.

Item: I will and bequeath unto Richard Macniel [McNeal] of Montreal, merchant, the sum of fifty pounds, lawful money of the Provience of Quebec, in testimony of my grateful acknowledgement of his kind and friendly attention to me in my weak and low estate.

Item: I will that all my household furniture, books, plate, linnen, and all my moveables, not before especialy bequeathed, be sold to the highest bidder; and the moneys arising therefrom, as well as the moneys due to me, may be disposed of by my executors in trust for the following purposes:

Whereas my wife is now *enceint* ["pregnant"] by me, I do will, give, and bequeath all the residue of my estate so above described unto Richard Macniel and Samuel Judah, of Montreal, merchants, in trust, to be by them employed for the best use and behoof of the child whereof my said wife is now *enceint,* if it should be born with life; and my will is that the interest of the said residue should be added to the principal and be paid to the said child on the day it shall attain the age of twenty one years; and in the event that the said child shall not be born with life, or shall not attain the age of twenty one years, then I give the said residue and interest thereof to my said trustees, to be by them possessed on this farther trust; that is to say, to pay the same in equal portions to my dear brothers, Solomon Abraham and Hart Abraham, of Plimouth, in Great Britain, their executors, administrators, or assigns.

And for the due execution of this, my last will and testament, I do appoint Richard Macniel and Samuel Judah, of Montreal, merchants, to be my executors, with full power to do all lawful acts tending thereto.

In witness whereof, I have, to this my last will and testament, subscribed my name and affixed my seal, declaring and publishing this to be my last will and testament, at Montreal, in the Province of Quebec, the tenth day of March, in the year of the world, five thousand seven hundred and eighty seven [*sic!* It should be 5543].

Kaufman Abram [in Hebrew script]

Signed, sealed, published, and declared by Chapman Abraham, the above named testator, as and for his last will and testament before us, who, at his request, in his presence, and in the presence of each other, have subscribed our names as witnesses thereto.

I. W. Kenney, N. Bayard, Wm. Dummer Powel

B [NO. 177]

10th April, 1783.

Inventory of sundries, the goods and chattels, belonging to the estate of Chapman Abrams, late of the city of Montreal, in the Province of Quebec, merchant, deceased, made and taken at the request of Richard McNeal and Samuel Judah, of the same place, merchants, testamentary executors named in the last will and testament of the said late Chapman Abrams, made at Montreal aforesaid, dated the tenth of March, one thousand seven hundred and eighty three. This inventory made and taken by me, John Gerbrand Beek, of the said city and district of Montreal, notary and tabellion [scrivener] public, being thereunto lawfully authorised, sworn, and admitted, in the presence of the said Richard McNeal and Samuel Judah, as follows:

In the parlor:

One oval looking glass, gild frame
One pair window curtains, compleat to draw up, cords, tassels, and four
  brass screws
One large walnut dining table
Six common painted chairs
One pair andirons with brass knobs
One four post bedsted
One traveling bodet [bidet? bath]
Five Hebrew books

In the hall:

One oval looking glass with gild frame
One pair window curtains, compleat to draw up, cords, tassels, and four
  brass screws
Two mahogany chairs
Six common chairs
One large walnut dinning table
One small pine table
One Japaned oval tea tray
One pair large andirons, brass fender, shovel, and tongs
Twelve cups and ten saucers, blue china
Six silver table spoons

Five silver tea spoons and one pair silver sugar tongs
One tea pott, sugar dish, and creamer, black ware
Twelve green handle knives and twelve ditto forks with silver ferrel [ferrule]
One slop bason and milk pott, china
One feather bed and bolster
One ditto bolster and pillow
One mahogany old shaving box, one rasor strap, with two basons, and old shaving box
Four fine cutt salts with three pearl spoons
One large china bowl
Two cutt decanters
Two water bottles
One dozen wine glasses
Five tumblers
One pewter inkstand
One Japaned water
One pair new boots
Twenty four men's shirts, good and bad
Thirteen pair silk hose, do. " do
Four pair thread do. " "
Five pair worsted do.
One pair shoe and one pair knee buckles, silver
One tin tea canister
One fowling piece

In the kitchin:

One wooden dresser
Twenty three queens ware [cream-colored Wedgewood] flat plates

Twelve	ditto	soup ditto
Six	ditto	sorted dishes
One	ditto	fish plate
Twelve	ditto	dessert do.

One china soup tureen and dish
Two butter tureens, queens ware
One Japaned bread basket
Two pair metal candlesticks
One Japaned gallon jugg
Two frying pans
One gridiron
Two copper sauce pans
One iron pott
Four smoothing irons

One pair kitchin tongs and shovel
One water bucket
Three washing tubs
One brass teaketle
One pewter collender
One pair snuffers
One dozen common knives and forks
One double iron stove pipe and stone [stove?]

In the yard:

One high runner cariole [sleigh], cushions and harness
One cow
Three milk pans
One roasting jack
Seven blankets
Three good sails and one bad one
Four tin kettles and two soups
Four parcels roap [rope]
One market basket

Thus done and inventorised at Montreal aforesaid, in the house of Joseph Perrinault, lately occupied by the deceased Chapman Abrams, in St. Francis Street, this tenth day of April, one thousand seven hundred and eighty three; and did the said executors promise, as they do hereby, that if anything should come to their knowledge wherewith this inventory ought to be augmented or deminished, they will give due notice thereof where it doth belong.

And after being duly read, have thereunto sett their names with the aforesaid notary,

Richard McNeall, Samuel Judah

J. G. Beek, notary public.

No. 178   London Merchants Solicit American Business After the Revolution—1783

The Revolutionary War, as might be expected, disrupted trade between England and her North American colonies. To be sure, the merchants on both sides of the ocean engaged in clandestine trade, but the British blockade and American privateers made such commerce hazardous. As soon as the preliminary treaty of peace between the United States and Britain had been signed in 1782, the English merchants naturally sought to resume their relations with prospective American customers.

The following letter, a printed circular, is the attempt of a London agent to induce Aaron Lopez to do business with an Anglo-Spanish firm in Cadiz. Lopez, of course, would have been a choice customer. Unfortunately for the writer, however, the Newport shipper had died by drowning in May, 1782.

SOURCE. Newport Historical Society Library, Lopez Letters.

London, 17 March, 1783.

Sir:

Permit me to congratulate you on the return of peace and the honourable manner in which it has been settled for your states, the happy results of which will, I hope, be productive of every satisfaction to you and your connexions.

As your trade to Spain henceforward will naturally become much more extensive, may I take the liberty of making you a tender of the services of my house of Butlers and Mathew in Cadiz, well known on your continent from their numerous connexions for many years past, and particularly during the late troubles. I can venture to assure you, they will transact your business on the most favourable terms, and pay every attention to promote your interest and encourage your correspondence.

At foot you will find a note of some of their principal friends here, connected with your continent, who will readily give you any information you may require concerning them.

I propose going to Cadiz soon, and from thence shall, under the firm [official signature] of the house, take the liberty of handing you a price current [price list] of our imports and exports, for your government [guidance].

I am, with greatest regard, sir,

Your most obedient servant,
Patrick Kincaid

Messrs. Berwickes and Mourgue;
Lane, Son, and Fraser;
Champion, Dickason, & Co.;
Kirkpatrick, Escott, Reed, & Co.

No. 179   An Army Supplyman Tries to Collect a Bill from an Officer—1783

When the Hessians came to America with the British troops during the Revolution, they brought their own sutlers with them. Some of them were Jews, including Alexander Zuntz, a commissary and agent for the general staff.

Zuntz, a native of Westphalia, arrived in 1779 and soon married the twenty-three-year-old daughter of Abraham I. Abrahams, a well-known merchant and religious functionary in the New York congregation. The fact that Zuntz, then thirty-seven, married here would seem to indicate that he liked the looks of the country and intended to remain in America.

During the war Zuntz not only served the German mercenaries in New York, but also opened a store on his own account. In his later years he manufactured starch and hair powder and, when that enterprise failed, became a broker.

An observant Jew, Zuntz helped to keep Congregation Shearith Israel alive, in spite of the fact that the majority of its members were Whigs who fled New York on the approach of the British forces. After the war the erstwhile sutler remained in the city and was cordially accepted by the returning Jews. He was obviously a fine person who had no difficulty in gaining the respect of the Jewish community, which documented its confidence in him by thrice electing him president during the 1790's.

In July, 1783, some of the officers of the British occupation forces were preparing to return to Europe without paying their bills. Zuntz, naturally enough, wanted his accounts settled at once and, as we see in the following letter, appealed to General Sir Guy Carleton for aid in recovering what one of the departing officers owed him.

SOURCE. Colonial Williamsburg, The British Headquarters [Carleton] Papers.

To His Excellency, Sir Guy Carleton, K. B. [Knight of the Bath], General and Commander in Chief, etc., etc., etc.:

Alexander Zuntz, of the city of New York, begs leave most humbly to represent,

That Lieut. Conrady, of the Hanau Free Corps, is indebted to him in the sum of £12 19s. 9d.;

That the said corps is soon about to embark for Europe;

That he has made application to his Excellency, Lieut. Gen. Losberg, to order payment of the said sum, who informed your memorialist that, with respect to such office[r]s as belonged to this corps, application must be made to Your Excellency.

Your memorialist therefore most humbly prays that Your Excellency will be pleased to order that Lieut. Conrady pay to him the amount of his demand which he acknowledges to be just, or give such order, relative to stopping his pay for that purpose, as to Your Excellency shall seem meet.

And, as in duty bound, shall ever pray.

Alexander Zuntz

New York, 7th July, 1783.

———

No. 180   Isaac DaCosta, Jr., Notifies Michael Gratz About Some Defaulting Debtors—1784

During the Revolutionary period two Isaac DaCostas lived in Charleston, South Carolina. The elder, a well-known merchant and ardent patriot, died in 1783. His widow Sarah Pimenta DaCosta is mentioned in the postscript of the following letter. Her husband's nephew, Isaac DaCosta, Jr. (1746–1809), also was a merchant but, as far as we can determine, left no impress on the local Jewish community. Like his uncle, the young man spent some time in Philadelphia during the war and was among the émigrés who joined Mikveh Israel in that city.

By February, 1784, Isaac DaCosta, Jr., was back in Charleston, writing thank-you notes to his friend Michael Gratz. The latter had asked the Charlestonian to inquire into the financial status of a Mr. Braidford and of William Kelsall & Co., who had signed some bills of exchange in the possession of the Gratzes.

Businessmen frequently accorded social courtesies to visitors from other places and did not hesitate to ask their friends for advice on such matters as prevailing prices and defaulting debtors. Whether the admixture of the amenities and the mutual interchange of commercial data were more prevalent among Jews in relation to one another than among non-Jews in their own circles is difficult to determine.

SOURCE. The Historical Society of Pennsylvania, Etting Papers.

Charleston, 2d February, 1784.

Mr. Michael Gratz, Merchant,
Per Capt. Allebone,
Philadelphia.

Dear Sir:

I have the pleasure of informing you that I arrived safe, after a passage of nine days, but in a poor state of health. Permit me to return you and your good spouse my most cordial thanks for your great attention while in Philadelphia, and shall be happy to have it in my power to render you or yours every service in my power.

Agreable to promise, have made every inquiry respecting the drawer and indorsers of the two protested bills of exchange, and sorry I am to add that, from the minutest inquiry, Braidford has no property in this country, and that he only came out here as an agent for a number of gentlemen who possessed a large quantity of land in this state. It therefore will require a stricter inquiry, which I shall fully do after my arrival from Savannah, Georgia, where I am going after a very great villian, who has taken me in for a very large sum. It's in that state I shall get information respecting William Kelsall & Co.; and on my return, shall inform you with my success. No effort shall be wanting on my part to procure information and, if possible, satisfaction.

Please make my most respectfull compliments to Mr. Barnet Gratz and his vaulable [valuable?] daughter, Miss Ratchel, and your worthy spouse and dear children, and am, with respect, dear sir,

Your obedient and very humble servant,

Isaac Da Costa

P.S. My aunt, Mrs. Sarah DaCosta, and sons begs to be remembered to you, Mrs. Gratz, and to every branch of your esteemed family.

No. 181   Joseph Lopez Returns from London with Assorted Goods—1784

Expecting a choice assortment of spring goods, the Providence firm of Brown & Benson, in a letter of March, 1784, solicited the patronage of the Newport merchants, including Jacob Rodriguez Rivera (Document A). In his answer, printed below, Rivera informed the Providence house that he himself expected a shipment of goods, and that Joseph Lopez (1754–1822), the son of Aaron Lopez, would not be in the market for anything, since he was in London making purchases (Document B).

Merchants in the colonial and early national periods bought their stocks wherever they could, from American jobbers or from London commission houses (through resident buyers) or wholesalers. Occasionally an American went to England to bring back a bride, to see his family, to settle an estate, or to fight a case before the Privy Council, etc., and on his return brought back goods for his shop. It is doubtful whether any American Jewish merchants went abroad solely for the purpose of buying goods.

SOURCE. The John Carter Brown Library, Brown Papers.

A [NO. 181]

Providence, March 22d, 1784.

We expect, in the first arrival from London, a very large and well chosen assortment of spring goods, with which we shall be happy to supply you on as good terms as any importer in the state. We shall deem ourselves [grateful?] for the preferences you may give us, and are, with due esteem,

Your obedient friends,
B. & B.

Coppy to:
Jacob Rodrigues Rivera
Moses Seixas
Thomas Green
Walter Easton
Simeon Martin
Nathan Bebee
} Newport

B [NO. 181]

Newport, March 28th, 1784.

Messrs. Brown & Benson.
My dear Gentlemen:

I thank you very sincerly for your kind favour of the 22d current, which I have now in hand, and for the kind offer it contains of supplying me, from the general and large assortment of goods you expect this spring, with any I may have occasion for, on as good terms as any importer in this state, which [I] should certainly accept, as I wish (from a great inclination I have) to give your new house the prefference of any I know. But I expect myself a general and well assorted cargo by first ships, which will prevent my gratifying, for the present, with your request. But whenever occasion requires it, you need not doubt of my first applicacion.

I have also delivered your message to Mrs. Lopez, who desires I woud inform you with her thanks, that as Mr. Joseph Lopez is now in London, and expected this spring, she expects he will supply the shop from the goods he may bring.

With sentiments of true esteem and respect, and offers of my best services, I very sincerly am, dear gentlemen,

Your friend and humble servant,
Jacob Rodrigues Rivera

No. 182   Daniel Boone Writes to Cohen & Isaacs About Their Kentucky Lands—1784

The largest Jewish mercantile house in Richmond, Virginia, during the Revolutionary period was that of Cohen & Isaacs. Isaiah Isaacs (1747–1806), a silversmith, came to Virginia about 1769, and probably was the first Jew to settle permanently in the Old Dominion. For a while he lived in Charlottesville, but most of his time was spent in Richmond, where he entered local politics and in 1785 was appointed Clerk of the Market.

Jacob I. Cohen, a German Jew, arrived in Pennsylvania in the early 1770's. For a while he traded with the Indians. During the Revolution he joined the army, and finally settled in Richmond, entering into partnership with Isaiah Isaacs in or before 1781.

Firms such as Cohen & Isaacs speculated extensively in land warrants, usually military bounties, which were picked up for cash or goods. In 1781 the firm was already doing business with Daniel Boone of Kentucky. Document A is a brief note by Boone, acknowledging receipt of warrants for 10,000 acres of land which he was to survey. Document B is a letter by Boone, written in 1784, informing the partners that he had located some land for them on the Licking River in Kentucky, and asking them for payment for services rendered.

SOURCE. Document A: The Library of Congress, Division of Manuscripts; Document B: Historical Society of Pennsylvania, Simon Gratz Collection.

A [NO. 182]

Desember the 24, 1781.

Received of Jacub Cohan 12 warrants consising of 5,000 akers of Land and the same for Iasiah Isec, and six pound specia, for which I promis to locate the said lands on as good as the cuntry will admit of.

Gevn under my hand this 24 day of Desember, 1781.

Daniel Boone

B [NO. 182]

Aprael the 28, 1784.

Mr. Jacob Cohons,
Merchant in Richmond.
(Favored by Mr. Grant.)
Sir:

No doubt you are desireous your land bisniss should be dunn but that is a thing inposible without money, and yours and Mr. Isaacs' will amount to a smart sum: 24 warrants (1 [s.] 3 [d.] pur warrant) [totaling] £1 10s. 0 d., and enterry [entry fee] 2[s.] 6[d.] and copys 2[s.] 6[d.]. The hole [whole] amounts to [£]1 15 0[d.] shilings. This sum I advanced the minet I made the enterrys [entries] which you will pleas to rayimburs. Survayors' fees [£]10 0[s.] 6[d.], registers' fees [£]3 15[s.] 1 2/2[d.], returning the 2 plots to Marekell's ofis [office] 7[s.] 2/2[d.], cha[i]n men and markers £6 0 s. 0 d., finding purvistions [provisions] for this bisness £1 0 s. 0 d. pound.

Now, sir, you will pleas to show this bill to Col. Henry or Capt. Chapmon Auston [Austin], who has ben out here a survaying, and see if I am right or not and send the money by the first opertunety.

Mr. Samuel Grant, my sister's sun, will lykly hand you this later [letter]. If so, he will be a good hand to send by, and I will bee acountable for any money put into his hands inless kild by the Indins. The hole [whole] a mount, I think, is £22 10s. 8d. 2/2.

Your land lyes on Lickeng Rever, on the south side, a bout 50 milds from the Ohigho [River] by water, and a bout 20 by land. Large bouts [boats] may come up to your doore.

I am, sir, your most obedent, omble sarvent,

Daniel Boone

N.B. Sir: Pleas send me 3 or 4 quire of paper by the bearer, Samuel Grant, if he will bring it. D.B.

———

No. 183   Finances and Banking—1784–1796

The postwar period presented the newly independent nation with a host of economic problems. Until the adoption of the Federal Constitution and of the fiscal program of Alexander Hamilton, there was considerable economic uncertainty and distress, accompanied by extensive speculation in stocks, loan certificates, and the like. Business failures were relatively frequent. In the years between 1787 and 1791 over 300 Philadelphia merchants became insolvent, among them four Jews.

Document A, printed below, reflects this period of uncertainty and fear: Joseph Nourse, the Register of the United States Treasury, writing from Annapolis, the temporary capital of the country, sought to withdraw the funds he had on deposit or on loan with Haym Salomon, the Philadelphia broker. Nourse's correspondent, James Milligan, the Comptroller of the United States Treasury, had once been a partner of the Lancaster merchant, Joseph Simon, in the fur trade at Fort Pitt.

Brokers such as Haym Salomon, who served also as moneylenders and bankers, now appear on the scene. We know of at least seven Philadelphia Jews who were in that business in the 1780's.

Among the businessmen conscious of the changes in the financial world was the Newport merchant and Mason, Moses Seixas (1744– 1809). When the Bank of Rhode Island was established in 1795, Seixas was appointed cashier, a position he retained until his death. The bank was located in his home, where Seixas as cashier and his son as teller transacted business five days a week. On the Sabbath, when neither of them worked, they gave the keys to a Gentile boy, who in turn handed them to a Gentile clerk. For his labors the boy was rewarded with some unleavened bread on Passover and "Haman's ears" (bonbons in this case) on Purim.

Document B, a brief and formal note from Cashier Seixas to Brown, Benson, and Ives, of Providence, although of no importance in its contents, is significant because it testifies to the presence of Jewish businessmen in this country in the field of commercial banking in the late eighteenth century. After the Revolution, more and more firms, such as banks, insurance, turnpike companies, and the like, organized as corporations whose securities appeared on the market. Some towns even showed the first signs of the beginning of the factory system. These were the first faint intimations of the Industrial Revolution in the United States.

The new departures in finance, commerce, and industry are foreshadowed faintly in the activity of Haym Salomon in Philadelphia, Moses Seixas in Newport, and others.

SOURCE. Document A: Bendiner Collection of Milligan Papers, Philadelphia; Document B: The John Carter Brown Library, Brown Papers.

A [NO. 183]

Annapolis, 24th December, 1784.

Dear Sir:

Since writing the letter that will be delivered you herewith, I have seen Quaker Brown of Philadelphia, who acquaints us that Mr. [George?] Meade hath failed, and that some Jew brokers have also broke, that people appear dubious and look strange at each other.

It therefore seems a matter of prudence that I owe my family to withdraw what money I have in Mr. Salomon's hands. For this purpose, I enclose a draft on him at three days sight in your favor for nine hundred and forty dollars, accompanied with a letter of advice. This money I request the favour of you to lodge with your own in the Bank [of North America].

I do not imagine that any difficulty will attend the payment from the want of Mr. Salomon's promisory note to me for sixteen hundred dollars, but should any appear, my brother John can open my trunk and take it out, it being in my bank book together with a note of Isaac Franks for five hundred dollars at 90 days sight. Mr. Jenefer [Jenifer], I understand, purposes to decline [to meet his obligations?].

I hope, sir, you will excuse the trouble I give you. If I know myself, I should be happy in the opportunity of making a suitable return for this and other favors conferred on, sir, with great regard,

Your most obedient friend and humble servant,
Joseph Nourse

James Milligan, Esq.

B [NO. 183]

Bank of Rhode Island, December 26th, 1796.

Gentlemen :

Inclosed you have the certificates for the 10 shares in the stock of this bank, standing in the name of Brown, Benson, & Ives. Transfering cannot be done until after the 2d of next month, and then either personally in [the] bank or by virtue of a power [of attorney], similar to that which is required at the Bank of the United States.

I am very respectfully, gentlemen,

Your most humble servant,
M. Seixas, cashier

Messrs. Brown & Ives

No. 184 Bernard Hart Leases a House in Montreal—1785

Bernard Hart (1764–1855), of Bavarian ancestry, was born in London. He came to America when he was about thirteen years of age and for many years transacted business in Canada. There, in 1799, he married Catherine Brett. Their grandson was Bret Harte, the American writer.

Later Hart settled permanently in New York City, where he became an important figure on the Stock Exchange. He was also one of the pillars of Congregation Shearith Israel.

In the following document Hart leased a building for a year. The vaults described were used either for sales purposes or for storage. Solomon Mittleberger, the lessor, was not a Jew.

SOURCE. Montreal Old Courthouse, Municipal Records.

13th April, 1785.

On this thirteenth day of April, in the year of our Lord one thousand seven hundred and eighty five, before me, John Gerbrand Beek, notary public, dwelling in the city of Montreal, in the Province of Quebec, by lawfull authority admitted and sworn, and in presence of the underwritten witnesses, personally came and appeared Mr. Solomon Mittleberger of the said city, baker, who declared that for and in consideration of the yearly rent and covenants herein mentioned and reserved, hath demised, granted site, and to farm lete [farm let], and by these presents doth demise, grant site, and to farm lete unto Mr. Barnard Hart, of the same place, merchant, also present, and accepting all that part of his house and tenement [near?] the market place in the said city of Montreal, as was formerly occupied by Christy Cramer of said city of Montreal, merchant, containing four appartements on the first floor, and the same number of appartements on the second floor, with the vaults underneath, and garret above said appartements, as also one vaulted passage or gateway under said house;

To have and to hold the said appartements, vaults, and garrets, and half passage herein before mentioned, as heretofore occupied by the said Christy Cramer, unto the said Barnard Hart, his executors, and administrators, from the first day of May next, for and during the term of one year thence next ensuing, and fully to be complete and ended, he, the said Bernard Hart, his executors and administrators yealding and paying therefore, during the said term, the yearly rent or sum of eighty three pounds, six shillings, and eight pence, Quebec currency, by even and equal quarterly payments, that is to say, a quarter rent at the expiration of every three months to be paid unto the said Solomon Mittleberger, his heirs, executors, administrators, and assignes, during the said term; which said sum of eighty three pounds, six shillings, and eight pence currency aforesaid, he, the said Bernard Hart, promised and obliged himself, his heirs, and assigns to pay or cause to be paid unto the said Solomon Mittleberger, his heirs and assigns, in manner and at the time herein prefixed;

And it is particularly agreed upon that the said Bernard Hart shall not lete [let] the said house to any tavern keeper whatever, all or any part of the term of one year, without licence and consent in writing first had and obtained for that purpose;

And at the expiration of the said term, he, the said Bernard Hart, shall peaceably and quietly yield up and return the said premises in the like order as when he received them in his possession, which will be on the first day of May, one thousand seven [hundred] and eighty six;

And he, the said Solomon Mittleberger, doth hereby for himself, his heirs, and assignes promise and agree that the said Bernard Hart, his executors and administrators, paying the yearly rent aforesaid, and performing the covenants herein before mentioned, may peaceably and quietly have, hold, and enjoy the said appartements, vaults, garret, and premisses, as herein before mentioned.

Thus done at Montreal aforesaid, the day, month, and year first above written, in the office of the underwritten notary, in the presence of Samuel Burch and David Lukin as witnesses, and signed by the said parties, notary, and witnesses, after being duly read.

David Lukin   Solomon Mittleberger
Samuel Burch   Bernard Hart
                 J. G. Beek, Notary Public

No. 185   Jacob Rodriguez Rivera Writes to the Captain of One of His Slave Ships—1785

Jacob Rodriguez Rivera and his son-in-law Aaron Lopez, who died in 1782, were active in the slave trade. Ever since 1764, if not earlier, Lopez and Rivera sent their ships to the coast of Africa to trade in human chattels. From that time, until about 1775, the partners nearly always had at least one ship engaged in the trade, and in 1772 and 1773 Lopez dispatched four slavers to Africa. Rivera may have been his partner in these ventures.

The letter printed below was sent by Rivera to Captain Nathaniel Briggs, who was then on the African coast, picking up a cargo of Negroes. The captain had been working for Lopez and Rivera since at least 1765. In 1789, several years after the enactment of a Massachusetts statute against the slave trade, Briggs became the defendant in an action instituted against him for running a cargo of slaves into the West Indian island of Martinique. His flight to another state, however, put an end to the prosecution.

The letter was sent to Africa through the courtesy of Captain James Duncan (Jr.?), who was there on the same business. Its primary purpose was to warn Briggs to stay away from the French island of Saint Lucia, whose officials were confiscating vessels that had entered without proper authorization.

The postscript (in the handwriting of Moses Seixas) listed the ships that were soon to sail for the African slave coast.

Note the pious wish at the end of the letter: "God bless you."

SOURCE. Yale University Library.

Newport, Sept. 13th, 1785.

Capt. Nathaniel Briggs.

Sir:

We hope that when Capt. Duncan arrives on the coast, [he] will find you safe arrived and as forward in your trade as you had reason to expect from the prospect we were flattered with at your departure, and [we hope that] at the end, your voyage may in every respect answer our most sanguine expectations.

We have now the pleasure to inform you that, three days after your departure, we had the agreeable news that Capt. Sherman [Ebenezer Shearman?], in our brigantine *Betsey*, had stopt at Eustatious [West Indies] from the coast, and not having met a market for his slaves there, had proceeded to South Carolina, where we have since received advice of his safe arrival there, and carried in 140 very good slaves for cargoe, 133 of which Mr. Russel (on whom he valued himself) had disposed and avaraged £53 sterling a head. (The remaining 7 were ruffage; their fate we have not yett heard.) But [he] was obliged, in order to obtain that price, to take bonds for the whole, one half payable in 1786, and the other 1787. And, Mr. Russel assures us, it's in safe hands and does not expects there will be any bad debts. We are daily expecting him [Sherman] home, and hope [he] will arrive before Duncan sails.

It's not very agreeable to have a vessell come home without as much as will pay her portage bill, but hope [that] when we receive the proceeds, it will leave us a very handsom proffit. As Champlin arrived there [in Africa] so much earlier in the season then [than] he [Sherman], [Champlin] was able to obtain a better price and shorter credit. Our brigantine, being already fitted with Guinea stores, and may be fitted out for the same voyage with little expence. We propose to fitt her out for the coast as soon as she arrives with all posible dispatch. By that time, we hope, you'll have left the coast with good success.

Capt. Sherman wrote us that he had called at St. Lucea to try the markets, but was informed by our friends there that several vessell[s] had been seized there and in several other islands for comming into port without first obtaining permission, and advised him immediately to goe away, to prevent his sharing the same fate. And Capt. Sherman advises us that, if we had any vessells on the [African] coast, to inform them of this, that they may act with great caution in calling at any of the West India Island[s], which we think proper to inform you for your government [guidance].

We have nothing further at present to add, save that your family, we understand, are well, and so is all ours, who join in our kind respects to you, and are

Your friends and owners,
Jacob Rodrigues Rivera & Co.

The following vessells, it is said, are intended for the coast, but none have as yet begun to fitt [be outfitted], but make no doubt will, and sail in a month or 8 weeks:

Capt. Wolf in a brigantine belonging to Cook and Lassells.

Capt. Benj. Hicks in a brigantine belonging to Providence, owned by Sterry & Co.

Capt. Peleg Clark says he is determined to go. Has his rum in the stills, but no vessell yet.

Capt. Sherman in our brigantine, *Betsey.*

Caleb Gardner talks of sending his brigantine when she gets home from Copenhagen. No news as yet of Daniel Gardner's arrival in the West Indies.

Col. Cook's sloop, *Borden Mart,* arrived last Saturday. The molasses all gone in the distill house. Wood is got home and brought the pay for Lassell's bill. Taggart [is] daily expected, when we are promised a few hogsheads molasses.

We have got your [insurance] policy reduced to £675 LMY, taking in the notes you gave for the premium and gave our own on interest. The inclosed paper we forgot to give you. Don't fail writing by all opportunity and let us know how the ship proves. God bless you.

No. 186.   Commercial Chaos in the Post-Revolutionary
Period—1786

During the years before the federal constitution went into effect and when the Articles of Confederation were still in force (1781–89), each state exercised a great deal of autonomy in matters of foreign and domestic commerce. Some of the states had their own tariff regulations and engaged in mutually retaliatory commercial warfare. In September, 1786, a convention met in Annapolis to consider the problems of interstate commerce. Out of this meeting grew the Constitutional Convention of 1787.

The following petition reflects the dissensions then existing among the thirteen states. Moses Homberg, a merchant of Philadelphia and New York, received in Philadelphia a shipment sent from New York destined for Baltimore. The goods were being held in the Quaker

City and, before they could be shipped on to Baltimore, Homberg had to secure the permission of the highest Pennsylvania authorities. Almost exactly a year later Philadelphia newspapers carried the information that Homberg was bankrupt.

SOURCE. Pennsylvania Historical and Museum Commission, P.R.P. XXVI, 33, 2.

To His Excellency the President and the Honorable the Vice President of the Supreme Executive Council of the State of Pennsylvania:

The humble remonstrance of Moses Homberg, merchant, of the city of Philadelphia, most respectfully sheweth:

That, in the beginning of this present month of March, there arrived into this port from the city of New-York six barrels of merchandize, consigned to your remonstrant and destined for the port of Baltimore, under his firm [name]; but he, the said Moses Homberg, not then being in this city, on account of urgent business which occasioned his presence abroad, his friend, Mr. Moses D. Nathan, broker and merchant of this city, entered into bond at the Custom House for this port, agreeable to law, for said goods, during the absence of Your Honours' remonstrant;

And as soon as Your Honors' remonstrant returned again, his friend, Mr. Moses D. Nathan, informed him, with his agency, respecting this matter, who immediately made all diligent enquiry for an opportunity [to] send off said goods to the destined port of Baltimore, but could meet with none since for near three weeks past, except a present one, and that is only a sloop called the *Dove* (Alexander Graves, master), bound for Christeen [Christiana, Delaware], where said goods from there may be sent off for Baltimore.

Therefore, your humble remonstrant requests of this honorable board the favor that by them leave may be granted him to send off by said sloop *Dove* the aforesaid goods unto Christeen, without incumbrance, in order that the same may be from thence transported to the port of Baltimore.

And Your Honors' humble remonstrant shall ever pray, etc.

Moses Homberg

Philadelphia, March 17, 1786.

No. 187   A Petition to Congress to Confirm Title to Land
Purchased from the Indians—1787

The question of titles to lands was a complicated one. As a rule, purchasers were expected to receive some sort of title from the Indians and then to obtain confirmation from the colonial or state authorities. Even in colonial times individuals were not encouraged to buy land directly from the Indians.

In the following petition two men who had already purchased land derived from Indian title turned to Congress for confirmation of their claim. One of the petitioners, Samuel Judah (1725–89), was a member of the Hart and Judah clan of Canada; his partner Isaac Melcher was not a Jew. Samuel Judah, a Montreal merchant, made occasional business trips to Detroit during and after the Revolutionary War. His grandson of the same name, a Vincennes lawyer, was speaker of the Indiana House of Representatives in 1840.

SOURCE. The Library of Congress, Division of Manuscripts, Papers of the Continental Congress, 41, VI, 481–82.

To the Honorable the Representatives of the United States in Congress assembled. The memorial of the subscribers humbly sheweth:

That the principal chiefs and leaders of the Pottawatamy nation of Indians, at Detroit, for themselves and the whole of the said nation, on the 23th day of September, 1780, conveyed unto Thomas Finchly of Detroit, merchant, a tract of land discribed in the conveyance (a copy of which is hereunto annexed, and the original ready to be produced), beginning at Swan Creek, a river running thence along the banks of Lake Erie to a little river or creek called Stroney Creek, one hundred and fifty acres in depth;

That your memorialists are now the proprietors thereof; and that by the late treaty [of Paris, 1783], concluded between the United States of America and the King [George III] of Great Britain, the aforesaid tract of land is included in the territory ceded to the United States.

Your memorialists have no doubt of the justice of their claim; but ever disposed to acquiesce in the just arrangements of Congress (whose measures we have always aided), humbly pray that the Honorable the Congress will confirm unto your memorialists the aforesaid tract of land, by such ways and means as you may direct, upon your memorialists' paying a reasonable compensation for the confirmation of the grant thereof.

And your memorialists, as in duty bound, etc.

Isaac Melcher, for himself and Samuel Judah

New York, March 29th, 1787.

————

No. 188   Trade with Prussia—1787

As early as 1756, Frederick II, King of Prussia, entertained the idea of bartering American tobacco for Prussian textiles. In 1783, when it was obvious that Great Britain would recognize the new United States, the Prussians began to negotiate a commercial treaty with the Americans. They were no longer afraid of British reprisals. In the same year the famous Jewish magician, Jacob Philadelphia, tried to interest the Prussians in establishing a trading company that would exchange American hides, furs, and tobacco for German textiles, ironware, dyes, porcelain, and glassware. Nothing came of that proposal (Jacob R. Marcus, *Early American Jewry*, II, 85–90). Finally a treaty of commerce and amity with Prussia was ratified by Congress in May, 1786.

In the spring of 1787, Posen-born Judah Moses, a Richmond merchant, approached the office of commerce and manufactures of the Royal Prussian Department of Finance, War, and Interior *(General Direktorium)* in Berlin with an offer: he asked for permission to barter American raw materials, primarily tobacco, for German manufactures: textiles, hardware, and porcelain. It was his hope that he would be allowed to establish a factor's office in Stettin, Pomerania, where he himself would be stationed; his children in the United States would handle the other end of the business.

His proposals, made in writing, were subjected to an analysis by competent German civil servants in the Department of Commerce and Manufactures. (Marginal notes made by one or both of the rapporteurs are enclosed in parentheses, but not all such glosses are included in this translation.) On the whole, as we see in the subjoined report the two experts made to their superiors, they were favorably inclined to Moses' project. Unfortunately, we do not know whether this scheme to further trade between the two countries was ever implemented.

Judah Moses' plans are interesting in that they reflect the enterprising spirit of an American merchant eager to take advantage of the new trade treaty. It is a striking commentary on the difference between Prussia and the United States that the laws and privileges of Stettin permitted its citizenry to exclude Jews from their midst. Prussia was still rooted in medievalism. It was not until 1871 that the Jews of the German Empire were finally emancipated. As early as 1787 Judah Moses, an American, had insisted that he be given equal rights in Prussia with Christians. As a citizen of the world's newest and largest republic, he was well aware that his country was open for settlement to all men, irrespective of creed.

SOURCE. Ehemaliges Preussisches Geheim Staatsarchiv, heute

Deutsches Zentralarchiv, Abteilung Merseburg, Generaldirektorium, Manufactur- und Kommerzienkollegium, Kommerziensachen, Generalia, Titel XIX, Nr. 1.

Documents of the Department of Commerce in matters pertaining to the American Jewish merchant, Judah Moses, concerning the establishment of a reciprocal direct agreement between the Prussian and American States.

A general royal and honorable committee of the *General Direktorium* dealing with industry and trade, as well as excise and customs, has referred to us [the undersigned officials] an application of the American merchant Judah Moses, and has asked us for our opinion concerning the plans of the petitioner, who wishes to establish himself in our country and to develop a reciprocal direct exchange of American products for our manufactured goods. We have discussed the matter on the basis of the original documents of the committee, consisting of fifteen pages, and are not amiss obediently to present them to you together with the original application of the petitioner, which was handed to us on condition that we return it.

The reason for his proposition, so he states, p. 13 of the committee's documents, is the fact that he had an opportunity to buy up, little by little, a tract of land which had originally been given to the officers and men of the united (Continental) army in lieu of pay, and who, as the result of the actual surveying and distribution, was later allotted the advantageous location along the Ohio in Virginia. The land itself, however, had always been a dead investment for him because Congress had made the reservation that his shares of land were to be offered for sale before anybody else's. The only way to make immediate and profitable use of his investments was to make a deal with a planter, exchanging the whole tract of land for agricultural products instead of for cash. The result, however, was the same, for the agricultural products were of as little use to him as the land itself. He, therefore, was compelled to find a way to dispose of these products at a profit. In England he found that trading companies had a monopoly in these very products; France and Denmark supplied their needs from their own colonies; in Holland and Hamburg the competition was too great. For these reasons he has come here, where as yet no restrictions and prohibitions limit the freedom of trade in American products, intending to establish himself in the Prussian states in order to set up a reciprocal direct commercial exchange of overseas products for our domestic manufactures.

It is his present plan, according to his own documentary depositions, pp. 2–3 of the committee's documents, and a later supplement, submitted by him, p. 15, to take up residence in Stettin, together with the value of his products which represent his present fortune, which he assesses at 200,000 rthlr. [Reichsthaler]. With this, his own fortune, he intends to establish a wholesale commission business, import 200,000 Reichsthaler worth of products, and export in return the equivalent amount of domestic manufactures. Subsequent reciprocal trade relations are to be based on this initial arrangement, which he intends to do by establishing his own office in Stettin, and by dealing through the business houses of his children in America.

For the execution of this plan he has set the following conditions for himself:

1. The establishment of his residence in Stettin, with all the civil rights and privileges of a Christian citizen.

2. Importation of 50 per cent of his stated fortune, free of excise and customs.

3. An export bounty [drawback?] on all domestic manufactures which he can prove to have disposed of abroad. He is willing to accept the drawback in chinaware (at 5 per cent on all articles, as determined by the bank) with the usual discount. (Both of these bounties he expects to obtain only gradually in the space of four to five years, to the extent to which he gradually imports his products and in turn exports in the same ratio domestic manufactures.)

So much for the idea of the petitioner. As far as our unprejudiced opinion is concerned, we believe that the matter, taken generally, is exceedingly interesting to the Prussian State. For the whole country, and especially for the place where he sets up his establishment, there will develop an entirely new branch of commerce of which as yet the Prussian State has not taken advantage, and which hitherto has been entirely in the hands of the Dutch and Hamburg merchants. Until now we have been receiving, third hand, the products which we are now to receive first hand, and this, in view of the prices of the goods, is an essential advantage.

Virginia, the province where his offices are located, also is so favorably situated for a direct exchange of products that the expectation of a favorable outcome cannot easily fail. Her connections with the English, French, and Spanish colonies and the [West India] Islands give her the best opportunity to purchase the goods selectively and at the cheapest prices, and all these advantages are directly in the hands of the petitioner.

Another but very essential advantage, particularly since we are not permitted to open up markets over there, is that we shall have a market for American goods in the country. Our domestic manufactures have, for this reason, been retarded, and this prospective barter of our manufactured goods for imported raw materials is incontestably beneficial to the Prussian states.

Neither are there any objections to this petition as far as the constitution of our country is concerned. The goods which he has designated for import, p. 4, are as yet not restricted by prohibitions, monopolies etc. And among the goods which he wishes to export, p. 5, are some which hitherto have enjoyed little or no sale outside this country, and others, which at least did not go as far as America through direct major trade channels. Besides, nobody will suffer any losses through this barter except the foreigner who until now has had a monopoly on trade with these products. And it must be advantageous even for the local merchants, in the place where our petitioner sets up his establishment, to have these goods delivered to their front doors, without any compulsion, without monopoly, or any other pressure, when purchasing them from this wholesaler who in no way interferes with the retail business of the local merchant.

It remains for us merely to consider the special conditions which he has made. But these also seem to be reasonable. The selection of Stettin surely was made by him as carefully as possible. It is a place which is provided with everything that can interest a merchant, where a thriving trade already exists, and whose flourishing commerce proves its suitability for trade. Commerce, favored by location, is most likely sufficiently attractive to a man seeking to establish a business in a foreign country. His demands for export concessions likewise seem to us to be well justified, since all states which desire an extensive trade for their industries and their manufactures have granted and are still granting such export bounties. Some day we will have to grant such drawbacks anyway, at least for such goods as are being sent overseas. This will enable the patriotic domestic merchant to endure the losses from an unsuccessful speculation, and also to meet the competition of domestic goods with foreign goods (and particularly with foreign trading centers). We would thus merely be initiating with the petitioner what would be accorded to other merchants in the future also, and this might well be an encouraging example for other enterprising individuals. We, therefore, should not turn him down, especially since his demands, which propose a mere consideration of 5 per cent payable through the bank, are so reasonable. His assurance of his willingness to accept also another condition with respect to the bounty, as well as the nature of the drawback itself, which he asks in the form of porcelain and not in cash, seems to us to speak even more favorably for him.

What matters now is the third of his conditions, namely, the free importation of one half of his declared fortune, free of excise and duties. However, even this condition appears to us as not unreasonable. Besides, he is asking that this, as well as the drawback, be granted only gradually, over a period of from four to five years, and is asking for the free importation of only half of his present, actual fortune valued at 200,000 Reichsthaler, without extending the importation benefits to his subsequent imports. In the future, we may possibly reach the point where we must grant to every domestic merchant certain favors for similar raw materials that are brought across the sea at such risks. In this respect also, we would merely initiate this procedure with him, and only with respect to a certain amount of his fortune.

According to our unprejudiced opinion, there are, therefore, no weighty objections in this respect to the petitioner's request. Under certain circumstances, however, his request might require a closer scrutiny. The objection might be made that no merchant of the Jewish nation has been hitherto permitted to establish himself here. Nor can the petitioner prove with certainty the true state of his fortune, for want of a local counting-house that knows him. He seems to have foreseen the difficulty, as far as the first point is concerned, by asking for the same privileges as Christian citizens. If one were to grant a Jew the rights reserved for Christian merchants, and allow him to reside in Stettin, the question would then rise whether that could be brought into harmony with the present constitution. Perhaps the applicant could be persuaded to establish himself in another place without having to forego the advantages of the Stettin location. Cammin, Demmin, or Anklam [all in Pomerania] would be favorable to his establishment in that he would be enabled to share the property-ownership rights with all the inhabitants of the town with regard to owning land and ships. And at Cammin, particularly, he would retain direct connections with Stettin and Berlin by water. Both of these advantages recommend the location at Cammin most highly for his establishment there. This place, however, still has to struggle with the greatest inconveniences, as long as the navigable channel from the sea is not considerably deepened.

We, therefore, most obediently find that Judah Moses should in this case be permitted a stay in Stettin for himself and for his family, as a commission agent for the American trade.

To be sure, as far as the other circumstance is concerned, he has not been able to prove the state of his fortune other than by a letter from his associates, pp. 6–10, and by a bill of lading of a cargo that General Green is supposed to have on board for the petitioner's account, pp. 11–12. However, there seems to be no need for this, since all the concessions for which he has asked depend solely on his establishment in this country and on the actual importation of his wealth. Not until he shall have fulfilled on his part all the offers made by him will he be granted the favors applied for, and on this premise it is, therefore, a matter of indifference to the State with what sum he establishes his business. This difficulty could, therefore, in all likelihood be overcome also.

We believe that the whole plan of the petitioner could become of the utmost importance to our country, once the location of his business is assured. However, we most obediently leave it to Your Excellency to decide further in this matter with regard to the importance of the enterprise itself.

Grothe   Philippi

Berlin, April 26, 1787.

––––––

No. 189   Manuel Jacob Monsanto Sells Two Negro Slaves—1787

A traveler who visited the Spanish town of Natchez, on the Mississippi, in 1789 reported that he had been most hospitably entertained by a couple whom he believed to be Spanish Jews. These people were Benjamin and Clara Monsanto. Benjamin's parents were born in The Hague; Clara's family came from Curaçao. Both of them were Jews, although at Natchez they lived as nominal Roman Catholics. In a sense they were Marranos, although the authorities doubtless knew that they were Jews. The officials, however, did not have the least desire to disturb them. The Spanish Inquisition was a long way off from Fort Panmure at Natchez.

Benjamin Monsanto planted tobacco near the fort, but he seems to have engaged in the buying and selling of slaves as well. His brother Manuel Jacob Monsanto, of New Orleans, was his partner. Benjamin died in that city in 1795. The following document is a deed to two Negro slaves, sold by Manuel Jacob Monsanto to one James Saunders.

Monsanto was not an uncommon name. Families by that name lived in Surinam and the Virgin Islands in the eighteenth century, and one Isaac Monsanto traded in English Pensacola in 1771.

SOURCE. Office of the Chancery Clerk, Adams County, Natchez, Mississippi.

Be it known to all to whom these presents shall come, that I, Manuel Jacob Monsanto, do really and effectually sell to James Saunders a Negro man named Polidor, aged twenty five years, and a Negro woman named Lucy, aged twenty six years, both natives of Guinea, for the sum of eight hundred and fifty dollars in silver, payable at the end of the month of December, in the year one thousand seven hundred and eighty eight, the said seller not being in any manner responsible for any accident that may happen to said slaves, John Lum, planter, being surety therefor.

For which said consideration I do hereby resign all right, title, possession, interest, and claim in and to the said slaves, the whole of which I transfer and convey to the purchaser aforesaid, and his assigns, to be, as his own, possessed and enjoyed, sold, exchanged, or otherwise alienated at pleasure, in virtue of these presents granted in his favor in token of real delivery, without other proof of purchase and possession being required, hereby binding myself to maintain the validity of this present sale and conveyance in full right in favor of the purchaser aforesaid, and granting authority to the justices of his Majesty [King Charles III of Spain] to compel me to the execution of the same, as if judgment had already been given therein, renouncing all laws, rights, and privileges, general or special, in my favor whatsoever.

And I, the said James Saunders, being present at the granting thereof, do hereby accept the foregoing sale and conveyance of said slaves in my favor, in the form, and for the consideration therein mentioned and contained, granting formal acknowledgment of the same, and renouncing the laws respecting delivery, things not seen nor received, *fraud,* or other exceptions in the case, general or special, whatsoever.

Done and executed, in testimony thereof, in Fort Panmur, at Natchez, this seventh day of the month of November, in the year one thousand seven hundred and eighty seven.

I, Don Carlos De Grand Pré, Lieutenant Colonel of the Royal [Spanish] Armies and Civil and Military Commandant of the fort and district aforesaid, acting as notary public, there being none in the said district, certify that the parties contracting have acknowledged and signed the foregoing, with Don Antonio Soler, and Juan Carreras, witnesses present.

Monsanto, frère	Juan Carreras
Antonio Soler	James Saunders
Carlos De Grand Pré	

No. 190 Levy Solomons and Judah Williams Barter Horses for Hogs—1790

The following contract between Levy Solomons, a merchant, and Judah Williams, a farmer, calls for the exchange of two hundred hogs for ten horses.

Levy Solomons (*ca.* 1730–92) doubtless came to Canada from England during the period of the conquest (1759–60). He was one of five entrepreneurs who joined together as purveyors to the British army. After the French and Indian War he became a fur merchant and was considered by some to be the largest dealer in that commodity in all Montreal. He had commercial connections in Albany, an important point on the route between the St. Lawrence River and New York.

Solomons sympathized with the Whigs, in spite of the fact that most of his Canadian friends and associates were Loyalists. Although prosecuted for aiding the Continental forces during their invasion of Canada, he managed to remain in the province. In later years he was highly respected in both the Jewish and the general community, his earlier Whig leanings notwithstanding.

The name of Levy Solomons occurs frequently in the oldest known records of Congregation Shearith Israel in Montreal. He was one of the leaders, if not the chief figure, in the local Jewish religious community. His Jewish interests, however, did not deter him from dealing in hogs.

SOURCE. Montreal Old Courthouse, Municipal Records.

Before the underwritten notaries, residing in the city of Montreal, in the Province of Quebec, personally came and appeared Judah Williams, of Troy, in the County of Albany, State of New York, farmer, of the one part, and Levy Solomons of Montreal aforesaid, merchant, of the other part, which parties declared to have agreed and covenanted in manner of following, that is to say:

The said Judah Williams binds and obliges himself to furnish and deliver unto the said Levy Solomons, on or before the tenth day of August next, two hundred male cut hogs, weighing on an average one hundred pounds weight or thereabouts, as near as possible [as] can be expected, which weight shall be ascertained by the certificates of credable people from whom the said Judah Williams shall purchase the said hogs, and to be reckoned and computed at the rate of two pence halfpenny lawful money of the province aforesaid, per pound weight.

And the said Levy Solomons did, and hereby doth, bind and oblige himself to receive the said two hundred male cut hogs, and to pay or cause to be paid unto the said Judah Williams the said sum of two pence halfpenny lawful money for every pound the said hogs shall weigh, and be ascertained by the said certificates.

Also, [he] binds and obliges himself to furnish and deliver unto the said Judah Williams ten horses (equal to five horses now in the said Levy Solomons's stables, and which have been seen by the said Judah Williams) at twenty five Spanish dollars of five shillings currency each, the amount of which being deducted from the amount of the produce of the hogs, the said Levy Solomons bind[s] and obliges himself to pay or cause to be paid unto the said Judah Williams such remainder as then shall be due to him within three days after the said hogs shall be delivered.

And for the true performance of all and singular the covenants and agreements above set down, the said parties did, and hereby do, bind themselves, the one to the other, their, and either of their, executors, administrators, and assigns, in the penal sum of one hundred pounds, lawful money aforesaid.

Thus done and passed at Montreal aforesaid, in the office of John Gerbrand Beek, notary, on the twenty second day of June, in the year of our Lord, one thousand seven hundred and ninety, and signed, the said parties with us notaries, being first duly read.

Judah Williams	J. G. Beek, notary public
Levy Solomons	B'te [Jean-Baptiste] Desève, notaire

No. 191 Samuel and Moses Myers, of Virginia, Trade with Stephen Girard—1791–1792

Stephen Girard (1750–1831), the Philadelphia merchant, frequently wrote to Samuel Myers (1755–1836), of Petersburg, on business matters. The latter, a son of the silversmith Myer Myers, was a native New Yorker. During the Revolution he was a partner in the very successful firm of Isaac Moses & Company, which acquired great wealth during the war by running the British blockade. Once the peace was signed and normal trade relations with England were resumed, however, the firm went into bankruptcy and the partnership was dissolved. Myers, then the senior partner of S. & M. Myers, spent some time in Norfolk, moved on to Petersburg, and finally settled in Richmond. It was during Myers' stay in Petersburg that Girard began to do business with him (Document A).

The third member of the firm of Isaac Moses & Company was Moses Myers (ca. 1752–1835), no relative of Samuel. Moses was the son of Hyam Myers, a New York merchant who for years had lived in Canada. As a member of the firm of S. & M. Myers, Moses, in 1787, settled in Norfolk, where he remained for the rest of his life. He was one of the outstanding merchants and leaders of the city, ultimately becoming the president of the Common Council. After his friend and former partner introduced him to Girard, Moses also served as the Philadelphian's agent.

In Girard's letter to Moses Myers (Document B), the former refers briefly but bitterly to his differences with a Mr. Kendall. His adversary occupied some of Girard's property in Northampton County on the eastern shore of Virginia. Girard had made repeated efforts to dispossess Kendall, but all to no avail. Finally Girard wrote that Myers should burn Kendall out. The instructions need not be taken literally; the owner merely wanted Myers to accomplish a speedy and effective solution to his difficulties with the recalcitrant debtor.

SOURCE. Girard College, Philadelphia, Pa.; Stephen Girard Papers.

A [NO. 191]

Philadelphia, 7 November, 1791.

Mr. Samuel Myers,
Petersburg.
Dear Sir:

I have duly received your esteemed favour of the 28 instant, adviseing me of your declining to take up my proposals respecting the purchasse of 100 hogsheads of tobacco. I should have been happy to find my terms had suited you, but hope that in futer times your arra[n]gements will unable [enable] you to accomodate your friend.

As my presente imbarassement (which is princepaly occasioned by the lownese of the exchange on France which prevents to draw) obliges me to use every means in my power to procure the cargo of the ship *Le Père de Famille* ["The Father of the Family"], I have this day taken the liberty to draw on you, order of Messrs. William and James Douglas, for £580 2s. 3d. Pennsylvania currency, payable on the 12 day of January next, which is for the coffee and other articles sold to you on the twelvth day of last September, at four months' credit. Beg you will honor my draft.

I am with esteem,
[Stephen Girard]

B [NO. 191]

Philadelphia, 23 January, 1792.

Mr. Moses Myers,
Norfolk.
Dear Sir:

I have just received a letter from Mr. Thomas Filchett, the copy of which I here inclose for your governe[ment, guidance].

I am sorry to find that the possession of my land, etc. on the Eastern Shore is not yet obtained. I earnestly beg that you will take every means to have Mr. Kendall turned out, even by seting fire to all the buildings.

You may realy [rely] that I aproave before hand every step which you will [take] for the closure of that business. Messrs. W. and J. Douglas have creditted me of £ 50 12s. 5d. Virginia currency received from you.

I am respectfully,
[Stephen Girard]

No. 192 Starting Life Anew in the Postwar World—1791–1792

Aaron Lopez, who had carried on a world-wide trade, died insolvent in 1782. One of his sons, Joseph, was still engaged in settling his father's estate more than twenty years after the latter's death. No capital was available to Joseph, who turned to the manufacture of kosher cheese for export to the islands (Document A).

Two other Lopezes of the second generation who had to shift for themselves were David, Jr., and Aaron, Jr.

It was probably in the 1780's that the younger Aaron Lopez moved to Charleston, South Carolina, where he engaged in business as an auctioneer. There, on November 27, 1791, Aaron was joined by brother David, Jr. Their success in the prosperous and growing metropolis of South Carolina is recounted in a letter sent northward by David (Document B). The letters of both Joseph and David were addressed to Uriah Hendricks, a successful merchant in New York City.

In his letter to Hendricks, Joseph asked about the fate of a lottery ticket that both he and David had purchased. New York Jews were then all elated because a group of them had won £30,000 on a lucky ticket, and a portion of this money had been turned over to the synagogue.

SOURCE. American Jewish Archives, Uriah Hendricks Papers.

A [NO. 192]

New Port, November 24th, 1791.

Mr. Uriah Hendricks.
Dear Sir:

It's sometime since I have had the pleasure of meriting a line from your goodself, and sincerely lament that nothing should occur mutually to keep alive a correspondence I shall always be happy to cherish. And wish it was in my power to promote an intercourse in some kind of bussiness, but my embarrassed state in the settlement of my late parent's affairs still continues to preclude me from entering into trade. Therefore I must exercise further patience, and wait the event of things.

This will be handed you by Uncle David, who is determined to spend the winter at New York. Any civilities you may be pleased to extend towards him shall be esteemed as tho' confered on me, and permit me to crave your acceptance of a casher [kosher] cheese delivered into his care, which I hope will prove of a good quality. Suffer me, my dear sir, to entreat you'll be so obliging as to write to your friends in England to procure and send about the value of half a guinea's worth of cardo [cardoon], the blossoms of an herb, which is made use of altogether in Europe for the making of cheese instead of the strong, disagreable runnett [rennet] we make use of here. Its cost shall be thankfully reimbursed you, and I will promise to solicit your acceptance of the first good cheese that is made with the cardo. I have in view next summer, please God, to make a considerable quantity of cheese for exportation to the Israelites inhabiting the West India Islands, as what I have hitherto shipped to that market has amply paid me for the undertaking.

Please to tribute my best love to my dear sister Becky, and respectfull salutations to your amiable family, and believe me to be with sincerest esteem and respect, dear sir,

Your affectionate brother,
Joseph Lopes

P.S. Brother David embarked for Charleston the 9th [?] instant. Fine winds succeeded his departure, and I presume he will have a short passage. I am interested in a small part of the Dutch lottery ticket you sold him, and I will thank you to inform me its fate.

B [NO. 192]

Charleston, 6th February, 1792.

Mr. Uriah Hendricks.
Dear Sir:

I have not since my last respects had the pleasure of a line from you, yet will not omit this good oppertunity, altho overcharged with a multiplicity of business, to impart to you the plan I advised you I had in contemplation, which I now have the satisfaction to tell you is effected with a success beyond my most sanguine expectations.

Having discovered from my first observations an opening to a branch of business, the most profitable of any in this quarter, that of an auctioneer, and finding my brother Aaron perfectly versed therein, having served seven years with one of the first masters, well acquainted with characters [notables], and posesing the esteem and confidence of all ranks of people here, it occured to me the most eligible employment I could adopt, as well for him as myself. Therefore, without much hesitation, we announced the matter to our friends who imediately strengthened our ideas and promised their support and countenance [approval]. The same we have found realized in the most ample and liberall manner.

We opened on the 17th ultimo with a property to the amount of £1,000 sterling, [a] great part of which was knocked of[f] at our first sales, since which, our stores and vaults have been continualy crowded with all kinds of goods, and our sales respectable. Business daily encreaces, and we esteem ourselves not second to any other auctioneer in the city, being patronized by many merchants of the first respectability and influence.

In addition to that branch, I also at [the] same time commenced that of a commission store, in order to avail of the advantages offered me by many of my nortward friends in the shipping line, and in case I determined to fix [settle] here. I have wrote them on the subject and now hourly anticipate returns thereto.

The advantages we can afford our friends, beyond what other commission stores can, is that of recuring to the vendue [auction] to facilitate the vent [sale] of their goods without an aditicnal comission, as we propose not charging but a single comission wither disposed of at publick or private sale, whereas others, when obliged to recur to the auction, generally saddle the goods consigned them with a commission added to that of the vendue; besides, having it allways in our power to make the essay will tend to accelerate the sales to as good or better advantage than at private.

In order to avail of these two branches, we have found it necessary to carry them on under our seperate names, the vendue under the firm [signature] of my brother, and the store under my own, there existing a law of this state precluding vendue masters entering any vessel or goods at the customs house in his own name. We can, however, assist at both, and our particular friends know us to be as one.

Having now announced to you my new avocations, it only remains to tender you my best services therein, and to assure you that I shall ever execute your commands with the same zeal and pleasure I have bestowed on those transactions I hitherto have had the pleasure of being favoured with from you.

I beg you to present my best affections to my dear sister and famly, and beleive me to rest with sincere esteem, dear sir,

Your brother and humble servant,
David Lopez, Jr.

Price Currency, viz.:
Rice 9s. 6d. a [to] 10s.
Tobacco 11s. 6d.–12s.
Indigo 2s. 9d.–6s. 3d. in great demand
N.[ew] E.[ngland] rum 2s. 9d.

W.[est] I.[ndia] d[itt]o 4s.
Spirits 4s. 1d.
Muscovado sugars 50s. a 70s. neat hundred
Loaf d[itt]o 14d.
Madeira wine £22 a £70 p[er] pipe
Coffee 10d. a 12d.
Baltimore flour fine six and a half dollars p[er] barrel

No. 193   Solomon Hays Engages to Clerk in the Upper Country—1794

Six Hays brothers came from Holland to New York in the first part of the eighteenth century. Some drifted to Canada in the 1760's; others were Loyalists during the Revolution and settled in that northern province after the war. Among the Hayses who lived in Canada in the 1790's was a Solomon Hays, of Montreal.

In the following indenture Solomon bound himself to work for three years at the Indian trade in the Upper Country, roughly the equivalent of present-day Ontario. If, as we believe, Solomon Hays was the son of Michael Solomon Hays, he was twenty-four years of age in 1794.

After spending several years clerking on the frontier, a young man was sure to learn the business. And if he had competence, some capital, and a good name, he could engage in the trade for himself. Probably that was Solomon's hope and is what his cousin John was doing at the time. John Hays, after working in the Upper Country for an eastern Canadian firm, moved south to Illinois, where in 1798 he became sheriff of St. Clair County.

SOURCE. Montreal Old Courthouse, Municipal Records.

Before the underwritten notaries, residing in the city of Montreal, in the Province of Lower Canada, duly admitted and sworn, personally came and appeared Salomon Hays, of the same place, who voluntarily did, and hereby doth, bind and engage himself to Messrs. Grant, Campion & Company, merchants, trading at Montreal aforesaid, and carrying on the Upper Country trade with the Indians present, and accepting thereof Mr. Samuel Gerrard, one of the copartners of the said firm, to serve, abide, and continue with the said Grant, Campion, & Co., or either of them or their representatives, in the Upper Countries aforesaid (except at the Illenois), in such capacity as he, the said Salomon Hays, shall be able to serve, for the term of three years, fully to be compleat and ended.

And for that purpose, at the first requisition of the said Grant, Campion, & Company, any or either of them, [he is] to depart from this city for the said Upper Countries in one of their canoes, and there, during the said term of three years, [he] well and faithfully shall serve, his said employers' secrets keep, their lawful commands every where gladly do. Hurt to his said employers he shall not do, nor willingly suffer to be done by others, but the same, to his power, shall let [hinder] or forthwith give notice thereof. The goods wherewith he shall at any time be intrusted, he shall not imbezil or waste, nor lend them without consent, and render true and faithful accounts thereof. He shall not depart or absent himself from the said service without leave, but in all things, as a good and faithful clerk, shall and will demean himself towards his said employers during the abovesaid term.

This engagement is thus made for and in consideration that the said Grant, Campion & Co., some of them, or their representatives, shall find and provide for the said Salomon Hays, during the said term of three years, meat, drink, and all necessary wearing apparel, as is customary and usual in the said Upper Countries and Indian trade abovesaid.

Thus done and passed at Montreal aforesaid, in the office of John Gerbrand Beek, notary, on the fourth day of March, one thousand seven hundred and ninety four, and signed by the said parties and notaries after being duly read.

Solomon Hays
Grant, Campion & Co.
J. G. Beek, notary public 1794.
B'te [Jean-Baptiste] Desève, notary

No. 194 David Nassy in North America—1794–1796

David de Isaac Cohen Nassy, a native of Surinam in South America, was one of the most distinguished Jews of that Dutch province. Among his many activities were those of physician, pharmacist, Jewish communal leader, and publicist. In all likelihood he was one of the authors of the *Essai historique sur la Colonie de Surinam, etc.* ("Historical Essay on the Colony of Surinam"), a study of the Jews in that country. This work was prepared in 1788 at the request of Christian Wilhelm von Dohm, an enlightened German civil servant interested in enfranchising the Jews of Europe, who was the author of *Ueber die buergerliche Verbesserung der Juden* ("On the Civil Improvement of the Jews").

Resenting certain injustices, perhaps political disabilities, that he had experienced at home, Nassy left Surinam about 1792 and settled in Philadelphia. Soon after his arrival he was elected to membership in the American Philosophical Society. A year later, during the pestilence, he wrote *Observations on the Cause, Nature, and Treatment of the Epidemic Disorder Prevalent in Philadelphia.* Nassy, widely employed as physician by the victims of the disease, disagreed with Dr. Benjamin Rush on the nature and treatment of the illness.

Within a year after his arrival in the United States, Nassy began his correspondence with the Providence firm of Brown, Benson & Ives. The Browns had long enjoyed close commercial relations with Surinam, and Nassy turned to them to forward his letters to his native country. On June 14, 1794, he wrote to the company, recommending to their attention a friend in Surinam who desired to get in touch with an American house (Document A).

In July, Nassy informed his Rhode Island correspondents that he had written to influential friends at home, asking them to keep a beneficent eye on the firm's interests. By that time, having found that he did not like the North American climate, he had decided to return home and made inquiries about passage. He was eager to know whether he could secure accommodations out of Philadelphia or whether he had to embark from Providence (Document B).

The following February, after an exchange of letters, Nassy advised Brown, Benson & Ives that he intended to establish a commission house in Surinam and would like to serve as the correspondent for the Providence firm (Document C).

Political events impeded Nassy's return. By April, having heard that the French forces had taken Holland, that the Batavian Republic had been proclaimed, and that there was a possibility that Surinam might come under French domination, Nassy decided to remain in Philadelphia for the time being (Document D). Later in the month, however, he received the reassuring news that should any change take place in Surinam, it would be for the better. That decided him: he would go home (Document E). During the summer of 1795 Nassy sailed for South America.

In January, 1796, some months after his safe arrival in Surinam, Nassy once more wrote to Brown, Benson & Ives, informing them that he was in business and asking for their patronage (Document F). In some of his earlier letters to the Providence house Nassy evidently had an aide prepare the final copy. Most, but not all, of his letters are fairly intelligible. This last one, however, he must have written altogether by himself: it is less comprehensible and its spelling is certainly unique. It is followed by a paraphrase to make it more intelligible.

Some time after he had re-established himself in Surinam, Nassy wrote the *Lettre Politico-Theologico-Morale sur les Juifs* ("Politico-Theological-Moral Letter on the Jews"), an attempt to justify the enfranchisement which the Dutch Jews had already received. In a letter accompanying a copy of his publication which he sent to the American Philosophical Society, he wrote that his work reflected the teachings of liberty and equality so characteristically exemplified by the United States. As a naturalized citizen of the United States, and impressed by its egalitarian concepts, Nassy, we may be sure, preached its doctrines in the land to which he had returned.

SOURCE. The John Carter Brown Library, Brown Papers.

A [NO. 194]

Philadelphia, June the 14th, 1794.

Gentlemen:

I am highly obliged to you for the kindness you have favored me with in sending my letters. I did send you one lately, which I beg you to have conveyed as soon as you can.

One of my friends in Surinam, my correspondent, Mr. Mordecai de la Parra, a rich man and of an unquestionable character, writes me that by the death of Mr. Brandon, a merchant of a considerable fortune in our colony, he had determined himself to follow intirely the trade with America and to associate himself with another gentleman, Mr. Lobo. Therefore, he desires me to direct him a merchant who could send cargoes, whether by commission or in partnership. As this place [Philadelphia] do not make any business with Surinam, I take the liberty, gentlemen, of recommending to you my friend, Mr. De La Para. In case you would make any speculation on our colony, be assured, and I pass my word for it, that you will be pleased with his uprightness and honesty. Being acquainted besides with a number of the grand planters of Surinam, and being much regarded by the governor, he is in such situation as to be of a great advantage to you, supposed you favor him with your orders.

I desire to be excused for the trouble I am continually giving to you. Be pleased to continue your favors to me and to believe that I am, with much consideration, gentlemen,

Your most humble, obedient servant,
David Nassy

M. M. [Messieurs] Brown, Benson, & Ives,
Providence, R. Island.

B [NO. 194]

Philadelphia, July 14, 1794.

Gentlemen:

I received the letter you have favoured me with [of] the date of 27 June. My nephew['s] departure for Hispaniola [Haiti] with a medecinal cargo for my own account has hindered me from writing sooner to you. I am very glad that you relate to me about my friends of Surinam.

Be assured, gentlemen, they will make all their endeavours respecting every thing you want as a prove [proof] they honour my own recommendation. I have written to them by the same opportunity on that matter and also to the governor, to which I have requested to grant his special protection to your vessels from Rhode Island. The favour that honourable gentleman has granted to Captain Robert G. Burchan of this city on my recommendation makes me hope that he will deal towards your vessels in the same manner that he formerly did.

The said governor and my friends by their last letters I have received call me home, for which I am very much inclined, because the climate of this continent is unwholesome for me, and although [notwithstanding] my success in the medecine practice and the best intimate acquaintances I have acquired here, chiefly among the principal persons of this country, I have determined to go back about the end of this year.

In that case, may I find a good opportunity [ship] in your place? Or would you think that you will have some advantages in sending here a vessel, which you would load with flour and boards? If you met yourselves [agree] with my opinion, I will be ready to take a passage on it with my family and all that I should pick up, provided the freight should be paid to you according to the use. I own to you, gentlemen, that was I obliged to go and embark my self, my family, and goods in your place, it should be too trouble some and cost a great deal money, although the city [Philadelphia] has no, or very few conexions with my country.

In such hypothesy, gentlemen, could I rely on your recommendation about your friends of Rhode Island, from which, I am doubtless, I could get confidence and trust for every thing that may concern them to Surinam? In which place I could help them by many usefull ways, either in a mercantile branch and commerce acquaintances, planters, and our government, with which I have got good authority by friendship.

I should be, gentlemen, veriwell disposed to undertake a travel for your country this summer, in the very desiring [?] to make your personal acquaintance, of what I am very desirous. Independently I could have your answer by word on every thing I have been bold to ask of you. But as the number of my patients increases every day, I am compelled to stay here for the present, where I expect a letter from you about it. 'Tis a favour that I hope to receive of your kindness, provided that you don't take amiss my asking, and you would have [to] do it at your leisure, in order to dress [establish] my business in consequence.

You may believe, gentlemen, how much I should be grateful to you, for I mete the heaviness of the trouble I give to you, and you may consider that I should never find to serve you any how, in order to prove the esteem I have for you and the good disposition I am for your availing.

Here I join [enclose] some letters for Surinam.

I am, with a highly esteem, gentlemen,

Your most obedient servant,
David Nassy

P.S. Sir, you will do well if you give to your captain the letter for the governor, that he may deliver it himself into the hands of his Excellency.
Messrs. Brown, Benzon, & Yves, Marchant,
Providence, Rhode Island.

C [NO. 194]

Philadelphia, February 25, 1795.

Gentlemen:

As I hope under the Divine Providence to depart from hence for Surinam in the course of April next, agreably to the last letter I had the honour of writing you, I take the liberty of communicating to you my intentions of establishing there a house of commerce with some merchant here, for the purpose of receiving on commission such cargoes as may be found expedient to consign to me from this continent.

To that end I will sail from this place with a cargo consigned to me. But having observed that salted provisions, etc., are much dearer here than with you, I thought if I could established that commerce with you, under such conditions as you may deem suitable and as are usual amongst merchants, the speculation would be more easily carried on owing to the frequent intercourse between your city and Surinam, and more advantageous owing to the price of the goods to be exported.

I then propose to you to be concerned with me in that establishment, and to consign me on commission such cargoes as you shall send to the colony. My near connections with the government of my country and with my other friends, yet [also] the knowledge of the place, will enable me to store your goods and thereby obtain the same price as the merchants of the country get from the planters, after the low price they commonly pay to your captains. Besides, I will be able to send your vessels back with the produce of the country in the shortest time possible, which circumstance cannot fail being advantageous to you, were it only by saving the considerable expences incurred by the long staying of your vessels in the colony, whilst I could clear them within four, or at the furthest six, weeks.

Confident that you will agree [accept] my proposal, I send you a list of such articles as are now the most wanted at Surinam, agreably to the last letter I have just received from my friends. I will be able afterwards to write you from the place itself what the garrison shall stand in need of, since the governor, who favours me with his friendship, writes me that being my self employed in the government, I will easily obtain the privilege to supply the public stores with every necessary article, at the same price as other merchants.

Such are, gentlemen, the proposals I submit to your consideration, which may in time prove very advantageous. I am conscious that in such cases mutual confidence is indispensably necessary, and I assure you that nothing shall be wanted on my part to deserve yours. I can only mention [to] you that my probity and punctuality did always command at Surinam the general esteem and confidence, and the particular friendship of the governor. And since three years I have resided in this city, I have acquired such consideration that I would never quit it were [not] the climate so contrary to my health.

I beg you would favour me with your answer as soon as possible, that I may know how to act here with several merchants who have applied to me for the purposes I propose to you. At all events, whatever may be your determination, you may depend, gentlemen, upon my rendering you at Surinam all services in my power, and, as often as your captains will apply to me for advice, I will be very happy in giving them, as a grateful friend, the most useful directions.

I have the honor to be, gentlemen,

Your obedient, humble servant and friend,

David Nassy

I beg you would forward the inclosed by the first opportunity for Surinam:

List of goods, etc.
All sorts of salted provisions
Best spermacati oil
Fish or train [whale] oil
Potatos, onions, barley, butter, and cheese
Boards of all kinds, assorted oars of different sizes
Small quantity of common and superfine flour

D [NO. 194]

Philadelphia, April 11th, 1795.

Gentlemen:

The surprising news lately arived, respecting the fate of Holland, and the consideration that it may probably affect the colony of Surinam, has induced me for the present to suspend my intended return to that place, until we receive more certain intelligence upon this subject. I have for this reason taken the liberty to inclose a letter, which I shall esteem at [as] a particular favor if you'll be so obliging as to forward, as addressed, by the earliest opportunity, and if you do not meet with an immediate conveyance, shall thank you to forward it by way of Boston, it being of considerable consequence to the colony [Surinam] as well as myself.

I received yours of March 20th, and if I have the good fortune to return to Surinam, you may be assured that it will afford me particular pleasure to render your captains every service in my power, and shall ever retain a grateful remembrance of your kindness.

I remain with esteem,

Your much obliged, humble servant and friend,

David Nassy

E [NO. 194]

Philadelphia, 26 April, 1795.

Gentlemen:

I have taken the liberty of writing to you the 9th instant about my delaying my departure for Surinam, but as I have since received letters from that place via New Yorke, where by I am informed every thing is there in the greatest tranquillity, and they hope that the revolution even of Holland will do more good than evil to the colony, I intend to go there, but as the wessel in which I expected to sail could not wait, I am forced to trouble you again and to desire you would be kind enough to inform me the soonest possible whether I can find a passage in your port on board a good vessel with conveniencies for my family, four in number, and room enough for my goods. I prequist [beg] that favour of your friendship and will remember it with gratitude for ever.

I therefore beg you would inform me precisely of the time I must be with you, that I m[a]y send my effects by water and go by land with my family. I hope, gentlemen, and I trust in your goodness, that you will set a reasonable price on my passage, considering that it is a whole family and I have many things I will pay the usual freight for.

As to my person, I have nothing to fear from the privateers, since I am [a] good while ago naturalized before the [Pennsylvania] Supreme Court, a citizen of the United States, and I will take the greatest care to procure a passaport from the Minister [Secretary] of State for my self and family. On the receipt of your answer informing me of the time the wessel shall sail, I will prepare to set out for your place. Other wise the expences of my journey would be useless. I am ashamed to give you so much trouble. You may depend on my gratitude.

I am with much esteem, gentlemen,

Your obedient, humble servant and friend,

David Nassy

F [NO. 194]

Suriname, January 27th, 1796.

Gentelman:

By may arrival at St. Thomas, I had the honor to writhe your and to aquanted your of may determination to part from thence to Suriname, and now by may arrivall I can nott neglated by aquanted you, and likewice to retourn may tanks to you for all the kaind favors and frindschap I resived of your during the times I waas att Philadelphia. I hoop resiproklick to be able to sarved your in this collonie, wich will be a greed satisfaction for may. In cace any of your captins or master of vessels will come to this poort, your maid faile recomand them to may. I will do may indaver to adsist them in all watt lays in may power. I have at presant tread in marchandice bisnes to purchace cargos and renter consignation of vessels and marchandice goods. If any of your frinds send any consignemand to me, I will be obliged to your for a recomendation and hoope to give them a quick and good dispatch. Recomanding may especialy in your frindschap, and have the honor to remain, gentelman,

Your most humble servant,

David Nassy

[Paraphrase of Document F—No. 194]

Gentlemen:

On my arrival at St. Thomas, I had the honor to write you and to acquaint you with my determination to depart thence to Surinam. And now, on my arrival, I can not neglect acquainting you, and likewise returning my thanks to you for all the kind favors and friendship I received of you during the time I was at Philadelphia. I hope, reciprocally, to be able to serve you in this colony, which will be a great satisfaction to me.

In case any of your captains or masters of vessels will come to this port, you must not fail to recommend them to me. I will endeavour to do all that lies in my power. I have at present entered into the merchandise business, purchasing cargos and accepting consignments of goods coming in on vessels. If any of your friends send any consignment to me, I will be obliged to you for a recommendation, and hope to give them quick and good service.

Recommending myself especially to your friendship, I have the honor to remain, gentlemen, etc.

———

No. 195   Abraham Nunez Cardozo Becomes a Clerk in the Coal Business—1797

Benjamin Nathan Cardozo (1870–1938), an associate justice of the United States Supreme Court, came from a Spanish-Portuguese family that had been in this country since about 1750. It was then that Aaron Nunez Cardozo, the first of his American ancestors, came to New York. One of Aaron's sons, Abraham Nunez Cardozo (1758–1816), settled in Richmond about 1790. Other members of the family had already moved to Virginia.

In 1797, as we see from the following document, Abraham agreed to work as a clerk in the coal business. His employer was Henry (Harry) Heth, a veteran of the Revolutionary War and a member of a well-known Virginia family. The firm, Nicolson, Heth & Co., was located in Manchester, across the river from Richmond.

The contract stipulated that Cardozo was to eat with the Heths. We may be sure that the food was not kosher. It was difficult for Jews living in the country to remain "Jewish." America was a great melting pot even in those days.

This member of the Cardozo family never married. He died in Richmond, leaving a farm in the Bowling Green area.

SOURCE. University of Virginia Library, Charlottesville, Heth Collection.

I have this day agreed with Harry Heth to live with him as a clerk in the coal business, from the first day of January, one thousand seven hundred and ninety eight, at the rate of two hundred pounds per year and my board for the term of one year, from the said first day of January, 1798, under the penalty of five hundred pounds,

As witness, my hand, in Manchester, this twentieth day of February, one thousand seven hundred and ninety seven.

A. Cardozo

Feb. 20, 1797.
Attest:
John Stewart, W. Claiberne

No. 196 Lazarus Hays Is Apprenticed to a Merchant—1798

Andrew Hays, of Montreal, was a member of a widespread New York family of Dutch origin and the husband of Branney (Abigail) David. Their son Lazarus was named after his maternal grandfather, Lazarus David, a Welsh Jew, who was among the Canadian pioneers. Lazarus probably entered Canada with the British troops about 1760. He died a relatively young man of forty-two in 1776.

When young Lazarus was ready to start out in life, his parents apprenticed the fourteen-year-old boy to his uncle Samuel David, a merchant. Uncle Samuel, who was then thirty-two years of age, had already made progress in what was to be a very successful and distinguished career. The articles of apprenticeship binding uncle and nephew together for a period of four years are set forth in the following document.

SOURCE. Montreal Old Courthouse, Municipal Records.

Before the subscribing public notaries for the city and district of Montreal, in the Province of Lower Canada, residing in said city, personally appeared Lazerus Hays (son of Mr. Andrew Hays, of this city, silversmith, and Mrs. Branney David [Hays], his wife), who, being on or about the age of fourteen years, by virtue of these presents, and for the considerations hereinafter mentioned, declared to have of his own free and voluntary will, as well as by the will and consent of his said father and mother (parties to these presents and accepting thereof), placed and bound himself as an apprentice to Mr. Samuel David of the same place, merchant, also present and accepting, to be taught in the said trade and business of a merchant, which the said Samuel David now useth, and with him, in the manner of an apprentice, to dwell, continue, and serve from the day of the date hereof, for and during the term of four years, and fully to be complete and ended.

During all which term the said apprentice his said master well and faithfully shall serve, his secrets keep, his lawful commands every where gladly do, hurt to his said master he shall not do, nor willingly suffer to be done by others, but the same, to his power, shall let [hinder] or forthwith give notice thereof to his said master. The goods of his said master he shall not imbezil or waste, nor lend them without his consent to any. From the service of his said master he shall not at any time depart or absent himself without his said master's leave, but in all things, as a good and faithful apprentice, shall and will behave and demean himself towards his said master and all his during the said term.

And the said master his said apprentice the said trade and business of a merchant which he now useth, with all things thereto belonging, shall and will teach and instruct or otherwise cause to be well and sufficiently taught and instructed, after the best way and manner that he can. And shall and will also find and allow unto his said apprentice meat, drink, washing, lodging, and apparel, both linen and woolen, and all other necessaries in sickness and in health, meet and convenient for such an apprentice, during the term aforesaid.

And at the expiration of the said term, shall and will give to his said apprentice, over and above his then cloathing, one new suit of apparel, to wit, coat, waistcoat and breeches, hat, shoes and stockings, with suitable linen, as is fit and usual for such an apprentice, for so the said parties to these presents have agreed.

For thus, etc., promising, etc., obliging, etc., done and passed at the said city of Montreal, in the office of Jonathan Abraham Gray, one of us the said notaries, in the year of our Lord one thousand seven hundred and ninety eight, the twenty eighth day of September, in the afternoon, and signed by the said parties, with us notaries, these presents having first been duly read.

Lazarus Hays   Branney David [Hays]
Andrew Hays   Samuel David

J. A. Gray, notary public
1798.
B'te [Jean-Baptiste] Desève, notaire

Index

476